Mary gives birth to Jesus
Luke 2:1–7

The boy Jesus teaches in the Temple
Luke 2:41-52

John baptizes Jesus
Matthew 3:13–17

© WBTC 2011

Jesus chooses followers
Mark 1:16-20

© WBTC 2011

CHILDREN'S

NEW TESTAMENT

LEAFWOOD
PUBLISHERS

World Bible Translation Center

Children's New Testament: Easy-to-Read Version™

Co-published by Leafwood Publishers and World Bible Translation Center

Illustrations by Paul Trice

Free Downloads

Download free electronic copies of World Bible Translation Center's Bibles and New Testaments at: www.wbtc.org

Addresses

Leafwood Publishers
1626 Campus Court
Abilene, Texas 79601
1-877-816-4455
www.leafwoodpublishers.com

World Bible Translation Center, Inc.
P.O. Box 820648
Fort Worth, Texas 76182
Email: bibles@wbtc.org
Web: www.wbtc.org

ISBN-13: 978-0-89112-291-3

Mfr: Dickinson Press Inc., Grand Rapids, MI USA, Job #3934200, 09/21/2011

Contents

Abbreviations

New Testament names are in *italics*.

Acts	*Acts*	Judges	Judges
Amos	Amos	1 Kings	1 Kings
1 Chronicles	1 Chron.	2 Kings	2 Kings
2 Chronicles	2 Chron.	Lamentations	Lam.
Colossians	*Col.*	Leviticus	Lev.
1 Corinthians	*1 Cor.*	*Luke*	*Lk.*
2 Corinthians	*2 Cor.*	Malachi	Mal.
Daniel	Dan.	*Mark*	*Mk.*
Deuteronomy	Deut.	*Matthew*	*Mt.*
Ecclesiastes	Ecc.	Micah	Micah
Ephesians	*Eph.*	Nahum	Nahum
Esther	Esther	Nehemiah	Neh.
Exodus	Ex.	Numbers	Num.
Ezekiel	Ezek.	Obadiah	Obad.
Ezra	Ezra	*1 Peter*	*1 Pet.*
Galatians	*Gal.*	*2 Peter*	*2 Pet.*
Genesis	Gen.	*Philemon*	*Phm.*
Habakkuk	Hab.	*Philippians*	*Php.*
Haggai	Hag.	Proverbs	Prov.
Hebrews	*Heb.*	Psalms	Ps.
Hosea	Hos.	*Revelation*	*Rev.*
Isaiah	Isa.	*Romans*	*Rom.*
James	*Jas.*	Ruth	Ruth
Jeremiah	Jer.	1 Samuel	1 Sam.
Job	Job	2 Samuel	2 Sam.
Joel	Joel	Song of Songs	S. of S.
John	*Jn.*	*1 Thessalonians*	*1 Th.*
1 John	*1 Jn.*	*2 Thessalonians*	*2 Th.*
2 John	*2 Jn.*	*1 Timothy*	*1 Tim.*
3 John	*3 Jn.*	*2 Timothy*	*2 Tim.*
Jonah	Jonah	*Titus*	*Titus*
Joshua	Josh.	Zechariah	Zech.
Jude	*Jude*	Zephaniah	Zeph.

Preface

This special version of the New Testament is for those who want an English translation that accurately expresses the full meaning of the original text in a style that is clear and easy to understand. It is especially helpful to those who have limited experience with English, including children and people who are just learning English. It is designed to help such people overcome or avoid the most common difficulties in reading with understanding.

The writers of Scripture, especially those who produced the New Testament writings, showed by the language style they used that they were interested in good communication. The translators of this English version considered this an important example to follow. So they worked to express the meaning of the Biblical text in a form that would be simple and natural. They used language that, instead of working as a barrier to understanding, would provide a key to unlock the truths of the Scriptures for a large segment of the English-speaking world.

The translation is based directly on the original languages of Scripture. In the case of the Old Testament, the translators followed the Hebrew Masoretic Text as it is found in the latest printed edition of *Biblia Hebraica Stuttgartensia* (1984), while referring occasionally to some earlier readings in the Dead Sea Scrolls. In some cases, they also followed the *Septuagint (LXX)*, the Greek translation of the Old Testament, where it has readings that are actually earlier than any known Hebrew manuscript. For the New Testament, the source text was that which is found in both the United Bible Societies' *Greek New Testament* (fourth revised edition, 1993) and the Nestle-Aland *Novum Testamentum Graece* (twenty-seventh edition, 1993). The occasional variation from these printed editions was guided by reference to the findings of more recent scholarship.

Several special features are used to aid understanding. Brief explanations or synonyms (italicized within parentheses) sometimes follow difficult or unusual words in the text. If a word or phrase needs fuller explanation, it is specially marked in one of two ways: (1) If its usage is unique or unusual, it is marked by a letter of the alphabet (ᵃ) linking it to a footnote that provides an explanation or important information. Included in such footnotes are references to Scripture quotations and information about alternate readings when significant differences occur in the ancient manuscripts. (2) If it is a word that occurs frequently with the same meaning, its first occurrence in a section is marked with an asterisk (*) indicating that an explanation can be found in a Word List at the end of the Bible.

As in all translations, words that are implied by the context are often supplied in the text to make the meaning clear. For example, the phrase that in Greek is simply "David of Jesse" is always translated into English as "David the son of Jesse." If such explanatory words or phrases are extensive or unusual, they may be marked by half brackets. For example, in the translation, "The Lord gave this command to Moses ⌊for the people⌋," the phrase in half brackets is added to avoid any misunderstanding that the Lord's command was intended only for Moses and not for all the people.

Finally, in the Gospels, the first four books of the New Testament, the section headings are often followed by cross references. These identify where the same or similar material is found in one or more of the other Gospels.

Introduction

New Testament is a name that has been used for centuries to describe a group of writings or "books" that make up the second major part of the Bible. So the Bible is actually two collections of books. In fact, the word Bible comes from a Greek word meaning "books." The word translated "testament" was used to mean a covenant or agreement. It refers to God's promise to bless his people. The Old Testament is the collection of writings that relate to the agreement God made with the descendants of Jacob (also called Israel) in the time of Moses. The New Testament is the collection of writings that relate to the agreement God made with all people who believe in Jesus Christ.

The Old Testament writings tell about the great things God did for the people of Israel and his plan for them as his chosen people to bring his blessings to the whole world. These writings look forward to the coming of a savior or "Messiah" (see "CHRIST" in the Word List). The New Testament writings continue the Old Testament story. They describe the coming of that savior (Jesus Christ) and the meaning of his coming for all people. The Old Testament is important for understanding the New Testament, because it provides the necessary background. And the New Testament completes the story of salvation that began in the Old Testament.

THE OLD TESTAMENT

The Old Testament writings are a collection of thirty-nine different books produced by many different authors. They were written mainly in Hebrew, the language of ancient Israel. There are a few sections in Aramaic, an international language in Bible times. Portions of the Old Testament were written over 3500 years ago, and more than 1000 years passed between the writing of the first book and the last. In this collection there are books of law, history, prose, songs, poetry, and wise sayings.

The Old Testament is often divided into three main sections: the Law, the Prophets, and the Holy Writings. The Law contains five books called "The Five Books of Moses." The first book is *Genesis*. It tells about the beginning of the world as we know it, the first man and woman, and their first sin against God. It tells about the Great Flood and the family God saved through that flood, and it tells about the beginnings of the nation of Israel, the people God chose to use for a special purpose.

THE STORY OF ABRAHAM

God made an agreement with Abraham, a great man of faith. In that agreement God promised to make Abraham the father of a great nation and to give him and his descendants the land of Canaan. Abraham was circumcised to show that he had accepted the agreement, and circumcision became the proof of the agreement between God and his people. Abraham did not know how God would do what he had promised but trusted him to make it happen. This pleased God very much.

God told Abraham to leave his home in Mesopotamia and led him to Canaan (later called the land of Israel, which was approximately the same geographical area known today as Palestine). In his old age Abraham had a son named Isaac, who had a son named Jacob. Jacob (also called Israel) had twelve sons and a daughter. This family became the nation of Israel, but it never forgot its tribal origin. It continued to refer to itself as the twelve tribes of Israel—descendants of the twelve sons of Jacob: Reuben, Simeon, Levi, Judah, Dan, Naphtali, Gad, Asher, Issachar, Zebulun, Joseph, and Benjamin. The three main ancestors—Abraham, Isaac, and Jacob (Israel)—are known as the "fathers" or "patriarchs" of Israel.

Abraham was also a "father" of another kind. Many times in ancient Israel, God called certain people to speak for him. These special people, or prophets, were God's representatives to the rest of his people. Through the prophets God gave the people of Israel promises, warnings, laws, teachings, lessons drawn from past experiences, and lessons based on future events. Abraham "the Hebrew" is the first prophet mentioned in the Scriptures.

ISRAEL SET FREE FROM SLAVERY

The family of Jacob (Israel) grew to include about 70 of his direct descendants. One of his sons, Joseph, became a high official in Egypt. Times were hard, so Jacob and his family moved to Egypt, where there was plenty of food and life was easier. This tribe of Hebrews grew to be a small nation, and the Pharaoh (the title or name of the king of

Egypt) made them serve as slaves. The book of *Exodus* tells about how finally, after 400 years, God used the prophet Moses to free the people of Israel from slavery and lead them eventually to settle again in Palestine. The price for freedom was high, but the Egyptians were the ones who had to pay. God punished them with a series of ten plagues, demanding with each one that his chosen people be set free. But following each disaster, the king stubbornly refused to free them. The final plague, however, brought about the death of the firstborn sons of all the families of Egypt, including the Pharaoh's son. This caused the king finally to agree to let the Israelites go free.

The people of Israel had been given special preparations to make for their trip to freedom. Dressed and ready for the escape, each family killed and roasted a lamb. They put the blood from the lamb on their doorposts as a special sign to God. They hurriedly baked bread without yeast and ate their meal. That night the Lord went through the land. If the blood of the lamb was not on the doorposts, the firstborn of that family died. This is why the firstborn sons of the Egyptians were put to death, while the Lord "passed over" the homes of his people. This night and the events surrounding it were later remembered in many ways in the worship and sacrifices of the people of Israel.

After the Israelite slaves were set free and were leaving Egypt, the Pharaoh changed his mind again. He sent his army to catch them and bring them back, but God saved his people. He divided the Red Sea, making a path through it to lead them to freedom on the other side. Then he released the waters to destroy the army of Egyptians that was following them. After Moses led the people in a song of praise to God for his protection and kindness, he led them on a long and difficult journey. Finally, they came to a mountain in the desert of Sinai on the Arabian Peninsula, where God made a special agreement with his people.

THE LAW OF MOSES

God's rescue of the people of Israel and his agreement with them at Mount Sinai set this nation apart from all others. This agreement contained promises and laws for the people of Israel. A part of this agreement, known as the Ten Commandments, was written by God on two stone tablets and given to the people. These commands contain the basic principles for the kind of life God wanted the people of Israel to live, including their duty to God, family, and others.

The Ten Commandments and the rest of the rules and teachings given at Mount Sinai became known as "the Law of Moses" or simply "the law." Many times these terms are used to refer to the first five books of the Scriptures and often to the entire Old Testament.

Besides the Ten Commandments and other rules of conduct, the Law of Moses contains rules about priests, sacrifices, worship, and holy days. These rules are found in the book of *Leviticus*. According to the Law of Moses, all priests and their helpers came from the tribe of Levi. These helpers were called "Levites." The most important priest was called the high priest.

The Law of Moses included instructions for building the Holy Tent ("Tabernacle"), or Meeting Tent, the place where the people of Israel went to worship God. It also has instructions for making all the things to be used in their worship. This prepared the Israelites for the building of the Temple, the holy building in Jerusalem on Mount Zion, where the people would later go to worship God. The rules about sacrifices and worship forced the people to see that they sinned against each other and against God. But they also gave the people a way to be forgiven and to be reunited with one another and with God. These sacrifices prepared the way for a better understanding of the sacrifice God was preparing to give for all the people of the world.

The Law of Moses also contained instructions for celebrating a number of holy days or festivals. Each festival had its own special meaning. Some festivals were happy occasions to celebrate special times of the year, especially harvest times. These included the Festival of Weeks in the spring and the Festival of Shelters in the fall. (See these terms in the Word List.)

Other festivals were for remembering the wonderful things God had done for his people. Passover was this kind of holy day. Each family relived the escape from Egypt, gathering in their homes to remember this part of Israel's history and to sing songs of praise to God. A lamb was slaughtered and the meal prepared. Each cup of wine and piece of food reminded the people of the things God had done to save them from a life of pain and sadness. One holy day, in particular, was very serious. Every year, on the Day of Atonement, the people had to remember the many wrong things they had done to others and to God. This was a day of sadness, and the people did not eat. But on that day the high priest offered special sacrifices to "cover over" or atone for their sins.

The agreement between God and Israel was very important to

the writers of the Old Testament. Almost all the books of the Prophets and Holy Writings are based on the fact that the nation of Israel, and every citizen of Israel, had made a very special agreement with their God. They called it the "agreement of the Lord" or simply "the agreement." Their books of history interpret events in light of the agreement: If the individual or nation was faithful to God and the agreement, then God rewarded them. If the people abandoned the agreement, then God punished them. God sent his prophets to remind the people of their agreement with him. The poets of Israel sang of the wonderful things God did for his obedient people, and they mourned the pain and punishments that came to those who disobeyed. These writers based their concepts of right and wrong on the teaching of the agreement. And when innocent people suffered, the poets struggled to understand why.

THE KINGDOM OF ISRAEL
The story of ancient Israel is the story of people who were always leaving God, God rescuing the people, the people turning back to God and eventually leaving him again. This cycle began almost as soon as the people had accepted God's agreement, and it was repeated again and again. At Mount Sinai the people of Israel agreed to follow God, and then they rebelled and were forced to wander 40 years in the desert. Finally, Moses' helper, Joshua, led the people into the promised land. Then came the battles to gain control of the different areas and settle the first parts of what later came to be known as the land of Israel. For the first few centuries after this settlement, the people were governed by local leaders called judges.

Eventually, the people wanted a king. The first king God appointed for them was Saul. But Saul did not obey God, so God chose a shepherd boy named David to be the new king. The prophet Samuel came and poured oil on his head, anointing him king of Israel. God promised David that the future kings of Israel would be his descendants from the tribe of Judah. David conquered the city of Jerusalem and made it his capital and the future site of the Temple. He organized the priests, prophets, songwriters, musicians, and singers for the Temple worship. David even wrote many of the songs (or psalms) himself, but God did not let him build the Temple.

When David was old and about to die, with God's blessing he made his son Solomon king of Israel. David warned his son to always follow God and obey the agreement. As king, Solomon built the Temple in Jerusalem that David had planned, and he expanded Israel's borders. At this time Israel was at the high point of its power. Solomon became famous, and Israel became strong.

JUDAH AND ISRAEL—THE DIVIDED KINGDOM

At Solomon's death there was disagreement and a struggle among the people, and the nation was divided. The northern ten tribes called themselves Israel. The southern tribes called themselves Judah. (The modern term "Jew" comes from this name.) Judah remained loyal to the agreement, and David's dynasty (family of kings) continued ruling in Jerusalem for several hundred years.

In the northern kingdom (Israel) numerous kings and dynasties came and went, because the people did not follow the agreement. The kings of Israel had several capital cities at various times, the last of which was Samaria. In order to strengthen their hold on the people, the kings of Israel changed the way to worship God. They chose new priests and built two new temples—one at Dan (on the northern border of Israel) and the other at Bethel (along Israel's border with Judah). There were many wars between Israel and Judah.

During this time of civil war and troubles, God sent many prophets to Judah and Israel. Some of the prophets were priests; others were farmers. Some were advisors to kings; others lived a much simpler life. Some of the prophets wrote their teachings or prophecies; many others did not. But all the prophets spoke for justice, fairness, and the need to depend on God for help.

Many prophets warned that the people would be defeated and scattered if they did not turn back to God. Some prophets saw visions of future glories as well as future punishments. Many of them looked forward to the time when a new king would come to rule the kingdom. Some saw this king as a descendant of David who would lead the people of God into a new Golden Age. Some spoke of this king as ruling forever over an eternal kingdom. Others saw him as a servant who would suffer many things in order to bring his people back to God. But all of them saw him as the Messiah, the one anointed (chosen) by God to bring in a new age.

THE DESTRUCTION OF ISRAEL AND JUDAH

The people of Israel did not listen to God's warnings. So in 722/721 B.C. Samaria fell to the invading Assyrians. The people of Israel were taken from their homes and scattered throughout the Assyrian Empire, lost forever to their brothers and sisters in Judah. Then the Assyrians brought in foreigners to resettle the land of Israel. These people were taught about the religion of Judah and Israel, and many of them tried to follow the agreement. These people came to be known as the Samaritans. The Assyrians tried to invade Judah. Many cities fell to the invaders, but God saved Jerusalem. The defeated king of Assyria returned to his homeland, and there he was murdered by two of his sons. So Judah was saved.

For a while the people of Judah changed. They began to obey God, but only for a short time. They, too, were finally defeated and scattered. The nation of Babylon rose to power and invaded Judah. At first they took only a few important people away as captives. But a few years later, in 587/586 b.c., they returned to destroy Jerusalem and the Temple. Some of the people escaped to Egypt, but most of them were taken as slaves to Babylon. Again God sent prophets to the people, and they began to listen. It seems that the destruction of the Temple and Jerusalem and the exile in Babylon brought about a real change in the people. The prophets spoke more and more about the new king and his kingdom. One of the prophets, Jeremiah, even spoke of a new agreement—an agreement that would not be written on tablets of stone, but would be in the hearts of God's people.

THE RETURN TO PALESTINE

Meanwhile, Cyrus came to power over the Persian Empire and conquered Babylon. Cyrus allowed people to return to their homelands. So after 70 years of exile, many of the people of Judah went back home. The people tried to rebuild their nation, but Judah remained small and weak. The people rebuilt the Temple, although it was not as beautiful as the one Solomon had built. Many of the people truly turned to God and began studying the Law, the writings of the prophets, and the other holy writings. Many men became scribes (special scholars), who made copies of the Scriptures. Eventually, these men organized schools for studying the Scriptures. The people began meeting together on the Sabbath (Saturday) to study, pray, and worship God together. In their synagogues (meetings) they studied the Scriptures, and many people began looking for the Messiah to come. In the West, Alexander the Great gained control of Greece and soon conquered the world. He spread the Greek language as well as the customs and culture of Greece to many parts of the world. When he died, his kingdom was divided. Soon another empire grew and gained control of a large part of the known world, including Palestine, where the people of Judah lived.

The new rulers, the Romans, were often cruel and harsh, and the Jewish people were proud and not willing to submit to Roman rule. In these troubled times there were many Jews who were looking for the Messiah to come in their own lifetime. They wanted to be ruled only by God and the Messiah who God had promised to send them. They did not understand that God planned to save the world through the Messiah. They thought that God's plan was to save the Jews from the world! Some were content to wait for God to send his Messiah. Others thought that they should "help" God establish his new kingdom by making sure that the Law of Moses was observed and that the Temple, the land, and the Jewish people were kept pure. In order to make this happen, they were willing to suffer, to die, or to kill anyone, foreigners or other Jews, who threatened these goals. Such Jews eventually came to be known as "Zealots."

THE JEWISH RELIGIOUS GROUPS

By the first century B.C., the Law of Moses had become extremely important to the Jews. They had studied and argued over it for centuries. The people understood the law in different ways, but many Jews were ready to die for that law. There were three major religious groups among the Jews, and there were scribes (scholars or experts in the law) in each group.

The Sadducees

One of the groups was called the Sadducees. This name probably comes from the name Zadok, the high priest in King David's time. Many of the priests and the people in authority were Sadducees. These men accepted only the law (the five books of Moses) as their authority in religious matters. The Law of Moses taught many things about the priests and sacrifices, but it did not teach about life after death. So the Sadducees did not believe that people would ever be raised from death.

The Pharisees

Another group was called the Pharisees. This name comes from a Hebrew word meaning "to interpret (explain)" or "to separate." These men tried to teach or interpret the Law of Moses to the common people. The Pharisees believed that there was an oral tradition going back to Moses' time. They believed that people of each generation could interpret the law in a way that would allow it to meet the needs of that generation. This meant that the Pharisees could accept not only the Law of Moses as their authority, but also the Prophets, the Holy Writings, and even their own traditions. These men tried very hard to follow the law and their traditions. So they were very careful about what they ate and what they touched. They were careful about washing their hands and bathing. They also believed that people would be raised from death, because they understood many of the prophets to say that would happen.

The Essenes
The third major group was the Essenes. Many of the priests in Jerusalem did not live the way God wanted them to. Also, the Romans had appointed many of the high priests, and some of these men were not qualified according to the Law of Moses. Because of this, the Essenes did not think that the worship and sacrifices in the Jerusalem Temple were being done properly. So they moved out into the Judean desert to live. They formed their own community, where only other Essenes could come and live. They fasted, prayed, and waited for God to send the Messiah to purify the temple and the priesthood. Many scholars believe that the Essenes were connected in some way with the Qumran Community and the many ancient writings (including the Dead Sea Scrolls) found at Qumran and other places in that area of the Judean desert.

THE NEW TESTAMENT
God had begun his plan. He had chosen a special nation. He had made an agreement with those people that would prepare them to understand his justice and his goodness. Through prophets and poets he had revealed his plan to bless the world by establishing a perfect spiritual "kingdom" based on a new and better agreement. This plan would begin with the coming of the promised Messiah. The prophets had spoken of his coming in great detail. They had told where the Messiah would be born, the kind of person he would be, and the work he would have to do. It was now time for the Messiah to come and begin the new agreement.

    The writings of the New Testament describe how God's new agreement was revealed and put into effect by Jesus, who was the Christ (meaning "the Anointed One," the Messiah). They teach that this agreement was to be for all people. And they tell how people in the first century responded to God's kind offer of love and became a part of the new agreement. Many things that were part of the first agreement are given new meaning under the new agreement, especially ideas related to Israelite worship, such as temple, priesthood, and sacrifice. These writings give instructions to God's people about how to live in this world. They also describe the blessings that God promises his people for a full and meaningful life here and for life with him after death.

The New Testament writings include twenty-seven different "books" by at least eight different writers. All of them wrote in Greek, which was widely spoken in the first-century world. More than half of the total writing was done by four "apostles," men chosen by Jesus to be his special representatives or helpers. Three of these, Matthew, John, and Peter, were among the twelve closest followers of Jesus during his life on earth. The fourth, Paul, was chosen as an apostle later by Jesus through a miraculous appearance.

The first four books, called "Gospels," are separate accounts of the life and death of Jesus Christ. Generally, these books emphasize Jesus' teaching, the purpose of his appearance on earth, and the special significance of his death, rather than just the historical facts of his life. This is especially true of the fourth book, the *Gospel of John*. The first three Gospels are very similar in content. In fact, much of the material in one is found in one or both of the others. There are differing points of emphasis in each one, however, and each writer seems to have been addressing a different audience, with perhaps a different goal or goals in view.

The four Gospels are followed by *Acts*, a history of the events following the death of Jesus. It describes how God's offer of love to all people was announced throughout the world by Jesus' followers. It tells how the proclaiming of this "gospel" or "Good News" resulted in the conversion of thousands of people throughout Palestine and the Roman world to faith in Jesus Christ. The book of *Acts* was written by a medical doctor named Luke, an eyewitness of much that he recorded. Luke was also the author of the third Gospel. His two books make a logical unit with *Acts* being the natural sequel to his account of the life of Jesus.

Following *Acts*, there is a collection of letters written to individuals or groups of believers in Christ. These letters were sent from leaders in the faith, such as Paul and Peter, two of Jesus' apostles. These letters were written to help the people of that time deal with problems they were facing. They serve to inform, correct, teach, and encourage not only those people but all who become followers of Jesus in regard to their faith, their life together, and their life in the world.

The final book of the New Testament, *Revelation*, is very different from all the others, although its purpose is similar to that of other letters to churches. It begins with words of criticism, encouragement, and instruction addressed to groups of believers in seven different cities of Asia Minor (modern Turkey). But it continues with a picture of spiritual warfare that is of interest to all followers of Christ. It uses highly figurative language and tells of visions seen by the author, the apostle John. Many of the figures and images are from the Old Testament and can best be understood by comparing them to the Old Testament writings. This last book of the New Testament is a message of hope given to God's people through the Holy Spirit. This message assures believers in Jesus Christ of ultimate victory over the forces of evil.

THE BOOKS OF THE NEW TESTAMENT

The following additional information on each of the New Testament books should be helpful in preparation for reading each book:

Matthew. Matthew is the name of one of Jesus' twelve closest followers. Matthew was a Jewish tax collector when Jesus chose him as one of his apostles. Matthew's writing shows the influence of his Jewish background and interests. He seems especially interested in the fulfillment of Old Testament prophecies in the life of Jesus. Matthew really centers his book, however, around the teaching of Jesus.

Mark. John Mark was a young companion to some of the apostles. Mark's style of writing is brief and full of action. Unlike Matthew and Luke, he shows very little interest in Jesus' teachings. Mark apparently aimed his writing at the Roman, non-Jewish mind and centers on the actions of Jesus that prove him to be the Son of God. Mark seems mainly interested in people knowing that Jesus came to earth for the purpose of saving them from the consequences of sin.

Luke. This is one of two books written by a traveling companion of the apostle Paul. Luke was a well-educated medical doctor and a talented writer. He seems familiar with Mark's Gospel and much of the material in the Gospel of Matthew, but he chooses to include mainly the parts that would be attractive and understandable to his non-Jewish audience. More than the other Gospel writers, he seems interested in an orderly account of Jesus' life as a historical reality.

Emphasis, however, is not on the events in Jesus' life, but on Jesus himself as a loving, caring person who taught people the real meaning of life and who reached out to the needs of all people with power to help and save.

John. This Gospel is very different from the first three. This is seen immediately from the beautiful but profound introduction. John introduces much material that is not found in the other Gospels. His main interest is in proving Jesus to be the Messiah (Christ), the divine Son of God and savior of the world.

Acts. This book, written by Luke, takes up where his first book ends. It begins with Jesus' instructions to his followers to go throughout the world announcing the "Good News," a message about God's love for all people. Jesus wanted them to tell what they now knew about his divine mission to save people from the consequences of their wrongdoing. Luke traces the exciting fulfillment of this assignment, centering on the activities of two main characters, Peter and Paul. He shows how the movement that began shortly after the death and resurrection of Jesus spread rapidly from a small beginning in Jerusalem into the surrounding regions of Judea and Samaria, and eventually to the farthest areas of the Roman empire.

The next group of New Testament writings consists of the Letters of Paul. The apostle Paul (originally named Saul) was a well-educated Jew from Tarsus in Cilicia (Southeast Turkey). Educated in Jerusalem, he was a leader among the Pharisees, and he was violently opposed to the movement made up of followers of Jesus Christ. Jesus appeared to him in a vision, however, and changed the whole direction of his life. About ten years later, he began traveling all over the Roman world to proclaim the message about Christ. During this period he wrote many letters to churches (groups of believers in Christ) and to individuals. Thirteen of these letters are included in the New Testament.

Paul's letter to the **Romans** is the longest and fullest of all his letters. Most of his letters are to groups of believers in cities where he had pioneered in teaching people about Christ and forming churches. However, when he wrote this letter to "Christ followers" living in Rome, he had never been there. He was in Greece about 57 A.D., and not being able to travel on to Rome as he had wanted, he wrote his teaching in this letter. Besides dealing with a number of other issues, he includes a carefully-written presentation of the fundamental truths regarding faith in Jesus.

The letters of **1 Corinthians** and **2 Corinthians** are two of several that Paul wrote to the believers in Corinth, a city in southern Greece. In the first of these two letters, Paul deals with some problems that had developed among the believers there and answers questions that some of them had sent to him. Among the many subjects Paul covers are unity, marriage, sexual sin, divorce, and Jewish customs. Of particular interest is chapter 13, Paul's famous writing on love, which he sees as the solution to their problems. The second letter follows up on the Corinthians' response to the first letter.

Paul's letter to the **Galatians** deals with a problem of a different kind among the believers in Galatia. Paul had proclaimed the message about Christ there and had formed some churches. Then a group of Jewish teachers went there and taught some ideas that were very different from the true teaching of Christ. The problem was a crucial one, because it involved the basis for a person's good relationship with God. Being unable to travel to Galatia at the time, Paul strongly confronted the problem in this letter. Like his letter to the Romans, it also includes a presentation of the basics of faith in Jesus, but for a different reason.

Paul wrote the letter to the **Ephesians** while he was in prison, but it is not certain where or when. The theme of this letter is God's plan to bring all people together under the rule of Christ. Paul encourages believers to live their lives in harmony with each other and with complete commitment to God's purpose for them.

Paul's letter to the **Philippians** was also written from prison, probably from Rome. Paul was facing many troubles at the time, but he trusted God, and this letter is full of confidence and joy. Paul wrote to encourage the believers in Philippi and to thank them for some financial help they had sent to him.

Paul wrote the letter to the **Colossians** to confront some false teachings that were troubling the church in Colossae, a city in Asia Minor (modern Turkey). Parts of this letter are similar to the letter to the Ephesians. Paul gives some practical lessons for living the way a follower of Christ should.

The letters of **1 Thessalonians** and **2 Thessalonians** were probably among the first of Paul's letters. On Paul's first trip to Macedonia (northern Greece), he told the people of Thessalonica the message about Christ. Many people believed, but Paul had to leave after a short time. Paul wrote to encourage the people in their new faith. He also discusses some things the people did not understand, especially concerning Christ's expected return. The second letter continues this discussion.

The letters of **1 Timothy**, **2 Timothy**, and **Titus** were written toward the end of Paul's life to two of his close companions. Paul had left Timothy in Ephesus and Titus in Crete to help with some problems about the organization and function of the churches there. Apparently Timothy and Titus were to help the churches in these places prepare for independent leadership and operation. In the first letter to Timothy and the letter to Titus, Paul gives some guidelines for the selection of leaders as well as instructions for dealing with various problems and situations. The second letter to Timothy, written from prison as Paul faced what he felt was the end of his life, is very personal. The letter is full of advice and encouragement as he urges Timothy to follow his own example of faith, courage, and endurance.

Philemon is a short letter written by Paul at the same time he wrote the letter to the Colossians. Philemon, a believer in Colossae, was the master of a runaway slave Onesimus, who had become a follower of Christ through Paul's influence. The letter is Paul's appeal to Philemon to forgive Onesimus and welcome him back.

In addition to the letters of Paul, there are eight letters written by other followers of Jesus. The author of **Hebrews** is unknown, but it is clear that is was written to Jewish believers in Christ. They were in danger of being pulled away from their belief in Jesus. This letter was written to encourage and strengthen the faith of these believers. The writer emphasizes the superiority of Jesus Christ over all other beings and persons. He teaches that the eternal priesthood of Jesus Christ and the "better agreement" are superior to the Old Testament priesthood and the "first agreement." The writer closes by encouraging the people to trust in God and to live for Him.

The word "practical" is almost always used in describing the letter of **James**, "a servant" of God and Jesus. Some people think this is one of Jesus' brothers. The Jewish background of James is clear as he teaches about fairness and justice, helping the poor, friendship with the world, wisdom, self-control, trials and temptations, doing and hearing, and faith and works. He also encourages people to pray and be patient.

The letters of **1 Peter** and **2 Peter** were written by the apostle Peter to followers of Christ who were living in many different places. Peter teaches such believers about their living hope and their real home in heaven. Because of the hard times they are facing, Peter assures them that God has not forgotten them. They will be better because of their suffering. He reminds them that God has blessed them and has forgiven their sins through Jesus Christ. They should respond by living right. In his second letter, the apostle confronts false teachers. He teaches about true knowledge and the second coming of Christ.

The letters of **1 John**, **2 John**, and **3 John** were written by the apostle John. John's letters of love assure the believers that God will always accept them. John teaches that people show their love to God by loving the people around them and by doing the things God wants them to do. The second and third letters appeal to Christ's followers to love one another, and they warn against false teachers and ungodly behavior.

The writer of the letter **Jude** is a brother of James and probably a brother of Jesus. This letter encourages faithfulness and speaks out against troublemakers and false teachers.

The **Revelation** of the apostle John begins with words of criticism, encouragement, and instruction addressed to groups of believers in seven different cities of Asia Minor (modern Turkey). But it continues with a picture of spiritual warfare that is of interest to all followers of Christ. It uses highly figurative language as it tells of visions seen by the author. Many of the figures and images are from the Old Testament and can best be understood by comparing them to Old Testament writings. This last book of the New Testament writings assures believers of ultimate victory over the forces of evil through the power of God and Jesus Christ, their leader and helper.

THE BIBLE AND TODAY'S READER

Today's reader of the Bible should keep in mind that these books were written thousands of years ago for people who lived in cultures very different from ours today. Many of the historical accounts, illustrations, and references they contain can only be understood with some knowledge of the time and culture in which the writers lived. Generally, however, the writings focus on principles that are universally true. For example, Jesus told a story about a man sowing grain in a field that had different types of soil conditions. Those exact conditions may be unfamiliar to a person today, but the lesson Jesus draws from the example is appropriate for people in any time or place.

The modern reader may find the world of the Bible somewhat strange. The customs, the attitudes, and the way people talk may be quite unfamiliar. It is only reasonable to judge these things by their experience and ideals, not by today's standards. It is also important to note that the Bible was not written as a book of science. It was written mainly to describe historical events and present the significance of those events in ways that relate to all people. Its teachings present universal truths that are beyond the realm of science. It remains relevant even in our own time, because it deals with people's basic spiritual needs, which never change.

If you read the Bible with an open mind, you can expect to receive many benefits. You will gain knowledge about the history and culture of the ancient world. You will learn about the life and teachings of Jesus Christ and what it means to be his follower. You will gain basic spiritual insights and learn practical lessons for living a dynamic and joy-filled life. You will find answers to life's most difficult questions. There are, therefore, many good reasons for reading this book, and if you read it with a sincere and receptive spirit, you may well discover God's purpose for your life.

Matthew

The Family History of Jesus the Messiah
(Lk. 3:23b–38)

1 ¹This is the family history of Jesus the Messiah.* He came from the family of David,* who was from the family of Abraham.* ² Abraham was the father of Isaac.

Isaac was the father of Jacob.*
Jacob was the father of Judah and his brothers.
³ Judah was the father of Perez and Zerah. (Their mother was Tamar.)
Perez was the father of Hezron.
Hezron was the father of Ram.
⁴ Ram was the father of Amminadab.
Amminadab was the father of Nahshon.
Nahshon was the father of Salmon.
⁵ Salmon was the father of Boaz. (His mother was Rahab.)
Boaz was the father of Obed. (His mother was Ruth.)
Obed was the father of Jesse.
⁶ Jesse was the father of King David.
David was the father of Solomon. (His mother had been Uriah's wife.)
⁷ Solomon was the father of Rehoboam.
Rehoboam was the father of Abijah.
Abijah was the father of Asa.
⁸ Asa was the father of Jehoshaphat.
Jehoshaphat was the father of Jehoram.
Jehoram was the father of Uzziah.
⁹ Uzziah was the father of Jotham.
Jotham was the father of Ahaz.
Ahaz was the father of Hezekiah.
¹⁰ Hezekiah was the father of Manasseh.
Manasseh was the father of Amon.
Amon was the father of Josiah.
¹¹ Josiah was the grandfather of Jehoiachin*ᵃ* and his brothers, who lived during the time that the people were taken away to Babylon.
¹² After they were taken to Babylon:
Jehoiachin was the father of Shealtiel.
Shealtiel was the grandfather of Zerubbabel.
¹³ Zerubbabel was the father of Abiud.
Abiud was the father of Eliakim.
Eliakim was the father of Azor.
¹⁴ Azor was the father of Zadok.
Zadok was the father of Achim.
Achim was the father of Eliud.
¹⁵ Eliud was the father of Eleazar.
Eleazar was the father of Matthan.

ᵃ 1:11 Jehoiachin Literally, "Jechoniah," another name for Jehoiachin.

Matthan was the father of Jacob.

16 Jacob was the father of Joseph.
Joseph was the husband of Mary,
and Mary was the mother of Jesus, who is called the Messiah.

17So there were fourteen generations from Abraham to David. There were also fourteen generations from David until the people were taken away to Babylon. And there were fourteen more from the time the people were taken to Babylon until the Messiah was born.

The Birth of Jesus the Messiah
(Lk. 2:1–7)

18This is how the birth of Jesus the Messiah* happened. His mother Mary was engaged to marry Joseph. But before they married, he learned that she was expecting a baby. (She was pregnant by the power of the Holy Spirit.*) 19Mary's husband, Joseph, was a good man. He did not want to cause her public disgrace, so he planned to divorce her secretly.

20But after Joseph thought about this, an angel from the Lord came to him in a dream. The angel said, "Joseph, son of David,* don't be afraid to accept Mary to be your wife. The baby inside her is from the Holy Spirit. 21She will give birth to a son. You will name him Jesus.ᵈ Give him that name because he will save his people from their sins."

22All this happened to make clear the full meaning of what the Lord said through the prophet*: 23"The virgin* will be pregnant and will give birth to a son. They will name him Immanuel."ᵇ (Immanuel means "God with us.")

24When Joseph woke up, he did what the Lord's angel told him to do. He married Mary. 25But Joseph did not have sexual relations with her until her son was born. And he named him Jesus.

Wise Men Come to Visit Jesus

2 ¹Jesus was born in the town of Bethlehem in Judea during the time when Herod* was king. After Jesus was born, some wise men* from the east came to Jerusalem. 2They asked people, "Where is the child who has been born to be the king of the Jews? We saw the star that shows he was born. We saw it rise in the sky in the east and have come to worship him."

3When King Herod heard about this, it upset him as well as everyone else in Jerusalem. 4Herod called a meeting of all the leading Jewish priests and teachers of the law. He asked them where the Messiah* would be born. 5They answered, "In the town of Bethlehem in Judea, just as the prophet* wrote:

6 'Bethlehem, in the land of Judah,
    you are important among
        the rulers of Judah.
Yes, a ruler will come from you,
    and that ruler will lead
        Israel, my people.'"   *Micah 5:2*

7Then Herod had a private meeting with the wise men from the east. He learned from them the exact time they first saw the star. 8Then he sent them to Bethlehem. He said, "Go and look carefully for the child. When you find

---

ᵈ 1:21 **Jesus** The name Jesus means "the LORD (YAHWEH) saves."

ᵇ 1:23 Quote from Isa. 7:14.

him, come tell me. Then I can go worship him too."

⁹After the wise men heard the king, they left. They saw the same star they had seen in the east, and they followed it. The star went before them until it stopped above the place where the child was. ¹⁰They were very happy and excited to see the star.

¹¹The wise men came to the house where the child was with his mother Mary. They bowed down and worshiped him. Then they opened the boxes of gifts they had brought for him. They gave him treasures of gold, frankincense,* and myrrh.* ¹²But God warned the wise men in a dream not to go back to Herod. So they went home to their own country a different way.

Jesus' Parents Take Him to Egypt

¹³After the wise men* left, an angel from the Lord came to Joseph in a dream. The angel said, "Get up! Take the child with his mother and escape to Egypt. Herod* wants to kill the child and will soon start looking for him. Stay in Egypt until I tell you to come back."

¹⁴So Joseph got ready and left for Egypt with the child and the mother. They left during the night. ¹⁵Joseph stayed in Egypt until Herod died. This gave full meaning to what the Lord said through the prophet*: "I called my son to come out of Egypt."ᵃ

Herod Kills the Baby Boys in Bethlehem

¹⁶Herod* saw that the wise men* had fooled him, and he was very angry. So he gave an order to kill all the baby boys in Bethlehem and the whole area around Bethlehem. Herod had learned

from the wise men the time the baby was born. It was now two years from that time. So he said to kill all the boys who were two years old and younger. ¹⁷This gave full meaning to what God said through the prophet* Jeremiah:

¹⁸ "A sound was heard in
  Ramah—
  bitter crying and great
  sadness.
Rachel cries for her children,
  and she cannot be comforted,
  because her children are
  gone."   *Jeremiah 31:15*

Joseph and Mary Return From Egypt

¹⁹While Joseph was in Egypt, Herod* died. An angel from the Lord came to Joseph in a dream ²⁰and said, "Get up! Take the child with his mother and go to Israel. Those who were trying to kill the child are now dead."

²¹So Joseph took the child and the mother and went to Israel. ²²But he heard that Archelaus was now king in Judea. Archelaus became king when his father Herod died. So Joseph was afraid to go there. Then, after being warned in a dream, he went away to the area of Galilee. ²³He went to a town called Nazareth and lived there. This gave full meaning to what God said through the prophets.* God said the Messiahᵇ would be called a Nazarene.ᶜ

John Prepares the Way for Jesus

(Mk. 1:1–8; Lk. 3:1–9, 15–17; Jn. 1:19–28)

3 ¹When it was the right time, John the Baptizer* began

ᵃ **2:15** Quote from Hos. 11:1.

ᵇ **2:23 the Messiah** Literally, "he." See "MESSIAH" in the Word List.

ᶜ **2:23 Nazarene** A person from the city of Nazareth. This name sounds like the Hebrew word for "branch." So Matthew may be referring to the promise of a "branch" of David's family. See Isa. 11:1.

telling people a message from God. This was out in the desert area of Judea. ²John said, "Change your hearts and lives, because God's kingdom* is now very near.*" ³John is the one Isaiah the prophet* was talking about when he said,

"There is someone shouting in the desert:

'Prepare the way for the Lord.
Make the road straight for
    him.'"   *Isaiah 40:3*

⁴John's clothes were made from camel's hair, and he had a leather belt around his waist. For food, he ate locusts* and wild honey. ⁵People came to John from Jerusalem and the rest of Judea and from all the areas along the Jordan River. ⁶They confessed the bad things they had done, and John baptized* them in the Jordan.

⁷Many Pharisees* and Sadducees* came to where John was baptizing people. When John saw them, he said, "You are all snakes! Who warned you to run from God's judgment that is coming? ⁸Change your hearts! And show by the way you live that you have changed. ⁹I know what you are thinking. You want to say, 'but Abraham* is our father!' That means nothing. I tell you, God could make children for Abraham from these rocks. ¹⁰The ax is now ready to cut down the trees.*b* Every tree that does not produce good fruit will be cut down and thrown into the fire.

¹¹"I baptize you with water to show that you have changed your hearts and lives. But there is someone coming later who is able to do more than I can. I am not good enough to be the slave who takes off his sandals. He will baptize you with the Holy Spirit* and with fire. ¹²He will come ready to clean the grain.*c* He will separate the good grain from the straw, and he will put the good part into his barn. Then he will burn the useless part with a fire that cannot be stopped."

Jesus Is Baptized by John
(Mk. 1:9–11; Lk. 3:21–22)

¹³Then Jesus came from Galilee to the Jordan River. He came to John, wanting John to baptize* him. ¹⁴But John tried to stop him. John said, "Why do you come to me to be baptized? I should be baptized by you!"

¹⁵Jesus answered, "Let it be this way for now. We should do whatever God says is right." Then John agreed.

¹⁶So Jesus was baptized. As soon as he came up out of the water, the sky opened, and he saw God's Spirit coming down on him like a dove. ¹⁷A voice from heaven said, "This is my Son, the one I love. I am very pleased with him."

The Temptation of Jesus
(Mk. 1:12–13; Lk. 4:1–13)

4 ¹Then the Spirit* led Jesus into the desert. He was taken there to be tempted by the devil. ²Jesus ate nothing for 40 days and nights. After this, he was very hungry. ³The devil*d* came to tempt him and said, "If you are the Son of God, tell these rocks to become bread."

---

a **3:2 is now very near** Or "is coming soon" or "has come."
b **3:10 trees** The people who don't obey God. They are like "trees" that will be cut down.

c **3:12 clean the grain** Meaning that Jesus will separate the good people from those who are bad.
d **4:3 The devil** Literally, "The tempter."

[4]Jesus answered him, "The Scriptures* say,

'It is not just bread that keeps people alive.
Their lives depend on what God says.'"   *Deuteronomy 8:3*

[5]Then the devil led Jesus to the holy* city of Jerusalem and put him on a high place at the edge of the Temple* area. [6]He said to Jesus, "If you are the Son of God, jump off, because the Scriptures say,

'God will command his angels to help you,
and their hands will catch you,
so that you will not hit your foot on a rock.'"   *Psalm 91:11–12*

[7]Jesus answered, "The Scriptures also say,

'You must not test the Lord your God.'"   *Deuteronomy 6:16*

[8]Then the devil led Jesus to the top of a very high mountain and showed him all the kingdoms of the world and all the wonderful things in them. [9]The devil said, "If you will bow down and worship me, I will give you all these things."

[10]Jesus said to him, "Get away from me, Satan*! The Scriptures say,

'You must worship the Lord your God.
Serve only him!'"
     Deuteronomy 6:13

[11]So the devil left him. Then some angels came to Jesus and helped him.

Jesus Begins His Work in Galilee
(Mk. 1:14–15; Lk. 4:14–15)

[12]Jesus heard that John was put in prison, so he went back to Galilee. [13]But he did not stay in Nazareth. He went to live in Capernaum, a town near Lake Galilee in the area near Zebulun and Naphtali. [14]He did this to give full meaning to what the prophet* Isaiah said:

[15] "Listen, land of Zebulun and land of Naphtali,
lands by the road that goes to the sea, the area past the Jordan River—
Galilee, where those from other nations live.
[16] The people who live in spiritual darkness
have seen a great light.
The light has shined for those who live in the land that is as dark as a grave."   *Isaiah 9:1–2*

[17]From that time Jesus began to tell people his message: "Change your hearts and lives, because God's kingdom* is now very near.[a]"

Jesus Chooses Some Followers
(Mk. 1:16–20; Lk. 5:1–11)

[18]As Jesus was walking by Lake Galilee, he saw two brothers, Simon (called Peter) and Simon's brother Andrew. These brothers were fishermen, and they were fishing in the lake with a net. [19]Jesus said to them, "Come, follow me, and I will make you a different kind of fishermen. You will bring in people, not fish." [20]Simon and Andrew immediately left their nets and followed him.

[21]Jesus continued walking by Lake Galilee. He saw two other brothers, James and John, the sons of Zebedee. They were in a boat with their father Zebedee. They were preparing their nets to catch fish. Jesus told the brothers to come with him. [22]So they immediately left the boat and their father, and they followed Jesus.

a 4:17 is now very near Or "is coming soon" or "has come."

Jesus Teaches and Heals the People
(Lk. 6:17–19)

23Jesus went everywhere in the country of Galilee. He taught in the synagogues* and told the Good News about God's kingdom.* And he healed all the people's diseases and sicknesses. 24The news about Jesus spread all over Syria, and people brought to him all those who were sick. They were suffering from different kinds of diseases and pain. Some had demons* inside them, some suffered from seizures, and some were paralyzed. Jesus healed them all. 25Large crowds followed him—people from Galilee, the Ten Towns,* Jerusalem, Judea, and the area across the Jordan River.

Jesus Teaches the People
(Lk. 6:20–23)

5 1When Jesus saw the crowds of people there, he went up on a hill and sat down. His followers came and sat next to him. 2Then Jesus began teaching the people. He said,

3 "Great blessings belong to
    those who know they are
    spiritually in need.*a*
God's kingdom* belongs to
    them.
4 Great blessings belong to those
    who are sad now.
God will comfort them.
5 Great blessings belong to
    those who are humble.
They will be given the land
    God promised.*b*

6 Great blessings belong to those
    who want to do right more
    than anything else.*c*
God will fully satisfy them.
7 Great blessings belong to
    those who show mercy to
    others.
Mercy will be given to them.
8 Great blessings belong to those
    whose thoughts are pure.
They will be with God.
9 Great blessings belong to
    those who work to bring
    peace.
God will call them his sons
    and daughters.
10 Great blessings belong
    to those who suffer
    persecution for doing what
    is right.
God's kingdom belongs to
    them.

11"People will insult you and hurt you. They will lie and say all kinds of evil things about you because you follow me. But when they do that, know that great blessings belong to you. 12Be happy about it. Be very glad because you have a great reward waiting for you in heaven. People did these same bad things to the prophets* who lived before you.

You Are Like Salt and Light
(Mk. 9:50; 4:21; Lk. 14:34–35; 8:16)

13"You are the salt of the earth. But if the salt loses its taste, it cannot be made salty again. Salt is useless if it loses its salty taste. It will be thrown out where people will just walk on it.
14"You are the light that shines for the world to see. You are like a city built on a hill that cannot be hidden. 15People don't hide a

---

a **5:3 those ... in need** Literally, "the poor in spirit."

b **5:5 They will ... promised** This is the meaning of these words in Ps. 37:11. Here, they probably refer to a spiritual "promised land," but they can also mean "The earth will belong to them."

c **5:6 want ... more than anything else** Literally, "hunger and thirst for righteousness."

7 MATTHEW 5:32

lamp under a bowl. They put it on a lampstand. Then the light shines for everyone in the house. ¹⁶In the same way, you should be a light for other people. Live so that they will see the good things you do and praise your Father in heaven.

Jesus and the Old Testament Writings

¹⁷"Don't think that I have come to destroy the Law of Moses* or the teaching of the prophets.* I have come not to destroy their teachings but to give full meaning to them. ¹⁸I assure you that nothing will disappear from the law until heaven and earth are gone. The law will not lose even the smallest letter or the smallest part of a letter until it has all been done.

¹⁹"A person should obey every command in the law, even one that does not seem important. Whoever refuses to obey any command and teaches others not to obey it will be the least important in God's kingdom.* But whoever obeys the law and teaches others to obey it will be great in God's kingdom. ²⁰I tell you that you must do better than the teachers of the law and the Pharisees.* If you are not more pleasing to God than they are, you will never enter God's kingdom.

Jesus Teaches About Anger

²¹"You have heard that it was said to our people long ago, 'You must not murder anyone.ᵃ Any person who commits murder will be judged.' ²²But I tell you, don't be angry with anyone. If you are angry with others, you will be judged. And if you insult someone, you will be judged by the high court. And if you call someone a

fool, you will be in danger of the fire of hell.

²³"So, what if you are offering your gift at the altar* and remember that someone has something against you? ²⁴Leave your gift there and go make peace with that person. Then come and offer your gift.

²⁵"If anyone wants to take you to court, make friends with them quickly. Try to do that before you get to the court. If you don't, they might hand you over to the judge. And the judge will hand you over to a guard, who will throw you into jail. ²⁶I assure you that you will not leave there until you have paid everything you owe.

Jesus Teaches About Sexual Sin

²⁷"You have heard that it was said, 'You must not commit adultery.*'ᵇ ²⁸But I tell you that if a man looks at a woman and wants to sin sexually with her, he has already committed that sin with her in his mind. ²⁹If your right eye makes you sin, take it out and throw it away. It is better to lose one part of your body than to have your whole body thrown into hell. ³⁰If your right hand makes you sin, cut it off and throw it away. It is better to lose one part of your body than for your whole body to go into hell.

Jesus Teaches About Divorce
(Mt. 19:9; Mk. 10:11–12; Lk. 16:18)

³¹"It was also said, 'Any man who divorces his wife must give her a written notice of divorce.'ᶜ ³²But I tell you that any man who divorces his wife, except for the problem of sexual sin, is causing his wife to be guilty of adultery.*

ᵃ **5:21** Quote from Ex. 20:13; Deut. 5:17.
ᵇ **5:27** Quote from Ex. 20:14; Deut. 5:18.
ᶜ **5:31** Quote from Deut. 24:1.

And whoever marries a divorced woman is guilty of adultery.

Jesus Teaches About Making Promises

33"You have heard that it was said to our people long ago, 'When you make a vow,* you must not break your promise. Keep the vows that you make to the Lord.'*a* 34But I tell you, when you make a promise, don't try to make it stronger with a vow. Don't make a vow using the name of heaven, because heaven is God's throne. 35Don't make a vow using the name of the earth, because the earth belongs to him.*b* Don't make a vow using the name of Jerusalem, because it also belongs to him, the great King. 36And don't even say that your own head is proof that you will keep your promise. You cannot make one hair on your head white or black. 37Say only 'yes' if you mean 'yes,' and say only 'no' if you mean 'no.' If you say more than that, it is from the Evil One.*

Jesus Teaches About Fighting Back

(Lk. 6:29–30)

38"You have heard that it was said, 'An eye for an eye, and a tooth for a tooth.'*c* 39But I tell you, don't fight back against someone who wants to do harm to you. If they hit you on the right cheek, let them hit the other cheek too. 40If anyone wants to sue you in court and take your shirt, let them have your coat too. 41If a soldier forces you to walk with him one mile,*d* go with him two. 42Give to anyone who asks you for something. Don't refuse to give to anyone who wants to borrow from you.

Love Your Enemies

(Lk. 6:27–28, 32–36)

43"You have heard that it was said, 'Love your neighbor*e* and hate your enemy.' 44But I tell you, love your enemies. Pray for those who treat you badly. 45If you do this, you will be children who are truly like your Father in heaven. He lets the sun rise for all people, whether they are good or bad. He sends rain to those who do right and to those who do wrong. 46If you love only those who love you, why should you get a reward for that? Even the tax collectors* do that. 47And if you are nice only to your friends, you are no better than anyone else. Even the people who don't know God are nice to their friends. 48What I am saying is that you must be perfect, just as your Father in heaven is perfect.

Jesus Teaches About Giving

6 1"Be careful! When you do something good, don't do it in front of others so that they will see you. If you do that, you will have no reward from your Father in heaven.

2"When you give to those who are poor, don't announce that you are giving. Don't be like the hypocrites.* When they are in the synagogues* and on the streets, they blow trumpets before they give so that people will see them. They want everyone to praise them. The truth is, that's all the reward they will get. 3So when you give to the poor, don't let anyone know what you are doing.*f* 4Your giving

---

a **5:33** See Lev. 19:12; Num. 30:2; Deut. 23:21.

b **5:35 the earth . . . him** Literally, "it is the footstool of his feet."

c **5:38** Quote from Ex. 21:24; Lev. 24:20.

d **5:41 one mile** Literally, "one *milion*," about 1.5 km.

e **5:43** Quote from Lev. 19:18.

f **6:3 don't . . . doing** Literally, "don't let your left hand know what your right hand is doing."

should be done in private. Your Father can see what is done in private, and he will reward you.

Jesus Teaches About Prayer
(Lk. 11:2–4)

⁵"When you pray, don't be like the hypocrites.* They love to stand in the synagogues* and on the street corners and pray loudly. They want people to see them. The truth is, that's all the reward they will get. ⁶But when you pray, you should go into your room and close the door. Then pray to your Father. He is there in that private place. He can see what is done in private, and he will reward you.

⁷"And when you pray, don't be like the people who don't know God. They say the same things again and again. They think that if they say it enough, their god will hear them. ⁸Don't be like them. Your Father knows what you need before you ask him. ⁹So this is how you should pray:

'Our Father in heaven,
    we pray that your name will
    always be kept holy.*
¹⁰ We pray that your kingdom*
    will come—
    that what you want will be
    done here on earth, the
    same as in heaven.
¹¹ Give us the food we need for
    today.
¹² Forgive our sins,
    just as we have forgiven
    those who did wrong to us.
¹³ Don't let us be tempted,
    but save us from the Evil
    One.*'ᵃ

¹⁴Yes, if you forgive others for the wrongs they do to you, then your Father in heaven will also forgive your wrongs. ¹⁵But if you don't forgive others, then your Father in heaven will not forgive the wrongs you do.

Jesus Teaches About Fasting

¹⁶"When you fast,* don't make yourselves look sad like the hypocrites.* They put a look of suffering on their faces so that people will see they are fasting. The truth is, that's all the reward they will get. ¹⁷So when you fast, wash your face and make yourself look nice. ¹⁸Then no one will know you are fasting, except your Father, who is with you even in private. He can see what is done in private, and he will reward you.

You Cannot Serve Two Masters
(Lk. 12:33–34; 11:34–36; 16:13)

¹⁹"Don't save treasures for yourselves here on earth. Moths and rust will destroy them. And thieves can break into your house and steal them. ²⁰Instead, save your treasures in heaven, where they cannot be destroyed by moths or rust and where thieves cannot break in and steal them. ²¹Your heart will be where your treasure is.

²²"The only source of light for the body is the eye. If you look at people and want to help them, you will be full of light.* ²³But if you look at people in a selfish way, you will be full of darkness.* And if the only light you have is really darkness, you have the worst kind of darkness.ᵇ

²⁴"You cannot serve two masters at the same time. You will

ᵃ **6:13** Some Greek copies add: "For the kingdom and the power and the glory belong to you forever and ever. Amen."

ᵇ **6:23** Literally, "²²The lamp of the body is the eye. So, if your eye is pure, your whole body will be full of light. ²³But if your eye is evil, your whole body will be dark. So, if the light in you is darkness, how much is the darkness."

hate one and love the other, or you will be loyal to one and not care about the other. You cannot serve God and Money*a* at the same time.

Put God's Kingdom First
(Lk. 12:22–34)

25"So I tell you, don't worry about the things you need to live—what you will eat, drink, or wear. Life is more important than food, and the body is more important than what you put on it. 26Look at the birds. They don't plant, harvest, or save food in barns, but your heavenly Father feeds them. Don't you know you are worth much more than they are? 27You cannot add any time to your life by worrying about it.

28"And why do you worry about clothes? Look at the wildflowers in the field. See how they grow. They don't work or make clothes for themselves. 29But I tell you that even Solomon, the great and rich king, was not dressed as beautifully as one of these flowers. 30If God makes what grows in the field so beautiful, what do you think he will do for you? It's just grass—one day it's alive, and the next day someone throws it into a fire. But God cares enough to make it beautiful. Surely he will do much more for you. Your faith is so small!

31"Don't worry and say, 'What will we eat?' or 'What will we drink?' or 'What will we wear?' 32That's what those people who don't know God are always thinking about. Don't worry, because your Father in heaven knows that you need all these things. 33What you should want most is God's kingdom* and doing what he wants you to do. Then he will give you all these other things you need. 34So don't worry about tomorrow. Each day has enough trouble of its own. Tomorrow will have its own worries.

Be Careful About Criticizing Others
(Lk. 6:37–38, 41–42)

7 1"Don't judge others, and God will not judge you. 2If you judge others, you will be judged the same way you judge them. God will treat you the same way you treat others.

3"Why do you notice the small piece of dust that is in your friend's eye, but you don't notice the big piece of wood that is in your own? 4Why do you say to your friend, 'Let me take that piece of dust out of your eye'? Look at yourself first! You still have that big piece of wood in your own eye. 5You are a hypocrite*! First, take the wood out of your own eye. Then you will see clearly to get the dust out of your friend's eye.

6"Don't give something that is holy* to dogs. They will only turn and hurt you. And don't throw your pearls to pigs. They will only step on them.

Ask God for What You Need
(Lk. 11:9–13)

7"Continue to ask, and God will give to you. Continue to search, and you will find. Continue to knock, and the door will open for you. 8Yes, whoever continues to ask will receive. Whoever continues to look will find. And whoever continues to knock will have the door opened for them.

9"Do any of you have a son? If he asked for bread, would you give him a rock? 10Or if he asked for a fish, would you give him a

a **6:24 Money** Or "*mamona*," an Aramaic word meaning "wealth."

snake? Of course not! [11]You people are so bad, but you still know how to give good things to your children. So surely your heavenly Father will give good things to those who ask him.

A Very Important Rule

[12]"Do for others what you would want them to do for you. This is the meaning of the Law of Moses* and the teaching of the prophets.*

The Way to Heaven and the Way to Hell

(Lk. 13:24)

[13]"You can enter true life only through the narrow gate. The gate to hell is very wide, and there is plenty of room on the road that leads there. Many people go that way. [14]But the gate that opens the way to true life is narrow. And the road that leads there is hard to follow. Only a few people find it.

What People Do Shows What They Are

(Lk. 6:43–44; 13:25–27)

[15]"Be careful of false prophets.* They come to you and look gentle like sheep. But they are really dangerous like wolves. [16]You will know these people because of what they do. Good things don't come from people who are bad, just as grapes don't come from thornbushes, and figs don't come from thorny weeds. [17]In the same way, every good tree produces good fruit, and bad trees produce bad fruit. [18]A good tree cannot produce bad fruit, and a bad tree cannot produce good fruit. [19]Every tree that does not produce good fruit is cut down and thrown into the fire. [20]You will know these false people by what they do.[a]

[21]"Not everyone who calls me Lord will enter God's kingdom.*

a 7:20 by what they do Literally, "by their fruits."

The only people who will enter are those who do what my Father in heaven wants. [22]On that last Day* many will call me Lord. They will say, 'Lord, Lord, by the power of your name we spoke for God. And by your name we forced out demons* and did many miracles.*' [23]Then I will tell those people clearly, 'Get away from me, you people who do wrong. I never knew you.'

Two Kinds of People

(Lk. 6:47–49)

[24]"Whoever hears these teachings of mine and obeys them is like a wise man who built his house on rock. [25]It rained hard, the floods came, and the winds blew and beat against that house. But it did not fall because it was built on rock.

[26]"Whoever hears these teachings of mine and does not obey them is like a foolish man who built his house on sand. [27]It rained hard, the floods came, and the winds blew and beat against that house. And it fell with a loud crash."

[28]When Jesus finished speaking, the people were amazed at his teaching. [29]He did not teach like their teachers of the law. He taught like someone who has authority.

Jesus Heals a Sick Man

(Mk. 1:40–45; Lk. 5:12–16)

8 [1]Jesus came down from the hill, and a large crowd followed him. [2]Then a man sick with leprosy* came to him. The man bowed down before Jesus and said, "Lord, you have the power to heal me if you want."

[3]Jesus touched the man. He said, "I want to heal you. Be healed!" Immediately the man was healed

from his leprosy. ⁴Then Jesus said to him, "Don't tell anyone about what happened. But go and let the priest look at you.ᵃ And offer the gift that Moses* commanded for people who are made well. This will show everyone that you are healed."

Jesus Heals an Officer's Servant
(Lk. 7:1–10; Jn. 4:43–54)

⁵Jesus went to the city of Capernaum.* When he entered the city, an army officer* came to him and begged for help. ⁶The officer said, "Lord, my servant is very sick at home in bed. He can't move his body and has much pain."

⁷Jesus said to the officer, "I will go and heal him."

⁸The officer answered, "Lord, I am not good enough for you to come into my house. You need only to give the order, and my servant will be healed. ⁹I know this, because I understand authority. There are people who have authority over me, and I have soldiers under my authority. I tell one soldier, 'Go,' and he goes. I tell another soldier, 'Come,' and he comes. I say to my servant, 'Do this,' and my servant obeys me."

¹⁰When Jesus heard this, he was amazed. He said to those who were with him, "The truth is, this man has more faith than anyone I have found, even in Israel.* ¹¹Many people will come from the east and from the west. These people will sit and eat with Abraham,* Isaac,* and Jacob* in God's kingdom.* ¹²And those who should have the kingdom will be thrown out. They will be thrown outside into the darkness, where people will cry and grind their teeth with pain."

¹³Then Jesus said to the officer, "Go home. Your servant will be healed the way you believed he would." Right then his servant was healed.

Jesus Heals Many People
(Mk. 1:29–34; Lk. 4:38–41)

¹⁴Jesus went to Peter's house. He saw that Peter's mother-in-law was in bed with a high fever. ¹⁵He touched her hand, and the fever left her. Then she stood up and began to serve him.

¹⁶That evening people brought to Jesus many people who had demons* inside them. He spoke and the demons left the people. He healed all those who were sick. ¹⁷So Jesus made clear the full meaning of what Isaiah the prophet* said:

"He took away our diseases
and carried away our
sicknesses."   *Isaiah 53:4*

Following Jesus
(Lk. 9:57–62)

¹⁸When Jesus saw the crowd around him, he told his followers to go to the other side of the lake. ¹⁹Then a teacher of the law came to him and said, "Teacher, I will follow you any place you go."

²⁰Jesus said to him, "The foxes have holes to live in. The birds have nests. But the Son of Man* has no place to rest."

²¹Another of Jesus' followers said to him, "Lord, I will follow you too, but let me go and bury my father first."

²²But Jesus said to him, "Follow me, and let those who are dead bury their own dead."

Jesus' Followers See His Power
(Mk. 4:35–41; Lk. 8:22–25)

²³Jesus got into a boat, and his followers went with him. ²⁴After

---

a **8:4 let the priest look at you** The Law of Moses said a priest must decide when a person with leprosy was well.

the boat left the shore, a very bad storm began on the lake. The waves covered the boat. But Jesus was sleeping. 25The followers went to him and woke him. They said, "Lord, save us! We will drown!" 26Jesus answered, "Why are you afraid? You don't have enough faith." Then he stood up and gave a command to the wind and the water. The wind stopped, and the lake became very calm. 27The men were amazed. They said, "What kind of man is this? Even the wind and the water obey him!"

Jesus Sends Demons Out of Two Men
(Mk. 5:1–20; Lk. 8:26–39)

28Jesus arrived at the other side of the lake in the country of the Gadarene*a* people. There, two men who had demons* inside them came to him. They lived in the burial caves and were so dangerous that no one could use the road by those caves. 29They came to Jesus and shouted, "What do you want with us, Son of God? Did you come here to punish us before the right time?"

30Near that place there was a large herd of pigs feeding. 31The demons begged Jesus, "If you make us leave these men, please send us into that herd of pigs." 32Jesus said to them, "Go!" So the demons left the men and went into the pigs. Then the whole herd of pigs ran down the hill into the lake, and all were drowned. 33The men who had the work of caring for the pigs ran away. They went into town and told the people everything

a 8:28 Gadarene From Gadara, an area southeast of Lake Galilee.

that happened, especially about the men who had the demons. 34Then the whole town went out to see Jesus. When the people saw him, they begged him to leave their area.

Jesus Heals a Crippled Man
(Mk. 2:1–12; Lk. 5:17–26)

9 1Jesus got into a boat and went back across the lake to his own town. 2Some people brought to him a man who was paralyzed and was lying on a mat. Jesus saw that these people had much faith. So he said to the paralyzed man, "Young man, you will be glad to hear this. Your sins are forgiven." 3Some of the teachers of the law heard what Jesus said. They said to themselves, "What an insult to God for this man to say that!" 4Jesus knew what they were thinking. So he said, "Why are you thinking such evil thoughts? 5-6The Son of Man* has power on earth to forgive sins. But how can I prove this to you? Maybe you are thinking it was easy for me to say, 'Your sins are forgiven.' There's no proof that it really happened. But what if I say to the man, 'Stand up and walk'? Then you will be able to see that I really have this power." So Jesus said to the paralyzed man, "Stand up. Take your mat and go home." 7The man stood up and went home. 8The people saw this and they were amazed. They praised God for letting someone have such power.

Matthew (Levi) Follows Jesus
(Mk. 2:13–17; Lk. 5:27–32)

9When Jesus was leaving, he saw a man named Matthew sitting at the place for collecting taxes. Jesus said to him, "Follow me." So he got up and followed Jesus.

10Jesus ate dinner at Matthew's house. Many tax collectors* and others with bad reputations came and ate with him and his followers. 11The Pharisees* saw that Jesus was eating with these people. They asked his followers, "Why does your teacher eat with tax collectors and other sinners?"

12Jesus heard them say this. So he said to them, "It is the sick people who need a doctor, not those who are healthy. 13You need to go and learn what this Scripture means: 'I don't want animal sacrifices; I want you to show kindness to people.'ᵃ I did not come to invite good people. I came to invite sinners."

Jesus Is Not Like Other Religious Leaders
(Mk. 2:18–22; Lk. 5:33–39)

14Then the followers of John* came to Jesus and said, "We and the Pharisees* fast* often, but your followers don't ever fast. Why?"

15Jesus answered, "At a wedding the friends of the bridegroom* are not sad while he is with them. They cannot fast then. But the time will come when the bridegroom will be taken from them. Then they will fast.

16"When someone sews a patch over a hole in an old coat, they never use a piece of cloth that has not already been shrunk. If they do, the patch will shrink and pull away from the coat. Then the hole will be worse. 17Also, people never pour new wine into old wineskins.* They would break, the wine would spill out, and the wineskins would be ruined. People always put new wine into new wineskins, which won't break, and the wine stays good."

Jesus Gives Life to a Dead Girl and Heals a Sick Woman
(Mk. 5:21–43; Lk. 8:40–56)

18While Jesus was still talking, a leader of the synagogue* came to him. The leader bowed down before him and said, "My daughter has just died. But if you will come and touch her with your hand, she will live again."

19So Jesus and his followers went with the man.

20On the way, there was a woman who had been bleeding for twelve years. She came close behind Jesus and touched the bottom of his coat. 21She was thinking, "If I can touch his coat, I will be healed."

22Jesus turned and saw the woman. He said, "Be happy, dear woman. You are made well because you believed." Then the woman was healed.

23Jesus continued going with the Jewish leader and went into the leader's house. He saw people there who make music for funerals. And he saw a crowd of people crying loudly. 24Jesus said, "Go away. The girl is not dead. She is only sleeping." But the people laughed at him. 25After the people were put out of the house, Jesus went into the girl's room. He held the girl's hand, and the girl stood up. 26The news about this spread all around the area.

Jesus Heals More People

27As Jesus was going away from there, two blind men followed him. They said loudly, "Show kindness to us, Son of David.*"

28Jesus went inside, and the blind men went with him. He asked them, "Do you believe that

a 9:13 Quote from Hos. 6:6.

I am able to make you see again?" They answered, "Yes, Lord, we believe."

29Then Jesus touched their eyes and said, "You believe that I can make you see again, so it will happen." 30Then the men were able to see. Jesus gave them a strong warning. He said, "Don't tell anyone about this." 31But they left and spread the news about Jesus all around that area.

32As these two men were leaving, some people brought another man to Jesus. This man could not talk because he had a demon* inside him. 33Jesus forced the demon out, and the man was able to talk. The people were amazed and said, "We have never seen anything like this in Israel.*"

34But the Pharisees* said, "The ruler of demons is the one that gives him power to force demons out."

Jesus Feels Sorry for the People

35Jesus traveled through all the towns and villages. He taught in their synagogues* and told people the Good News about God's kingdom.* He healed all kinds of diseases and sicknesses. 36Jesus saw the many people and felt sorry for them because they were worried and helpless—like sheep without a shepherd to lead them. 37Jesus said to his followers, "There is such a big harvest of people to bring in. But there are only a few workers to help harvest them. 38God owns the harvest. Ask him to send more workers to help gather his harvest."

Jesus Sends His Apostles on a Mission
(Mk. 3:13–19; 6:7–13; Lk. 6:12–16; 9:1–6)

10 1Jesus called his twelve followers together. He gave them power over evil spirits and

power to heal every kind of disease and sickness. 2These are the names of the twelve apostles*:
  Simon (also called Peter),
  Andrew, the brother of Peter,
  James, the son of Zebedee,
  John, the brother of James,
3 Philip,
  Bartholomew,
  Thomas,
  Matthew, the tax collector,*
  James, the son of Alphaeus,
  Thaddaeus,
4 Simon, the Zealot,*
  Judas Iscariot (the one who handed Jesus over to his enemies).

5Jesus sent the twelve men out with these instructions: "Don't go to the non-Jewish people. And don't go into any town where the Samaritans* live. 6But go to the people of Israel.* They are like sheep that are lost. 7When you go, tell them this: 'God's kingdom* is now very near.ª' 8Heal the sick. Bring the dead back to life. Heal the people who have leprosy.* And force demons* out of people. I give you these powers freely, so help others freely. 9Don't carry any money with you—gold or silver or copper. 10Don't carry a bag. Take only the clothes and sandals you are wearing. And don't take a walking stick. A worker should be given what he needs.

11"When you enter a city or town, find some worthy person there and stay in his home until you leave. 12When you enter that home, say, 'Peace be with you.' 13If the people in that home welcome you, they are worthy of your peace. May they have the peace

ª 10:7 is now very near Or "is coming soon" or "has come."

you wished for them. But if they don't welcome you, they are not worthy of your peace. Take back the peace you wished for them. ¹⁴And if the people in a home or a town refuse to welcome you or listen to you, then leave that place and shake the dust off your feet.ᵃ ¹⁵I can assure you that on the judgment day it will be worse for that town than for the people of Sodom* and Gomorrah.*

Jesus Warns About Troubles

(Mk. 13:9–13; Lk. 21:12–17)

¹⁶"Listen! I am sending you, and you will be like sheep among wolves. So be smart like snakes. But also be like doves and don't hurt anyone. ¹⁷Be careful! There are people who will arrest you and take you to be judged. They will whip you in their synagogues.* ¹⁸You will be taken to stand before governors and kings. People will do this to you because you follow me. You will tell about me to those kings and governors and to the non-Jewish people. ¹⁹When you are arrested, don't worry about what to say or how you should say it. At that time you will be given the words to say. ²⁰It will not really be you speaking; the Spirit of your Father will be speaking through you.

²¹"Brothers will turn against their own brothers and hand them over to be killed. Fathers will hand over their own children to be killed. Children will fight against their own parents and will have them killed. ²²Everyone will hate you because you follow me. But the one who remains faithful to the end will

be saved. ²³When you are treated badly in one city, go to another city. I promise you that you will not finish going to all the cities of Israel before the Son of Man* comes again.

²⁴"Students are not better than their teacher. Servants are not better than their master. ²⁵Students should be happy to be treated the same as their teacher. And servants should be happy to be treated the same as their master. If those people call me 'the ruler of demons,' and I am the head of the family,ᵇ then it is even more certain that they will insult you, the members of the family!

Fear God, Not People

(Lk. 12:2–7)

²⁶"So don't be afraid of those people. Everything that is hidden will be shown. Everything that is secret will be made known. ²⁷I tell you all this secretly,ᶜ but I want you to tell it publicly.ᵈ Whatever I tell you privately,ᵉ you should shout for everyone to hear.ᶠ

²⁸"Don't be afraid of people. They can kill the body, but they cannot kill the soul. The only one you should fear is God, the one who can send the body and the soul to be destroyed in hell. ²⁹When birds are sold, two small birds cost only a penny. But not even one of those little birds can die without your Father knowing it. ³⁰God even knows how many hairs are on your head. ³¹So don't

---

ᵃ 10:14 **shake the dust off your feet** A warning. It would show that they were finished talking to these people.

ᵇ 10:25 **call me ... family** Literally, "call the head of the household Beelzebul." See verse 9:34.

ᶜ 10:27 **secretly** Literally, "in the dark."

ᵈ 10:27 **publicly** Literally, "in the light."

ᵉ 10:27 **privately** Literally, "in the ear."

ᶠ 10:27 **for everyone to hear** Literally, "on the housetops."

be afraid. You are worth more than a whole flock of birds.

Don't Be Ashamed of Your Faith
(Lk. 12:8–9)

32"If you stand before others and are willing to say you believe in me, then I will tell my Father in heaven that you belong to me. 33But if you stand before others and say you do not believe in me, then I will tell my Father in heaven that you do not belong to me.

Following Jesus May Bring You Trouble
(Lk. 12:51–53; 14:26–27)

34"Do not think that I have come to bring peace to the earth. I did not come to bring peace. I came to bring trouble.ᵃ 35I have come to make this happen:
'A son will turn against his father.
A daughter will turn against her mother.
A daughter-in-law will turn against her mother-in-law.
36 Even members of your own family will be your enemies.'   *Micah 7:6*
37"Those who love their father or mother more than they love me are not worthy of me. And those who love their son or daughter more than they love me are not worthy of me. 38Those who will not accept the cross* that is given to them when they follow me are not worthy of me. 39Those who try to keep the life they have will lose it. But those who give up their life for me will find true life.

God Will Bless Those Who Welcome You
(Mk. 9:41)

40"Whoever accepts you also accepts me. And whoever accepts me accepts the one who sent me. 41Whoever accepts a prophet* because he is a prophet will get the same reward a prophet gets. And whoever accepts a godly person just because that person is godly will get the same reward a godly person gets. 42Whoever helps any of these little ones because they are my followers will definitely get a reward, even if they only give them a cup of cold water."

John Sends Men to Ask Jesus a Question
(Lk. 7:18–35)

11 1When Jesus finished these instructions for his twelve followers, he left there. He went to the towns in Galilee to teach the people and tell them God's message.

2When John was in prison, he heard about the things that were happening—things the Messiah* would do. So he sent some of his followers to Jesus. 3They asked him, "Are you the one we have been expecting, or should we wait for someone else?"

4Jesus answered, "Go tell John what you have heard and seen: 5The blind can see. The crippled can walk. People with leprosy* are healed. The deaf can hear. The dead are brought back to life. And the Good News* is being told to the poor. 6Great blessings belong to those who don't have a problem accepting me."

7When John's followers left, Jesus began talking to the people about John. He said, "What did you people go out to the desert to see? Someone who is weak, like a stem of grassᵇ blowing in the wind? 8Really, what did you expect to see? Someone dressed in fine clothes? Of course not. People

ᵃ **10:34 trouble** Literally, "a sword."

ᵇ **11:7 stem of grass** Literally, "reed."

who wear fine clothes are all in kings' palaces. 9So what did you go out to see? A prophet*? Yes, John is a prophet. But I tell you, he is more than that. 10This Scripture* was written about him:

> 'Listen! I will send my
> messenger ahead of you.
> He will prepare the way for
> you.'   *Malachi 3:1*

11"The truth is that John the Baptizer* is greater than anyone who has ever come into this world. But even the least important person in God's kingdom* is greater than John. 12Since the time John the Baptizer came until now, God's kingdom has been going forward strongly.a And people have been trying to take control of it by force. 13Before John came, the Law of Moses* and all the prophets told about the things that would happen. 14And if you believe what they said, then John is Elijah.b He is the one they said would come. 15You people who hear me, listen!

16"What can I say about the people who live today? What are they like? The people today are like children sitting in the marketplace. One group of children calls to the other group,

> 17 'We played flute music for you,
> but you did not dance;
> we sang a funeral song,
> but you were not sad.'

18Why do I say people are like that? Because John came, not eating like other people or drinking wine, and people say, 'He has a demon* inside him.' 19The Son of Man* came eating and drinking, and people say, 'Look at him!

---

a **11:12 has been ... strongly** Or "has suffered violence."
b **11:14 Elijah** See Mal. 4:5–6.

He eats too much and drinks too much wine. He's a friend of tax collectors* and other sinners.' But wisdom is shown to be right by what it does."

Jesus Warns People Who Refuse to Believe
(Lk. 10:13–15)

20Then Jesus criticized the cities where he did most of his miracles.* He criticized these cities because the people there did not change their lives and stop sinning. 21Jesus said, "It will be bad for you Chorazin*! It will be bad for you Bethsaida*! I did many miracles in you. If these same miracles had happened in Tyre* and Sidon,* the people there would have changed their lives a long time ago. They would have worn sackcloth* and put ashes on themselves to show that they were sorry for their sins. 22But I tell you, on the day of judgment it will be worse for you than for Tyre and Sidon.

23"And you, Capernaum,* will you be lifted up to heaven? No! You will be thrown down to the place of death. I did many miracles in you. If these same miracles had happened in Sodom,* the people there would have stopped sinning, and it would still be a city today. 24But I tell you, it will be worse for you in the day of judgment than for Sodom."

Jesus Offers Rest to His People
(Lk. 10:21–22)

25Then Jesus said, "I praise you, Father, Lord of heaven and earth. I am thankful that you have hidden these things from those who are so wise and so smart. But you have shown them to people who are like little children. 26Yes, Father, you did this because it's what you really wanted to do.

²⁷"My Father has given me everything. No one knows the Son—only the Father knows the Son. And no one knows the Father—only the Son knows the Father. And the only people who will know about the Father are those the Son chooses to tell. ²⁸"Come to me all of you who are tired from the heavy burden you have been forced to carry. I will give you rest. ²⁹Accept my teaching.ᵃ Learn from me. I am gentle and humble in spirit. And you will be able to get some rest. ³⁰Yes, the teaching that I ask you to accept is easy. The load I give you to carry is light."

Jesus Is Lord Over the Sabbath Day
(Mk. 2:23–28; Lk. 6:1–5)

12 ¹About that same time, Jesus was walking through the fields of grain on a Sabbath* day. His followers were with him, and they were hungry. So they began to pick the grain and eat it. ²The Pharisees* saw this. They said to Jesus, "Look! Your followers are doing something that is against the law to do on the Sabbath day."

³Jesus said to them, "You have read what David* did when he and those with him were hungry. ⁴David went into God's house. He and those with him ate the bread that was offered to God. It was against the law for David or those with him to eat that bread. Only the priests were allowed to eat it. ⁵And you have read in the Law of Moses* that on every Sabbath day the priests at the Temple* break the law about the Sabbath

day. But they are not wrong for doing that. ⁶I tell you that there is something here that is greater than the Temple. ⁷The Scriptures* say, 'I don't want animal sacrifices; I want you to show kindness to people.'ᵇ You don't really know what that means. If you understood it, you would not judge those who have done nothing wrong.

⁸"The Son of Man* is Lord over the Sabbath day."

Jesus Heals a Man on the Sabbath Day
(Mk. 3:1–6; Lk. 6:6–11)

⁹Jesus went from there to their synagogue.* ¹⁰In the synagogue there was a man with a crippled hand. Some Jews there were looking for a reason to accuse Jesus of doing wrong. So they asked him, "Is it right to heal on the Sabbath* day?"ᶜ

¹¹Jesus answered, "If any of you has a sheep and it falls into a ditch on the Sabbath day, you will take the sheep and help it out of the ditch. ¹²Surely a man is more important than a sheep. So it is right to do good on the Sabbath day."

¹³Then Jesus said to the man with the crippled hand, "Hold out your hand." The man held out his hand, and it became well again, the same as the other hand. ¹⁴But the Pharisees* left and made plans to kill Jesus.

Jesus Is God's Chosen Servant
¹⁵Jesus knew what the Pharisees* were planning. So he left that place, and many people followed him. He healed all who were sick, ¹⁶but he warned them not to tell others who he was. ¹⁷This was to

ᵃ **11:29 Accept my teaching** Literally, "Take my yoke upon you." A yoke was put on the neck of a work animal for pulling a load. It was a Jewish symbol for the law. See Acts 15:10; Gal. 5:1.

ᵇ **12:7** Quote from Hos. 6:6.
ᶜ **12:10 "Is it right … day"** It was against Jewish law to work on the Sabbath day.

give full meaning to what Isaiah the prophet* said when he spoke for God:

18 "Here is my servant,
  the one I have chosen.
He is the one I love,
  and I am very pleased with him.
I will fill him with my Spirit,*
  and he will bring justice to the nations.
19 He will not argue or shout;
  no one will hear his voice in the streets.
20 He will not break off even a bent stem of grass.*a
He will not put out even the weakest flame.
He will not give up until he has made justice victorious.
21 All people will hope in him."

Isaiah 42:1-4

Jesus' Power Is From God
(Mk. 3:20-30; Lk. 11:14-23; 12:10)

22Then some people brought a man to Jesus. This man was blind and could not talk, because he had a demon* inside him. Jesus healed the man, and he could talk and see. 23All the people were amazed at what Jesus did. They said, "Maybe he is the promised Son of David*!"

24When the Pharisees* heard this, they said, "This man uses the power of Satanb to force demons out of people. Satan is the ruler of demons."

25Jesus knew what the Pharisees were thinking. So he said to them, "Every kingdom that fights against itself will be destroyed. And every city or family that is divided against itself will not survive. 26So if Satan* forces out his own demons,c then he is fighting against himself, and his kingdom will not survive. 27You say that I use the power of Satan to force out demons. If that is true, then what power do your people use when they force out demons? So your own people will prove that you are wrong. 28But I use the power of God's Spirit to force out demons, and this shows that God's kingdom* has come to you. 29Whoever wants to enter a strong man's house and steal his things must first tie him up. Then they can steal the things from his house. 30Whoever is not with me is against me. And anyone who does not work with me is working against me.

31"So I tell you, people can be forgiven for every sinful thing they do and for every bad thing they say against God. But anyone who speaks against the Holy Spirit* will not be forgiven. 32You can even speak against the Son of Man* and be forgiven. But anyone who speaks against the Holy Spirit will never be forgiven—not now or in the future.

What You Do Shows What You Are
(Lk. 6:43-45)

33"If you want good fruit, you must make the tree good. If your tree is not good, it will have bad fruit. A tree is known by the kind of fruit it produces. 34You snakes! You are so evil. How can you say anything good? What people say with their mouths comes from what fills their hearts. 35Those who are good have good things saved in their hearts. That's why

---

a 12:20 **stem of grass** Literally, "reed."
b 12:24 **Satan** Literally, "Beelzebul" (the devil). Also in verse 27.

c 12:26 **if Satan ... demons** Literally, "if Satan forces out Satan."

they say good things. But those who are evil have hearts full of evil, and that's why they say things that are evil. ³⁶I tell you that everyone will have to answer for all the careless things they have said. This will happen on the day of judgment. ³⁷Your words will be used to judge you. What you have said will show whether you are right or whether you are guilty."

Some People Doubt Jesus' Authority
(Mk. 8:11–12; Lk. 11:29–32)

³⁸Then some of the Pharisees* and teachers of the law answered Jesus. They said, "Teacher, we want to see you do a miracle* as a sign from God."

³⁹Jesus answered, "Evil and sinful people are the ones who want to see a miracle as a sign. But no miracle will be done to prove anything to them. The only sign will be the miracle that happened to the prophet* Jonah.[a] ⁴⁰Jonah was in the stomach of the big fish for three days and three nights. In the same way, the Son of Man* will be in the grave three days and three nights. ⁴¹On the judgment day, you people who live now will be compared with the people from Nineveh,[b] and they will be witnesses who show how guilty you are. Why do I say this? Because when Jonah preached to those people, they changed their lives. And you are listening to someone greater than Jonah, but you refuse to change!

⁴²"On the judgment day, you people who live now will also be compared with the queen of the South,[c] and she will be a witness who shows how guilty you are. I say this because she traveled from far, far away to listen to Solomon's wise teaching. And I tell you that someone greater than Solomon is right here, but you won't listen!

The Danger of Emptiness
(Lk. 11:24–26)

⁴³"When an evil spirit comes out of a person, it travels through dry places looking for a place to rest, but it finds none. ⁴⁴So it says, 'I will go back to the home I left.' When it comes back, it finds that home still empty. It is all neat and clean. ⁴⁵Then the evil spirit goes out and brings seven other spirits more evil than itself. They all go and live there, and that person has even more trouble than before. It is the same way with the evil people who live today."

Jesus' Followers Are His True Family
(Mk. 3:31–35; Lk. 8:19–21)

⁴⁶While Jesus was talking to the people, his mother and brothers stood outside. They wanted to talk to him. ⁴⁷Someone told him, "Your mother and brothers are waiting for you outside. They want to talk to you."

⁴⁸Jesus answered, "Who is my mother? Who are my brothers?" ⁴⁹Then he pointed to his followers and said, "See! These people are my mother and my brothers. ⁵⁰Yes, anyone who does what my Father in heaven wants is my true brother and sister and mother."

A Story About a Farmer Sowing Seed
(Mk. 4:1–9; Lk. 8:4–8)

13 ¹That same day Jesus went out of the house and sat by

---

[a] **12:39 Jonah** The story of Jonah is found in the Old Testament book of Jonah.
[b] **12:41 Nineveh** City where Jonah preached. See Jonah 3.

[c] **12:42 queen of the South** Or "queen of Sheba." She traveled about 1000 miles (1600 km) to learn God's wisdom from Solomon. See 1 Kings 10:1–13.

the lake. ²A large crowd gathered around him. So he got into a boat and sat down. All the people stayed on the shore. ³Then Jesus used stories to teach them many things. He told them this story:

"A farmer went out to sow seed. ⁴While he was scattering the seed, some of it fell by the road. The birds came and ate all that seed. ⁵Other seed fell on rocky ground, where there was not enough dirt. It grew very fast there, because the soil was not deep. ⁶But when the sun rose, it burned the plants. The plants died because they did not have deep roots. ⁷Some other seed fell among thorny weeds. The weeds grew and stopped the good plants from growing. ⁸But some of the seed fell on good ground. There it grew and made grain. Some plants made 100 times more grain, some 60 times more, and some 30 times more. ⁹You people who hear me, listen!"

Why Jesus Used Stories to Teach
(Mk. 4:10–12; Lk. 8:9–10)

¹⁰The followers came to Jesus and asked, "Why do you use these stories to teach the people?"

¹¹Jesus answered, "Only you can know the secret truths about God's kingdom.* Those other people cannot know these secret truths. ¹²The people who have some understanding will be given more. And they will have even more than they need. But those who do not have much understanding will lose even the little understanding that they have. ¹³This is why I use these stories to teach the people: They see, but they don't really see. They hear, but they don't really hear or understand. ¹⁴So they show that what Isaiah said about them is true:

'You people will listen and
    listen,
    but you will not understand.
You will look and look,
    but you will not really see.
¹⁵ Yes, the minds of these people
    are now closed.
They have ears, but they
    don't listen.
They have eyes, but they
    refuse to see.
If their minds were not closed,
    they might see with their
    eyes;
    they might hear with their
    ears;
    they might understand with
    their minds.
Then they might turn back
    to me and be healed.'
    Isaiah 6:9–10

¹⁶But God has blessed you. You understand what you see with your eyes. And you understand what you hear with your ears. ¹⁷I can assure you, many prophets* and godly people wanted to see what you now see. But they did not see it. And many prophets and godly people wanted to hear what you now hear. But they did not hear it.

Jesus Explains the Story About Seed
(Mk. 4:13–20; Lk. 8:11–15)

¹⁸"So listen to the meaning of that story about the farmer:

¹⁹"What about the seed that fell by the path? That is like the people who hear the teaching about God's kingdom* but do not understand it. The Evil One* comes and takes away what was planted in their hearts.

²⁰"And what about the seed that fell on rocky ground? That is like the people who hear the teaching and quickly and gladly accept it. ²¹But they do not let the teaching go deep into their lives. They

keep it only a short time. As soon as trouble or persecution* comes because of the teaching they accepted, they give up.

²²"And what about the seed that fell among the thorny weeds? That is like the people who hear the teaching but let worries about this life and love for money stop it from growing. So it does not produce a crop in their lives.

²³"But what about the seed that fell on the good ground? That is like the people who hear the teaching and understand it. They grow and produce a good crop, sometimes 100 times more, sometimes 60 times more, and sometimes 30 times more."

A Story About Wheat and Weeds

²⁴Then Jesus used another story to teach them. Jesus said, "God's kingdom* is like a man who planted good seed in his field. ²⁵That night, while everyone was asleep, the man's enemy came and planted weeds among the wheat and then left. ²⁶Later, the wheat grew, and heads of grain grew on the plants. But at the same time the weeds also grew. ²⁷Then the man's servants came to him and said, 'You planted good seed in your field. Where did the weeds come from?'

²⁸"The man answered, 'An enemy planted weeds.'

"The servants asked, 'Do you want us to go and pull up the weeds?'

²⁹"He answered, 'No, because when you pull up the weeds, you might also pull up the wheat. ³⁰Let the weeds and the wheat grow together until the harvest time. At the harvest time I will tell the workers this: First, gather the weeds and tie them together

to be burned. Then gather the wheat and bring it to my barn.'"

What Is God's Kingdom Like?

(Mk. 4:30–34; Lk. 13:18–21)

³¹Then Jesus told the people another story: "God's kingdom* is like a mustard seed that a man plants in his field. ³²It is the smallest of all seeds. But when it grows, it is the largest of all garden plants. It becomes a tree big enough for the birds to come and make nests in its branches."

³³Then Jesus told them another story: "God's kingdom is like yeast that a woman mixes into a big bowl of flour to make bread. The yeast makes all the dough rise."

³⁴Jesus used stories to tell all these things to the people. He always used stories to teach them. ³⁵This was to make clear the full meaning of what the prophet* said:

"I will speak using stories;
  I will tell things that have
    been secrets since the
    world was made."   *Psalm 78:2*

Jesus Explains a Hard Story

³⁶Then Jesus left the people and went into the house. His followers came to him and said, "Explain to us the meaning of the story about the weeds in the field."

³⁷He answered, "The man who planted the good seed in the field is the Son of Man.* ³⁸The field is the world. The good seed are the people in God's kingdom.* The weeds are the people who belong to the Evil One.* ³⁹And the enemy who planted the bad seed is the devil. The harvest is the end of time. And the workers who gather are God's angels.

⁴⁰"The weeds are pulled up and burned in the fire. It will be the

same at the end of time. 41The Son of Man will send his angels, and they will find the people who cause sin and all those who do evil. The angels will take those people out of his kingdom.* 42They will throw them into the place of fire. There the people will be crying and grinding their teeth with pain. 43Then the godly people will shine like the sun. They will be in the kingdom of their Father. You people who hear me, listen!

Stories About a Treasure and a Pearl

44"God's kingdom* is like a treasure hidden in a field. One day a man found the treasure. He hid it again and was so happy that he went and sold everything he owned and bought the field.

45"Also, God's kingdom is like a merchant* looking for fine pearls. 46One day he found a very fine pearl. He went and sold everything he had to buy it.

A Story About a Fishing Net

47"Also, God's kingdom* is like a net that was put into the lake. The net caught many different kinds of fish. 48It was full, so the fishermen pulled it to the shore. They sat down and put all the good fish in baskets. Then they threw away the bad fish. 49It will be the same at the end of time. The angels will come and separate the evil people from the godly people. 50They will throw the evil people into the place of fire. There the people will cry and grind their teeth with pain."

51Then Jesus asked his followers, "Do you understand all these things?"

They said, "Yes, we understand."

52Then Jesus said to the followers, "So every teacher of the law who has learned about God's kingdom has some new things to teach. He is like the owner of a house. He has new things and old things saved in that house. And he brings out the new with the old."

Jesus Goes to His Hometown

(Mk. 6:1–6; Lk. 4:16–30)

53When Jesus finished teaching with these stories, he left there. 54He went to the town where he grew up. He taught the people in the synagogue,* and they were amazed. They said, "Where did this man get such wisdom and this power to do miracles*? 55Isn't he just the son of the carpenter we know? Isn't his mother's name Mary, and aren't his brothers James, Joseph, Simon, and Judas? 56And don't all his sisters still live here in town? How is he able to do these things?" 57So they had a problem accepting him.

But Jesus said to them, "People everywhere give honor to a prophet,* but in his own town or in his own home a prophet does not get any honor." 58Jesus did not do many miracles there, because the people did not believe in him.

Herod Thinks Jesus Is John the Baptizer

(Mk. 6:14–29; Lk. 9:7–9)

14 1About that time, Herod,* the ruler of Galilee, heard what the people were saying about Jesus. 2So he said to his servants, "This man is really John the Baptizer.* He must have risen from death, and that is why he can do these miracles.*"

How John the Baptizer Was Killed

3Before this time, Herod* had arrested John.* He had him chained and put in prison. He arrested John because of Herodias, the wife of Philip, Herod's brother. 4John

had told him, "It is not right for you to be married to Herodias."
⁵Herod wanted to kill him, but he was afraid of the people. They believed that John was a prophet.*
⁶On Herod's birthday, the daughter of Herodias danced for him and his group. Herod was very pleased with her. ⁷So he promised that he would give her anything she wanted. ⁸Herodias told her daughter what to ask for. So she said to Herod, "Give me the head of John the Baptizer* here on this plate."
⁹King Herod was very sad. But he had promised to give the daughter anything she wanted. And the people eating with Herod had heard his promise. So he ordered what she asked to be done. ¹⁰He sent men to the prison, where they cut off John's head. ¹¹And the men brought John's head on a plate and gave it to the girl. Then she took the head to her mother, Herodias. ¹²John's followers came and got his body and buried it. Then they went and told Jesus what happened.

Jesus Feeds More Than 5000
(Mk. 6:30–44; Lk. 9:10–17; Jn. 6:1–14)

¹³When Jesus heard what happened to John,* he left in a boat. He went alone to a place where no one lived. But the people heard that Jesus had left. So they left their towns and followed him. They went by land to the same place he went. ¹⁴When Jesus got out of the boat, he saw a large crowd of people. He felt sorry for them, and he healed the ones who were sick.
¹⁵Late that afternoon, the followers came to Jesus and said, "No one lives in this place. And it is already late. Send the people away so they can go to the towns and buy food for themselves."
¹⁶Jesus said, "The people don't need to go away. You give them some food to eat."
¹⁷The followers answered, "But we have only five loaves of bread and two fish."
¹⁸Jesus said, "Bring the bread and the fish to me." ¹⁹Then he told the people to sit down on the grass. He took the five loaves of bread and the two fish. He looked into the sky and thanked God for the food. Then he broke the bread into pieces, which he gave to the followers, and they gave the food to the people. ²⁰Everyone ate until they were full. When they finished eating, the followers filled twelve baskets with the pieces of food that were not eaten. ²¹There were about 5000 men there who ate. There were also women and children who ate.

Jesus Walks on Water
(Mk. 6:45–52; Jn. 6:16–21)

²²Then Jesus made the followers get into the boat. He told them to go to the other side of the lake. He said he would come later. He stayed there to tell everyone they could go home. ²³After Jesus said goodbye to the people, he went up into the hills by himself to pray. It was late, and he was there alone. ²⁴By this time the boat was already a long way from shore. Since the wind was blowing against it, the boat was having trouble because of the waves.
²⁵Between three and six o'clock in the morning, Jesus' followers were still in the boat. Jesus came to them. He was walking on the water. ²⁶When they saw him walking on the water, it scared

them. "It's a ghost!" they said, screaming in fear.

27But Jesus quickly spoke to them. He said, "Don't worry! It's me! Don't be afraid."

28Peter said, "Lord, if that is really you, tell me to come to you on the water."

29Jesus said, "Come, Peter."

Then Peter left the boat and walked on the water to Jesus. 30But while Peter was walking on the water, he saw the wind and the waves. He was afraid and began sinking into the water. He shouted, "Lord, save me!"

31Then Jesus caught Peter with his hand. He said, "Your faith is small. Why did you doubt?"

32After Peter and Jesus were in the boat, the wind stopped. 33Then the followers in the boat worshiped Jesus and said, "You really are the Son of God."

Jesus Heals Many Sick People
(Mk. 6:53–56)

34After they crossed the lake, they came to the shore at Gennesaret. 35Some men there saw Jesus and knew who he was. So they sent word to the other people throughout that area that Jesus had come. The people brought all their sick people to him. 36They begged Jesus to let them only touch the edge of his coat to be healed. And all the sick people who touched his coat were healed.

God's Law and Human Traditions
(Mk. 7:1–23)

15 1Then some Pharisees* and teachers of the law came to Jesus. They came from Jerusalem and asked him, 2"Why do your followers not obey the traditions we have from our great leaders who lived long ago? Your followers don't wash their hands before they eat!"

3Jesus answered, "And why do you refuse to obey God's command so that you can follow those traditions you have? 4God said, 'You must respect your father and mother.'a And God also said, 'Whoever says anything bad to their father or mother must be killed.'b 5But you teach that a person can say to their father or mother, 'I have something I could use to help you. But I will not use it for you. I will give it to God.' 6You are teaching them not to respect their father. So you are teaching that it is not important to do what God said. You think it is more important to follow those traditions you have. 7You are hypocrites*! Isaiah was right when he spoke for God about you:

8 'These people honor me with
    their words,
but I am not really
    important to them.
9 Their worship of me is
    worthless.
The things they teach
    are only human rules.'"

Isaiah 29:13

10Jesus called the people to him. He said, "Listen and understand what I am saying. 11It is not what people put in their mouth that makes them wrong.c It is what comes out of their mouth that makes them wrong."

12Then the followers came to Jesus and asked, "Do you know that the Pharisees are upset about what you said?"

---

a **15:4** Quote from Ex. 20:12; Deut. 5:16.
b **15:4** Quote from Ex. 21:17.
c **15:11 wrong** Literally, "unclean" or "not pure," meaning unacceptable to God. Also in verse 18.

13Jesus answered, "Every plant that my Father in heaven has not planted will be pulled up by the roots. 14Stay away from the Pharisees. They lead the people, but they are like blind men leading other blind men. And if a blind man leads another blind man, both of them will fall into a ditch."

15Peter said, "Explain to us what you said earlier to the people."

16Jesus said, "Do you still have trouble understanding? 17Surely you know that all the food that enters the mouth goes into the stomach. Then it goes out of the body. 18But the bad things people say with their mouth come from the way they think. And that's what can make people wrong. 19All these bad things begin in the mind: evil thoughts, murder, adultery,* sexual sins, stealing, lying, and insulting people. 20These are the things that make people wrong. Eating without washing their hands will never make people unacceptable to God."

Jesus Helps a Non-Jewish Woman
(Mk. 7:24–30)

21Jesus went from there to the area of Tyre and Sidon. 22A Canaanite woman from that area came out and began shouting, "Lord, Son of David,* please help me! My daughter has a demon* inside her, and she is suffering very much."

23But Jesus did not answer her. So the followers came to him and said, "Tell her to go away. She keeps crying out and will not leave us alone."

24Jesus answered, "God sent me only to the lost people*a* of Israel.*"

a **15:24 people** Literally, "sheep."

25Then the woman came over to Jesus and bowed before him. She said, "Lord, help me!"

26He answered her with this saying: "It is not right to take the children's bread and give it to the dogs."

27The woman said, "Yes, Lord, but even the dogs eat the pieces of food that fall from their master's table."

28Then Jesus answered, "Woman, you have great faith! You will get what you asked for." And right then the woman's daughter was healed.

Jesus Heals Many People

29Then Jesus went from there to the shore of Lake Galilee. He went up on a hill and sat down.

30A large crowd of people came to him. They brought many other sick people and put them before him. There were people who could not walk, people who were blind, crippled, or deaf, and many others. Jesus healed them all. 31People were amazed when they saw that those who could not speak were now able to speak. Crippled people were made strong. Those who could not walk were now able to walk. The blind were able to see. Everyone thanked the God of Israel* for this.

Jesus Feeds More Than 4000
(Mk. 8:1–10)

32Jesus called his followers to him and said, "I feel sorry for these people. They have been with me three days, and now they have nothing to eat. I don't want to send them away hungry. They might faint while going home."

33The followers asked Jesus, "Where can we get enough bread to feed all these people? We are a long way from any town."

34Jesus asked, "How many loaves of bread do you have?"

They answered, "We have seven loaves of bread and a few small fish."

35Jesus told the people to sit on the ground. 36He took the seven loaves of bread and the fish. Then he gave thanks to God for the food. He broke the bread into pieces, which he gave to the followers, and they gave the food to the people. 37All the people ate until they were full. After this, the followers filled seven baskets with the pieces of food that were not eaten. 38There were about 4000 men there who ate. There were also some women and children. 39After they all ate, Jesus told the people they could go home. He got into the boat and went to the area of Magadan.

Some People Doubt Jesus' Authority
(Mk. 8:11–13; Lk. 12:54–56)

16 1The Pharisees* and Sadducees* came to Jesus. They wanted to test him. So they asked him to show them a miracle* as a sign from God.

2Jesus answered, "When you people see the sunset, you know what the weather will be. If the sky is red, you say we will have good weather. 3And in the morning, if the sky is dark and red, you say that it will be a rainy day. These are signs of the weather. You see these signs in the sky and know what they mean. In the same way, you see the things that are happening now. These are also signs, but you don't know their meaning. 4It is the evil and sinful people who want to see a miracle as a sign from God. But no miracle will be done to prove anything to them. The only sign will be the miracle that happened to Jonah.*a*"

Then Jesus went away from there.

Jesus' Followers Misunderstand Him
(Mk. 8:14–21)

5Jesus and his followers went across the lake. But the followers forgot to bring bread. 6Jesus said to the followers, "Be careful! Guard against the yeast* of the Pharisees* and the Sadducees.*"

7The followers discussed the meaning of this. They said, "Did Jesus say this because we forgot to bring bread?"

8Jesus knew that they were talking about this. So he asked them, "Why are you talking about not having bread? Your faith is small. 9Do you still not understand? Remember the five loaves of bread that fed the 5000 people and the many baskets you filled with the bread that was left? 10And remember the seven loaves of bread that fed the 4000 people and the many baskets you filled that time? 11So how could you think that I am concerned about bread? I am telling you to be careful and guard against the yeast of the Pharisees and the Sadducees."

12Then the followers understood what Jesus meant. He was not telling them to guard against the yeast used in bread. He was telling them to guard against the teaching of the Pharisees and the Sadducees.

Peter Says Jesus Is the Messiah
(Mk. 8:27–30; Lk. 9:18–21)

13Jesus went to the area of Caesarea Philippi. He said to his followers, "Who do people say I am*b*?"

---

a **16:4 Jonah** A prophet in the Old Testament. After three days in a big fish he came out alive, just as Jesus would come out from the tomb on the third day.

b **16:13 I am** Literally, "the Son of Man is."

[14]They answered, "Some people say you are John the Baptizer.* Others say you are Elijah.* And some say you are Jeremiah* or one of the prophets.*"

[15]Then Jesus said to his followers, "And who do you say I am?"

[16]Simon Peter answered, "You are the Messiah,* the Son of the living God."

[17]Jesus answered, "You are blessed, Simon son of Jonah. No one taught you that. My Father in heaven showed you who I am. [18]So I tell you, you are Peter.[d] And I will build my church* on this rock. The power of death[b] will not be able to defeat my church. [19]I will give you the keys to God's kingdom.* When you speak judgment here on earth, that judgment will be God's judgment. When you promise forgiveness here on earth, that forgiveness will be God's forgiveness."[c]

[20]Then Jesus warned his followers not to tell anyone he was the Messiah.

Jesus Says He Must Die
(Mk. 8:31–9:1; Lk. 9:22–27)

[21]From that time Jesus began telling his followers that he must go to Jerusalem. He explained that the older Jewish leaders, the leading priests, and the teachers of the law would make him suffer many things. And he told his followers that he must be killed. Then, on the third day, he would be raised from death.

[22]Peter took Jesus away from the other followers to talk to him alone. He began to criticize him. He said, "God save you from those sufferings, Lord! That will never happen to you!"

[23]Then Jesus said to Peter, "Get away from me, Satan[d]! You are not helping me! You don't care about the same things God does. You care only about things that people think are important."

[24]Then Jesus said to his followers, "If any of you want to be my follower, you must stop thinking about yourself and what you want. You must be willing to carry the cross* that is given to you for following me. [25]Any of you who try to save the life you have will lose it. But you who give up your life for me will find true life. [26]It is worth nothing for you to have the whole world if you yourself are lost. You could never pay enough to buy back your life. [27]The Son of Man* will come again with his Father's glory* and with his angels. And he will reward everyone for what they have done. [28]Believe me when I say that there are some people standing here who will see the Son of Man coming with his kingdom before they die."

Jesus Is Seen With Moses and Elijah
(Mk. 9:2–13; Lk. 9:28–36)

17 [1]Six days later, Jesus took Peter, James, and John the brother of James and went up on a high mountain. They were all alone there. [2]While these followers watched him, Jesus was changed. His face became bright like the sun, and his clothes became white as light. [3]Then two

a **16:18 Peter** The Greek name "Peter," like the Aramaic name "Cephas," means "rock."
b **16:18 power of death** Literally, "gates of Hades."
c **16:19 When you speak … God's forgiveness** Literally, "Whatever you bind on earth will have been bound in heaven, and whatever you loose on earth will have been loosed in heaven."
d **16:23 Satan** Name for the devil meaning "the enemy." Jesus means that Peter was talking like Satan.

men were there, talking with him. They were Moses* and Elijah.*

⁴Peter said to Jesus, "Lord, it is good that we are here. If you want, I will put three tents here—one for you, one for Moses, and one for Elijah."

⁵While Peter was talking, a bright cloud came over them. A voice came from the cloud and said, "This is my Son, the one I love. I am very pleased with him. Obey him!"

⁶The followers with Jesus heard this voice. They were very afraid, so they fell to the ground. ⁷But Jesus came to them and touched them. He said, "Stand up. Don't be afraid." ⁸The followers looked up, and they saw that Jesus was now alone.

⁹As Jesus and the followers were coming down the mountain, he gave them this command: "Don't tell anyone about what you saw on the mountain. Wait until the Son of Man* has been raised from death. Then you can tell people about what you saw."

¹⁰The followers asked Jesus, "Why do the teachers of the law say that Elijah must come*ᵃ* before the Messiah* comes?"

¹¹Jesus answered, "They are right to say Elijah is coming. And it is true that Elijah will make all things the way they should be. ¹²But I tell you, Elijah has already come. People did not know who he was, and they treated him badly, doing whatever they wanted to do. It is the same with the Son of Man. Those same people will make the Son of Man suffer." ¹³Then the followers understood that when Jesus said Elijah,

he was really talking about John the Baptizer.*

Jesus Frees a Boy From an Evil Spirit
(Mk. 9:14–29; Lk. 9:37–43a)

¹⁴Jesus and the followers went back to the people. A man came to Jesus and bowed before him. ¹⁵The man said, "Lord, be kind to my son. He suffers so much from the seizures he has. He often falls into the fire or into the water. ¹⁶I brought him to your followers, but they could not heal him."

¹⁷Jesus answered, "You people today have no faith. Your lives are so wrong! How long must I stay with you? How long must I continue to be patient with you? Bring the boy here." ¹⁸Jesus gave a strong command to the demon* inside the boy. The demon came out of the boy, and the boy was healed.

¹⁹Then the followers came to Jesus alone. They said, "We tried to force the demon out of the boy, but we could not. Why were we not able to make the demon go out?"

²⁰Jesus answered, "You were not able to make the demon go out, because your faith is too small. Believe me when I tell you, if your faith is only as big as a mustard* seed you can say to this mountain, 'Move from here to there,' and it will move. You will be able to do anything." ²¹ᵇ

Jesus Talks About His Death
(Mk. 9:30–32; Lk. 9:43b–45)

²²Later, the followers met together in Galilee. Jesus said to them, "The Son of Man* will be handed over to the control of other men, ²³who will kill him. But on the third day

ᵃ **17:10 Elijah must come** See Mal. 4:5–6.

ᵇ **17:21** Some Greek copies add verse 21: "But that kind of spirit comes out only with prayer and fasting."

he will be raised from death." The followers were very sad to hear that Jesus would be killed.

Jesus Teaches About Paying Taxes

24Jesus and his followers went to Capernaum.* There the men who collect the two-drachma Temple* tax came to Peter and asked, "Does your teacher pay the Temple tax?"

25Peter answered, "Yes, he does." Peter went into the house where Jesus was. Before Peter could speak, Jesus said to him, "The kings on the earth get different kinds of taxes from people. But who are those who pay the taxes? Are they the king's children? Or do other people pay the taxes? What do you think?"

26Peter answered, "The other people pay the taxes."

Jesus said, "Then the children of the king don't have to pay taxes. 27But we don't want to upset these tax collectors.* So do this: Go to the lake and fish. After you catch the first fish, open its mouth. Inside its mouth you will find a four-drachma coin. Take that coin and give it to the tax collectors. That will pay the tax for you and me."

Who Is the Greatest?
(Mk. 9:33–37; Lk. 9:46–48)

18 1About that time the followers came to Jesus and asked, "Who is the greatest in God's kingdom*?"

2Jesus called a little child to come to him. He stood the child in front of the followers. 3Then he said, "The truth is, you must change your thinking and become like little children. If you don't do this, you will never enter God's kingdom. 4The greatest person in God's kingdom is the one who makes himself humble like this child.

5"Whoever accepts a little child like this in my name is accepting me.

Jesus Warns About Causes of Sin
(Mk. 9:42–48; Lk. 17:1–2)

6"If one of these little children believes in me, and someone causes that child to sin, it will be very bad for that person. It would be better for them to have a millstone* tied around their neck and be drowned in the deep sea. 7I feel sorry for the people in the world because of the things that make people sin. These things must happen, but it will be very bad for anyone who causes them to happen.

8"If your hand or your foot makes you sin, cut it off and throw it away. It is better for you to lose part of your body and have eternal life than to have two hands and two feet and be thrown into the fire that burns forever. 9If your eye makes you sin, take it out and throw it away. It is better for you to have only one eye and have eternal life than to have two eyes and be thrown into the fire of hell.

Jesus Uses a Story About a Lost Sheep
(Lk. 15:3–7)

10"Be careful. Don't think these little children are not important. I tell you that these children have angels in heaven. And those angels are always with my Father in heaven. 11a

12"If a man has 100 sheep, but one of the sheep is lost, what will he do? He will leave the other 99 sheep on the hill and go look for the lost sheep. Right? 13And if he finds the lost sheep, he is happier

a 18:11 Some Greek copies add verse 11: "The Son of Man came to save lost people." See Lk. 19:10.

about that one sheep than about the 99 sheep that were never lost. I can assure you, [14]in the same way your Father in heaven does not want any of these little children to be lost.

When Someone Hurts You
(Lk. 17:3)

[15]"If your brother or sister in God's family does something wrong, go and tell them what they did wrong. Do this when you are alone with them. If they listen to you, then you have helped them to be your brother or sister again. [16]But if they refuse to listen, go to them again and take one or two people with you. Then there will be two or three people who will be able to tell all that happened.[a] [17]If they refuse to listen to them, tell the church.* And if they refuse to listen to the church, treat them as you would treat someone who does not know God or who is a tax collector.*

[18]"I can assure you that when you speak judgment here on earth, it will be God's judgment. And when you promise forgiveness here on earth, it will be God's forgiveness.[b] [19]To say it another way, if two of you on earth agree on anything you pray for, my Father in heaven will do what you ask. [20]Yes, if two or three people are together believing in me, I am there with them."

A Story About Forgiveness

[21]Then Peter came to Jesus and asked, "Lord, when someone[c]

won't stop doing wrong to me, how many times must I forgive them? Seven times?"

[22]Jesus answered, "I tell you, you must forgive them more than seven times. You must continue to forgive them even if they do wrong to you seventy-seven times.[d]

[23]"So God's kingdom* is like a king who decided to collect the money his servants owed him. [24]The king began to collect his money. One servant owed him several thousand pounds[e] of silver. [25]He was not able to pay the money to his master, the king. So the master ordered that he and everything he owned be sold, even his wife and children. The money would be used to pay the king what the servant owed.

[26]"But the servant fell on his knees and begged, 'Be patient with me. I will pay you everything I owe.' [27]The master felt sorry for him. So he told the servant he did not have to pay. He let him go free.

[28]"Later, that same servant found another servant who owed him a hundred silver coins.* He grabbed him around the neck and said, 'Pay me the money you owe me!'

[29]"The other servant fell on his knees and begged him, 'Be patient with me. I will pay you everything I owe.'

[30]"But the first servant refused to be patient. He told the judge

---

[a] **18:16 Then … happened** See Deut. 19:15.
[b] **18:18 when you speak … God's forgiveness** Literally, "whatever you bind on earth will have been bound in heaven, and whatever you loose on earth will have been loosed in heaven."
[c] **18:21 someone** Literally, "my brother."

[d] **18:22 seventy-seven times** Or "seventy times seven," a very large number, meaning there should be no limit to forgiveness.
[e] **18:24 several thousand pounds** Literally, "10,000 *talanta*" or "talents." A talent was about 27 to 36 kg (60 to 80 pounds) of gold, silver, or copper coins.

that the other servant owed him money, and that servant was put in jail until he could pay everything he owed. ³¹All the other servants saw what happened. They felt very sorry for the man. So they went and told their master everything that happened.

³²"Then the master called his servant in and said, 'You evil servant. You begged me to forgive your debt, and I said you did not have to pay anything! ³³So you should have given that other man who serves with you the same mercy I gave you.' ³⁴The master was very angry, so he put the servant in jail to be punished. And he had to stay in jail until he could pay everything he owed.

³⁵"This king did the same as my heavenly Father will do to you. You must forgive your brother or sister with all your heart, or my heavenly Father will not forgive you."

Jesus Teaches About Divorce
(Mk. 10:1–12)

19 ¹After Jesus said all these things, he left Galilee. He went into the area of Judea on the other side of the Jordan River. ²Many people followed him. Jesus healed the sick people there.

³Some Pharisees* came to Jesus. They tried to make him say something wrong. They asked him, "Is it right for a man to divorce his wife for any reason he chooses?"

⁴Jesus answered, "Surely you have read this in the Scriptures*: When God made the world, 'he made people male and female.'ᵃ ⁵And God said, 'That is why a man will leave his father and mother and be joined to his wife. And the

two people will become one.'ᵇ ⁶So they are no longer two, but one. God has joined them together, so no one should separate them."

⁷The Pharisees asked, "Then why did Moses* give a command allowing a man to divorce his wife by writing a certificate of divorceᶜ?"

⁸Jesus answered, "Moses allowed you to divorce your wives because you refused to accept God's teaching. But divorce was not allowed in the beginning. ⁹I tell you that whoever divorces his wife, except for the problem of sexual sin, and marries another woman is guilty of adultery.*"

¹⁰The followers said to Jesus, "If that is the only reason a man can divorce his wife, it is better not to marry."

¹¹He answered, "This statement is true for some, but not for everyone—only for those who have been given this gift. ¹²There are different reasons why some men don't marry.ᵈ Some were born without the ability to produce children. Others were made that way later in life. And others have given up marriage because of God's kingdom.* This is for anyone who is able to accept it."

Jesus Welcomes Children
(Mk. 10:13–16; Lk. 18:15–17)

¹³Then the people brought their little children to Jesus so that he could lay his hands on* them to bless them and pray for them. When the followers saw this, they told the people to stop bringing their children to him. ¹⁴But Jesus

ᵃ **19:4** Quote from Gen. 1:27; 5:2.
ᵇ **19:5** Quote from Gen. 2:24.
ᶜ **19:7 a command … certificate of divorce** See Deut. 24:1.
ᵈ **19:12 some men don't marry** Literally, "there are eunuchs."

said, "Let the little children come to me. Don't stop them, because God's kingdom* belongs to people who are like these children." ¹⁵After Jesus blessed the children, he left there.

A Rich Man Refuses to Follow Jesus
(Mk. 10:17–31; Lk. 18:18–30)

¹⁶A man came to Jesus and asked, "Teacher, what good thing must I do to have eternal life?"

¹⁷Jesus answered, "Why do you ask me about what is good? Only God is good. But if you want to have eternal life, obey the law's commands."

¹⁸The man asked, "Which ones?"

Jesus answered, "'You must not murder anyone, you must not commit adultery,* you must not steal, you must not tell lies about others, ¹⁹you must respect your father and mother,'ᵃ and 'love your neighborᵇ the same as you love yourself.'ᶜ"

²⁰The young man said, "I have obeyed all these commands. What else do I need?"

²¹Jesus answered, "If you want to be perfect, then go and sell all that you own. Give the money to the poor, and you will have riches in heaven. Then come and follow me!"

²²But when the young man heard Jesus tell him to give away his money, he was sad. He didn't want to do this, because he was very rich. So he left.

²³Then Jesus said to his followers, "The truth is, it will be very hard for a rich person to enter God's kingdom.* ²⁴Yes, I tell you, it is easier for a camel to go through the eye of a needle than for a rich person to enter God's kingdom."

²⁵The followers were amazed to hear this. They asked, "Then who can be saved?"

²⁶Jesus looked at them and said, "This is something that people cannot do. But God can do anything."

²⁷Peter said to him, "We left everything we had and followed you. So what will we have?"

²⁸Jesus said to them, "When the time of the new world comes, the Son of Man* will sit on his great and glorious throne. And I can promise that you who followed me will sit on twelve thrones, and you will judge the twelve tribes of Israel.* ²⁹Everyone who has left houses, brothers, sisters, father, mother, children, or farms to follow me will get much more than they left. And they will have eternal life. ³⁰Many people who are first now will be last in the future. And many who are last now will be first in the future.

Jesus Uses a Story About Farm Workers

20 ¹"God's kingdom* is like a man who owned some land. One morning, the man went out very early to hire some people to work in his vineyard.* ²He agreed to pay the workers one silver coin* for working that day. Then he sent them into the vineyard to work.

³"About nine o'clock the man went to the marketplace and saw some other people standing there. They were doing nothing. ⁴So he said to them, 'If you go and work in my field, I will pay you what your work is worth.' ⁵So they went to work in the vineyard.

ᵃ **19:19** Quote from Ex. 20:12–16; Deut. 5:16–20.
ᵇ **19:19 your neighbor** Or "others." Jesus' teaching in Lk. 10:25–37 makes clear that this includes anyone in need.
ᶜ **19:19** Quote from Lev. 19:18.

"The man went out again about twelve o'clock and again at three o'clock. Both times he hired some others to work in his vineyard. 6About five o'clock the man went to the marketplace again. He saw some other people standing there. He asked them, 'Why did you stand here all day doing nothing?'

7"They said, 'No one gave us a job.'

"The man said to them, 'Then you can go and work in my vineyard.'

8"At the end of the day, the owner of the field said to the boss of all the workers, 'Call the workers and pay them all. Start by paying the last people I hired. Then pay all of them, ending with the ones I hired first.'

9"The workers who were hired at five o'clock came to get their pay. Each worker got one silver coin. 10Then the workers who were hired first came to get their pay. They thought they would be paid more than the others. But each one of them also received one silver coin. 11When they got their silver coin, they complained to the man who owned the land. 12They said, 'Those people were hired last and worked only one hour. But you paid them the same as us. And we worked hard all day in the hot sun.'

13"But the man who owned the field said to one of them, 'Friend, I am being fair with you. You agreed to work for one silver coin. Right? 14So take your pay and go. I want to give the man who was hired last the same pay I gave you. 15I can do what I want with my own money. Why would you be jealous because I am generous?'

16"So those who are last now will be first in the future. And those who are first now will be last in the future."

Jesus Talks Again About His Death
(Mk. 10:32–34; Lk. 18:31–34)

17Jesus was going to Jerusalem. His twelve followers were with him. While they were walking, he gathered the followers together and spoke to them privately. He said to them, 18"We are going to Jerusalem. The Son of Man* will be handed over to the leading priests and the teachers of the law, and they will say he must die. 19They will hand him over to the foreigners, who will laugh at him and beat him with whips, and then they will kill him on a cross. But on the third day after his death, he will be raised to life again."

A Mother Asks a Special Favor
(Mk. 10:35–45)

20Then Zebedee's wife came to Jesus and brought her sons. She bowed before Jesus and asked him to do something for her.

21Jesus said, "What do you want?"

She said, "Promise that one of my sons will sit at your right side in your kingdom and the other at your left."

22So Jesus said to the sons, "You don't understand what you are asking. Can you drink from the cup*a* that I must drink from?"

The sons answered, "Yes, we can!"

23Jesus said to them, "It is true that you will drink from the cup that I drink from. But it is not for me to say who will sit at my right or my left. My Father has decided

---

a **20:22 cup** A symbol of suffering. Jesus used the idea of drinking from a cup to mean accepting the suffering he would face in the terrible events that were soon to come. Also in verse 23.

who will do that. He has prepared those places for them."

24The other ten followers heard this and were angry with the two brothers. 25So Jesus called the followers together. He said, "You know that the rulers of the non-Jewish people love to show their power over the people. And their important leaders love to use all their authority over the people. 26But it should not be that way with you. Whoever wants to be your leader must be your servant. 27Whoever wants to be first must serve the rest of you like a slave. 28Do as I did: The Son of Man* did not come for people to serve him. He came to serve others and to give his life to save many people."

Jesus Heals Two Blind Men
(Mk. 10:46–52; Lk. 18:35–43)

29When Jesus and his followers were leaving Jericho, a large crowd followed him. 30There were two blind men sitting by the road. They heard that Jesus was coming by. So they shouted, "Lord, Son of David,* please help us!"

31The people there criticized the blind men and told them to be quiet. But they shouted more and more, "Lord, Son of David, please help us!"

32Jesus stopped and said to them, "What do you want me to do for you?"

33They answered, "Lord, we want to be able to see."

34Jesus felt sorry for the blind men. He touched their eyes, and immediately they were able to see. Then they became followers of Jesus.

Jesus Enters Jerusalem Like a King
(Mk. 11:1–11; Lk. 19:28–38; Jn. 12:12–19)

21 1Jesus and his followers were coming closer to Jerusalem. But first they stopped at Bethphage at the hill called the Mount of Olives.* From there Jesus sent two of his followers into town. 2He said to them, "Go to the town you can see there. When you enter it, you will find a donkey with her colt. Untie them both, and bring them to me. 3If anyone asks you why you are taking the donkeys, tell them, 'The Master needs them. He will send them back soon.'"

4This showed the full meaning of what the prophet* said:

5 "Tell the people of Zion,a
   'Now your king is coming to you.
He is humble and riding on a donkey.
He is riding on a young donkey, born from a work animal.'"   Zechariah 9:9

6The followers went and did what Jesus told them to do. 7They brought the mother donkey and the young donkey to him. They covered the donkeys with their coats, and Jesus sat on them. 8On the way to Jerusalem, many people spread their coats on the road for Jesus. Others cut branches from the trees and spread them on the road. 9Some of the people were walking ahead of Jesus. Others were walking behind him. They all shouted,

   "Praiseb to the Son of David*!
   'Welcome! God bless the one who comes in the name of the Lord!'   Psalm 118:25–26

---

a 21:5 people of Zion Literally, "daughter of Zion," meaning the city of Jerusalem.
b 21:9 Praise Literally, "Hosanna," a Hebrew word used in praying to God for help. Here, it was probably a shout of celebration used in praising God or his Messiah. Also in the last line of this verse and in verse 15.

Praise to God in heaven!"

¹⁰Then Jesus went into Jerusalem. All the people in the city were confused. They asked, "Who is this man?" ¹¹The crowds following Jesus answered, "This is Jesus. He is the prophet from the town of Nazareth in Galilee."

Jesus Goes to the Temple
(Mk. 11:15–19; Lk. 19:45–48; Jn. 2:13–22)

¹²Jesus went into the Temple* area. He threw out all those who were selling and buying things there. He turned over the tables that belonged to those who were exchanging different kinds of money. And he turned over the benches of those who were selling doves. ¹³Jesus said to them, "The Scriptures* say, 'My Temple will be called a house of prayer.'ᵃ But you are changing it into a 'hiding place for thieves.'ᵇ"

¹⁴Some blind people and some who were crippled came to Jesus in the Temple area. Jesus healed them. ¹⁵The leading priests and the teachers of the law saw the wonderful things he was doing. And they saw the children praising him in the Temple area. The children were shouting, "Praise to the Son of David.*" All this made the priests and the teachers of the law angry.

¹⁶They asked Jesus, "Do you hear what these children are saying?"

He answered, "Yes. The Scriptures say, 'You have taught children and babies to give praise.'ᶜ Have you not read that Scripture?" ¹⁷Then Jesus left them and went out of the city to Bethany, where he spent the night.

ᵃ **21:13** Quote from Isa. 56:7.
ᵇ **21:13** Quote from Jer. 7:11.
ᶜ **21:16** Quote from Ps. 8:2 (Greek version).

Jesus Shows the Power of Faith
(Mk. 11:12–14, 20–24)

¹⁸Early the next morning, Jesus was going back to the city. He was very hungry. ¹⁹He saw a fig tree beside the road and went to get a fig from it. But there were no figs on the tree. There were only leaves. So Jesus said to the tree, "You will never again produce fruit!" The tree immediately dried up and died.

²⁰When the followers saw this, they were very surprised. They asked, "How did the fig tree dry up and die so quickly?"

²¹Jesus answered, "The truth is, if you have faith and no doubts, you will be able to do the same as I did to this tree. And you will be able to do more. You will be able to say to this mountain, 'Go, mountain, fall into the sea.' And if you have faith, it will happen. ²²If you believe, you will get anything you ask for in prayer."

Jewish Leaders Doubt Jesus' Authority
(Mk. 11:27–33; Lk. 20:1–8)

²³Jesus went into the Temple* area. While Jesus was teaching there, the leading priests and the older leaders of the people came to him. They said, "Tell us! What authority do you have to do these things you are doing? Who gave you this authority?"

²⁴Jesus answered, "I will ask you a question too. If you answer me, then I will tell you what authority I have to do these things. ²⁵Tell me: When John baptized* people, did his authority come from God, or was it only from other people?"

The priests and the Jewish leaders talked about Jesus' question. They said to each other, "If we answer, 'John's baptism was from

God,' then he will say, 'Then why didn't you believe John?' ²⁶But we can't say John's baptism was from someone else. We are afraid of the people, because they all believe John was a prophet.*"

²⁷So they told Jesus, "We don't know the answer."

Jesus said, "Then I will not tell you who gave me the authority to do these things.

Jesus Uses a Story About Two Sons

²⁸"Tell me what you think about this: There was a man who had two sons. He went to the first son and said, 'Son, go and work today in the vineyard.*'

²⁹"The son answered, 'I will not go.' But later he decided he should go, and he went.

³⁰"Then the father went to the other son and said, 'Son, go and work today in the vineyard.' He answered, 'Yes, sir, I will go and work.' But he did not go.

³¹"Which of the two sons obeyed his father?"

The Jewish leaders answered, "The first son."

Jesus said to them, "The truth is, you are worse than the tax collectors* and the prostitutes. In fact, they will enter God's kingdom* before you enter. ³²John came showing you the right way to live, and you did not believe him. But the tax collectors and prostitutes believed John. You saw that happening, but you would not change. You still refused to believe him.

God Sends His Son

(Mk. 12:1–12; Lk. 20:9–19)

³³"Listen to this story: There was a man who owned a vineyard.* He put a wall around the field and dug a hole for a winepress.* Then he built a tower. He leased the land to some farmers and then left on a trip. ³⁴Later, it was time for the grapes to be picked. So the man sent his servants to the farmers to get his share of the grapes.

³⁵"But the farmers grabbed the servants and beat one. They killed another one and then stoned to death a third servant. ³⁶So the man sent some other servants to the farmers. He sent more servants than he sent the first time. But the farmers did the same thing to them that they did the first time. ³⁷So the man decided to send his son to the farmers. He said, 'The farmers will respect my son.'

³⁸"But when the farmers saw the son, they said to each other, 'This is the owner's son. This vineyard will be his. If we kill him, it will be ours.' ³⁹So the farmers took the son, threw him out of the vineyard, and killed him.

⁴⁰"So what will the owner of the vineyard do to these farmers when he comes?"

⁴¹The Jewish priests and leaders said, "He will surely kill those evil men. Then he will lease the land to other farmers, who will give him his share of the crop at harvest time."

⁴²Jesus said to them, "Surely you have read this in the Scriptures*:

'The stone that the builders
   refused to accept became
   the cornerstone.*
The Lord did this, and
   it is wonderful to us.'

Psalm 118:22–23

⁴³"So I tell you that God's kingdom* will be taken away from you. It will be given to people who do what God wants in his kingdom. ⁴⁴Whoever falls on this stone will

be broken. And it will crush anyone it falls on."[a]

45When the leading priests and the Pharisees* heard these stories, they knew that Jesus was talking about them. 46They wanted to find a way to arrest Jesus. But they were afraid to do anything, because the people believed that Jesus was a prophet.*

A Story About
People Invited to a Dinner
(Lk. 14:15-24)

22 1Jesus used some more stories to teach the people. He said, 2"God's kingdom* is like a king who prepared a wedding feast for his son. 3He invited some people to the feast. When it was ready, the king sent his servants to tell the people to come. But they refused to come to the king's feast.

4"Then the king sent some more servants. He said to them, 'I have already invited the people. So tell them that my feast is ready. I have killed my best bulls and calves to be eaten. Everything is ready. Come to the wedding feast.'

5"But when the servants told the people to come, they refused to listen. They all went to do other things. One went to work in his field, and another went to his business. 6Some of the other people grabbed the servants, beat them, and killed them. 7The king was very angry. He sent his army to kill those who murdered his servants. And the army burned their city.

8"After that the king said to his servants, 'The wedding feast is ready. I invited those people, but they were not good enough to come to my feast. 9So go to the street corners and invite everyone you see. Tell them to come to my feast.' 10So the servants went into the streets. They gathered all the people they could find, good and bad alike, and brought them to where the wedding feast was ready. And the place was filled with guests.

11"When the king came in to meet the guests, he saw a man there who was not dressed in the right clothes for a wedding. 12The king said, 'Friend, how were you allowed to come in here? You are not wearing the right clothes.' But the man said nothing. 13So the king told some servants, 'Tie this man's hands and feet. Throw him out into the darkness, where people are crying and grinding their teeth with pain.'

14"Yes, many people are invited. But only a few are chosen."

The Jewish Leaders Try to Trick Jesus
(Mk. 12:13-17; Lk. 20:20-26)

15Then the Pharisees* left the place where Jesus was teaching. They made plans to catch him saying something wrong. 16They sent some men to Jesus. They were some of their own followers and some from the group called Herodians.* They said, "Teacher, we know you are an honest man. We know you teach the truth about God's way. You are not afraid of what others think about you. All people are the same to you. 17So tell us what you think. Is it right to pay taxes to Caesar* or not?"

18But Jesus knew that these men were trying to trick him. So he said, "You hypocrites*! Why are you trying to catch me saying

---

a **21:44** Some Greek copies do not have verse 44.

something wrong? ¹⁹Show me a coin used for paying the tax." They showed Jesus a silver coin.* ²⁰Then he asked, "Whose picture is on the coin? And whose name is written on the coin?"

²¹They answered, "It is Caesar's picture and Caesar's name."

Then Jesus said to them, "Give to Caesar what belongs to Caesar, and give to God what belongs to God."

²²When they heard what Jesus said, they were amazed. They left him and went away.

Some Sadducees Try to Trick Jesus
(Mk. 12:18–27; Lk. 20:27–40)

²³That same day some Sadducees* came to Jesus. (Sadducees believe that no one will rise from death.) The Sadducees asked Jesus a question. ²⁴They said, "Teacher, Moses* told us that if a married man dies and had no children, his brother must marry the woman. Then they will have children for the dead brother.ᵃ ²⁵There were seven brothers among us. The first brother married but died. He had no children. So his brother married the woman. ²⁶Then the second brother also died. The same thing happened to the third brother and all the other brothers. ²⁷The woman was the last to die. ²⁸But all seven men had married her. So when people rise from death, whose wife will she be?"

²⁹Jesus answered, "You are so wrong! You don't know what the Scriptures* say. And you don't know anything about God's power. ³⁰At the time when people rise from death, there will be no marriage. People will not be married

to each other. Everyone will be like the angels in heaven. ³¹Surely you have read what God said to you about people rising from death. ³²God said, 'I am the God of Abraham,* the God of Isaac,* and the God of Jacob.'*ᵇ So they were not still dead, because he is the God only of living people."

³³When the people heard this, they were amazed at Jesus' teaching.

Which Command Is the Most Important?
(Mk. 12:28–34; Lk. 10:25–28)

³⁴The Pharisees* learned that Jesus had made the Sadducees* look so foolish that they stopped trying to argue with him. So the Pharisees had a meeting. ³⁵Then one of them, an expert in the Law of Moses,* asked Jesus a question to test him. ³⁶He said, "Teacher, which command in the law is the most important?"

³⁷Jesus answered, "'Love the Lord your God with all your heart, all your soul, and all your mind.'ᶜ ³⁸This is the first and most important command. ³⁹And the second command is like the first: 'Love your neighborᵈ the same as you love yourself.'ᵉ ⁴⁰All of the law and the writings of the prophets* take their meaning from these two commands."

Is the Messiah David's Son or David's Lord?
(Mk. 12:35–37; Lk. 20:41–44)

⁴¹So while the Pharisees* were together, Jesus asked them a question. ⁴²He said, "What do you

---

ᵃ **22:24 if ... dead brother** See Deut. 25:5, 6.

ᵇ **22:32** Quote from Ex. 3:6.
ᶜ **22:37** Quote from Deut. 6:5.
ᵈ **22:39 your neighbor** Or "others." Jesus' teaching in Lk. 10:25–37 makes clear that this includes anyone in need.
ᵉ **22:39** Quote from Lev. 19:18.

think about the Messiah*? Whose son is he?"

The Pharisees answered, "The Messiah is the Son of David.*"

43Jesus said to them, "Then why did David call him 'Lord'? David was speaking by the power of the Spirit.* He said,

44'The Lord God said to my Lord:
Sit by me at my right side,
and I will put your enemies
under your control.ᵃ'

Psalm 110:1

45David calls the Messiah 'Lord.' So how can he be David's son?"

46None of the Pharisees could answer Jesus' question. And after that day, no one was brave enough to ask him any more questions.

Jesus Criticizes the Religious Leaders
(Mk. 12:38–40; Lk. 11:37–52; 20:45–47)

23 ¹Then Jesus spoke to the people and to his followers. He said, ²"The teachers of the law and the Pharisees* have the authority to tell you what the Law of Moses* says. ³So you should obey them. Do everything they tell you to do. But their lives are not good examples for you to follow. They tell you to do things, but they don't do those things themselves. ⁴They make strict rules that are hard for people to obey. They try to force others to obey all their rules. But they themselves will not try to follow any of those rules.

⁵"The only reason they do what they do is for other people to see them. They make the little Scripture* boxesᵇ they wear bigger and bigger. And they make the tasselsᶜ on their prayer clothes long enough for people to notice them. ⁶These men love to have the places of honor at banquets and the most important seats in the synagogues.* ⁷They love for people to show respect to them in the marketplaces and to call them 'Teacher.'

⁸"But you must not be called 'Teacher.' You are all equal as brothers and sisters. You have only one Teacher. ⁹And don't call anyone on earth 'Father.' You have one Father. He is in heaven. ¹⁰And you should not be called 'Master.' You have only one Master, the Messiah.* ¹¹Whoever serves you like a servant is the greatest among you. ¹²People who think they are better than others will be made humble. But people who humble themselves will be made great.

¹³"It will be bad for you teachers of the law and you Pharisees! You are hypocrites*! You close the way for people to enter God's kingdom.* You yourselves don't enter, and you stop those who are trying to enter. ¹⁴ᵈ

¹⁵"It will be bad for you teachers of the law and you Pharisees! You are hypocrites. You travel across the seas and across different countries to find one person who will follow your ways. When

---

ᵃ **22:44 control** Literally, "feet."

ᵇ **23:5 Scripture boxes** Small leather boxes containing four important Scriptures. Some Jews tied these to the forehead and left arm to show their devotion to God and his word. Many Pharisees made these bigger to show that they were more religious than others.

ᶜ **23:5 tassels** Decorations made from wool threads that hung down from the four corners of the clothing or prayer shawls worn by Jews. They were supposed to be reminders of God's commands (see Num. 15:38–41).

ᵈ **23:14** Some Greek copies add verse 14: "It will be bad for you, teachers of the law and you Pharisees. You are hypocrites. You cheat widows and take their homes. Then you make long prayers so that people can see you. So you will have a worse punishment." See Mk. 12:40; Lk. 20:47.

you find that person, you make him worse than you are. And you are so bad that you belong in hell! ¹⁶"It will be bad for you teachers of the law and you Pharisees! You guide the people, but you are blind. You say, 'If anyone uses the name of the Temple* to make a promise, that means nothing. But anyone who uses the gold that is in the Temple to make a promise must keep that promise.' ¹⁷You are blind fools! Can't you see that the Temple is greater than the gold on it? It's the Temple that makes the gold holy*! ¹⁸"And you say, 'If anyone uses the altar* to make a promise, that means nothing. But anyone who uses the gift on the altar to make a promise must keep that promise.' ¹⁹You are blind! Can't you see that the altar is greater than any gift on it? It's the altar that makes the gift holy! ²⁰Whoever uses the altar to make a promise is really using the altar and everything on the altar. ²¹And anyone who uses the Temple to make a promise is really using the Temple and God, who lives in it. ²²Whoever uses heaven to make a promise is using God's throne and the one who is seated on it.

²³"It will be bad for you teachers of the law and you Pharisees! You are hypocrites! You give God a tenth of the food you get, even your mint, dill, and cumin.ᵃ But you don't obey the really important teachings of the law—being fair, showing mercy, and being faithful. These are the things you should do. And you should also continue to do those other things. ²⁴You guide the people, but you are blind! Think about a man picking a little fly out of his drink and then swallowing a camel! You are like that.ᵇ

²⁵"It will be bad for you teachers of the law and you Pharisees! You are hypocrites! You wash clean the outside of your cups and dishes. But inside they are full of what you got by cheating others and pleasing yourselves. ²⁶Pharisees, you are blind! First make the inside of the cup clean and good. Then the outside of the cup will also be clean.

²⁷"It will be bad for you teachers of the law and you Pharisees! You are hypocrites! You are like tombs* that are painted white. Outside they look fine, but inside they are full of dead people's bones and all kinds of filth. ²⁸It is the same with you. People look at you and think you are godly. But on the inside you are full of hypocrisy* and evil.

²⁹"It will be bad for you teachers of the law and you Pharisees! You are hypocrites! You build tombs for the prophets.* And you show honor to the graves of the godly people who were killed. ³⁰And you say, 'If we had lived during the time of our ancestors,* we would not have helped them kill these prophets.' ³¹So you give proof that you are descendants of those who

---

a **23:23 You give … cumin** Literally, "You tithe mint, dill, and cumin." The Law of Moses required Israelites to share their food supply by dedicating a tenth of their field crops and livestock to God (see Lev. 27:30–32; Deut. 26:12). This did not include such small garden plants as those mentioned here. So these Pharisees were giving more than required to be sure they were not breaking the Law.

b **23:24 You are like that** Meaning "You worry about the smallest mistakes but commit the biggest sin."

Jesus heals a crippled man
Mark 2:1-12

Jesus gives life to a dead girl
Mark 5:21-43

© WBTC 2011

killed the prophets. 32And you will finish the sin that your ancestors started!

33"You are snakes! You are from a family of poisonous snakes! You will not escape God. You will all be judged guilty and go to hell! 34So I tell you this: I send to you prophets and teachers who are wise and know the Scriptures. You will kill some of them. You will hang some of them on crosses. You will beat some of them in your synagogues. You will chase them from town to town.

35"So you will be guilty for the death of all the good people who have been killed on earth. You will be guilty for the killing of that godly man Abel. And you will be guilty for the killing of Zechariah*d* son of Berachiah. He was killed between the Temple and the altar. You will be guilty for the killing of all the good people who lived between the time of Abel and the time of Zechariah. 36Believe me when I say that all these things will happen to you people who are living now.

Jesus Warns the People of Jerusalem
(Lk. 13:34–35)

37"O Jerusalem, Jerusalem! You kill the prophets.* You stone to death those that God has sent to you. Many, many times I wanted to help your people. I wanted to gather them together as a hen gathers her chicks under her wings. But you did not let me. 38Now your house will be left completely empty. 39I tell you, you will not see me again until that time when you will say, 'Welcome! God

bless the one who comes in the name of the Lord.'*b*"

Jesus Warns About the Future
(Mk. 13:1–31; Lk. 21:5–33)

24 1Jesus left the Temple* area and was walking away. But his followers came to him to show him the Temple's buildings. 2He asked them, "Are you looking at these buildings? The fact is, they will be destroyed. Every stone will be thrown down to the ground. Not one stone will be left on another."

3Later, Jesus was sitting at a place on the Mount of Olives.* The followers came to be alone with him. They said, "Tell us when these things will happen. And what will happen to prepare us for your coming and the end of time?"

4Jesus answered, "Be careful! Don't let anyone fool you. 5Many people will come and use my name. They will say, 'I am the Messiah.*' And they will fool many people. 6You will hear about wars that are being fought. And you will hear stories about other wars beginning. But don't be afraid. These things must happen before the end comes. 7Nations will fight against other nations. Kingdoms will fight against other kingdoms. There will be times when there is no food for people to eat. And there will be earthquakes in different places. 8These things are only the beginning of troubles, like the first pains of a woman giving birth.

9"Then you will be arrested and handed over to be punished and killed. People all over the world will hate you because you believe in me. 10During that time many

---

a **23:35 Abel, Zechariah** In the Hebrew Old Testament, these are the first and last persons murdered.

b **23:39** Quote from Ps. 118:26.

believers will lose their faith. They will turn against each other and hate each other. [11]Many false prophets* will come and cause many people to believe things that are wrong. [12]There will be so much more evil in the world that the love of most believers will grow cold. [13]But the one who remains faithful to the end will be saved. [14]And the Good News I have shared about God's kingdom* will be told throughout the world. It will be spread to every nation. Then the end will come.

[15]"Daniel the prophet* spoke about 'the terrible thing that causes destruction.'[a] You will see this terrible thing standing in the holy place." (You who read this should understand what it means.) [16]"The people in Judea at that time should run away to the mountains. [17]They should run away without wasting time to stop for anything. If they are on the roof of their house, they must not go down to get anything out of the house. [18]If they are in the field, they must not go back to get a coat.

[19]"During that time it will be hard for women who are pregnant or have small babies! [20]Pray that it will not be winter or a Sabbath* day when these things happen and you have to run away, [21]because it will be a time of great trouble. There will be more trouble than has ever happened since the beginning of the world. And nothing as bad as that will ever happen again.

[22]"But God has decided to make that terrible time short. If it were not made short, no one would continue living. But God will make that time short to help the people he has chosen.

[23]"Someone might say to you at that time, 'Look, there is the Messiah!' Or someone else might say, 'There he is!' But don't believe them. [24]False messiahs and false prophets will come and do great miracles and wonders,[b] trying to fool the people God has chosen, if that is possible. [25]Now I have warned you about this before it happens.

[26]"Someone might tell you, 'The Messiah is there in the desert!' But don't go into the desert to look for him. Someone else might say, 'There is the Messiah in that room!' But don't believe it. [27]When the Son of Man* comes, everyone will see him. It will be like lightning flashing in the sky that can be seen everywhere. [28]It's like looking for a dead body: You will find it where the vultures* are gathering above.

[29]"Right after the trouble of those days, this will happen:
'The sun will become dark,
    and the moon will not give
    light.
The stars will fall from the sky,
    and everything in the sky
    will be changed.'[c]
[30]"Then there will be something in the sky that shows the Son of Man is coming. All the people of the world will cry. Everyone will see the Son of Man coming on the clouds in the sky. He will come with power and great glory.* [31]He will use a loud trumpet to send his angels all around the earth.

---

a **24:15 'the terrible thing ... destruction'** See Dan. 9:27; 12:11 (also Dan. 11:31).

b **24:24 miracles and wonders** Here, amazing acts done by Satan's power.
c **24:29** See Isa. 13:10; 34:4.

They will gather his chosen people from every part of the earth.

³²"The fig tree teaches us a lesson: When its branches become green and soft, and new leaves begin to grow, then you know that summer is very near. ³³In the same way, when you see all these things happening, you will know that the time*a* is very near, already present. ³⁴I assure you that all these things will happen while some of the people of this time are still living. ³⁵The whole world, earth and sky, will be destroyed, but my words will last forever.

Only God Knows When the Time Will Be
(Mk. 13:32–37; Lk. 17:26–30, 34–36)

³⁶"No one knows when that day or time will be. The Son and the angels in heaven don't know when it will be. Only the Father knows.

³⁷"When the Son of Man* comes, it will be the same as what happened during Noah's time. ³⁸In those days before the flood, people were eating and drinking, marrying and giving their children to be married right up to the day Noah entered the boat. ³⁹They knew nothing about what was happening until the flood came and destroyed them all.

"It will be the same when the Son of Man comes. ⁴⁰Two men will be working together in the field. One will be taken and the other will be left. ⁴¹Two women will be grinding grain with a mill.* One will be taken and the other will be left.

⁴²"So always be ready. You don't know the day your Lord will come. ⁴³What would a homeowner do if he knew when a thief was coming? You know he would be ready and not let the thief break in. ⁴⁴So you also must be ready. The Son of Man will come at a time when you don't expect him.

Good Servants and Bad Servants
(Lk. 12:41–48)

⁴⁵"Who is the wise and trusted servant? The master trusts one servant to give the other servants their food at the right time. Who is the one the master trusts to do that work? ⁴⁶When the master comes and finds that servant doing the work he gave him, it will be a day of blessing for that servant. ⁴⁷I can tell you without a doubt, the master will choose that servant to take care of everything he owns.

⁴⁸"But what will happen if that servant is evil and thinks his master will not come back soon? ⁴⁹He will begin to beat the other servants. He will eat and drink with others who are drunk. ⁵⁰Then the master will come when the servant is not ready, at a time when the servant is not expecting him. ⁵¹Then the master will punish that servant. He will send him away to be with the hypocrites,* where people will cry and grind their teeth with pain.

A Story About Ten Girls

25 ¹"At that time God's kingdom* will be like ten girls who went to wait for the bridegroom.* They took their lamps with them. ²Five of the girls were foolish, and five were wise. ³The foolish girls took their lamps with them, but they did not take extra oil for the lamps. ⁴The wise girls took their lamps and more oil in jars. ⁵When the bridegroom was very late, the girls could not keep

a **24:33 time** The time Jesus has been talking about when something important will happen. See Lk. 21:31, where Jesus says that this is the time for God's kingdom to come.

their eyes open, and they all fell asleep.

6"At midnight someone announced, 'The bridegroom is coming! Come and meet him!'

7"Then all the girls woke up. They made their lamps ready. 8But the foolish girls said to the wise girls, 'Give us some of your oil. The oil in our lamps is all gone.'

9"The wise girls answered, 'No! The oil we have might not be enough for all of us. But go to those who sell oil and buy some for yourselves.'

10"So the foolish girls went to buy oil. While they were gone, the bridegroom came. The girls who were ready went in with the bridegroom to the wedding feast. Then the door was closed and locked.

11"Later, the other girls came. They said, 'Sir, sir! Open the door to let us in.'

12"But the bridegroom answered, 'Certainly not! I don't even know you.'

13"So always be ready. You don't know the day or the time when the Son of Man* will come.

A Story About Three Servants
(Lk. 19:11–27)

14"At that time God's kingdom* will also be like a man leaving home to travel to another place for a visit. Before he left, he talked with his servants. He told his servants to take care of his things while he was gone. 15He decided how much each servant would be able to care for. The man gave one servant five bags of money.*a He

gave another servant two bags. And he gave a third servant one bag. Then he left. 16The servant who got five bags went quickly to invest the money. Those five bags of money earned five more. 17It was the same with the servant who had two bags. That servant invested the money and earned two more. 18But the servant who got one bag of money went away and dug a hole in the ground. Then he hid his master's money in the hole.

19"After a long time the master came home. He asked the servants what they did with his money. 20The servant who got five bags brought that amount and five more bags of money to the master. The servant said, 'Master, you trusted me to care for five bags of money. So I used them to earn five more.'

21"The master answered, 'You did right. You are a good servant who can be trusted. You did well with that small amount of money. So I will let you care for much greater things. Come and share my happiness with me.'

22"Then the servant who got two bags of money came to the master. The servant said, 'Master, you gave me two bags of money to care for. So I used your two bags to earn two more.'

23"The master answered, 'You did right. You are a good servant who can be trusted. You did well with a small amount of money. So I will let you care for much greater things. Come and share my happiness with me.'

24"Then the servant who got one bag of money came to the master. The servant said, 'Master, I knew you were a very hard

---

a **25:15 bags of money** Literally, "talanta" or "talents." A talent was about 27 to 36 kg (60 to 80 pounds) of gold, silver, or copper coins. Also in verses 20, 22, 24, 28.

man. You harvest what you did not plant. You gather crops where you did not put any seed. ²⁵So I was afraid. I went and hid your money in the ground. Here is the one bag of money you gave me.'

²⁶"The master answered, 'You are a bad and lazy servant! You say you knew that I harvest what I did not plant and that I gather crops where I did not put any seed. ²⁷So you should have put my money in the bank. Then, when I came home, I would get my money back. And I would also get the interest that my money earned.'

²⁸"So the master told his other servants, 'Take the one bag of money from that servant and give it to the servant who has ten bags. ²⁹Everyone who uses what they have will get more. They will have much more than they need. But people who do not use what they have will have everything taken away from them.' ³⁰Then the master said, 'Throw that useless servant outside into the darkness, where people will cry and grind their teeth with pain.'

The Son of Man Will Judge All People

³¹"The Son of Man* will come again with divine greatness,* and all his angels will come with him. He will sit as king on his great and glorious throne. ³²All the people of the world will be gathered before him. Then he will separate everyone into two groups. It will be like a shepherd separating his sheep from his goats. ³³He will put the sheep on his right and the goats on his left.

³⁴"Then the king will say to the godly people on his right, 'Come, my Father has great blessings for you. The kingdom* he promised is now yours. It has been prepared for you since the world was made. ³⁵It is yours because when I was hungry, you gave me food to eat. When I was thirsty, you gave me something to drink. When I had no place to stay, you welcomed me into your home. ³⁶When I was without clothes, you gave me something to wear. When I was sick, you cared for me. When I was in prison, you came to visit me.'

³⁷"Then the godly people will answer, 'Lord, when did we see you hungry and give you food? When did we see you thirsty and give you something to drink? ³⁸When did we see you with no place to stay and welcome you into our home? When did we see you without clothes and give you something to wear? ³⁹When did we see you sick or in prison and care for you?'

⁴⁰"Then the king will answer, 'The truth is, anything you did for any of my people here,[a] you also did for me.'

⁴¹"Then the king will say to the evil people on his left, 'Get away from me. God has already decided that you will be punished. Go into the fire that burns forever—the fire that was prepared for the devil and his angels. ⁴²You must go away because when I was hungry, you gave me nothing to eat. When I was thirsty, you gave me nothing to drink. ⁴³When I had no place to stay, you did not welcome me into your home. When I was without clothes, you gave me nothing to wear. When I was sick and in prison, you did not care for me.'

[a] 25:40 any of my people here Literally, "one of the least of these brothers of mine." Also in verse 45.

⁴⁴"Then those people will answer, 'Lord, when did we see you hungry or thirsty? When did we see you without a place to stay? Or when did we see you without clothes or sick or in prison? When did we see any of this and not help you?'

⁴⁵"The king will answer, 'The truth is, anything you refused to do for any of my people here, you refused to do for me.'

⁴⁶"Then these evil people will go away to be punished forever. But the godly people will go and enjoy eternal life."

The Jewish Leaders Plan to Kill Jesus
(Mk. 14:1–2; Lk. 22:1–2; Jn. 11:45–53)

26 ¹After Jesus finished saying all these things, he said to his followers, ²"You know that the day after tomorrow is Passover.* On that day the Son of Man* will be handed over to his enemies to be killed on a cross."

³Then the leading priests and the older Jewish leaders had a meeting at the palace where the high priest* lived. The high priest's name was Caiaphas. ⁴In the meeting they tried to find a way to arrest and kill Jesus without anyone knowing what they were doing. They planned to arrest Jesus and kill him. ⁵They said, "We cannot arrest Jesus during Passover. We don't want the people to become angry and cause a riot."

A Woman Does Something Special
(Mk. 14:3–9; Jn. 12:1–8)

⁶Jesus was in Bethany at the house of Simon the leper.* ⁷While he was there, a woman came to him. She had an alabaster* jar filled with expensive perfume. She poured the perfume on Jesus' head while he was eating.

⁸The followers saw the woman do this and were upset at her. They said, "Why waste that perfume? ⁹It could be sold for a lot of money, and the money could be given to those who are poor."

¹⁰But Jesus knew what happened. He said, "Why are you bothering this woman? She did a very good thing for me. ¹¹You will always have the poor with you.ᵃ But you will not always have me. ¹²This woman poured perfume on my body. She did this to prepare me for burial after I die. ¹³The Good News* will be told to people all over the world. And I can assure you that everywhere the Good News is told, the story of what this woman did will also be told, and people will remember her."

Judas Agrees to Help Jesus' Enemies
(Mk. 14:10–11; Lk. 22:3–6)

¹⁴Then one of the twelve followers went to talk to the leading priests. This was the follower named Judas Iscariot. ¹⁵He said, "I will hand Jesus over to you. What will you pay me for doing this?" The priests gave him 30 silver coins. ¹⁶After that Judas waited for the best time to hand Jesus over to them.

The Passover Meal
(Mk. 14:12–21; Lk. 22:7–14, 21–23; Jn. 13:21–30)

¹⁷On the first day of the Festival of Unleavened Bread,* the followers came to Jesus. They said, "We will prepare everything for you to eat the Passover* meal. Where do you want us to have the meal?"

¹⁸Jesus answered, "Go into the city. Go to a man I know. Tell him that the Teacher says, 'The chosen

ᵃ **26:11 You will ... with you** See Deut. 15:11.

time is near. I will have the Passover meal with my followers at your house.'" ¹⁹They obeyed and did what Jesus told them to do. They prepared the Passover meal. ²⁰In the evening Jesus was at the table with the twelve followers. ²¹They were all eating. Then Jesus said, "Believe me when I say that one of you twelve here will hand me over to my enemies." ²²The followers were very sad to hear this. Each one said, "Lord, surely I am not the one!" ²³Jesus answered, "One who has dipped his bread in the same bowl with me will be the one to hand me over. ²⁴The Son of Man* will suffer what the Scriptures* say will happen to him. But it will be very bad for the one who hands over the Son of Man to be killed. It would be better for him if he had never been born." ²⁵Then Judas, the very one who would hand him over, said to Jesus, "Teacher, surely I am not the one you are talking about, am I?"

Jesus answered, "Yes, it is you."

The Lord's Supper
(Mk. 14:22–26; Lk. 22:15–20; 1 Cor. 11:23–25)

²⁶While they were eating, Jesus took some bread and thanked God for it. He broke off some pieces, gave them to his followers and said, "Take this bread and eat it. It is my body." ²⁷Then he took a cup of wine, thanked God for it, and gave it to them. He said, "Each one of you drink some of it. ²⁸This wine is my blood, which will be poured out to forgive the sins of many and begin the new agreement* from God to his people. ²⁹I want you to know, I will not drink this wine again until that day when we are together in my Father's kingdom* and the wine is new. Then I will drink it again with you."

³⁰They all sang a song and then went out to the Mount of Olives.*

Jesus Says His Followers Will Leave Him
(Mk. 14:27–31; Lk. 22:31–34; Jn. 13:36–38)

³¹Jesus told the followers, "Tonight you will all lose your faith in me. The Scriptures* say,

'I will kill the shepherd,
and the sheep will run away.'
Zechariah 13:7

³²But after I am killed, I will rise from death. Then I will go into Galilee. I will be there before you go there."

³³Peter answered, "All the other followers may lose their faith in you. But my faith will never be shaken."

³⁴Jesus answered, "The truth is, tonight you will say you don't know me. You will deny me three times before the rooster crows."

³⁵But Peter answered, "I will never say I don't know you! I will even die with you!" And all the other followers said the same thing.

Jesus Prays Alone
(Mk. 14:32–42; Lk. 22:39–46)

³⁶Then Jesus went with his followers to a place called Gethsemane. He said to them, "Sit here while I go there and pray." ³⁷He told Peter and the two sons of Zebedee to come with him. Then he began to be very sad and troubled. ³⁸Jesus said to Peter and the two sons of Zebedee, "My heart is so heavy with grief, I feel as if I am dying. Wait here and stay awake with me."

³⁹Then Jesus went on a little farther away from them. He fell to the ground and prayed, "My

Father, if it is possible, don't make me drink from this cup.*a* But do what you want, not what I want." ⁴⁰Then he went back to his followers and found them sleeping. He said to Peter, "Could you men not stay awake with me for one hour? ⁴¹Stay awake and pray for strength against temptation. Your spirit wants to do what is right, but your body is weak."

⁴²Then Jesus went away a second time and prayed, "My Father, if I must do this*b* and it is not possible for me to escape it, then I pray that what you want will be done."

⁴³Then he went back to the followers. Again he found them sleeping. They could not stay awake. ⁴⁴So he left them and went away one more time and prayed. This third time he prayed, he said the same thing.

⁴⁵Then Jesus went back to the followers and said, "Are you still sleeping and resting? The time has come for the Son of Man* to be handed over to the control of sinful men. ⁴⁶Stand up! We must go. Here comes the one who will hand me over."

Jesus Is Arrested
(Mk. 14:43–50; Lk. 22:47–53; Jn. 18:3–12)

⁴⁷While Jesus was still speaking, Judas, one of the twelve apostles* came there. He had a big crowd of people with him, all carrying swords and clubs. They had been sent from the leading priests and the older leaders of the people.

⁴⁸Judas*c* planned to do something to show them which one was Jesus. He said, "The one I kiss will be Jesus. Arrest him." ⁴⁹So he went to Jesus and said, "Hello, Teacher!" Then Judas kissed him.

⁵⁰Jesus answered, "Friend, do the thing you came to do."

Then the men came and grabbed Jesus and arrested him. ⁵¹When that happened, one of the followers with Jesus grabbed his sword and pulled it out. He swung it at the servant of the high priest* and cut off his ear.

⁵²Jesus said to the man, "Put your sword back in its place. People who use swords will be killed with swords. ⁵³Surely you know I could ask my Father and he would give me more than twelve armies of angels. ⁵⁴But it must happen this way to show the truth of what the Scriptures* said."

⁵⁵Then Jesus said to the crowd, "Why do you come to get me with swords and clubs as if I were a criminal. Every day I sat in the Temple* area teaching. You did not arrest me there. ⁵⁶But all these things have happened to show the full meaning of what the prophets* wrote." Then all of Jesus' followers left him and ran away.

Jesus Before the Jewish Leaders
(Mk. 14:53–65; Lk. 22:54–55, 63–71; Jn. 18:13–14, 19–24)

⁵⁷The men who arrested Jesus led him to the house of Caiaphas the high priest.* The teachers of the law and the older Jewish leaders were gathered there. ⁵⁸Peter followed Jesus but stayed back at a distance. He followed him to the

a 26:39 cup A symbol of suffering. Jesus used the idea of drinking from a cup to mean accepting the suffering he would face in the terrible events that were soon to come.
b 26:42 do this Literally, "drink this," referring to the "cup," the symbol of suffering in verse 39.
c 26:48 Judas Literally, "the one who handed him over."

yard of the high priest's house. Peter went in and sat with the guards. He wanted to see what would happen to Jesus.

⁵⁹The leading priests and the high council tried to find something against Jesus so that they could kill him. They tried to find people to lie and say that Jesus had done wrong. ⁶⁰Many people came and told lies about him. But the council could find no real reason to kill him. Then two people came ⁶¹and said, "This man*ᵃ* said, 'I can destroy the Temple* of God and build it again in three days.'"

⁶²Then the high priest stood up and said to Jesus, "Don't you have anything to say about these charges against you? Are they telling the truth?" ⁶³But Jesus said nothing.

Again the high priest said to Jesus, "You are now under oath.* I command you by the power of the living God to tell us the truth. Tell us, are you the Messiah,* the Son of God?"

⁶⁴Jesus answered, "Yes, that's right. But I tell you, in the future you will see the Son of Man* sitting at the right side of God. And you will see the Son of Man coming on the clouds of heaven."

⁶⁵When the high priest heard this, he tore his clothes in anger. He said, "This man has said things that insult God! We don't need any more witnesses. You all heard his insulting words. ⁶⁶What do you think?"

The Jewish leaders answered, "He is guilty, and he must die."

⁶⁷Then some there spit in Jesus' face, and they hit him with their fists. Others slapped him. ⁶⁸They said, "Show us that you are a prophet,*ᵇ* Messiah! Tell us who hit you!"

Peter Is Afraid to Say He Knows Jesus
(Mk. 14:66–72; Lk. 22:56–62; Jn. 18:15–18, 25–27)

⁶⁹While Peter was sitting outside in the yard, a servant girl came up to him. She said, "You were with Jesus, that man from Galilee."

⁷⁰But Peter told everyone there that this was not true. "I don't know what you are talking about," he said.

⁷¹Then he left the yard. At the gate another girl saw him and said to the people there, "This man was with Jesus of Nazareth."

⁷²Again, Peter said he was never with Jesus. He said, "I swear to God I don't know the man!"

⁷³A short time later those standing there went to Peter and said, "We know you are one of them. It's clear from the way you talk."

⁷⁴Then Peter began to curse. He said, "I swear to God, I don't know the man!" As soon as he said this, a rooster crowed. ⁷⁵Then he remembered what Jesus had told him: "Before the rooster crows, you will say three times that you don't know me." Then Peter went outside and cried bitterly.

Jesus Is Taken to Governor Pilate
(Mk. 15:1; Lk. 23:1–2; Jn. 18:28–32)

27 ¹Early the next morning, all the leading priests and older leaders of the people met and decided to kill Jesus. ²They tied him, led him away, and handed him over to Pilate,* the governor.

ᵃ **26:61 This man** That is, Jesus. His enemies avoided saying his name.

ᵇ **26:68 prophet** A prophet often knows things that are hidden to other people.

Judas Kills Himself
(Acts 1:18–19)

3Judas saw that they had decided to kill Jesus. He was the one who had handed him over. When he saw what happened, he was very sorry for what he had done. So he took the 30 silver coins back to the priests and the older leaders. 4Judas said, "I sinned. I handed over to you an innocent man to be killed."

The Jewish leaders answered, "We don't care! That's a problem for you, not us."

5So Judas threw the money into the Temple.* Then he went out from there and hanged himself.

6The leading priests picked up the silver coins in the Temple. They said, "Our law does not allow us to keep this money with the Temple money, because this money has paid for a man's death." 7So they decided to use the money to buy a field called Potter's Field. This field would be a place to bury people who died while visiting in Jerusalem. 8That is why that field is still called the Field of Blood. 9This showed the full meaning of what Jeremiah the prophet* said:

"They took 30 silver coins.
That was how much the people of Israel* decided to pay for his life. 10They used those 30 silver coins to buy the potter's field, as the Lord commanded me."*a*

Governor Pilate Questions Jesus
(Mk. 15:2–5; Lk. 23:3–5; Jn. 18:33–38)

11Jesus stood before Pilate,* the governor, who asked him, "Are you the king of the Jews?"

Jesus answered, "Yes, that's right."

12Then, when the leading priests and the older Jewish leaders made their accusations against Jesus, he said nothing.

13So Pilate said to him, "Don't you hear all these charges they are making against you? Why don't you answer?"

14But Jesus did not say anything, and this really surprised the governor.

Pilate Tries but Fails to Free Jesus
(Mk. 15:6–15; Lk. 23:13–25; Jn. 18:39–19:16)

15Every year at Passover* time the governor would free one prisoner—whichever one the people wanted him to free. 16At that time there was a man in prison who was known to be very bad. His name was Barabbas.*b*

17When a crowd gathered, Pilate* said to them, "I will free one man for you. Which one do you want me to free: Barabbas or Jesus who is called the Messiah*?" 18Pilate knew that they had handed Jesus over to him because they were jealous of him.

19While Pilate was sitting there in the place for judging, his wife sent a message to him. It said, "Don't do anything with that man. He is not guilty. Last night I had a dream about him, and it troubled me very much."

20But the leading priests and older Jewish leaders told the people to ask for Barabbas to be set free and for Jesus to be killed.

21Pilate said, "I have Barabbas and Jesus. Which one do you want me to set free for you?"

a 27:10 "They took ... me" See Zech. 11:12–13; Jer. 32:6–9.

b 27:16 Barabbas In some Greek copies the name is Jesus Barabbas.

The people answered, "Barabbas!"

22Pilate asked, "So what should I do with Jesus, the one called the Messiah?"

All the people said, "Kill him on a cross!"

23Pilate asked, "Why do you want me to kill him? What wrong has he done?"

But they shouted louder, "Kill him on a cross!"

24Pilate saw that there was nothing he could do to make the people change. In fact, it looked as if there would be a riot. So he took some water and washed his hands[a] in front of them all. He said, "I am not guilty of this man's death. You are the ones who are doing it!"

25The people answered, "We will take full responsibility for his death. You can blame us and even our children!"

26Then Pilate set Barabbas free. And he told some soldiers to beat Jesus with whips. Then he handed him over to the soldiers to be killed on a cross.

Pilate's Soldiers Make Fun of Jesus
(Mk. 15:16–20; Jn. 19:2–3)

27Then Pilate's* soldiers took Jesus into the governor's palace. All the soldiers gathered around him. 28They took off Jesus' clothes and put a red robe on him. 29Then they made a crown from thorny branches and put it on his head, and they put a stick in his right hand. Then they bowed before him, making fun of him. They said, "We salute you, king of the Jews!" 30They spit on him. Then they took his stick and kept hitting him on the head with it. 31After they finished making fun of him, the soldiers took off the robe and put his own clothes on him again. Then they led him away to be killed on a cross.

Jesus Is Nailed to a Cross
(Mk. 15:21–32; Lk. 23:26–39; Jn. 19:17–19)

32The soldiers were going out of the city with Jesus. They saw a man from Cyrene named Simon, and they forced him to carry Jesus' cross. 33They came to the place called Golgotha. (Golgotha means "The Place of the Skull.") 34There the soldiers gave Jesus some wine mixed with gall.[b] But when he tasted it, he refused to drink it.

35The soldiers nailed Jesus to a cross. Then they threw dice to divide his clothes between them. 36The soldiers stayed there to guard him. 37They put a sign above his head with the charge against him written on it: "THIS IS JESUS, THE KING OF THE JEWS."

38Two criminals were nailed to crosses beside Jesus—one on the right and the other on the left. 39People walked by and shouted insults at Jesus. They shook their heads 40and said, "You said you could destroy the Temple* and build it again in three days. So save yourself! Come down from that cross if you really are the Son of God!"

41The leading priests, the teachers of the law, and the older Jewish leaders were also there. They made fun of Jesus the same as the other people did. 42They said, "He saved others, but he can't save himself! People say he is the king of Israel.* If he is the king, he

---

[a] **27:24 washed his hands** Pilate did this as a sign to show that he wanted no part in what the people did.

[b] **27:34 gall** Probably used as a drug to relieve pain.

should come down now from the cross. Then we will believe in him. 43He trusted God. So let God save him now, if God really wants him. He himself said, 'I am the Son of God.'" 44And in the same way, the criminals on the crosses beside Jesus also insulted him.

Jesus Dies
(Mk. 15:33–41; Lk. 23:44–49; Jn. 19:28–30)
45At noon the whole country became dark. The darkness continued for three hours. 46About three o'clock Jesus cried out loudly, "Eli, Eli, lema sabachthani?" This means "My God, my God, why have you left me alone?"[a]
47Some of the people standing there heard this. They said, "He is calling Elijah."[b] 48Quickly, one of them ran and got a sponge. He filled the sponge with sour wine and tied the sponge to a stick. Then he used the stick to give the sponge to Jesus to get a drink from it. 49But the others said, "Don't bother him. We want to see if Elijah will come to save him."
50Again Jesus cried out loudly and then died.[c]
51When Jesus died, the curtain* in the Temple* was torn into two pieces. The tear started at the top and tore all the way to the bottom. Also, the earth shook and rocks were broken. 52The graves opened, and many of God's people who had died were raised from death. 53They came out of the graves. And after Jesus was raised from

death, they went into the holy city, and many people saw them. 54The army officer* and the soldiers guarding Jesus saw this earthquake and everything that happened. They were very afraid and said, "He really was the Son of God!"
55Many women were standing away from the cross, watching. These were the women who had followed Jesus from Galilee to care for him. 56Mary Magdalene, Mary the mother of James and Joseph, and the mother of James and John[d] were there.

Jesus Is Buried
(Mk. 15:42–47; Lk. 23:50–56; Jn. 19:38–42)
57That evening a rich man named Joseph came to Jerusalem. He was a follower of Jesus from the town of Arimathea. 58He went to Pilate* and asked to have Jesus' body. Pilate gave orders for the soldiers to give Jesus' body to him. 59Then Joseph took the body and wrapped it in a new linen cloth. 60He put Jesus' body in a new tomb* that he had dug in a wall of rock. Then he closed the tomb by rolling a very large stone to cover the entrance. After he did this, he went away. 61Mary Magdalene and the other woman named Mary were sitting near the tomb.

The Tomb of Jesus Is Guarded
62That day was the day called Preparation day.* The next day, the leading priests and the Pharisees* went to Pilate.* 63They said, "Sir, we remember that while that liar was still alive he said, 'I will rise from death in three days.' 64So give the order for the tomb* to be guarded well for three days.

a 27:46 Quote from Ps. 22:1.
b 27:47 "He is calling Elijah" The word for "My God" (Eli in Hebrew or Eloi in Aramaic) sounded to the people like the name of Elijah, a famous man who spoke for God about 850 B.C.
c 27:50 died Literally, "let his spirit leave."
d 27:56 James and John Literally, "the sons of Zebedee."

55

His followers might come and try to steal the body. Then they could tell everyone that he has risen from death. That lie will be even worse than what they said about him before."

65Pilate said, "Take some soldiers and go guard the tomb the best way you know." 66So they all went to the tomb and made it safe from thieves. They did this by sealing the stone in the entrance and putting soldiers there to guard it.

News That Jesus Has Risen From Death
(Mk. 16:1–8; Lk. 24:1–12; Jn. 20:1–10)

28 1The day after the Sabbath* day was the first day of the week. That day at dawn Mary Magdalene and the other woman named Mary went to look at the tomb.*

2Suddenly an angel of the Lord came from the sky, and there was a huge earthquake. The angel went to the tomb and rolled the stone away from the entrance. Then he sat on top of the stone. 3The angel was shining as bright as lightning. His clothes were as white as snow. 4The soldiers guarding the tomb were very afraid of the angel. They shook with fear and then became like dead men.

5The angel said to the women, "Don't be afraid. I know you are looking for Jesus, the one who was killed on the cross. 6But he is not here. He has risen from death, as he said he would. Come and see the place where his body was. 7And go quickly and tell his followers, 'Jesus has risen from death. He is going into Galilee and will be there before you. You will see him there.'" Then the angel said, "Now I have told you."

8So the women left the tomb quickly. They were afraid, but they were also very happy. They ran to tell his followers what happened. 9Suddenly, Jesus was there in front of them. He said, "Hello!" The women went to him and, holding on to his feet, worshiped him. 10Then Jesus said to them, "Don't be afraid. Go tell my followers*a* to go to Galilee. They will see me there."

Report to the Jewish Leaders
11The women went to tell the followers. At the same time, some of the soldiers who were guarding the tomb* went into the city. They went to tell the leading priests everything that happened. 12Then the priests met with the older Jewish leaders and made a plan. They paid the soldiers a lot of money 13and said to them, "Tell the people that Jesus' followers came during the night and stole the body while you were sleeping. 14If the governor hears about this, we will talk to him and keep you out of trouble." 15So the soldiers kept the money and obeyed the priests. And that story is still spread among the Jews even today.

Jesus Talks to His Followers
(Mk. 16:14–18; Lk. 24:36–49; Jn. 20:19–23; Acts 1:6–8)

16The eleven followers went to Galilee, to the mountain where Jesus told them to go. 17On the mountain the followers saw Jesus. They worshiped him. But some of the followers did not believe that it was really Jesus. 18So he came to them and said, "All authority in heaven and on earth is given to me. 19So go and make followers

a 28:10 followers Literally, "brothers."

of all people in the world. Baptize* them in the name of the Father and the Son and the Holy Spirit.* ²⁰Teach them to obey everything that I have told you to do. You can be sure that I will be with you always. I will continue with you until the end of time."

Mark

John Prepares the Way for Jesus
(Mt. 3:1–12; Lk. 3:1–9, 15–17; Jn. 1:19–28)

1 ¹The Good News* about Jesus the Messiah,* the Son of God,ᵃ begins ²with what the prophet* Isaiah said would happen. He wrote:

"Listen! I will send my
    messenger ahead of you.
He will prepare the way for
    you."   *Malachi 3:1*

³ "There is someone shouting in
    the desert:
'Prepare the way for the Lord.
Make the road straight for
    him.'"   *Isaiah 40:3*

⁴So John the Baptizer* came and was baptizing* people in the desert area. He told them to be baptized to show that they wanted to change their lives, and then their sins would be forgiven. ⁵All the people from Judea, including everyone from Jerusalem, came out to John. They confessed the bad things they had done, and he baptized them in the Jordan River.

⁶John wore clothes made from camel's hair and a leather belt around his waist. He ate locusts* and wild honey.

⁷This is what John told the people: "There is someone coming later who is able to do more than I can. I am not good enough to be the slave who stoops down to untie his sandals. ⁸I baptize you with water, but the one who is coming will baptize you with the Holy Spirit.*"

Jesus Is Baptized by John
(Mt. 3:13–17; Lk. 3:21–22)

⁹About that time Jesus came from the town of Nazareth in Galilee to the place where John was. John baptized* Jesus in the Jordan River. ¹⁰As Jesus was coming up out of the water, he saw the sky torn open. The Spirit* came down on him like a dove. ¹¹A voice came from heaven and said, "You are my Son, the one I love. I am very pleased with you."

Jesus Goes Away to Be Tempted
(Mt. 4:1–11; Lk. 4:1–13)

¹²Then the Spirit* sent Jesus into the desert alone. ¹³He was there for 40 days, being tempted by Satan.* During this time he was out among the wild animals. Then angels came and helped him.

Jesus Begins His Work in Galilee
(Mt. 4:12–17; Lk. 4:14–15)

¹⁴After John was put in prison, Jesus went into Galilee and told people the Good News* from God. ¹⁵He said, "The right time is now here. God's kingdom* is very near.ᵇ Change your hearts and lives, and believe the Good News!"

ᵃ 1:1 the Son of God Some Greek copies do not have these words.

ᵇ 1:15 is very near Or "is coming soon" or "has come."

Jesus Chooses Some Followers
(Mt. 4:18–22; Lk. 5:1–11)

16Jesus was walking by Lake Galilee. He saw Simon*a* and his brother Andrew. These two men were fishermen, and they were throwing a net into the lake to catch fish. 17Jesus said to them, "Come, follow me, and I will make you a different kind of fishermen. You will bring in people, not fish." 18So they immediately left their nets and followed Jesus.

19Jesus continued walking by Lake Galilee. He saw two more brothers, James and John, the sons of Zebedee. They were in their boat, preparing their nets to catch fish. 20Their father Zebedee and the men who worked for him were in the boat with the brothers. When Jesus saw the brothers, he told them to come. They left their father and followed Jesus.

Jesus Frees a Man From an Evil Spirit
(Lk. 4:31–37)

21Jesus and his followers went to Capernaum.* On the Sabbath* day, Jesus went into the synagogue* and taught the people. 22They were amazed at his teaching. He did not teach like their teachers of the law. He taught like someone with authority. 23While Jesus was in the synagogue, a man was there who had an evil spirit inside him. The man shouted, 24"Jesus of Nazareth! What do you want with us? Did you come to destroy us? I know who you are—God's Holy One!"

25Jesus, his voice full of warning, said, "Be quiet, and come out of him!" 26The evil spirit made the man shake. Then the spirit made a loud noise and came out of him.

27The people were amazed. They asked each other, "What is happening here? This man is teaching something new, and he teaches with authority! He even commands evil spirits, and they obey him." 28So the news about Jesus spread quickly everywhere in the area of Galilee.

Jesus Heals Many People
(Mt. 8:14–17; Lk. 4:38–41)

29Jesus and the followers left the synagogue.* They all went with James and John to the home of Simon and Andrew. 30Simon's mother-in-law was very sick. She was in bed and had a fever. The people there told Jesus about her. 31So he went to her bed. Jesus held her hand and helped her stand up. The fever left her, and she was healed. Then she began serving them.

32That night, after the sun went down, the people brought to Jesus many who were sick. They also brought those who had demons* inside them. 33Everyone in the town gathered at the door of that house. 34Jesus healed many of those who had different kinds of sicknesses. He also forced many demons out of people. But he would not allow the demons to speak, because they knew who he was.*b*

Jesus Goes to Other Towns
(Lk. 4:42–44)

35The next morning Jesus woke up very early. He left the house while it was still dark and went to a place where he could be alone

---

a **1:16 Simon** Simon's other name was Peter. Also in verses 29, 30, 36.

b **1:34 who he was** Meaning that the demons knew that Jesus was the Messiah, the Son of God.

and pray. 36Later, Simon and his friends went to look for Jesus. 37They found him and said, "Everyone is looking for you!"

38Jesus answered, "We should go to another place. We can go to other towns around here, and I can tell God's message to those people too. That is why I came." 39So Jesus traveled everywhere in Galilee. He spoke in the synagogues,* and he forced demons* out of people.

Jesus Heals a Sick Man
(Mt. 8:1–4; Lk. 5:12–16)

40A man who had leprosy* came to Jesus. The man bowed on his knees and begged him, "You have the power to heal me if you want."

41These last words made Jesus angry.*a* But he touched him and said, "I want to heal you. Be healed!" 42Immediately the leprosy disappeared, and the man was healed.

43Jesus told the man to go, but he gave him a strong warning: 44"Don't tell anyone about what I did for you. But go and let the priest look at you.*b* And offer a gift to God because you have been healed. Offer the gift that Moses* commanded.*c* This will show everyone that you are healed." 45The man left there and told everyone he saw that Jesus had healed him. So the news about Jesus spread. And that is why he could not enter a town if people saw him.

a **1:41 These … angry** Most Greek copies have "Moved with pity …." But it is hard to explain why some good Greek copies and Latin versions have "Filled with anger …," so many scholars now consider it to be the original reading.
b **1:44 let the priest look at you** The Law of Moses said a priest must decide when a person with leprosy was well.
c **1:44 Moses commanded** See Lev. 14:1–32.

He stayed in places where people did not live. But people came from all the towns to the places where he was.

Jesus Heals a Crippled Man
(Mt. 9:1–8; Lk. 5:17–26)

2 1A few days later, Jesus came back to Capernaum.* The news spread that he was back home. 2A large crowd gathered to hear him speak. The house was so full that there was no place to stand, not even outside the door. While Jesus was teaching, 3some people brought a paralyzed man to see him. He was being carried by four of them. 4But they could not get the man inside to Jesus because the house was so full of people. So they went to the roof above Jesus and made a hole in it. Then they lowered the mat with the paralyzed man on it. 5When Jesus saw how much faith they had, he said to the paralyzed man, "Young man, your sins are forgiven."

6Some of the teachers of the law were sitting there. They saw what Jesus did, and they said to themselves, 7"Why does this man say things like that? What an insult to God! No one but God can forgive sins."

8Jesus knew immediately what these teachers of the law were thinking. So he said to them, "Why do you have these questions in your minds? 9–10The Son of Man* has power on earth to forgive sins. But how can I prove this to you? Maybe you are thinking it was easy for me to say to the crippled man, 'Your sins are forgiven.' There's no proof it really happened. But what if I say to the man, 'Stand up. Take your mat and walk'? Then you will be able to see if I really have this power or not." So Jesus said to the paralyzed man, [11]"I tell you, stand up. Take your mat and go home."

[12]Immediately the paralyzed man stood up. He picked up his mat and walked out of the room. Everyone could see him. They were amazed and praised God. They said, "This is the most amazing thing we have ever seen!"

Levi (Matthew) Follows Jesus
(Mt. 9:9–13; Lk. 5:27–32)

[13]Jesus went to the lake again, and many people followed him there. So Jesus taught them. [14]He was walking beside the lake, and he saw a man named Levi, son of Alphaeus. Levi was sitting at his place for collecting taxes. Jesus said to him, "Follow me." Then Levi stood up and followed Jesus.

[15]Later that day, Jesus and his followers ate at Levi's house. There were also many tax collectors* and others with bad reputations eating with them. (There were many of these people who followed Jesus.) [16]When some teachers of the law who were Pharisees* saw Jesus eating with such bad people, they asked his followers, "Why does he eat with tax collectors and sinners?"

[17]When Jesus heard this, he said to them, "It is the sick people who need a doctor, not those who are healthy. I did not come to invite good people. I came to invite sinners."

Jesus Is Not Like Other Religious Leaders
(Mt. 9:14–17; Lk. 5:33–39)

[18]The followers of John* and the Pharisees* were fasting.* Some people came to Jesus and said, "John's followers fast, and the followers of the Pharisees fast. But your followers don't fast. Why?"

[19]Jesus answered, "At a wedding the friends of the bridegroom* are not sad while he is with them. They cannot fast while the bridegroom is still there. [20]But the time will come when the bridegroom will be taken from them. Then they will fast.

[21]"When someone sews a patch over a hole in an old coat, they never use a piece of cloth that is not yet shrunk. If they do, the patch will shrink and pull away from the coat. Then the hole will be worse. [22]Also, no one ever pours new wine into old wineskins.* The wine would break them, and the wine would be ruined along with the wineskins. You always put new wine into new wineskins."

Jesus Is Lord Over the Sabbath Day
(Mt. 12:1–8; Lk. 6:1–5)

[23]On the Sabbath* day, Jesus and his followers were walking through some grain fields. The followers picked some grain to eat. [24]Some Pharisees* said to Jesus, "Why are your followers doing this? It is against the law to pick grain on the Sabbath."

[25]Jesus answered, "You have read what David* did when he and the people with him were hungry and needed food. [26]It was during the time of Abiathar the high priest.* David went into God's house and ate the bread that was offered to God. And the Law of Moses* says that only priests can eat that bread. David also gave some of the bread to the people with him."

[27]Then Jesus said to the Pharisees, "The Sabbath day was made to help people. People were not made to be ruled by the Sabbath.

²⁸So the Son of Man* is Lord of every day, even the Sabbath."

Jesus Heals a Man on the Sabbath Day
(Mt. 12:9–14; Lk. 6:6–11)

3 ¹Another time Jesus went into the synagogue.* In the synagogue there was a man with a crippled hand. ²Some Jews there were watching Jesus closely. They were waiting to see if he would heal the man on a Sabbath* day. They wanted to see Jesus do something wrong so that they could accuse him. ³Jesus said to the man with the crippled hand, "Stand up here so that everyone can see you."

⁴Then Jesus asked the people, "Which is the right thing to do on the Sabbath day: to do good or to do evil? Is it right to save a life or to destroy one?" The people said nothing to answer him.

⁵Jesus looked at the people. He was angry, but he felt very sad because they were so stubborn. He said to the man, "Hold out your hand." The man held out his hand, and it was healed. ⁶Then the Pharisees* left and made plans with the Herodians* about a way to kill Jesus.

Many Follow Jesus

⁷Jesus went away with his followers to the lake. A large crowd of people from Galilee followed them. ⁸Many also came from Judea, from Jerusalem, from Idumea, from the area across the Jordan River, and from the area around Tyre and Sidon. These people came because they heard about all that Jesus was doing. ⁹Jesus saw how many people there were, so he told his followers to get a small boat and make it ready for him. He wanted the boat so that the crowds of people could not push against him. ¹⁰He had healed many of them, so all the sick people were pushing toward him to touch him. ¹¹Some people had evil spirits inside them. When the evil spirits saw Jesus, they bowed before him and shouted, "You are the Son of God!" ¹²But Jesus gave the spirits a strong warning not to tell anyone who he was.

Jesus Chooses His Twelve Apostles
(Mt. 10:1–4; Lk. 6:12–16)

¹³Then Jesus went up on a hill and invited those he wanted to go with him. So they joined him there. ¹⁴And he chose twelve men and called them apostles.* He wanted these twelve men to be with him, and he wanted to send them to other places to tell people God's message. ¹⁵He also wanted them to have the power to force demons* out of people. ¹⁶These are the names of the twelve men Jesus chose:

Simon (the one Jesus named Peter),
¹⁷ James and his brother John, the sons of Zebedee (the ones Jesus named Boanerges, which means "Sons of Thunder"),
¹⁸ Andrew,
Philip,
Bartholomew,
Matthew,
Thomas,
James, the son of Alphaeus,
Thaddaeus,
Simon, the Zealot,*
¹⁹ Judas Iscariot (the one who handed Jesus over to his enemies).

Jesus' Power Is From God
(Mt. 12:22–32; Lk. 11:14–23; 12:10)

²⁰Then Jesus went home, but again a large crowd gathered

there. There were so many people that he and his followers could not eat. ²¹His family heard about all these things. They went to get him because people said he was crazy.

²²And the teachers of the law from Jerusalem said, "Satan*ᵃ* is living inside him! He uses power from the ruler of demons* to force demons out of people."

²³So Jesus called them together and talked to them using some stories. He said, "Satan* will not force his own demons out of people. ²⁴A kingdom that fights against itself will not survive. ²⁵And a family that is divided will not survive. ²⁶If Satan is against himself and is fighting against his own people, he will not survive. That would be the end of Satan.

²⁷"Whoever wants to enter a strong man's house and steal his things must first tie him up. Then they can steal the things from his house.

²⁸"I want you to know that people can be forgiven for all the sinful things they do. They can even be forgiven for the bad things they say against God. ²⁹But anyone who speaks against the Holy Spirit* will never be forgiven. They will always be guilty of that sin."

³⁰Jesus said this because the teachers of the law had accused him of having an evil spirit inside him.

Jesus' Followers Are His True Family
(Mt. 12:46–50; Lk. 8:19–21)

³¹Then Jesus' mother and brothers came. They stood outside and sent someone in to tell him to come out. ³²Many people were sitting around Jesus. They said to him, "Your mother and brothers are waiting for you outside."

³³Jesus asked, "Who is my mother? Who are my brothers?" ³⁴Then he looked at the people sitting around him and said, "These people are my mother and my brothers! ³⁵My true brother and sister and mother are those who do what God wants."

A Story About a Farmer Sowing Seed
(Mt. 13:1–9; Lk. 8:4–8)

4 ¹Another time Jesus began teaching by the lake, and a large crowd gathered around him. He got into a boat so that he could sit and teach from the lake. All the people stayed on the shore near the water. ²Jesus used stories to teach them many things. One of his lessons included this story:

³"Listen! A farmer went out to sow seed. ⁴While he was scattering the seed, some of it fell by the road. The birds came and ate all that seed. ⁵Other seed fell on rocky ground, where there was not enough dirt. It grew quickly there because the soil was not deep. ⁶But then the sun rose and the plants were burned. They died because they did not have deep roots. ⁷Some other seed fell among thorny weeds. The weeds grew and stopped the good plants from growing. So they did not make grain. ⁸But some of the seed fell on good ground. There it began to grow, and it made grain. Some plants made 30 times more grain, some 60 times more, and some 100 times more."

⁹Then Jesus said, "You people who hear me, listen!"

ᵃ **3:22 Satan** Literally, "Beelzebul" (the devil).

Why Jesus Used Stories to Teach
(Mt. 13:10–17; Lk. 8:9–10)

[10]Later, Jesus was away from the people. The twelve apostles* and his other followers asked him about the stories.

[11]Jesus said, "Only you can know the secret truth about God's kingdom.* But to those other people I tell everything by using stories. [12]I do this so that,

'They will look and look but
never really see;
they will listen and listen
but never understand.
If they saw and understood,
they might change and be
forgiven.'"   *Isaiah 6:9–10*

Jesus Explains the Story About Seed
(Mt. 13:18–23; Lk. 8:11–15)

[13]Then Jesus said to the followers, "Do you understand this story? If you don't, how will you understand any story? [14]The farmer is like someone who plants God's teaching in people. [15]Sometimes the teaching falls on the path. That is like some people who hear the teaching of God. As soon as they hear it, Satan* comes and takes away the teaching that was planted in them.

[16]"Other people are like the seed planted on rocky ground. They hear the teaching, and they quickly and gladly accept it. [17]But they don't allow it to go deep into their lives. They keep it only a short time. As soon as trouble or persecution* comes because of the teaching they accepted, they give up.

[18]"Others are like the seed planted among the thorny weeds. They hear the teaching, [19]but their lives become full of other things: the worries of this life, the love of money, and everything else they want. This keeps the teaching from growing, and it does not produce a crop[a] in their lives.

[20]"And others are like the seed planted on the good ground. They hear the teaching and accept it. Then they grow and produce a good crop—sometimes 30 times more, sometimes 60 times more, and sometimes 100 times more."

Use the Understanding You Have
(Lk. 8:16–18)

[21]Then Jesus said to them, "You don't take a lamp and hide it under a bowl or a bed, do you? Of course not. You put it on a lampstand. [22]Everything that is hidden will be made clear. Every secret thing will be made known. [23]You people who hear me, listen! [24]Think carefully about what you are hearing. God will know how much to give you by how much you understand now. But he will give you more than you deserve. [25]The people who have some understanding will receive more. But those who do not have much will lose even the small amount they have."

Jesus Uses a Story About Seed

[26]Then Jesus said, "God's kingdom* is like a man who plants seed in the ground. [27]The seed begins to grow. It grows night and day. It doesn't matter whether the man is sleeping or awake, the seed still grows. He doesn't know how it happens. [28]Without any help the ground produces grain. First the plant grows, then the head, and then all the grain in the head. [29]When the grain is ready, the man cuts it. This is the harvest time."

---

a **4:19 produce a crop** Meaning to do the good things God wants his people to do.

What Is God's Kingdom Like?

(Mt. 13:31–32, 34–35; Lk. 13:18–19)

30Then Jesus said, "What can I use to show you what God's kingdom* is like? What story can I use to explain it? 31God's kingdom is like a mustard seed, which is smaller than any other seed on earth that you can plant. 32But when you plant it, it grows and becomes the largest of all the plants in your garden. It has branches that are very big. The wild birds can come and make nests there and be protected from the sun."

33Jesus used many stories like these to teach the people. He taught them all they could understand. 34He always used stories to teach them. But when he was alone with his followers, Jesus explained everything to them.

Jesus' Followers See His Power

(Mt. 8:23–27; Lk. 8:22–25)

35That day, at evening, Jesus said to his followers, "Come with me across the lake." 36So they left the crowd behind and went with Jesus in the boat he was already in. There were also other boats that went with them. 37A very bad wind came up on the lake. The waves were coming over the sides and into the boat, and it was almost full of water. 38Jesus was inside the boat, sleeping with his head on a pillow. The followers went and woke him. They said, "Teacher, don't you care about us? We are going to drown!"

39Jesus stood up and gave a command to the wind and the water. He said, "Quiet! Be still!" Then the wind stopped, and the lake became calm.

40He said to his followers, "Why are you afraid? Do you still have no faith?"

41They were very afraid and asked each other, "What kind of man is this? Even the wind and the water obey him!"

Jesus Frees a Man From Evil Spirits

(Mt. 8:28–34; Lk. 8:26–39)

5 1Jesus and his followers went across the lake to the area where the Gerasene people lived. 2When Jesus got out of the boat, a man came to him from the caves where the dead are buried. This man had an evil spirit living inside him. 3He lived in the burial caves. No one could keep him tied up, even with chains. 4Many times people had put chains on his hands and feet, but he broke the chains. No one was strong enough to control him. 5Day and night he stayed around the burial caves and on the hills. He would scream and cut himself with rocks.

6While Jesus was still far away, the man saw him. He ran to Jesus and bowed down before him. 7-8As Jesus was saying, "You evil spirit, come out of this man," the man shouted loudly, "What do you want with me, Jesus, Son of the Most High God? I beg you in God's name not to punish me!"

9Then Jesus asked the man, "What is your name?"

The man answered, "My name is Legion,a because there are many spirits inside me." 10The spirits inside the man begged Jesus again and again not to send them out of that area.

11A large herd of pigs was eating on a hill near there. 12The evil spirits begged Jesus, "Send us to the pigs. Let us go into them." 13So

a **5:9 Legion** This name means very many. A legion was about 6000 men in the Roman army.

Jesus allowed them to do this. The evil spirits left the man and went into the pigs. Then the herd of pigs ran down the hill and into the lake. They were all drowned. There were about 2000 pigs in that herd.

[14]The men who had the work of caring for the pigs ran away. They ran to the town and to the farms and told everyone what happened. The people went out to see. [15]They came to Jesus, and they saw the man who had the many evil spirits. He was sitting down and was wearing clothes. He was in his right mind again. When they saw this, they were afraid. [16]Those who had seen what Jesus did told the others what happened to the man who had the demons* living in him. And they also told about the pigs. [17]Then the people began to beg Jesus to leave their area.

[18]Jesus was preparing to leave in the boat. The man who was now free from the demons begged to go with him. [19]But Jesus did not allow the man to go. He said, "Go home to your family and friends. Tell them about all that the Lord did for you. Tell them how the Lord was good to you."

[20]So the man left and told the people in the Ten Towns* about the great things Jesus did for him. Everyone was amazed.

Jesus Gives Life to a Dead Girl and Heals a Sick Woman

(Mt. 9:18–26; Lk. 8:40–56)

[21]Jesus went back to the other side of the lake in the boat. There, a large crowd of people gathered around him on the shore. [22]A leader of the synagogue* came. His name was Jairus. He saw Jesus and bowed down before him. [23]He begged Jesus again and again, saying, "My little daughter is dying. Please come and lay your hands on* her. Then she will be healed and will live."

[24]So Jesus went with Jairus. Many people followed Jesus. They were pushing very close around him.

[25]There among the people was a woman who had been bleeding for the past twelve years. [26]She had suffered very much. Many doctors had tried to help her, and all the money she had was spent, but she was not improving. In fact, her sickness was getting worse.

[27]The woman heard about Jesus, so she followed him with the other people and touched his coat. [28]She thought, "If I can just touch his clothes, that will be enough to heal me." [29]As soon as she touched his coat, her bleeding stopped. She felt that her body was healed from all the suffering. [30]Jesus immediately felt power go out from him, so he stopped and turned around. "Who touched my clothes?" he asked.

[31]The followers said to Jesus, "There are so many people pushing against you. But you ask, 'Who touched me?'"

[32]But Jesus continued looking for the one who touched him. [33]The woman knew that she was healed, so she came and bowed at Jesus' feet. She was shaking with fear. She told Jesus the whole story. [34]He said to her, "Dear woman, you are made well because you believed. Go in peace. You will not suffer anymore."

[35]While Jesus was still there speaking, some men came from the house of Jairus, the synagogue leader. They said, "Your daughter

is dead. There is no need to bother the Teacher."

36But Jesus did not care what the men said. He said to the synagogue leader, "Don't be afraid; just believe."

37Jesus let only Peter, James, and John the brother of James go with him. 38They went to the synagogue leader's house, where Jesus saw many people crying loudly. There was a lot of confusion. 39He entered the house and said, "Why are you people crying and making so much noise? This child is not dead. She is only sleeping." 40But everyone laughed at him.

Jesus told the people to leave the house. Then he went into the room where the child was. He brought the child's father and mother and his three followers into the room with him. 41Then Jesus held the girl's hand and said to her, *"Talitha, koum!"* (This means "Little girl, I tell you to stand up!") 42The girl immediately stood up and began walking. (She was twelve years old.) The father and mother and the followers were amazed. 43Jesus gave the father and mother very strict orders not to tell people about this. Then he told them to give the girl some food to eat.

Jesus Goes to His Hometown
(Mt. 13:53–58; Lk. 4:16–30)

6 1Jesus left and went back to his hometown. His followers went with him. 2On the Sabbath* day Jesus taught in the synagogue,* and many people heard him. They were amazed and said, "Where did this man get this teaching? How did he get such wisdom? Who gave it to him? And where did he get the power to do miracles*? 3Isn't he just the carpenter we know—Mary's son, the brother of James, Joses, Judas, and Simon? And don't his sisters still live here in town?" So they had a problem accepting him.

4Then Jesus said to them, "People everywhere give honor to a prophet,* except in his own town, with his own people, or in his home." 5Jesus was not able to do any miracles there except the healing of some sick people by laying his hands on* them. 6He was surprised that the people there had no faith. Then he went to other villages in that area and taught.

Jesus Sends His Apostles on a Mission
(Mt. 10:1, 5–15; Lk. 9:1–6)

7Jesus called his twelve apostles* together. He sent them out in groups of two and gave them power over evil spirits. 8This is what he told them: "Take nothing for your trip except a stick for walking. Take no bread, no bag, and no money. 9You can wear sandals, but don't take extra clothes. 10When you enter a house, stay there until you leave that town. 11If any town refuses to accept you or refuses to listen to you, then leave that town and shake the dust off your feet*a* as a warning to them."

12The apostles left and went to other places. They talked to the people and told them to change their hearts and lives. 13They forced many demons* out of people and put olive oil on*b* many who were sick and healed them.

a 6:11 shake the dust off your feet A warning. It would show that they were finished talking to these people.
b 6:13 put olive oil on Olive oil was used like a medicine.

Herod Thinks Jesus Is John the Baptizer
(Mt. 14:1–12; Lk. 9:7–9)

¹⁴King Herod* heard about Jesus, because Jesus was now famous. Some people said, "He is John the Baptizer.* He must have risen from death, and that is why he can do these miracles.*"

¹⁵Other people said, "He is Elijah.*"

And others said, "He is a prophet.* He is like the prophets who lived long ago."

¹⁶Herod heard these things about Jesus. He said, "I killed John by cutting off his head. Now he has been raised from death!"

How John the Baptizer Was Killed

¹⁷Herod* himself had ordered his soldiers to arrest John and put him in prison. Herod did this to please his wife Herodias. She had been married to Herod's brother Philip, but then Herod married her. ¹⁸John told Herod, "It is not right for you to be married to your brother's wife." ¹⁹So Herodias hated John. She wanted him dead, but she was not able to persuade Herod to kill him. ²⁰Herod was afraid to kill John, because he knew that he was a good and holy* man. So he protected him. He liked listening to John, although what John said left him with so many questions.

²¹Then the right time came for Herodias to cause John's death. It happened on Herod's birthday. Herod gave a dinner party for the most important government leaders, the commanders of his army, and the most important people in Galilee. ²²The daughter of Herodias came to the party and danced. When she danced, Herod and the people eating with him were very pleased.

So King Herod said to the girl, "I will give you anything you want." ²³He promised her, "Anything you ask for I will give to you—even half of my kingdom."

²⁴The girl went to her mother and asked, "What should I ask King Herod to give me?"

Her mother answered, "Ask for the head of John the Baptizer.*"

²⁵So right then the girl went back in to the king. She said to him, "Please give me the head of John the Baptizer. Bring it to me now on a plate."

²⁶King Herod was very sad, but he didn't want to break the promise he had made to her in front of his guests. ²⁷So he sent a soldier to cut off John's head and bring it to him. The soldier went and cut off John's head in the prison. ²⁸He brought the head back on a plate and gave it to the girl, and the girl gave it to her mother. ²⁹John's followers heard about what happened, so they came and got John's body and put it in a tomb.*

Jesus Feeds More Than 5000
(Mt. 14:13–21; Lk. 9:10–17; Jn. 6:1–14)

³⁰The apostles* Jesus had sent out came back to him. They gathered around him and told him about all they had done and taught. ³¹Jesus and his followers were in a very busy place. There were so many people that he and his followers did not even have time to eat. He said to them, "Come with me. We will go to a quiet place to be alone. There we will get some rest."

³²So Jesus and his followers went away alone. They went in a boat to a place where no one lived. ³³But many people saw them leave and knew who they were.

So people from every town ran to the place where they were going and got there before Jesus. ³⁴As Jesus stepped out of the boat, he saw a large crowd waiting. He felt sorry for them, because they were like sheep without a shepherd to care for them. So he taught the people many things.

³⁵It was now very late in the day. Jesus' followers came to him and said, "No one lives around here, and it is already very late. ³⁶So send the people away. They need to go to the farms and towns around here to buy some food to eat."

³⁷But Jesus answered, "You give them some food to eat."

They said to Jesus, "We can't buy enough bread to feed all these people. We would all have to work a month to earn enough to buy that much bread!"

³⁸Jesus asked them, "How many loaves of bread do you have now? Go and see."

They counted their loaves of bread. They came to Jesus and said, "We have five loaves of bread and two fish."

³⁹Then Jesus said to them, "Tell everyone to sit in groups on the green grass." ⁴⁰So all the people sat in groups. There were about 50 or 100 people in each group.

⁴¹Jesus took the five loaves and two fish. He looked up to the sky and thanked God for the food. Then he broke the bread into pieces, which he gave to his followers to distribute to the people. Then he divided the two fish among everyone there.

⁴²They all ate until they were full. ⁴³After they finished eating, the followers filled twelve baskets with the pieces of bread and fish that were left. ⁴⁴There were about 5000 men there who ate.

Jesus Walks on Water
(Mt. 14:22–33; Jn. 6:16–21)

⁴⁵Then Jesus told the followers to get into the boat. He told them to go to the other side of the lake to Bethsaida. He said he would come later. He stayed there to tell everyone they could go home. ⁴⁶After he said goodbye to them, he went up into the hills to pray.

⁴⁷That night, the boat was still in the middle of the lake. Jesus was alone on the land. ⁴⁸He saw the boat far away on the lake. And he saw the followers working hard to row the boat. The wind was blowing against them. Sometime between three and six o'clock in the morning, Jesus went out to the boat, walking on the water. He continued walking until he was almost past the boat. ⁴⁹But the followers saw Jesus walking on the water. They thought he was a ghost, and they started screaming. ⁵⁰It scared them all to see him. But he spoke to them and said, "Don't worry! It's me! Don't be afraid." ⁵¹When he got into the boat with the followers, the wind stopped. The followers were completely amazed. ⁵²They could not believe what happened. It was like the miracle he did with the bread. They still didn't understand what that meant.

Jesus Heals Many Sick People
(Mt. 14:34–36)

⁵³Jesus and his followers went across the lake and came to shore at Gennesaret. They tied the boat there. ⁵⁴When they were out of the boat, the people there saw Jesus. They knew who he was, ⁵⁵so they ran to tell others throughout that area. They

brought sick people on mats to every place Jesus went. 56Jesus went into towns, cities, and farms around that area. And every place he went, the people brought sick people to the marketplaces. They begged him to let them touch any part of his coat. And all those who touched him were healed.

God's Law and Human Traditions
(Mt. 15:1–20)

7 1Some Pharisees* and some teachers of the law came from Jerusalem and gathered around Jesus. 2They saw that some of his followers ate food with hands that were not clean, meaning that they did not wash their hands in a special way. 3The Pharisees and all the other Jews never eat before washing their hands in this special way. They do this to follow the traditions they have from their great leaders who lived long ago. 4And when these Jews buy something in the market, they never eat it until they wash it in a special way. They also follow other rules from their people who lived before them. They follow rules like the washing of cups, pitchers, and pots.*a*

5The Pharisees and teachers of the law said to Jesus, "Your followers don't follow the traditions we have from our great leaders who lived long ago. They eat their food with hands that are not clean. Why do they do this?"

6Jesus answered, "You are all hypocrites.* Isaiah was right when he wrote these words from God about you:

'These people honor me with their words,

but I am not really important to them.

7 Their worship of me is worthless.

The things they teach are only human rules.' *Isaiah 29:13*

8You have stopped following God's commands, preferring instead the man-made rules you got from others."

9Then he said, "You show great skill in avoiding the commands of God so that you can follow your own teachings! 10Moses* said, 'You must respect your father and mother.'*b* He also said, 'Whoever says anything bad to their father or mother must be killed.'*c* 11But you teach that people can say to their father or mother, 'I have something I could use to help you, but I will not use it for you. I will give it to God.' 12You are telling people that they do not have to do anything for their father or mother. 13So you are teaching that it is not important to do what God said. You think it is more important to follow those traditions you have, which you pass on to others. And you do many things like that."

14Jesus called the people to him again. He said, "Everyone should listen to me and understand what I am saying. 15There is nothing people can put in their mouth that will make them wrong.*d* People are made wrong by what comes from inside them." 16*e*

17Then Jesus left the people and went into the house. The

---

a **7:4 pots** Some Greek copies add "and couches."

b **7:10** Quote from Ex. 20:12; Deut. 5:16.

c **7:10** Quote from Ex. 21:17.

d **7:15 wrong** Literally, "unclean" or "not pure," meaning unacceptable to God. Also in verse 20.

e **7:16** Some Greek copies add verse 16: "You people who hear me, listen!"

followers asked Jesus about what he had told the people. [18]He said, "Do you still have trouble understanding? Surely you know that nothing that enters the mouth from the outside can make people unacceptable to God. [19]Food does not go into a person's mind. It goes into the stomach. Then it goes out of the body." (When Jesus said this, he meant there is no food that is wrong for people to eat.)

[20]And Jesus said, "The things that make people wrong are the things that come from the inside. [21]All these bad things begin inside a person, in the mind: bad thoughts, sexual sins, stealing, murder, [22]adultery,* greed, doing bad things to people, lying, doing things that are morally wrong, jealousy, insulting people, proud talking, and foolish living. [23]These evil things come from inside a person. And these are the things that make people unacceptable to God."

Jesus Helps a Non-Jewish Woman
(Mt. 15:21–28)

[24]Jesus went from there to the area around Tyre. He did not want the people in that area to know he was there, so he went into a house. But he could not stay hidden. [25]A woman heard that he was there. Her little daughter had an evil spirit inside her. So the woman came to Jesus and bowed down near his feet. [26]She was not a Jew. She was born in Phoenicia, an area in Syria. She begged Jesus to force the demon* out of her daughter. [27]Jesus told the woman, "It is not right to take the children's bread and give it to the dogs. First let the children eat all they want."

[28]She answered, "That is true, Lord. But the dogs under the table can eat the pieces of food that the children don't eat."

[29]Then he told her, "That is a very good answer. You may go. The demon has left your daughter."

[30]The woman went home and found her daughter lying on the bed. The demon was gone.

Jesus Heals a Deaf Man

[31]Then Jesus left the area around Tyre and went through Sidon. On his way to Lake Galilee he went through the area of the Ten Towns.* [32]While he was there, some people brought a man to him who was deaf and could not talk clearly. The people begged Jesus to put his hand on the man to heal him.

[33]Jesus led the man away from the people to be alone with him. He put his fingers in the man's ears. Then he spit on a finger and put it on the man's tongue. [34]Jesus looked up to the sky and with a loud sigh he said, "*Ephphatha!*" (This means "Open!") [35]As soon as Jesus did this, the man was able to hear. He was able to use his tongue, and he began to speak clearly.

[36]Jesus told the people not to tell anyone about this. But the more he told them not to say anything, the more people they told. [37]They were all completely amazed. They said, "Look at what he has done. It's all good. He makes deaf people able to hear and gives a new voice to people who could not talk."

Jesus Feeds More Than 4000
(Mt. 15:32–39)

8 [1]Another time there were many people with Jesus. The people had nothing to eat. So he called his followers to him and said, 2"I feel sorry for these people. They have been with me for three days, and now they have nothing to eat. 3I should not send them home hungry. If they leave without eating, they will faint on the way home. Some of them live a long way from here."

4Jesus' followers answered, "But we are far away from any towns. Where can we get enough bread to feed all these people?"

5Then Jesus asked them, "How many loaves of bread do you have?"

They answered, "We have seven loaves of bread."

6Jesus told the people to sit on the ground. Then he took the seven loaves and gave thanks to God. He broke the bread into pieces and gave them to his followers. He told them to give the bread to the people, and they did as he said. 7The followers also had a few small fish. Jesus gave thanks for the fish and told them to give the fish to the people.

8They all ate until they were full. Then the followers filled seven baskets with the pieces of food that were left. 9There were about 4000 men who ate. After they ate, Jesus told them to go home. 10Then he went in a boat with his followers to the area of Dalmanutha.

Some People Doubt Jesus' Authority
(Mt. 16:1–4; Lk. 11:16, 29)

11The Pharisees* came to Jesus and asked him questions. They wanted to test him. So they asked him to do a miracle* as a sign from God. 12Jesus sighed deeply and said, "Why do you people ask to see a miracle as a sign? I want you to know that no miracle will be done to prove anything to you."

13Then Jesus left them and went in the boat to the other side of the lake.

Jesus' Followers Misunderstand Him
(Mt. 16:5–12)

14The followers had only one loaf of bread with them in the boat. They forgot to bring more bread. 15Jesus warned them, "Be careful! Guard against the yeast* of the Pharisees* and the yeast of Herod.*"

16The followers discussed the meaning of this. They said, "He said this because we have no bread."

17Jesus knew that the followers were talking about this. So he asked them, "Why are you talking about having no bread? Do you still not see or understand? Are you not able to understand? 18Do you have eyes that can't see? Do you have ears that can't hear? Remember what I did before, when we did not have enough bread? 19I divided five loaves of bread for 5000 people. Remember how many baskets you filled with pieces of food that were not eaten?"

The followers answered, "We filled twelve baskets."

20"And when I divided seven loaves of bread for 4000 people, how many baskets did you fill with the leftover pieces?"

They answered, "We filled seven baskets."

21Then he said to them, "You remember these things I did, but you still don't understand?"

Jesus Heals a Blind Man in Bethsaida
22Jesus and his followers came to Bethsaida. Some people brought a blind man to him and begged him to touch the man. 23So Jesus held the blind man's hand and led him

out of the village. Then he spit on the man's eyes. He laid his hands on* him and asked, "Can you see now?"

²⁴The man looked up and said, "Yes, I see people. They look like trees walking around."

²⁵Again Jesus laid his hands on the man's eyes, and the man opened them wide. His eyes were healed, and he was able to see everything clearly. ²⁶Jesus told him to go home. He said, "Don't go into the town."

Peter Says Jesus Is the Messiah
(Mt. 16:13–20; Lk. 9:18–21)

²⁷Jesus and his followers went to the towns in the area of Caesarea Philippi. While they were traveling, Jesus asked the followers, "Who do people say I am?"

²⁸They answered, "Some people say you are John the Baptizer.* Others say you are Elijah.* And others say you are one of the prophets.*"

²⁹Then Jesus asked, "Who do you say I am?"

Peter answered, "You are the Messiah.*"

³⁰Jesus told the followers, "Don't tell anyone who I am."

Jesus Says He Must Die
(Mt. 16:21–28; Lk. 9:22–27)

³¹Then Jesus began to teach his followers that the Son of Man* must suffer many things. He taught that the Son of Man would not be accepted by the older Jewish leaders, the leading priests, and the teachers of the law. He said that the Son of Man must be killed and then rise from death after three days. ³²Jesus told them everything that would happen. He did not keep anything secret. Peter took Jesus away from the other followers to talk to him alone. Peter criticized him for saying these things. ³³But Jesus turned and looked at his followers. Then he criticized Peter. He said to Peter, "Get away from me, Satan*ᵃ*! You don't care about the same things God does. You care only about things that people think are important."

³⁴Then Jesus called the crowd and his followers to him. He said, "Any of you who want to be my follower must stop thinking about yourself and what you want. You must be willing to carry the cross* that is given to you for following me. ³⁵Any of you who try to save the life you have will lose it. But you who give up your life for me and for the Good News* will save it. ³⁶It is worth nothing for you to have the whole world if you yourself are lost. ³⁷You could never pay enough to buy back your life. ³⁸People today are so sinful. They have not been faithful to God. As you live among them, don't be ashamed of me and my teaching. If that happens, Iᵇ will be ashamed of you when I come with the glory* of my Father and the holy* angels."

9 ¹Then Jesus said, "Believe me when I say that some of you people standing here will see God's kingdom* come with power before you die."

Jesus Is Seen With Moses and Elijah
(Mt. 17:1–13; Lk. 9:28–36)

²Six days later, Jesus took Peter, James, and John and went up on a high mountain. They were all alone there. While these followers watched him, Jesus was changed. ³His clothes became

ᵃ 8:33 **Satan** Name for the devil meaning "the enemy." Jesus means that Peter was talking like Satan.
ᵇ 8:38 **I** Literally, "the Son of Man" (Jesus).

shining white—whiter than anyone on earth could make them. 4Then two men were there talking with Jesus. They were Elijah* and Moses.*

5Peter said to Jesus, "Teacher, it is good that we are here. We will put three tents here—one for you, one for Moses, and one for Elijah." 6Peter did not know what to say, because he and the other two followers were so afraid.

7Then a cloud came and covered them. A voice came from the cloud and said, "This is my Son, the one I love. Obey him!"

8The followers looked, but they saw only Jesus there alone with them.

9As Jesus and the followers were walking back down the mountain, he gave them these instructions: "Don't tell anyone about what you saw on the mountain. Wait until after the Son of Man* rises from death. Then you can tell people what you saw."

10So the followers waited to say anything about what they saw. But they discussed among themselves what Jesus meant about rising from death. 11They asked him, "Why do the teachers of the law say that Elijah must come*a* first?"

12Jesus answered, "They are right to say that Elijah must come first. Elijah makes all things the way they should be. But why do the Scriptures* say that the Son of Man will suffer much and that people will think he is worth nothing? 13I tell you that Elijah has already come. And people did to him all the bad things they wanted to do. The Scriptures said this would happen to him."

a **9:11 Elijah must come** See Mal. 4:5–6.

Jesus Frees a Boy From an Evil Spirit
(Mt. 17:14–20; Lk. 9:37–43a)

14Then Jesus, Peter, James, and John went to the other followers. They saw many people around them. The teachers of the law were arguing with the followers. 15When the people saw Jesus, they were very surprised and ran to welcome him.

16Jesus asked, "What are you arguing about with the teachers of the law?"

17A man answered, "Teacher, I brought my son to you. He is controlled by an evil spirit that keeps him from talking. 18The spirit attacks him and throws him on the ground. He foams at the mouth, grinds his teeth, and becomes very stiff. I asked your followers to force the evil spirit out, but they could not."

19Jesus answered, "You people today don't believe! How long must I stay with you? How long must I be patient with you? Bring the boy to me!"

20So the followers brought the boy to Jesus. When the evil spirit saw Jesus, it attacked the boy. The boy fell down and rolled on the ground. He was foaming at the mouth.

21Jesus asked the boy's father, "How long has this been happening to him?"

The father answered, "Since he was very young. 22The spirit often throws him into a fire or into water to kill him. If you can do anything, please have pity on us and help us."

23Jesus said to the father, "Why did you say 'if you can'? All things are possible for the one who believes."

24Immediately the father shouted, "I do believe. Help me to believe more!"

25Jesus saw that all the people were running there to see what was happening. So he spoke to the evil spirit. He said, "You evil spirit that makes this boy deaf and stops him from talking—I command you to come out of him and never enter him again!"

26The evil spirit screamed. It caused the boy to fall on the ground again, and then it came out. The boy looked as if he was dead. Many people said, "He is dead!" 27But Jesus took hold of his hand and helped him stand up.

28Then Jesus went into the house. His followers were alone with him there. They said, "Why weren't we able to force that evil spirit out?"

29Jesus answered, "That kind of spirit can be forced out only with prayer.a"

Jesus Talks About His Death
(Mt. 17:22–23; Lk. 9:43b–45)

30Then Jesus and his followers left there and went through Galilee. Jesus did not want the people to know where they were. 31He wanted to teach his followers alone. He said to them, "The Son of Man* will be handed over to the control of other men, who will kill him. After three days, he will rise from death." 32But the followers did not understand what he meant, and they were afraid to ask him.

Who Is the Greatest?
(Mt. 18:1–5; Lk. 9:46–48)

33Jesus and his followers went to Capernaum.* They went into

a **9:29 prayer** Some Greek copies have "prayer and fasting."

a house, and Jesus said to them, "I heard you arguing on the way here today. What were you arguing about?" 34But the followers did not answer, because their argument on the road was about which one of them was the greatest.

35Jesus sat down and called the twelve apostles* to him. He said, "Whoever wants to be the most important must make others more important than themselves. They must serve everyone else."

36Then Jesus took a small child and stood the child in front of the followers. He held the child in his arms and said, 37"Whoever accepts children like these in my name is accepting me. And anyone who accepts me is also accepting the one who sent me."

Whoever Is Not Against Us Is For Us
(Lk. 9:49–50)

38Then John said, "Teacher, we saw a man using your name to force demons* out of someone. He is not one of us. So we told him to stop, because he does not belong to our group."

39Jesus said, "Don't stop him. Whoever uses my name to do powerful things will not soon say bad things about me. 40Whoever is not against us is with us. 41I can assure you that anyone who helps you by giving you a drink of water because you belong to the Messiah* will definitely get a reward.

Jesus Warns About Causes of Sin
(Mt. 18:6–9; Lk. 17:1–2)

42"If one of these little children believes in me, and someone causes that child to sin, it will be very bad for that person. It would be better for them to have a millstone* tied around their neck and be drowned in the sea. 43If your hand makes you sin, cut it off. It is better for you to lose part of your body and have eternal life than to have two hands and go to hell. There the fire never stops. [44a] [45]If your foot makes you sin, cut it off. It is better for you to lose part of your body and have eternal life than to have two feet and be thrown into hell. [46b] [47]If your eye makes you sin, take it out. It is better for you to have only one eye and enter God's kingdom* than to have two eyes and be thrown into hell. [48]The worms that eat the people in hell never die. The fire there is never stopped.

[49]"Everyone will be salted with fire.[c]

[50]"Salt is good. But if it loses its salty taste, you can't make it good again. So, don't lose that good quality of salt you have. And live in peace with each other."

Jesus Teaches About Divorce
(Mt. 19:1–12)

10 [1]Then Jesus left there and went into the area of Judea and across the Jordan River. Again, many people came to him, and Jesus taught them as he always did.

[2]Some Pharisees* came to Jesus and tried to make him say something wrong. They asked him, "Is it right for a man to divorce his wife?"

[3]Jesus answered, "What did Moses* command you to do?"

[4]The Pharisees said, "Moses allowed a man to divorce his wife by writing a certificate of divorce."[d]

[5]Jesus said, "Moses wrote that command for you because you refused to accept God's teaching. [6]But when God made the world, 'he made people male and female.'[e] [7]That is why a man will leave his father and mother and be joined to his wife. [8]And the two people will become one.'[f] So they are no longer two, but one. [9]God has joined them together, so no one should separate them."

[10]Later, when the followers and Jesus were in the house, they asked him again about the question of divorce. [11]He said, "Whoever divorces his wife and marries another woman has sinned against his wife. He is guilty of adultery.* [12]And the woman who divorces her husband and marries another man is also guilty of adultery."

Jesus Welcomes Children
(Mt. 19:13–15; Lk. 18:15–17)

[13]People brought their small children to Jesus so that he could lay his hands on* them to bless them. But the followers told the people to stop bringing their children to him. [14]Jesus saw what happened. He did not like his followers telling the children not to come. So he said to them, "Let the little children come to me. Don't stop them, because God's kingdom* belongs to people who are like these little children. [15]The truth is, you must accept God's kingdom like a little child accepts things, or you

---

[a] **9:44** Some Greek copies add verse 44, which is the same as verse 48.
[b] **9:46** Some Greek copies add verse 46, which is the same as verse 48.
[c] **9:49** Some Greek copies add, "and every sacrifice will be salted with salt." In the Old Testament salt was put on sacrifices. This verse could mean that Jesus' followers will be tested by suffering and that they must offer themselves to God as sacrifices.

[d] **10:4 "Moses … certificate of divorce"** See Deut. 24:1.
[e] **10:6** Quote from Gen. 1:27; 5:2.
[f] **10:8** Quote from Gen. 2:24.

will never enter it." [16] Then Jesus held the children in his arms. He laid his hands on them and blessed them.

A Rich Man Refuses to Follow Jesus
(Mt. 19:16–30; Lk. 18:18–30)

[17] Jesus started to leave, but a man ran to him and bowed down on his knees before him. The man asked, "Good Teacher, what must I do to get the life that never ends?"

[18] Jesus answered, "Why do you call me good? Only God is good. [19] And you know his commands: 'You must not murder anyone, you must not commit adultery,* you must not steal, you must not lie, you must not cheat, you must respect your father and mother ....'*a*"

[20] The man said, "Teacher, I have obeyed all these commands since I was a boy."

[21] Jesus looked at the man in a way that showed how much he cared for him. He said, "There is still one thing you need to do. Go and sell everything you have. Give the money to those who are poor, and you will have riches in heaven. Then come and follow me."

[22] The man was upset when Jesus told him to give away his money. He didn't want to do this, because he was very rich. So he went away sad.

[23] Then Jesus looked at his followers and said to them, "It will be very hard for a rich person to enter God's kingdom*!"

[24] The followers were amazed at what Jesus said. But he said again, "My children, it is very hard to enter God's kingdom! [25] It is easier for a camel to go through the eye of a needle than for a rich person to enter God's kingdom!"

[26] The followers were even more amazed and said to each other, "Then who can be saved?"

[27] Jesus looked at them and said, "That is something people cannot do, but God can. He can do anything."

[28] Peter said to Jesus, "We left everything to follow you!"

[29] Jesus said, "I can promise that everyone who has left their home, brothers, sisters, mother, father, children, or farm for me and for the Good News* about me [30] will get a hundred times more than they left. Here in this world they will get more homes, brothers, sisters, mothers, children, and farms. And with these things they will have persecutions.* But in the world that is coming they will also get the reward of eternal life. [31] Many people who have the highest place now will have the lowest place in the future. And the people who have the lowest place now will have the highest place then."

Jesus Talks Again About His Death
(Mt. 20:17–19; Lk. 18:31–34)

[32] Jesus and those with him were on their way to Jerusalem. He was at the front of the group. His followers were wondering what was happening, and the people who followed behind them were feeling afraid. Jesus gathered the twelve apostles* again and talked with them alone. He told them what would happen in Jerusalem. [33] He said, "We are going to Jerusalem. The Son of Man* will be handed over to the leading priests and teachers of the law. They will say that he must die and will hand him over to the foreigners,

a **10:19** Quote from Ex. 20:12–16; Deut. 5:16–20.

34who will laugh at him and spit on him. They will beat him with whips and kill him. But on the third day after his death, he will rise to life again."

James and John Ask for a Favor
(Mt. 20:20–28)

35Then James and John, sons of Zebedee, came to Jesus and said, "Teacher, we want to ask you to do something for us."

36Jesus asked, "What do you want me to do for you?"

37The sons answered, "Let us share the great honor you will have as king. Let one of us sit at your right side and the other at your left."

38Jesus said, "You don't understand what you are asking. Can you drink from the cup*a* that I must drink from? Can you be baptized with the same baptism*b* that I must go through?"

39The sons answered, "Yes, we can!"

Jesus said to the sons, "It is true that you will drink from the cup that I drink from. And you will be baptized with the same baptism that I must go through. 40But it is not for me to say who will sit at my right or my left. God has prepared those places for the ones he chooses."

41When the other ten followers heard this, they were angry with James and John. 42Jesus called all the followers together. He said,

"The non-Jewish people have men they call rulers. You know that those rulers love to show their power over the people. And their important leaders love to use all their authority over the people. 43But it should not be that way with you. Whoever wants to be your leader must be your servant. 44Whoever wants to be first must serve the rest of you like a slave. 45Follow my example: Even the Son of Man* did not come for people to serve him. He came to serve others and to give his life to save many people."

Jesus Heals a Blind Man
(Mt. 20:29–34; Lk. 18:35–43)

46Then they came to the town of Jericho. When Jesus left there with his followers, a large crowd was with them. A blind man named Bartimaeus (meaning "son of Timaeus") was sitting by the road. He was always begging for money. 47He heard that Jesus from Nazareth was walking by. So he began shouting, "Jesus, Son of David,* please help me!"

48Many people criticized the blind man and told him to be quiet. But he shouted more and more, "Son of David, please help me!"

49Jesus stopped and said, "Tell him to come here."

So they called the blind man and said, "You can be happy now. Stand up! Jesus is calling you." 50The blind man stood up quickly. He left his coat there and went to Jesus.

51Jesus asked the man, "What do you want me to do for you?"

He answered, "Teacher, I want to see again."

52Jesus said, "Go. You are healed because you believed."

---

a **10:38 cup** A symbol of suffering. Jesus used the idea of drinking from a cup to mean accepting the suffering he would face in the terrible events that were soon to come. Also in verse 39.

b **10:38 baptized with the same baptism** Baptism, which usually means to be immersed in water, has a special meaning here—being covered or "buried" in troubles. Also in verse 39.

Immediately the man was able to see again. He followed Jesus down the road.

Jesus Enters Jerusalem Like a King
(Mt. 21:1–11; Lk. 19:28–40; Jn. 12:12–19)

11 ¹Jesus and his followers were coming closer to Jerusalem. They came to the towns of Bethphage and Bethany at the Mount of Olives.* There Jesus sent two of his followers to do something. ²He said to them, "Go to the town you can see there. When you enter it, you will find a young donkey that no one has ever ridden. Untie it and bring it here to me. ³If anyone asks you why you are taking the donkey, tell them, 'The Master needs it. He will send it back soon.'"

⁴The followers went into the town. They found a young donkey tied in the street near the door of a house, and they untied it. ⁵Some people were standing there and saw this. They asked, "What are you doing? Why are you untying that donkey?" ⁶The followers answered the way Jesus told them, and the people let them take the donkey.

⁷The followers brought the donkey to Jesus. They put their coats on it, and Jesus sat on it. ⁸Many people spread their coats on the road for Jesus. Others cut branches in the fields and spread the branches on the road. ⁹Some of them were walking ahead of Jesus. Others were walking behind him. Everyone shouted,

"'Praise*ᵃ* Him!'

'Welcome! God bless the one who comes in the name of the Lord!'   *Psalm 118:25–26*

¹⁰ "God bless the kingdom of our father David.*
That kingdom is coming!
Praise to God in heaven!'"

¹¹Jesus entered Jerusalem and went to the Temple.* He looked at everything in the Temple area, but it was already late. So he went to Bethany with the twelve apostles.*

Jesus Says a Fig Tree Will Die
(Mt. 21:18–19)

¹²The next day, Jesus was leaving Bethany. He was hungry. ¹³He saw a fig tree with leaves. So he went to the tree to see if it had any figs growing on it. But he found no figs on the tree. There were only leaves, because it was not the right time for figs to grow. ¹⁴So Jesus said to the tree, "People will never eat fruit from you again." His followers heard him say this.

Jesus Goes to the Temple
(Mt. 21:12–17; Lk. 19:45–48; Jn. 2:13–22)

¹⁵Jesus went to Jerusalem and entered the Temple* area. He began driving out the people who were buying and selling things there. He turned over the tables that belonged to those who were exchanging different kinds of money. And he turned over the benches of those who were selling doves. ¹⁶He refused to allow anyone to carry things through the Temple area. ¹⁷Then Jesus began teaching the people and said, "It is written in the Scriptures,* 'My Temple will be called a house of prayer for all nations.'ᵇ But you

ᵃ **11:9 Praise** Literally, "Hosanna," a Hebrew word used in praying to God for help. Here, it was probably a shout of celebration used in praising God or his Messiah. Also in verse 10.

ᵇ **11:17** Quote from Isa. 56:7.

have changed it into a 'hiding place for thieves.'[a]"

18When the leading priests and the teachers of the law heard what Jesus said, they began trying to find a way to kill him. They were afraid of him because all the people were amazed at his teaching. 19That night Jesus and his followers left the city.

Jesus Shows the Power of Faith
(Mt. 21:20–22)

20The next morning Jesus was walking with his followers. They saw the fig tree that he spoke to the day before. The tree was dry and dead, even the roots. 21Peter remembered the tree and said to Jesus, "Teacher, look! Yesterday, you told that fig tree to die. Now it is dry and dead!"

22Jesus answered, "Have faith in God. 23The truth is, you can say to this mountain, 'Go, mountain, fall into the sea.' And if you have no doubts in your mind and believe that what you say will happen, then God will do it for you. 24So I tell you to ask for what you want in prayer. And if you believe that you have received those things, then they will be yours. 25When you are praying and you remember that you are angry with another person about something, forgive that person. Forgive them so that your Father in heaven will also forgive your sins." 26 b

Jewish Leaders Doubt Jesus' Authority
(Mt. 21:23–27; Lk. 20:1–8)

27Jesus and his followers went again to Jerusalem. Jesus was walking in the Temple* area. The leading priests, the teachers of the law, and the older Jewish leaders came to him. 28They said, "Tell us! What authority do you have to do these things? Who gave you this authority?"

29Jesus answered, "I will ask you a question. You answer my question. Then I will tell you whose authority I use to do these things. 30Tell me: When John baptized* people, did his authority come from God or was it only from other people? Answer me."

31These Jewish leaders talked about Jesus' question. They said to each other, "If we answer, 'John's baptism was from God,' then he will say, 'Then why didn't you believe John?' 32But we can't say that John's baptism was from someone else." (These leaders were afraid of the people, because the people believed that John was a prophet.*)

33So the leaders answered Jesus, "We don't know the answer."

Jesus said, "Then I will not tell you who gave me the authority to do these things."

God Sends His Son
(Mt. 21:33–46; Lk. 20:9–19)

12 1Jesus used stories to teach the people. He said, "A man planted a vineyard.* He put a wall around the field and dug a hole for a winepress.* Then he built a tower. He leased the land to some farmers and left for a trip.

2"Later, it was time for the grapes to be picked. So the man sent a servant to the farmers to get his share of the grapes. 3But the farmers grabbed the servant and beat him. They sent him away with nothing. 4Then the man sent another servant to the farmers. They hit this servant on the head, showing no respect for

---

a 11:17 Quote from Jer. 7:11.
b 11:26 Some early Greek copies add verse 26: "But if you don't forgive others, then your Father in heaven will not forgive your sins."

him. ⁵So the man sent another servant. The farmers killed this servant. The man sent many other servants to the farmers. The farmers beat some of them and killed the others.

⁶"The man had only one person left to send to the farmers. It was his son. He loved his son, but he decided to send him. He said, 'The farmers will respect my son.'

⁷"But the farmers said to each other, 'This is the owner's son, and this vineyard will be his. If we kill him, it will be ours.' ⁸So they took the son, threw him out of the vineyard, and killed him.

⁹"So what will the man who owns the vineyard do? He will go and kill those farmers. Then he will lease the land to others. ¹⁰Surely you have read this in the Scriptures*:

'The stone that the builders
    refused to accept became
    the cornerstone.*
¹¹ The Lord did this, and it
    is wonderful to us.'"

Psalm 118:22–23

¹²When these Jewish leaders heard this story, they knew it was about them. They wanted to find a way to arrest Jesus, but they were afraid of what the crowd would do. So they left him and went away.

The Jewish Leaders Try to Trick Jesus
(Mt. 22:15–22; Lk. 20:20–26)

¹³Later, the Jewish leaders sent some Pharisees* and some men from the group called Herodians* to Jesus. They wanted to catch him saying something wrong. ¹⁴They went to Jesus and said, "Teacher, we know that you are an honest man. You are not afraid of what others think about you. All people are the same to you. And

you teach the truth about God's way. Tell us, is it right to pay taxes to Caesar*? Should we pay them or not?"

¹⁵But Jesus knew that these men were really trying to trick him. He said, "Why are you trying to catch me saying something wrong? Bring me a silver coin.* Let me see it." ¹⁶They gave Jesus a coin and he asked, "Whose picture is on the coin? And whose name is written on it?" They answered, "It is Caesar's picture and Caesar's name."

¹⁷Then Jesus said to them, "Give to Caesar what belongs to Caesar, and give to God what belongs to God." The men were amazed at what Jesus said.

Some Sadducees Try to Trick Jesus
(Mt. 22:23–33; Lk. 20:27–40)

¹⁸Then some Sadducees* came to Jesus. (Sadducees believe that no one will rise from death.) They asked him a question: ¹⁹"Teacher, Moses* wrote that if a married man dies and had no children, his brother must marry the woman. Then they will have children for the dead brother.ᵃ ²⁰There were seven brothers. The first brother married but died. He had no children. ²¹So the second brother married the woman. But he also died and had no children. The same thing happened with the third brother. ²²All seven brothers married the woman and died. None of the brothers had any children with her. And she was the last to die. ²³But all seven brothers had married her. So at the time when people rise from death, whose wife will she be?"

ᵃ 12:19 if ... dead brother See Deut. 25:5, 6.

24Jesus answered, "How could you be so wrong? It's because you don't know what the Scriptures* say. And you don't know anything about God's power. 25When people rise from death, there will be no marriage. People will not be married to each other. All people will be like angels in heaven. 26Surely you have read what God said about people rising from death. In the book where Moses wrote about the burning bush,*a* it says that God told Moses this: 'I am the God of Abraham,* the God of Isaac,* and the God of Jacob.'*b* 27So they were not still dead, because he is the God only of living people. You Sadducees are so wrong!"

Which Command Is the Most Important?

(Mt. 22:34–40; Lk. 10:25–28)

28One of the teachers of the law came to Jesus. He heard Jesus arguing with the Sadducees* and the Pharisees.* He saw that Jesus gave good answers to their questions. So he asked him, "Which of the commands is the most important?"

29Jesus answered, "The most important command is this: 'People of Israel,* listen! The Lord our God is the only Lord. 30Love the Lord your God with all your heart, all your soul, all your mind, and all your strength.'*c* 31The second most important command is this: 'Love your neighbor*d* the same as you love yourself.'*e* These

two commands are the most important."

32The man answered, "That was a good answer, Teacher. You are right in saying that God is the only Lord and that there is no other God. 33And you must love God with all your heart, all your mind, and all your strength. And you must love others the same as you love yourself. These commands are more important than all the animals and sacrifices we offer to God."

34Jesus saw that the man answered him wisely. So he said to him, "You are close to God's kingdom.*" And after that time, no one was brave enough to ask Jesus any more questions.

Is the Messiah David's Son or David's Lord?

(Mt. 22:41–46; Lk. 20:41–44)

35Jesus was teaching in the Temple* area. He asked, "Why do the teachers of the law say that the Messiah* is the son of David*? 36With the help of the Holy Spirit,* David himself says,

'The Lord God said to my Lord:
Sit by me at my right side,
and I will put your enemies
under your control.*f*'

Psalm 110:1

37David himself calls the Messiah 'Lord.' So how can the Messiah be David's son?" Many people listened to Jesus and were very pleased.

Jesus Criticizes the Teachers of the Law

(Mt. 23:1–36; Lk. 20:45–47)

38Jesus continued teaching. He said, "Be careful of the teachers of the law. They like to walk around wearing clothes that look important. And they love for people to

a **12:26 burning bush** See Ex. 3:1–12.
b **12:26** Quote from Ex. 3:6.
c **12:29–30** Quote from Deut. 6:4–5.
d **12:31 your neighbor** Or "others." Jesus' teaching in Lk. 10:25–37 makes clear that this includes anyone in need.
e **12:31** Quote from Lev. 19:18.

f **12:36 control** Literally, "feet."

show respect to them in the marketplaces. ³⁹They love to have the most important seats in the synagogues* and the places of honor at banquets. ⁴⁰But they cheat widows and take their homes. Then they try to make themselves look good by saying long prayers. God will punish them very much."

True Giving
(Lk. 21:1–4)

⁴¹Jesus sat near the Temple* collection box*ᵃ* and watched as people put money into it. Many rich people put in a lot of money. ⁴²Then a poor widow came and put in two very small copper coins, worth less than a penny.

⁴³Jesus called his followers to him and said, "This poor widow put in only two small coins. But the truth is, she gave more than all those rich people. ⁴⁴They have plenty, and they gave only what they did not need. This woman is very poor, but she gave all she had. It was money she needed to live on."

Jesus Warns About the Future
(Mt. 24:1–44; Lk. 21:5–33)

13 ¹Jesus was leaving the Temple* area. One of his followers said to him, "Teacher, look how big those stones are! What beautiful buildings!"

²Jesus said, "Do you see these great buildings? They will all be destroyed. Every stone will be thrown down to the ground. Not one stone will be left on another."

³Later, Jesus was sitting at a place on the Mount of Olives.* He was alone with Peter, James, John, and Andrew. They could all see the Temple, and they said to Jesus, ⁴"Tell us when these things will happen. And what will show us it is time for them to happen?"

⁵Jesus said to them, "Be careful! Don't let anyone fool you. ⁶Many people will come and use my name. They will say, 'I am the Messiah,*ᵇ*' and they will fool many people. ⁷You will hear about wars that are being fought. And you will hear stories about other wars beginning. But don't be afraid. These things must happen before the end comes. ⁸Nations will fight against other nations. Kingdoms will fight against other kingdoms. There will be times when there is no food for people to eat. And there will be earthquakes in different places. These things are only the beginning of troubles, like the first pains of a woman giving birth.

⁹"You must be careful! There are people who will arrest you and take you to be judged for being my followers. They will beat you in their synagogues.* You will be forced to stand before kings and governors. You will tell them about me. ¹⁰Before the end comes, the Good News* must be told to all nations. ¹¹Even when you are arrested and put on trial, don't worry about what you will say. Say whatever God tells you at the time. It will not really be you speaking. It will be the Holy Spirit.*

¹²"Brothers will turn against their own brothers and hand them over to be killed. Fathers will hand over their own children to be killed. Children will fight against their own parents

---

ᵃ **12:41 collection box** A special box in the Jewish place for worship where people put their gifts to God.

ᵇ **13:6 the Messiah** Literally "the one," meaning the chosen one sent by God. See Mt. 24:5 and "Messiah" in the Word List.

and have them killed. [13]All people will hate you because you follow me. But those who remain faithful to the end will be saved.

[14]"You will see 'the terrible thing that causes destruction.'[a] You will see this thing standing in the place where it should not be." (Reader, I trust you understand what this means.) "Everyone in Judea at that time should run away to the mountains. [15]They should run away without wasting time to stop for anything. If someone is on the roof of their house, they must not go down to take things out of the house. [16]If someone is in the field, they must not go back to get a coat.

[17]"During that time it will be hard for women who are pregnant or have small babies. [18]Pray that these things will not happen in winter, [19]because those days will be full of trouble. There will be more trouble than has ever happened since the beginning, when God made the world. And nothing that bad will ever happen again. [20]But the Lord has decided to make that terrible time short. If it were not made short, no one could survive. But the Lord will make that time short to help the special people he has chosen.

[21]"Someone might say to you at that time, 'Look, there is the Messiah[*]!' Or another person might say, 'There he is!' But don't believe them. [22]False messiahs and false prophets[*] will come and do miracles and wonders,[b] trying to fool the people God has chosen, if that is possible. [23]So be careful.

Now I have warned you about all this before it happens.

[24]"During the days following that time of trouble,

'The sun will become dark,
 and the moon will not give light.
[25] The stars will fall from the sky,
 and everything in the sky will be changed.'[c]

[26]"Then people will see the Son of Man[*] coming in the clouds with great power and glory.[*] [27]He will send his angels all around the earth. They will gather his chosen people from every part of the earth.

[28]"The fig tree teaches us a lesson: When its branches become green and soft, and new leaves begin to grow, then you know that summer is very near. [29]In the same way, when you see all these things happening, you will know that the time[d] is very near, already present. [30]I assure you that all these things will happen while some of the people of this time are still living. [31]The whole world, earth and sky, will be destroyed, but my words will last forever.

[32]"No one knows when that day or time will be. The Son and the angels in heaven don't know when that day or time will be. Only the Father knows. [33]Be careful! Always be ready. You don't know when that time will be.

[34]"It's like a man who goes on a trip and leaves his house in the care of his servants. He gives each one a special job to do. He tells

---

[a] **13:14 'the terrible thing ... destruction'** See Dan. 9:27; 12:11 (also Dan. 11:31).
[b] **13:22 miracles and wonders** Here, amazing acts done by Satan's power.
[c] **13:24–25** See Isa. 13:10; 34:4.
[d] **13:29 time** The time Jesus has been talking about when something important will happen. See Lk. 21:31, where Jesus says that this is the time for God's kingdom to come.

the servant guarding the door to always be ready. And this is what I am telling you now. 35You must always be ready. You don't know when the owner of the house will come back. He might come in the afternoon, or at midnight, or in the early morning, or when the sun rises. 36If you are always ready, he will not find you sleeping, even if he comes back earlier than expected. 37I tell you this, and I say it to everyone: 'Be ready!'"

The Jewish Leaders Plan to Kill Jesus
(Mt. 26:1–5; Lk. 22:1–2; Jn. 11:45–53)

14 1It was now only two days before the Passover* and the Festival of Unleavened Bread.* The leading priests and teachers of the law were trying to find a way to arrest Jesus without the people seeing it. Then they could kill him. 2They said, "But we cannot arrest Jesus during the festival. We don't want the people to be angry and cause a riot."

A Woman Does Something Special
(Mt. 26:6–13; Jn. 12:1–8)

3Jesus was in Bethany at the house of Simon the leper.* While he was eating there, a woman came to him. She had an alabaster* jar filled with expensive perfume made of pure nard.* She opened the jar and poured the perfume on Jesus' head.

4Some of the followers there saw this. They were upset and complained to each other. They said, "Why waste that perfume? 5It was worth a full year's pay.*a It could have been sold and the money given to those who are poor." And they told the woman what a bad thing she had done.

6Jesus said, "Leave her alone. Why are you giving her such trouble? She did a very good thing for me. 7You will always have the poor with you,b and you can help them any time you want. But you will not always have me. 8This woman did the only thing she could do for me. She poured perfume on my body before I die to prepare it for burial. 9The Good News* will be told to people all over the world. And I can assure you that everywhere the Good News is told, the story of what this woman did will also be told, and people will remember her."

Judas Agrees to Help Jesus' Enemies
(Mt. 26:14–16; Lk. 22:3–6)

10Then Judas Iscariot, one of the twelve apostles,* went to talk to the leading priests about handing Jesus over to them. 11They were very happy about this, and they promised to pay him. So he waited for the best time to hand Jesus over to them.

The Passover Meal
(Mt. 26:17–25; Lk. 22:7–14, 21–23; Jn. 13:21–30)

12It was now the first day of the Festival of Unleavened Bread*— the day the lambs were killed for the Passover.* Jesus' followers came to him and said, "We will go and prepare everything for you to eat the Passover meal. Where do you want us to have the meal?"

13Jesus sent two of his followers into the city. He said to them, "Go into the city. You will see a man carrying a jar of water. He will come to you. Follow him. 14He will go into a house. Tell the owner of

---

a **14:5 a full year's pay** Literally, "300 denarii." One Roman denarius, a silver coin, was the average pay for one day's work.

b **14:7 You will . . . with you** See Deut. 15:11.

the house, 'The Teacher asks that you show us the room where he and his followers can eat the Passover meal.' [15]The owner will show you a large room upstairs that is ready for us. Prepare the meal for us there."

[16]So the followers left and went into the city. Everything happened the way Jesus said. So the followers prepared the Passover meal.

[17]In the evening Jesus went to that house with the twelve apostles.* [18]While they were all at the table eating, he said, "Believe me when I say that one of you will hand me over to my enemies— one of you eating with me now."

[19]The followers were very sad to hear this. Each one said to Jesus, "Surely I am not the one!"

[20]Jesus answered, "It is one of you twelve—the one who is dipping his bread in the same bowl with me. [21]The Son of Man* will suffer what the Scriptures* say will happen to him. But it will be very bad for the one who hands over the Son of Man to be killed. It would be better for him if he had never been born."

The Lord's Supper
(Mt. 26:26–30; Lk. 22:15–20; 1 Cor. 11:23–25)

[22]While they were eating, Jesus took some bread and thanked God for it. He broke off some pieces, gave them to his followers and said, "Take and eat this bread. It is my body."

[23]Then he took a cup of wine, thanked God for it, and gave it to them. They all drank from the cup. [24]Then he said, "This wine is my blood, which will be poured out for many to begin the new agreement* from God to his people. [25]I want you to know, I will not drink this wine again until that day when I drink it in God's kingdom* and the wine is new."

[26]They all sang a song and then went out to the Mount of Olives.*

Jesus Says His Followers Will Leave Him
(Mt. 26:31–35; Lk. 22:31–34; Jn. 13:36–38)

[27]Then Jesus told the followers, "You will all lose your faith. The Scriptures* say,

'I will kill the shepherd,
   and the sheep will run away.'
                        Zechariah 13:7

[28]But after I am killed, I will rise from death. Then I will go to Galilee. I will be there before you come."

[29]Peter said, "All the other followers may lose their faith. But my faith will never be shaken."

[30]Jesus answered, "The truth is, tonight you will say you don't know me. You will say it three times before the rooster crows twice."

[31]But Peter strongly protested, "I will never say I don't know you! I will even die with you!" And all the other followers said the same thing.

Jesus Prays Alone
(Mt. 26:36–46; Lk. 22:39–46)

[32]Jesus and his followers went to a place named Gethsemane. He said to them, "Sit here while I pray." [33]But he told Peter, James, and John to come with him. He began to be very distressed and troubled, [34]and he said to them, "My heart is so heavy with grief, I feel as if I am dying. Wait here and stay awake."

[35]Jesus went on a little farther away from them, fell to the ground, and prayed. He asked that, if possible, he would not have this time of suffering. [36]He

said, "*Abba*,[a] Father! You can do all things. Don't make me drink from this cup.[b] But do what you want, not what I want."

[37]Then he went back to his followers and found them sleeping. He said to Peter, "Simon, why are you sleeping? Could you not stay awake with me for one hour? [38]Stay awake and pray for strength against temptation. Your spirit wants to do what is right, but your body is weak."

[39]Again Jesus went away and prayed the same thing. [40]Then he went back to the followers and again found them sleeping. They could not stay awake. They did not know what they should say to him.

[41]After Jesus prayed a third time, he went back to his followers. He said to them, "Are you still sleeping and resting? That's enough! The time has come for the Son of Man* to be handed over to the control of sinful men. [42]Stand up! We must go. Here comes the man who is handing me over to them."

Jesus Is Arrested

(Mt. 26:47–56; Lk. 22:47–53; Jn. 18:3–12)

[43]While Jesus was still speaking, Judas, one of the twelve apostles,* came there. He had a big crowd of people with him, all carrying swords and clubs. They had been sent from the leading priests, the teachers of the law, and the older Jewish leaders.

[44]Judas[c] planned to do something to show them which one was Jesus. He said, "The one I kiss will be Jesus. Arrest him and guard him while you lead him away." [45]So Judas went over to Jesus and said, "Teacher!" Then he kissed him. [46]The men grabbed Jesus and arrested him. [47]One of the followers standing near Jesus grabbed his sword and pulled it out. He swung it at the servant of the high priest* and cut off his ear.

[48]Then Jesus said, "Why do you come to get me with swords and clubs as if I were a criminal? [49]Every day I was with you teaching in the Temple* area. You did not arrest me there. But all these things have happened to show the full meaning of what the Scriptures* said." [50]Then all of Jesus' followers left him and ran away.

[51]One of those following Jesus was a young man wearing only a linen cloth. When the people tried to grab him, [52]he left the cloth in their hands and ran away naked.

Jesus Before the Jewish Leaders

(Mt. 26:57–68; Lk. 22:54–55,
63–71; Jn. 18:13–14, 19–24)

[53]Those who arrested Jesus led him to the house of the high priest.* All the leading priests, the older Jewish leaders, and the teachers of the law were gathered there. [54]Peter followed Jesus but stayed back at a distance. He followed him to the yard of the high priest's house. He went into the yard and sat there with the guards, warming himself by their fire.

---

a **14:36 Abba** An Aramaic word that was used by Jewish children as a name for their fathers.

b **14:36 cup** A symbol of suffering. Jesus used the idea of drinking from a cup to mean accepting the suffering he would face in the terrible events that were soon to come.

c **14:44 Judas** Literally, "the one who handed him over."

55The leading priests and the whole high council tried to find something that Jesus had done wrong so they could kill him. But the council could find no proof that would allow them to kill Jesus. 56Many people came and told lies against Jesus, but they all said different things. None of them agreed.

57Then some others stood up and told more lies against Jesus. They said, 58"We heard this man*a* say, 'I will destroy this Temple* built by human hands. And three days later, I will build another Temple not made by human hands.'" 59But also what these people said did not agree.

60Then the high priest stood up before everyone and said to Jesus, "These people said things against you. Do you have something to say about their charges? Are they telling the truth?" 61But Jesus said nothing to answer him.

The high priest asked Jesus another question: "Are you the Messiah,* the Son of the blessed God?" 62Jesus answered, "Yes, I am the Son of God. And in the future you will see the Son of Man* sitting at the right side of God All-Powerful. And you will see the Son of Man coming on the clouds of heaven."

63When the high priest heard this, he tore his clothes in anger. He said, "We don't need any more witnesses! 64You all heard these insults to God. What do you think?"

Everyone agreed that Jesus was guilty and must be killed. 65Some of the people there spit at him. They covered his eyes and hit him with their fists. They said, "Be a prophet*b* and tell us who hit you!" Then the guards led Jesus away and beat him.

Peter Is Afraid to Say He Knows Jesus
(Mt. 26:69–75; Lk. 22:56–62; Jn. 18:15–18, 25–27)

66While Peter was still in the yard, a servant girl of the high priest* came there. 67She saw him warming himself by the fire. She looked closely at him and said, "You were with Jesus, that man from Nazareth."

68But Peter said this was not true. "That makes no sense," he said. "I don't know what you are talking about!" Then he left and went to the entrance of the yard, and a rooster crowed.*c*

69When the servant girl saw him there, she began saying again to the people standing around, "This man is one of them." 70Again Peter said it was not true.

A short time later, the people standing there said, "We know you are one of them, because you are from Galilee."

71Then Peter began to curse. He said, "I swear to God, I don't know this man you are talking about!"

72As soon as Peter said this, the rooster crowed the second time. Then he remembered what Jesus had told him: "Before the rooster crows twice, you will say three times that you don't know me." Then Peter began to cry.

Governor Pilate Questions Jesus
(Mt. 27:1–2, 11–14; Lk. 23:1–5; Jn. 18:28–38)

15 1Very early in the morning, the leading priests, the older

---

a **14:58 this man** That is, Jesus. His enemies avoided saying his name.

b **14:65 prophet** A prophet often knows things that are hidden to other people.

c **14:68** Some Greek copies do not have "and a rooster crowed."

Jewish leaders, the teachers of the law, and the whole high council decided what to do with Jesus. They tied him, led him away, and handed him over to Governor Pilate.*

2Pilate asked Jesus, "Are you the king of the Jews?"

Jesus answered, "Yes, that is right."

3The leading priests accused Jesus of many things. 4So Pilate asked Jesus another question. He said, "You can see that these people are accusing you of many things. Why don't you answer?" 5But Jesus still did not answer, and this really surprised Pilate.

Pilate Tries but Fails to Free Jesus
(Mt. 27:15–31; Lk. 23:13–25; Jn. 18:39–19:16)

6Every year at the Passover* time the governor would free one prisoner—whichever one the people wanted. 7There was a man in prison at that time named Barabbas. He and the rebels with him had been put in prison for committing murder during a riot.

8The people came to Pilate* and asked him to free a prisoner as he always did. 9Pilate asked them, "Do you want me to free the king of the Jews?" 10Pilate knew that the leading priests had handed Jesus over to him because they were jealous of him. 11But the leading priests persuaded the people to ask Pilate to free Barabbas, not Jesus.

12Pilate asked the people again, "So what should I do with this man you call the king of the Jews?" 13The people shouted, "Kill him on a cross!"

14Pilate asked, "Why? What wrong has he done?"

But the people shouted louder and louder, "Kill him on a cross!"

15Pilate wanted to please the people, so he set Barabbas free for them. And he told the soldiers to beat Jesus with whips. Then he handed him over to the soldiers to be killed on a cross.

16Pilate's soldiers took Jesus into the governor's palace (called the Praetorium). They called all the other soldiers together. 17They put a purple robe on Jesus, made a crown from thorny branches, and put it on his head. 18Then they began shouting, "Welcome, king of the Jews!" 19They kept on beating his head with a stick and spitting on him. Then they bowed down on their knees and pretended to honor him as a king. 20After they finished making fun of him, they took off the purple robe and put his own clothes on him again. Then they led him out of the palace to be killed on a cross.

Jesus Is Nailed to a Cross
(Mt. 27:32–44; Lk. 23:26–39; Jn. 19:17–19)

21There was a man from Cyrene named Simon walking into the city from the fields. He was the father of Alexander and Rufus. The soldiers forced him to carry Jesus' cross. 22They led Jesus to the place called Golgotha. (Golgotha means "The Place of the Skull.") 23There they gave him some wine mixed with myrrh,* but he refused to drink it. 24The soldiers nailed Jesus to a cross. Then they divided his clothes among themselves, throwing dice to see who would get what.

25It was nine o'clock in the morning when they nailed Jesus to the cross. 26There was a sign with the charge against him written on it. It said, "THE KING OF THE JEWS." 27They also nailed two criminals to crosses beside Jesus—one on the right and the other on the left. 28 *a*

29People walked by and said bad things to Jesus. They shook their heads and said, "You said you could destroy the Temple* and build it again in three days. 30So save yourself! Come down from that cross!"

31The leading priests and the teachers of the law were also there. They made fun of Jesus the same as the other people did. They said to each other, "He saved others, but he can't save himself! 32If he is really the Messiah,* the king of Israel,* he should come down from the cross now. When we see this, then we will believe in him." The criminals on the crosses beside Jesus also said bad things to him.

Jesus Dies
(Mt. 27:45–56; Lk. 23:44–49; Jn. 19:28–30)

33At noon the whole country became dark. This darkness continued until three o'clock. 34At three o'clock Jesus cried out loudly, *"Eloi, Eloi, lama sabachthani."* This means "My God, my God, why have you left me alone?" *b*

35Some of the people standing there heard this. They said, "Listen! He is calling Elijah." *c*

36One man there ran and got a sponge. He filled the sponge with sour wine and tied it to a stick. Then he used the stick to give the sponge to Jesus to get a drink from it. The man said, "We should wait now and see if Elijah will come to take him down from the cross."

37Then Jesus cried out loudly and died.

38When Jesus died, the curtain* in the Temple* was torn into two pieces. The tear started at the top and tore all the way to the bottom. 39The army officer* who was standing there in front of the cross saw what happened when Jesus died. The officer said, "This man really was the Son of God!"

40Some women were standing away from the cross, watching. Among these women were Mary Magdalene, Salome, and Mary the mother of James and Joses. (James was her youngest son.) 41These were the women who had followed Jesus in Galilee and cared for him. Many other women who had come with Jesus to Jerusalem were also there.

Jesus Is Buried
(Mt. 27:57–61; Lk. 23:50–56; Jn. 19:38–42)

42This day was called Preparation day. (That means the day before the Sabbath* day.) It was becoming dark. 43A man named Joseph from Arimathea was brave enough to go to Pilate* and ask for Jesus' body. Joseph was an important member of the high council. He was one of the people who wanted God's kingdom* to come. 44Pilate was surprised to hear that Jesus was already dead. So he called for the army officer* in charge and asked him if Jesus was already dead. 45When Pilate heard it from the officer, he told Joseph he could have the body.

46Joseph bought some linen cloth. He took the body from the

---

a **15:28** Some Greek copies add verse 28: "And this showed the full meaning of the Scripture that says, 'They put him with criminals.'"

b **15:34** Quote from Ps. 22:1.

c **15:35 He is calling Elijah** The word for "My God" (*Eli* in Hebrew or *Eloi* in Aramaic) sounded to the people like the name of Elijah, a famous man who spoke for God about 850 B.C.

cross, wrapped it in the linen, and put the body in a tomb* that was dug in a wall of rock. Then he closed the tomb by rolling a large stone to cover the entrance. ⁴⁷Mary Magdalene and Mary the mother of Joses saw the place where Jesus was put.

News That Jesus Has Risen From Death
(Mt. 28:1–8; Lk. 24:1–12; Jn. 20:1–10)

16 ¹The next day after the Sabbath* day, Mary Magdalene, Salome, and Mary the mother of James bought some sweet-smelling spices to put on Jesus' body. ²Very early on that day, the first day of the week, the women were going to the tomb.* It was very early after sunrise. ³The women said to each other, "There is a large stone covering the entrance of the tomb. Who will move the stone for us?"

⁴Then the women looked and saw that the stone was moved. The stone was very large, but it was moved away from the entrance. ⁵The women walked into the tomb and saw a young man there wearing a white robe. He was sitting on the right side of the tomb. The women were afraid. ⁶But the man said, "Don't be afraid. You are looking for Jesus from Nazareth, the one who was killed on a cross. He has risen from death! He is not here. Look, here is the place they put him when he was dead. ⁷Now go and tell his followers. And be sure to tell Peter. Tell them, 'Jesus is going into Galilee and will be there before you come. You will see him there, as he told you before.'"

⁸The women were very afraid and confused. They left the tomb and ran away. They did not tell about what happened, because they were afraid.ᵃ

Some Followers See Jesus
(Mt. 28:9–10; Jn. 20:11–18; Lk. 24:13–35)

⁹Jesus rose from death early on the first day of the week. He appeared first to Mary Magdalene. One time in the past Jesus had forced seven demons* out of Mary. ¹⁰After Mary saw Jesus, she went and told his followers. They were very sad and were crying. ¹¹But Mary told them that Jesus was alive. She said that she had seen Jesus, but they did not believe her.

¹²Later, Jesus appeared to two followers while they were walking in the country. But Jesus did not look the same as before he was killed. ¹³These followers went back to the other followers and told them what happened. Again, the followers did not believe them.

Jesus Talks to His Followers
(Mt. 28:16–20; Lk. 24:36–49; Jn. 20:19–23; Acts 1:6–8)

¹⁴Later, Jesus appeared to the eleven followers while they were eating. He criticized them because they had so little faith. They were stubborn and refused to believe the people who said Jesus had risen from death.

¹⁵He said to them, "Go everywhere in the world. Tell the Good News* to everyone. ¹⁶Whoever believes and is baptized* will be

---

a **16:8** Some of the oldest Greek copies end the book here. A few later copies have this shorter ending: "But they soon gave all the instructions to Peter and those with him. After that Jesus himself sent them out from east to west with the holy message that will never change—that people can be saved forever."

saved. But those who do not believe will be judged guilty. [17]And the people who believe will be able to do these things as proof: They will use my name to force demons* out of people. They will speak in languages they never learned. [18]If they pick up snakes or drink any poison, they will not be hurt. They will lay their hands on sick people, and they will get well."

Jesus Goes Back to Heaven

(Lk. 24:50–53; Acts 1:9–11)

[19]After the Lord Jesus said these things to his followers, he was carried up into heaven. There, Jesus sat at the right side of God. [20]The followers went everywhere in the world telling people the Good News,* and the Lord helped them. By giving them power to do miracles* the Lord proved that their message was true.

Luke

Luke Writes About the Life of Jesus

1 [1] Most Honorable Theophilus: Many others have tried to give a report of the things that happened among us to complete God's plan. [2] What they have written agrees with what we learned from the people who saw those events from the beginning. They also served God by telling people his message. [3] I studied it all carefully from the beginning. Then I decided to write it down for you in an organized way. [4] I did this so that you can be sure that what you have been taught is true.

Zechariah and Elizabeth

[5] During the time when Herod* ruled Judea, there was a priest named Zechariah. He belonged to Abijah's group.[a] His wife came from the family of Aaron. Her name was Elizabeth. [6] Zechariah and Elizabeth were both good people who pleased God. They did everything the Lord commanded, always following his instructions completely. [7] But they had no children. Elizabeth could not have a baby, and both of them were very old.

[8] Zechariah was serving as a priest before God for his group. It was his group's time to serve. [9] The priests always chose one priest to offer the incense,* and Zechariah was the one chosen this time. So he went into the Temple* of the Lord to offer the incense. [10] There was a large crowd outside praying at the time the incense was offered.

[11] Then, on the right side of the incense table, an angel of the Lord came and stood before Zechariah. [12] When he saw the angel, Zechariah was upset and very afraid. [13] But the angel said to him, "Zechariah, don't be afraid. Your prayer has been heard by God. Your wife Elizabeth will give birth to a baby boy, and you will name him John. [14] You will be very happy, and many others will share your joy over his birth. [15] He will be a great man for the Lord. He will never drink wine or beer. Even before he is born, he will be filled with the Holy Spirit.*

[16] "John will help many people of Israel* return to the Lord their God. [17] John himself will go ahead of the Lord and make people ready for his coming. He will be powerful like Elijah* and will have the same spirit. He will make peace between fathers and their children. He will cause people who are not obeying God to change and start thinking the way they should."

[18] Zechariah said to the angel, "How can I know that what you say is true? I am an old man, and my wife is also old."

---

a **1:5 Abijah's group** Jewish priests were divided into 24 groups. See 1 Chron. 24.

[19]The angel answered him, "I am Gabriel, the one who always stands ready before God. He sent me to talk to you and to tell you this good news. [20]Now, listen! You will not be able to talk until the day when these things happen. You will lose your speech because you did not believe what I told you. But everything I said will really happen."

[21]Outside, the people were still waiting for Zechariah. They were surprised that he was staying so long in the Temple. [22]Then Zechariah came outside, but he could not speak to them. So the people knew that he had seen a vision* inside the Temple. He was not able to speak, so he could only make signs to the people. [23]When his time of service was finished, he went home.

[24]Later, Zechariah's wife Elizabeth became pregnant. So she did not go out of her house for five months. She said, [25]"Look what the Lord has done for me! He decided to help me. Now people will stop thinking there is something wrong with me."

The Virgin Mary

[26-27]During Elizabeth's sixth month of pregnancy, God sent the angel Gabriel to a virgin* girl who lived in Nazareth, a town in Galilee. She was engaged to marry a man named Joseph from the family of David.* Her name was Mary. [28]The angel came to her and said, "Greetings! The Lord is with you; you are very special to him."

[29]But Mary was very confused about what the angel said. She wondered, "What does this mean?"

[30]The angel said to her, "Don't be afraid, Mary, because God is very pleased with you. [31]Listen! You will become pregnant and have a baby boy. You will name him Jesus. [32]He will be great. People will call him the Son of the Most High God, and the Lord God will make him king like his ancestor David. [33]He will rule over the people of Jacob* forever; his kingdom will never end."

[34]Mary said to the angel, "How will this happen? I am still a virgin."

[35]The angel said to Mary, "The Holy Spirit* will come to you, and the power of the Most High God will cover you. The baby will be holy and will be called the Son of God. [36]And here's something else: Your relative Elizabeth is pregnant. She is very old, but she is going to have a son. Everyone thought she could not have a baby, but she has been pregnant now for six months. [37]God can do anything!"

[38]Mary said, "I am the servant of the Lord God. Let this thing you have said happen to me!" Then the angel went away.

Mary Visits Zechariah and Elizabeth

[39]Mary got up and went quickly to a town in the hill country of Judea. [40]She went into Zechariah's house and greeted Elizabeth. [41]When Elizabeth heard Mary's greeting, the unborn baby inside her jumped, and she was filled with the Holy Spirit.* [42]In a loud voice she said to Mary, "God has blessed you more than any other woman. And God has blessed the baby you will have. [43]You are the mother of my Lord, and you have come to me! Why has something so good happened to me? [44]When I heard your voice, the baby inside me jumped with

joy. 45Great blessings are yours because you believed what the Lord said to you! You believed this would happen."

Mary Praises God

46Then Mary said,

"I praise the Lord with all my
heart.
47 I am very happy because God
is my Savior.
48 I am not important,
but he has shown his care
for me, his lowly servant.
From now until the end of
time,
people will remember how
much God blessed me.
49 Yes, the Powerful One has
done great things for me.
His name is very holy.
50 He always gives mercy to
those who worship him.
51 He reached out his arm and
showed his power.
He scattered those who
are proud and think great
things about themselves.
52 He brought down rulers from
their thrones
and raised up the humble
people.
53 He filled the hungry with good
things,
but he sent the rich away
with nothing.
54 God has helped Israel—the
people he chose to serve
him.
He did not forget his
promise to give us his
mercy.
55 He has done what he
promised to our ancestors,*
to Abraham* and his
children forever."

56Mary stayed with Elizabeth for about three months and then went home.

The Birth of John

57When it was time for Elizabeth to give birth, she had a boy. 58Her neighbors and relatives heard that the Lord was very good to her, and they were happy for her. 59When the baby was eight days old, they came to circumcise* him. They wanted to name him Zechariah because this was his father's name. 60But his mother said, "No, he will be named John."

61The people said to Elizabeth, "But no one in your family has that name." 62Then they made signs to his father, "What would you like to name him?"

63Zechariah asked for something to write on. Then he wrote, "His name is John." Everyone was surprised. 64Then Zechariah could talk again, and he began praising God. 65And all their neighbors were afraid. In all the hill country of Judea, people continued talking about these things. 66Everyone who heard about these things wondered about them. They thought, "What will this child be?" They could see that the Lord was with him.

Zechariah Praises God

67Then Zechariah, John's father, was filled with the Holy Spirit* and told the people a message from God:

68 "Praise to the Lord God of
Israel.*
He has come to help his
people and has given them
freedom.
69 He has given us a powerful
Savior
from the family of his
servant David.*
70 This is what he promised
through his holy* prophets*
long ago.

71 He will save us from our
enemies
and from the power of all
those who hate us.
72 God said he would show mercy
to our fathers,*
and he remembered his holy
agreement.*
73 This was the promise he
made to our father
Abraham,*
74 a promise to free us from the
power of our enemies,
so that we could serve him
without fear
75 in a way that is holy and
right for as long as we live.

76 "Now you, little boy, will be
called a prophet of the Most
High God.
You will go first before the
Lord to prepare the way for
him.
77 You will make his people
understand that they will
be saved by having their
sins forgiven.

78 "With the loving mercy of our
God,
a new day*a* from heaven will
shine on us.
79 It will bring light to those who
live in darkness, in the fear
of death.
It will guide us into the way
that brings peace."
80 And so the little boy John
grew up and became stronger in
spirit. Then he lived in areas away
from other people until the time
when he came out to tell God's
message to the people of Israel.

a 1:78 new day Literally, "dawn," used here
as a symbol, probably meaning the Lord's
Messiah.

The Birth of Jesus Christ
(Mt. 1:18–25)

2 ¹It was about that same time
that Augustus Caesar* sent
out an order to all people in the
countries that were under Roman
rule. The order said that everyone's name must be put on a list.
²This was the first counting of all
the people while Quirinius was
governor of Syria. ³Everyone traveled to their own hometowns to
have their name put on the list.
⁴So Joseph left Nazareth, a town
in Galilee, and went to the town
of Bethlehem in Judea. It was
known as the town of David.* Joseph went there because he was
from the family of David. ⁵Joseph
registered with Mary because
she was engaged to marry him.
(She was now pregnant.) ⁶While
Joseph and Mary were in Bethlehem, the time came for her to
have the baby. ⁷She gave birth to
her first son. She wrapped him up
well and laid him in a box where
cattle are fed. She put him there
because the guest room was full.

Some Shepherds Hear About Jesus
⁸That night, some shepherds were
out in the fields near Bethlehem
watching their sheep. ⁹An angel
of the Lord appeared to them, and
the glory* of the Lord was shining around them. The shepherds
were very afraid. ¹⁰The angel said
to them, "Don't be afraid. I have
some very good news for you—
news that will make everyone
happy. ¹¹Today your Savior was
born in David's town. He is the
Messiah,* the Lord. ¹²This is how
you will know him: You will find
a baby wrapped in pieces of cloth
and lying in a feeding box."
¹³Then a huge army of angels
from heaven joined the first angel,

and they were all praising God, saying,

14 "Praise God in heaven,
    and on earth let there be
    peace to the people who
    please him."

15 The angels left the shepherds and went back to heaven. The shepherds said to each other, "Let's go to Bethlehem and see this great event the Lord has told us about."

16 So they went running and found Mary and Joseph. And there was the baby, lying in the feeding box. 17 When they saw the baby, they told what the angels said about this child. 18 Everyone was surprised when they heard what the shepherds told them. 19 Mary continued to think about these things, trying to understand them. 20 The shepherds went back to their sheep, praising God and thanking him for everything they had seen and heard. It was just as the angel had told them.

21 When the baby was eight days old, he was circumcised,* and he was named Jesus. This name was given by the angel before the baby began to grow inside Mary.

Jesus Is Presented in the Temple

22 The time came for Mary and Joseph to do the things the Law of Moses* taught about being made pure.*a They brought Jesus to Jerusalem so that they could present him to the Lord. 23 It is written in the law of the Lord: "When a mother's first baby is a boy, he shall be called 'special for the Lord.'"*b 24 The law of the Lord also says that people must give a sacrifice*: "You must sacrifice two doves or two young pigeons."*c So Joseph and Mary went to Jerusalem to do this.

Simeon Sees Jesus

25 A man named Simeon lived in Jerusalem. He was a good man who was devoted to God. He was waiting for the time when God would come to help Israel.* The Holy Spirit* was with him. 26 The Holy Spirit told him that he would not die before he saw the Messiah* from the Lord. 27 The Spirit led Simeon to the Temple.* So he was there when Mary and Joseph brought the baby Jesus to do what the Jewish law said they must do. 28 Simeon took the baby in his arms and thanked God:

29 "Now, Lord, you can let me,
    your servant, die in peace
    as you said.
30 I have seen with my own eyes
    how you will save your
    people.
31   Now all people can see your
    plan.
32 He is a light to show your way
    to the other nations.
    And he will bring honor to
    your people Israel."

33 Jesus' father and mother were amazed at what Simeon said about him. 34 Then Simeon blessed them and said to Mary, "Many Jews will fall and many will rise because of this boy. He will be a sign from God that some will not accept. 35 So the secret thoughts of many will be made known. And the things that happen will

---

a **2:22 pure** The Law of Moses said that 40 days after a Jewish woman gave birth to a baby, she must be made ritually clean by a ceremony at the Temple. See Lev. 12:2–8.

b **2:23 "When . . . 'special for the Lord'"** See Ex. 13:2, 12.

c **2:24** Quote from Lev. 12:8.

be painful for you—like a sword cutting through your heart."

Anna Sees Jesus

³⁶Anna, a prophetess,* was there at the Temple.* She was from the family of Phanuel in the tribe of Asher. She was now very old. She had lived with her husband seven years ³⁷before he died and left her alone. She was now 84 years old. Anna was always at the Temple; she never left. She worshiped God by fasting* and praying day and night.

³⁸Anna was there when Joseph and Mary came to the Temple. She praised God and talked about Jesus to all those who were waiting for God to free Jerusalem.

Joseph and Mary Return Home

³⁹Joseph and Mary finished doing all the things that the law of the Lord commanded. Then they went home to Nazareth, their own town in Galilee. ⁴⁰The little boy Jesus was developing into a mature young man, full of wisdom. God was blessing him.

Jesus as a Boy

⁴¹Every year Jesus' parents went to Jerusalem for the Passover* festival. ⁴²When Jesus was twelve years old, they went to the festival as usual. ⁴³When the festival was over, they went home, but Jesus stayed in Jerusalem. His parents did not know about it. ⁴⁴They traveled for a whole day thinking that Jesus was with them in the group. They began looking for him among their family and close friends, ⁴⁵but they did not find him. So they went back to Jerusalem to look for him there.

⁴⁶After three days they found him. Jesus was sitting in the Temple* area with the religious teachers, listening and asking

them questions. ⁴⁷Everyone who heard him was amazed at his understanding and wise answers. ⁴⁸When his parents saw him, they wondered how this was possible. And his mother said, "Son, why did you do this to us? Your father and I were very worried about you. We have been looking for you."

⁴⁹Jesus said to them, "Why did you have to look for me? You should have known that I must be where my Father's work is.ᵃ" ⁵⁰But they did not understand the meaning of what he said to them.

⁵¹Jesus went with them to Nazareth and obeyed them. His mother was still thinking about all these things. ⁵²As Jesus grew taller, he continued to grow in wisdom. God was pleased with him and so were the people who knew him.

John Prepares the Way for Jesus
(Mt. 3:1–12; Mk. 1:1–8; Jn. 1:19–28)

3 ¹It was the 15th year of the rule of Tiberius Caesar.* These men were under Caesar:
Pontius Pilate,* the governor of Judea;
Herod,* the ruler of Galilee;
Philip, Herod's brother, the ruler of Iturea and Trachonitis;
Lysanias, the ruler of Abilene. ²Annas and Caiaphas were the high priests.* During this time, John, the son of Zechariah, was living in the desert, and he received a message from God. ³So he went through the whole area around the Jordan River and told the people God's message. He told them to be baptized* to show that they wanted to change their

ᵃ **2:49 where … work is** Or "in my Father's house."

lives, and then their sins would be forgiven. [4]This is like the words written in the book of Isaiah the prophet*:

"There is someone shouting in the desert:
  'Prepare the way for the Lord.
  Make the road straight for him.
[5] Every valley will be filled,
  and every mountain and hill will be made flat.
Crooked roads will be made straight,
  and rough roads will be made smooth.
[6] Then everyone will see how God will save his people!'"

  Isaiah 40:3–5

[7]Crowds of people came to be baptized by John. But he said to them, "You are all snakes! Who warned you to run from God's judgment that is coming? [8]Change your hearts! And show by your lives that you have changed. I know what you are about to say—'but Abraham* is our father!' That means nothing. I tell you that God can make children for Abraham from these rocks! [9]The ax is now ready to cut down the trees.[a] Every tree that does not produce good fruit will be cut down and thrown into the fire."

[10]The people asked John, "What should we do?"

[11]He answered, "If you have two shirts, share with someone who does not have one. If you have food, share that too."

[12]Even the tax collectors* came to John. They wanted to be baptized. They said to him, "Teacher, what should we do?"

[13]He told them, "Don't take more taxes from people than you have been ordered to collect."

[14]The soldiers asked him, "What about us? What should we do?"

He said to them, "Don't use force or lies to make people give you money. Be happy with the pay you get."

[15]Everyone was hoping for the Messiah* to come, and they wondered about John. They thought, "Maybe he is the Messiah."

[16]John's answer to this was, "I baptize you in water, but there is someone coming later who is able to do more than I can. I am not good enough to be the slave who unties his sandals. He will baptize you with the Holy Spirit* and with fire. [17]He will come ready to clean the grain.[b] He will separate the good grain from the straw, and he will put the good part into his barn. Then he will burn the useless part with a fire that cannot be stopped." [18]John said many other things like this to encourage the people to change, and he told them the Good News.*

How John's Work Later Ended

[19]John criticized Herod* the ruler for what he had done with Herodias, the wife of Herod's brother, as well as for all the other bad things he had done. [20]So Herod added another bad thing to all his other wrongs: He put John in jail.

Jesus Is Baptized by John

(Mt. 3:13–17; Mk. 1:9–11)

[21]When all the people were being baptized,* Jesus came and was baptized too. And while he was praying, the sky opened, [22]and the Holy Spirit* came down on

---

[a] **3:9 trees** Meaning the people who don't obey God. They are like "trees" that will be cut down.

[b] **3:17 clean the grain** Meaning that Jesus will separate the good people from those who are bad.

him. The Spirit looked like a real dove. Then a voice came from heaven and said, "You are my Son, the one I love. I am very pleased with you."

The Family History of Joseph
(Mt. 1:1–17)

23When Jesus began to teach, he was about 30 years old. People thought that Jesus was Joseph's son.

Joseph was the son of Eli.
24 Eli was the son of Matthat.
Matthat was the son of Levi.
Levi was the son of Melchi.
Melchi was the son of Jannai.
Jannai was the son of Joseph.
25 Joseph was the son of Mattathias.
Mattathias was the son of Amos.
Amos was the son of Nahum.
Nahum was the son of Esli.
Esli was the son of Naggai.
26 Naggai was the son of Maath.
Maath was the son of Mattathias.
Mattathias was the son of Semein.
Semein was the son of Josech.
Josech was the son of Joda.
27 Joda was the son of Joanan.
Joanan was the son of Rhesa.
Rhesa was the son of Zerubbabel.
Zerubbabel was the son of Shealtiel.
Shealtiel was the son of Neri.
28 Neri was the son of Melchi.
Melchi was the son of Addi.
Addi was the son of Cosam.
Cosam was the son of Elmadam.
Elmadam was the son of Er.
29 Er was the son of Joshua.
Joshua was the son of Eliezer.
Eliezer was the son of Jorim.
Jorim was the son of Matthat.
Matthat was the son of Levi.
30 Levi was the son of Simeon.
Simeon was the son of Judah.
Judah was the son of Joseph.
Joseph was the son of Jonam.
Jonam was the son of Eliakim.
31 Eliakim was the son of Melea.
Melea was the son of Menna.
Menna was the son of Mattatha.
Mattatha was the son of Nathan.
Nathan was the son of David.
32 David was the son of Jesse.
Jesse was the son of Obed.
Obed was the son of Boaz.
Boaz was the son of Salmon.
Salmon was the son of Nahshon.
33 Nahshon was the son of Amminadab.
Amminadab was the son of Admin.
Admin was the son of Arni.
Arni was the son of Hezron.
Hezron was the son of Perez.
Perez was the son of Judah.
34 Judah was the son of Jacob.
Jacob was the son of Isaac.
Isaac was the son of Abraham.
Abraham was the son of Terah.
Terah was the son of Nahor.
35 Nahor was the son of Serug.
Serug was the son of Reu.
Reu was the son of Peleg.
Peleg was the son of Eber.
Eber was the son of Shelah.
36 Shelah was the son of Cainan.
Cainan was the son of Arphaxad.
Arphaxad was the son of Shem.
Shem was the son of Noah.
Noah was the son of Lamech.
37 Lamech was the son of Methuselah.
Methuselah was the son of Enoch.
Enoch was the son of Jared.

Jared was the son of
Mahalaleel.
Mahalaleel was the son of
Cainan.
38 Cainan was the son of Enos.
Enos was the son of Seth.
Seth was the son of Adam.
Adam was the son of God.

Jesus Is Tempted by the Devil
(Mt. 4:1–11; Mk. 1:12–13)

4 1Now filled with the Holy Spirit,* Jesus returned from the Jordan River. And then the Spirit led him into the desert. 2There the devil tempted Jesus for 40 days. Jesus ate nothing during this time, and when it was finished, he was very hungry.

3The devil said to him, "If you are the Son of God, tell this rock to become bread."

4Jesus answered, "The Scriptures* say,

'It is not just bread that keeps
people alive.'"   Deuteronomy 8:3

5Then the devil took Jesus and in a moment of time showed him all the kingdoms of the world. 6The devil said to him, "I will make you king over all these places. You will have power over them, and you will get all the glory.* It has all been given to me. I can give it to anyone I want. 7I will give it all to you, if you will only worship me."

8Jesus answered, "The Scriptures say,

'You must worship the Lord
your God.
Serve only him.'"
              Deuteronomy 6:13

9Then the devil led Jesus to Jerusalem and put him on a high place at the edge of the Temple* area. He said to him, "If you are the Son of God, jump off! 10The Scriptures say,

'God will command his angels
to take care of you.'   Psalm 91:11
11It is also written,
'Their hands will catch you
so that you will not hit your
foot on a rock.'"   Psalm 91:12

12Jesus answered, "But the Scriptures also say,

'You must not test the Lord
your God.'"   Deuteronomy 6:16

13The devil finished tempting Jesus in every way and went away to wait until a better time.

Jesus Begins His Work in Galilee
(Mt. 4:12–17; Mk. 1:14–15)

14Jesus went back to Galilee with the power of the Spirit.* Stories about him spread all over the area around Galilee. 15He began to teach in the synagogues,* and everyone praised him.

Jesus Goes to His Hometown
(Mt. 13:53–58; Mk. 6:1–6)

16Jesus traveled to Nazareth, the town where he grew up. On the Sabbath* day he went to the synagogue* as he always did. He stood up to read. 17The book of Isaiah the prophet* was given to him. He opened the book and found the place where this is written:

18 "The Spirit of the Lord is on me.
He has chosen me to tell good
news to the poor.
He sent me to tell prisoners
that they are free
and to tell the blind that
they can see again.
He sent me to free those who
have been treated badly
19 and to announce that the
time has come for the
Lord to show his kindness."
              Isaiah 61:1–2; 58:6

20Jesus closed the book, gave it back to the helper, and sat down. As everyone in the synagogue watched him closely, 21he began to speak to them. He said, "While you heard me reading these words just now, they were coming true!"

22Everyone there said good things about Jesus. They were amazed to hear him speak such wonderful words. They said, "How is this possible? Isn't he Joseph's son?"

23Jesus said to them, "I know you will tell me the old saying: 'Doctor, heal yourself.' You want to say, 'We heard about the things you did in Capernaum.* Do those same things here in your own hometown!'" 24Then he said, "The truth is, a prophet is not accepted in his own hometown.

25-26"During the time of Elijah* it did not rain in Israel for three and a half years. There was no food anywhere in the whole country. There were many widows in Israel during that time. But the fact is, Elijah was sent to none of those widows in Israel. He was sent only to a widow in Zarephath, a town in Sidon.

27"And there were many people with leprosy* living in Israel during the time of the prophet Elisha.* But none of them were healed; the only one was Naaman. And he was from the country of Syria, not Israel."

28When the people in the synagogue heard this, they were very angry. 29They got up and forced Jesus to go out of town. Their town was built on a hill. They took Jesus to the edge of the hill to throw him off. 30But he walked through the middle of the crowd and went away.

Jesus Frees a Man From an Evil Spirit
(Mk. 1:21–28)

31Jesus went to Capernaum, a city in Galilee. On the Sabbath* day he taught the people. 32They were amazed at his teaching because he spoke with authority.

33In the synagogue* there was a man who had an evil spirit from the devil inside him. The man shouted loudly, 34"Jesus of Nazareth! What do you want with us? Did you come here to destroy us? I know who you are—God's Holy One!" 35But Jesus warned the evil spirit to stop. He said, "Be quiet! Come out of the man!" The evil spirit threw the man down on the ground in front of everyone. Then the evil spirit left the man and did not hurt him.

36The people were amazed. They said to each other, "What does this mean? With authority and power he commands evil spirits and they come out." 37And so the news about Jesus spread to every place in the whole area.

Jesus Heals Peter's Mother-in-Law
(Mt. 8:14–17; Mk. 1:29–34)

38Jesus left the synagogue* and went to Simon's*d* house. Simon's mother-in-law was very sick. She had a high fever. They asked Jesus to do something to help her. 39He stood very close to her and ordered the sickness to go away. The sickness left her, and she got up and began serving them.

Jesus Heals Many Others

40When the sun went down, the people brought their sick friends to Jesus. They had many different kinds of sicknesses. Jesus laid his hands on* each sick person and healed them all. 41Demons* came out of many people. The demons shouted, "You are the Son of God." But Jesus gave a strong

---

a **4:38 Simon** Simon's other name was Peter. Also in 5:3, 4, 5, 10.

command for the demons not to speak, because they knew he was the Messiah.*

Jesus Goes to Other Towns
(Mk. 1:35–39)

42The next day Jesus went to a place to be alone. The people looked for him. When they found him, they tried to stop him from leaving. 43But he said to them, "I must tell the Good News* about God's kingdom* to other towns too. This is why I was sent." 44Then Jesus told the Good News in the synagogues* in Judea.

Jesus Chooses Some Followers
(Mt. 4:18–22; Mk. 1:16–20)

5 1As Jesus stood beside Lake Galilee,*a* a crowd of people pushed to get closer to him and to hear the teachings of God. 2Jesus saw two boats at the shore of the lake. The fishermen were washing their nets. 3Jesus got into the boat that belonged to Simon. He asked Simon to push off a little from the shore. Then he sat down in the boat and taught the people on the shore.

4When Jesus finished speaking, he said to Simon, "Take the boat into the deep water. If all of you will put your nets into the water, you will catch some fish."

5Simon answered, "Master, we worked hard all night trying to catch fish and caught nothing. But you say I should put the nets into the water, so I will." 6The fishermen put their nets into the water. Their nets were filled with so many fish that they began to break. 7They called to their friends in the other boat to come and help them. The friends came, and both boats were filled so full of fish that they were almost sinking.

8-9The fishermen were all amazed at the many fish they caught. When Simon Peter saw this, he bowed down before Jesus and said, "Go away from me, Lord. I am a sinful man!" 10James and John, the sons of Zebedee, were amazed too. (James and John worked together with Simon.)

Jesus said to Simon, "Don't be afraid. From now on your work will be to bring in people, not fish!"

11The men brought their boats to the shore. They left everything and followed Jesus.

Jesus Heals a Sick Man
(Mt. 8:1–4; Mk. 1:40–45)

12One time Jesus was in a town where a very sick man lived. This man was covered with leprosy.* When the man saw Jesus, he bowed before Jesus and begged him, "Lord, you have the power to heal me if you want."

13Jesus said, "I want to heal you. Be healed!" Then he touched the man, and immediately the leprosy disappeared. 14Then Jesus said, "Don't tell anyone about what happened. But go and let the priest look at you.*b* And offer a gift to God for your healing as Moses* commanded. This will show people that you are healed."

15But the news about Jesus spread more and more. Many people came to hear him and to be healed of their sicknesses. 16Jesus often went away to other places to be alone so that he could pray.

a 5:1 Galilee Literally, "Gennesaret."

b 5:14 let the priest look at you The Law of Moses said a priest must decide when a person with leprosy was well.

Jesus Heals a Crippled Man
(Mt. 9:1–8; Mk. 2:1–12)

17One day Jesus was teaching the people. The Pharisees* and teachers of the law were sitting there too. They had come from every town in Galilee and Judea and from Jerusalem. The Lord was giving Jesus the power to heal people. 18There was a man who was paralyzed, and some other men were carrying him on a mat. They tried to bring him and put him down before Jesus. 19But there were so many people that they could not find a way to Jesus. So they went up on the roof and lowered the crippled man down through a hole in the ceiling. They lowered the mat into the room so that the crippled man was lying before Jesus. 20Jesus saw how much faith they had and said to the sick man, "Friend, your sins are forgiven."

21The Jewish teachers of the law and the Pharisees thought to themselves, "Who is this man who dares to say such things? What an insult to God! No one but God can forgive sins."

22But Jesus knew what they were thinking and said, "Why do you have these questions in your minds? 23-24The Son of Man* has power on earth to forgive sins. But how can I prove this to you? Maybe you are thinking it was easy for me to say, 'Your sins are forgiven.' There's no proof that it really happened. But what if I say to the man, 'Stand up and walk'? Then you will be able to see that I really have this power." So Jesus said to the paralyzed man, "I tell you, stand up! Take your mat and go home!"

25The man immediately stood up in front of everyone. He picked up his mat and walked home, praising God. 26Everyone was completely amazed and began to praise God. They were filled with great respect for God's power. They said, "Today we saw amazing things!"

Levi (Matthew) Follows Jesus
(Mt. 9:9–13; Mk. 2:13–17)

27After this Jesus went out and saw a tax collector* sitting at his place for collecting taxes. His name was Levi. Jesus said to him, "Follow me!" 28Levi got up, left everything, and followed Jesus.

29Then Levi gave a big dinner at his house for Jesus. At the table there were many tax collectors and some other people too. 30But the Pharisees* and those who taught the law for the Pharisees began to complain to the followers of Jesus, "Why do you eat and drink with tax collectors and other sinners?"

31Jesus answered them, "It is the sick people who need a doctor, not those who are healthy. 32I have not come to ask good people to change. I have come to ask sinners to change the way they live."

Jesus Is Not Like Other Religious Leaders
(Mt. 9:14–17; Mk. 2:18–22)

33They said to Jesus, "John's followers often fast* and pray, the same as the followers of the Pharisees.* But your followers eat and drink all the time."

34Jesus said to them, "At a wedding you can't ask the friends of the bridegroom* to be sad and fast while he is still with them. 35But the time will come when the groom will be taken away from them. Then his friends will fast."

36Jesus told them this story: "No one takes cloth off a new coat to cover a hole in an old coat. That would ruin the new coat, and the cloth from the new coat would not be the same as the old cloth. [37]Also, no one ever pours new wine into old wineskins.* The new wine would break them. The wine would spill out, and the wineskins would be ruined. [38]You always put new wine into new wineskins. [39]No one who drinks old wine wants new wine. They say, 'The old wine is just fine.' "

Jesus Is Lord Over the Sabbath Day
(Mt. 12:1–8; Mk. 2:23–28)

6 [1]One time on a Sabbath* day, Jesus was walking through some grain fields. His followers picked the grain, rubbed it in their hands, and ate it. [2]Some Pharisees* said, "Why are you doing that? It is against the Law of Moses* to do that on the Sabbath day."

[3]Jesus answered, "You have read about what David* did when he and the people with him were hungry. [4]David went into God's house. He took the bread that was offered to God and ate it. And he gave some of the bread to the people with him. This was against the Law of Moses, which says that only the priests can eat that bread." [5]Then Jesus said to the Pharisees, "The Son of Man* is Lord over the Sabbath day."

Jesus Heals a Man on the Sabbath Day
(Mt. 12:9–14; Mk. 3:1–6)

[6]On another Sabbath* day Jesus went into the synagogue* and taught the people. A man with a crippled right hand was there. [7]The teachers of the law and the Pharisees* were watching Jesus closely. They were waiting to see if he would heal on the Sabbath day. They wanted to see him do something wrong so that they could accuse him. [8]But Jesus knew what they were thinking. He said to the man with the crippled hand, "Get up and stand here where everyone can see." The man got up and stood there. [9]Then Jesus said to them, "I ask you, which is the right thing to do on the Sabbath day: to do good or to do evil? Is it right to save a life or to destroy one?"

[10]Jesus looked around at all of them and then said to the man, "Hold out your hand." The man held out his hand, and it was healed. [11]The Pharisees and the teachers of the law got so mad they couldn't think straight. They talked to each other about what they could do to Jesus.

Jesus Chooses His Twelve Apostles
(Mt. 10:1–4; Mk. 3:13–19)

[12]A few days later, Jesus went out to a mountain to pray. He stayed there all night praying to God. [13]The next morning he called his followers. He chose twelve of them and called them apostles.* These are the ones he chose:

[14] Simon (Jesus named him
      Peter),
   Andrew, brother of Peter,
   James,
   John,
   Philip,
   Bartholomew,
[15] Matthew,
   Thomas,
   James, the son of Alphaeus,
   Simon, called the Zealot,*
[16] Judas, the son of James,
   Judas Iscariot (the one who
      turned against Jesus).

Jesus Teaches and Heals the People
(Mt. 4:23–25; 5:1–12)

[17]Jesus and the apostles* came down from the mountain. Jesus stood on a flat place. A large crowd

of his followers was there. Also, there were many people from all around Judea, Jerusalem, and the seacoast cities of Tyre* and Sidon.* ¹⁸They all came to hear Jesus teach and to be healed of their sicknesses. He healed the people who were troubled by evil spirits. ¹⁹Everyone was trying to touch him, because power was coming out from him. Jesus healed them all.

²⁰Jesus looked at his followers and said,

"Great blessings belong to you who are poor.
God's kingdom* belongs to you.
²¹ Great blessings belong to you who are hungry now.
You will be filled.
Great blessings belong to you who are crying now.
You will be happy and laughing.

²²"People will hate you because you belong to the Son of Man.* They will make you leave their group. They will insult you. They will think it is wrong even to say your name. When these things happen, know that great blessings belong to you. ²³You can be happy then and jump for joy, because you have a great reward in heaven. The ancestors* of those people did the same things to the prophets.*

²⁴ "But how bad it will be for you rich people,
because you had your easy life.
²⁵ How bad it will be for you people who are full now,
because you will be hungry.
How bad it will be for you people who are laughing now,
because you will be sad and cry.

²⁶"How bad it is when everyone says nothing but good about you. Just look at the false prophets.* Their ancestors always said good things about them.

Love Your Enemies
(Mt. 5:38–48; 7:12a)

²⁷"But I say to you people who are listening to me, love your enemies. Do good to those who hate you. ²⁸Ask God to bless the people who ask for bad things to happen to you. Pray for the people who are mean to you. ²⁹If someone hits you on the side of your face, let them hit the other side too. If someone takes your coat, don't stop them from taking your shirt too. ³⁰Give to everyone who asks you for something. When someone takes something that is yours, don't ask for it back. ³¹Do for others what you want them to do for you.

³²"If you love only those who love you, should you get any special praise for doing that? No, even sinners love those who love them! ³³If you do good only to those who do good to you, should you get any special praise for doing that? No, even sinners do that! ³⁴If you lend things to people, always expecting to get something back, should you get any special praise for that? No, even sinners lend to other sinners so that they can get back the same amount!

³⁵"I'm telling you to love your enemies and do good to them. Lend to people without expecting to get anything back. If you do this, you will have a great reward. You will be children of the Most High God. Yes, because God is good even to the people who are

full of sin and not thankful. [36]Give love and mercy the same as your Father gives love and mercy.

Be Careful About Criticizing Others
(Mt. 7:1-5)

[37]"Don't judge others, and God will not judge you. Don't condemn others, and you will not be condemned. Forgive others, and you will be forgiven. [38]Give to others, and you will receive. You will be given much. It will be poured into your hands—more than you can hold. You will be given so much that it will spill into your lap. The way you give to others is the way God will give to you."

[39]Jesus told them this story: "Can a blind man lead another blind man? No. Both of them will fall into a ditch. [40]Students are not better than their teacher. But when they have been fully taught, they will be like their teacher.

[41]"Why do you notice the small piece of dust that is in your friend's eye, but you don't see the big piece of wood that is in your own eye? [42]You say to your friend, 'Let me get that little piece of dust out of your eye.' Why do you say this? Can't you see that big piece of wood in your own eye? You are a hypocrite.* First, take the wood out of your own eye. Then you will see clearly to get the dust out of your friend's eye.

Only Good Trees Produce Good Fruit
(Mt. 7:17-20; 12:34b-35)

[43]"A good tree does not produce bad fruit. And a bad tree does not produce good fruit. [44]Every tree is known by the kind of fruit it produces. You won't find figs on thorny weeds. And you can't pick grapes from thornbushes! [45]Good people have good things saved in their hearts. That's why they say good things. But those who are evil have hearts full of evil, and that's why they say things that are evil. What people say with their mouths comes from what fills their hearts.

Two Kinds of People
(Mt. 7:24-27)

[46]"Why do you call me, 'Lord, Lord,' but you don't do what I say? [47]The people who come to me, who listen to my teachings and obey them—I will show you what they are like: [48]They are like a man building a house. He digs deep and builds his house on rock. The floods come, and the water crashes against the house. But the flood cannot move the house, because it was built well.

[49]"But the people who hear my words and do not obey are like a man who builds a house without preparing a foundation. When the floods come, the house falls down easily and is completely destroyed."

Jesus Heals an Officer's Servant
(Mt. 8:5-13; Jn. 4:43-54)

7 [1]Jesus finished saying all these things to the people. Then he went into Capernaum.* [2]In Capernaum there was an army officer.* He had a servant who was very sick; he was near death. The officer loved the servant very much. [3]When he heard about Jesus, he sent some older Jewish leaders to him. He wanted the men to ask Jesus to come and save the life of his servant. [4]The men went to Jesus. They begged Jesus to help the officer. They said, "This officer is worthy to have your help. [5]He loves our people and he built the synagogue* for us."

[6]So Jesus went with them. He was coming near the officer's

Jesus feeds a large crowd
John 6:1-15

© WBTC 2011

Jesus walks on water
Matthew 14:22-33

house when the officer sent friends to say, "Lord, you don't need to do anything special for me. I am not good enough for you to come into my house. [7]That is why I did not come to you myself. You need only to give the order, and my servant will be healed. [8]I know this because I am a man under the authority of other men. And I have soldiers under my authority. I tell one soldier, 'Go,' and he goes. And I tell another soldier, 'Come,' and he comes. And I say to my servant, 'Do this,' and my servant obeys me."

[9]When Jesus heard this, he was amazed. He turned to the people following him and said, "I tell you, this is the most faith I have seen anywhere, even in Israel.*"

[10]The group that was sent to Jesus went back to the house. There they found that the servant was healed.

Jesus Brings a Woman's Son Back to Life

[11]The next day Jesus and his followers went to a town called Nain. A big crowd was traveling with them. [12]When Jesus came near the town gate, he saw some people carrying a dead body. It was the only son of a woman who was a widow. Walking with her were many other people from the town. [13]When the Lord saw the woman, he felt very sorry for her and said, "Don't cry." [14]He walked to the open coffin and touched it. The men who were carrying the coffin stopped. Jesus spoke to the dead son: "Young man, I tell you, get up!" [15]Then the boy sat up and began to talk, and Jesus gave him back to his mother.

[16]Everyone was filled with fear. They began praising God and said, "A great prophet* is here with us!"

and "God is taking care of his people."

[17]This news about Jesus spread all over Judea and to all the other places around there.

John Sends Men to Ask Jesus a Question
(Mt. 11:2–19)

[18]John's followers told him about all these things. John called for two of his followers. [19]He sent them to the Lord to ask, "Are you the one we heard was coming, or should we wait for someone else?"

[20]So the men came to Jesus. They said, "John the Baptizer* sent us to you with this question: 'Are you the one who is coming, or should we wait for someone else?'"

[21]Right then Jesus healed many people of their sicknesses and diseases. He healed those who had evil spirits and made many who were blind able to see again. [22]Then he said to John's followers, "Go tell John what you have seen and heard: The blind can see. The crippled can walk. People with leprosy* are healed. The deaf can hear. The dead are brought back to life. And the Good News* is being told to the poor. [23]Great blessings belong to those who don't have a problem accepting me."

[24]When John's followers left, Jesus began talking to the people about John: "What did you people go out into the desert to see? Someone who is weak, like a stem of grass[a] blowing in the wind? [25]Really, what did you expect to see? Someone dressed in fine clothes? Of course not. People who wear fancy clothes and live in luxury are all in kings' palaces. [26]So what did you go out to see? A prophet*? Yes, John is a prophet. But I tell you, he

a **7:24 stem of grass** Literally, "reed."

is more than that. ²⁷This Scripture* was written about him:

'Listen! I will send my
    messenger ahead of you.
He will prepare the way for
    you.'   *Malachi 3:1*

²⁸I tell you, no one ever born is greater than John. But even the least important person in God's kingdom* is greater than John."

²⁹(When the people heard this, they all agreed that God's teaching was good. Even the tax collectors* agreed. These were the people who were baptized* by John. ³⁰But the Pharisees* and experts in the law refused to accept God's plan for themselves; they did not let John baptize them.)

³¹"What shall I say about the people of this time? What can I compare them to? What are they like? ³²They are like children sitting in the marketplace. One group of children calls to the other children and says,

'We played flute music for you,
    but you did not dance;
we sang a sad song,
    but you did not cry.'

³³John the Baptizer came and did not eat the usual food or drink wine. And you say, 'He has a demon* inside him.' ³⁴The Son of Man* came eating and drinking. And you say, 'Look at him! He eats too much and drinks too much wine! He is a friend of tax collectors and other sinners!' ³⁵But wisdom is shown to be right by those who accept it."

Simon the Pharisee

³⁶One of the Pharisees* asked Jesus to eat with him. Jesus went into the Pharisee's house and took a place at the table.

³⁷There was a sinful woman in that town. She knew that Jesus was eating at the Pharisee's house. So the woman brought some expensive perfume in an alabaster* jar. ³⁸She stood at Jesus' feet, crying. Then she began to wash his feet with her tears. She dried his feet with her hair. She kissed his feet many times and rubbed them with the perfume.

³⁹When the Pharisee who asked Jesus to come to his house saw this, he thought to himself, "If this man were a prophet,ᵃ he would know that the woman who is touching him is a sinner!"

⁴⁰In response, Jesus said to the Pharisee, "Simon, I have something to say to you."

Simon said, "Let me hear it, Teacher."

⁴¹Jesus said, "There were two men. Both men owed money to the same banker. One man owed him 500 silver coins.* The other man owed him 50 silver coins. ⁴²The men had no money, so they could not pay their debt. But the banker told the men that they did not have to pay him. Which one of those two men will love him more?"

⁴³Simon answered, "I think it would be the one who owed him the most money."

Jesus said to him, "You are right." ⁴⁴Then he turned to the woman and said to Simon, "Do you see this woman? When I came into your house, you gave me no water for my feet. But she washed my feet with her tears and dried my feet with her hair. ⁴⁵You did not greet me with a kiss, but she has been kissing my feet since I came in. ⁴⁶You did not honor me with

ᵃ **7:39 prophet** A prophet often knows things that are hidden to other people.

oil for my head, but she rubbed my feet with her sweet-smelling oil. ⁴⁷I tell you that her many sins are forgiven. This is clear, because she showed great love. People who are forgiven only a little will love only a little."

⁴⁸Then Jesus said to her, "Your sins are forgiven."

⁴⁹The people sitting at the table began to think to themselves, "Who does this man think he is? How can he forgive sins?"

⁵⁰Jesus said to the woman, "Because you believed, you are saved from your sins. Go in peace."

The Group With Jesus

8 ¹The next day, Jesus traveled through some cities and small towns. Jesus told the people a message from God, the Good News about God's kingdom.* The twelve apostles* were with him. ²There were also some women with him. Jesus had healed these women of sicknesses and evil spirits. One of them was Mary, who was called Magdalene. Seven demons had come out of her. ³Also with these women were Joanna, the wife of Chuza (the manager of Herod's* property), Suzanna, and many other women. These women used their own money to help Jesus and his apostles.

A Story About a Farmer Sowing Seed
(Mt. 13:1–17; Mk. 4:1–12)

⁴A large crowd came together. People came to Jesus from every town, and he told them this story: ⁵"A farmer went out to sow seed. While he was scattering the seed, some of it fell beside the road. People walked on the seed, and the birds ate it all. ⁶Other seed fell on rock. It began to grow but then died because it had no water. ⁷Some other seed fell among thorny weeds. This seed grew, but later the weeds stopped the plants from growing. ⁸The rest of the seed fell on good ground. This seed grew and made 100 times more grain."

Jesus finished the story. Then he called out, "You people who hear me, listen!"

⁹Jesus' followers asked him, "What does this story mean?"

¹⁰He said, "You have been chosen to know the secret truths about God's kingdom.* But I use stories to speak to other people. I do this so that,
'They will look,
but they will not see,
and they will listen,
but they will not
understand.'   *Isaiah 6:9*

Jesus Explains the Story About Seed
(Mt. 13:18–23; Mk. 4:13–20)

¹¹"This is what the story means: The seed is God's teaching. ¹²Some people are like the seed that fell beside the path. They hear God's teaching, but then the devil comes and causes them to stop thinking about it. This keeps them from believing it and being saved. ¹³Others are like the seed that fell on rock. That is like the people who hear God's teaching and gladly accept it. But they don't have deep roots. They believe for a while. But when trouble comes, they turn away from God.

¹⁴"What about the seed that fell among the thorny weeds? That is like the people who hear God's teaching, but they let the worries, riches, and pleasures of this life stop them from growing. So they never produce a crop.ᵃ ¹⁵And

---

a 8:14 **produce a crop** Meaning to do the good things God wants his people to do.

what about the seed that fell on the good ground? That is like the people who hear God's teaching with a good, honest heart. They obey it and patiently produce a good crop.

Use the Understanding You Have
(Mk. 4:21–25)

16"No one lights a lamp and then covers it with a bowl or hides it under a bed. Instead, they put the lamp on a lampstand so that the people who come in will have enough light to see. 17Everything that is hidden will become clear. Every secret thing will be made known, and everyone will see it. 18So think carefully about what you are hearing. The people who have some understanding will receive more. But those who do not have understanding will lose even what they think they have."

Jesus' Followers Are His True Family
(Mt. 12:46–50; Mk. 3:31–35)

19Jesus' mother and brothers came to visit him. But they could not get close to him, because there were so many people. 20Someone said to Jesus, "Your mother and your brothers are standing outside. They want to see you."

21Jesus answered them, "My mother and my brothers are those who listen to God's teaching and obey it."

Jesus' Followers See His Power
(Mt. 8:23–27; Mk. 4:35–41)

22One day Jesus and his followers got into a boat. He said to them, "Come with me across the lake." And so they started across. 23While they were sailing, Jesus slept. A big storm blew across the lake, and the boat began to fill with water. They were in danger. 24The followers went to Jesus and woke him. They said, "Master!

Master! We will drown!"

Jesus got up. He gave a command to the wind and the waves. The wind stopped, and the lake became calm. 25He said to his followers, "Where is your faith?"

They were afraid and amazed. They said to each other, "What kind of man is this? He commands the wind and the water, and they obey him."

Jesus Frees a Man From Evil Spirits
(Mt. 8:28–34; Mk. 5:1–20)

26Jesus and his followers sailed on across the lake. They sailed to the area where the Gerasene people live, across from Galilee. 27When Jesus got out of the boat, a man from that town came to him. This man had demons* inside him. For a long time he had worn no clothes. He did not live in a house but in the caves where the dead are buried.

28-29The demon inside the man had often seized him, and he had been put in jail with his hands and feet in chains. But he would always break the chains. The demon inside him would force him to go out to the places where no one lived. Jesus commanded the evil spirit to come out of the man. When the man saw Jesus, he fell down before him, shouting loudly, "What do you want with me, Jesus, Son of the Most High God? Please, don't punish me!"

30Jesus asked him, "What is your name?"

The man answered, "Legion."[a] (He said his name was "Legion" because many demons had gone into him.) 31The demons begged Jesus not to send them into the

a 8:30 "Legion" This name means very many. A legion was about 6000 men in the Roman army.

bottomless pit.*a* ³²On that hill there was a big herd of pigs eating. The demons begged Jesus to allow them to go into the pigs. So he allowed them to do this. ³³Then the demons came out of the man and went into the pigs. The herd of pigs ran down the hill into the lake, and all were drowned.

³⁴The men who were caring for the pigs ran away and told the story in the fields and in the town. ³⁵People went out to see what had happened. They came to Jesus and found the man sitting there at the feet of Jesus. The man had clothes on and was in his right mind again; the demons were gone. This made the people afraid. ³⁶The men who saw these things happen told the others all about how Jesus made the man well. ³⁷All those who lived in the area around Gerasa asked Jesus to go away because they were afraid. So Jesus got into the boat to go back to Galilee. ³⁸The man he had healed begged to go with him. But Jesus sent him away, saying, ³⁹"Go back home and tell people what God did for you."

So the man went all over town telling what Jesus had done for him.

Jesus Gives Life to a Dead Girl and Heals a Sick Woman
(Mt. 9:18–26; Mk. 5:21–43)

⁴⁰When Jesus went back to Galilee, the people welcomed him. Everyone was waiting for him. ⁴¹⁻⁴²A man named Jairus came to him. He was a leader of the synagogue.* He had only one daughter. She was twelve years old, and she was dying. So Jairus bowed down at the feet of Jesus and begged him to come to his house.

While Jesus was going to Jairus' house, the people crowded all around him. ⁴³A woman was there who had been bleeding for twelve years. She had spent all her money on doctors,*b* but no doctor was able to heal her. ⁴⁴The woman came behind Jesus and touched the bottom of his coat. At that moment, her bleeding stopped. ⁴⁵Then Jesus said, "Who touched me?"

They all said they had not touched him. And Peter said, "Master, people are all around you, pushing against you."

⁴⁶But Jesus said, "Someone touched me. I felt power go out from me." ⁴⁷When the woman saw that she could not hide, she came forward, shaking. She bowed down before Jesus. While everyone listened, she told why she touched him. Then she said that she was healed immediately when she touched him. ⁴⁸Jesus said to her, "My daughter, you are made well because you believed. Go in peace."

⁴⁹While Jesus was still speaking, someone came from the house of the synagogue leader and said, "Your daughter has died! Don't bother the Teacher anymore."

⁵⁰Jesus heard this and said to Jairus, "Don't be afraid! Just believe and your daughter will be well."

⁵¹Jesus went to the house. He let only Peter, John, James, and the girl's father and mother go inside with him. ⁵²Everyone was crying and feeling sad because the girl

---

a **8:31 bottomless pit** Literally, "the abyss," something like a deep hole where evil spirits are kept.

b **8:43 She had spent ... doctors** Some Greek copies do not have these words.

was dead. But Jesus said, "Don't cry. She is not dead. She is only sleeping."

⁵³The people laughed at him, because they knew that the girl was dead. ⁵⁴But Jesus held her hand and called to her, "Little girl, stand up!" ⁵⁵Her spirit came back into her, and she stood up immediately. Jesus said, "Give her something to eat." ⁵⁶The girl's parents were amazed. He told them not to tell anyone about what happened.

Jesus Sends His Apostles on a Mission
(Mt. 10:5–15; Mk. 6:7–13)

9 ¹Jesus called his twelve apostles* together. He gave them power to heal sicknesses and power to force demons* out of people. ²He sent them to tell about God's kingdom* and to heal the sick. ³He said to them, "When you travel, don't take a walking stick. Also, don't carry a bag, food, or money. Take for your trip only the clothes you are wearing. ⁴When you go into a house, stay there until it is time to leave. ⁵If the people in the town will not welcome you, go outside the town and shake the dust off your feet as a warning to them."

⁶So the apostles went out. They traveled through all the towns. They told the Good News* and healed people everywhere.

Herod Is Confused About Jesus
(Mt. 14:1–12; Mk. 6:14–29)

⁷Herod* the ruler heard about all these things that were happening. He was confused because some people said, "John the Baptizer has risen from death." ⁸Others said, "Elijah* has come to us." And some others said, "One of the prophets* from long ago has risen from death." ⁹Herod said, "I cut off John's head. So who is this man I hear these things about?" Herod continued trying to see Jesus.

Jesus Feeds More Than 5000
(Mt. 14:13–21; Mk. 6:30–44; Jn. 6:1–14)

¹⁰When the apostles* came back, they told Jesus what they had done on their trip. Then he took them away to a town called Bethsaida. There, he and his apostles could be alone together. ¹¹But the people learned where Jesus went and followed him. He welcomed them and talked with them about God's kingdom.* He healed the people who were sick.

¹²Late in the afternoon, the twelve apostles came to Jesus and said, "No one lives in this place. Send the people away. They need to find food and places to sleep in the farms and towns around here."

¹³But Jesus said to the apostles, "You give them something to eat."

They said, "We have only five loaves of bread and two fish. Do you want us to go buy food for all these people?" There are too many! ¹⁴(There were about 5000 men there.)

Jesus said to his followers, "Tell the people to sit in groups of about 50 people."

¹⁵So the followers did this and everyone sat down. ¹⁶Then Jesus took the five loaves of bread and two fish. He looked up into the sky and thanked God for the food. Then he broke it into pieces, which he gave to the followers to give to the people. ¹⁷They all ate until they were full. And there was a lot of food left. Twelve baskets were filled with the pieces of food that were not eaten.

Peter Says Jesus Is the Messiah
(Mt. 16:13–19; Mk. 8:27–29)

¹⁸One time Jesus was praying alone. His followers came together

there, and he asked them, "Who do the people say I am?"

¹⁹They answered, "Some people say you are John the Baptizer. Others say you are Elijah.* And some people say you are one of the prophets* from long ago that has come back to life."

²⁰Then Jesus said to his followers, "And who do you say I am?"

Peter answered, "You are the Messiah* from God."

²¹Jesus warned them not to tell anyone.

Jesus Says He Must Die
(Mt. 16:21–28; Mk. 8:30–9:1)

²²Then Jesus said, "The Son of Man* must suffer many things. He will be rejected by the older Jewish leaders, the leading priests, and teachers of the law. And he will be killed. But after three days he will be raised from death."

²³Jesus continued to say to all of them, "Any of you who want to be my follower must stop thinking about yourself and what you want. You must be willing to carry the cross* that is given to you every day for following me. ²⁴Any of you who try to save the life you have will lose it. But you who give up your life for me will save it. ²⁵It is worth nothing for you to have the whole world if you yourself are destroyed or lost. ²⁶Don't be ashamed of me and my teaching. If that happens, I *a* will be ashamed of you when I come with my divine greatness* and that of the Father and the holy angels. ²⁷Believe me when I say that some of you people standing here will see God's kingdom* before you die."

Jesus Is Seen With Moses and Elijah
(Mt. 17:1–8; Mk. 9:2–8)

²⁸About eight days after Jesus said these things, he took Peter, John, and James and went up on a mountain to pray. ²⁹While Jesus was praying, his face began to change. His clothes became shining white. ³⁰Then two men were there, talking with him. They were Moses* and Elijah.* ³¹They also looked bright and glorious. They were talking with Jesus about his death that would happen in Jerusalem. ³²Peter and the others were asleep. But they woke up and saw the glory* of Jesus. They also saw the two men who were standing with him. ³³When Moses and Elijah were leaving, Peter said, "Master, it is good that we are here. We will put three tents here—one for you, one for Moses, and one for Elijah." (He did not know what he was saying.)

³⁴While Peter was saying these things, a cloud came all around them. Peter, John, and James were afraid when the cloud covered them. ³⁵A voice came from the cloud and said, "This is my Son. He is the one I have chosen. Obey him."

³⁶When the voice stopped, only Jesus was there. Peter, John, and James said nothing. And for a long time after that, they told no one about what they had seen.

Jesus Frees a Boy From an Evil Spirit
(Mt. 17:14–18; Mk. 9:14–27)

³⁷The next day, Jesus, Peter, John, and James came down from the mountain. A large group of people met Jesus. ³⁸A man in the group shouted to him, "Teacher, please come and look at my son. He is the only child I have. ³⁹An evil spirit comes into him, and then

---

a **9:26** I Literally, "the Son of Man" (Jesus).

he shouts. He loses control of himself and foams at the mouth. The evil spirit continues to hurt him and almost never leaves him. 40I begged your followers to make the evil spirit leave my son, but they could not do it."

41Jesus answered, "You people today have no faith. Your lives are all wrong. How long must I be with you and be patient with you?" Then Jesus said to the man, "Bring your son here."

42While the boy was coming, the demon* threw the boy to the ground. The boy lost control of himself. But Jesus gave a strong command to the evil spirit. Then the boy was healed, and Jesus gave him back to his father. 43All the people were amazed at the great power of God.

Jesus Talks About His Death
(Mt. 17:22-23; Mk. 9:30-32)

The people were still amazed about all the things Jesus did. He said to his followers, 44"Don't forget what I will tell you now: The Son of Man* will soon be handed over to the control of other men." 45But the followers did not understand what he meant. The meaning was hidden from them so that they could not understand it. But they were afraid to ask Jesus about what he said.

Who Is the Greatest?
(Mt. 18:1-5; Mk. 9:33-37)

46Jesus' followers began to have an argument about which one of them was the greatest. 47Jesus knew what they were thinking, so he took a little child and stood the child beside him. 48Then he said to the followers, "Whoever accepts a little child like this in my name is accepting me. And anyone who accepts me is also accepting the one who sent me. The one among you who is the most humble—this is the one who is great."

Whoever Is Not Against You Is for You
(Mk. 9:38-40)

49John answered, "Master, we saw someone using your name to force demons* out of people. We told him to stop because he does not belong to our group."

50Jesus said to him, "Don't stop him. Whoever is not against you is for you."

A Samaritan Town

51The time was coming near when Jesus would leave and go back to heaven. He decided to go to Jerusalem. 52He sent some men ahead of him. They went into a town in Samaria to make everything ready for him. 53But the people there would not welcome Jesus because he was going toward Jerusalem. 54James and John, the followers of Jesus, saw this. They said, "Lord, do you want us to call fire down from heaven and destroy those people?"a

55But Jesus turned and criticized them for saying this.b 56Then he and his followers went to another town.

Following Jesus
(Mt. 8:19-22)

57They were all traveling along the road. Someone said to Jesus, "I will follow you anywhere you go."

58He answered, "The foxes have holes to live in. The birds have nests. But the Son of Man* has no place where he can rest his head."

a 9:54 Some Greek copies add "as Elijah did?"
b 9:55 Some Greek copies add "And he said, 'You don't know what kind of spirit you belong to. 56The Son of Man did not come to destroy people's lives but to save them.'"

⁵⁹Jesus said to another man, "Follow me!"

But the man said, "Lord, let me go and bury my father first."

⁶⁰But Jesus said to him, "Let the people who are dead bury their own dead. You must go and tell about God's kingdom.*"

⁶¹Another man said, "I will follow you, Lord, but first let me go and say goodbye to my family."

⁶²Jesus said, "Anyone who begins to plow a field but looks back is not prepared for God's kingdom."

Jesus Sends Out 72 of His Followers

10 ¹After this, the Lord chose 72ᵈ more followers. He sent them out in groups of two. He sent them ahead of him into every town and place where he planned to go. ²He said to them, "There is such a big harvest of people to bring in. But there are only a few workers to help harvest them. God owns the harvest. Ask him to send more workers to help bring in his harvest.

³"You can go now. But listen! I am sending you, and you will be like sheep among wolves. ⁴Don't carry any money, a bag, or sandals. Don't stop to talk with people on the road. ⁵Before you go into a house, say, 'Peace be with this home.' ⁶If the people living there love peace, your blessing of peace will stay with them. But if not, your blessing of peace will come back to you. ⁷Stay in the peace-loving house. Eat and drink what the people there give you. A worker should be given his pay. Don't leave that house to stay in another house.

⁸"If you go into a town and the people welcome you, eat the food they give you. ⁹Heal the sick people who live there, and tell them, 'God's kingdom* is now very near youᵇ!'

¹⁰"But if you go into a town and the people don't welcome you, then go out into the streets of that town and say, ¹¹'Even the dirt from your town that sticks to our feet we wipe off against you. But remember that God's kingdom is coming soon.' ¹²I tell you, on the judgment day it will be worse for the people of that town than for the people of Sodom.*

Jesus Warns People Who Refuse to Believe
(Mt. 11:20–24)

¹³"It will be bad for you, Chorazin*! It will be bad for you, Bethsaida*! I did many miracles* in you. If those same miracles had happened in Tyre* and Sidon,* then the people in those cities would have changed their lives and stopped sinning a long time ago. They would have worn sackcloth* and sat in ashes to show that they were sorry for their sins. ¹⁴But on the judgment day it will be worse for you than for Tyre and Sidon. ¹⁵And you, Capernaum,* will you be lifted up to heaven? No, you will be thrown down to the place of death!

¹⁶"When anyone listens to you my followers, they are really listening to me. But when anyone refuses to accept you, they are really refusing to accept me. And when anyone refuses to accept me, they are refusing to accept the one who sent me."

ᵈ **10:1 72** Some Greek copies say 70. Also in verse 17.

ᵇ **10:9 is now very near you** Or "is coming to you soon" or "has come to you."

Satan Falls

¹⁷When the 72 followers came back from their trip, they were very happy. They said, "Lord, even the demons* obeyed us when we used your name!" ¹⁸Jesus said to them, "I saw Satan* falling like lightning from the sky. ¹⁹He is the enemy, but know that I have given you more power than he has. I have given you power to crush his snakes and scorpions under your feet. Nothing will hurt you. ²⁰Yes, even the spirits obey you. And you can be happy, not because you have this power, but because your names are written in heaven."

Jesus Prays to the Father
(Mt. 11:25–27; 13:16–17)

²¹Then the Holy Spirit* made Jesus feel very happy. Jesus said, "I praise you, Father, Lord of heaven and earth. I am thankful that you have hidden these things from those who are so wise and so smart. But you have shown them to people who are like little children. Yes, Father, you did this because it's what you really wanted to do. ²²"My Father has given me all things. No one knows who the Son is—only the Father knows. And only the Son knows who the Father is. The only people who will know about the Father are those the Son chooses to tell."

²³Then Jesus turned to his followers. They were there alone with him. He said, "It is a great blessing for you to see what you now see! ²⁴I tell you, many prophets* and kings wanted to see what you now see, but they could not. And they wanted to hear what you now hear, but they could not."

A Story About the Good Samaritan

²⁵Then an expert in the law stood up to test Jesus. He said, "Teacher, what must I do to get eternal life?" ²⁶Jesus said to him, "What is written in the law? What do you understand from it?" ²⁷The man answered, "'Love the Lord your God with all your heart, all your soul, all your strength, and all your mind.'^a Also, 'Love your neighbor the same as you love yourself.'^b" ²⁸Jesus said, "Your answer is right. Do this and you will have eternal life."

²⁹But the man wanted to show that the way he was living was right. So he said to Jesus, "But who is my neighbor?" ³⁰To answer this question, Jesus said, "A man was going down the road from Jerusalem to Jericho. Some robbers surrounded him, tore off his clothes, and beat him. Then they left him lying there on the ground almost dead. ³¹"It happened that a Jewish priest was going down that road. When he saw the man, he did not stop to help him. He walked away. ³²Next, a Levite* came near. He saw the hurt man, but he went around him. He would not stop to help him either. He just walked away. ³³"Then a Samaritan* man traveled down that road. He came to the place where the hurt man was lying. He saw the man and felt very sorry for him. ³⁴The Samaritan went to him and poured olive oil and wine^c on his wounds. Then he covered the man's

^a 10:27 Quote from Deut. 6:5.
^b 10:27 Quote from Lev. 19:18.
^c 10:34 olive oil and wine These were used like medicine to soften and clean wounds.

wounds with cloth. The Samaritan had a donkey. He put the hurt man on his donkey, and he took him to an inn. There he cared for him. 35The next day, the Samaritan took out two silver coins* and gave them to the man who worked at the inn. He said, 'Take care of this hurt man. If you spend more money on him, I will pay it back to you when I come again.'"

36Then Jesus said, "Which one of these three men do you think was really a neighbor to the man who was hurt by the robbers?"

37The teacher of the law answered, "The one who helped him." Jesus said, "Then you go and do the same."

Mary and Martha

38While Jesus and his followers were traveling, he went into a town, and a woman named Martha let him stay at her house. 39She had a sister named Mary. Mary was sitting at Jesus' feet and listening to him teach. 40But her sister Martha was busy doing all the work that had to be done. Martha went in and said, "Lord, don't you care that my sister has left me to do all the work by myself? Tell her to help me!"

41But the Lord answered her, "Martha, Martha, you are getting worried and upset about too many things. 42Only one thing is important. Mary has made the right choice, and it will never be taken away from her."

Jesus Teaches About Prayer
(Mt. 6:9–15)

11 1One time Jesus was out praying, and when he finished, one of his followers said to him, "John* taught his followers how to pray. Lord, teach us how to pray too."

2Jesus said to the followers, "This is how you should pray:
'Father, we pray that your
  name will always be kept
  holy.
We pray that your kingdom*
  will come.
3 Give us the food we need for
  each day.
4 Forgive our sins,
  just as we forgive everyone
  who has done wrong to us.
And don't let us be tempted.'"

Ask God for What You Need
(Mt. 7:7–11)

5–6Then Jesus said to them, "Suppose one of you went to your friend's house very late at night and said to him, 'A friend of mine has come into town to visit me. But I have nothing for him to eat. Please give me three loaves of bread.' 7Your friend inside the house answers, 'Go away! Don't bother me! The door is already locked. My children and I are in bed. I cannot get up and give you the bread now.' 8I tell you, maybe friendship is not enough to make him get up to give you the bread. But he will surely get up to give you what you need if you continue to ask. 9So I tell you, continue to ask, and God will give to you. Continue to search, and you will find. Continue to knock, and the door will open for you. 10Yes, whoever continues to ask will receive. Whoever continues to look will find. And whoever continues to knock will have the door opened for them. 11Do any of you have a son? What would you do if your son asked you for a fish? Would any father give him a snake? 12Or, if he asked for an egg, would you give him a scorpion? Of course not! 13Even you who are bad know how to give good things to your children. So surely your heavenly Father knows how to give the Holy Spirit* to the people who ask him."

Jesus' Power Is From God
(Mt. 12:22–30; Mk. 3:20–27)

14One time Jesus was sending a demon* out of a man who could not talk. When the demon came out, the man was able to speak. The crowds were amazed. 15But some of the people said, "He uses the power of Satan*a* to force demons out of people. Satan is the ruler of demons."

16Some others there wanted to test Jesus. They asked him to do a miracle as a sign from God. 17But he knew what they were thinking. So he said to them, "Every kingdom that fights against itself will be destroyed. And a family that fights against itself will break apart. 18So if Satan* is fighting against himself, how will his kingdom survive? You say that I use the power of Satan to force out demons. 19But if I use Satan's power to force out demons, then what power do your people use when they force out demons? So your own people will prove that you are wrong. 20But I use the power of God to force out demons. This shows that God's kingdom* has now come to you.

21"When a strong man with many weapons guards his own house, the things in his house are safe. 22But suppose a stronger man comes and defeats him. The stronger man will take away the weapons that the first man trusted to keep his house safe. Then the stronger man will do what he wants with the other man's things.

23"Whoever is not with me is against me. And anyone who does not work with me is working against me.

The Danger of Emptiness
(Mt. 12:43–45)

24"When an evil spirit comes out of someone, it travels through dry places, looking for a place to rest. But it finds no place to rest. So it says, 'I will go back to the home I left.' 25When it comes back, it finds that home all neat and clean. 26Then the evil spirit goes out and brings back seven other spirits more evil than itself. They all go and live there, and that person has even more trouble than before."

The People God Blesses

27As Jesus was saying these things, a woman with the people there called out to him, "Blessings from God belong to the woman who gave birth to you and fed you!"

28But Jesus said, "The people who hear the teaching of God and obey it—they are the ones who have God's blessing."

Some People Doubt Jesus' Authority
(Mt. 12:38–42; Mk. 8:12)

29The crowd grew larger and larger. Jesus said, "The people who live today are evil. They ask for a miracle* as a sign from God. But no miracle will be done to prove anything to them. The only sign will be the miracle that happened to Jonah.*b* 30Jonah was a sign for those who lived in Nineveh.*c* It is

b **11:29 Jonah** A prophet in the Old Testament. After three days in a big fish he came out alive, just as Jesus would come out from the tomb on the third day.
c **11:30 Nineveh** City where Jonah preached. See Jonah 3.

a **11:15 Satan** Literally, "Beelzebul" (the devil). Also in verses 18, 19.

the same with the Son of Man.* He will be a sign for the people of this time.

³¹"On the judgment day, you people who live now will be compared with the queen of the South,ᵃ and she will be a witness who shows how guilty you are. Why do I say this? Because she traveled from far, far away to listen to Solomon's wise teaching. And I tell you that someoneᵇ greater than Solomon is right here, but you won't listen!

³²"On the judgment day, you people who live now will also be compared with the people from Nineveh, and they will be witnesses who show how guilty you are. I say this because when Jonah preached to those people, they changed their hearts and lives. And you are listening to someone greater than Jonah, but you refuse to change!

Be a Light for the World
(Mt. 5:15; 6:22–23)

³³"No one takes a light and puts it under a bowl or hides it. Instead, they put it on a lampstand so that the people who come in can see. ³⁴The only source of light for the body is the eye. When you look at people and want to help them, you are full of light. But when you look at people in a selfish way, you are full of darkness.ᶜ ³⁵So be careful! Don't let the light in you become darkness. ³⁶If you are full of

light, and there is no part of you that is dark, then you will be all bright, as though you have the light of a lamp shining on you."

Jesus Criticizes the Religious Leaders
(Mt. 23:1–36; Mk. 12:38–40; Lk. 20:45–47)

³⁷After Jesus had finished speaking, a Pharisee* asked Jesus to eat with him. So he went and took a place at the table. ³⁸But the Pharisee was surprised when he saw that Jesus did not wash his handsᵈ first before the meal. ³⁹The Lord said to him, "The washing you Pharisees do is like cleaning only the outside of a cup or a dish. But what is inside you? You want only to cheat and hurt people. ⁴⁰You are foolish! The same one who made what is outside also made what is inside. ⁴¹So pay attention to what is inside. Give to the people who need help. Then you will be fully clean.

⁴²"But it will be bad for you Pharisees! You give God a tenth of the food you get, even your mint, your rue, and every other little plant in your garden.ᵉ But you forget to be fair to others and to love God. These are the things you should do. And you should also continue to do those other things.

⁴³"It will be bad for you Pharisees because you love to have the most important seats in the

---

ᵃ **11:31 queen of the South** Or "queen of Sheba." She traveled about 1000 miles (1600 km) to learn God's wisdom from Solomon. See 1 Kings 10:1–13.
ᵇ **11:31 someone** Literally, "something." Also in verse 32.
ᶜ **11:34** Literally, "The lamp of the body is your eye. When your eye is pure, your whole body is full of light. But if it is evil, your body is dark."
ᵈ **11:38 wash his hands** Washing the hands was a Jewish religious custom that the Pharisees thought was very important.
ᵉ **11:42 You give ... garden** Literally, "You tithe mint, rue, and every herb." The Law of Moses required Israelites to share their food supply by dedicating a tenth of their field crops and livestock to God (see Lev. 27:30–32; Deut. 26:12). This did not include such small garden plants as those mentioned here. So these Pharisees were giving more than required to be sure they were not breaking the Law.

synagogues.* And you love for people to show respect to you in the marketplaces. 44It will be bad for you, because you are like hidden graves. People walk on them without knowing it."

45One of the experts in the law said to Jesus, "Teacher, when you say these things about the Pharisees, you are criticizing our group too."

46Jesus answered, "It will be bad for you, you experts in the law! You make strict rules that are very hard for people to obey.d You try to force others to obey your rules. But you yourselves don't even try to follow any of those rules. 47It will be bad for you, because you build tombs* for the prophets.* But these are the same prophets your ancestors* killed! 48And now you show all people that you agree with what your ancestors did. They killed the prophets, and you build tombs for the prophets! 49This is why God in his wisdom said, 'I will send prophets and apostlesb to them. Some of my prophets and apostles will be killed by evil men. Others will be treated badly.'

50"So you people who live now will be punished for the deaths of all the prophets who were killed since the beginning of the world. 51You will be punished for the killing of Abel.c And you will be punished for the killing of Zechariah,d

who was killed between the altar* and the Temple.* Yes, I tell you that you people will be punished for them all.

52"It will be bad for you, you experts in the law! You have taken away the key to learning about God. You yourselves would not learn, and you stopped others from learning too."

53When Jesus went out, the teachers of the law and the Pharisees began to give him much trouble. They tried to make him answer questions about many things. 54They were trying to find a way to catch Jesus saying something wrong.

Don't Be Like the Pharisees

12 1Many thousands of people came together. There were so many people that they were stepping on each other. Before Jesus spoke to the people, he said to his followers, "Be careful of the yeast* of the Pharisees.* I mean that they are hypocrites.* 2Everything that is hidden will be shown, and everything that is secret will be made known. 3What you say in the dark will be told in the light. And what you whisper in a private room will be shouted from the top of the house."

Fear Only God
(Mt. 10:28–31)

4Then Jesus said to the people, "I tell you, my friends, don't be afraid of people. They can kill the body, but after that they can do nothing more to hurt you. 5I will show you the one to fear. You should fear God, who has the power to kill you and also to throw you into hell. Yes, he is the one you should fear.

6"When birds are sold, five small birds cost only two pennies. But

---

a **11:46 You make ... obey** Literally, "You put heavy burdens on people that are hard for them to carry."

b **11:49 prophets and apostles** People chosen by God to tell his Good News to the world.

c **11:51 Abel** In the Hebrew Old Testament, the first person to be murdered.

d **11:51 Zechariah** In the Hebrew Old Testament, the last person to be murdered.

God does not forget any of them. [7]Yes, God even knows how many hairs you have on your head. Don't be afraid. You are worth much more than many birds.

Don't Be Ashamed of Your Faith
(Mt. 10:32–33; 12:32; 10:19–20)

[8]"I tell you, if you stand before others and are willing to say you believe in me, then I[a] will say that you belong to me. I will say this in the presence of God's angels. [9]But if you stand before others and say you do not believe in me, then I will say that you do not belong to me. I will say this in the presence of God's angels.

[10]"Whoever says something against the Son of Man* can be forgiven. But whoever speaks against the Holy Spirit* will not be forgiven.

[11]"When men bring you into the synagogues* before the leaders and other important men, don't worry about what you will say. [12]The Holy Spirit will teach you at that time what you should say."

Jesus Warns Against Selfishness

[13]One of the men in the crowd said to Jesus, "Teacher, our father just died and left some things for us. Tell my brother to share them with me."

[14]But Jesus said to him, "Who said I should be your judge or decide how to divide your father's things between you two?" [15]Then Jesus said to them, "Be careful and guard against all kinds of greed. People do not get life from the many things they own."

[16]Then Jesus used this story: "There was a rich man who had some land. His land grew a very good crop of food. [17]He thought to himself, 'What will I do? I have no place to keep all my crops.'

[18]"Then he said, 'I know what I will do. I will tear down my barns and build bigger barns! I will put all my wheat and good things together in my new barns. [19]Then I can say to myself, I have many good things stored. I have saved enough for many years. Rest, eat, drink, and enjoy life!'

[20]"But God said to that man, 'Foolish man! Tonight you will die. So what about the things you prepared for yourself? Who will get those things now?'

[21]"This is how it will be for anyone who saves things only for himself. To God that person is not rich."

Put God's Kingdom First
(Mt. 6:25–34; 19–21)

[22]Jesus said to his followers, "So I tell you, don't worry about the things you need to live—what you will eat or what you will wear. [23]Life is more important than food, and the body is more important than what you put on it. [24]Look at the birds. They don't plant, harvest, or save food in houses or barns, but God feeds them. And you are worth much more than crows. [25]None of you can add any time to your life by worrying about it. [26]And if you can't do the little things, why worry about the big things?

[27]"Think about how the wildflowers grow. They don't work or make clothes for themselves. But I tell you that even Solomon, the great and rich king, was not dressed as beautifully as one of these flowers. [28]If God makes what grows in the field so beautiful, what do you think he will do for you? That's just grass—one day

---

[a] 12:8 | Literally, "the Son of Man" (Jesus).

it's alive, and the next day someone throws it into a fire. But God cares enough to make it beautiful. Surely he will do much more for you. Your faith is so small! 29"So don't always think about what you will eat or what you will drink. Don't worry about it. 30That's what all those people who don't know God are always thinking about. But your Father knows that you need these things. 31What you should be thinking about is God's kingdom.* Then he will give you all these other things you need.

Don't Trust in Money

32"Don't fear, little flock. Your Father wants to share his kingdom with you. 33Sell the things you have and give that money to those who need it. This is the only way you can keep your riches from being lost. You will be storing treasure in heaven that lasts forever. Thieves can't steal that treasure, and moths can't destroy it. 34Your heart will be where your treasure is.

Always Be Ready

(Mt. 24:42-44)

35"Be ready! Be fully dressed and have your lights shining. 36Be like servants who are waiting for their master to come home from a wedding party. The master comes and knocks, and the servants immediately open the door for him. 37When their master sees that they are ready and waiting for him, it will be a great day for those servants. I can tell you without a doubt, the master will get himself ready to serve a meal and tell the servants to sit down. Then he will serve them. 38Those servants might have to wait until midnight or later for their master. But they will be glad they did when he comes in and finds them still waiting. 39"What would a homeowner do if he knew when a thief was coming? You know he would not let the thief break in. 40So you also must be ready, because the Son of Man* will come at a time when you don't expect him!"

Who Is the Trusted Servant?

(Mt. 24:45-51)

41Peter said, "Lord, did you tell this story for us or for all people?"

42The Lord said, "Who is the wise and trusted servant? The master trusts one servant to give the other servants their food at the right time. Who is the servant that the master trusts to do that work? 43When the master comes and finds him doing the work he gave him, it will be a day of blessing for that servant! 44I can tell you without a doubt, the master will choose that servant to take care of everything he owns.

45"But what will happen if that servant is evil and thinks his master will not come back soon? He will begin to beat the other servants, men and women. He will eat and drink until he has had too much. 46Then the master will come when the servant is not ready, at a time when the servant is not expecting him. Then the master will punish that servant and send him away to be with the other people who don't obey.

47"That servant knew what his master wanted him to do. But he did not make himself ready or try to do what his master wanted. So that servant will be punished very much! 48But what about the servant who does not know what his master wants? He also does things that deserve punishment. But he will get less punishment than the servant who knew what he should do. Whoever has been given much will be responsible for much. Much more will be expected from the one who has been given more."

Following Jesus May Bring You Trouble
(Mt. 10:34–36)

49Jesus continued speaking: "I came to bring fire to the world. I wish it were already burning! 50There is a kind of baptism*a* that I must suffer through. I feel very troubled until it is finished. 51Do you think I came to give peace to the world? No, I came to divide the world! 52From now on, a family of five will be divided, three against two, and two against three.

53 A father and son will be
divided:
The son will turn against his
father.
The father will turn against
his son.
A mother and her daughter
will be divided:
The daughter will turn
against her mother.
The mother will turn against
her daughter.
A mother-in-law and her
daughter-in-law will be
divided:
The daughter-in-law
will turn against her
mother-in-law.
The mother-in-law
will turn against her
daughter-in-law."

a 12:50 baptism This word, which usually means to be immersed in water, has a special meaning here—being covered or "buried" in troubles.

Understanding the Times
(Mt. 16:2–3)

54Then Jesus said to the people, "When you see clouds growing bigger in the west, you say, 'A rainstorm is coming.' And soon it begins to rain. 55When you feel the wind begin to blow from the south, you say, 'It will be a hot day.' And you are right. 56You hypocrites*! You can understand the weather. Why don't you understand what is happening now?

Settle Your Problems
(Mt. 5:25–26)

57"Why can't you decide for yourselves what is right? 58Suppose someone is suing you, and you are both going to court. Try hard to settle it on the way. If you don't settle it, you may have to go before the judge. And the judge will hand you over to the officer, who will throw you into jail. 59I tell you, you will not get out of there until you have paid every cent you owe."

Change Your Hearts

13 1Some people there with Jesus at that time told him about what had happened to some worshipers from Galilee. Pilate* had them killed. Their blood was mixed with the blood of the animals they had brought for sacrificing.* 2Jesus answered, "Do you think this happened to those people because they were more sinful than all other people from Galilee? 3No, they were not. But if you don't decide now to change your lives, you will all be destroyed like those people! 4And what about those 18 people who died when the tower of Siloam fell on them? Do you think they were more sinful than everyone else in Jerusalem? 5They were not. But I tell you if you don't decide now to change your lives, you will all be destroyed too!"

The Useless Tree

6Jesus told this story: "A man had a fig tree. He planted it in his garden. He came looking for some fruit on it, but he found none. 7He had a servant who took care of his garden. So he said to his servant, 'I have been looking for fruit on this tree for three years, but I never find any. Cut it down! Why should it waste the ground?' 8But the servant answered, 'Master, let the tree have one more year to produce fruit. Let me dig up the dirt around it and fertilize it. 9Maybe the tree will have fruit on it next year. If it still does not produce, then you can cut it down.'"

Jesus Heals a Woman on the Sabbath

10Jesus taught in one of the synagogues* on the Sabbath* day. 11A woman was there who had an evil spirit inside her. It had made the woman crippled for 18 years. Her back was always bent; she could not stand up straight. 12When Jesus saw her, he called to her, "Woman, you have been made free from your sickness!" 13He laid his hands on* her, and immediately she was able to stand up straight. She began praising God.

14The synagogue leader was angry because Jesus healed on the Sabbath day. He said to the people, "There are six days for work. So come to be healed on one of those days. Don't come for healing on the Sabbath day."

15The Lord answered, "You people are hypocrites*! All of you untie your work animals and lead them to drink water every day—even on the Sabbath day. 16This woman that I healed is a true descendant of Abraham.ᵃ But Satan* has held her for 18 years. Surely it is not wrong for her to be made free from her sickness on a Sabbath day!" 17When Jesus said this, all those who were criticizing him felt ashamed of themselves. And all the people were happy for the wonderful things he was doing.

What Is God's Kingdom Like?

(Mt. 13:31–33; Mk. 4:30–32)

18Then Jesus said, "What is God's kingdom* like? What can I compare it to? 19God's kingdom is like the seed of the mustard* plant. Someone plants this seed in their garden. The seed grows and becomes a tree, and the birds build nests on its branches."

20Jesus said again, "What can I compare God's kingdom with? 21It is like yeast that a woman mixes into a big bowl of flour to make bread. The yeast makes all the dough rise."

The Narrow Door

(Mt. 7:13–14, 21–23)

22Jesus was teaching in every town and village. He continued to travel toward Jerusalem. 23Someone said to him, "Lord, how many people will be saved? Only a few?"

Jesus said, 24"The door to heaven is narrow. Try hard to enter it. Many people will want to enter there, but they will not be able to go in. 25If a man locks the door of his house, you can stand outside and knock on the door, but he won't open it. You can say, 'Sir, open the door for us.' But he will answer, 'I don't know you. Where did you come from?' 26Then you will say, 'We ate and drank with you. You taught in the streets of

---

a **13:16 true descendant of Abraham** Literally, "daughter of Abraham."

our town.' 27Then he will say to you, 'I don't know you. Where did you come from? Get away from me! You are all people who do wrong!'

28"You will see Abraham,* Isaac,* Jacob,* and all the prophets* in God's kingdom.* But you will be left outside. There you will cry and grind your teeth with pain. 29People will come from the east, west, north, and south. They will sit down at the table in God's kingdom. 30People who have the lowest place in life now will have the highest place in God's kingdom. And people who have the highest place now will have the lowest place in God's kingdom."

Jesus Will Die in Jerusalem
(Mt. 23:37–39)

31Just then some Pharisees* came to Jesus and said, "Go away from here and hide. Herod* wants to kill you!"

32Jesus said to them, "Go tell that fox,*a* 'Today and tomorrow I am forcing demons* out of people and finishing my work of healing. Then, the next day, the work will be finished.' 33After that I must go, because all prophets* should die in Jerusalem.

34"Jerusalem, Jerusalem! You kill the prophets. You stone to death the people God has sent to you. How many times I wanted to help your people. I wanted to gather them together as a hen gathers her chicks under her wings. But you did not let me. 35Now your home will be left completely empty. I tell you, you will not see me again until that time when you will say, 'Welcome! God bless the one who comes in the name of the Lord.'*b*"

Is It Right to Heal on the Sabbath Day?

14 1On a Sabbath* day, Jesus went to the home of a leading Pharisee* to eat with him. The people there were all watching him very closely. 2A man with a bad disease*c* was there in front of him. 3Jesus said to the Pharisees and experts in the law, "Is it right or wrong to heal on the Sabbath day?" 4But they would not answer his question. So he took the man and healed him. Then he sent the man away. 5Jesus said to the Pharisees and teachers of the law, "If your son or work animal falls into a well on the Sabbath day, you know you would pull him out immediately." 6The Pharisees and teachers of the law could say nothing against what he said.

Don't Make Yourself Important

7Then Jesus noticed that some of the guests were choosing the best places to sit. So he told this story: 8"When someone invites you to a wedding, don't sit in the most important seat. They may have invited someone more important than you. 9And if you are sitting in the most important seat, they will come to you and say, 'Give this man your seat!' Then you will have to move down to the last place and be embarrassed.

10"So when someone invites you, go sit in the seat that is not important. Then they will come to you and say, 'Friend, move up here to this better place!' What an honor this will be for you in front of all the other guests. 11Everyone

b **13:35** Quote from Ps. 118:26.
c **14:2 disease** The man had dropsy, a sickness that causes the body to swell larger and larger.

a **13:32 fox** Jesus means that Herod is clever and sly like a fox.

who makes themselves important will be made humble. But everyone who makes themselves humble will be made important."

You Will Be Rewarded

¹²Then Jesus said to the Pharisee* who had invited him, "When you give a lunch or a dinner, don't invite only your friends, brothers, relatives, and rich neighbors. At another time they will pay you back by inviting you to eat with them. ¹³Instead, when you give a feast, invite the poor, the crippled, and the blind. ¹⁴Then you will have great blessings, because these people cannot pay you back. They have nothing. But God will reward you at the time when all godly people rise from death."

A Story About People Invited to a Dinner
(Mt. 22:1–10)

¹⁵One of the men sitting at the table with Jesus heard these things. The man said to him, "It will be a great blessing for anyone to eat a meal in God's kingdom*!"

¹⁶Jesus said to him, "A man gave a big dinner. He invited many people. ¹⁷When it was time to eat, he sent his servant to tell the guests, 'Come. The food is ready.' ¹⁸But all the guests said they could not come. Each one made an excuse. The first one said, 'I have just bought a field, so I must go look at it. Please excuse me.' ¹⁹Another man said, 'I have just bought five pairs of work animals; I must go and try them out. Please excuse me.' ²⁰A third man said, 'I just got married; I can't come.'

²¹"So the servant returned and told his master what happened. The master was angry. He said, 'Hurry! Go into the streets and alleys of the town. Bring me the poor, the crippled, the blind, and the lame.'

²²"Later, the servant said to him, 'Master, I did what you told me to do, but we still have places for more people.' ²³The master said to the servant, 'Go out to the highways and country roads. Tell the people there to come. I want my house to be full! ²⁴None of those people I invited first will get to eat any of this food.'"

Decide if You Can Follow Me
(Mt. 10:37–38)

²⁵Many people were traveling with Jesus. He said to them, ²⁶"If you come to me but will not leave your family, you cannot be my follower. You must love me more than your father, mother, wife, children, brothers, and sisters— even more than your own life! ²⁷Whoever will not carry the cross* that is given to them when they follow me cannot be my follower.

²⁸"If you wanted to build a building, you would first sit down and decide how much it would cost. You must see if you have enough money to finish the job. ²⁹If you don't do that, you might begin the work, but you would not be able to finish. And if you could not finish it, everyone would laugh at you. ³⁰They would say, 'This man began to build, but he was not able to finish.'

³¹"If a king is going to fight against another king, first he will sit down and plan. If he has only 10,000 men, he will try to decide if he is able to defeat the other king who has 20,000 men. ³²If he thinks he cannot defeat the other king, he will send some men to ask for peace while that king's army is still far away.

33"It is the same for each of you. You must leave everything you have to follow me. If not, you cannot be my follower.

Don't Lose Your Influence
(Mt. 5:13; Mk. 9:50)

34"Salt is a good thing. But if the salt loses its salty taste, you can't make it salty again. 35It is worth nothing. You can't even use it as dirt or dung. People just throw it away.

"You people who hear me, listen!"

Joy in Heaven
(Mt. 18:12–14)

15 1Many tax collectors* and sinners came to listen to Jesus. 2Then the Pharisees* and the teachers of the law began to complain, "Look, this man*a* welcomes sinners and even eats with them!"

3Then Jesus told them this story: 4"Suppose one of you has 100 sheep, but one of them gets lost. What will you do? You will leave the other 99 sheep there in the field and go out and look for the lost sheep. You will continue to search for it until you find it. 5And when you find it, you will be very happy. You will carry it 6home, go to your friends and neighbors and say to them, 'Be happy with me because I found my lost sheep!' 7In the same way, I tell you, heaven is a happy place when one sinner decides to change. There is more joy for that one sinner than for 99 good people who don't need to change.

8"Suppose a woman has ten silver coins,*b* but she loses one of them. She will take a light and clean the house. She will look carefully for the coin until she finds it. 9And when she finds it, she will call her friends and neighbors and say to them, 'Be happy with me because I have found the coin that I lost!' 10In the same way, it's a happy time for the angels of God when one sinner decides to change."

Story About Two Sons

11Then Jesus said, "There was a man who had two sons. 12The younger son said to his father, 'Give me now the part of your property that I am supposed to receive someday.' So the father divided his wealth between his two sons.

13"A few days later the younger son gathered up all that he had and left. He traveled far away to another country, and there he wasted his money living like a fool. 14After he spent everything he had, there was a terrible famine throughout the country. He was hungry and needed money. 15So he went and got a job with one of the people who lived there. The man sent him into the fields to feed pigs. 16He was so hungry that he wanted to eat the food the pigs were eating. But no one gave him anything.

17"The son realized that he had been very foolish. He thought, 'All my father's hired workers have plenty of food. But here I am, almost dead because I have nothing to eat. 18I will leave and go to my father. I will say to him: Father, I have sinned against God and have done wrong to you. 19I am no longer worthy to be called your son. But let me be like one of your hired workers.' 20So he left and went to his father.

a **15:2 this man** That is, Jesus. His enemies avoided saying his name.
b **15:8 silver coins** Each coin, a Greek drachma, was worth the average pay for one day's work.

The Younger Son Returns

"While the son was still a long way off, his father saw him coming and felt sorry for him. So he ran to him and hugged and kissed him. 21The son said, 'Father, I have sinned against God and have done wrong to you. I am no longer worthy to be called your son.'

22"But the father said to his servants, 'Hurry! Bring the best clothes and put them on him. Also, put a ring on his finger and good sandals on his feet. 23And bring our best calf and kill it so that we can celebrate with plenty to eat. 24My son was dead, but now he is alive again! He was lost, but now he is found!' So they began to have a party.

The Older Son Complains

25"The older son had been out in the field. When he came near the house, he heard the sound of music and dancing. 26So he called to one of the servant boys and asked, 'What does all this mean?' 27The boy said, 'Your brother has come back, and your father killed the best calf to eat. He is happy because he has his son back safe and sound.'

28"The older son was angry and would not go in to the party. So his father went out and begged him to come in. 29But he said to his father, 'Look, for all these years I have worked like a slave for you. I have always done what you told me to do, and you never gave me even a young goat for a party with my friends. 30But then this son of yours comes home after wasting your money on prostitutes, and you kill the best calf for him!'

31"His father said to him, 'Oh, my son, you are always with me, and everything I have is yours.

32But this was a day to be happy and celebrate. Your brother was dead, but now he is alive. He was lost, but now he is found.'"

True Wealth

16 1Jesus said to his followers, "Once there was a rich man. He hired a manager to take care of his business. Later, he learned that his manager was cheating him. 2So he called the manager in and said to him, 'I have heard bad things about you. Give me a report of what you have done with my money. You can't be my manager anymore.'

3"So, the manager thought to himself, 'What will I do? My master is taking my job away from me. I am not strong enough to dig ditches. I am too proud to beg. 4I know what I will do! I will do something to make friends, so that when I lose my job, they will welcome me into their homes.'

5"So the manager called in each person who owed the master some money. He asked the first one, 'How much do you owe my master?' 6He answered, 'I owe him 100 jars*a* of olive oil.' The manager said to him, 'Here is your bill. Hurry! Sit down and make the bill less. Write 50 jars.'

7"Then the manager asked another one, 'How much do you owe my master?' He answered, 'I owe him 100 measures*b* of wheat.' Then the manager said to him, 'Here is your bill; you can make it less. Write 80 measures.'

8"Later, the master told the dishonest manager that he had done a smart thing. Yes, worldly people

a 16:6 jars Greek *batous*, from the Hebrew *bath*, about 20 quarts or 22 liters.
b 16:7 measures Greek *korous*, from the Hebrew *cor*, about 200 quarts or 220 liters.

are smarter in their business with each other than spiritual people are.

⁹"I tell you, use the worldly things you have now to make 'friends' for later. Then, when those things are gone, you will be welcomed into a home that lasts forever. ¹⁰Whoever can be trusted with small things can also be trusted with big things. Whoever is dishonest in little things will be dishonest in big things too. ¹¹If you cannot be trusted with worldly riches, you will not be trusted with the true riches. ¹²And if you cannot be trusted with the things that belong to someone else, you will not be given anything of your own.

¹³"You cannot serve two masters at the same time. You will hate one master and love the other. Or you will be loyal to one and not care about the other. You cannot serve God and Money*ᵃ* at the same time."

God's Law Cannot Be Changed
(Mt. 11:12–13)

¹⁴The Pharisees* were listening to all these things. They criticized Jesus because they all loved money. ¹⁵Jesus said to them, "You make yourselves look good in front of people. But God knows what is really in your hearts. What people think is important is worth nothing to God.

¹⁶"Before John the Baptizer* came, people were taught the Law of Moses* and the writings of the prophets.* But since the time of John, the Good News* about God's kingdom* is being told. And everyone is trying hard to get into

it. ¹⁷But even the smallest part of a letter in the law cannot be changed. It would be easier for heaven and earth to pass away.

Divorce and Remarriage

¹⁸"Any man who divorces his wife and marries another woman is guilty of adultery.* And the man who marries a divorced woman is also guilty of adultery."

The Rich Man and Lazarus

¹⁹Jesus said, "There was a rich man who always dressed in the finest clothes. He was so rich that he was able to enjoy all the best things every day. ²⁰There was also a very poor man named Lazarus. Lazarus' body was covered with sores. He was often put by the rich man's gate. ²¹Lazarus wanted only to eat the scraps of food left on the floor under the rich man's table. And the dogs came and licked his sores.

²²"Later, Lazarus died. The angels took him and placed him in the arms of Abraham.* The rich man also died and was buried. ²³He was sent to the place of death*ᵇ* and was in great pain. He saw Abraham far away with Lazarus in his arms. ²⁴He called, 'Father Abraham, have mercy on me! Send Lazarus to me so that he can dip his finger in water and cool my tongue. I am suffering in this fire!'

²⁵"But Abraham said, 'My child, remember when you lived? You had all the good things in life. But Lazarus had nothing but problems. Now he is comforted here, and you are suffering. ²⁶Also, there is a big pit between you and us. No one can cross over to help you, and no one can come here from there.'

ᵃ **16:13 Money** Or "mamona," an Aramaic word meaning "wealth."

ᵇ **16:23 place of death** Literally, "Hades."

27"The rich man said, 'Then please, father Abraham, send Lazarus to my father's house on earth. 28I have five brothers. He could warn my brothers so that they will not come to this place of pain.'

29"But Abraham said, 'They have the Law of Moses* and the writings of the prophets* to read; let them learn from that.'

30"The rich man said, 'No, father Abraham! But if someone came to them from the dead, then they would decide to change their lives.'

31"But Abraham said to him, 'If your brothers won't listen to Moses and the prophets, they won't listen to someone who comes back from the dead.'"

Sin and Forgiveness

(Mt. 18:6–7, 21–22; Mk. 9:42)

17 1Jesus said to his followers, "Things will surely happen that will make people sin. But it will be very bad for anyone who makes this happen. 2It will be very bad for anyone who makes one of these little children sin. It would be better for them to have a millstone* tied around their neck and be drowned in the sea. 3So be careful!

"If your brother or sister in God's family does something wrong, warn them. If they are sorry for what they did, forgive them. 4Even if they do something wrong to you seven times in one day, but they say they are sorry each time, you should forgive them."

How Big Is Your Faith?

5The apostles* said to the Lord, "Give us more faith!"

6The Lord said, "If your faith is as big as a mustard* seed, you can say to this mulberry tree, 'Dig yourself up and plant yourself in the ocean!' And the tree will obey you.

Be Good Servants

7"Suppose one of you has a servant who has been working in the field, plowing or caring for the sheep. When he comes in from work, what would you say to him? Would you say, 'Come in, sit down and eat'? 8Of course not! You would say to your servant, 'Prepare something for me to eat. Then get ready and serve me. When I finish eating and drinking, then you can eat.' 9The servant should not get any special thanks for doing his job. He is only doing what his master told him to do. 10It is the same with you. When you finish doing all that you are told to do, you should say, 'We are not worthy of any special thanks. We have only done the work we should do.'"

Be Thankful

11Jesus was traveling to Jerusalem. He went from Galilee to Samaria. 12He came into a small town, and ten men met him there. They did not come close to him, because they all had leprosy.* 13But the men shouted, "Jesus! Master! Please help us!"

14When Jesus saw the men, he said, "Go and show yourselves to the priests."[a]

While the ten men were going to the priests, they were healed. 15When one of them saw that he was healed, he went back to Jesus. He praised God loudly. 16He bowed down at Jesus' feet and thanked him. (He was a Samaritan.*) 17Jesus said, "Ten men

---

a **17:14 show yourselves to the priests** The Law of Moses said a priest must decide when a person with leprosy was well.

were healed; where are the other nine? ¹⁸This man is not even one of our people. Is he the only one who came back to give praise to God?" ¹⁹Then Jesus said to the man, "Stand up! You can go. You were healed because you believed."

The Coming of God's Kingdom
(Mt. 24:23–28, 37–41)

²⁰Some of the Pharisees* asked Jesus, "When will God's kingdom* come?"

Jesus answered, "God's kingdom is coming, but not in a way that you can see it. ²¹People will not say, 'Look, God's kingdom is here!' or 'There it is!' No, God's kingdom is here with you.[a]"

²²Then Jesus said to his followers, "The time will come when you will want very much to see one of the days of the Son of Man,* but you will not be able to. ²³People will say to you, 'Look, there it is!' or 'Look, here it is!' Stay where you are; don't go away and search.

When Jesus Comes Again

²⁴"When the Son of Man* comes again, you will know it. On that day he will shine like lightning flashes across the sky. ²⁵But first, the Son of Man must suffer many things. The people of today will refuse to accept him.

²⁶"When the Son of Man comes again, it will be the same as it was when Noah lived. ²⁷People were eating, drinking, and getting married even on the day when Noah entered the boat. Then the flood came and killed them all.

²⁸"It will be the same as during the time of Lot, when God destroyed Sodom.* Those people were eating, drinking, buying, selling, planting, and building

houses for themselves. ²⁹They were doing these things even on the day when Lot left town. Then fire and sulfur rained down from the sky and killed them all. ³⁰This is exactly how it will be when the Son of Man comes again.

³¹"On that day if a man is on his roof, he will not have time to go inside and get his things. If a man is in the field, he cannot go back home. ³²Remember what happened to Lot's wife[b]!

³³"Whoever tries to keep the life they have will lose it. But whoever gives up their life will save it. ³⁴That night there may be two people sleeping in one room. One will be taken and the other will be left. ³⁵There may be two women working together. One will be taken and the other will be left." ³⁶[c]

³⁷The followers asked Jesus, "Where will this be, Lord?"

Jesus answered, "It's like looking for a dead body—you will find it where the vultures* are gathering above."

God Will Answer His People

18 ¹Then Jesus taught the followers that they should always pray and never lose hope. He used this story to teach them: ²"Once there was a judge in a town. He did not care about God. He also did not care what people thought about him. ³In that same town there was a woman whose husband had died. She came many times to this judge and said, 'There is a man who is doing bad

---

b 17:32 Lot's wife The story about Lot's wife is found in Gen. 19:15–17, 26.

c 17:36 A few Greek copies add verse 36: "Two men will be in the same field. One man will be taken, but the other man will be left behind."

a 17:21 here with you Or "inside you."

things to me. Give me my rights!' ⁴But the judge did not want to help the woman. After a long time, the judge thought to himself, 'I don't care about God. And I don't care about what people think. ⁵But this woman is bothering me. If I give her what she wants, then she will leave me alone. But if I don't give her what she wants, she will bother me until I am sick.'"

⁶The Lord said, "Listen, there is meaning in what the bad judge said. ⁷God's people shout to him night and day, and he will always give them what is right. He will not be slow to answer them. ⁸I tell you, God will help his people quickly. But when the Son of Man* comes again, will he find people on earth who believe in him?"

Being Right With God

⁹There were some people who thought they were very good and looked down on everyone else. Jesus used this story to teach them: ¹⁰"One time there was a Pharisee* and a tax collector.* One day they both went to the Temple* to pray. ¹¹The Pharisee stood alone, away from the tax collector. When the Pharisee prayed, he said, 'O God, I thank you that I am not as bad as other people. I am not like men who steal, cheat, or commit adultery.* I thank you that I am better than this tax collector. ¹²I fast* twice a week, and I give a tenth of everything I get!'

¹³"The tax collector stood alone too. But when he prayed, he would not even look up to heaven. He felt very humble before God. He said, 'O God, have mercy on me. I am a sinner!' ¹⁴I tell you, when this man finished his prayer and went home, he was right with God. But the Pharisee, who felt

that he was better than others, was not right with God. People who make themselves important will be made humble. But those who make themselves humble will be made important."

Jesus Welcomes Children
(Mt. 19:13–15; Mk. 10:13–16)

¹⁵Some people brought their small children to Jesus so that he could lay his hands on* them to bless them. But when the followers saw this, they told the people not to do this. ¹⁶But Jesus called the little children to him and said to his followers, "Let the little children come to me. Don't stop them, because God's kingdom* belongs to people who are like these little children. ¹⁷The truth is, you must accept God's kingdom like a little child accepts things, or you will never enter it."

A Rich Man Refuses to Follow Jesus
(Mt. 19:16–30; Mk. 10:17–31)

¹⁸A religious leader asked Jesus, "Good Teacher, what must I do to get eternal life?"

¹⁹Jesus said to him, "Why do you call me good? Only God is good. ²⁰And you know his commands: 'You must not commit adultery,* you must not murder anyone, you must not steal, you must not tell lies about others, you must respect your father and mother ....'ᵃ"

²¹But the leader said, "I have obeyed all these commands since I was a boy."

²²When Jesus heard this, he said to the leader, "But there is still one thing you need to do. Sell everything you have and give the money to those who are poor. You will have riches in heaven. Then

ᵃ 18:20 Quote from Ex. 20:12–16; Deut. 5:16–20.

come and follow me." 23But when the man heard Jesus tell him to give away his money, he was sad. He didn't want to do this, because he was very rich.

24When Jesus saw that the man was sad, he said, "It will be very hard for rich people to enter God's kingdom.* 25It is easier for a camel to go through the eye of a needle than for a rich person to enter God's kingdom."

Who Can Be Saved?

26When the people heard this, they said, "Then who can be saved?"

27Jesus answered, "God can do things that are not possible for people to do."

28Peter said, "Look, we left everything we had and followed you."

29Jesus said, "I can promise that everyone who has left their home, wife, brothers, parents, or children for God's kingdom* 30will get much more than they left. They will get many times more in this life. And in the world that is coming they will get the reward of eternal life."

Jesus Talks Again About His Death
(Mt. 20:17–19; Mk. 10:32–34)

31Then Jesus talked to the twelve apostles* alone. He said to them, "Listen, we are going to Jerusalem. Everything that God told the prophets* to write about the Son of Man* will happen. 32He will be handed over to the foreigners, who will laugh at him, insult him, and spit on him. 33They will beat him with whips and then kill him. But on the third day after his death, he will rise to life again." 34The apostles tried to understand this, but they could not; the meaning was hidden from them.

Jesus Heals a Blind Man
(Mt. 20:29–34; Mk. 10:46–52)

35Jesus came near the city of Jericho. There was a blind man sitting beside the road. He was begging people for money. 36When he heard the people coming down the road, he asked, "What is happening?"

37They told him, "Jesus, the one from Nazareth, is coming here."

38The blind man was excited and said, "Jesus, Son of David,* please help me!"

39The people who were in front leading the group criticized the blind man. They told him to be quiet. But he shouted more and more, "Son of David, please help me!"

40Jesus stopped there and said, "Bring that man to me!" When he came close, Jesus asked him, 41"What do you want me to do for you?"

He said, "Lord, I want to see again."

42Jesus said to him, "You can see now. You are healed because you believed."

43Then the man was able to see. He followed Jesus, thanking God. Everyone who saw this praised God for what happened.

Zacchaeus

19 1Jesus was going through the city of Jericho. 2In Jericho there was a man named Zacchaeus. He was a wealthy, very important tax collector.* 3He wanted to see who Jesus was. There were many others who wanted to see Jesus too. Zacchaeus was too short to see above the people. 4So he ran to a place where he knew Jesus would come. Then he climbed a sycamore tree so he could see him.

⁵When Jesus came to where Zacchaeus was, he looked up and saw him in the tree. Jesus said, "Zacchaeus, hurry! Come down! I must stay at your house today."

⁶Zacchaeus hurried and came down. He was happy to have Jesus in his house. ⁷Everyone saw this. They began to complain, "Look at the kind of man Jesus is staying with. Zacchaeus is a sinner!"

⁸Zacchaeus said to the Lord, "I want to do good. I will give half of my money to the poor. If I have cheated anyone, I will pay them back four times more."

⁹Jesus said, "Today is the day for this family to be saved from sin. Yes, even this tax collector is one of God's chosen people.ᵃ ¹⁰The Son of Man* came to find lost people and save them."

Use What God Gives You

(Mt. 25:14–30)

¹¹As the crowd listened to what he was saying, Jesus went on to tell a story. He was now near Jerusalem and knew that the people thought it was almost time for God's kingdom* to come. ¹²So he said, "A very important man was preparing to go to a country far away to be made a king. Then he planned to return home and rule his people. ¹³So he called ten of his servants together. He gave a bag of moneyᵇ to each servant. He said, 'Do business with this money until I come back.' ¹⁴But the people in the kingdom hated the man. They sent a group to follow him to the other country. There they said, 'We don't want this man to be our king.'

¹⁵"But the man was made king. When he came home, he said, 'Call those servants who have my money. I want to know how much more money they earned with it.' ¹⁶The first servant came and said, 'Sir, I earned ten bags of money with the one bag you gave me.' ¹⁷The king said to him, 'That's great! You are a good servant. I see that I can trust you with small things. So now I will let you rule over ten of my cities.'

¹⁸"The second servant said, 'Sir, with your one bag of money I earned five bags.' ¹⁹The king said to this servant, 'You can rule over five cities.'

²⁰"Then another servant came in and said to the king, 'Sir, here is your bag of money. I wrapped it in a piece of cloth and hid it. ²¹I was afraid of you because you are a hard man. You even take money that you didn't earn and gather food that you didn't grow.'

²²"Then the king said to him, 'What a bad servant you are! I will use your own words to condemn you. You said that I am a hard man. You said that I even take money that I didn't earn and gather food that I didn't grow. ²³If that is true, you should have put my money in the bank. Then, when I came back, my money would have earned some interest.' ²⁴Then the king said to the men who were watching, 'Take the bag of money away from this servant and give it to the servant who earned ten bags of money.'

²⁵"The men said to the king, 'But sir, that servant already has ten bags of money.'

ᵃ **19:9 one of God's chosen people** Literally, "a son of Abraham."

ᵇ **19:13 bag of money** One bag of money was a Greek mina, enough to pay a person for working three months. Also in verses 16, 18, 20, 24, 25.

26"The king said, 'People who use what they have will get more. But those who do not use what they have will have everything taken away from them. 27Now where are my enemies? Where are the people who did not want me to be king? Bring my enemies here and kill them. I will watch them die.'"

Jesus Enters Jerusalem Like a King
(Mt. 21:1–11; Mk. 11:1–11; Jn. 12:12–19)

28After Jesus said these things, he continued traveling toward Jerusalem. 29He came near Bethphage and Bethany, towns near the hill called the Mount of Olives.* He sent out two of his followers. 30He said, "Go into the town you can see there. When you enter the town, you will find a young donkey tied there that no one has ever ridden. Untie it, and bring it here to me. 31If anyone asks you why you are taking the donkey, you should say, 'The Master needs it.'"

32The two followers went into town. They found the donkey exactly like Jesus told them. 33They untied it, but its owners came out. They said to the followers, "Why are you untying our donkey?"

34The followers answered, "The Master needs it." 35So the followers brought the donkey to Jesus. They put their coats on its back. Then they put Jesus on the donkey. 36He rode along the road toward Jerusalem. The followers spread their coats on the road before him. 37Jesus was coming close to Jerusalem. He was already near the bottom of the Mount of Olives. The whole group of followers was happy. They were very excited and praised God. They thanked God for all the powerful things they had seen. 38They said,

"'Welcome! God bless the king who comes in the name of the Lord.'   *Psalm 118:26*

Peace in heaven and glory* to God!"

39Some of the Pharisees* said to Jesus, "Teacher, tell your followers not to say these things."

40But Jesus answered, "I tell you, if my followers didn't say them, these stones would shout them."

Jesus Cries for Jerusalem

41Jesus came near Jerusalem. Looking at the city, he began to cry for it 42and said, "I wish you knew today what would bring you peace. But it is hidden from you now. 43A time is coming when your enemies will build a wall around you and hold you in on all sides. 44They will destroy you and all your people. Not one stone of your buildings will stay on top of another. All this will happen because you did not know the time when God came to save you."

Jesus Goes to the Temple
(Mt. 21:12–17; Mk. 11:15–19; Jn. 2:13–22)

45Jesus went into the Temple* area. He began to throw out the people who were selling things there. 46He said, "The Scriptures* say, 'My Temple will be a house of prayer.'ᵃ But you have changed it into a 'hiding place for thieves.'ᵇ"

47Jesus taught the people in the Temple area every day. The leading priests, the teachers of the law, and some of the leaders of the people wanted to kill him. 48But they did not know how they could do it, because everyone was listening to him. The people were very interested in what Jesus said.

a **19:46** Quote from Isa. 56:7.
b **19:46** Quote from Jer. 7:11.

Jewish Leaders Doubt Jesus' Authority
(Mt. 21:23–27; Mk. 11:27–33)

20 ¹One day Jesus was in the Temple* area teaching the people. He was telling them the Good News.* The leading priests, teachers of the law, and older Jewish leaders came to talk to Jesus. ²They said, "Tell us what authority you have to do these things. Who gave you this authority?"

³Jesus answered, "I will ask you a question too. Tell me: ⁴When John* baptized* people, did his authority come from God or was it only from other people?"

⁵The priests, the teachers of the law, and the Jewish leaders all talked about this. They said to each other, "If we answer, 'John's baptism was from God,' then he will say, 'Then why did you not believe John?' ⁶But if we say that John's baptism was from someone else, the people will stone us to death. They all believe that John was a prophet.*" ⁷So they answered, "We don't know the answer."

⁸So Jesus said to them, "Then I will not tell you who gave me the authority to do these things."

God Sends His Son
(Mt 21:33–46; Mk. 12:1–12)

⁹Then Jesus told the people this story: "A man planted a vineyard.* He leased the land to some farmers. Then he went away for a long time. ¹⁰Later, it was time for the grapes to be picked. So the man sent a servant to those farmers so that they would give him his share of the grapes. But they beat the servant and sent him away with nothing. ¹¹So the man sent another servant. They beat this servant too and showed no respect for him. They sent the servant away with nothing. ¹²So the man sent a third servant to the farmers. They hurt this servant badly and threw him out.

¹³"The owner of the vineyard said, 'What will I do now? I will send my son. I love my son very much. Maybe the farmers will respect my son.' ¹⁴When the farmers saw the son, they said to each other, 'This is the owner's son. This vineyard will be his. If we kill him, it will be ours.' ¹⁵So the farmers threw the son out of the vineyard and killed him.

"What will the owner of the vineyard do? ¹⁶He will come and kill those farmers. Then he will lease the land to some other farmers."

When the people heard this story, they said, "This should never happen!" ¹⁷But Jesus looked into their eyes and said, "Then what does this verse mean:

'The stone that the builders
   refused to accept became
   the cornerstone*'?   *Psalm 118:22*
¹⁸Everyone who falls on that stone will be broken. If that stone falls on you, it will crush you!"

¹⁹When the teachers of the law and the leading priests heard this story, they knew it was about them. So they wanted to arrest Jesus right then, but they were afraid of what the people would do.

The Jewish Leaders Try to Trick Jesus
(Mt. 22:15–22; Mk. 12:13–17)

²⁰So the Jewish leaders waited for the right time to get Jesus. They sent some men to him, who pretended to be sincere. They wanted to find something wrong with what Jesus said. (If they found something wrong, then they

could hand him over to the governor, who had the authority to arrest him.) ²¹So the men said to Jesus, "Teacher, we know that what you say and teach is true. It doesn't matter who is listening—you teach the same to all people. You always teach the truth about God's way. ²²Tell us, is it right for us to pay taxes to Caesar* or not?"

²³But Jesus knew that these men were trying to trick him. He said to them, ²⁴"Show me a silver coin.* Whose name and picture are on it?"

They said, "Caesar's."

²⁵He said to them, "Then give to Caesar what belongs to Caesar, and give to God what belongs to God."

²⁶The men were amazed at his wise answer. They could say nothing. They were not able to trick Jesus there in front of the people. He said nothing they could use against him.

Some Sadducees Try to Trick Jesus
(Mt. 22:23–33; Mk. 12:18–27)

²⁷Some Sadducees* came to Jesus. (Sadducees believe that people will not rise from death.) They asked him, ²⁸"Teacher, Moses* wrote that if a married man dies and had no children, his brother must marry his widow. Then they will have children for the dead brother.^a ²⁹One time there were seven brothers. The first brother married a woman but died. He had no children. ³⁰Then the second brother married the woman, and he died. ³¹And the third brother married the woman, and he died. The same thing happened with all the other brothers. They all died and had no children. ³²The

woman was the last to die. ³³But all seven brothers married her. So when people rise from death, whose wife will this woman be?"

³⁴Jesus said to the Sadducees, "On earth, people marry each other. ³⁵Some people will be worthy to be raised from death and live again after this life. In that life they will not marry. ³⁶In that life people are like angels and cannot die. They are children of God, because they have been raised from death. ³⁷Moses clearly showed that people are raised from death. When Moses wrote about the burning bush,^b he said that the Lord is 'the God of Abraham,* the God of Isaac,* and the God of Jacob.'*^c ³⁸So they were not still dead, because he is the God only of living people. Yes, to God they are all still living."

³⁹Some of the teachers of the law said, "Teacher, your answer was very good." ⁴⁰No one was brave enough to ask him another question.

Is the Messiah David's Son or David's Lord?
(Mt. 22:41–46; Mk. 12:35–37)

⁴¹Then Jesus said, "Why do people say that the Messiah* is the Son of David*? ⁴²In the book of Psalms, David* himself says,

'The Lord God said to my Lord:
   Sit by me at my right side,
⁴³ and I will put your enemies
     under your power.'^d *Psalm 110:1*
⁴⁴David calls the Messiah 'Lord.' So how can the Messiah also be David's son?"

---

^a **20:28 if ... dead brother** See Deut. 25:5, 6.

^b **20:37 burning bush** See Ex. 3:1–12.
^c **20:37 'the God of ... Jacob'** Words taken from Ex. 3:6.
^d **20:43 and I ... power** Literally, "until I make your enemies a footstool for your feet."

Warning Against the Teachers of the Law

(Mt. 23:1–36; Mk. 12:38–40; Lk. 11:37–54)

45While all the people were listening to Jesus, he said to his followers, 46"Be careful of the teachers of the law. They like to walk around wearing clothes that look important. And they love for people to show respect to them in the marketplaces. They love to have the most important seats in the synagogues* and the places of honor at banquets. 47But they cheat widows and take their homes. Then they try to make themselves look good by saying long prayers. God will punish them very much."

True Giving

(Mk. 12:41–44)

21 1Jesus looked up and saw some rich people putting their gifts to God into the Temple* collection box. 2Then he saw a poor widow put two small copper coins into the box. 3He said, "This poor widow gave only two small coins. But the truth is, she gave more than all those rich people. 4They have plenty, and they gave only what they did not need. This woman is very poor, but she gave all she had to live on."

Jesus Warns About the Future

(Mt. 24:1–14; Mk. 13:1–13)

5Some of the followers were talking about the Temple.* They said, "This is a beautiful Temple, built with the best stones. Look at the many good gifts that have been offered to God."

6But Jesus said, "The time will come when all that you see here will be destroyed. Every stone of these buildings will be thrown down to the ground. Not one stone will be left on another."

7Some followers asked Jesus, "Teacher, when will these things happen? What will show us that it is time for these things to happen?"

8Jesus said, "Be careful! Don't be fooled. Many people will come using my name. They will say, 'I am the Messiah*a*' and 'The right time has come!' But don't follow them. 9When you hear about wars and riots, don't be afraid. These things must happen first. Then the end will come later."

10Then Jesus said to them, "Nations will fight against other nations. Kingdoms will fight against other kingdoms. 11There will be great earthquakes, sicknesses, and other bad things in many places. In some places there will be no food for the people to eat. Terrible things will happen, and amazing things will come from heaven to warn people.

12"But before all these things happen, people will arrest you and do bad things to you. They will judge you in their synagogues* and put you in jail. You will be forced to stand before kings and governors. They will do all these things to you because you follow me. 13But this will give you an opportunity to tell about me. 14Decide now not to worry about what you will say. 15I will give you the wisdom to say things that none of your enemies can answer. 16Even your parents, brothers, relatives, and friends will turn against you. They will have some of you killed. 17Everyone will hate you because you follow me. 18But none of these

a **21:8 the Messiah** Literally "the one," meaning the chosen one sent by God. See Mt. 24:5 and "MESSIAH" in the Word List.

things can really harm you. [19]You will save yourselves by continuing strong in your faith through all these things.

The Destruction of Jerusalem

(Mt. 24:15–21; Mk. 13:14–19)

[20]"You will see armies all around Jerusalem. Then you will know that the time for its destruction has come. [21]The people in Judea at that time should run away to the mountains. The people in Jerusalem must leave quickly. If you are near the city, don't go in! [22]The prophets* wrote many things about the time when God will punish his people. The time I am talking about is when all these things must happen. [23]During that time it will be hard for women who are pregnant or have small babies, because very bad times will come to this land. God will be angry with these people. [24]Some of the people will be killed by soldiers. Others will be made prisoners and taken to all the different countries. The holy city of Jerusalem will be under the control of foreigners until their time is completed.

Don't Fear

(Mt. 24:29–31; Mk. 13:24–27)

[25]"Amazing things will happen to the sun, moon, and stars. And people all over the earth will be upset and confused by the noise of the sea and its crashing waves. [26]They will be afraid and worried about what will happen to the world. Everything in the sky will be changed. [27]Then people will see the Son of Man* coming in a cloud with power and great glory.* [28]When these things begin to happen, stand up tall and don't be afraid. Know that it is almost time for God to free you!"

My Words Will Live Forever

(Mt. 24:32–35; Mk. 13:28–31)

[29]Then Jesus told this story: "Look at all the trees. The fig tree is a good example. [30]When it turns green, you know that summer is very near. [31]In the same way, when you see all these things happening, you will know that God's kingdom* is very near.

[32]"I assure you that all these things will happen while some of the people of this time are still living. [33]The whole world, earth and sky, will be destroyed, but my words will last forever.

Be Ready All the Time

[34]"Be careful not to spend your time having parties and getting drunk or worrying about this life. If you do that, you won't be able to think straight, and the end might come when you are not ready. [35]It will come as a surprise to everyone on earth. [36]So be ready all the time. Pray that you will be able to get through all these things that will happen and stand safe before the Son of Man.*"

[37]During the day Jesus taught the people in the Temple* area. At night he went out of the city and stayed all night on the Mount of Olives.* [38]Every morning all the people got up early to go listen to Jesus at the Temple.

The Jewish Leaders Plan to Kill Jesus

(Mt. 26:1–5, 14–16; Mk. 14:1–2, 10–11; Jn. 11:45–53)

22 [1]It was almost time for the Jewish Festival of Unleavened Bread,* called the Passover.* [2]The leading priests and teachers of the law wanted to kill Jesus. But they were trying to find a quiet way to do it, because they were afraid of what the people would do.

Judas Agrees to Help Jesus' Enemies
(Mt. 26:14–16; Mk. 14:10–11)

3One of Jesus' twelve apostles* was named Judas Iscariot. Satan* entered him, 4and he went and talked with the leading priests and some of the soldiers who guarded the Temple.* He talked to them about a way to hand Jesus over to them. 5The priests were very happy about this. They promised to give Judas money for doing this. 6He agreed. Then he waited for the best time to hand him over to them. He wanted to do it when no one was around to see it.

The Passover Meal
(Mt. 26:17–25; Mk. 14:12–21; Jn. 13:21–30)

7The Day of Unleavened Bread[a] came. This was the day when the Jews always killed the lambs for the Passover.* 8Jesus said to Peter and John, "Go and prepare the Passover meal for us to eat."

9They said to him, "Where do you want us to prepare the meal?"

He said to them, 10"When you go into the city, you will see a man carrying a jar of water. Follow him. He will go into a house. 11Tell the owner of the house, 'The Teacher asks that you please show us the room where he and his followers can eat the Passover meal.' 12Then the owner will show you a large room upstairs that is ready for us. Prepare the meal there."

13So Peter and John left. Everything happened the way Jesus said. So they prepared the Passover meal.

The Lord's Supper
(Mt. 26:26–30; Mk. 14:22–26; 1 Cor. 11:23–25)

14The time came for them to eat the Passover* meal. Jesus and the apostles* were together at the table. 15Jesus said to them, "I wanted very much to eat this Passover meal with you before I die. 16I will never eat another Passover meal until it is given its full meaning in God's kingdom.*"

17Then Jesus took a cup of wine. He gave thanks to God for it and said, "Take this cup and give it to everyone here. 18I will never drink wine again until God's kingdom comes."

19Then he took some bread and thanked God for it. He broke off some pieces, gave them to the apostles and said, "This bread is my body that I am giving for you. Eat this to remember me." 20In the same way, after supper, Jesus took the cup of wine and said, "This wine represents the new agreement* from God to his people. It will begin when my blood is poured out for you."[b]

Who Will Turn Against Jesus?

21Jesus said, "But here on this table is the hand of the one who will hand me over to my enemies. 22The Son of Man* will do what God has planned. But it will be very bad for the one who hands over the Son of Man to be killed."

23Then the apostles* asked each other, "Which one of us would do that?"

Be Like a Servant

24Later, the apostles* began to argue about which one of them was the most important. 25But Jesus said to them, "The kings of the world rule over their people, and those who have authority over others want to be called 'the

---

a **22:7 Day of Unleavened Bread** Same as Passover.

b **22:20** A few Greek copies do not have Jesus' words in the last part of verse 19 and all of verse 20.

great providers for the people.' [26]But you must not be like that. The one with the most authority among you should act as if he is the least important. The one who leads should be like one who serves. [27]Who is more important: the one serving or the one sitting at the table being served? Everyone thinks it's the one being served, right? But I have been with you as the one who serves. [28]"You men have stayed with me through many struggles. [29]So I give you authority to rule with me in the kingdom the Father has given me. [30]You will eat and drink at my table in that kingdom. You will sit on thrones and judge the twelve tribes of Israel.*

Peter Will Be Tested and Fail
(Mt. 26:31–35; Mk. 14:27–31; Jn. 13:36–38)

[31]"Satan* has asked to test you men like a farmer tests his wheat. O Simon, Simon,[a] [32]I have prayed that you will not lose your faith! Help your brothers be stronger when you come back to me."

[33]But Peter said to Jesus, "Lord, I am ready to go to jail with you. I will even die with you!"

[34]But Jesus said, "Peter, before the rooster crows tomorrow morning, you will say you don't know me. You will say this three times."

Be Ready for Trouble

[35]Then Jesus said to the apostles,* "Remember when I sent you out without money, a bag, or sandals? Did you need anything?"

The apostles said, "No."

[36]Jesus said to them, "But now if you have money or a bag, carry that with you. If you don't have a sword, sell your coat and buy one. [37]The Scriptures* say,

'He was considered a criminal.'
Isaiah 53:12

This Scripture must happen. It was written about me, and it is happening now."

[38]The followers said, "Look, Lord, here are two swords."

Jesus said to them, "That's enough."[b]

Jesus Prays Alone
(Mt. 26:36–46; Mk. 14:32–42)

[39-40]Jesus left the city and went to the Mount of Olives.* His followers went with him. (He went there often.) He said to his followers, "Pray for strength against temptation."

[41]Then Jesus went about 50 steps away from them. He knelt down and prayed, [42]"Father, if you are willing, please don't make me drink from this cup.[c] But do what you want, not what I want." [43]Then an angel from heaven came to help him. [44]Jesus was full of pain; he struggled hard in prayer. Sweat dripped from his face like drops of blood falling to the ground.[d] [45]When he finished praying, he went to his followers. He found them asleep, worn out from their grieving. [46]Jesus said to them, "Why are you sleeping? Get up and pray for strength against temptation."

---

b **22:38 "That's enough"** Or "Enough of that!" meaning "Don't talk anymore about such things."

c **22:42 cup** A symbol of suffering. Jesus used the idea of drinking from a cup to mean accepting the suffering he would face in the terrible events that were soon to come.

d **22:44** Some Greek copies do not have verses 43 and 44.

a **22:31 Simon** Simon's other name was Peter.

Jesus Is Arrested

(Mt. 26:47–56; Mk. 14:43–50; Jn. 18:3–11)

47While Jesus was speaking, a crowd came up. It was led by Judas, one of the twelve apostles.* He came over to Jesus to kiss him.

48But Jesus said to him, "Judas, are you using the kiss of friendship to hand over the Son of Man* to his enemies?" 49The followers of Jesus were standing there too. They saw what was happening and said to Jesus, "Lord, should we use our swords?" 50And one of them did use his sword. He cut off the right ear of the servant of the high priest.*

51Jesus said, "Stop!" Then he touched the servant's ear and healed him.

52Jesus spoke to the group that came to arrest him. They were the leading priests, the older Jewish leaders, and the Jewish soldiers. He said to them, "Why did you come out here with swords and clubs? Do you think I am a criminal? 53I was with you every day in the Temple* area. Why didn't you try to arrest me there? But this is your time—the time when darkness rules."

Peter Is Afraid to Say He Knows Jesus

(Mt. 26:57–58, 69–75; Mk. 14:53–54, 66–72; Jn. 18:12–18, 25–27)

54They arrested Jesus and took him away to the house of the high priest.* Peter followed Jesus but stayed back at a distance. 55The soldiers started a fire in the middle of the yard and sat together. Peter sat with them. 56A servant girl saw him sitting there. She could see because of the light from the fire. She looked closely at Peter's face. Then she said, "This man was also with Jesus."

57But Peter said this was not true. He said, "Lady, I don't know him." 58A short time later, someone else saw Peter and said, "You are also one of them."

But Peter said, "Man, I am not!"

59About an hour later, another man said, "It's true. I'm sure this man was with him, because he is from Galilee."

60But Peter said, "Man, I don't know what you are talking about!"

Immediately, while he was still speaking, a rooster crowed. 61Then the Lord turned and looked into Peter's eyes. And Peter remembered what the Lord had said, "Before the rooster crows in the morning, you will say three times that you don't know me." 62Then Peter went outside and cried bitterly.

The Guards Treat Jesus Badly

(Mt. 26:67–68; Mk. 14:65)

63The men guarding Jesus made fun of him and beat him. 64They covered his eyes so that he could not see them. Then they hit him and said, "Be a prophet[a] and tell us who hit you!" 65And they shouted all kinds of insults at him.

Jesus Before the Jewish Leaders

(Mt. 26:59–66; Mk. 14:55–64; Jn. 18:19–24)

66The next morning, the older leaders of the people, the leading priests, and the teachers of the law came together. They led Jesus away to their high council. 67They said, "If you are the Messiah,* then tell us that you are."

Jesus said to them, "If I tell you I am the Messiah, you will not believe me. 68And if I ask you, you will not answer. 69But beginning now, the Son of Man* will sit at the right side of God All-Powerful."

---

a **22:64 prophet** A prophet often knows things that are hidden to other people.

70They all said, "Then are you the Son of God?" Jesus said to them, "You are right in saying that I am."

71They said, "Why do we need witnesses now? We all heard what he said!"

Governor Pilate Questions Jesus
(Mt. 27:1–2, 11–14; Mk. 15:1–5; Jn. 18:28–38)

23 1Then the whole group stood up and led Jesus away to Pilate.* 2They began to accuse Jesus and said to Pilate, "We caught this man trying to change the thinking of our people. He says we should not pay taxes to Caesar.* He calls himself the Messiah,* a king."

3Pilate asked Jesus, "Are you the king of the Jews?"

Jesus answered, "Yes, what you say is true."

4Pilate said to the leading priests and the people, "I find nothing wrong with this man."

5But they kept on saying, "His teaching is causing trouble all over Judea. He began in Galilee, and now he is here!"

Pilate Sends Jesus to Herod

6Pilate* heard this and asked if Jesus was from Galilee. 7He learned that Jesus was under Herod's* authority. Herod was in Jerusalem at that time, so Pilate sent Jesus to him.

8When Herod saw Jesus, he was very happy. He had heard all about him and had wanted to meet him for a long time. Herod wanted to see a miracle,* so he was hoping that Jesus would do one. 9He asked him many questions, but Jesus said nothing. 10The leading priests and teachers of the law were standing there shouting things against Jesus. 11Then Herod and his soldiers laughed at him.

They made fun of him by dressing him in clothes like kings wear. Then Herod sent him back to Pilate. 12In the past Pilate and Herod had always been enemies. But on that day they became friends.

Pilate Tries but Fails to Free Jesus
(Mt. 27:15–26; Mk. 15:6–15; Jn. 18:39–19:16)

13Pilate* called all the people together with the leading priests and the Jewish leaders. 14He said to them, "You brought this man to me. You said he was trying to change the people. But I judged him before you all and have not found him guilty of the things you say he has done. 15Herod* didn't find him guilty either. He sent him back to us. Look, he has done nothing bad enough for the death penalty. 16So, after I punish him a little, I will let him go free." 17a

18But they all shouted, "Kill him! Let Barabbas go free!" 19(Barabbas was a man who was in jail for starting a riot in the city and for murder.)

20Pilate wanted to let Jesus go free. So again Pilate told them that he would let him go. 21But they shouted again, "Kill him! Kill him on a cross!"

22A third time Pilate said to the people, "Why? What wrong has he done? He is not guilty. I can find no reason to kill him. So I will let him go free after I punish him a little."

23But the people continued to shout. They demanded that Jesus be killed on a cross. Their shouting got so loud that 24Pilate decided to give them what they wanted. 25They wanted Barabbas to go free—the one who was in jail

---

a **23:17** A few Greek copies add verse 17: "Every year at the Passover festival, Pilate had to release one prisoner to the people."

for starting a riot and for murder. Pilate let Barabbas go free. And he handed Jesus over to be killed. This is what the people wanted.

Jesus Is Nailed to a Cross
(Mt. 27:32–44; Mk. 15:21–32; Jn. 19:17–19)

26The soldiers led Jesus away. At that same time there was a man from Cyrene named Simon coming into the city from the fields. The soldiers forced him to carry Jesus' cross and walk behind him. 27A large crowd followed Jesus. Some of the women were sad and crying. They felt sorry for him. 28But Jesus turned and said to the women, "Women of Jerusalem, don't cry for me. Cry for yourselves and for your children too. 29The time is coming when people will say, 'The women who cannot have babies are the ones God has blessed. It's really a blessing that they have no children to care for.' 30Then the people will say to the mountains, 'Fall on us!' They will say to the hills, 'Cover us!'a 31If this can happen to someone who is good, what will happen to those who are guilty?b"

32There were also two criminals led out with Jesus to be killed. 33They were led to a place called "The Skull." There the soldiers nailed Jesus to the cross. They also nailed the criminals to crosses beside Jesus—one on the right and the other on the left. 34Jesus said, "Father, forgive them. They don't know what they are doing."c

The soldiers threw dice to divide Jesus' clothes between them. 35The people stood there watching everything. The Jewish leaders laughed at Jesus. They said, "If he is God's Chosen One, the Messiah,* then let him save himself. He saved others, didn't he?"

36Even the soldiers laughed at Jesus and made fun of him. They came and offered him some sour wine. 37They said, "If you are the king of the Jews, save yourself!" 38(At the top of the cross these words were written: "THIS IS THE KING OF THE JEWS.")

39One of the criminals hanging there began to shout insults at Jesus: "Aren't you the Messiah? Then save yourself, and save us too!"

40But the other criminal stopped him. He said, "You should fear God. All of us will die soon. 41You and I are guilty. We deserve to die because we did wrong. But this man has done nothing wrong." 42Then he said, "Jesus, remember me when you begin ruling as king!"

43Then Jesus said to him, "I promise you, today you will be with me in paradise.*"

Jesus Dies
(Mt. 27:45–56; Mk. 15:33–41; Jn. 19:28–30)

44It was about noon, but it turned dark throughout the land until three o'clock in the afternoon, 45because the sun stopped shining. The curtain* in the Temple* was torn into two pieces. 46Jesus shouted, "Father, I put my life in your hands!"d After Jesus said this, he died.

47The army officer* there saw what happened. He praised God,

---

a 23:30 Quote from Hos. 10:8.

b 23:31 If this can happen ... guilty Literally, "If they do these things in the green tree, what will happen in the dry?"

c 23:34 Jesus said, "Father ... doing" Some early copies of Luke do not have these words.

d 23:46 "I put ... hands" Literally, "I put my spirit in your hands." Quote from Ps. 31:5.

saying, "I know this man was a good man!"

⁴⁸Many people had come out of the city to see all this. When they saw it, they felt very sorry and left. ⁴⁹The people who were close friends of Jesus were there. Also, there were some women who had followed Jesus from Galilee. They all stood far away from the cross and watched these things.

Jesus Is Buried
(Mt. 27:57–61; Mk. 15:42–47; Jn. 19:38–42)

⁵⁰⁻⁵¹A man named Joseph was there from the Jewish town of Arimathea. He was a good man, who lived the way God wanted. He was waiting for God's kingdom* to come. Joseph was a member of the Jewish council. But he did not agree when the other Jewish leaders decided to kill Jesus. ⁵²He went to Pilate* and asked for the body of Jesus. ⁵³He took the body down from the cross and wrapped it in cloth. Then he put it in a tomb* that was dug in a wall of rock. This tomb had never been used before. ⁵⁴It was late on Preparation day.* When the sun went down, the Sabbath* day would begin.

⁵⁵The women who had come from Galilee with Jesus followed Joseph. They saw the tomb. Inside they saw where he put Jesus' body. ⁵⁶Then they left to prepare some sweet-smelling spices to put on the body.

On the Sabbath day they rested, as commanded in the Law of Moses.*

News That Jesus Has Risen From Death
(Mt. 28:1–10; Mk. 16:1–8; Jn. 20:1–10)

24 ¹Very early Sunday morning, the women came to the tomb* where Jesus' body was laid. They brought the sweet-smelling spices they had prepared. ²They saw that the heavy stone that covered the entrance had been rolled away. ³They went in, but they did not find the body of the Lord Jesus. ⁴They did not understand this. While they were wondering about it, two men in shining clothes stood beside them. ⁵The women were very afraid. They bowed down with their faces to the ground. The men said to them, "Why are you looking for a living person here? This is a place for dead people. ⁶Jesus is not here. He has risen from death. Do you remember what he said in Galilee? ⁷He said the Son of Man* must be handed over to the control of sinful men, be killed on a cross, and rise from death on the third day." ⁸Then the women remembered what Jesus had said.

⁹The women left the tomb and went to the eleven apostles* and the other followers. They told them everything that happened at the tomb. ¹⁰These women were Mary Magdalene, Joanna, Mary, the mother of James, and some others. They told the apostles everything that happened. ¹¹But the apostles did not believe what they said. It sounded like nonsense. ¹²But Peter got up and ran to the tomb to see. He looked in, but he saw only the cloth that Jesus' body had been wrapped in. It was just lying there. Peter went away to be alone, wondering what had happened.[a]

On The Road to Emmaus
(Mk. 16:12–13)

¹³That same day two of Jesus' followers were going to a town

[a] 24:12 A few Greek copies do not have this verse.

named Emmaus. It is about seven miles[a] from Jerusalem. [14]They were talking about everything that had happened. [15]While they were talking, discussing these things, Jesus himself came near and walked with them. [16](But the two men were not allowed to recognize Jesus.) [17]He asked them, "What's this I hear you discussing with each other as you walk?"

The two men stopped, their faces looking very sad. [18]The one named Cleopas said, "You must be the only person in Jerusalem who doesn't know what has just happened there."

[19]Jesus said, "What are you talking about?"

They said, "It's about Jesus, the one from Nazareth. To God and to all the people he was a great prophet.* He said and did many powerful things. [20]But our leaders and the leading priests handed him over to be judged and killed. They nailed him to a cross. [21]We were hoping that he would be the one to free Israel.* But then all this happened.

"And now something else: It has been three days since he was killed, [22]but today some of our women told us an amazing thing. Early this morning they went to the tomb* where the body of Jesus was laid. [23]But they did not find his body there. They came and told us they had seen some angels in a vision.* The angels told them Jesus was alive! [24]So some of our group went to the tomb too. It was just as the women said. They saw the tomb, but they did not see Jesus."

[25]Then Jesus said to the two men, "You are foolish and slow to realize what is true. You should believe everything the prophets said. [26]The prophets said the Messiah* must suffer these things before he begins his time of glory.*" [27]Then he began to explain everything that had been written about himself in the Scriptures.* He started with the books of Moses* and then he talked about what the prophets had said about him.

[28]They came near the town of Emmaus, and Jesus acted as if he did not plan to stop there. [29]But they wanted him to stay. They begged him, "Stay with us. It's almost night. There's hardly any daylight left." So he went in to stay with them.

[30]Joining them at the supper table, Jesus took some bread and gave thanks. Then he broke some off and gave it to them. [31]Just then the men were allowed to recognize him. But when they saw who he was, he disappeared. [32]They said to each other, "When he talked to us on the road, it felt like a fire burning in us. How exciting it was when he explained to us the true meaning of the Scriptures!"

[33]So the two men got up then and went back to Jerusalem. There they found the followers of Jesus meeting together. The eleven apostles* and the people with them [34]said, "The Lord really has risen from death! He appeared to Simon."

[35]Then the two men told what had happened on the road. They talked about how they recognized Jesus when he shared the bread with them.

---

a **24:13 seven miles** Literally, "60 *stadious*," almost 12 km.

Jesus Appears to His Followers

(Mt. 28:16–20; Mk. 16:14–18;
Jn. 20:19–23; Acts 1:6–8)

36While the two men were saying these things to the other followers, Jesus himself came and stood among them. He said to them, "Peace be with you." 37This surprised the followers. They were afraid. They thought they were seeing a ghost. 38But Jesus said, "Why are you troubled? Why do you doubt what you see? 39Look at my hands and my feet. It's really me. Touch me. You can see that I have a living body; a ghost does not have a body like this."

40After Jesus told them this, he showed them his hands and his feet. 41The followers were amazed and very, very happy to see that Jesus was alive. They still could not believe what they saw. He said to them, "Do you have any food here?" 42They gave him a piece of cooked fish. 43While the followers watched, he took the fish and ate it.

44Jesus said to them, "Remember when I was with you before? I said that everything written about me must happen—everything written in the Law of Moses,* the books of the prophets,* and the Psalms."

45Then Jesus helped the followers understand these Scriptures* about him. 46Jesus said to them, "It is written that the Messiah* would be killed and rise from death on the third day. 47–48You saw these things happen—you are witnesses. You must go and tell people that they must change and turn to God, which will bring them his forgiveness. You must start from Jerusalem and tell this message in my name to the people of all nations. 49Remember that I will send you the one my Father promised. Stay in the city until you are given that power from heaven."

Jesus Goes Back to Heaven

(Mk. 16:19–20; Acts 1:9–11)

50Jesus led his followers out of Jerusalem almost to Bethany. He raised his hands and blessed his followers. 51While he was blessing them, he was separated from them and carried into heaven. 52They worshiped him and went back to Jerusalem very happy. 53They stayed at the Temple* all the time, praising God.

John

Christ Comes to the World

1 ¹Before the world began, the Word[a] was there. The Word was with God, and the Word was God. ²He was there with God in the beginning. ³Everything was made through him, and nothing was made without him. ⁴In him there was life, and that life was a light for the people of the world. ⁵The light[b] shines in the darkness,* and the darkness has not defeated[c] it.

⁶There was a man named John,* who was sent by God. ⁷He came to tell people about the light. Through him all people could hear about the light and believe. ⁸John was not the light. But he came to tell people about the light. ⁹The true light was coming into the world. This is the true light that gives light to all people.

¹⁰The Word was already in the world. The world was made through him, but the world did not know him. ¹¹He came to the world that was his own. And his own people did not accept him. ¹²But some people did accept him.

They believed in him, and he gave them the right to become children of God. ¹³They became God's children, but not in the way babies are usually born. It was not because of any human desire or plan. They were born from God himself.

¹⁴The Word became a man and lived among us. We saw his divine greatness*—the greatness that belongs to the only Son of the Father. The Word was full of grace* and truth. ¹⁵John told people about him. He said loudly, "This is the one I was talking about when I said, 'The one who is coming after me is greater than I am, because he was living before I was even born.'"

¹⁶Yes, the Word was full of grace and truth, and from him we all received one blessing after another.[d] ¹⁷That is, the law was given to us through Moses,* but grace and truth came through Jesus Christ. ¹⁸No one has ever seen God. The only Son is the one who has shown us what God is like. He is himself God and is very close to the Father.[e]

---

a **1:1 Word** The Greek word is "*logos*," meaning any kind of communication. It could be translated "message." Here, it describes Jesus Christ before he was sent to earth as a human being, which is the way God chose to tell the world about himself. Also in verses 10, 14, 16.

b **1:5 light** Meaning Christ, the Word, who brought to the world understanding about God. Also in verse 7.

c **1:5 defeated** Or "understood."

d **1:16 one blessing after another** Literally, "grace in place of grace."

e **1:18 The only Son ... Father** Or more literally, "The one and only *Son*, God, who is very close to the Father, has shown us what he is like." Some other Greek copies say, "The only Son is very close to the Father and has shown us what he is like."

John Tells About the Messiah

(Mt. 3:1–12; Mk. 1:1–8; Lk. 3:1–9, 15–17)

19The Jewish leaders in Jerusalem sent some priests and Levites* to John* to ask him, "Who are you?" He told them the truth. 20Without any hesitation he said openly and plainly, "I am not the Messiah.*"

21They asked him, "Then who are you? Are you Elijah*?"

He answered, "No, I am not Elijah."

They asked, "Are you the Prophet*a*?"

He answered, "No, I am not the Prophet."

22Then they said, "Who are you? Tell us about yourself. Give us an answer to tell the people who sent us. What do you say about yourself?"

23John told them the words of the prophet* Isaiah:

"I am the voice of someone
　shouting in the desert:
'Make a straight road ready
　for the Lord.'"　　　*Isaiah 40:3*

24These Jews were sent from the Pharisees.* 25They said to John, "You say you are not the Messiah. You say you are not Elijah or the Prophet. Then why do you baptize* people?"

26John answered, "I baptize people with water. But there is someone here with you that you don't know. 27He is the one who is coming later. I am not good enough to be the slave who unties the strings on his sandals."

28These things all happened at Bethany on the other side of the Jordan River. This is where John was baptizing people.

Jesus, the Lamb of God

29The next day John saw Jesus coming toward him and said, "Look, the Lamb* of God. He takes away the sins of the world! 30This is the one I was talking about when I said, 'There is a man coming after me who is greater than I am, because he was living even before I was born.' 31I did not know who he was. But I came baptizing people with water so that Israel* could know that he is the Messiah.*b*"

32–34Then John said this for everyone to hear: "I also did not know who the Messiah was. But the one who sent me to baptize* with water told me, 'You will see the Spirit* come down and rest on a man. He is the one who will baptize with the Holy Spirit.' I have seen this happen. I saw the Spirit come down from heaven like a dove and rest on this man. So this is what I tell people: 'He is the Son of God.'*c*"

The First Followers of Jesus

35The next day John was there again and had two of his followers with him. 36He saw Jesus walking by and said, "Look, the Lamb* of God!"

37The two followers heard him say this, so they followed Jesus. 38Jesus turned and saw the two men following him. He asked, "What do you want?"

They said, "Rabbi, where are you staying?" ("Rabbi" means "Teacher.")

---

a **1:21 Prophet** They probably meant the prophet that God told Moses he would send. See Deut. 18:15–19. Also in verse 24.

b **1:31 so that ... the Messiah** Literally, "so that he might be revealed ⌊as the Messiah⌋ to Israel." See "MESSIAH" in the Word List.

c **1:32–34 He is the Son of God** Some very early Greek copies have "He is the chosen one of God."

[39] He answered, "Come with me and you will see." So the two men went with him. They saw the place where he was staying, and they stayed there with him that day. It was about four o'clock. [40] These men followed Jesus after they had heard about him from John. One of them was Andrew, the brother of Simon Peter. [41] The first thing Andrew did was to go and find his brother Simon. Andrew said to him, "We have found the Messiah.*" ("Messiah" means "Christ.*")

[42] Then Andrew brought Simon to Jesus. Jesus looked at him and said, "You are Simon, the son of John. You will be called Cephas." ("Cephas" means "Peter.*")

[43] The next day Jesus decided to go to Galilee. He met Philip and said to him, "Follow me." [44] Philip was from the town of Bethsaida, the same as Andrew and Peter. [45] Philip found Nathanael and told him, "We have found the man that Moses* wrote about in the law. The prophets* wrote about him too. He is Jesus, the son of Joseph. He is from Nazareth."

[46] But Nathanael said to Philip, "Nazareth! Can anything good come from Nazareth?"

Philip answered, "Come and see."

[47] Jesus saw Nathanael coming toward him and said, "This man coming is a true Israelite,* one you can trust.*"

[48] Nathanael asked, "How do you know me?"

Jesus answered, "I saw you when you were under the fig tree, before Philip told you about me."

[49] Then Nathanael said, "Teacher, you are the Son of God. You are the King of Israel.*"

[50] Jesus said to him, "Do you believe this just because I said I saw you under the fig tree? You will see much greater things than that!" [51] Then he said, "Believe me when I say that you will all see heaven open. You will see 'angels of God going up and coming down'*c on the Son of Man.*"

The Wedding at Cana

2 [1] Two days later there was a wedding in the town of Cana in Galilee, and Jesus' mother was there. [2] Jesus and his followers were also invited. [3] At the wedding there was not enough wine, so Jesus' mother said to him, "They have no more wine."

[4] Jesus answered, "Dear woman, why are you telling me this? It is not yet time for me to begin my work."

[5] His mother said to the servants, "Do what he tells you."

[6] There were six large stone waterpots there that were used by the Jews in their washing ceremonies.*d Each one held about 20 or 30 gallons.*e

[7] Jesus said to the servants, "Fill the waterpots with water." So they filled them to the top.

---

a **1:42 Peter** The Greek name "Peter," like the Aramaic name "Cephas," means "rock."
b **1:47 one you can trust** Literally, "in whom is no deceit." In the Old Testament, Israel's other name, Jacob, is explained with words that mean "deceit" or "trickery," for which he was well known. See Gen. 27:35, 36.

c **1:51** Quote from Gen. 28:12.
d **2:6 washing ceremonies** The Jews had religious rules about washing in special ways before eating, before worshiping in the Temple, and at other special times.
e **2:6 20 or 30 gallons** Literally, "2 or 3 *metretas*," about 80 to 120 liters.

8Then he said to them, "Now dip out some water and take it to the man in charge of the feast." So they did what he said. 9Then the man in charge tasted it, but the water had become wine. He did not know where the wine had come from, but the servants who brought the water knew. He called the bridegroom* 10and said to him, "People always serve the best wine first. Later, when the guests are drunk, they serve the cheaper wine. But you have saved the best wine until now."

11This was the first of all the miraculous signs* Jesus did. He did it in the town of Cana in Galilee. By this he showed his divine greatness,* and his followers believed in him.

12Then Jesus went to the town of Capernaum.* His mother and brothers and his followers went with him. They all stayed there a few days.

Jesus at the Temple
(Mt. 21:12–13; Mk. 11:15–17; Lk. 19:45–46)
13It was almost time for the Jewish Passover,* so Jesus went to Jerusalem. 14There in the Temple* area he saw men selling cattle, sheep, and doves. He saw others sitting at tables, exchanging and trading people's money. 15Jesus made a whip with some pieces of rope. Then he forced all these men and the sheep and cattle to leave the Temple area. He turned over the tables of the money traders and scattered their money. 16Then he said to those who were selling pigeons, "Take these things out of here! Don't make my Father's house a place for buying and selling!"

17When this happened, his followers remembered what was written in the Scriptures*:
"My strong devotion to your Temple will destroy me."
Psalm 69:9

18Some Jews said to Jesus, "Show us a miracle* as a sign from God. Prove that you have the right to do these things."

19Jesus answered, "Destroy this temple and I will build it again in three days."

20They answered, "People worked 46 years to build this Temple! Do you really believe you can build it again in three days?"

21But the temple Jesus meant was his own body. 22After he was raised from death, his followers remembered that he had said this. So they believed the Scriptures, and they believed the words Jesus said.

23Jesus was in Jerusalem for the Passover festival. Many people believed in him because they saw the miraculous signs* he did. 24But Jesus did not trust them, because he knew how all people think. 25He did not need anyone to tell him what a person was like. He already knew.

Jesus and Nicodemus
3 1There was a man named Nicodemus, one of the Pharisees.* He was an important Jewish leader. 2One night he came to Jesus and said, "Teacher, we know that you are a teacher sent from God. No one can do these miraculous signs* that you do unless they have God's help."

3Jesus answered, "I assure you, everyone must be born again. Anyone who is not born again cannot be in God's kingdom.*"

4Nicodemus said, "How can a man who is already old be born again? Can he go back into his mother's womb and be born a second time?"

⁵Jesus answered, "Believe me when I say that everyone must be born from water and the Spirit.* Anyone who is not born from water and the Spirit cannot enter God's kingdom. ⁶The only life people get from their human parents is physical. But the new life that the Spirit gives a person is spiritual. ⁷Don't be surprised that I told you, 'You must be born again.' ⁸The wind blows wherever it wants to. You hear it, but you don't know where it is coming from or where it is going. It is the same with everyone who is born from the Spirit."

⁹Nicodemus asked, "How is all this possible?"

¹⁰Jesus said, "You are an important teacher of Israel,* and you still don't understand these things? ¹¹The truth is, we talk about what we know. We tell about what we have seen. But you people don't accept what we tell you. ¹²I have told you about things here on earth, but you do not believe me. So I'm sure you will not believe me if I tell you about heavenly things! ¹³The only one who has ever gone up to heaven is the one who came down from heaven—the Son of Man.*

¹⁴"Moses lifted up the snake in the desert.ᵃ It is the same with the Son of Man. He must be lifted up too. ¹⁵Then everyone who believes in him can have eternal life."ᵇ

¹⁶Yes, God loved the world so much that he gave his only Son, so that everyone who believes in him would not be lost but have eternal life. ¹⁷God sent his Son into the world. He did not send him to judge the world guilty, but to save the world through him. ¹⁸People who believe in God's Son are not judged guilty. But people who do not believe are already judged, because they have not believed in God's only Son. ¹⁹They are judged by this fact: The lightᶜ has come into the world. But they did not want light. They wanted darkness,* because they were doing evil things. ²⁰Everyone who does evil hates the light. They will not come to the light, because the light will show all the bad things they have done. ²¹But anyone who follows the true way comes to the light. Then the light will show that whatever they have done was done through God.

Jesus and John the Baptizer

²²After this, Jesus and his followers went into the area of Judea. There he stayed with his followers and baptized* people. ²³John was also baptizing people in Aenon, a place near Salim with plenty of water. People were going there to be baptized. ²⁴This was before John was put in prison.

²⁵Some of John's followers had an argument with another Jew about religious washing.ᵈ ²⁶Then they came to John and said, "Teacher, remember the man who

---

ᵃ 3:14 Moses lifted ... desert When God's people were dying from snake bites, God told Moses to put a brass snake on a pole for them to look at and be healed. See Num. 21:4–9.
ᵇ 3:15 Some scholars think that Jesus' words to Nicodemus continue through verse 21.
ᶜ 3:19 light This means Christ, the Word, who brought to the world understanding about God.
ᵈ 3:25 religious washing The Jews had religious rules about washing in special ways before eating, before worshiping in the Temple, and at other special times.

was with you on the other side of the Jordan River? He is the one you were telling everyone about. He is also baptizing people, and many are going to him."

27John answered, "A person can receive only what God gives. 28You yourselves heard me say, 'I am not the Messiah.* I am only the one God sent to prepare the way for him.' 29The bride always belongs to the bridegroom.* The friend who helps the bridegroom just waits and listens. He is happy just to hear the bridegroom talk. That's how I feel now. I am so happy that he is here. 30He must become more and more important, and I must become less important.

The One Who Comes From Heaven

31"The one who comes from above is greater than all others. The one who is from the earth belongs to the earth. He talks about things that are on the earth. But the one who comes from heaven is greater than all others. 32He tells what he has seen and heard, but people don't accept what he says. 33Whoever accepts what he says has given proof that God speaks the truth. 34God sent him, and he tells people what God says. God gives him the Spirit* fully. 35The Father loves the Son and has given him power over everything. 36Whoever believes in the Son has eternal life. But those who do not obey the Son will never have that life. They cannot get away from God's anger."

Jesus Talks to a Woman in Samaria

4 1Jesus learned that the Pharisees* had heard the report that he was making and baptizing* more followers than John. 2(But really, Jesus himself did not baptize anyone; his followers baptized

people for him.) 3So he left Judea and went back to Galilee. 4On the way to Galilee, he had to go through the country of Samaria.

5In Samaria Jesus came to the town called Sychar, which is near the field that Jacob gave to his son Joseph. 6Jacob's well was there. Jesus was tired from his long trip, so he sat down beside the well. It was about noon. 7A Samaritan* woman came to the well to get some water, and Jesus said to her, "Please give me a drink." 8This happened while his followers were in town buying some food.

9The woman answered, "I am surprised that you ask me for a drink! You are a Jew and I am a Samaritan woman!" (Jews have nothing to do with Samaritans.*a*)

10Jesus answered, "You don't know what God can give you. And you don't know who I am, the one who asked you for a drink. If you knew, you would have asked me, and I would have given you living water."

11The woman said, "Sir, where will you get that living water? The well is very deep, and you have nothing to get water with. 12Are you greater than our ancestor Jacob*? He is the one who gave us this well. He drank from it himself, and his sons and all his animals drank from it too."

13Jesus answered, "Everyone who drinks this water will be thirsty again. 14But anyone who drinks the water I give will never be thirsty again. The water I give people will be like a spring flowing inside them. It will bring them eternal life."

a **4:9 Jews have nothing to do with Samaritans** Or "Jews don't use things that Samaritans have used."

15The woman said to Jesus, "Sir, give me this water. Then I will never be thirsty again and won't have to come back here to get more water."

16Jesus told her, "Go get your husband and come back."

17The woman answered, "But I have no husband."

Jesus said to her, "You are right to say you have no husband. 18That's because, although you have had five husbands, the man you live with now is not your husband. That much was the truth."

19The woman said, "Sir, I can see that you are a prophet.a 20Our fathers worshiped on this mountain. But you Jews say that Jerusalem is the place where people must worship."

21Jesus said, "Believe me, woman! The time is coming when you will not have to be in Jerusalem or on this mountain to worship the Father. 22You Samaritans worship something you don't understand. We Jews understand what we worship, since salvation comes from the Jews. 23But the time is coming when the true worshipers will worship the Father in spirit and truth. In fact, that time is now here. And these are the kind of people the Father wants to be his worshipers. 24God is spirit. So the people who worship him must worship in spirit and truth."

25The woman said, "I know that the Messiah* is coming." (He is the one called Christ.*) "When he comes, he will explain everything to us."

26Then Jesus said, "He is talking to you now—I am the Messiah."

27Just then Jesus' followers came back from town. They were surprised because they saw Jesus talking with a woman. But none of them asked, "What do you want?" or "Why are you talking with her?"

28Then the woman left her water jar and went back to town. She told the people there, 29"A man told me everything I have ever done. Come see him. Maybe he is the Messiah." 30So the people left the town and went to see Jesus.

31While the woman was in town, Jesus' followers were begging him, "Teacher, eat something!"

32But Jesus answered, "I have food to eat that you know nothing about."

33So the followers asked themselves, "Did someone already bring him some food?"

34Jesus said, "My food is to do what the one who sent me wants me to do. My food is to finish the work that he gave me to do. 35When you plant, you always say, 'Four more months to wait before we gather the grain.' But I tell you, open your eyes, and look at the fields. They are ready for harvesting now. 36Even now, the people who harvest the crop are being paid. They are gathering crops for eternal life. So now the people who plant can be happy together with those who harvest. 37It is true when we say, 'One person plants, but another person harvests the crop.' 38I sent you to harvest a crop that you did not work for. Others did the work, and you get the profit from their work."

39Many of the Samaritan people in that town believed in Jesus. They believed because of what

---

a 4:19 prophet A prophet often knows things that are hidden to other people.

the woman had told them about him. She had told them, "He told me everything I have ever done." ⁴⁰The Samaritans went to Jesus. They begged him to stay with them. So he stayed there two days. ⁴¹Many more people became believers because of the things he said.

⁴²The people said to the woman, "First we believed in Jesus because of what you told us. But now we believe because we heard him ourselves. We know now that he really is the one who will save the world."

Jesus Heals an Official's Son
(Mt. 8:5–13; Lk. 7:1–10)

⁴³Two days later Jesus left and went to Galilee. ⁴⁴(Jesus had said before that a prophet* is not respected in his own country.) ⁴⁵When he arrived in Galilee, the people there welcomed him. They had been at the Passover* festival in Jerusalem and had seen everything he did there.

⁴⁶Jesus went to visit Cana in Galilee again. Cana is where he had changed the water into wine. One of the king's important officials lived in the city of Capernaum.* This man's son was sick. ⁴⁷The man heard that Jesus had come from Judea and was now in Galilee. So he went to Jesus and begged him to come to Capernaum and heal his son, who was almost dead. ⁴⁸Jesus said to him, "You people must see miraculous signs* and wonders* before you will believe in me."

⁴⁹The king's official said, "Sir, come before my little son dies."

⁵⁰Jesus answered, "Go. Your son will live."

The man believed what Jesus told him and went home. ⁵¹On the way home, the man's servants came and met him. They said, "Your son is well."

⁵²The man asked, "What time did my son begin to get well?"

They answered, "It was about one o'clock yesterday when the fever left him."

⁵³The father knew that one o'clock was the same time that Jesus had said, "Your son will live." So the man and everyone in his house believed in Jesus.

⁵⁴That was the second miraculous sign that Jesus did after coming from Judea to Galilee.

Jesus Heals a Man at a Pool

5 ¹Later, Jesus went to Jerusalem for a special Jewish festival. ²In Jerusalem there is a pool with five covered porches. In Aramaic* it is called Bethzatha.ᵃ This pool is near the Sheep Gate. ³Many sick people were lying on the porches beside the pool. Some of them were blind, some were crippled, and some were paralyzed.ᵇ ⁴ᶜ ⁵One of the men lying there had been sick for 38 years. ⁶Jesus saw him lying there and knew that he had been sick for a very long time. So he asked him, "Do you want to be well?"

⁷The sick man answered, "Sir, there is no one to help me get into the water when it starts moving. I try to be the first one into the

---

ᵃ **5:2 Bethzatha** Also called Bethsaida or Bethesda, a pool of water north of the Temple in Jerusalem.
ᵇ **5:3** At the end of verse 3, some Greek copies add "and they waited for the water to move."
ᶜ **5:4** A few later copies add verse 4: "Sometimes an angel of the Lord came down to the pool and shook the water. After this, the first person to go into the pool was healed from any sickness he had."

water. But when I try, someone else always goes in before I can."

⁸Then Jesus said, "Stand up! Pick up your mat and walk." ⁹Immediately the man was well. He picked up his mat and started walking.

The day all this happened was a Sabbath* day. ¹⁰So some Jews said to the man who had been healed, "Today is the Sabbath. It is against our law for you to carry your mat on the Sabbath day."

¹¹But he answered, "The man who made me well told me, 'Pick up your mat and walk.'"

¹²They asked him, "Who is the man who told you to pick up your mat and walk?"

¹³But the man who had been healed did not know who it was. There were many people there, and Jesus had left.

¹⁴Later, Jesus found the man at the Temple* and said to him, "See, you are well now. But stop sinning or something worse may happen to you!"

¹⁵Then the man left and went back to the Jews who questioned him. He told them that Jesus was the one who made him well. ¹⁶Jesus was doing all this on the Sabbath day. So these Jews began trying to make him stop. ¹⁷But he said to them, "My Father never stops working, and so I work too."

¹⁸This made them try harder to kill him. They said, "First this man was breaking the law about the Sabbath day. Then he said that God is his Father! He is making himself equal with God!"

Jesus Has God's Authority

¹⁹But Jesus answered, "I assure you that the Son can do nothing alone. He does only what he sees his Father doing. The Son does the same things that the Father does. ²⁰The Father loves the Son and shows him everything he does. This man was healed. But the Father will show the Son greater things than this to do. Then you will all be amazed. ²¹The Father raises the dead and gives them life. In the same way, the Son gives life to those he wants to.

²²"Also, the Father judges no one. He has given the Son power to do all the judging. ²³God did this so that all people will respect the Son the same as they respect the Father. Anyone who does not respect the Son does not respect the Father. He is the one who sent the Son.

²⁴"I assure you, anyone who hears what I say and believes in the one who sent me has eternal life. They will not be judged guilty. They have already left death and have entered into life. ²⁵Believe me, an important time is coming. That time is already here. People who are dead will hear the voice of the Son of God. And those who listen will live. ²⁶Life comes from the Father himself. So the Father has also allowed the Son to give life. ²⁷And the Father has given him the power to judge all people because he is the Son of Man.*

²⁸"Don't be surprised at this. A time is coming when all people who are dead and in their graves will hear his voice. ²⁹Then they will come out of their graves. Those who did good in this life will rise and have eternal life. But those who did evil will rise to be judged guilty.

³⁰"I can do nothing alone. I judge only the way I am told. And my judgment is right, because I am not trying to please myself. I

want only to please the one who sent me.

Jesus Says More to the Jewish Leaders

31"If I tell people about myself, they cannot be sure that what I say is true. 32But there is someone else who tells people about me, and I know that what he says about me is true.

33"You sent men to John,* and he told you what is true. 34I don't need anyone to tell people about me, but I remind you of what John said so that you can be saved. 35John was like a lamp that burned and gave light, and you were happy to enjoy his light for a while.

36"But I have a proof about myself that is greater than anything John said. The things I do are my proof. These are what my Father gave me to do. They show that the Father sent me. 37And the Father who sent me has given proof about me himself. But you have never heard his voice. You have never seen what he looks like. 38The Father's teaching does not live in you, because you don't believe in the one the Father sent. 39You carefully study the Scriptures.* You think that they give you eternal life. These same Scriptures tell about me! 40But you refuse to come to me to have that life.

41"I don't want praise from you or any other human. 42But I know you—I know that you have no love for God. 43I have come from my Father and speak for him, but you don't accept me. But when other people come speaking only for themselves, you accept them. 44You like to have praise from each other. But you never try to get the praise that comes

from the only God. So how can you believe? 45Don't think that I will be the one to stand before the Father and accuse you. Moses* is the one to accuse you. And he is the one you hoped would save you. 46If you really believed Moses, you would believe me, because he wrote about me. 47But you don't believe what he wrote, so you can't believe what I say."

Jesus Feeds More Than 5000

(Mt. 14:13–21; Mk. 6:30–44; Lk. 9:10–17)

6 1Later, Jesus went across Lake Galilee (also known as Lake Tiberias). 2A great crowd of people followed him because they saw the miraculous signs* he did in healing the sick. 3Jesus went up on the side of the hill and sat there with his followers. 4It was almost the time for the Jewish Passover* festival.

5Jesus looked up and saw a crowd of people coming toward him. He said to Philip, "Where can we buy enough bread for all these people to eat?" 6He asked Philip this question to test him. Jesus already knew what he planned to do.

7Philip answered, "We would all have to work a month to buy enough bread for each person here to have only a little piece!"

8Another follower there was Andrew, the brother of Simon Peter. Andrew said, 9"Here is a boy with five loaves of barley bread and two little fish. But that is not enough for so many people."

10Jesus said, "Tell everyone to sit down." This was a place with a lot of grass, and about 5000 men sat down there. 11Jesus took the loaves of bread and gave thanks for them. Then he gave them to the people who were waiting to eat. He did the same with the fish. He gave them as much as they wanted. ¹²They all had plenty to eat. When they finished, Jesus said to his followers, "Gather the pieces of fish and bread that were not eaten. Don't waste anything." ¹³So they gathered up the pieces that were left. The people had started eating with only five loaves of barley bread. But the followers filled twelve large baskets with the pieces of food that were left.

¹⁴The people saw this miraculous sign that Jesus did and said, "He must be the Prophet[a] who is coming into the world."

¹⁵Jesus knew that the people planned to come get him and make him their king. So he left and went into the hills alone.

Jesus Walks on Water
(Mt. 14:22–27; Mk. 6:45–52)

¹⁶That evening Jesus' followers went down to the lake. ¹⁷It was dark now, and Jesus had not yet come back to them. They got into a boat and started going across the lake to Capernaum.* ¹⁸The wind was blowing very hard. The waves on the lake were becoming bigger. ¹⁹They rowed the boat about three or four miles.[b] Then they saw Jesus. He was walking on the water, coming to the boat. They were afraid. ²⁰But he said to them, "Don't be afraid. It's me." ²¹When he said this, they were glad to take him into the boat. And then the boat reached the shore at the place they wanted to go.

---

a **6:14 Prophet** They probably meant the prophet that God told Moses he would send. See Deut. 18:15–19.
b **6:19 three or four miles** Literally, "25 or 30 *stadia*," about 5 or 6 km.

The People Look for Jesus

²²The next day came. Some people had stayed on the other side of the lake. They knew that Jesus did not go with his followers in the boat. They knew that the followers had left in the boat alone. And they knew it was the only boat that was there. ²³But then some boats from Tiberias came and landed near the place where the people had eaten the day before. This was where they had eaten the bread after the Lord gave thanks. ²⁴The people saw that Jesus and his followers were not there now. So they got into the boats and went to Capernaum* to find Jesus.

Jesus, the Bread of Life

²⁵The people found Jesus on the other side of the lake. They asked him, "Teacher, when did you come here?"

²⁶He answered, "Why are you looking for me? Is it because you saw miraculous signs*? The truth is, you are looking for me because you ate the bread and were satisfied. ²⁷But earthly food spoils and ruins. So don't work to get that kind of food. But work to get the food that stays good and gives you eternal life. The Son of Man* will give you that food. He is the only one qualified by God the Father to give it to you."

²⁸The people asked Jesus, "What does God want us to do?"

²⁹Jesus answered, "The work God wants you to do is this: to believe in the one he sent."

³⁰So the people asked, "What miraculous sign will you do for us? If we can see you do a miracle, then we will believe you. What will you do? ³¹Our ancestors* were given manna* to eat in the desert.

As the Scriptures* say, 'He gave them bread from heaven to eat.'*[a]

32Jesus said, "I can assure you that Moses* was not the one who gave your people bread from heaven. But my Father gives you the true bread from heaven. 33God's bread is the one who comes down from heaven and gives life to the world."

34The people said, "Sir, from now on give us bread like that."

35Then Jesus said, "I am the bread that gives life. No one who comes to me will ever be hungry. No one who believes in me will ever be thirsty. 36I told you before that you have seen me, and still you don't believe. 37The Father gives me my people. Every one of them will come to me. I will always accept them. 38I came down from heaven to do what God wants, not what I want. 39I must not lose anyone God has given me. But I must raise them up on the last day. This is what the one who sent me wants me to do. 40Everyone who sees the Son and believes in him has eternal life. I will raise them up on the last day. This is what my Father wants."

41Some Jews began to complain about Jesus because he said, "I am the bread that comes down from heaven." 42They said, "This is Jesus. We know his father and mother. He is only Joseph's son. How can he say, 'I came down from heaven'?"

43But Jesus said, "Stop complaining to each other. 44The Father is the one who sent me, and he is the one who brings people to me. I will raise them up on the last day. Anyone the Father does not bring to me cannot come to me. 45It is written in the prophets*: 'God will teach them all.'[b] People listen to the Father and learn from him. They are the ones who come to me. 46I don't mean that there is anyone who has seen the Father. The only one who has ever seen the Father is the one who came from God. He has seen the Father.

47"I can assure you that anyone who believes has eternal life. 48I am the bread that gives life. 49Your ancestors ate the manna God gave them in the desert, but it didn't keep them from dying. 50Here is the bread that comes down from heaven. Whoever eats this bread will never die. 51I am the living bread that came down from heaven. Whoever eats this bread will live forever. This bread is my body. I will give my body so that the people in the world can have life."

52Then the Jews began to argue among themselves. They said, "How can this man give us his body to eat?"

53Jesus said, "Believe me when I say that you must eat the body of the Son of Man, and you must drink his blood. If you don't do this, you have no real life. 54Those who eat my body and drink my blood have eternal life. I will raise them up on the last day. 55My body is true food, and my blood is true drink. 56Those who eat my body and drink my blood live in me, and I live in them. 57"The Father sent me. He lives, and I live because of him. So everyone who eats me will live because of me. 58I am not like the bread that your ancestors ate.

a 6:31 Quote from Ps. 78:24.   b 6:45 Quote from Isa. 54:13.

They ate that bread, but they still died. I am the bread that came down from heaven. Whoever eats this bread will live forever."

59Jesus said all this while he was teaching in the synagogue* in the city of Capernaum.*

Many Followers Leave Jesus

60When Jesus' followers heard this, many of them said, "This teaching is hard. Who can accept it?"

61Jesus already knew that his followers were complaining about this. So he said, "Is this teaching a problem for you? 62Then what will you think when you see the Son of Man* going up to where he came from? 63It is the Spirit* that gives life. The body is of no value for that. But the things I have told you are from the Spirit, so they give life. 64But some of you don't believe." (Jesus knew the people who did not believe. He knew this from the beginning. And he knew the one who would hand him over to his enemies.) 65Jesus said, "That is why I said, 'Anyone the Father does not help to come to me cannot come.'"

66After Jesus said these things, many of his followers left and stopped following him.

67Jesus asked the twelve apostles,* "Do you want to leave too?"

68Simon Peter answered him, "Lord, where would we go? You have the words that give eternal life. 69We believe in you. We know that you are the Holy One from God."

70Then Jesus answered, "I chose all twelve of you. But one of you is a devil." 71He was talking about Judas, the son of Simon Iscariot. Judas was one of the twelve apostles, but later he would hand Jesus over to his enemies.

Jesus and His Brothers

7 1After this, Jesus traveled around the country of Galilee. He did not want to travel in Judea, because the Jewish leaders there wanted to kill him. 2It was time for the Jewish Festival of Shelters.* 3So his brothers said to him, "You should leave here and go to the festival in Judea. Then your followers there can see the miracles* you do. 4If you want to be well known, you must not hide what you do. So, if you can do such amazing things, let the whole world see you do them." 5Jesus' brothers said this because even they did not believe in him.

6Jesus said to them, "The right time for me has not yet come, but any time is right for you to go. 7The world cannot hate you. But the world hates me, because I tell the people in the world that they do evil things. 8So you go to the festival. I will not go now, because the right time for me has not yet come." 9After Jesus said this, he stayed in Galilee.

10So his brothers left to go to the festival. After they left, Jesus went too, but he did not let people see him. 11At the festival the Jewish leaders were looking for him. They said, "Where is that man?"

12There was a large group of people there. Many of them were talking secretly to each other about Jesus. Some people said, "He is a good man." But others said, "No, he fools the people." 13But no one was brave enough to talk about him openly. They were afraid of the Jewish leaders.

Jesus Teaches in Jerusalem

14When the festival was about half finished, Jesus went to the Temple* area and began to teach.

15The Jewish leaders were amazed and said, "How did this man learn so much? He never had the kind of teaching we had!" 16Jesus answered, "What I teach is not my own. My teaching comes from the one who sent me. 17People who really want to do what God wants will know that my teaching comes from God. They will know that this teaching is not my own. 18If I taught my own ideas, I would just be trying to get honor for myself. But if I am trying to bring honor to the one who sent me, I can be trusted. Anyone doing that is not going to lie. 19Moses* gave you the law,* right? But you don't obey that law. If you do, then why are you trying to kill me?"

20The people answered, "A demon* is making you crazy! We are not trying to kill you."

21Jesus said to them, "I did one miracle* on a Sabbath* day, and you were all surprised. 22But you obey the law Moses gave you about circumcision*—and sometimes you do it on a Sabbath day. (Really, Moses is not the one who gave you circumcision. It came from our ancestors* who lived before Moses.) Yes, you often circumcise baby boys on a Sabbath day. 23This shows that someone can be circumcised on a Sabbath day to obey the Law of Moses. So why are you angry with me for healing a person's whole body on the Sabbath day? 24Stop judging by the way things look. Be fair and judge by what is really right."

People Wonder if Jesus Is the Messiah

25Then some of the people who lived in Jerusalem said, "This is the man they are trying to kill. 26But he is teaching where everyone can see and hear him. And no one is trying to stop him from teaching. Maybe the leaders have decided that he really is the Messiah.* 27But when the real Messiah comes, no one will know where he comes from. And we know where this man's home is."

28Jesus was still teaching in the Temple* area when he said loudly, "Do you really know me and where I am from? I am here, but not by my own decision. I was sent by one who is very real. But you don't know him. 29I know him because I am from him. He is the one who sent me."

30When Jesus said this, the people tried to grab him. But no one was able even to touch him, because the right time for him had not yet come. 31But many of the people believed in Jesus. They said, "We are waiting for the Messiah to come. When he comes, will he do more miraculous signs* than this man has done?"

The Jewish Leaders Try to Arrest Jesus

32The Pharisees* heard what the people were saying about Jesus. So the leading priests and the Pharisees sent some Temple* police to arrest him. 33Then Jesus said, "I will be with you a little while longer. Then I will go back to the one who sent me. 34You will look for me, but you will not find me. And you cannot come where I am."

35These Jews said to each other, "Where will this man go that we cannot find him? Will he go to the Greek cities where our people live? Will he teach the Greek people there? 36He says, 'You will look for me, but you will not find me.' He also says, 'You cannot come where I am.' What does this mean?"

Jesus Talks About the Holy Spirit

37The last day of the festival came. It was the most important day. On that day Jesus stood up and said loudly, "Whoever is thirsty may come to me and drink. 38If anyone believes in me, rivers of living water will flow out from their heart. That is what the Scriptures* say." 39Jesus was talking about the Spirit.* The Spirit had not yet been given to people, because Jesus had not yet been raised to glory.* But later, those who believed in Jesus would receive the Spirit.

The People Argue About Jesus

40When the people heard the things that Jesus said, some of them said, "This man really is the Prophet.a"

41Other people said, "He is the Messiah.*"

And others said, "The Messiah will not come from Galilee. 42The Scriptures* say that the Messiah will come from the family of David.* And they say that he will come from Bethlehem, the town where David lived." 43So the people did not agree with each other about Jesus. 44Some of the people wanted to arrest him. But no one tried to do it.

The Jewish Leaders Refuse to Believe

45The Temple* police went back to the leading priests and the Pharisees.* The priests and the Pharisees asked, "Why didn't you bring Jesus?"

46The Temple police answered, "We have never heard anyone say such amazing things!"

47The Pharisees answered, "So he has fooled you too! 48You don't see any of the leaders or any of us Pharisees believing in him, do you? 49But those people out there know nothing about the law.* They are under God's curse!"

50But Nicodemus was there in that group. He was the one who had gone to see Jesus before.b He said, 51"Our law will not let us judge anyone without first hearing them and finding out what they have done."

52The Jewish leaders answered, "You must be from Galilee too! Study the Scriptures.* You will find nothing about a prophetc coming from Galilee."

A Woman Caught in Adultery

53Then they all left and went home.

8 1Jesus went to the Mount of Olives.* 2Early in the morning he went back to the Temple* area. The people all came to him, and he sat and taught them.

3The teachers of the law and the Pharisees* brought a woman they had caught in bed with a man who was not her husband. They forced her to stand in front of the people. 4They said to Jesus, "Teacher, this woman was caught in the act of adultery.* 5The Law of Moses* commands us to stone to death any such woman. What do you say we should do?"

6They were saying this to trick Jesus. They wanted to catch him saying something wrong so that they could have a charge against him. But Jesus stooped

---

a 7:40 Prophet They probably meant the prophet that God told Moses he would send. See Deut. 18:15-19.

b 7:50 He was the one ... before The story about Nicodemus going and talking to Jesus is in Jn. 3:1–21.

c 7:52 a prophet Two early Greek copies have "the Prophet," which would mean the "prophet like Moses" mentioned in Deut. 18:15. In Acts 3:22 and 7:37 this is understood to be the Messiah, as in verse 40 above.

Jesus tells about a good Samaritan
Luke 10:25–37

© WBTC 2011

Jesus tells about a lost sheep
Luke 15:1–7

down and started writing on the ground with his finger. [7]The Jewish leaders continued to ask him their question. So he stood up and said, "Anyone here who has never sinned should throw the first stone at her." [8]Then Jesus stooped down again and wrote on the ground.

[9]When they heard this, they began to leave one by one. The older men left first, and then the others. Jesus was left alone with the woman standing there in front of him. [10]He looked up again and said to her, "Where did they all go? Did no one judge you guilty?"

[11]She answered, "No one, sir."

Then Jesus said, "I don't judge you either. You can go now, but don't sin again."[a]

Jesus Is the Light of the World

[12]Later, Jesus talked to the people again. He said, "I am the light of the world. Whoever follows me will never live in darkness.* They will have the light that gives life."

[13]But the Pharisees* said to Jesus, "When you talk about yourself, you are the only one to say that these things are true. So we cannot accept what you say."

[14]Jesus answered, "Yes, I am saying these things about myself. But people can believe what I say, because I know where I came from. And I know where I am going. But you don't know where I came from or where I am going. [15]You judge me the way people judge other people. I don't judge anyone. [16]But if I judge, my judging is true, because when I judge I am not alone. The Father who sent me is

with me. [17]Your own law says that when two witnesses say the same thing, you must accept what they say. [18]I am one of the witnesses who speaks about myself. And the Father who sent me is my other witness."

[19]The people asked, "Where is your father?"

Jesus answered, "You don't know me or my Father. But if you knew me, you would know my Father too." [20]Jesus said these things while he was teaching in the Temple* area, near the room where the Temple offerings were kept. But no one arrested him, because the right time for him had not yet come.

Some Jews Don't Understand Jesus

[21]Again, Jesus said to the people, "I will leave you. You will look for me, but you will die in your sin. You cannot come where I am going."

[22]So the Jewish leaders asked themselves, "Will he kill himself? Is that why he said, 'You cannot come where I am going'?"

[23]But Jesus said to them, "You people are from here below, but I am from above. You belong to this world, but I don't belong to this world. [24]I told you that you would die in your sins. Yes, if you don't believe that I Am,[b] you will die in your sins."

[25]They asked, "Then who are you?"

Jesus answered, "I am what I have told you from the beginning. [26]I have much more I could say to judge you. But I tell people only

[b] 8:24 I Am This is like the name of God used in the Old Testament. See Isa. 41:4; 43:10; Ex. 3:14. However, it can also mean "I am he," meaning "I am the Messiah." Also in verses 28, 58.

[a] 8:11 The oldest and best Greek copies do not have verses 7:53–8:11. Other copies have this section in different places.

what I have heard from the one who sent me, and he speaks the truth."

27They did not understand who he was talking about. He was telling them about the Father. 28So he said to them, "You will lift up*a* the Son of Man.* Then you will know that I Am. You will know that whatever I do is not by my own authority. You will know that I say only what the Father has taught me. 29The one who sent me is with me. I always do what pleases him. So he has not left me alone." 30While he was saying these things, many people believed in him.

Jesus Talks About Freedom From Sin

31So Jesus said to the Jews who believed in him, "If you continue to accept and obey my teaching, you are really my followers. 32You will know the truth, and the truth will make you free."

33They answered, "We are Abraham's* descendants. And we have never been slaves. So why do you say that we will be free?"

34Jesus said, "The truth is, everyone who sins is a slave—a slave to sin. 35A slave does not stay with a family forever. But a son belongs to the family forever. 36So if the Son makes you free, you are really free. 37I know you are Abraham's descendants. But you want to kill me, because you don't want to accept my teaching. 38I am telling you what my Father has shown me. But you do what your father has told you."

39They said, "Our father is Abraham."

Jesus said, "If you were really Abraham's descendants, you would do what Abraham did. 40I am someone who has told you the truth I heard from God. But you are trying to kill me. Abraham did nothing like that. 41So you are doing what your own father did."

But they said, "We are not like children who never knew who their father was. God is our Father. He is the only Father we have."

42Jesus said to them, "If God were really your Father, you would love me. I came from God, and now I am here. I did not come by my own authority. God sent me. 43You don't understand the things I say, because you cannot accept my teaching. 44Your father is the devil. You belong to him. You want to do what he wants. He was a murderer from the beginning. He was always against the truth. There is no truth in him. He is like the lies he tells. Yes, the devil is a liar. He is the father of lies.

45"I am telling you the truth, and that's why you don't believe me. 46Can any of you prove that I am guilty of sin? If I tell the truth, why don't you believe me? 47Whoever belongs to God accepts what he says. But you don't accept what God says, because you don't belong to God."

Jesus Talks About Himself and Abraham

48The Jews there answered, "We say you are a Samaritan.* We say a demon* is making you crazy! Are we not right when we say this?"

49Jesus answered, "I have no demon in me. I give honor to my Father, but you give no honor to me. 50I am not trying to get honor for myself. There is one who wants this honor for me. He is the judge. 51I promise you, whoever

a 8:28 lift up Meaning to be nailed to a cross and "lifted up" on it to die. It may also have a second meaning: to be "lifted up" from death to heaven.

continues to obey my teaching will never die."

⁵²The Jews said to Jesus, "Now we know that you have a demon in you! Even Abraham* and the prophets* died. But you say, 'Whoever obeys my teaching will never die.' ⁵³Do you think you are greater than our father Abraham? He died, and so did the prophets. Who do you think you are?"

⁵⁴Jesus answered, "If I give honor to myself, that honor is worth nothing. The one who gives me honor is my Father. And you say that he is your God. ⁵⁵But you don't really know him. I know him. If I said I did not know him, I would be a liar like you. But I do know him, and I obey what he says. ⁵⁶Your father* Abraham was very happy that he would see the day when I came. He saw that day and was happy."

⁵⁷The Jews said to Jesus, "What? How can you say you have seen Abraham? You are not even 50 years old!"

⁵⁸Jesus answered, "The fact is, before Abraham was born, I Aм."
⁵⁹When he said this, they picked up stones to throw at him. But Jesus hid, and then he left the Temple* area.

Jesus Heals a Man Born Blind

9 ¹While Jesus was walking, he saw a man who had been blind since the time he was born. ²Jesus' followers asked him, "Teacher, why was this man born blind? Whose sin made it happen? Was it his own sin or that of his parents?"

³Jesus answered, "It was not any sin of this man or his parents that caused him to be blind. He was born blind so that he could be used to show what great things God can do. ⁴While it is daytime, we must continue doing the work of the one who sent me. The night is coming, and no one can work at night. ⁵While I am in the world, I am the light of the world."

⁶After Jesus said this, he spit on the dirt, made some mud and put it on the man's eyes. ⁷Jesus told him, "Go and wash in Siloam pool." (Siloam means "Sent.") So the man went to the pool, washed and came back. He was now able to see.

⁸His neighbors and some others who had seen him begging said, "Look! Is this the same man who always sits and begs?"

⁹Some people said, "Yes! He is the one." But others said, "No, he can't be the same man. He only looks like him."

So the man himself said, "I am that same man."

¹⁰They asked, "What happened? How did you get your sight?"

¹¹He answered, "The man they call Jesus made some mud and put it on my eyes. Then he told me to go to Siloam and wash. So I went there and washed. And then I could see."

¹²They asked him, "Where is this man?"

He answered, "I don't know."

Some Pharisees Have Questions

¹³Then the people brought the man to the Pharisees.* ¹⁴The day Jesus had made mud and healed the man's eyes was a Sabbath* day. ¹⁵So the Pharisees asked the man, "How did you get your sight?"

He answered, "He put mud on my eyes. I washed, and now I can see."

¹⁶Some of the Pharisees said, "That man does not obey the law about the Sabbath day. So he is not from God."

Others said, "But someone who is a sinner cannot do these miraculous signs.*" So they could not agree with each other.

17They asked the man again, "Since it was your eyes he healed, what do you say about him?"

He answered, "He is a prophet.*"

18The Jewish leaders still did not believe that this really happened to the man—that he was blind and was now healed. But later they sent for his parents. 19They asked them, "Is this your son? You say he was born blind. So how can he see?"

20His parents answered, "We know that this man is our son. And we know that he was born blind. 21But we don't know why he can see now. We don't know who healed his eyes. Ask him. He is old enough to answer for himself." 22They said this because they were afraid of the Jewish leaders. The leaders had already decided that they would punish anyone who said Jesus was the Messiah.* They would stop them from coming to the synagogue.* 23That is why his parents said, "He is old enough. Ask him."

24So the Jewish leaders called the man who had been blind. They told him to come in again. They said, "You should honor God by telling the truth. We know that this man is a sinner."

25The man answered, "I don't know if he is a sinner. But I do know this: I was blind, and now I can see."

26They asked, "What did he do to you? How did he heal your eyes?"

27He answered, "I have already told you that. But you would not listen to me. Why do you want to hear it again? Do you want to be his followers too?"

28At this they shouted insults at him and said, "You are his follower, not us! We are followers of Moses.* 29We know that God spoke to Moses. But we don't even know where this man comes from!"

30The man answered, "This is really strange! You don't know where he comes from, but he healed my eyes. 31We all know that God does not listen to sinners, but he will listen to anyone who worships and obeys him. 32This is the first time we have ever heard of anyone healing the eyes of someone born blind. 33This man must be from God. If he were not from God, he could not do anything like this."

34The Jewish leaders answered, "You were born full of sin! Are you trying to teach us?" And they told the man to get out of the synagogue and to stay out.

Spiritual Blindness

35When Jesus heard that they had forced the man to leave, he found him and asked him, "Do you believe in the Son of Man*?"

36The man said, "Tell me who he is, sir, so I can believe in him."

37Jesus said to him, "You have already seen him. The Son of Man is the one talking with you now."

38The man answered, "Yes, I believe, Lord!" Then he bowed and worshiped Jesus.

39Jesus said, "I came into this world so that the world could be judged. I came so that people who are blind*a* could see. And I came

---

a **9:39 people who are blind** Jesus is talking about people who are spiritually blind (without understanding), not physically blind.

so that people who think they see would become blind."

40Some of the Pharisees* were near Jesus. They heard him say this. They asked, "What? Are you saying that we are blind too?"

41Jesus said, "If you were really blind, you would not be guilty of sin. But you say that you see, so you are still guilty."

The Shepherd and His Sheep

10 1Jesus said, "It is certainly true that when a man enters the sheep pen, he should use the gate. If he climbs in some other way, he is a robber. He is trying to steal the sheep. 2But the man who takes care of the sheep enters through the gate. He is the shepherd. 3The man who guards the gate opens the gate for the shepherd. And the sheep listen to the voice of the shepherd. He calls his own sheep, using their names, and he leads them out. 4He brings all of his sheep out. Then he goes ahead of them and leads them. The sheep follow him, because they know his voice. 5But sheep will never follow someone they don't know. They will run away from him, because they don't know his voice."

6Jesus told the people this story, but they did not understand what it meant.

Jesus Is the Good Shepherd

7So Jesus said again, "I assure you, I am the gate for the sheep. 8All those who came before me were thieves and robbers. The sheep did not listen to them. 9I am the gate. Whoever enters through me will be saved. They will be able to come in and go out. They will find everything they need. 10A thief comes to steal, kill, and destroy. But I came to give life—life that is full and good.

11"I am the good shepherd, and the good shepherd gives his life for the sheep. 12The worker who is paid to keep the sheep is different from the shepherd. The paid worker does not own the sheep. So when he sees a wolf coming, he runs away and leaves the sheep alone. Then the wolf attacks the sheep and scatters them. 13The man runs away because he is only a paid worker. He does not really care for the sheep.

14-15"I am the shepherd who cares for the sheep. I know my sheep just as the Father knows me. And my sheep know me just as I know the Father. I give my life for these sheep. 16I have other sheep too. They are not in this flock here. I must lead them also. They will listen to my voice. In the future there will be one flock and one shepherd.a 17The Father loves me because I give my life. I give my life so that I can get it back again. 18No one takes my life away from me. I give my own life freely. I have the right to give my life, and I have the right to get it back again. This is what the Father told me."

19Again the Jews were divided over what Jesus was saying. 20Many of them said, "A demon* has come into him and made him crazy. Why listen to him?" 21But others said, "These aren't the words of someone controlled by a demon. A demon cannot heal the eyes of a blind man."

a **10:16 I have other sheep ... shepherd** Jesus means he has followers who are not Jews. See Jn. 11:52.

The Jewish Leaders Against Jesus

22It was winter, and the time came for the Festival of Dedication[a] at Jerusalem. 23Jesus was in the Temple* area at Solomon's Porch.* 24The Jewish leaders gathered around him. They said, "How long will you make us wonder about you? If you are the Messiah,* then tell us clearly."

25Jesus answered, "I told you already, but you did not believe. I do miracles* in my Father's name. These miracles show who I am. 26But you do not believe, because you are not my sheep. 27My sheep listen to my voice. I know them, and they follow me. 28I give my sheep eternal life. They will never die, and no one can take them out of my hand. 29My Father is the one who gave them to me, and he is greater than all.[b] No one can steal my sheep out of his hand. 30The Father and I are one."

31Again the Jews there picked up stones to kill Jesus. 32But he said to them, "The many wonderful things you have seen me do are from the Father. Which of these good things are you killing me for?"

33They answered, "We are not killing you for any good thing you did. But you say things that insult God. You are only a man, but you say you are the same as God! That is why we are trying to kill you!"

34Jesus answered, "It is written in your law that God said, 'I said

you are gods.'[c] 35This Scripture* called those people gods—the people who received God's message. And Scripture is always true. 36So why do you accuse me of insulting God for saying, 'I am God's Son'? I am the one God chose and sent into the world. 37If I don't do what my Father does, then don't believe what I say. 38But if I do what my Father does, you should believe in what I do. You might not believe in me, but you should believe in the things I do. Then you will know and understand that the Father is in me and I am in the Father."

39They tried to get Jesus again, but he escaped from them.

40Then he went back across the Jordan River to the place where John* began his work of baptizing* people. Jesus stayed there, 41and many people came to him. They said, "John never did any miraculous signs,* but everything John said about this man is true." 42And many people there believed in Jesus.

The Death of Lazarus

11 1There was a man named Lazarus who was sick. He lived in the town of Bethany, where Mary and her sister Martha lived. 2(Mary is the same woman who put perfume on the Lord and wiped his feet with her hair.) Mary's brother was Lazarus, the man who was now sick. 3So Mary and Martha sent someone to tell Jesus, "Lord, your dear friend Lazarus is sick."

4When Jesus heard this he said, "The end of this sickness will not be death. No, this sickness is for the glory* of God. This has

a 10:22 Festival of Dedication Hanukkah, or "Festival of Lights," a special week in December celebrating the time in 165 B.C. when the Jerusalem Temple was made pure and ready again for Jewish worship. Before then it had been under the control of a foreign (Greek) army and used for pagan worship.
b 10:29 he ... than all Some Greek copies have "they are greater than all."
c 10:34 Quote from Ps. 82:6.

happened to bring glory to the Son of God." [5]Jesus loved Martha and her sister and Lazarus. [6]So when he heard that Lazarus was sick, he stayed where he was two more days [7]and then said to his followers, "We should go back to Judea."

[8]They answered, "But Teacher, those Jews there tried to stone you to death. That was only a short time ago. Now you want to go back there?"

[9]Jesus answered, "There are twelve hours of light in the day. Whoever walks in the day will not stumble and fall because they can see with the light from the sun.[a] [10]But whoever walks at night will stumble because there is no light."

[11]Then Jesus said, "Our friend Lazarus is now sleeping, but I am going there to wake him."

[12]The followers answered, "But, Lord, if he can sleep, he will get well." [13]They thought Jesus meant that Lazarus was literally sleeping, but he really meant that Lazarus was dead.

[14]So then Jesus said plainly, "Lazarus is dead. [15]And I am glad I was not there. I am happy for you because now you will believe in me. We will go to him now."

[16]Then Thomas, the one called "Twin," said to the other followers, "We will go too. We will die there with Jesus."

Jesus in Bethany

[17]Jesus arrived in Bethany and found that Lazarus had already been dead and in the tomb* for four days. [18]Bethany was about two miles[b] from Jerusalem. [19]Many Jews had come to see Martha and Mary. They came to comfort them about their brother Lazarus.

[20]When Martha heard that Jesus was coming, she went out to greet him. But Mary stayed home. [21]Martha said to Jesus, "Lord, if you had been here, my brother would not have died. [22]But I know that even now God will give you anything you ask."

[23]Jesus said, "Your brother will rise and be alive again."

[24]Martha answered, "I know that he will rise to live again at the time of the resurrection* on the last day."

[25]Jesus said to her, "I am the resurrection. I am life. Everyone who believes in me will have life, even if they die. [26]And everyone who lives and believes in me will never really die. Martha, do you believe this?"

[27]Martha answered, "Yes, Lord. I believe that you are the Messiah,* the Son of God. You are the one who was coming to the world."

Jesus Cries

[28]After Martha said these things, she went back to her sister Mary. She talked to Mary alone and said, "The Teacher is here. He is asking for you." [29]When Mary heard this, she stood up and went quickly to Jesus. [30]He had not yet come into the village. He was still at the place where Martha met him. [31]The Jews who were in the house comforting Mary saw her get up and leave quickly. They thought she was going to the tomb* to cry there. So they followed her. [32]Mary went to the place where Jesus was. When she saw him, she bowed at his feet and said, "Lord, if you had been here, my brother would not have died."

a **11:9 from the sun** Literally, "of this world."
b **11:18 two miles** Literally, "15 *stadia*," almost 3 km.

³³When Jesus saw Mary crying and the people with her crying too, he was very upset and deeply troubled. ³⁴He asked, "Where did you put him?"

They said, "Lord, come and see."

³⁵Jesus cried.

³⁶And the Jews said, "Look! He loved Lazarus very much!"

³⁷But some of them said, "Jesus healed the eyes of the blind man. Why didn't he help Lazarus and stop him from dying?"

Jesus Raises Lazarus From Death

³⁸Again feeling very upset, Jesus came to the tomb.* It was a cave with a large stone covering the entrance. ³⁹He said, "Move the stone away."

Martha said, "But, Lord, it has been four days since Lazarus died. There will be a bad smell." Martha was the sister of the dead man.

⁴⁰Then Jesus said to her, "Remember what I told you? I said that if you believed, you would see God's divine greatness.*"

⁴¹So they moved the stone away from the entrance. Then Jesus looked up and said, "Father, I thank you that you heard me. ⁴²I know that you always hear me. But I said these things because of the people here around me. I want them to believe that you sent me."

⁴³After Jesus said this he called in a loud voice, "Lazarus, come out!" ⁴⁴The dead man came out. His hands and feet were wrapped with pieces of cloth. He had a handkerchief covering his face.

Jesus said to the people, "Take off the cloth and let him go."

The Jewish Leaders Plan to Kill Jesus

(Mt. 26:1–5; Mk. 14:1–2; Lk. 22:1–2)

⁴⁵There were many Jews who came to visit Mary. When they saw what Jesus did, many of them believed in him. ⁴⁶But some of them went to the Pharisees* and told them what Jesus did. ⁴⁷Then the leading priests and Pharisees called a meeting of the high council. They said, "What should we do? This man is doing many miraculous signs.* ⁴⁸If we let him continue doing these things, everyone will believe in him. Then the Romans will come and take away our Temple* and our nation."

⁴⁹One of the men there was Caiaphas. He was the high priest* that year. He said, "You people know nothing! ⁵⁰It is better for one man to die for the people than for the whole nation to be destroyed. But you don't realize this."

⁵¹Caiaphas did not think of this himself. As that year's high priest, he was really prophesying* that Jesus would die for the Jewish people. ⁵²Yes, he would die for the Jewish people. But he would also die for God's other children scattered all over the world. He would die to bring them all together and make them one people.

⁵³That day the Jewish leaders began planning to kill Jesus. ⁵⁴So Jesus stopped traveling around openly among the Jews. He went away to a town called Ephraim in an area near the desert. He stayed there with his followers.

⁵⁵It was almost time for the Jewish Passover* festival. Many people from the country went to Jerusalem before the Passover. They went to do the special things to make themselves pure for the festival. ⁵⁶The people looked for Jesus. They stood in the Temple area and asked each other, "Is he coming to the festival? What do you think?" ⁵⁷But the leading

priests and the Pharisees had given a special order about Jesus. They said that anyone who knew where he was must tell them so that they could arrest him.

Jesus in Bethany With His Friends
(Mt. 26:6–13; Mk. 14:3–9)

12 ¹Six days before the Passover* festival, Jesus went to Bethany. That is where Lazarus lived, the man Jesus raised from death. ²There they had a dinner for Jesus. Martha served the food, and Lazarus was one of the people eating with Jesus. ³Mary brought in a pint*a* of expensive perfume made of pure nard.* She poured the perfume on Jesus' feet. Then she wiped his feet with her hair. And the sweet smell from the perfume filled the whole house.

⁴Judas Iscariot, one of Jesus' followers, was there—the one who would later hand Jesus over to his enemies. Judas said, ⁵"That perfume was worth a full year's pay.*b* It should have been sold, and the money should have been given to the poor people." ⁶But Judas did not really care about the poor. He said this because he was a thief. He was the one who kept the moneybag for the group of followers. And he often stole money from the bag.

⁷Jesus answered, "Don't stop her. It was right for her to save this perfume for today—the day for me to be prepared for burial. ⁸You will always have those who are poor with you.*c* But you will not always have me."

The Plot Against Lazarus
⁹Many of the Jews heard that Jesus was in Bethany, so they went there to see him. They also went there to see Lazarus, the one Jesus raised from death. ¹⁰So the leading priests made plans to kill Lazarus too. ¹¹Because of him, many Jews were leaving them and believing in Jesus. That is why they wanted to kill Lazarus too.

Jesus Enters Jerusalem Like a King
(Mt. 21:1–11; Mk. 11:1–11; Lk. 19:28–40)

¹²The next day the people in Jerusalem heard that Jesus was coming there. These were the crowds of people who had come to the Passover* festival. ¹³They took branches of palm trees and went out to meet Jesus. They shouted,

"'Praise*d* Him!'
'Welcome! God bless the one
    who comes in the name of
    the Lord!'   *Psalm 118:25–26*

God bless the King of Israel!"
¹⁴Jesus found a donkey and rode on it, as the Scriptures* say,
¹⁵ "Do not be afraid, people of
    Zion*e*!
    Look! Your king is coming.
    He is riding on a young
    donkey."   *Zechariah 9:9*

¹⁶The followers of Jesus did not understand at that time what was happening. But after he was raised to glory,* they understood that this was written about him. Then they remembered that they had done these things for him.

---

a **12:3 pint** Literally, "*litra*," a Roman pound, equal to 327 grams (11.5 ounces).
b **12:5 a full year's pay** Literally, "300 denarii." One Roman denarius, a silver coin, was the average pay for one day's work.
c **12:8 You will ... with you** See Deut. 15:11.
d **12:13 Praise** Literally, "Hosanna," a Hebrew word used in praying to God for help. Here, it was probably a shout of celebration used in praising God or his Messiah.
e **12:15 people of Zion** Literally, "daughter of Zion," meaning the city of Jerusalem. See "Zion" in the Word List.

17There were many people with Jesus when he raised Lazarus from death and told him to come out of the tomb.* Now they were telling others about what Jesus did. 18That's why so many people went out to meet him—because they had heard about this miraculous sign* he did. 19So the Pharisees* said to each other, "Look! Our plan is not working. The people are all following him!"

Jesus Talks About Life and Death

20There were some Greeks* there too. These were some of the people who went to Jerusalem to worship at the Passover* festival. 21They went to Philip, who was from Bethsaida in Galilee. They said, "Sir, we want to meet Jesus." 22Philip went and told Andrew. Then Andrew and Philip went and told Jesus.

23Jesus said to them, "The time has come for the Son of Man* to receive his glory.* 24It is a fact that a grain of wheat must fall to the ground and die before it can grow and produce much more wheat. If it never dies, it will never be more than a single seed. 25Whoever loves the life they have now will lose it. But whoever is willing to give up their life in this world will keep it. They will have eternal life. 26Whoever serves me must follow me. My servants must be with me everywhere I am. My Father will give honor to anyone who serves me.

Jesus Talks About His Death

27"Now I am very troubled. What should I say? Should I say, 'Father save me from this time of suffering'? No, I came to this time so that I could suffer. 28Father, do what will bring you glory*!"

Then a voice came from heaven, "I have already brought glory to myself. I will do it again."

29The people standing there heard the voice. They said it was thunder.

But others said, "An angel spoke to him!"

30Jesus said, "That voice was for you and not for me. 31Now is the time for the world to be judged. Now the ruler of this world* will be thrown out. 32I will be lifted up[a] from the earth. When that happens, I will draw all people to myself." 33Jesus said this to show how he would die.

34The people said, "But our law says that the Messiah* will live forever. So why do you say, 'The Son of Man* must be lifted up'? Who is this 'Son of Man'?"

35Then Jesus said, "The light[b] will be with you for only a short time more. So walk while you have the light. Then the darkness* will not catch you. People who walk in the darkness don't know where they are going. 36So put your trust in the light while you still have it. Then you will be children of light." When Jesus finished saying these things, he went away to a place where the people could not find him.

Some Jews Refuse to Believe in Jesus

37The people saw all these miraculous signs* Jesus did, but they still did not believe in him. 38This was to give full meaning to what Isaiah the prophet* said:

---

a 12:32 **lifted up** Meaning to be nailed to a cross and "lifted up" on it to die. It may also have a second meaning: to be "lifted up" from death to heaven. Also in verse 34.
b 12:35 **light** This means Christ, as in Jn. 1:5–9. Also, it is a symbol of goodness and truth, qualities associated with Christ and his kingdom.

"Lord, who believed what we
told them?
Who has seen the Lord's
power?" *Isaiah 53:1*

[39] This is why the people could not believe. Because Isaiah also said,

[40] "God made the people blind.
He closed their minds.
He did this so that they would
not see with their eyes
and understand with their
minds.
He did it so that they would
not turn and be healed."
Isaiah 6:10

[41] Isaiah said this because he saw Jesus' divine greatness.* So he spoke about him.

[42] But many people believed in Jesus. Even many of the Jewish leaders believed in him, but they were afraid of the Pharisees,* so they did not say openly that they believed. They were afraid they would be ordered to stay out of the synagogue.* [43] They loved praise from people more than praise from God.

Jesus' Teaching Will Judge People

[44] Then Jesus said loudly, "Everyone who believes in me is really believing in the one who sent me. [45] Everyone who sees me is really seeing the one who sent me. [46] I came into this world as a light. I came so that everyone who believes in me will not stay in darkness.

[47] "I did not come into the world to judge people. I came to save the people in the world. So I am not the one who judges those who hear my teaching and do not obey. [48] But there is a judge for all those who refuse to believe in me and do not accept what I say. The message I have spoken will judge them on the last day.

[49] That is because what I taught was not from myself. The Father who sent me told me what to say and what to teach. [50] And I know that whatever he says to do will bring eternal life. So the things I say are exactly what the Father told me to say."

Jesus Washes His Followers' Feet

13 [1] It was almost time for the Jewish Passover* festival. Jesus knew that the time had come for him to leave this world and go back to the Father. Jesus had always loved the people in the world who were his. Now was the time he showed them his love the most.

[2] Jesus and his followers were at the evening meal. The devil had already persuaded Judas Iscariot to hand Jesus over to his enemies. (Judas was the son of Simon.) [3] The Father had given Jesus power over everything. Jesus knew this. He also knew that he had come from God. And he knew that he was going back to God. [4] So while they were eating, Jesus stood up and took off his robe. He got a towel and wrapped it around his waist. [5] Then he poured water into a bowl and began to wash the followers' feet.*a* He dried their feet with the towel that was wrapped around his waist.

[6] He came to Simon Peter. But Peter said to him, "Lord, you should not wash my feet."

[7] Jesus answered, "You don't know what I am doing now. But later you will understand."

---

a **13:5 wash … feet** A social custom of the first century, because people wore open sandals on very dusty roads. It was a humble duty, usually done by a servant. Also in verses 6–14.

8Peter said, "No! You will never wash my feet."

Jesus answered, "If I don't wash your feet, you are not one of my people."

9Simon Peter said, "Lord, after you wash my feet, wash my hands and my head too!"

10Jesus said, "After a person has a bath, his whole body is clean. He needs only to wash his feet. And you are clean, but not all of you." 11Jesus knew who would hand him over to his enemies. That is why he said, "Not all of you are clean."

12When Jesus finished washing their feet, he put on his clothes and went back to the table. He asked, "Do you understand what I did for you? 13You call me 'Teacher.' And you call me 'Lord.' And this is right, because that is what I am. 14I am your Lord and Teacher. But I washed your feet. So you also should wash each other's feet. 15I did this as an example for you. So you should serve each other just as I served you. 16Believe me, servants are not greater than their master. Those who are sent to do something are not greater than the one who sent them. 17If you know these things, great blessings will be yours if you do them. 18"I am not talking about all of you. I know the people I have chosen. But what the Scriptures* say must happen: 'The man who shared my food has turned against me.'a 19I am telling you this now before it happens. Then when it happens, you will believe

that I AM.b 20I assure you, whoever accepts the person I send also accepts me. And whoever accepts me also accepts the one who sent me."

Jesus Tells Who Will Turn Against Him
(Mt. 26:20–25; Mk. 14:17–21; Lk. 22:21–23)

21After Jesus said these things, he felt very troubled. He said openly, "Believe me when I say that one of you will hand me over to my enemies."

22His followers all looked at each other. They did not understand who Jesus was talking about. 23One of the followers was next to Jesus and was leaning close to him. This was the one Jesus loved very much. 24Simon Peter made signs to this follower to ask Jesus who he was talking about.

25That follower leaned closer to Jesus and asked, "Lord, who is it?"

26Jesus answered him, "I will dip this bread into the dish. The man I give it to is the one." So Jesus took a piece of bread, dipped it, and gave it to Judas Iscariot, the son of Simon. 27When Judas took the bread, Satan* entered him. Jesus said to Judas, "What you will do—do it quickly!" 28No one at the table understood why Jesus said this to Judas. 29Since Judas was the one in charge of the money, some of them thought that Jesus meant for him to go and buy some things they needed for the feast. Or they thought that Jesus wanted him to go give something to the poor.

a **13:18 has turned against me** Literally, "has lifted up his heel against me." Quote from Ps. 41:9.

b **13:19 I AM** This is like the name of God used in the Old Testament. See Isa. 41:4; 43:10; Ex. 3:14. However, it can also mean "I am he," meaning "I am the Messiah."

[30]Judas ate the bread Jesus gave him. Then he immediately went out. It was night.

Jesus Talks About His Death

[31]When Judas was gone, Jesus said, "Now is the time for the Son of Man* to receive his glory.* And God will receive glory through him. [32]If God receives glory through him, he will give glory to the Son through himself. And that will happen very soon."

[33]Jesus said, "My children, I will be with you only a short time more. You will look for me, but I tell you now what I told the Jewish leaders: Where I am going you cannot come.

[34]"I give you a new command: Love each other. You must love each other just as I loved you. [35]All people will know that you are my followers if you love each other."

Jesus Says Peter Will Deny Him

(Mt. 26:31–35; Mk. 14:27–31; Lk. 22:31–34)

[36]Simon Peter asked Jesus, "Lord, where are you going?"

Jesus answered, "Where I am going you cannot follow now. But you will follow later."

[37]Peter asked, "Lord, why can't I follow you now? I am ready to die for you!"

[38]Jesus answered, "Will you really give your life for me? The truth is, before the rooster crows, you will say three times that you don't know me."

Jesus Comforts His Followers

14 [1]Jesus said, "Don't be troubled. Trust in God, and trust in me. [2]There are many rooms in my Father's house. I would not tell you this if it were not true. I am going there to prepare a place for you. [3]After I go and prepare a place for you, I will come back. Then I will take you with me, so that you can be where I am. [4]You know the way to the place where I am going."

[5]Thomas said, "Lord, we don't know where you are going, so how can we know the way?"

[6]Jesus answered, "I am the way, the truth, and the life. The only way to the Father is through me. [7]If you really knew me, you would know my Father too. But now you know the Father. You have seen him."

[8]Philip said to him, "Lord, show us the Father. That is all we need."

[9]Jesus answered, "Philip, I have been with you for a long time. So you should know me. Anyone who has seen me has seen the Father too. So why do you say, 'Show us the Father'? [10]Don't you believe that I am in the Father and the Father is in me? The things I have told you don't come from me. The Father lives in me, and he is doing his own work. [11]Believe me when I say that I am in the Father and the Father is in me. Or believe because of the miracles* I have done.

[12]"I can assure you that whoever believes in me will do the same things I have done. And they will do even greater things than I have done, because I am going to the Father. [13]And if you ask for anything in my name, I will do it for you. Then the Father's glory* will be shown through the Son. [14]If you ask me for anything in my name, I will do it.

The Promise of the Holy Spirit

[15]"If you love me, you will do what I command. [16]I will ask the Father, and he will give you another Helper[a] to be with you

a **14:16 Helper** Or "Comforter," the Holy Spirit (see "HOLY SPIRIT" in the Word List). Also in verse 26.

forever. ¹⁷The Helper is the Spirit of truth.ᵃ The people of the world cannot accept him, because they don't see him or know him. But you know him. He lives with you, and he will be in you.

¹⁸"I will not leave you all alone like orphans. I will come back to you. ¹⁹In a very short time the people in the world will not see me anymore. But you will see me. You will live because I live. ²⁰On that day you will know that I am in the Father. You will know that you are in me and I am in you. ²¹Those who really love me are the ones who not only know my commands but also obey them. My Father will love such people, and I will love them. I will make myself known to them."

²²Then Judas (not Judas Iscariot) said, "Lord, how will you make yourself known to us, but not to the world?"

²³Jesus answered, "All who love me will obey my teaching. My Father will love them. My Father and I will come to them and live with them. ²⁴But anyone who does not love me does not obey my teaching. This teaching that you hear is not really mine. It is from my Father who sent me.

²⁵"I have told you all these things while I am with you. ²⁶But the Helper will teach you everything and cause you to remember all that I told you. This Helper is the Holy Spirit* that the Father will send in my name. ²⁷"I leave you peace. It is my own peace I give you. I give you peace in a different way than the world does. So don't be troubled. Don't be afraid. ²⁸You heard me say to you, 'I am leaving, but I will come back to you.' If you loved me, you would be happy that I am going back to the Father, because the Father is greater than I am. ²⁹I have told you this now, before it happens. Then when it happens, you will believe.

³⁰"I will not talk with you much longer. The ruler of this world* is coming. He has no power over me. ³¹But the world must know that I love the Father. So I do exactly what the Father told me to do. "Come now, let's go."

Jesus Is Like a Vine

15 ¹Jesus said, "I am the true vine, and my Father is the gardener. ²He cuts off every branchᵇ of mine that does not produce fruit.ᶜ He also trims every branch that produces fruit to prepare it to produce even more. ³You have already been prepared to produce more fruit by the teaching I have given you. ⁴Stay joined to me and I will stay joined to you. No branch can produce fruit alone. It must stay connected to the vine. It is the same with you. You cannot produce fruit alone. You must stay joined to me.

⁵"I am the vine, and you are the branches. If you stay joined to me, and I to you, you will produce plenty of fruit. But separated from me you won't be able to do anything. ⁶If you don't stay joined to me, you will be like a branch that has been thrown out and has dried up. All the dead

---

ᵃ **14:17 Spirit of truth** The Holy Spirit (see "HOLY SPIRIT" in the Word List). It was his work to help Jesus' followers understand God's truth. See Jn. 16:13.
ᵇ **15:2 branch** The "branches" are Jesus' followers. See verse 5.
ᶜ **15:2 produce fruit** Meaning the way Jesus' followers must live to show they belong to him. See verses 7–10.

branches like that are gathered up, thrown into the fire and burned. [7]Stay joined together with me, and follow my teachings. If you do this, you can ask for anything you want, and it will be given to you. [8]Show that you are my followers by producing much fruit. This will bring honor[a] to my Father.

[9]"I have loved you as the Father has loved me. Now continue in my love. [10]I have obeyed my Father's commands, and he continues to love me. In the same way, if you obey my commands, I will continue to love you. [11]I have told you these things so that you can have the true happiness that I have. I want you to be completely happy. [12]This is what I command you: Love each other as I have loved you. [13]The greatest love people can show is to die for their friends. [14]You are my friends if you do what I tell you to do. [15]I no longer call you servants, because servants don't know what their master is doing. But now I call you friends, because I have told you everything that my Father told me. [16]"You did not choose me. I chose you. And I gave you this work: to go and produce fruit—fruit that will last. Then the Father will give you anything you ask for in my name. [17]This is my command: Love each other.

Jesus Warns His Followers

[18]"If the world hates you, remember that they hated me first. [19]If you belonged to the world, the world would love you as it loves its own people. But I have chosen you to be different from those in the world. So you don't belong to the world, and that is why the world hates you.

[20]"Remember the lesson I told you: Servants are not greater than their master. If people treated me badly, they will treat you badly too. And if they obeyed my teaching, they will obey yours too. [21]They will do to you whatever they did to me, because you belong to me. They don't know the one who sent me. [22]If I had not come and spoken to the people of the world, they would not be guilty of sin. But now I have spoken to them. So they have no excuse for their sin.

[23]"Whoever hates me also hates my Father. [24]I did things among the people of the world that no one else has ever done. If I had not done those things, they would not be guilty of sin. But they have seen what I did, and still they hate me and my Father. [25]But this happened to make clear the full meaning of what is written in their law: 'They hated me for no reason.'[b]

[26]"I will send you the Helper[c] from the Father. The Helper is the Spirit of truth[d] who comes from the Father. When he comes, he will tell about me. [27]And you will tell people about me too, because you have been with me from the beginning.

16 [1]"I have told you all this so that you won't lose your

b **15:25 'They hated me for no reason'** These words could be from Ps. 35:19 or Ps. 69:4.
c **15:26 Helper** Or "Comforter." Also in 16:7, 8.
d **15:26 Spirit of truth** The Holy Spirit (see "Holy Spirit" in the Word List). It was his work to help Jesus' followers understand God's truth. See Jn. 16:13.

a **15:8 honor** Or "glory." See "Glory" in the Word List.

faith when you face troubles. ²People will tell you to leave their synagogues* and never come back. In fact, the time will come when they will think that killing you would be doing service for God. ³They will do this because they have not known the Father, and they have not known me. ⁴I have told you all this now to prepare you. So when the time comes for these things to happen, you will remember that I warned you.

The Work of the Holy Spirit

"I did not tell you these things at the beginning, because I was with you then. ⁵Now I am going back to the one who sent me. And none of you asks me, 'Where are you going?' ⁶But you are filled with sadness because I have told you all this. ⁷Let me assure you, it is better for you that I go away. I say this because when I go away I will send the Helper to you. But if I did not go, the Helper would not come.

⁸"When the Helper comes, he will show the people of the world how wrong they are about sin, about being right with God, and about judgment. ⁹He will prove that they are guilty of sin, because they don't believe in me. ¹⁰He will show them how wrong they are about how to be right with God. The Helper will do this, because I am going to the Father. You will not see me then. ¹¹And he will show them how wrong their judgment is, because their leader*a* has already been condemned.

¹²"I have so much more to tell you, but it is too much for you to accept now. ¹³But when the Spirit*

of truth comes, he will lead you into all truth. He will not speak his own words. He will speak only what he hears and will tell you what will happen in the future. ¹⁴The Spirit of truth will bring glory* to me by telling you what he receives from me. ¹⁵All that the Father has is mine. That is why I said that the Spirit will tell you what he receives from me.

Sadness Will Turn Into Happiness

¹⁶"After a short time you won't see me. Then after another short time you will see me again."

¹⁷Some of the followers said to each other, "What does he mean when he says, 'After a short time you won't see me. Then after another short time you will see me again'? And what does he mean when he says, 'Because I am going to the Father'?" ¹⁸They also asked, "What does he mean by 'a short time'? We don't understand what he is saying."

¹⁹Jesus saw that the followers wanted to ask him about this. So he said to them, "Are you asking each other what I meant when I said, 'After a short time you won't see me. Then after another short time you will see me again'? ²⁰The truth is, you will cry and be sad, but the world will be happy. You will be sad, but then your sadness will change to happiness. ²¹"When a woman gives birth to a baby, she has pain, because her time has come. But when her baby is born, she forgets the pain. She forgets because she is so happy that a child has been born into the world. ²²It is the same with you. Now you are sad, but I will see you again, and you will be happy. You will have a joy that no one can take away. ²³In

a **16:11 their leader** Literally, "the ruler of this world," meaning Satan. See "SATAN" in the Word List.

that day you will not have to ask me about anything. And I assure you, my Father will give you anything you ask him for in my name. 24You have never asked for anything in this way before. But ask in my name, and you will receive. And you will have the fullest joy possible.

Victory Over the World

25"I have told you these things, using words that hide the meaning. But the time will come when I will not use words like that to tell you things. I will speak to you in plain words about the Father. 26Then you will be able to ask the Father for things in my name. I'm not saying that I will have to ask the Father for you. 27The Father himself loves you because you have loved me. And he loves you because you have believed that I came from God. 28I came from the Father into the world. Now I am leaving the world and going back to the Father."

29Then his followers said, "You are already speaking plainly to us. You are not using words that hide the meaning. 30We can see now that you know all things. You answer our questions even before we ask them. This makes us believe that you came from God."

31Jesus said, "So now you believe? 32Listen to me. A time is coming when you will be scattered, each to his own home. In fact, that time is already here. You will leave me, and I will be alone. But I am never really alone, because the Father is with me.

33"I have told you these things so that you can have peace in me. In this world you will have troubles. But be brave! I have defeated the world!"

Jesus Prays for Himself and His Followers

17 1After Jesus said these things, he looked toward heaven and prayed, "Father, the time has come. Give glory* to your Son so that the Son can give glory to you. 2You gave the Son power over all people so that he could give eternal life to all those you have given to him. 3And this is eternal life: that people can know you, the only true God, and that they can know Jesus Christ, the one you sent. 4I finished the work you gave me to do. I brought you glory on earth. 5And now, Father, give me glory with you. Give me the glory I had with you before the world was made.

6"You gave me some people from the world. I have shown them what you are like. They belonged to you, and you gave them to me. They have obeyed your teaching. 7Now they know that everything I have came from you. 8I told them the words you gave me, and they accepted them. They realized the fact that I came from you and believed that you sent me. 9I pray for them now. I am not praying for the people in the world. But I am praying for these people you gave me, because they are yours. 10All I have is yours, and all you have is mine. And my glory is seen in them.

11"Now I am coming to you. I will not stay in the world, but these followers of mine are still in the world. Holy Father, keep them safe by the power of your name—the name you gave me. Then they will be one, just as you and I are one. 12While I was with them, I kept them safe by the power of your name—the name you gave me. I protected them. And only one of them was lost—the one who was sure to be lost. This was to show the truth of what the Scriptures* said would happen.

13"I am coming to you now. But I pray these things while I am still in the world. I say all this so that these followers can have the true happiness that I have. I want them to be completely happy. 14I have given them your teaching. And the world has hated them, because they don't belong to the world, just as I don't belong to the world.

15"I am not asking you to take them out of the world. But I am asking that you keep them safe from the Evil One.* 16They don't belong to the world, just as I don't belong to the world. 17Make them ready for your service through your truth. Your teaching is truth. 18I have sent them into the world, just as you sent me into the world. 19I am making myself completely ready to serve you. I do this for them, so that they also might be fully qualified for your service.

20"I pray not only for these followers but also for those who will believe in me because of their teaching. 21Father, I pray that all who believe in me can be one. You are in me and I am in you. I pray that they can also be one in us. Then the world will believe that you sent me. 22I have given them the glory that you gave me. I gave them this glory so that they can be one, just as you and I are one. 23I will be in them, and you will be in me. So they will be completely one. Then the world will know that you sent me and that you loved them just as you loved me.

24"Father, I want these people you have given me to be with me in every place I am. I want them to see my glory—the glory you gave me because you loved me before the world was made. 25Father, you are the one who always does what is right. The world does not know you, but I know you, and these followers of mine know that you sent me. 26I showed them what you are like, and I will show them again. Then they will have the same love that you have for me, and I will live in them."

Jesus Is Arrested

(Mt. 26:47–56; Mk. 14:43–50; Lk. 22:47–53)

18 1When Jesus finished praying, he left with his followers and went across the Kidron Valley. He went into a garden there, his followers still with him.

2Judas, the one responsible for handing Jesus over, knew where this place was. He knew because Jesus often met there with his followers. 3So Judas led a group of soldiers to the garden, along with some guards from the leading priests and the Pharisees.* They were carrying torches, lanterns, and weapons.

4Jesus already knew everything that would happen to him. So he went out and asked them, "Who are you looking for?"

5They answered, "Jesus from Nazareth."

He said, "I am Jesus."*a* (Judas, the one responsible for handing Jesus over, was standing there with them.) 6When Jesus said, "I am Jesus," the men moved back and fell to the ground.

a 18:5 **"I am Jesus"** Literally, "I am," which could have the same meaning here that it has in 8:24, 28, 58; 13:19. Also in verse 8.

⁷He asked them again, "Who are you looking for?"

They said, "Jesus from Nazareth." ⁸Jesus said, "I told you that I am Jesus. So if you are looking for me, let these other men go free." ⁹This was to show the truth of what Jesus said earlier: "I have not lost anyone you gave me."

¹⁰Simon Peter had a sword, which he pulled out. He struck the servant of the high priest* and cut off his right ear. (The servant's name was Malchus.) ¹¹Jesus said to Peter, "Put your sword back in its place! I must drink from the cup*a* the Father has given me."

Jesus Is Brought Before Annas
(Mt. 26:57–58; Mk. 14:53–54; Lk. 22:54)

¹²Then the soldiers with their commander and the Jewish guards arrested Jesus. They tied him ¹³and brought him to Annas, the father-in-law of Caiaphas. Caiaphas was the high priest* that year. ¹⁴He was also the one who had told the other Jewish leaders that it would be better if one man died for all the people.

Peter Lies About Knowing Jesus
(Mt. 26:69–70; Mk. 14:66–68; Lk. 22:55–57)

¹⁵Simon Peter and another one of Jesus' followers went with Jesus. This follower knew the high priest.* So he went with Jesus into the yard of the high priest's house. ¹⁶But Peter waited outside near the door. The follower who knew the high priest came back outside and spoke to the gatekeeper. Then he brought Peter inside. ¹⁷The girl at the gate said to Peter, "Are you

---

a **18:11 cup** A symbol of suffering. Jesus used the idea of drinking from a cup to mean accepting the suffering he would face in the terrible events that were soon to come.

also one of the followers of that man?"

Peter answered, "No, I am not!" ¹⁸It was cold, so the servants and guards had built a fire. They were standing around it, warming themselves, and Peter was standing with them.

The High Priest Questions Jesus
(Mt. 26:59–66; Mk. 14:55–64; Lk. 22:66–71)

¹⁹The high priest* asked Jesus questions about his followers and what he taught them. ²⁰Jesus answered, "I have always spoken openly to all people. I always taught in the synagogues* and in the Temple* area. All the Jews come together there. I never said anything in secret. ²¹So why do you question me? Ask the people who heard my teaching. They know what I said."

²²When Jesus said this, one of the guards standing there hit him. The guard said, "You should not talk to the high priest like that!" ²³Jesus answered, "If I said something wrong, tell everyone here what was wrong. But if what I said is right, then why do you hit me?"

²⁴So Annas sent Jesus to Caiaphas the high priest. He was still tied.

Peter Lies Again
(Mt. 26:71–75; Mk. 14:69–72; Lk. 22:58–62)

²⁵Simon Peter was standing at the fire, keeping himself warm. The other people said to Peter, "Aren't you one of the followers of that man?"

Peter denied it. He said, "No, I am not."

²⁶One of the servants of the high priest* was there. He was a relative of the man whose ear Peter had cut off. The servant said,

"I think I saw you with him in the garden!"

27But again Peter said, "No, I was not with him!" As soon as he said this, a rooster crowed.

Jesus Is Brought Before Pilate

(Mt. 27:1–2, 11–31; Mk. 15:1–20; Lk. 23:1–25)

28Then the guards took Jesus from Caiaphas' house to the Roman governor's palace. It was early in the morning. The Jews there would not go inside the palace. They did not want to make themselves unclean,*a* because they wanted to eat the Passover* meal. 29So Pilate* went outside to them and asked, "What do you say this man has done wrong?"

30They answered, "He is a bad man. That is why we brought him to you."

31Pilate said to them, "You take him yourselves and judge him by your own law."

The Jewish leaders answered, "But your law does not allow us to punish anyone by killing them." 32(This was to show the truth of what Jesus said about how he would die.)

33Then Pilate went back inside the palace. He called for Jesus and asked him, "Are you the king of the Jews?"

34Jesus said, "Is that your own question, or did other people tell you about me?"

35Pilate said, "I'm not a Jew! It was your own people and their leading priests who brought you before me. What have you done wrong?"

36Jesus said, "My kingdom does not belong to this world. If it did,

my servants would fight so that I would not be handed over to the Jewish leaders. No, my kingdom is not an earthly one."

37Pilate said, "So you are a king."

Jesus answered, "You are right to say that I am a king. I was born for this: to tell people about the truth. That is why I came into the world. And everyone who belongs to the truth listens to me."

38Pilate said, "What is truth?" Then he went out to the Jewish leaders again and said to them, "I can find nothing against this man. 39But it is one of your customs for me to free one prisoner to you at the time of the Passover. Do you want me to free this 'king of the Jews'?"

40They shouted back, "No, not him! Let Barabbas go free!" (Barabbas was a rebel.)

19 1Then Pilate ordered that Jesus be taken away and whipped. 2The soldiers made a crown from thorny branches and put it on his head. Then they put a purple robe around him. 3They kept coming up to him and saying, "Hail to the king of the Jews!" And they hit him in the face.

4Again Pilate came out and said to the Jewish leaders, "Look! I am bringing Jesus out to you. I want you to know that I find nothing I can charge him with." 5Then Jesus came out wearing the crown of thorns and the purple robe. Pilate said to the Jews, "Here is the man!"

6When the leading priests and the Jewish guards saw Jesus they shouted, "Kill him on a cross! Kill him on a cross!"

But Pilate answered, "You take him and nail him to a cross yourselves. I find nothing I can charge him with."

a 18:28 unclean Going into a non-Jewish place would ruin the special cleansing the Jews did to make themselves fit for worship. See Jn. 11:55.

[7]The Jewish leaders answered, "We have a law that says he must die, because he said he is the Son of God."

[8]When Pilate heard this, he was more afraid. [9]So he went back inside the palace and asked Jesus, "Where are you from?" But Jesus did not answer him. [10]Pilate said, "You refuse to speak to me? Remember, I have the power to make you free or to kill you on a cross."

[11]Jesus answered, "The only power you have over me is the power given to you by God. So the one who handed me over to you is guilty of a greater sin."

[12]After this, Pilate tried to let Jesus go free. But the Jewish leaders shouted, "Anyone who makes himself a king is against Caesar.* So if you let this man go free, that means you are not Caesar's friend."

[13]When Pilate heard this, he brought Jesus out to the place called "The Stone Pavement." (In Aramaic* the name is *Gabbatha*.) Pilate sat down on the judge's seat there. [14]It was now almost noon on Preparation day* of Passover week. Pilate said to the Jews, "Here is your king!"

[15]They shouted, "Take him away! Take him away! Kill him on a cross!"

Pilate asked them, "Do you want me to kill your king on a cross?"

The leading priests answered, "The only king we have is Caesar!"

[16]So Pilate handed Jesus over to them to be killed on a cross.

Jesus Is Nailed to a Cross

(Mt. 27:32–44; Mk. 15:21–32; Lk. 23:26–39)

The soldiers took Jesus. [17]He carried his own cross to a place called "The Place of the Skull." (In Aramaic* the name of this place is "Golgotha.") [18]There they nailed Jesus to the cross. They also nailed two other men to crosses. They put them on each side of Jesus with him in the middle.

[19]Pilate* told them to write a sign and put it on the cross. The sign said, "JESUS OF NAZARETH, THE KING OF THE JEWS." [20]The sign was written in Aramaic, in Latin, and in Greek. Many of the Jews read this sign, because the place where Jesus was nailed to the cross was near the city.

[21]The leading Jewish priests said to Pilate, "Don't write, 'The King of the Jews.' But write, 'This man said, I am the King of the Jews.'"

[22]Pilate answered, "I will not change what I have written."

[23]After the soldiers nailed Jesus to the cross, they took his clothes and divided them into four parts. Each soldier got one part. They also took his tunic.* It was all one piece of cloth woven from top to bottom. [24]So the soldiers said to each other, "We should not tear this into parts. Let's throw lots* to see who will get it." This happened to make clear the full meaning of what the Scriptures* say:

"They divided my clothes
    among them,
and they threw lots for what
    I was wearing."   *Psalm 22:18*

So the soldiers did this.

[25]Jesus' mother stood near his cross. Her sister was also standing there with Mary the wife of Clopas, and Mary Magdalene. [26]Jesus saw his mother. He also saw the follower he loved very much standing there. He said to his mother, "Dear woman, here

is your son." 27Then he said to the follower, "Here is your mother." So after that, this follower took Jesus' mother to live in his home.

Jesus Dies
(Mt. 27:45–56; Mk. 15:33–41; Lk. 23:44–49)

28Later, Jesus knew that everything had been done. To make the Scriptures* come true he said, "I am thirsty."*a 29There was a jar full of sour wine there, so the soldiers soaked a sponge in it. They put the sponge on a branch of a hyssop plant and lifted it to Jesus' mouth. 30When he tasted the wine, he said, "It is finished." Then he bowed his head and died.

31This day was Preparation day.* The next day was a special Sabbath* day. The Jewish leaders did not want the bodies to stay on the cross on the Sabbath day. So they asked Pilate* to order that the legs of the men be broken. And they asked that the bodies be taken down from the crosses. 32So the soldiers came and broke the legs*b of the two men on the crosses beside Jesus. 33But when the soldiers came close to Jesus, they saw that he was already dead. So they did not break his legs.

34But one of the soldiers stuck his spear into Jesus' side. Immediately blood and water came out. 35(The one who saw this happen has told about it. He told about it so that you also can believe. The things he says are true. He knows that he tells the truth.) 36These things happened to give full meaning to the Scriptures that said, "None of his bones will be broken"c 37and "People will look at the one they stabbed."d

Jesus Is Buried
(Mt. 27:57–61; Mk. 15:42–47; Lk. 23:50–56)

38Later, a man named Joseph from Arimathea asked Pilate* for the body of Jesus. (Joseph was a follower of Jesus, but he did not tell anyone, because he was afraid of the Jewish leaders.) Pilate said Joseph could take Jesus' body, so he came and took it away.

39Nicodemus went with Joseph. He was the man who had come to Jesus before and talked to him at night. He brought about 100 poundse of spices—a mixture of myrrh* and aloes.* 40These two men took Jesus' body and wrapped it in pieces of linen cloth with the spices. (This is how the Jews bury people.) 41In the place where Jesus was killed on the cross, there was a garden. In the garden there was a new tomb.* No one had ever been buried there before. 42The men put Jesus in that tomb because it was near, and the Jews were preparing to start their Sabbath* day.

News That Jesus Has Risen From Death
(Mt. 28:1–10; Mk. 16:1–8; Lk. 24:1–12)

20 1Early on Sunday morning, while it was still dark, Mary Magdalene went to the tomb.* She saw that the large stone was moved away from the entrance. 2So she ran to Simon Peter and the other follower (the one Jesus loved very much). She said, "They have taken the Lord

---

c 19:36 Quote from Ps. 34:20. The idea is from Ex. 12:46; Num. 9:12.
d 19:37 Quote from Zech. 12:10.
e 19:39 100 pounds Literally, "100 litras" (Roman pounds), equal to 32.7 kg (72 pounds).

a 19:28 "I am thirsty" See Ps. 22:15; 69:21.
b 19:32 broke the legs The legs were broken to make those on the crosses die more quickly.

out of the tomb, and we don't know where they put him."

³So Peter and the other follower started going to the tomb. ⁴They were both running, but the other follower ran faster than Peter and reached the tomb first. ⁵He bent down and looked in. He saw the pieces of linen cloth lying there, but he did not go in.

⁶Then Simon Peter finally reached the tomb and went in. He saw the pieces of linen lying there. ⁷He also saw the cloth that had been around Jesus' head. It was folded up and laid in a different place from the pieces of linen. ⁸Then the other follower went in—the one who had reached the tomb first. He saw what had happened and believed. ⁹(These followers did not yet understand from the Scriptures* that Jesus must rise from death.)

Jesus Appears to Mary Magdalene
(Mk. 16:9–11)

¹⁰Then the followers went back home. ¹¹But Mary stood outside the tomb,* crying. While she was crying, she bent down and looked inside the tomb. ¹²She saw two angels dressed in white sitting where Jesus' body had been. One was sitting where the head had been; the other was sitting where the feet had been.

¹³The angels asked Mary, "Woman, why are you crying?"

Mary answered, "They took away the body of my Lord, and I don't know where they put him." ¹⁴When Mary said this, she turned around and saw Jesus standing there. But she did not know that it was Jesus.

¹⁵He asked her, "Woman, why are you crying? Who are you looking for?"

She thought he was the man in charge of the garden. So she said to him, "Did you take him away, sir? Tell me where you put him. I will go and get him."

¹⁶Jesus said to her, "Mary."

She turned toward him and said in Aramaic,* "Rabboni," which means "Teacher."

¹⁷Jesus said to her, "You don't need to hold on to me! I have not yet gone back up to the Father. But go to my followersᵃ and tell them this: 'I am going back to my Father and your Father. I am going back to my God and your God.'"

¹⁸Mary Magdalene went to the followers and told them, "I saw the Lord!" And she told them what he had said to her.

Jesus Appears to His Followers
(Mt. 28:16–20; Mk. 16:14–18; Lk. 24:36–49)

¹⁹The day was Sunday, and that same evening the followers were together. They had the doors locked because they were afraid of the Jewish leaders. Suddenly, Jesus was standing there among them. He said, "Peace be with you!" ²⁰As soon as he said this, he showed them his hands and his side. When the followers saw the Lord, they were very happy.

²¹Then Jesus said again, "Peace be with you. It was the Father who sent me, and I am now sending you in the same way." ²²Then he breathed on them and said, "Receive the Holy Spirit.* ²³If you forgive the sins of anyone, their sins are forgiven. If there is anyone whose sins you don't forgive, their sins are not forgiven."

Jesus Appears to Thomas
²⁴Thomas (called Didymus) was one of the twelve, but he was not

ᵃ **20:17 followers** Literally, "brothers."

with the other followers when Jesus came. 25They told him, "We saw the Lord." Thomas said, "That's hard to believe. I will have to see the nail holes in his hands, put my finger where the nails were, and put my hand into his side. Only then will I believe it."

26A week later the followers were in the house again, and Thomas was with them. The doors were locked, but Jesus came and stood among them. He said, "Peace be with you!" 27Then he said to Thomas, "Put your finger here. Look at my hands. Put your hand here in my side. Stop doubting and believe."

28Thomas said to Jesus, "My Lord and my God!"

29Jesus said to him, "You believe because you see me. Great blessings belong to the people who believe without seeing me!"

Why John Wrote This Book

30Jesus did many other miraculous signs* that his followers saw, which are not written in this book. 31But these are written so that you can believe that Jesus is the Messiah,* the Son of God. Then, by believing, you can have life through his name.

Jesus Appears to Seven Followers

21 1Later, Jesus appeared again to his followers by Lake Galilee.ᵃ This is how it happened: 2Some of the followers were together—Simon Peter, Thomas (called Didymus), Nathanael from Cana in Galilee, the two sons of Zebedee, and two other followers. 3Simon Peter said, "I am going out to fish."

The other followers said, "We will go with you." So all of them went out and got into the boat. They fished that night but caught nothing.

4Early the next morning Jesus stood on the shore. But the followers did not know it was Jesus. 5Then he said to them, "Friends, have you caught any fish?"

They answered, "No."

6He said, "Throw your net into the water on the right side of your boat. You will find some fish there." So they did this. They caught so many fish that they could not pull the net back into the boat.

7The follower Jesus loved very much said to Peter, "That man is the Lord!" When Peter heard him say it was the Lord, he wrapped his coat around himself. (He had taken his clothes off to work.) Then he jumped into the water. 8The other followers went to shore in the boat. They pulled the net full of fish. They were not very far from shore, only about 100 yards.ᵇ 9When they stepped out of the boat and onto the shore, they saw a fire of hot coals. There were fish on the fire and some bread there too. 10Then Jesus said, "Bring some of the fish that you caught."

11Simon Peter got into the boat and pulled the net to the shore. It was full of big fish—153 of them! But even with that many fish, the net did not tear. 12Jesus said to them, "Come and eat." None of the followers would ask him, "Who are you?" They knew he was the Lord. 13Jesus walked over to

a 21:1 **Lake Galilee** Literally, "Lake of Tiberias," another name for Lake Galilee. See Jn. 6:1.

b 21:8 **100 yards** Literally, "200 cubits."

get the bread and gave it to them. He also gave them the fish.

¹⁴This was now the third time Jesus appeared to his followers after he was raised from death.

Jesus Talks to Peter

¹⁵When they finished eating, Jesus said to Simon Peter, "Simon, son of John, do you love me more than these other men love me?"

Peter answered, "Yes, Lord, you know that I love you."

Then Jesus said to him, "Take care of my lambs.ᵃ"

¹⁶Again Jesus said to him, "Simon, son of John, do you love me?"

Peter answered, "Yes, Lord, you know that I love you."

Then Jesus said, "Take care of my sheep."

¹⁷A third time Jesus said, "Simon, son of John, do you love me?"

Peter was sad because Jesus asked him three times, "Do you love me?" He said, "Lord, you know everything. You know that I love you!"

Jesus said to him, "Take care of my sheep. ¹⁸The truth is, when you were young, you tied your own belt and went where you wanted. But when you are old, you will put out your hands, and someone else

a **21:15 lambs** Jesus uses this word and the word "sheep" in verses 16 and 17 to mean his followers, as in Jn. 10.

will tie your belt. They will lead you where you don't want to go." ¹⁹(Jesus said this to show how Peter would die to give glory* to God.) Then he said to Peter, "Follow me!"

²⁰Peter turned and saw the follower Jesus loved very much walking behind them. (This was the follower who had leaned against Jesus at the supper and said, "Lord, who is it that will hand you over?") ²¹When Peter saw him behind them, he asked Jesus, "Lord, what about him?"

²²Jesus answered, "Maybe I want him to live until I come. That should not matter to you. You follow me!"

²³So a story spread among the followers of Jesus. They were saying that this follower would not die. But Jesus did not say he would not die. He only said, "Maybe I want him to live until I come. That should not matter to you."

²⁴That follower is the one who is telling these things. He is the one who has now written them all down. We know that what he says is true.

²⁵There are many other things that Jesus did. If every one of them were written down, I think the whole world would not be big enough for all the books that would be written.

Acts

Luke Writes Another Book

1 ¹Dear Theophilus,

The first book I wrote was about everything Jesus did and taught from the beginning ²until the day he was carried up into heaven. Before he went, he talked to the apostles* he had chosen. With the help of the Holy Spirit,* he told them what they should do. ³This was after his death, but he showed them that he was alive, proving it to them in many ways. The apostles saw Jesus many times during the 40 days after he was raised from death. He spoke to them about God's kingdom.* ⁴One time when Jesus was eating with them, he told them not to leave Jerusalem. He said, "Wait here until you receive what the Father promised to send. Remember, I told you about it before. ⁵John baptized* people with water, but in a few days you will be baptized with the Holy Spirit."

Jesus Is Carried Up Into Heaven

⁶The apostles* were all together. They asked Jesus, "Lord, is this the time for you to give the people of Israel* their kingdom again?"

⁷Jesus said to them, "The Father is the only one who has the authority to decide dates and times. They are not for you to know. ⁸But the Holy Spirit* will come on you and give you power. You will be my witnesses. You will tell people everywhere about me—in Jerusalem, in the rest of Judea, in Samaria, and in every part of the world."

⁹After Jesus said this, he was lifted up into the sky. While they were watching, he went into a cloud, and they could not see him. ¹⁰They were staring into the sky where he had gone. Suddenly two men wearing white clothes were standing beside them. ¹¹They said, "Men from Galilee, why are you standing here looking into the sky? You saw Jesus carried away from you into heaven. He will come back in the same way you saw him go."

A New Apostle Is Chosen

¹²Then the apostles* went back to Jerusalem from the Mount of Olives. This mountain is about a half mile *a* from Jerusalem. ¹³When they entered the city, they went to the upstairs room where they were staying. These are the ones who were there: Peter, John, James, Andrew, Philip, Thomas, Bartholomew, Matthew, James (the son of Alphaeus), Simon, the Zealot,* and Judas (the son of James).

¹⁴The apostles were all together. They were constantly praying with the same purpose. Some women, Mary the mother of Jesus,

---

a **1:12 half a mile** Literally, "a Sabbath day's journey."

and his brothers were there with the apostles.

15After a few days there was a meeting of the believers.* There were about 120 of them. Peter stood up and said, 16–17"Brothers and sisters, in the Scriptures* the Holy Spirit* said through David* that something must happen. He was talking about Judas, one of our own group. Judas served together with us. The Spirit said that Judas would lead men to arrest Jesus."

18(Judas was paid money for doing this. His money was used to buy him a field. But he fell on his head, his body broke open, and all his intestines poured out. 19And all the people of Jerusalem learned about this. That is why they named that field Akeldama, which in their language means "field of blood.")

20Peter said, "In the book of Psalms, this is written about Judas:

'People should not go near his
    land;
no one should live there.'

Psalm 69:25

And it is also written:

'Let another man have his
    work.'

Psalm 109:8

21–22"So now another man must join us and be a witness of Jesus' resurrection.* He must be one of those men who were part of our group during all the time the Lord Jesus was with us. He must have been with us from the time John was baptizing* people until the day when Jesus was carried up from us into heaven."

23They put two men before the group. One was Joseph Barsabbas. He was also called Justus. The other man was Matthias. 24–25They prayed, "Lord, you know

the minds of all people. Show us which one of these two men you choose to do this work. Judas turned away from it and went where he belongs. Lord, show us which man should take his place as an apostle!" 26Then they used lots* to choose one of the two men. The lots showed that Matthias was the one the Lord wanted. So he became an apostle with the other eleven.

The Coming of the Holy Spirit

2 1When the day of Pentecost* came, they were all together in one place. 2Suddenly a noise came from heaven. It sounded like a strong wind blowing. This noise filled the whole house where they were sitting. 3They saw something that looked like flames of fire. The flames were separated and stood over each person there. 4They were all filled with the Holy Spirit,* and they began to speak different languages. The Holy Spirit was giving them the power to do this.

5There were some godly Jews in Jerusalem at this time. They were from every country in the world. 6A large crowd came together because they heard the noise. They were surprised because, as the apostles* were speaking, everyone heard in their own language. 7They were all amazed at this. They did not understand how the apostles could do this. They said, "Look! These men we hear speaking are all from Galilee.ª 8But we hear them in our own languages. How is this possible? We are from all these different places: 9Parthia, Media, Elam, Mesopotamia, Judea,

ª 2:7 from Galilee The people thought men from Galilee could speak only their own language.

Cappadocia, Pontus, Asia,* ¹⁰Phrygia, Pamphylia, Egypt, the areas of Libya near the city of Cyrene, Rome, ¹¹Crete, and Arabia. Some of us were born Jews, and others have changed their religion to worship God like Jews. We are from these different countries, but we can hear these men in our own languages! We can all understand the great things they are saying about God."

¹²The people were all amazed and confused. They asked each other, "What is happening?" ¹³But others were laughing at the apostles, saying they were drunk from too much wine.

Peter Speaks to the People

¹⁴Then Peter stood up with the other eleven apostles.* He spoke loudly so that all the people could hear. He said, "My Jewish brothers and all of you who live in Jerusalem, listen to me. I will tell you something you need to know. Listen carefully. ¹⁵These men are not drunk as you think; it's only nine o'clock in the morning. ¹⁶But Joel the prophet* wrote about what you see happening here today. This is what he wrote:

¹⁷ 'God says:
In the last days I will pour out my Spirit* on all people.
Your sons and daughters will prophesy.*
Your young men will see visions.*
Your old men will have special dreams.
¹⁸ In those days I will pour out my Spirit on my servants, men and women, and they will prophesy.
¹⁹ I will work wonders* in the sky above.
I will cause miraculous signs* on the earth below.
There will be blood, fire, and thick smoke.
²⁰ The sun will be changed into darkness, and the moon will be as red as blood.
Then the great and glorious day of the Lord will come.
²¹ And everyone who trusts in the Lordᵃ will be saved.'
                              Joel 2:28–32

²²"My fellow Israelites,* listen to these words: Jesus from Nazareth was a very special man. God clearly showed this to you. He proved it by the miracles,* wonders, and miraculous signs he did through Jesus. You all saw these things, so you know this is true. ²³Jesus was handed over to you, and you killed him. With the help of evil men, you nailed him to a cross. But God knew all this would happen. It was his plan—a plan he made long ago. ²⁴Jesus suffered the pain of death, but God made him free. He raised him from death. There was no way for death to hold him. ²⁵David* said this about him:

'I saw the Lord before me always;
he is at my right side to keep me safe.
²⁶ So my heart is happy, and the words I speak are words of joy.
Yes, even my body will live with hope,
²⁷ because you will not leave me in the place of death.ᵇ

ᵃ **2:21 who trusts in the Lord** Literally, "who calls on the name of the Lord," meaning to show faith in him by worshiping him or praying to him for help.
ᵇ **2:27 place of death** Literally, "Hades." Also in verse 31.

You will not let the body of your Holy One rot in the grave.
28 You taught me how to live. You will come close to me and give me great joy.'

Psalm 16:8–11

29 "My brothers, I can tell you for sure about David, our great ancestor. He died, was buried, and his tomb* is still here with us today. 30 He was a prophet and knew something that God had said. God had promised David that someone from his own family would sit on David's throne as king.*a* 31 David knew this before it happened. That is why he said this about that future king:

'He was not left in the place of death.
His body did not rot in the grave.'

David was talking about the Messiah* rising from death. 32 So Jesus is the one God raised from death. We are all witnesses of this. We saw him. 33 Jesus was lifted up to heaven. Now he is with God, at God's right side. The Father has given the Holy Spirit to him, as he promised. So Jesus has now poured out that Spirit. This is what you see and hear. 34 David was not the one who was lifted up to heaven. David himself said,

'The Lord God said to my Lord:
Sit at my right side,
35   until I put your enemies under your power.'*b* *Psalm 110:1*

36 "So, all the people of Israel* should know this for certain: God has made Jesus to be Lord and Messiah. He is the man you nailed to the cross!"

37 When the people heard this, they felt very, very sorry. They asked Peter and the other apostles, "Brothers, what should we do?"

38 Peter said to them, "Change your hearts and lives and be baptized,* each one of you, in the name of Jesus Christ. Then God will forgive your sins, and you will receive the gift of the Holy Spirit. 39 This promise is for you. It is also for your children and for the people who are far away. It is for everyone the Lord our God calls to himself."

40 Peter warned them with many other words; he begged them, "Save yourselves from the evil of the people who live now!" 41 Then those who accepted what Peter said were baptized. On that day about 3000 people were added to the group of believers.

The Believers Share

42 The believers spent their time listening to the teaching of the apostles.* They shared everything with each other. They ate*c* together and prayed together. 43 Many wonders* and miraculous signs* were happening through the apostles, and everyone felt great respect for God. 44 All the believers stayed together and shared everything. 45 They sold their land and the things they owned. Then they divided the money and gave it to those who needed it. 46 The believers shared a common purpose, and every day they spent much of their time together in

---

a **2:30 God had promised ... as king** See 2 Sam. 7:12, 13 and Ps. 132:11.

b **2:35 until I put ... power** Literally, "until I make your enemies a footstool for your feet."

c **2:42 ate** Literally, "broke bread." This may mean a meal or the Lord's Supper, the special meal Jesus told his followers to eat to remember him. Also in verse 46. See Lk. 22:14–20.

the Temple* area. They also ate together in their homes. They were happy to share their food and ate with joyful hearts. 47The believers praised God and were respected by all the people. More and more people were being saved every day, and the Lord was adding them to their group.

Peter Heals a Crippled Man

3 1One day Peter and John went to the Temple* area. It was three o'clock in the afternoon, which was the time for the daily Temple prayer service. 2As they were entering the Temple area, a man was there who had been crippled all his life. He was being carried by some friends who brought him to the Temple every day. They put him by one of the gates outside the Temple. It was called Beautiful Gate. There he begged for money from the people going to the Temple. 3That day he saw Peter and John going into the Temple area. He asked them for money.

4Peter and John looked at the crippled man and said, "Look at us!" 5He looked at them; he thought they would give him some money. 6But Peter said, "I don't have any silver or gold, but I do have something else I can give you. By the power of Jesus Christ from Nazareth—stand up and walk!"

7Then Peter took the man's right hand and lifted him up. Immediately his feet and legs became strong. 8He jumped up, stood on his feet, and began to walk. He went into the Temple area with them. He was walking and jumping and praising God. 9-10All the people recognized him. They knew he was the crippled

man who always sat by the Beautiful Gate to beg for money. Now they saw this same man walking and praising God. They were amazed. They did not understand how this could happen.

Peter Speaks to the People

11The man was holding on to Peter and John. All the people were amazed. They ran to Peter and John at Solomon's Porch.*

12When Peter saw this, he said to the people, "My Jewish brothers, why are you surprised at this? You are looking at us as if it was our power that made this man walk. Do you think this was done because we are good? 13No, God did it! He is the God of Abraham,* the God of Isaac,* and the God of Jacob.* He is the God of all our fathers.* He gave glory* to Jesus, his special servant. But you handed him over to be killed. Pilate* decided to let him go free. But you told Pilate you did not want him. 14Jesus was holy* and good, but you said you did not want him. You told Pilate to give you a murderer*a* instead of Jesus. 15And so you killed the one who gives life! But God raised him from death. We are witnesses of this—we saw it with our own eyes.

16"This crippled man was healed because we trusted in Jesus. It was Jesus' power that made him well. You can see this man, and you know him. He was made completely well because of faith in Jesus. You all saw it happen!

17"My brothers, I know that what you did to Jesus was done because you did not understand what you were doing. And your

a **3:14 murderer** Barabbas, the man the Jews chose to let go free instead of Jesus. See Lk. 23:18.

leaders did not understand any more than you did. ¹⁸But God said these things would happen. Through the prophets* he said that his Messiah* would suffer and die. I have told you how God made this happen. ¹⁹So you must change your hearts and lives. Come back to God, and he will forgive your sins. ²⁰Then the Lord will give you times of spiritual rest. He will send you Jesus, the one he chose to be the Messiah.

²¹"But Jesus must stay in heaven until the time when all things will be made right again. God told about this time when he spoke long ago through his holy prophets. ²²Moses* said, 'The Lord your God will give you a prophet. That prophet will come from among your own people. He will be like me. You must obey everything he tells you. ²³And anyone who refuses to obey that prophet will die, separated from God's people.'ᵃ

²⁴"Samuel, and all the other prophets who spoke for God after Samuel, said that this time would come. ²⁵And what those prophets talked about is for you, their descendants. You have received the agreement that God made with your fathers. God said to your father Abraham, 'Every nation on earth will be blessed through your descendants.'ᵇ ²⁶God has sent his special servant Jesus. He sent him to you first. He sent him to bless you by causing each of you to turn away from your evil ways."

The Apostles and the Jewish High Council

4 ¹While Peter and John were speaking to the people, some Jewish leaders came up to them. There were some priests, the captain of the soldiers that guarded the Temple,* and some Sadducees.* ²They were upset because of what Peter and John were teaching the people. By telling people about Jesus, the apostles* were teaching that people will rise from death. ³The Jewish leaders arrested Peter and John and put them in jail. It was already night, so they kept them in jail until the next day. ⁴But many of the people who heard the apostles believed what they said. There were now about 5000 men in the group of believers.

⁵The next day the Jewish rulers, the older Jewish leaders, and the teachers of the law met in Jerusalem. ⁶Annas the high priest,* Caiaphas, John, and Alexander were there. Everyone from the high priest's family was there. ⁷They made Peter and John stand before all the people. They asked them over and over, "How did you make this crippled man well? What power did you use? By whose authority did you do this?"

⁸Then Peter was filled with the Holy Spirit* and said to them, "Rulers of the people and you older leaders, ⁹are you questioning us today about what we did to help this crippled man? Are you asking us what made him well? ¹⁰We want all of you and all the people of Israel* to know that this man was made well by the power of Jesus Christ from Nazareth. You nailed Jesus to a cross, but God raised him from death. This man was crippled, but he is now well. He is able to stand here before you because of the power of Jesus!

ᵃ 3:22–23 Quote from Deut. 18:15, 19.
ᵇ 3:25 Quote from Gen. 22:18; 26:24.

¹¹Jesus is

'the stoneᵃ that you builders
    thought was not important.
But this stone has become
    the cornerstone.*' *Psalm 118:22*

¹²Jesus is the only one who can save people. His name is the only power in the world that has been given to save anyone. We must be saved through him!"

¹³The Jewish leaders understood that Peter and John had no special training or education. But they also saw that they were not afraid to speak. So the leaders were amazed. They also realized that Peter and John had been with Jesus. ¹⁴They saw the crippled man standing there beside the apostles. They saw that he was healed, so they could say nothing against the apostles.

¹⁵The Jewish leaders told them to leave the council meeting. Then the leaders talked to each other about what they should do. ¹⁶They said, "What shall we do with these men? Everyone in Jerusalem knows about the miracle* they did as a sign from God. It's too obvious. We can't say it didn't happen. ¹⁷But we must make them afraid to talk to anyone again using that name.ᵇ Then this problem will not spread among the people."

¹⁸So the Jewish leaders called Peter and John in again. They told the apostles not to say anything or to teach anything in the name of Jesus. ¹⁹But Peter and John answered them, "What do you think is right? What would God want? Should we obey you or God? ²⁰We

ᵃ **4:11 stone** A picture or symbol meaning Jesus.
ᵇ **4:17 that name** That is, Jesus' name. The Jewish leaders avoided saying his name. See Lk. 15:2.

cannot be quiet. We must tell people about what we have seen and heard."

²¹⁻²²The Jewish leaders could not find a way to punish the apostles, because all the people were praising God for what had been done. This miracle was a sign from God. The man who was healed was more than 40 years old. So the Jewish leaders warned the apostles again and let them go free.

Peter and John Return to the Believers

²³Peter and John left the meeting of Jewish leaders and went to their own group. They told the group everything that the leading priests and the older Jewish leaders had said to them. ²⁴When the believers heard this, they all prayed to God with one purpose. They said, "Master, you are the one who made the sky, the earth, the sea, and everything in the world. ²⁵Our ancestor David* was your servant. With the help of the Holy Spirit* he wrote these words:

'Why are the nations shouting?
Why are the people planning
    such useless things?

²⁶'The kings of the earth prepare
    themselves to fight,
and the rulers all come
    together against the Lord
and against his Messiah.*' *Psalm 2:1-2*

²⁷That's what actually happened when Herod,* Pontius Pilate,* the other nations, and the people of Israel* all came together against Jesus here in Jerusalem. He is your holy* Servant, the one you made to be the Messiah. ²⁸These people who came together against Jesus made your plan happen. It was done because of your power and your will. ²⁹And now, Lord, listen

to what they are saying. They are trying to make us afraid. We are your servants. Help us to say what you want us to say without fear. 30Help us to be brave by showing us your power. Make sick people well. Cause miraculous signs* and wonders* to happen by the authority*a* of Jesus, your holy servant."

31After the believers prayed, the place where they were meeting shook. They were all filled with the Holy Spirit, and they continued to speak God's message* without fear.

The Believers Share

32The whole group of believers was united in their thinking and in what they wanted. None of them said that the things they had were their own. Instead, they shared everything. 33With great power the apostles* were making it known to everyone that the Lord Jesus was raised from death. And God blessed all the believers very much. 34None of them could say they needed anything. Everyone who owned fields or houses sold them. They brought the money they got 35and gave it to the apostles. Then everyone was given whatever they needed.

36One of the believers was named Joseph. The apostles called him Barnabas, a name that means "one who encourages others." He was a Levite* born in Cyprus. 37Joseph sold a field he owned. He brought the money and gave it to the apostles.

Ananias and Sapphira

5 1There was a man named Ananias. His wife's name was Sapphira. Ananias sold some land

a 4:30 **authority** Literally, "name."

he had, 2but he gave only part of the money to the apostles.* He secretly kept some of the money for himself. His wife knew this, and she agreed with it.

3Peter said, "Ananias, why did you let Satan* fill your mind with such an idea? You kept part of the money for yourself and lied about it to the Holy Spirit*! 4Before you sold the field, it belonged to you, right? And even after you sold it, you could have used the money any way you wanted. How could you even think of doing such a thing? You lied to God, not to us!"

5-6When Ananias heard this, he fell down and died. Some young men came and wrapped his body. They carried it out and buried it. And everyone who heard about this was filled with fear.

7About three hours later his wife came in. Sapphira did not know about what had happened to her husband. 8Peter said to her, "Tell me how much money you got for your field. Was it this much?"

Sapphira answered, "Yes, that was all we got for the field."

9Peter said to her, "Why did you and your husband agree to test the Spirit of the Lord? Listen! Do you hear those footsteps? The men who buried your husband are at the door. They will carry you out in the same way." 10At that moment Sapphira fell down by his feet and died. The young men came in and saw that she was dead. They carried her out and buried her beside her husband. 11The whole church* and all the other people who heard about this were filled with fear.

Proofs From God

12The apostles* were given the power to do many miraculous

signs* and wonders* among the people. They were together in Solomon's Porch,* and they all had the same purpose. 13None of the other people dared to stand with the apostles, but everyone was saying wonderful things about them. 14More and more people believed in the Lord, and many men and women were added to the group of believers. 15So the people brought those who were sick into the streets and put them on little beds and mats. They were hoping that Peter's shadow might fall on them as he walked by. 16People came from all the towns around Jerusalem. They brought those who were sick or troubled by evil spirits. All of them were healed.

The Apostles Are Arrested

17The high priest* and all his friends, a group called the Sadducees,* became very jealous. 18They grabbed the apostles* and put them in jail. 19But during the night, an angel of the Lord opened the doors of the jail. The angel led the apostles outside and said, 20"Go and stand in the Temple* area. Tell the people everything about this new life." 21When the apostles heard this, they did what they were told. They went into the Temple area about sunrise and began to teach the people.

The high priest and his friends came together and called a meeting of the high council and all the older Jewish leaders. They sent some men to the jail to bring the apostles to them. 22When the men went to the jail, they could not find the apostles there. So they went back and told the Jewish leaders about this. 23They said, "The jail was closed and locked. The guards were standing at the

doors. But when we opened the doors, the jail was empty!" 24The captain of the Temple guards and the leading priests heard this. They were confused and wondered what it all meant.

25Then another man came and told them, "Listen! The men you put in jail are standing in the Temple area teaching the people." 26The captain and his men went out and brought the apostles back. But the soldiers did not use force, because they were afraid of the people. They were afraid the people would stone them to death.

27The soldiers brought the apostles in and made them stand before the council. The high priest questioned them. 28He said, "We told you never again to teach using that name.ᵃ But look at what you have done! You have filled Jerusalem with your teaching. And you are trying to blame us for his death."

29Peter and the other apostles answered, "We must obey God, not you! 30You killed Jesus by nailing him to a cross. But God, the same God our fathers* had, raised Jesus up from death. 31Jesus is the one God honored by giving him a place at his right side. He made him our Leader and Savior. God did this to give all the people of Israel* the opportunity to change and turn to God to have their sins forgiven. 32We saw all these things happen, and we can say that they are true. The Holy Spirit* also shows that these things are true. God has given this Spirit to all those who obey him."

ᵃ 5:28 that name That is, Jesus' name. The Jewish leaders avoided saying his name. See Acts 4:17, 18.

[33]When the council members heard this, they became very angry. They began to plan a way to kill the apostles. [34]But one member of the council, a Pharisee* named Gamaliel, stood up. He was a teacher of the law, and all the people respected him. He told the men to make the apostles leave the meeting for a few minutes. [35]Then he said to them, "Men of Israel, be careful of what you are planning to do to these men. [36]Remember when Theudas appeared? He said he was an important man, and about 400 men joined him. But he was killed, and all who followed him were scattered and ran away. They were not able to do anything. [37]Later, during the time of the census, a man named Judas came from Galilee. Many people joined his group, but he was also killed, and all his followers were scattered. [38]And so now I tell you, stay away from these men. Leave them alone. If their plan is something they thought up, it will fail. [39]But if it is from God, you will not be able to stop them. You might even be fighting against God himself!"

The Jewish leaders agreed with what Gamaliel said. [40]They called the apostles in again. They beat them and told them not to speak anymore using the name of Jesus. Then they let them go free. [41]The apostles left the council meeting. They were happy because they were given the honor of suffering dishonor for Jesus. [42]The apostles did not stop teaching the people. They continued to tell the Good News*—that Jesus is the Messiah.* They did this every day in the Temple area and in people's homes.

Seven Men Chosen for a Special Work

6 [1]More and more people were becoming followers of Jesus. But during this same time, the Greek-speaking followers began to complain against the other Jewish followers. They said that their widows were not getting their share of what the followers received every day. [2]The twelve apostles* called the whole group of followers together.

The apostles said to them, "It would not be right for us to give up our work of teaching God's word in order to be in charge of getting food to people. [3]So, brothers and sisters, choose seven of your men who have a good reputation. They must be full of wisdom and the Spirit.* We will give them this work to do. [4]Then we can use all our time to pray and to teach the word of God."

[5]The whole group liked the idea. So they chose these seven men: Stephen (a man with great faith and full of the Holy Spirit), Philip,[a] Prochorus, Nicanor, Timon, Parmenas, and Nicolaus (a man from Antioch who had become a Jew). [6]Then they put these men before the apostles, who prayed and laid their hands on* them.

[7]The word of God was reaching more and more people. The group of followers in Jerusalem became larger and larger. Even a big group of Jewish priests believed and obeyed.

Some Jews Against Stephen

[8]Stephen received a great blessing. God gave him power to do great wonders* and miraculous signs* among the people. [9]But some

---

[a] **6:5 Philip** Not the apostle named Philip.

of the Jews there were from the synagogue* of Free Men,* as it was called. The group included Jews from Cyrene, Alexandria, Cilicia, and Asia.* They started arguing with Stephen. 10But the Spirit* was helping him speak with wisdom. His words were so strong that these Jews could not argue with him.

11So they told some men to say, "We heard Stephen say bad things against Moses* and against God!" 12By doing this, these Jews upset the people, the older Jewish leaders, and the teachers of the law. They became so angry that they came and grabbed Stephen and took him to a meeting of the high council.

13The Jews brought some men into the meeting to tell lies about Stephen. These men said, "This man is always saying things against this holy place and against the Law of Moses. 14We heard him say that Jesus from Nazareth will destroy this place and change what Moses told us to do." 15Everyone there in the council meeting was staring at Stephen. They saw that his face looked like the face of an angel.

Stephen's Speech

7 1The high priest* said to Stephen, "Is all this true?" 2Stephen answered, "My Jewish fathers and brothers, listen to me. Our great and glorious God appeared to Abraham, our ancestor,* when he was in Mesopotamia. This was before he lived in Haran. 3God said to him, 'Leave your country and your people, and go to the country I will show you.'a

4"So Abraham left the country of Chaldea.b He went to live in Haran. After his father died, God sent him to this place, where you live now. 5But God did not give Abraham any of this land, not even a foot of it. But God promised that in the future he would give Abraham this land for himself and for his children. This was before Abraham had any children.

6"This is what God said to him: 'Your descendants will live in another country. They will be strangers. The people there will make them slaves and mistreat them for 400 years. 7But I will punish the nation that made them slaves.'c And God also said, 'After those things happen, your people will come out of that country. Then they will worship me here in this place.'d

8"God made an agreement with Abraham; the sign for this agreement was circumcision.* And so when Abraham had a son, he circumcised him when he was eight days old. His son's name was Isaac. Isaac also circumcised his son Jacob. And Jacob did the same for his sons, who became the twelve great ancestors of our people.

9"These ancestors of ours became jealous of their brother Joseph and sold him to be a slave in Egypt. But God was with him 10and saved him from all his troubles. Pharaoh was the king of Egypt then. He liked Joseph and respected him because of the wisdom God gave him. Pharaoh gave Joseph the job of being a governor

a 7:3 Quote from Gen. 12:1.

b 7:4 Chaldea Or "Babylonia," a land in the southern part of Mesopotamia. See verse 2.
c 7:7 Quote from Gen. 15:13–14.
d 7:7 Quote from Gen. 15:14; Ex. 3:12.

of Egypt. He even let him rule over all the people in Pharaoh's house. ¹¹But all the land of Egypt and of Canaan* became dry. It became so dry that food could not grow, and the people suffered very much. Our people could not find anything to eat.

¹²"But Jacob heard that there was food in Egypt. So he sent our people there. This was their first trip to Egypt. ¹³Then they went there a second time. This time Joseph told his brothers who he was. And Pharaoh learned about Joseph's family. ¹⁴Then Joseph sent some men to tell Jacob, his father, to come to Egypt. He also invited all his relatives, a total of 75 people. ¹⁵So Jacob went down to Egypt. He and our other ancestors lived there until they died. ¹⁶Later, their bodies were moved to Shechem, where they were put in a tomb.* It was the same tomb that Abraham had bought in Shechem from the sons of Hamor. He paid them with silver.

¹⁷"The number of our people in Egypt grew. There were more and more of our people there. The promise that God made to Abraham was soon to come true. ¹⁸Then a different king began to rule Egypt, one who knew nothing about Joseph. ¹⁹This king tricked our people. He treated them badly, making them leave their children outside to die.

²⁰"This was the time when Moses* was born. He was a very beautiful child, and for three months his parents took care of him at home. ²¹When they put him outside, Pharaoh's daughter took him. She raised him as her own son. ²²The Egyptians taught Moses everything they knew. He was powerful in all he said and did.

²³"When Moses was about 40 years old, he decided to visit his own people, the people of Israel.* ²⁴He saw one of them being mistreated by an Egyptian, so he defended him. Moses hit the Egyptian to pay him back for hurting the man. He hit him so hard that it killed him. ²⁵Moses thought that his people would understand that God was using him to save them. But they did not understand.

²⁶"The next day, Moses saw two of his own people fighting. He tried to make peace between them. He said, 'Men, you are brothers! Why are you trying to hurt each other?' ²⁷The man who was hurting the other one pushed Moses away and said to him, 'Did anyone say you could be our ruler and judge? ²⁸Will you kill me just as you killed that Egyptian yesterday?'ᵃ ²⁹When Moses heard him say this, he left Egypt. He went to live in the land of Midian, where he was a stranger. During the time he lived there, he had two sons.

³⁰"Forty years later Moses was in the desert near Mount Sinai. An angel appeared to him in the flame of a burning bush. ³¹When Moses saw this, he was amazed. He went near to look closer at it. He heard a voice; it was the Lord's. ³²The Lord said, 'I am the same God your ancestors had—the God of Abraham,* the God of Isaac,* and the God of Jacob.*'ᵇ Moses began to shake with fear. He was afraid to look at the bush.

ᵃ 7:28 Quote from Ex. 2:14.
ᵇ 7:32 Quote from Ex. 3:6.

33"The Lord said to him, 'Take off your sandals, because the place where you are now standing is holy ground. 34I have seen my people suffer much in Egypt. I have heard my people crying and have come down to save them. Come now, Moses, I am sending you back to Egypt.'[a]

35"This Moses was the one his people said they did not want. They said, 'Did anyone say you could be our ruler and judge?'[b] But he is the one God sent to be a ruler and savior. God sent him with the help of an angel, the one Moses saw in the burning bush. 36So Moses led the people out of Egypt. He worked wonders* and miraculous signs* in Egypt, at the Red Sea, and then in the desert for 40 years.

37"This is the same Moses who said these words to the people of Israel: 'God will give you a prophet.* That prophet will come from among your own people. He will be like me.'[c] 38This same Moses was with the gathering of God's people in the desert. He was with the angel who spoke to him at Mount Sinai, and he was with our ancestors. He received life-giving words from God to give to us.

39"But our ancestors did not want to obey Moses. They rejected him. They wanted to go back to Egypt again. 40They said to Aaron, 'Moses led us out of the country of Egypt. But we don't know what has happened to him. So make some gods to go before us and lead us.'[d] 41So the people made an idol that looked like a calf. Then they brought sacrifices to it. They were very happy with what they had made with their own hands. 42But God turned against them and let them continue worshiping the army of false gods in the sky. This is what God says in the book that contains what the prophets wrote:

'People of Israel, you did not
　　bring me blood offerings
　　and sacrifices* in the desert
　　for 40 years;
43 You carried with you the tent
　　for worshiping Moloch
and the image of the star of
　　your god Rephan.
These were the idols you made
　　to worship.
So I will send you away
　　beyond Babylon.' *Amos 5:25-27*

44"The Holy Tent[e] was with our ancestors in the desert. God told Moses how to make this tent. He made it like the plan that God showed him. 45Later, Joshua led our ancestors to capture the lands of the other nations. Our people went in and God made the other people go out. When our people went into this new land, they took with them this same tent. Our people received this tent from their fathers, and our people kept it until the time of David.* 46God was very pleased with David. He asked God to let him build a Temple* for the people of Jacob.[f] 47But Solomon was the one who built the Temple.

48"But the Most High God does not live in houses built by human

a 7:34 Quote from Ex. 3:5–10.
b 7:35 Quote from Ex. 2:14.
c 7:37 Quote from Deut. 18:15.
d 7:40 Quote from Ex. 32:1.

e 7:44 Holy Tent Literally, "Tent of the Testimony." See "HOLY TENT" in the Word List.
f 7:46 for the people of Jacob Some Greek copies have "for the God of Jacob."

hands. This is what the prophet[a] writes:

⁴⁹ 'The Lord says,
Heaven is my throne,
   and the earth is where I rest
    my feet.
So do you think you can build
   a house for me?
   Do I need a place to rest?
⁵⁰ Remember, I made all these
    things!' "   *Isaiah 66:1–2*

⁵¹Then Stephen said, "You stubborn Jewish leaders! You refuse to give your hearts to God or even listen to him. You are always against what the Holy Spirit* wants you to do. That's how your ancestors were, and you are just like them! ⁵²They persecuted* every prophet who ever lived. They even killed those who long ago said that the Righteous One would come. And now you have turned against that Righteous One and killed him. ⁵³You are the people who received God's law, which he gave you through his angels. But you don't obey it!"

Stephen Is Killed

⁵⁴When those in the council meeting heard this, they became very angry. They were so mad they were grinding their teeth at him. ⁵⁵But Stephen was full of the Holy Spirit.* He looked up into heaven and saw the glory* of God. And he saw Jesus standing at God's right side. ⁵⁶Stephen said, "Look! I see heaven open. And I see the Son of Man* standing at God's right side."

⁵⁷Everyone there started shouting loudly, covering their ears with their hands. Together they all ran at Stephen. ⁵⁸They took him out of the city and began throwing stones at him. The men who told lies against Stephen gave their coats to a young man named Saul. ⁵⁹As they were throwing the stones at him, Stephen was praying. He said, "Lord Jesus, receive my spirit!" ⁶⁰He fell on his knees and shouted, "Lord, don't blame them for this sin!" These were his last words before he died.

8 ^{1–3}Saul agreed that the killing of Stephen was a good thing. Some godly men buried Stephen and cried loudly for him.

Trouble for the Believers

On that day the Jews began to persecute* the church* in Jerusalem, making them suffer very much. Saul was also trying to destroy the group. He went into their houses, dragged out men and women, and put them in jail. All the believers left Jerusalem. Only the apostles* stayed. The believers went to different places in Judea and Samaria. ⁴They were scattered everywhere, and in every place they went, they told people the Good News.*

Philip Tells the Good News in Samaria

⁵Philip[b] went to the city of Samaria and told people about the Messiah.* ⁶The people there heard Philip and saw the miraculous signs* he was doing. They all listened carefully to what he said. ⁷Many of these people had evil spirits inside them, but Philip made the evil spirits leave them. The spirits made a lot of noise as they came out. There were also many weak and crippled people there. Philip made these people well too. ⁸What a happy day this was for that city!

---

a **7:48 prophet** Isaiah, who spoke for God about 740–700 B.C.

b **8:5 Philip** Not the apostle named Philip.

9Now there was a man named Simon who lived in that city. Before Philip came there, Simon had been doing magic and amazing all the people of Samaria. He bragged and called himself a great man. 10All the people—the least important and the most important—believed what he said. They said, "This man has the power of God that is called 'the Great Power.'" 11Simon amazed the people with his magic for so long that the people became his followers. 12But Philip told the people the Good News* about God's kingdom* and the power of Jesus Christ. Men and women believed Philip and were baptized.* 13Simon himself also believed, and after he was baptized, he stayed close to Philip. When he saw the miraculous signs* and powerful things Philip did, he was amazed.

14The apostles* in Jerusalem heard that the people of Samaria had accepted the word of God. So they sent Peter and John to the people in Samaria. 15When Peter and John arrived, they prayed for the Samaritan believers to receive the Holy Spirit.* 16These people had been baptized in the name of the Lord Jesus, but the Holy Spirit had not yet come down on any of them. This is why Peter and John prayed. 17When the two apostles laid their hands on* the people, they received the Holy Spirit.

18Simon saw that the Spirit was given to people when the apostles laid their hands on them. So he offered the apostles money. 19He said, "Give me this power so that when I lay my hands on someone, they will receive the Holy Spirit." 20Peter said to Simon, "You and your money should both be destroyed because you thought you could buy God's gift with money. 21You cannot share with us in this work. Your heart is not right before God. 22Change your heart! Turn away from these evil thoughts and pray to the Lord. Maybe he will forgive you. 23I see that you are full of bitter jealousy and cannot stop yourself from doing wrong."

24Simon answered, "Both of you pray to the Lord for me, so that what you have said will not happen to me."

25Then the two apostles told the people what they had seen Jesus do. They told them the message* of the Lord. Then they went back to Jerusalem. On the way, they went through many Samaritan towns and told people the Good News.

Philip Teaches a Man From Ethiopia

26An angel of the Lord spoke to Philip. The angel said, "Get ready and go south on the road that leads down to Gaza from Jerusalem—the road that goes through the desert."

27So Philip got ready and went. On the road he saw a man from Ethiopia. He was a eunuch* and an important official in the service of Candace, the queen of the Ethiopians. He was responsible for taking care of all her money. This man had gone to Jerusalem to worship. 28Now he was on his way home. He was sitting in his chariot* reading from the book of Isaiah the prophet.* 29The Spirit* said to Philip, "Go to that chariot and stay near it." 30So he went toward the chariot, and he heard the man reading from Isaiah the prophet. Philip asked him, "Do you understand what you are reading?"

³¹The man answered, "How can I understand? I need someone to explain it to me." Then he invited Philip to climb in and sit with him. ³²The part of the Scriptures* that he was reading was this:

"He was like a sheep being led
  to the butcher.
He was like a lamb that makes
  no sound as its wool is
  being cut off.
He said nothing.
³³ He was shamed, and all his
  rights were taken away.
His life on earth has ended.
So there will be no story
  about his descendants."

Isaiah 53:7–8

³⁴The official[a] said to Philip, "Please, tell me, who is the prophet talking about? Is he talking about himself or about someone else?" ³⁵Philip began to speak. He started with this same Scripture and told the man the Good News* about Jesus.

³⁶While they were traveling down the road, they came to some water. The official said, "Look, here is water! What is stopping me from being baptized*?" ³⁷[b] ³⁸Then the official ordered the chariot to stop. Both Philip and the official went down into the water, and Philip baptized him. ³⁹When they came up out of the water, the Spirit of the Lord took Philip away; the official never saw him again. The official continued on his way home. He was very happy. ⁴⁰But Philip appeared in a city called Azotus. He was going to the city of Caesarea. He told people the Good News in all the towns on the way from Azotus to Caesarea.

Saul Becomes a Follower of Jesus

9 ¹In Jerusalem Saul was still trying to scare the followers of the Lord, even saying he would kill them. He went to the high priest* ²and asked him to write letters to the synagogues* in the city of Damascus. Saul wanted the high priest to give him the authority to find people in Damascus who were followers of the Way.* If he found any believers there, men or women, he would arrest them and bring them back to Jerusalem.

³So Saul went to Damascus. When he came near the city, a very bright light from heaven suddenly shined around him. ⁴He fell to the ground and heard a voice saying to him, "Saul, Saul! Why are you persecuting* me?"

⁵Saul said, "Who are you, Lord?"

The voice answered, "I am Jesus, the one you are persecuting. ⁶Get up now and go into the city. Someone there will tell you what you must do."

⁷The men traveling with Saul just stood there, unable to speak. They heard the voice, but they saw no one. ⁸Saul got up from the ground and opened his eyes, but he could not see. So the men with him held his hand and led him into Damascus. ⁹For three days, Saul could not see; he did not eat or drink.

¹⁰There was a follower of Jesus in Damascus named Ananias. In a vision* the Lord said to him, "Ananias!"

---

a **8:34 official** Literally, "eunuch." Also in verses 36, 38, 39.
b **8:37** Some late copies of Acts add verse 37: "Philip answered, 'If you believe with all your heart, you can.' The official said, 'I believe that Jesus Christ is the Son of God.'"

Ananias answered, "Here I am, Lord."

¹¹The Lord said to him, "Get up and go to the street called Straight Street. Find the house of Judas*a* and ask for a man named Saul from the city of Tarsus. He is there now, praying. ¹²He has seen a vision in which a man named Ananias came and laid his hands on* him so that he could see again."

¹³But Ananias answered, "Lord, many people have told me about this man. They told me about the many bad things he did to your holy people* in Jerusalem. ¹⁴Now he has come here to Damascus. The leading priests have given him the power to arrest all people who trust in you.*b*"

¹⁵But the Lord Jesus said to Ananias, "Go! I have chosen Saul for an important work. I want him to tell other nations, their rulers, and the people of Israel* about me. ¹⁶I will show him all that he must suffer for me."

¹⁷So Ananias left and went to the house of Judas. He laid his hands on Saul and said, "Saul, my brother, the Lord Jesus sent me. He is the one you saw on the road when you came here. He sent me so that you can see again and also be filled with the Holy Spirit.*" ¹⁸Immediately, something that looked like fish scales fell off Saul's eyes. He was able to see! Then he got up and was baptized.* ¹⁹After he ate, he began to feel strong again.

Saul Begins to Tell About Jesus

Saul stayed with the followers of Jesus in Damascus for a few days. ²⁰Soon he began to go to the synagogues* and tell people about Jesus. He told the people, "Jesus is the Son of God!"

²¹All the people who heard Saul were amazed. They said, "This is the same man who was in Jerusalem trying to destroy the people who trust in Jesus*c*! And that's why he has come here—to arrest the followers of Jesus and take them back to the leading priests."

²²But Saul became more and more powerful in proving that Jesus is the Messiah.* His proofs were so strong that the Jews who lived in Damascus could not argue with him.

Saul Escapes From Some Jews

²³After many days, some Jews made plans to kill Saul. ²⁴They were watching the city gates day and night. They wanted to kill Saul, but he learned about their plan. ²⁵One night some followers that Saul had taught helped him leave the city. They put him in a basket and lowered it down through a hole in the city wall.

Saul in Jerusalem

²⁶Then Saul went to Jerusalem. He tried to join the group of followers, but they were all afraid of him. They did not believe that he was really a follower of Jesus. ²⁷But Barnabas accepted Saul and took him to the apostles.* He told them how Saul had seen the Lord on the road and how the Lord had spoken to Saul. Then he told them how boldly Saul had spoken for the Lord in Damascus.

a **9:11 Judas** This is not either of the apostles named Judas.
b **9:14 who trust in you** Literally, "who call on your name," meaning to show faith in Jesus by worshiping him or praying to him for help.

c **9:21 who trust in Jesus** Literally, "who call on this name."

28And so Saul stayed with the followers and went all around Jerusalem speaking boldly for the Lord. 29He often had arguments with the Greek-speaking Jews, who began making plans to kill him. 30When the believers* learned about this, they took Saul to Caesarea, and from there they sent him to the city of Tarsus.

31The church* in Judea, Galilee, and Samaria had a time of peace. And with the help of the Holy Spirit,* these groups of believers became stronger in faith and showed their respect for the Lord by the way they lived. So the church everywhere grew in numbers.

Peter in Lydda and Joppa

32Peter was traveling through all the areas around Jerusalem, and he stopped to visit the believers*a* who lived in Lydda. 33There he met a man named Aeneas, who was paralyzed and had not been able to get out of bed for the past eight years. 34Peter said to him, "Aeneas, Jesus Christ heals you. Get up and make your bed!" He stood up immediately. 35All the people living in Lydda and on the plain of Sharon saw him, and they decided to follow the Lord.

36In the city of Joppa there was a follower of Jesus named Tabitha. Her Greek name, Dorcas, means "a deer." She was always doing good things for people and giving money to those in need. 37While Peter was in Lydda, Tabitha became sick and died. They washed her body and put it in an upstairs room. 38The followers in Joppa heard that Peter was in Lydda,

which was not far away. So they sent two men, who begged him, "Hurry, please come quickly!"

39Peter got ready and went with them. When he arrived, they took him to the upstairs room. All the widows stood around him. They were crying and showing him the coats and other clothes that Tabitha had made during her time with them. 40Peter sent all the people out of the room. He knelt down and prayed. Then he turned to Tabitha's body and said, "Tabitha, stand up!" She opened her eyes. When she saw Peter, she sat up. 41He gave her his hand and helped her stand up. Then he called the believers and the widows into the room. He showed them Tabitha; she was alive!

42People everywhere in Joppa learned about this, and many believed in the Lord. 43Peter stayed in Joppa for many days at the home of a man named Simon, who was a leatherworker.*

Peter and Cornelius

10 1In the city of Caesarea there was a man named Cornelius, a Roman army officer* in what was called the Italian Unit. 2He was a religious man. He and all the others who lived in his house were worshipers of the true God. He gave much of his money to help the poor people and always prayed to God. 3One afternoon about three o'clock, Cornelius had a vision.* He clearly saw an angel from God coming to him and saying, "Cornelius!"

4Staring at the angel and feeling afraid, Cornelius said, "What do you want, sir?"

The angel said to him, "God has heard your prayers and has seen your gifts to the poor. He

---

a **9:32 believers** Literally, "holy ones," a name for people who believe in Jesus. Also in verse 41.

remembers you and all you have done. 5Send some men now to the city of Joppa to get a man named Simon, who is also called Peter. 6He is staying with someone also named Simon, a leatherworker* who has a house beside the sea." 7The angel who spoke to Cornelius left. Then Cornelius called two of his servants and a soldier. The soldier was a religious man, one of his close helpers. 8Cornelius explained everything to these three men and sent them to Joppa.

9The next day they were coming near Joppa about noon, when Peter was going up to the roof to pray. 10He was hungry and wanted to eat. But while they were preparing the food for Peter to eat, he had a vision. 11He saw something coming down through the open sky. It looked like a big sheet being lowered to the ground by its four corners. 12In it were all kinds of animals, reptiles, and birds. 13Then a voice said to him, "Get up, Peter; kill anything here and eat it."

14But Peter said, "I can't do that, Lord! I have never eaten anything that is not pure or fit to be used for food."

15But the voice said to him again, "God has made these things pure. Don't say they are unfit to eat." 16This happened three times. Then the whole thing was taken back up into heaven. 17Peter wondered what this vision meant.

The men Cornelius sent had found Simon's house. They were standing at the door. 18They asked, "Is Simon Peter staying here?"

19While Peter was still thinking about the vision, the Spirit* said to him, "Listen, three men are looking for you. 20Get up and go downstairs. Go with these men without wondering if it's all right, because I sent them." 21So Peter went downstairs and said to them, "I think I'm the man you are looking for. Why did you come here?"

22The men said, "A holy* angel told Cornelius to invite you to his house. He is an army officer. He is a good man, one who worships God, and all the Jewish people respect him. The angel told him to invite you to his house so that he can listen to what you have to say." 23Peter asked the men to come in and stay for the night.

The next day Peter got ready and went away with the three men. Some of the believers* from Joppa went with him. 24The next day they came to the city of Caesarea. Cornelius was waiting for them and had already gathered his relatives and close friends at his house.

25When Peter entered the house, Cornelius met him. He fell down at Peter's feet and worshiped him. 26But Peter told him to get up. Peter said, "Stand up! I am only a man like you." 27Peter continued talking with Cornelius. Then Peter went inside and saw a large group of people gathered there.

28Peter said to the people, "You understand that it is against our law for a Jew to associate with or visit anyone who is not a Jew. But God has shown me that I should not consider anyone unfit or say they are not pure. 29That's why I didn't argue when your men asked me to come here. Now, please tell me why you sent for me."

30Cornelius said, "Four days ago, I was praying in my house. It was at this same time—three o'clock in the afternoon. Suddenly there was someone standing before me wearing bright, shiny clothes. [31]He said, 'Cornelius, God has heard your prayer and has seen your gifts to the poor. He remembers you and all you have done. [32]So send some men to the city of Joppa and tell Simon Peter to come. He is staying with another man named Simon, a leatherworker who has a house beside the sea.' [33]So I sent for you immediately. It was very good of you to come here. Now we are all here before God to hear everything the Lord has commanded you to tell us."

Peter Speaks in the House of Cornelius

[34]Peter began to speak: "I really understand now that God does not consider some people to be better than others. [35]He accepts anyone who worships him and does what is right. It is not important what nation they come from. [36]God has spoken to the people of Israel.* He sent them the Good News* that peace has come through Jesus Christ, the Lord of all people.

[37]"You know what has happened all over Judea. It began in Galilee after John* told the people they needed to be baptized.* [38]You know about Jesus from Nazareth. God made him the Messiah* by giving him the Holy Spirit* and power. Jesus went everywhere doing good for people. He healed those who were ruled by the devil, showing that God was with him. [39]"We saw all that Jesus did in Judea and in Jerusalem. But he was killed. They put him on a cross made of wood. [40]But on the third day after his death, God raised him to life and let him be

seen openly. [41]He was not seen by everyone, but only by us, the ones God had already chosen to be witnesses. We ate and drank with him after he was raised from death.

[42]"Jesus told us to go and speak to the people. He told us to tell them that he is the one God chose to be the Judge of all who are living and all who have died. [43]Everyone who believes in Jesus will have their sins forgiven through his name. All the prophets* agree that this is true."

God Shows That He Accepts All People

[44]While Peter was still speaking these words, the Holy Spirit* came down on all those who were listening to his speech. [45]The Jewish believers who came with Peter were amazed that the Holy Spirit had been poured out as a gift also to people who were not Jews. [46]They heard them speaking different languages and praising God. Then Peter said, [47]"How can anyone object to these people being baptized* in water? They have received the Holy Spirit the same as we did!" [48]So Peter told them to baptize Cornelius and his relatives and friends in the name of Jesus Christ. Then they asked Peter to stay with them for a few days.

Peter Returns to Jerusalem

11 [1]The apostles* and the believers* in Judea heard that non-Jewish people had accepted God's teaching too. [2]But when Peter came to Jerusalem, some Jewish believers[a] argued with him. [3]They

a 11:2 Jewish believers Literally, "those of circumcision." This may mean Jews who thought all followers of Christ must be circumcised and obey the Law of Moses. See Gal. 2:12.

said, "You went into the homes of people who are not Jews and are not circumcised,* and you even ate with them!"

4So Peter explained the whole story to them. 5He said, "I was in the city of Joppa. While I was praying, I had a vision.* I saw something coming down from heaven. It looked like a big sheet being lowered to the ground by its four corners. It came down close to me, 6and I looked inside. I saw all kinds of animals, including wild ones, as well as reptiles and birds. 7I heard a voice say to me, 'Get up, Peter. Kill anything here and eat it!'

8"But I said, 'I can't do that, Lord! I have never eaten anything that is not pure or fit to be used for food.'

9"But the voice from heaven answered again, 'God has made these things pure. Don't say they are unfit to eat!'

10"This happened three times. Then the whole thing was taken back into heaven. 11Suddenly there were three men standing outside the house where I was staying. They had been sent from Caesarea to get me. 12The Spirit* told me to go with them without wondering if it was all right. These six brothers here also went with me, and we went to the house of Cornelius. 13He told us about the angel he had seen standing in his house. The angel said, 'Send some men to Joppa to get Simon, the one who is also called Peter. 14He will speak to you, and what he tells you will save you and everyone living in your house.'

15"After I began speaking, the Holy Spirit came on them just as he came on us at the beginning.a 16Then I remembered the words of the Lord Jesus: 'John baptized* people in water, but you will be baptized in the Holy Spirit.' 17God gave these people the same gift he gave us who believed in the Lord Jesus Christ. So how could I object to what God wanted to do?"

18When the Jewish believers heard this, they stopped arguing. They praised God and said, "So God is also allowing even those who are not Jews to change their hearts so that they can have the life he gives!"

The Good News Comes to Antioch

19The believers were scattered by the persecutionb that began when Stephen was killed. Some of them went as far as Phoenicia, Cyprus, and Antioch. They told the Good News* in these places, but only to Jews. 20Some of these believers were men from Cyprus and Cyrene. When these men came to Antioch, they began speaking to people who were not Jews.c They told them the Good News about the Lord Jesus. 21The Lord was helping these men, and a large number of people believed and decided to follow the Lord.

22When the church* in Jerusalem heard about this, they sent

a 11:15 beginning The day of Pentecost described in Acts 2, when the Holy Spirit came on Jesus' first followers to give them power to begin their work of telling the world the Good News of salvation through Jesus.
b 11:19 persecution A time when the Jewish leaders in Jerusalem were punishing people who believed in Christ. See Acts 8:1–4.
c 11:20 people who were not Jews Literally, "Hellenists," meaning people who have been influenced by Greek culture. Some Greek copies have "Greeks."

Barnabas to Antioch. 23-24Barnabas was a good man, full of the Holy Spirit* and faith. When he went to Antioch and saw how God had blessed the believers there, he was very happy. He encouraged them all, saying, "Always be faithful to the Lord. Serve him with all your heart." Many more people became followers of the Lord.

25Then Barnabas went to the city of Tarsus to look for Saul. 26When he found him, he brought him to Antioch. They stayed there a whole year. Every time the church came together, Barnabas and Saul met with them and taught many people. It was in Antioch that the followers of the Lord Jesus were called "Christ-followers" for the first time.

27About that same time some prophets* went from Jerusalem to Antioch. 28One of them, named Agabus, stood up and spoke with the help of the Spirit. He said, "A very bad time is coming to the whole world. There will be no food for people to eat." (This time of famine happened when Claudius was emperor.*) 29The Lord's followers decided that they would each send as much as they could to help their brothers and sisters who lived in Judea. 30They gathered the money and gave it to Barnabas and Saul, who took it to the elders* in Judea.

More Trouble for the Believers

12 1During this same time, King Herod* began to do harm to some of those who were part of the church.* 2He ordered James, the brother of John, to be killed with a sword. 3Herod saw that many of the Jews liked this, so he decided to arrest Peter too. This happened during the Festival of Unleavened Bread.* 4He arrested Peter and put him in jail, where he was guarded by a group of 16 soldiers. Herod planned to bring Peter before the people, but he wanted to wait until after the Passover festival. 5So Peter was kept in jail, but the church was constantly praying to God for him.

Peter Is Led Out of the Jail

6One night, Peter, bound with two chains, was sleeping between two of the soldiers. More soldiers were guarding the door of the jail. Herod* was planning to bring Peter out before the people the next day. 7Suddenly an angel of the Lord was standing there, and the room was filled with light. The angel tapped Peter on the side and woke him up. The angel said, "Hurry, get up!" The chains fell off Peter's hands. 8The angel said, "Get dressed and put on your sandals." Peter did as he was told. Then the angel said, "Put on your coat and follow me."

9So the angel went out and Peter followed. He did not know if the angel was really doing this. He thought he might be seeing a vision.* 10Peter and the angel went past the first guard and the second guard. Then they came to the iron gate that separated them from the city. The gate opened for them by itself. After they went through the gate and walked about a block, the angel suddenly left.

11Peter realized then what had happened. He thought, "Now I know that the Lord really sent his angel to me. He rescued me from Herod and from everything those Jews thought would happen to me."

12When Peter realized this, he went to the home of Mary, the mother of John, who was also called Mark. Many people were gathered there and were praying. 13Peter knocked on the outside door. A servant girl named Rhoda came to answer it. 14She recognized Peter's voice, and she was very happy. She even forgot to open the door. She ran inside and told the group, "Peter is at the door!" 15The believers said to her, "You are crazy!" But she continued to say that it was true. So they said, "It must be Peter's angel."

16But Peter continued to knock. When the believers opened the door, they saw him. They were amazed. 17Peter made a sign with his hand to tell them to be quiet. He explained to them how the Lord led him out of the jail. He said, "Tell James and the other brothers what happened." Then he left and went to another place.

18The next day the soldiers were very upset. They wondered what happened to Peter. 19Herod looked everywhere for him but could not find him. So he questioned the guards and then ordered that they be killed.

The Death of Herod Agrippa

Later, Herod* moved from Judea. He went to the city of Caesarea and stayed there a while. 20Herod was very angry with the people from the cities of Tyre and Sidon. But these cities needed food from his country, so a group of them came to ask him for peace. They were able to get Blastus, the king's personal servant, on their side. 21Herod decided on a day to meet with them. On that day he was wearing a beautiful royal robe. He sat on his throne and made a speech to the people. 22The people shouted, "This is the voice of a god, not a man!" 23Herod did not give the glory* to God. So an angel of the Lord caused him to get sick. He was eaten by worms inside him, and he died.

24The message* of God was spreading, reaching more and more people.

25After Barnabas and Saul finished their work in Jerusalem, they returned to Antioch, taking John Mark with them.

Barnabas and Saul Given a Special Work

13 1In the church* at Antioch there were some prophets* and teachers. They were Barnabas, Simeon (also called Niger), Lucius (from the city of Cyrene), Manaen (who had grown up with King Herod[d]), and Saul. 2These men were all serving the Lord and fasting* when the Holy Spirit* said to them, "Appoint Barnabas and Saul to do a special work for me. They are the ones I have chosen to do it."

3So the church fasted and prayed. They laid their hands on* Barnabas and Saul and sent them out.

Barnabas and Saul in Cyprus

4Barnabas and Saul were sent out by the Holy Spirit.* They went to the city of Seleucia. Then they sailed from there to the island of Cyprus. 5When Barnabas and Saul came to the city of Salamis, they told the message* of God in the Jewish synagogues.* John Mark was with them to help.

6They went across the whole island to the city of Paphos. There they met a Jewish man named

---

a 13:1 **King Herod** Literally, "Herod the tetrarch." See "HEROD AGRIPPA I" in the Word List.

Jesus tells about a father and two sons
Luke 15:11–32

©WBTC 2011

Jesus welcomes children
Mark 10:13-16

©WBTC 2011

Barjesus who did magic. He was a false prophet.* [7]He always stayed close to Sergius Paulus, who was the governor and a very smart man. He invited Barnabas and Saul to come visit him, because he wanted to hear the message of God. [8]But the magician Elymas (as Barjesus was called in Greek) spoke against them, trying to stop the governor from believing in Jesus. [9]But Saul (also known as Paul), filled with the Holy Spirit, looked hard at Elymas [10]and said, "You son of the devil, full of lies and all kinds of evil tricks! You are an enemy of everything that is right. Will you never stop trying to change the Lord's truths into lies? [11]Now the Lord will touch you and you will be blind. For a time you will not be able to see anything—not even the light from the sun."

Then everything became dark for Elymas. He walked around lost. He was trying to find someone to lead him by the hand. [12]When the governor saw this, he believed. He was amazed at the teaching about the Lord.

Paul and Barnabas Go to Antioch in Pisidia

[13]Paul and the people with him sailed away from Paphos. They came to Perga, a city in Pamphylia. There John Mark left them and returned to Jerusalem. [14]They continued their trip from Perga and went to Antioch, a city near Pisidia.

On the Sabbath* day they went into the Jewish synagogue* and sat down. [15]The Law of Moses* and the writings of the prophets* were read. Then the leaders of the synagogue sent a message to Paul and Barnabas: "Brothers, if you have something to say that will help the people here, please speak."

[16]Paul stood up, raised his hand to get their attention, and said, "People of Israel* and all you others who worship the true God, please listen to me! [17]The God of Israel chose our ancestors.* And during the time our people lived in Egypt as foreigners, he made them great. Then he brought them out of that country with great power. [18]And he was patient with them for 40 years in the desert. [19]God destroyed seven nations in the land of Canaan* and gave their land to his people. [20]All this happened in about 450 years.

"After this, God gave our people judges until the time of Samuel* the prophet. [21]Then the people asked for a king. God gave them Saul, the son of Kish. Saul was from the tribe of Benjamin. He was king for 40 years. [22]After God took Saul away, God made David* their king. This is what God said about David: 'David, the son of Jesse, is the kind of person who does what pleases me. He will do everything I want him to do.'

[23]"As he promised, God has brought one of David's descendants to Israel to be their Savior. That descendant is Jesus. [24]Before he came, John* told all the people of Israel what they should do. He told them to be baptized* to show they wanted to change their lives. [25]When John was finishing his work, he said, 'Who do you think I am? I am not the Messiah.[a] He is coming later, and I am not worthy

---

a **13:25 the Messiah** Literally, "I" (that is, "he" or "the one"), meaning the chosen one sent by God. Compare Jn. 1:20. See "Messiah" in the Word List.

to be the slave who unties his sandals.'

26"My brothers, sons in the family of Abraham,* and you other people who also worship the true God, listen! The news about this salvation has been sent to us. 27The Jews living in Jerusalem and their leaders did not realize that Jesus was the Savior. The words the prophets wrote about him were read every Sabbath day, but they did not understand. They condemned Jesus. When they did this, they made the words of the prophets come true. 28They could not find any real reason why Jesus should die, but they asked Pilate* to kill him.

29"These Jews did all the bad things that the Scriptures* said would happen to Jesus. Then they took Jesus down from the cross and put him in a tomb.* 30But God raised him up from death! 31After this, for many days, those who had gone with Jesus from Galilee to Jerusalem saw him. They are now his witnesses to our people.

32"We tell you the Good News* about the promise God made to our ancestors. 33We are their descendants, and God has made this promise come true for us. God did this by raising Jesus from death. We also read about this in Psalm 2:

'You are my Son.
    Today I have become your
        Father.'   *Psalm 2:7*
34God raised Jesus from death. Jesus will never go back to the grave and become dust. So God said,

'I will give you the true and
    holy promises that I made
        to David.'   *Isaiah 55:3*
35But in another Psalm it says,

'You will not let your Holy One
    rot in the grave.'   *Psalm 16:10*
36"David did God's will during the time he lived. Then he died and was buried like all his ancestors. And his body did rot in the grave! 37But the one God raised from death did not rot in the grave. 38-39Brothers, understand what we are telling you. You can have forgiveness of your sins through this Jesus. The Law of Moses could not free you from your sins. But you can be made right with God if you believe in Jesus. 40So be careful! Don't let what the prophets said happen to you:

41'Listen, you people who doubt!
    You can wonder, but then go
        away and die;
because during your time,
    I will do something that you
        will not believe.
You will not believe it, even
    if someone explains it to
        you!'"   *Habakkuk 1:5*

42As Paul and Barnabas were leaving the synagogue, the people asked them to come again on the next Sabbath day and tell them more about these things. 43After the meeting, many of the people followed Paul and Barnabas, including many Jews and people who had changed their religion to be like Jews and worship the true God. Paul and Barnabas encouraged them to continue trusting in God's grace.*

44On the next Sabbath day, almost all the people in the city came together to hear the word of the Lord. 45When the Jews there saw all these people, they became very jealous. Shouting insults, they argued against everything Paul said. 46But Paul and

Barnabas spoke very boldly. They said, "We had to tell God's message* to you Jews first, but you refuse to listen. You have made it clear that you are not worthy of having eternal life. So we will now go to those who are not Jews. 47This is what the Lord told us to do:

'I have made you a light for the other nations,
to show people all over the world the way to be saved.'"

Isaiah 49:6

48When the non-Jewish people heard Paul say this, they were happy. They gave honor to the message of the Lord, and many of them believed it. These were the ones chosen to have eternal life. 49And so the message of the Lord was being told throughout the whole country. 50But the Jews there caused some of the important religious women and the leaders of the city to be angry and turn against Paul and Barnabas and throw them out of town. 51So Paul and Barnabas shook the dust off their feet.ᵃ Then they went to the city of Iconium. 52But the Lord's followers in Antioch were happy and filled with the Holy Spirit.*

Paul and Barnabas in Iconium

14 1Paul and Barnabas went to the city of Iconium. As they did in Antioch, they entered the Jewish synagogue.* They spoke to the people there. They spoke so well that many Jews and Greeks believed what they said. 2But some of the Jews did not believe. They said things that caused the non-Jewish people to be angry and turn against the believers.*

3So Paul and Barnabas stayed in Iconium a long time, and they spoke bravely for the Lord. They told the people about God's grace.* The Lord proved that what they said was true by causing miraculous signs* and wonders* to be done through them. 4But some of the people in the city agreed with the Jews who did not believe Paul and Barnabas. Others followed the apostles. So the city was divided.

5Some of the Jews there, as well as their leaders and some of the non-Jewish people, were determined to hurt Paul and Barnabas. They wanted to stone them to death. 6When Paul and Barnabas learned about this, they left the city. They went to Lystra and Derbe, cities in Lycaonia, and to the surrounding areas. 7They told the Good News* there too.

Paul in Lystra and Derbe

8In Lystra there was a man who had something wrong with his feet. He had been born crippled and had never walked. 9He was sitting and listening to Paul speak. Paul looked straight at him and saw that the man believed God could heal him. 10So Paul shouted, "Stand up on your feet!" The man jumped up and began walking around.

11When the people saw what Paul did, they shouted in their own Lycaonian language. They said, "The gods have come down to us in the form of humans!" 12The people began to call Barnabas "Zeus,*" and they called Paul "Hermes,*" because he was the main speaker. 13The temple of Zeus was near the city. The priest

---

ᵃ **13:51 shook the dust off their feet** A warning. It showed they were finished talking to these people.

of this temple brought some bulls and flowers to the city gates. The priest and the people wanted to offer a sacrifice to Paul and Barnabas.

14But when the apostles,* Barnabas and Paul, understood what the people were doing, they tore their own clothes.*a* Then they ran in among the people and shouted to them: 15"Men, why are you doing this? We are not gods. We are human just like you. We came to tell you the Good News.* We are telling you to turn away from these worthless things. Turn to the true living God, the one who made the sky, the earth, the sea, and everything that is in them.

16"In the past God let all the nations do what they wanted. 17But God was always there doing the good things that prove he is real. He gives you rain from heaven and good harvests at the right times. He gives you plenty of food and fills your hearts with joy."

18Even after saying all this, Paul and Barnabas still could hardly stop the people from offering sacrifices to them.

19Then some Jews came from Antioch and Iconium and persuaded the people to turn against Paul. So they threw stones at him and dragged him out of the town. They thought they had killed him. 20But when the followers of Jesus gathered around him, he got up and went back into the town. The next day he and Barnabas left and went to the city of Derbe.

The Return to Antioch in Syria

21They also told the Good News* in the city of Derbe, and many

people became followers of Jesus. Then Paul and Barnabas returned to the cities of Lystra, Iconium, and Antioch. 22In those cities they helped the followers grow stronger in their faith and encouraged them to continue trusting God. They told them, "We must suffer many things on our way into God's kingdom.*" 23They also chose elders* for each church* and stopped eating for a period of time to pray for them. These elders were men who had put their trust in the Lord Jesus, so Paul and Barnabas put them in his care.

24Paul and Barnabas went through the country of Pisidia. Then they came to the country of Pamphylia. 25They told people the message* of God in the city of Perga, and then they went down to the city of Attalia. 26And from there they sailed away to Antioch in Syria. This is the city where the believers had put them into God's care and sent them to do this work. Now they had finished it.

27When Paul and Barnabas arrived, they gathered the church together. They told them everything God had used them to do. They said, "God opened a door for the non-Jewish people to believe!" 28And they stayed there a long time with the Lord's followers.

The Meeting at Jerusalem

15 1Then some men came to Antioch from Judea and began teaching the non-Jewish believers*: "You cannot be saved if you are not circumcised* as Moses* taught us." 2Paul and Barnabas were against this teaching and argued with these men about it. So the group decided to send Paul, Barnabas, and some others

a **14:14 tore ... clothes** This showed they were very upset.

to Jerusalem to talk more about this with the apostles* and elders.*

³The church* helped them get ready to leave on their trip. The men went through the countries of Phoenicia and Samaria, where they told all about how the non-Jewish people had turned to the true God. This made all the believers very happy. ⁴When the men arrived in Jerusalem, the apostles, the elders, and the whole church welcomed them. Paul, Barnabas, and the others told about all that God had done with them. ⁵Some of the believers in Jerusalem had belonged to the Pharisees.* They stood up and said, "The non-Jewish believers must be circumcised. We must tell them to obey the Law of Moses!"

⁶Then the apostles and the elders gathered to study this problem. ⁷After a long debate, Peter stood up and said to them, "My brothers, I am sure you remember what happened in the early days. God chose me from among you to tell the Good News* to those who are not Jewish. It was from me that they heard the Good News and believed. ⁸God knows everyone, even their thoughts, and he accepted these non-Jewish people. He showed this to us by giving them the Holy Spirit* the same as he did to us. ⁹To God, those people are not different from us. When they believed, God made their hearts pure. ¹⁰So now, why are you putting a heavy burden*ᵃ* around the necks of the non-Jewish followers of Jesus? Are you trying to make God angry? We and our fathers* were not able to carry that burden. ¹¹No, we believe that we and these people will be saved the same way—by the grace* of the Lord Jesus."

¹²Then the whole group became quiet. They listened while Paul and Barnabas told about all the miraculous signs* and wonders* that God had done through them among the non-Jewish people. ¹³When they finished speaking, James said, "My brothers, listen to me. ¹⁴Simon Peter has told us how God showed his love for the non-Jewish people. For the first time, God accepted them and made them his people. ¹⁵The words of the prophets* agree with this too:

¹⁶ 'I will return after this.
  I will build David's* house
    again.
  It has fallen down.
  I will build again the parts of
    his house that have been
    pulled down.
  I will make his house new.
¹⁷ Then the rest of the world will
    look for the Lord God—
  all those of other nations
    who are my people too.
  The Lord said this.
  And he is the one who does
    all these things.'   *Amos 9:11–12*

¹⁸ 'All this has been known from
    the beginning of time.'ᵇ
¹⁹"So I think we should not make things hard for those who have turned to God from among the non-Jewish people. ²⁰Instead, we should send a letter telling them only the things they should not do:
  Don't eat food that has been
    given to idols.* This makes
    the food unclean.

ᵃ **15:10 burden** The Jewish law. Some of the Jews tried to make the non-Jewish believers follow this law.

ᵇ **15:18** See Isa. 45:21.

Don't be involved in sexual sin. Don't eat meat from animals that have been strangled or any meat that still has the blood in it. [21]They should not do any of these things, because there are still men in every city who teach the Law of Moses. The words of Moses have been read in the synagogue* every Sabbath* day for many years."

The Letter to the Non-Jewish Believers

[22]The apostles,* the elders,* and the whole church* wanted to send some men with Paul and Barnabas to Antioch. The group decided to choose some of their own men. They chose Judas (also called Barsabbas) and Silas, men who were respected by the believers.* [23]The group sent the letter with these men. The letter said:

From the apostles and elders, your brothers,
To all the non-Jewish brothers in the city of Antioch and in the countries of Syria and Cilicia.

Dear Brothers:

[24]We have heard that some men have come to you from our group. What they said troubled and upset you. But we did not tell them to do this. [25]We have all agreed to choose some men and send them to you. They will be with our dear friends, Barnabas and Paul. [26]Barnabas and Paul have given their lives to serve our Lord Jesus Christ. [27]So we have sent Judas and Silas with them. They will tell you the same things. [28]We agree with the Holy Spirit* that you should have no more burdens, except for these necessary things:
[29]Don't eat food that has been given to idols.*
Don't eat meat from animals that have been strangled or any meat that still has the blood in it.
Don't be involved in sexual sin.
If you stay away from these, you will do well.

We say goodbye now.

[30]So Paul, Barnabas, Judas, and Silas left Jerusalem and went to Antioch. There they gathered the group of believers together and gave them the letter. [31]When the believers read it, they were happy. The letter comforted them. [32]Judas and Silas, who were also prophets,* said many things to encourage the believers* and make them stronger in their faith. [33]After Judas and Silas stayed there for a while, they left. They received a blessing of peace from the believers.* Then they went back to those who had sent them. [34]ᵃ

[35]But Paul and Barnabas stayed in Antioch. They and many others taught the believers and told other people the Good News* about the Lord.

Paul and Barnabas Separate

[36]A few days later, Paul said to Barnabas, "We should go back to all the towns where we told people the message* of the Lord. We should visit the believers* to see how they are doing." [37]Barnabas wanted to bring John Mark with them too. [38]But on their first trip John Mark did

---

ᵃ 15:34 Some Greek copies add verse 34: "But Silas decided to remain there."

not continue with them in the work. He had left them at Pamphylia. So Paul did not think it was a good idea to take him this time. 39Paul and Barnabas had a big argument about this. It was so bad that they separated and went different ways. Barnabas sailed to Cyprus and took Mark with him. 40Paul chose Silas to go with him. The believers* in Antioch put Paul into the Lord's care and sent him out. 41Paul and Silas went through the countries of Syria and Cilicia, helping the churches* grow stronger.

Timothy Goes With Paul and Silas

16 1Paul went to the city of Derbe and then to Lystra, where a follower of Jesus named Timothy lived. Timothy's mother was a Jewish believer, but his father was a Greek. 2The believers* in the cities of Lystra and Iconium had only good things to say about him. 3Paul wanted Timothy to travel with him, but all the Jews living in that area knew that his father was a Greek. So Paul circumcised* Timothy to please the Jews.

4Then Paul and those with him traveled through other cities. They gave the believers the rules and decisions from the apostles* and elders* in Jerusalem. They told them to obey these rules. 5So the churches* were becoming stronger in their faith, and the number of believers was growing every day.

Paul Is Called to Macedonia

6Paul and those with him went through the areas of Phrygia and Galatia because the Holy Spirit* did not allow them to tell the Good News* in the province of Asia.* 7When they reached the border of Mysia, they tried to go on into Bithynia, but the Spirit of Jesus did not let them go there. 8So they passed by Mysia and went to the city of Troas.

9That night Paul saw a vision.* In it, a man from Macedonia* came to Paul. The man stood there and begged, "Come across to Macedonia and help us." 10After Paul had seen the vision, we*a* immediately prepared to leave for Macedonia. We understood that God had called us to tell the Good News to those people.

The Conversion of Lydia

11We left Troas in a ship and sailed to the island of Samothrace. The next day we sailed to the city of Neapolis. 12Then we went to Philippi, a Roman colony and the leading city in that part of Macedonia.* We stayed there for a few days.

13On the Sabbath* day we went out the city gate to the river. There we thought we might find a special place for prayer. Some women had gathered there, so we sat down and talked with them. 14There was a woman there named Lydia from the city of Thyatira. Her job was selling purple cloth. She was a worshiper of the true God. Lydia was listening to Paul, and the Lord opened her heart to accept what Paul was saying. 15She and all the people living in her house were baptized.* Then she invited us into her home. She said, "If you think I am a true believer in the Lord Jesus, come

---

a 16:10 we Luke, the writer, apparently went with Paul to Macedonia but did not leave Philippi with him. (See verse 40.) The first person pronoun occurs again in 20:5–21:18 and 27:1–28.

stay in my house." She persuaded us to stay with her.

Paul and Silas in Jail

¹⁶One day we were going to the place for prayer, and a servant girl met us. She had a spirit*a* in her that gave her the power to tell what would happen in the future. By doing this she earned a lot of money for the men who owned her. ¹⁷She started following Paul and the rest of us around. She kept shouting, "These men are servants of the Most High God! They are telling you how you can be saved!" ¹⁸She continued doing this for many days. This bothered Paul, so he turned and said to the spirit, "By the power of Jesus Christ, I command you to come out of her!" Immediately, the spirit came out.

¹⁹When the men who owned the servant girl saw this, they realized that they could no longer use her to make money. So they grabbed Paul and Silas and dragged them to the public square to meet with the authorities. ²⁰They brought Paul and Silas before the Roman officials and said, "These men are Jews, and they are making trouble in our city. ²¹They are telling people to do things that are not right for us as Romans to do."

²²The whole crowd turned against Paul and Silas. The officials tore the clothes off both men and ordered that they be beaten with rods. ²³They were beaten severely and thrown into jail. The officials told the jailer, "Guard them very carefully!" ²⁴When the jailer heard this special order, he put Paul and Silas far inside the jail and bound their feet between large blocks of wood.

²⁵About midnight Paul and Silas were praying and singing songs to God. The other prisoners were listening to them. ²⁶Suddenly there was an earthquake so strong that it shook the foundation of the jail. All the doors of the jail opened, and the chains on all the prisoners fell off. ²⁷The jailer woke up and saw that the jail doors were open. He thought that the prisoners had already escaped, so he got his sword and was ready to kill himself.*b* ²⁸But Paul shouted, "Don't hurt yourself! We are all here!"

²⁹The jailer told someone to bring a light. Then he ran inside and, shaking with fear, fell down in front of Paul and Silas. ³⁰Then he brought them outside and said, "Men, what must I do to be saved?"

³¹They said to him, "Believe in the Lord Jesus and you will be saved—you and all who live in your house." ³²So Paul and Silas told the message* of the Lord to the jailer and all the people who lived in his house. ³³It was late at night, but the jailer took Paul and Silas and washed their wounds. Then the jailer and all his people were baptized.* ³⁴After this the jailer took Paul and Silas home and gave them some food. All the people were very happy because they now believed in God.

³⁵The next morning the Roman officials sent some soldiers to tell the jailer, "Let these men go free." ³⁶The jailer said to Paul, "The officials have sent these soldiers

---

a **16:16 spirit** A spirit from the devil that gave special knowledge.

b **16:27 kill himself** He thought the leaders would kill him for letting the prisoners escape.

to let you go free. You can leave now. Go in peace."

³⁷But Paul said to the soldiers, "Those officials did not prove that we did anything wrong, but they beat us in public and put us in jail. And we are Roman citizens.^a Now they want us to go away quietly. No, they must come here themselves and lead us out!"

³⁸The soldiers told the officials what Paul said. When they heard that Paul and Silas were Roman citizens, they were afraid. ³⁹So they came and told them they were sorry. They led them out of the jail and asked them to leave the city. ⁴⁰But when Paul and Silas came out of the jail, they went to Lydia's house. They saw some of the believers* there and encouraged them. Then they left.

Paul and Silas in Thessalonica

17 ¹Paul and Silas traveled through the cities of Amphipolis and Apollonia. They came to the city of Thessalonica, where there was a Jewish synagogue.* ²Paul went into the synagogue to see the Jews as he always did. The next three weeks, on each Sabbath* day, he discussed the Scriptures* with them. ³He explained the Scriptures to show them that the Messiah* had to die and then rise from death. He said, "This Jesus that I am telling you about is the Messiah." ⁴Some of the Jews there believed Paul and Silas and decided to join them. Also, a large number of Greeks who were worshipers of the true God and many important women joined them.

⁵But the Jews who did not believe became jealous, so they got some bad men from around the city center to make trouble. They formed a mob and caused a riot in the city. They went to Jason's house, looking for Paul and Silas. They wanted to bring them out before the people. ⁶When they did not find them, they dragged Jason and some of the other believers to the city leaders. The people shouted, "These men have made trouble everywhere in the world, and now they have come here too! ⁷Jason is keeping them in his house. They all do things against the laws of Caesar.* They say there is another king called Jesus."

⁸When the city leaders and the other people heard this, they became very upset. ⁹They made Jason and the other believers deposit money to guarantee that there would be no more trouble. Then they let them go.

Paul and Silas Go to Berea

¹⁰That same night the believers* sent Paul and Silas to another city named Berea. When they arrived there, they went to the Jewish synagogue.* ¹¹The people in Berea were more open-minded than those in Thessalonica. They were so glad to hear the message Paul told them. They studied the Scriptures* every day to make sure that what they heard was really true. ¹²The result was that many of them believed, including many important Greek women and men.

¹³But when the Jews in Thessalonica learned that Paul was telling people God's message* in Berea, they came there too. They upset the people and made trouble. ¹⁴So the believers immediately sent Paul away to the coast, but Silas and Timothy stayed in Berea.

---

a **16:37 Roman citizens** Roman law said that Roman citizens must not be beaten before their trial.

15Those who went with Paul took him to the city of Athens. They returned with a message for Silas and Timothy to come and join him as soon as they could.

Paul in Athens

16While Paul was waiting for Silas and Timothy in Athens, he was upset because he saw that the city was full of idols.* 17In the synagogue* he talked with the Jews and with the Greeks who were worshipers of the true God. He also went to the public square every day and talked with everyone who came by. 18Some of the Epicurean and some of the Stoic philosophers* argued with him.

Some of them said, "This man doesn't really know what he is talking about. What is he trying to say?" Paul was telling them the Good News* about Jesus and the resurrection.* So they said, "He seems to be telling us about some other gods."

19They took Paul to a meeting of the Areopagus council.* They said, "Please explain to us this new idea that you have been teaching. 20The things you are saying are new to us. We have never heard this teaching before, and we want to know what it means." 21(The people of Athens and the foreigners who lived there spent all their time either telling or listening to all the latest ideas.)

22Then Paul stood up before the meeting of the Areopagus council and said, "Men of Athens, everything I see here tells me you are very religious. 23I was going through your city and I saw the things you worship. I found an altar that had these words written on it: 'TO AN UNKNOWN GOD.' You worship a god that you don't know. This is the God I want to tell you about.

24"He is the God who made the whole world and everything in it. He is the Lord of the land and the sky. He does not live in temples built by human hands. 25He is the one who gives people life, breath, and everything else they need. He does not need any help from them. He has everything he needs. 26God began by making one man, and from him he made all the different people who live everywhere in the world. He decided exactly when and where they would live.

27"God wanted people to look for him, and perhaps in searching all around for him, they would find him. But he is not far from any of us. 28It is through him that we are able to live, to do what we do, and to be who we are. As your own poets have said, 'We all come from him.'

29"That's right. We all come from God. So you must not think that he is like something people imagine or make. He is not made of gold, silver, or stone. 30In the past people did not understand God, and he overlooked this. But now he is telling everyone in the world to change and turn to him. 31He has decided on a day when he will judge all the people in the world in a way that is fair. To do this he will use a man he chose long ago. And he has proved to everyone that this is the man to do it. He proved it by raising him from death!"

32When the people heard about Jesus being raised from death, some of them laughed. But others said, "We will hear more about this from you later." 33So Paul left the council meeting. 34But some of the people joined with Paul and became believers. Among these were Dionysius, a member of the Areopagus council, a woman named Damaris, and some others.

Paul in Corinth

18 1Later, Paul left Athens and went to the city of Corinth. 2There he met a Jewish man named Aquila, who was born in the country of Pontus. But he and his wife, Priscilla, had recently moved to Corinth from Italy. They left Italy because Claudius* had given an order for all Jews to leave Rome. Paul went to visit Aquila and Priscilla. 3They were tentmakers, the same as Paul, so he stayed with them and worked with them. 4Every Sabbath* day Paul went to the synagogue* and talked with both Jews and Greeks, trying to persuade them to believe in Jesus. 5But after Silas and Timothy came from Macedonia,* Paul spent all his time telling God's message* to the Jews, trying to convince them that Jesus is the Messiah.* 6But they disagreed with what Paul was teaching and started insulting him. So Paul shook the dust from his clothes.a He said to them, "If you are not saved, it will be your own fault! I have done all I can do. After this I will go only to the non-Jewish people."

7Paul left the synagogue and moved into the home of Titius Justus, a man who was a worshiper of the true God. His house was next to the synagogue. 8Crispus was the leader of that synagogue. He and all the people living in his house believed in the Lord Jesus. Many other people in Corinth also listened to Paul. They, too, believed and were baptized.*

9During the night, Paul had a vision.* The Lord said to him, "Don't be afraid, and don't stop talking to people. 10I am with you, and no one will be able to hurt you. Many of my people are in this city." 11Paul stayed there for a year and a half teaching God's message to the people.

Paul Is Brought Before Gallio

12During the time that Gallio was the governor of Achaia,* some of the Jews came together against Paul. They took him to court. 13They said to Gallio, "This man is teaching people to worship God in a way that is against our law!" 14Paul was ready to say something, but Gallio spoke to the Jews. He said, "I would listen to you if your complaint was about a crime or other wrong. 15But it is only about words and names— arguments about your own law. So you must solve this problem yourselves. I don't want to be a judge of these matters." 16So Gallio made them leave the court.

17Then they all grabbed Sosthenes, the leader of the synagogue.* They beat him before the court. But this did not bother Gallio.

Paul Returns to Antioch

18Paul stayed with the believers* for many days. Then he left and sailed for Syria. Priscilla and Aquila were also with him. At Cenchrea Paul cut off his hair,b because he had made a promise

a 18:6 shook the dust from his clothes A warning. It showed Paul was finished talking to these Jews.

b 18:18 cut off his hair This may show that Paul was ending a Nazirite vow, a time of special dedication and service promised to God. See "NAZIRITE" in the Word List.

to God. ¹⁹Then they went to the city of Ephesus, where Paul left Priscilla and Aquila. While Paul was in Ephesus, he went into the synagogue* and talked with the Jews. ²⁰They asked him to stay longer, but he refused. ²¹He left them and said, "I will come back to you again if God wants me to." And so he sailed away from Ephesus.

²²When Paul arrived at Caesarea, he went to Jerusalem and visited the church* there. After that he went to Antioch. ²³Paul stayed in Antioch for a while. Then he left there and went through the countries of Galatia and Phrygia. He traveled from town to town in these countries, helping all the followers of Jesus grow stronger in their faith.

Apollos in Ephesus and Corinth

²⁴A Jew named Apollos came to Ephesus. Born in the city of Alexandria, he was an educated man who knew the Scriptures* well. ²⁵He had been taught about the Lord and was always excited*ᵃ* to talk to people about Jesus. What he taught was right, but the only baptism* he knew about was the baptism that John* taught. ²⁶Apollos began to speak very boldly in the synagogue.* When Priscilla and Aquila heard him speak, they took him to their home and helped him understand the way of God better.

²⁷Apollos wanted to go to Achaia.* So the believers* in Ephesus helped him. They wrote a letter to the Lord's followers in Achaia and asked them to accept Apollos. When he arrived there, he was a great help to those who

had believed in Jesus because of God's grace.* ²⁸He argued very strongly against the Jews before all the people. He clearly proved that the Jews were wrong. He used the Scriptures and showed that Jesus is the Messiah.*

Paul in Ephesus

19 ¹While Apollos was in the city of Corinth, Paul was visiting some places on his way to Ephesus. In Ephesus he found some other followers of the Lord. ²He asked them, "Did you receive the Holy Spirit* when you believed?"

These followers said to him, "We have never even heard of a Holy Spirit!"

³Paul asked them, "So what kind of baptism* did you have?"

They said, "It was the baptism that John* taught."

⁴Paul said, "John told people to be baptized to show they wanted to change their lives. He told people to believe in the one who would come after him, and that one is Jesus."

⁵When these followers heard this, they were baptized in the name of the Lord Jesus. ⁶Then Paul laid his hands on* them, and the Holy Spirit came on them. They began speaking different languages and prophesying.* ⁷There were about twelve men in this group.

⁸Paul went into the synagogue* and spoke very boldly. He continued doing this for three months. He talked with the Jews, trying to persuade them to accept what he was telling them about God's kingdom.* ⁹But some of them became stubborn and refused to believe. In front of everyone, they said bad things about the Way.*

ᵃ 18:25 excited Or "on fire with the Spirit."

So Paul left these Jews and took the Lord's followers with him. He went to a place where a man named Tyrannus had a school. There Paul talked with people every day. 10He did this for two years. Because of this work, everyone in Asia,* Jews and Greeks,* heard the word of the Lord.

The Sons of Sceva

11God used Paul to do some very special miracles.* 12Some people carried away handkerchiefs and clothes that Paul had used and put them on those who were sick. The sick people were healed, and evil spirits left them.

13-14Some Jews also were traveling around forcing evil spirits out of people. The seven sons of Sceva, one of the leading priests, were doing this. These Jews tried to use the name of the Lord Jesus to make the evil spirits go out of people. They all said, "By the same Jesus that Paul talks about, I order you to come out!"

15But one time an evil spirit said to these Jews, "I know Jesus, and I know about Paul, but who are you?"

16Then the man who had the evil spirit inside him jumped on these Jews. He was much stronger than all of them. He beat them up and tore their clothes off. They all ran away from that house.

17All the people in Ephesus, Jews and Greeks,* learned about this. They were all filled with fear and gave great honor to the Lord Jesus. 18Many of the believers began to confess, telling about all the evil things they had done. 19Some of them had used magic. These believers brought their magic books and burned them before everyone. These books were worth about 50,000 silver coins.ᵃ 20This is how the word of the Lord was spreading in a powerful way, causing more and more people to believe.

Paul Plans a Trip

21After this, Paul made plans to go to Jerusalem. He planned to go through the regions of Macedonia* and Achaia,* and then go to Jerusalem. He thought, "After I visit Jerusalem, I must also visit Rome." 22Timothy and Erastus were two of his helpers. Paul sent them ahead to Macedonia. But he stayed in Asia* for a while.

Trouble in Ephesus

23But during that time there was some trouble in Ephesus about the Way.* This is how it all happened: 24There was a man named Demetrius. He worked with silver. He made little silver models that looked like the temple of the goddess Artemis. The men who did this work made a lot of money.

25Demetrius had a meeting with these men and some others who did the same kind of work. He told them, "Men, you know that we make a lot of money from our business. 26But look at what this man Paul is doing. Listen to what he is saying. He has convinced many people in Ephesus and all over Asia* to change their religion. He says the gods that people make by hand are not real. 27I'm afraid this is going to turn people against our business. But there is also another problem. People will begin to think that the temple of the great goddess Artemis is not important. Her greatness will be destroyed. And Artemis is the goddess that

---

ᵃ **19:19 silver coins** Probably Greek drachmas. One coin was worth the average pay for one day's work.

everyone in Asia and the whole world worships."

²⁸When the men heard this, they became very angry. They shouted, "Great is Artemis, the goddess of Ephesus!" ²⁹The whole city was thrown into confusion. The people grabbed Gaius and Aristarchus, men from Macedonia* who were traveling with Paul, and rushed all together into the stadium. ³⁰Paul wanted to go in and talk to the people, but the Lord's followers did not let him go. ³¹Also, some leaders of the country who were friends of Paul sent him a message telling him not to go into the stadium.

³²Some people were shouting one thing and others were shouting something else. The meeting was very confused. Most of the people did not know why they had come there. ³³Some Jews made a man named Alexander stand before the crowd, and they told him what to say. Alexander waved his hand, trying to explain things to the people. ³⁴But when the people saw that Alexander was a Jew, they all began shouting the same thing. For two hours they continued shouting, "Great is Artemis of Ephesus! Great is Artemis of Ephesus! Great is Artemis …!"

³⁵Then the city clerk persuaded the people to be quiet. He said, "Men of Ephesus, everyone knows that Ephesus is the city that keeps the temple of the great goddess Artemis. Everyone knows that we also keep her holy rock.ᵃ ³⁶No one can deny this, so you should be quiet. You must stop and think before you do anything else.

³⁷"You brought these menᵇ here, but they have not said anything bad against our goddess. They have not stolen anything from her temple. ³⁸We have courts of law and there are judges. Do Demetrius and those men who work with him have a charge against anyone? They should go to the courts. Let them argue with each other there.

³⁹"Is there something else you want to talk about? Then come to the regular town meeting of the people. It can be decided there. ⁴⁰I say this because someone might see this trouble today and say we are rioting. We could not explain all this trouble, because there is no real reason for this meeting." ⁴¹After the city clerk said this, he told the people to go home.

Paul Goes to Macedonia and Greece

20 ¹When the trouble stopped, Paul invited the Lord's followers to come visit him. After encouraging them, he told them goodbye and left for Macedonia.* ²On his way through Macedonia he had many words of encouragement for the followers in various places. Then he went to Greece ³and stayed there three months.

Paul was ready to sail for Syria, but some Jews were planning something against him. So he decided to go back through Macedonia to Syria. ⁴These men were traveling with him: Sopater, the son of Pyrrhus, from the city of Berea; Aristarchus and Secundus, from the city of Thessalonica; Gaius, from the city of Derbe; Timothy; and two men from Asia,*

ᵃ **19:35 holy rock** Probably a meteorite or rock that the people thought looked like Artemis and worshiped.

ᵇ **19:37 men** Gaius and Aristarchus, the men traveling with Paul.

Tychicus and Trophimus. 5These men went first, ahead of Paul. They waited for us in the city of Troas. 6We sailed from the city of Philippi after the Festival of Unleavened Bread.* We met these men in Troas five days later and stayed there seven days.

Paul's Last Visit to Troas

7On Sunday*a* we all met together to eat the Lord's Supper.*b* Paul talked to the group. Because he was planning to leave the next day, he continued talking until midnight. 8We were all together in a room upstairs, and there were many lights in the room. 9There was a young man named Eutychus sitting in the window. Paul continued talking, and Eutychus became very, very sleepy. Finally, he went to sleep and fell out of the window. He fell to the ground from the third floor. When the people went down and lifted him up, he was dead. 10Paul went down to where Eutychus was, knelt down beside him, and put his arms around him. He said to the other believers, "Don't worry. He is alive now." 11Then Paul went upstairs again, broke off some pieces of bread and ate. He spoke to them a long time. It was early morning when he finished, and then he left. 12The Lord's followers took Eutychus home alive, and they were all greatly comforted.

a **20:7 Sunday** Literally, "first day of the week," which for the Jews began at sunset on Saturday. But if Luke is using Greek time here, then the meeting was Sunday night.
b **20:7 to eat the Lord's Supper** Literally, "to break bread." This may mean a meal or the Lord's Supper, the special meal Jesus told his followers to eat to remember him. See Lk. 22:14–20.

The Trip From Troas to Miletus

13We went on ahead of Paul and sailed for the city of Assos, planning to meet him there. This is what he told us to do because he wanted to go by land. 14When he caught up with us at Assos, we took him on board, and we all sailed to Mitylene. 15The next day, we sailed away from there and came to a place near the island of Chios. Then the next day, we sailed to the island of Samos. A day later, we came to the city of Miletus. 16Paul had already decided not to stop at Ephesus. He did not want to stay too long in Asia.* He was hurrying because he wanted to be in Jerusalem on the day of Pentecost* if possible.

Paul Speaks to the Elders From Ephesus

17In Miletus Paul sent a message back to Ephesus, telling the elders* of the church* in Ephesus to come to him.

18When they came, Paul said to them, "You know about my life from the first day I came to Asia.* You know the way I lived all the time I was with you. 19The Jews planned things against me, and this gave me much trouble. But you know that I always served the Lord, sometimes with tears. I never thought about myself first. 20I always did what was best for you. I told you the Good News* about Jesus in public before the people and also taught in your homes. 21I told everyone— Jewish and non-Jewish people— to change and turn to God. I told them all to believe in our Lord Jesus.

22"But now I must obey the Spirit* and go to Jerusalem. I don't know what will happen to me there. 23I know only that in every city the Holy Spirit tells me that troubles and even jail wait for me. ²⁴I don't care about my own life. The most important thing is that I finish my work. I want to finish the work that the Lord Jesus gave me to do—to tell people the Good News about God's grace.*

²⁵"And now listen to me. I know that none of you will ever see me again. All the time I was with you, I told you the Good News about God's kingdom.* ²⁶So today I can tell you one thing that I am sure of: God will not blame me if some of you are not saved. ²⁷I can say this because I know that I told you everything that God wants you to know. ²⁸Be careful for yourselves and for all the people God has given you. The Holy Spirit gave you the work of caring forᵃ this flock.ᵇ You must be shepherds to the church of God,ᶜ the people he bought with his own blood.ᵈ ²⁹I know that after I leave, some men will come into your group. They will be like wild wolves and will try to destroy the flock. ³⁰Also, men from your own group will begin to teach things that are wrong. They will lead some of the Lord's followers away from the truth to follow them. ³¹So be careful! And always remember what I did during the three years I was with you. I never stopped reminding each one of you how you should live, counseling you day and night and crying over you.

³²"Now I am putting you in God's care. I am depending on the message* about his grace to make you strong. That message is able to give you the blessings that God gives to all his holy people.* ³³When I was with you, I never wanted anyone's money or fine clothes. ³⁴You know that I always worked to take care of my own needs and the needs of the people who were with me. ³⁵I always showed you that you should work just as I did and help people who are weak. I taught you to remember the words of the Lord Jesus: 'You will have a greater blessing when you give than when you receive.'"

³⁶When Paul finished speaking, he knelt down, and they all prayed together. ³⁷⁻³⁸They cried and cried. They were especially sad because Paul had said they would never see him again. They hugged him and kissed him. Then they went with him to the ship to say goodbye.

Paul Goes to Jerusalem

21 ¹After we said goodbye to the elders,* we sailed away straight to Cos island. The next day we went to the island of Rhodes, and from there we went to Patara. ²There we found a ship that was going to the area of Phoenicia. We got on the ship and sailed away.

³We sailed near the island of Cyprus. We could see it on the north side, but we did not stop. We sailed to the country of Syria. We stopped at Tyre because the ship needed to unload its cargo there. ⁴We found the Lord's followers there and stayed with

---

ᵃ **20:28 gave … caring for** Literally, "made you overseers of."

ᵇ **20:28 flock** A flock is many sheep. Here, it means a group of God's people who follow their leaders (elders) like sheep following a shepherd.

ᶜ **20:28 of God** Some Greek copies say, "of the Lord."

ᵈ **20:28 his own blood** Or "the blood of his own Son."

them for seven days. They warned Paul not to go to Jerusalem because of what the Spirit* had told them. ⁵But when our time there was up, we returned to the ship to continue our trip. All the followers, even the women and children, came with us to the seashore. We all knelt down on the beach, prayed, ⁶and said goodbye. Then we got on the ship, and the followers went home.

⁷We continued our trip from Tyre and went to the city of Ptolemais. We greeted the believers* there and stayed with them one day. ⁸The next day we left Ptolemais and went to the city of Caesarea. We went into the home of Philip and stayed with him. He had the work of telling the Good News.* He was one of the seven helpers.ᵈ ⁹He had four unmarried daughters who had the gift of prophesying.*

¹⁰After we had been there for several days, a prophet* named Agabus came from Judea. ¹¹He came to us and borrowed Paul's belt. He used it to tie his own hands and feet. He said, "The Holy Spirit tells me, 'This is how the Jews in Jerusalem will tie up the man who wears this belt.ᵇ Then they will hand him over to people who don't know God.'"

¹²When we heard this, we and the other followers there begged Paul not to go to Jerusalem. ¹³But he said, "Why are you crying and making me feel so sad? I am willing to be put in jail in Jerusalem. I am even ready to die for the name of the Lord Jesus!"

¹⁴We could not persuade him to stay away from Jerusalem. So we stopped begging him and said, "We pray that what the Lord wants will be done."

¹⁵After this, we got ready and left for Jerusalem. ¹⁶Some of the followers of Jesus from Caesarea went with us. These followers took us to the home of Mnason, a man from Cyprus, who was one of the first people to be a follower of Jesus. They took us to his home so that we could stay with him.

Paul Visits James

¹⁷The brothers and sisters in Jerusalem were very happy to see us. ¹⁸The next day Paul went with us to visit James, and all the elders* were there. ¹⁹After greeting them, Paul told them point by point all that God had used him to do among the non-Jewish people.

²⁰When the leaders heard this, they praised God. Then they said to Paul, "Brother, you can see that thousands of Jews have become believers, but they think it is very important to obey the Law of Moses.* ²¹They have been told that you teach the Jews who live in non-Jewish regions to stop following the Law of Moses. They have heard that you tell them not to circumcise* their sons or follow our other customs.

²²"What should we do? The Jewish believers here will learn that you have come. ²³So we will tell you what to do: Four of our men have made a vowᶜ to God. ²⁴Take these men with you and share in

---

ᵃ **21:8 seven helpers** Men chosen for a special work. See Acts 6:1–6.
ᵇ **21:11 belt** Paul's belt; so Agabus means that the Jews in Jerusalem will tie Paul up (arrest him).
ᶜ **21:23 vow** Probably a Nazirite vow, a time of special dedication and service promised to God. See "Nazirite" in the Word List.

their cleansing ceremony.*a* Pay their expenses so that they can shave their heads.*b* This will prove to everyone that the things they have heard about you are not true. They will see that you obey the Law of Moses in your own life.

25"In regard to the non-Jewish believers, we have already sent a letter to them saying what we think they should do:

'Don't eat food that has been given to idols.*

Don't eat meat from animals that have been strangled or any meat that still has the blood in it.

Don't be involved in sexual sin.'"

Paul Is Arrested

26So Paul took the four men with him. The next day he shared in their cleansing ceremony. Then he went to the Temple* area and announced the time when the days of the cleansing ceremony would be finished. On the last day an offering would be given for each of the men.

27When the seven-day period was almost finished, some Jews from Asia* saw Paul in the Temple area. They stirred up everyone into an angry mob. They grabbed Paul 28and shouted, "Men of Israel,* help us! This is the man who is teaching things that are against the Law of Moses,* against our people, and against this Temple of ours. This is what he teaches people everywhere. And now he has brought some Greeks* into the Temple area and has made

this holy place unclean!" 29(The Jews said this because they had seen Trophimus with Paul in Jerusalem. Trophimus was a man from Ephesus. The Jews thought that Paul had taken him into the holy area of the Temple.)

30An angry reaction spread throughout the city, and everyone came running to the Temple. They grabbed Paul and dragged him out of the holy area, and the gates were closed immediately. 31While they were trying to kill Paul, the commander of the Roman army in Jerusalem got word that the whole city was in a state of riot. 32Immediately the commander ran to where the crowd had gathered, taking with him some army officers* and soldiers. When the people saw the commander and his soldiers, they stopped beating Paul.

33The commander went over to Paul and arrested him. He told his soldiers to tie him up with two chains. Then he asked, "Who is this man? What has he done wrong?" 34Some people there were shouting one thing, and others were shouting something else. Because of all this confusion and shouting, the commander could not learn the truth about what had happened. So he told the soldiers to take Paul to the army building. 35-36The whole crowd was following them. When the soldiers came to the steps, they had to carry Paul. They did this to protect him, because the people were ready to hurt him. The people were shouting, "Kill him!"

37When the soldiers were ready to take Paul into the army building, he asked the commander, "Can I say something to you?"

---

a **21:24 cleansing ceremony** The special things Jews did to end the Nazirite vow. Also in verse 26.

b **21:24 shave their heads** To show that their vow was finished.

The commander said, "Oh, you speak Greek? 38Then you are not the man I thought you were. I thought you were the Egyptian who started some trouble against the government not long ago and led four thousand terrorists out to the desert."

39Paul said, "No, I am a Jew from Tarsus in the country of Cilicia. I am a citizen of that important city. Please, let me speak to the people."

40The commander told Paul he could speak. So he stood on the steps and waved his hand so that the people would be quiet. The people became quiet and Paul spoke to them in Aramaic.*

Paul Speaks to the People

22 1Paul said, "My brothers and fathers, listen to me! I will make my defense to you."

2When the Jews heard Paul speaking Aramaic,* they became very quiet. Then Paul said,

3"I am a Jew, born in Tarsus in the country of Cilicia. I grew up in this city. I was a student of Gamaliel,a who carefully taught me everything about the law of our fathers.* I was very serious about serving God, the same as all of you here today. 4I persecuted* the people who followed the Way.* Some of them were killed because of me. I arrested men and women and put them in jail.

5"The high priest* and the whole council of older Jewish leaders can tell you that this is true. One time these leaders gave me some letters. The letters were to the Jewish brothers in the city of Damascus. I was going there to arrest the followers of Jesus and bring them back to Jerusalem for punishment.

Paul Tells About His Conversion

6"But something happened to me on my way to Damascus. It was about noon when I came close to Damascus. Suddenly a bright light from heaven shined all around me. 7I fell to the ground and heard a voice saying to me, 'Saul, Saul, why are you persecuting* me?'

8"I asked, 'Who are you, Lord?' The voice said, 'I am Jesus from Nazareth, the one you are persecuting.' 9The men who were with me did not understand the voice, but they saw the light.

10"I said, 'What shall I do, Lord?' The Lord answered, 'Get up and go into Damascus. There you will be told all that I have planned for you to do.' 11I could not see, because the bright light had made me blind. So the men led me into Damascus.

12"In Damascus a man named Ananiasb came to me. He was a man who was devoted to God and obeyed the Law of Moses.* All the Jews who lived there respected him. 13He came to me and said, 'Saul, my brother, look up and see again!' Immediately I was able to see him.

14"Ananias told me, 'The God of our fathers* chose you long ago to know his plan. He chose you to see the Righteous One and to hear words from him. 15You will be his witness to all people. You will tell them what you have seen and heard. 16Now, don't wait any longer. Get up, be baptized* and

---

a 22:3 **Gamaliel** A very important teacher of the Pharisees, a Jewish religious group. See Acts 5:34.

b 22:12 **Ananias** In Acts there are three men with this name. See Acts 5:1 and 23:2 for the other two.

wash away your sins, trusting in Jesus to save you.*ᵃ*'

¹⁷"Later, I came back to Jerusalem. I was praying in the Temple* area, and I saw a vision.* ¹⁸I saw Jesus, and he said to me, 'Hurry and leave Jerusalem now! The people here will not accept the truth you tell them about me.'

¹⁹"I said, 'But, Lord, the people know that I was the one who put the believers in jail and beat them. I went through all the synagogues* to find and arrest the people who believe in you. ²⁰The people also know that I was there when Stephen, your witness, was killed. I stood there and agreed that they should kill him. I even held the coats of the men who were killing him!'

²¹"But Jesus said to me, 'Leave now. I will send you far away to the non-Jewish people.'"

²²The people stopped listening when Paul said this last thing. They all shouted, "Get rid of this man! He doesn't deserve to live." ²³They kept on shouting, ripping off their clothes and throwing dust into the air.*ᵇ* ²⁴Then the commander told the soldiers to take Paul into the army building and beat him. He wanted to make Paul tell why the people were shouting against him like this. ²⁵So the soldiers were tying Paul, preparing to beat him. But he said to an army officer* there, "Do you have the right to beat a Roman citizen*ᶜ* who has not been proven guilty?"

²⁶When the officer heard this, he went to the commander and told him about it. The officer said, "Do you know what you are doing? This man is a Roman citizen!"

²⁷The commander came to Paul and said, "Tell me, are you really a Roman citizen?"

He answered, "Yes."

²⁸The commander said, "I paid a lot of money to become a Roman citizen."

But Paul said, "I was born a citizen."

²⁹The men who were preparing to question Paul moved away from him immediately. The commander was afraid because he had already put Paul in chains, and he was a Roman citizen.

Paul Speaks to the Jewish Leaders

³⁰The next day the commander decided to learn why the Jews were accusing Paul. So he ordered the leading priests and the whole high council to meet together. He had Paul's chains taken off and had him brought in to face the council.

23 ¹Paul looked at the council members and said, "Brothers, I have lived my life in a good way before God. I have always done what I thought was right." ²Ananias,*ᵈ* the high priest,* was there. When he heard this, he told the men who were standing near Paul to hit him in the mouth. ³Paul said to Ananias, "God will hit you too! You are like a dirty

---

ᵃ **22:16 trusting in Jesus to save you** Literally, "calling on his name," meaning to show faith in Jesus by worshiping him or praying to him for help.
ᵇ **22:23 ripping ... air** These actions were signs of very strong anger.

ᶜ **22:25 Roman citizen** Roman law said that Roman citizens must not be beaten before their trial. Also at 23:27.
ᵈ **23:2 Ananias** Not the same man named Ananias in Acts 22:12.

wall that has been painted white. You sit there and judge me, using the Law of Moses.* But you are telling them to hit me, and that is against the law."

⁴The men standing near Paul said to him, "Are you sure you want to insult God's high priest like that?"

⁵Paul said, "Brothers, I did not know this man was the high priest. The Scriptures* say, 'You must not say bad things about a leader of your people.'ᵃ"

⁶Paul knew that some of the men in the council meeting were Sadducees* and some were Pharisees.* So he shouted, "My brothers, I am a Pharisee and my father was a Pharisee! I am on trial here because I believe that people will rise from death."

⁷When Paul said this, a big argument started between the Pharisees and the Sadducees. The group was divided. ⁸(The Sadducees believe that after people die, they will not live again as an angel or as a spirit. But the Pharisees believe in both.) ⁹All these Jews began shouting louder and louder. Some of the teachers of the law, who were Pharisees, stood up and argued, "We find nothing wrong with this man. Maybe an angel or a spirit really did speak to him."

¹⁰The argument turned into a fight, and the commander was afraid that the Jews would tear Paul to pieces. So he told the soldiers to go down and take Paul away from these Jews and put him in the army building.

¹¹The next night the Lord Jesus came and stood by Paul. He said, "Be brave! You have told people in

Jerusalem about me. You must do the same in Rome."

Some Jews Plan to Kill Paul

¹²The next morning some of the Jews made a plan to kill Paul. They made a promise to themselves that they would not eat or drink anything until they had killed him. ¹³There were more than 40 of them who made this plan. ¹⁴They went and talked to the leading priests and the older Jewish leaders. They said, "We have promised ourselves that we will not eat or drink until we have killed Paul. ¹⁵So this is what we want you to do: Send a message to the commander from you and the high council. Tell him you want him to bring Paul out to you. Say that you want to ask him more questions. We will be waiting to kill him while he is on the way here."

¹⁶But Paul's nephew heard about this plan. He went to the army building and told Paul. ¹⁷Then Paul called one of the army officers* and said to him, "Take this young man to the commander. He has a message for him." ¹⁸So the army officer brought Paul's nephew to the commander. The officer said, "The prisoner Paul asked me to bring this young man to you. He has something to tell you."

¹⁹The commander led the young man to a place where they could be alone. The commander asked, "What do you want to tell me?"

²⁰The young man said, "Some Jews have decided to ask you to bring Paul down to their council meeting tomorrow. They want you to think that they plan to ask Paul more questions. ²¹But don't believe them! More than 40 of

ᵃ **23:5** Quote from Ex. 22:28.

them are hiding and waiting to kill him. They have all promised not to eat or drink until they have killed him. Now they are waiting for you to say yes."

²²The commander sent the young man away, telling him, "Don't tell anyone that you have told me about their plan."

Paul Is Sent to Caesarea

²³Then the commander called two army officers.* He said to them, "I need some men to go to Caesarea. Get 200 soldiers ready. Also, get 70 soldiers on horses and 200 men to carry spears. Be ready to leave at nine o'clock tonight. ²⁴Get some horses for Paul to ride so that he can be taken to Governor Felix safely." ²⁵The commander wrote a letter that said:

²⁶From Claudius Lysias,
To the Most Honorable Governor Felix.

Greetings:

²⁷Some Jews had taken this man and planned to kill him. But I learned that he is a Roman citizen, so I went with my soldiers and saved him. ²⁸I wanted to know why they were accusing him. So I brought him before their council meeting. ²⁹This is what I learned: The Jews said this man did some things that were wrong. But these charges were about their own Jewish laws, and there was nothing worthy of jail or death. ³⁰I was told that some of the Jews were making a plan to kill him. So I decided to send him to you. I also told those Jews to tell you what they have against him.

³¹The soldiers did what they were told. They got Paul and took him to the city of Antipatris that night. ³²The next day the soldiers on horses went with Paul to Caesarea, but the other soldiers and the spearmen went back to the army building in Jerusalem. ³³The soldiers on horses entered Caesarea, gave the letter to Governor Felix, and then turned Paul over to him.

³⁴The governor read the letter and asked Paul, "What country are you from?" The governor learned that Paul was from Cilicia. ³⁵The governor said, "I will hear your case when the Jews who are accusing you come here too." Then the governor gave orders for Paul to be kept in the palace built by Herod.*

Some Jews Accuse Paul

24 ¹Five days later Ananias, the high priest,* went to the city of Caesarea. He brought with him some of the older Jewish leaders and a lawyer named Tertullus. They went to Caesarea to make charges against Paul before the governor. ²⁻³Paul was called into the meeting, and Tertullus began to make his accusations.

Tertullus said, "Most Honorable Felix, our people enjoy much peace because of you, and many wrong things in our country are being made right through your wise help. For this we all continue to be very thankful. ⁴But I don't want to take any more of your time. So I will say only a few words. Please be patient. ⁵This man is a troublemaker. He causes trouble with the Jews everywhere in the world. He is a leader of the Nazarene group. ⁶⁻⁸Also, he was trying to make the Temple* unclean, but we stopped him.[a] You can decide if all this is true. Ask him some questions yourself." [9]The other Jews agreed and said it was all true.

Paul Defends Himself Before Felix

[10]The governor made a sign for Paul to speak. So Paul answered, "Governor Felix, I know that you have been a judge over this nation for a long time. So I am happy to defend myself before you. [11]I went to worship in Jerusalem only twelve days ago. You can learn for yourself that this is true. [12]These Jews who are accusing me did not find me arguing with anyone at the Temple* or making trouble with the people. And I was not making trouble or arguing in the synagogues* or any other place in the city. [13]These men cannot prove the things they are saying against me now.

[14]"But I will tell you this: I worship the God of our fathers* as a follower of the Way,* which these Jews say is not the right way, and I believe everything that is taught in the Law of Moses* and all that is written in the books of the prophets.* [15]I have the same hope in God that these Jews have—the hope that all people, good and bad, will be raised from death. [16]This is why I always try to do what I believe is right before God and before everyone.

[17-18]"I was away from Jerusalem for many years. I went back there to take money to help my people. I also had some gifts to offer at the Temple. I was doing this when some Jews saw me there. I had finished the cleansing ceremony.[b] I had not made any trouble, and no one was gathering around me. [19]But some Jews from Asia* were there. They should be here, standing before you. If I have really done anything wrong, they are the ones who should accuse me. They were there! [20]Ask these men here if they found any wrong in me when I stood before the high council meeting in Jerusalem. [21]I did say one thing when I stood before them and shouted, 'You are judging me today because I believe that people will rise from death!'"

[22]Felix already understood a lot about the Way. He stopped the trial and said, "When commander Lysias comes here, I will decide what to do with you." [23]Felix told the army officer* to keep Paul guarded but to give him some freedom and to let his friends bring whatever he needed.

Paul Speaks to Felix and His Wife

[24]After a few days Felix came with his wife Drusilla, who was a Jew. Felix asked for Paul to be brought to him. He listened to Paul talk about believing in Christ Jesus. [25]But Felix became afraid when Paul spoke about things like doing right, self-control, and the judgment that will come in the future. He said, "Go away now. When I have more time, I will call for you." [26]But Felix had another reason for talking with Paul. He hoped Paul would pay him a bribe, so he sent for Paul often and talked with him.

---

a **24:6-8** Some Greek copies add 6b-8a: "And we wanted to judge him by our own law. [7]But the officer Lysias came and used great force to take him from us. [8]And Lysias ordered those who wanted to accuse him to come to you."

b **24:17-18 cleansing ceremony** The special things Jews did to end the Nazirite vow. See "Nazirite" in the Word List.

27But after two years, Porcius Festus became governor. So Felix was no longer governor. But he left Paul in prison to please the Jews.

Paul Asks to See Caesar

25 1Festus became governor, and three days later he went from Caesarea to Jerusalem. 2The leading priests and the important Jewish leaders made charges against Paul before Festus. 3They asked Festus to do them a favor. They wanted him to send Paul back to Jerusalem because they had a plan to kill Paul on the way. 4But Festus answered, "No, Paul will be kept in Caesarea. I will be going there soon myself, 5and your leaders can go with me. If this man has really done anything wrong, they can accuse him there."

6Festus stayed in Jerusalem another eight or ten days and then went back to Caesarea. The next day Festus told the soldiers to bring Paul before him. Festus was seated on the judgment seat. 7Paul came into the room, and the Jews who had come from Jerusalem stood around him. They made many serious charges against him, but they could not prove anything. 8Paul defended himself, saying, "I have done nothing wrong against the Jewish law, against the Temple,* or against Caesar.*"

9But Festus wanted to please the Jews. So he asked Paul, "Do you want to go to Jerusalem for me to judge you there on these charges?"

10Paul said, "I am standing at Caesar's judgment seat now. This is where I should be judged. I have done nothing wrong to the Jews, and you know it. 11If I have done something wrong and the law says I must die, then I agree that I should die. I don't ask to be saved from death. But if these charges are not true, then no one can hand me over to these people. No, I want Caesar to hear my case!"

12Festus talked about this with his advisors. Then he said, "You have asked to see Caesar, so you will go to Caesar!"

Festus Asks King Agrippa About Paul

13A few days later King Agrippa* and Bernice* came to Caesarea to visit Festus. 14They stayed there many days, and Festus told the king about Paul's case. Festus said, "There is a man that Felix left in prison. 15When I went to Jerusalem, the leading priests and the older Jewish leaders there made charges against him. They wanted me to order his death. 16But I told them, 'When a man is accused of doing something wrong, Romans don't hand him over for others to judge. First, he must face the people accusing him. And then he must be allowed to defend himself against their charges.'

17"So when these Jews came here for the trial, I did not waste time. The next day I sat on the judgment seat and ordered Paul to be brought in. 18The Jews stood up and accused him. But they did not accuse him of the kind of crimes I thought they would. 19Their charges were all about their own religion and about a man named Jesus. Jesus died, but Paul said that he is still alive. 20I did not have any idea about how to judge these matters. So I asked Paul, 'Do you want to go to Jerusalem and be judged there?' 21But Paul asked to be kept in Caesarea.

He wants a decision from the emperor.* So I ordered that he be held until I could send him to Caesar* in Rome."

²²Agrippa said to Festus, "I would like to hear this man too."

Festus said, "Tomorrow you can hear him."

²³The next day Agrippa and Bernice came to the meeting with great show, acting like very important people. They entered the room with military leaders and important men of the city. Festus ordered the soldiers to bring Paul in.

²⁴Festus said, "King Agrippa and all of you gathered here with us, you see this man. All the Jewish people, here and in Jerusalem, have complained to me about him. When they complain about him, they shout that he should be killed. ²⁵When I judged him, I did not find him guilty of any crime worthy of death. But he asked to be judged by Caesar, so I decided to send him to Rome. ²⁶However, I don't really know what to tell Caesar that this man has done wrong. So I have brought him before all of you—especially you, King Agrippa. I hope that you can question him and give me something to write to Caesar. ²⁷I think it is foolish to send a prisoner to Caesar without making some charges against him."

Paul Before King Agrippa

26 ¹Agrippa* said to Paul, "You may now speak to defend yourself." Paul raised his hand to get their attention and began to speak. ²He said, "King Agrippa, I feel fortunate that I can stand here before you today and answer all the charges these Jews have made against me. ³I am very happy to talk to you, because you know so much about all the Jewish customs and the things the Jews argue about. Please listen to me patiently.

⁴"All the Jews know about my whole life. They know the way I lived from the beginning in my own country and later in Jerusalem. ⁵These Jews have known me for a long time. If they want to, they can tell you that I was a good Pharisee.* And the Pharisees obey the laws of the Jewish religion more carefully than any other group. ⁶Now I am on trial because I hope for the promise that God made to our fathers.* ⁷This is the promise that all the twelve tribes of our people hope to receive. For this hope the Jews serve God day and night. My king, the Jews have accused me because I hope for this same promise. ⁸Why do you people think it is impossible for God to raise people from death?

⁹"I used to think that I should do everything I could against Jesus from Nazareth. ¹⁰And that's what I did, beginning in Jerusalem. The leading priests gave me the authority to put many of God's people in jail. And when they were being killed, I agreed that it was a good thing. ¹¹I visited all the synagogues* and punished them, trying to make them curse*ᵃ* Jesus. My anger against these people was so strong that I went to other cities to find them and punish them.

Paul Tells About Seeing Jesus

¹²"One time the leading priests gave me permission and the authority to go to the city of

---

ᵃ **26:11 curse** Literally, "blaspheme," the same as saying they did not believe in Jesus.

Damascus. [13]On the way there, at noon, I saw a light from heaven, brighter than the sun. It shined all around me and those traveling with me. [14]We all fell to the ground. Then I heard a voice talking to me in Aramaic.* The voice said, 'Saul, Saul, why are you persecuting* me? You are only hurting yourself by fighting me.'

[15]"I said, 'Who are you, Lord?'

"The Lord said, 'I am Jesus. I am the one you are persecuting. [16]Stand up! I have chosen you to be my servant. You will tell people about me—what you have seen today and what I will show you. This is why I have come to you. [17]I will keep you safe from your own people and from the non-Jewish people, the ones I am sending you to. [18]You will make them able to understand the truth. They will turn away from darkness to the light. They will turn away from the power of Satan, and they will turn to God. Then their sins can be forgiven, and they can be given a place among God's people—those who have been made holy* by believing in me.'"

Paul Tells About His Work

[19]Paul continued speaking: "King Agrippa,* after I had this vision* from heaven, I obeyed it. [20]I began telling people to change their hearts and lives and turn back to God. And I told them to do what would show that they had really changed. I went first to people in Damascus. Then I went to Jerusalem and to every part of Judea and told the people there. I also went to the non-Jewish people.

[21]"This is why the Jews grabbed me and were trying to kill me at the Temple.* [22]But God helped me, and he is still helping me today. With God's help I am standing here today and telling all people what I have seen. But I am saying nothing new. I am saying only what Moses* and the prophets* said would happen. [23]They said that the Messiah* would die and be the first to rise from death. They said that he would bring the light of God's saving truth[a] to the Jewish people and to the non-Jewish people."

Paul Tries to Persuade Agrippa

[24]While Paul was still defending himself, Festus shouted, "Paul, you are out of your mind! Too much study has made you crazy."

[25]Paul said, "Most Honorable Festus, I am not crazy. What I am saying is true. It all makes perfect sense. [26]King Agrippa* knows about all this, and I can speak freely to him. I know that he has heard about these things, because they happened where everyone could see them. [27]King Agrippa, do you believe what the prophets* wrote? I know you believe!"

[28]King Agrippa said to Paul, "Do you think you can persuade me to become a 'Christ-follower' so easily?"

[29]Paul said, "It is not important if it is easy or if it is hard. I pray to God that not only you but that everyone listening to me today could be saved and be just like me—except for these chains I have!"

[30]King Agrippa, Governor Festus, Bernice,* and all the people sitting with them stood up [31]and left the room. They were talking

---

a **26:23 bring ... truth** Literally, "proclaim light."

to each other. They said, "This man has done nothing worthy of being put to death or even put in jail." ³²And Agrippa said to Festus, "We could let him go free, but he has asked to see Caesar.*"

Paul Sails for Rome

27 ¹It was decided that we would sail for Italy. An army officer* named Julius, who served in the emperor's* special army, was put in charge of guarding Paul and some other prisoners on the trip. ²We got on a ship from the city of Adramyttium that was ready to sail to different places in Asia.* Aristarchus, a man from Thessalonica in Macedonia,* went with us.

³The next day we came to the city of Sidon. Julius was very good to Paul and gave him freedom to go visit his friends there, who gave him whatever he needed. ⁴We left that city and sailed close to the island of Cyprus because the wind was blowing against us. ⁵We went across the sea by Cilicia and Pamphylia. Then we came to the city of Myra in Lycia. ⁶There the army officer found a ship from the city of Alexandria that was going to Italy. So he put us on it.

⁷We sailed slowly for many days. It was hard for us to reach the city of Cnidus because the wind was blowing against us. We could not go any farther that way, so we sailed by the south side of the island of Crete near Salmone. ⁸We sailed along the coast, but the sailing was hard. Then we came to a place called Safe Harbors, near the city of Lasea.

⁹We had lost much time, and it was now dangerous to sail, because it was already after the Jewish day of fasting.ᵃ So Paul warned them, ¹⁰"Men, I can see that there will be a lot of trouble on this trip. The ship, everything in it, and even our lives may be lost!" ¹¹But the captain and the owner of the ship did not agree with Paul. So the army officer accepted what they said instead of believing Paul. ¹²Also, that harbor was not a good place for the ship to stay for the winter, so most of the men decided that we should leave there. They hoped we could reach Phoenix, where the ship could stay for the winter. Phoenix was a city on the island of Crete. It had a harbor that faced southwest and northwest.

The Storm

¹³Then a good wind began to blow from the south. The men on the ship thought, "This is the wind we wanted, and now we have it!" So they pulled up the anchor. We sailed very close to the island of Crete. ¹⁴But then a very strong wind called the "Northeaster" came from across the island. ¹⁵This wind took the ship and carried it away. The ship could not sail against the wind, so we stopped trying and let the wind blow us.

¹⁶We went below a small island named Cauda. With the island protecting us from the wind, we were able to bring in the lifeboat, but it was very hard to do. ¹⁷After the men brought the lifeboat in, they tied ropes around the ship to hold it together. The men were afraid that the ship would hit the sandbanks of Syrtis.* So they

ᵃ **27:9 day of fasting** The Day of Atonement, an important Jewish holy day in the fall of the year. This was the time of year that bad storms happened on the sea.

lowered the sail and let the wind carry the ship.

[18]The next day the storm was blowing against us so hard that the men threw some things out of the ship.[a] [19]A day later they threw out the ship's equipment. [20]For many days we could not see the sun or the stars. The storm was very bad. We lost all hope of staying alive—we thought we would die.

[21]The men did not eat for a long time. Then one day Paul stood up before them and said, "Men, I told you not to leave Crete. You should have listened to me. Then you would not have all this trouble and loss. [22]But now I tell you to be happy. None of you will die, but the ship will be lost. [23]Last night an angel came to me from God—the God I worship and belong to. [24]The angel said, 'Paul, don't be afraid! You must stand before Caesar.* And God has given you this promise: He will save the lives of all those sailing with you.' [25]So men, there is nothing to worry about. I trust God, and I am sure everything will happen just as his angel told me. [26]But we will crash on an island."

[27]On the fourteenth night we were still being blown around in the Adriatic Sea.* The sailors thought we were close to land. [28]They threw a rope into the water with a weight on the end of it. They found that the water was 120 feet[b] deep. They went a little farther and threw the rope in again. It was 90 feet[c] deep. [29]The sailors were afraid that we would hit the rocks, so they threw four anchors into the water. Then they prayed for daylight to come. [30]Some of the sailors wanted to leave the ship, and they lowered the lifeboat to the water. They wanted the other men to think that they were throwing more anchors from the front of the ship. [31]But Paul told the army officer* and the other soldiers, "If these men do not stay in the ship, you will lose all hope of survival." [32]So the soldiers cut the ropes and let the lifeboat fall into the water.

[33]Just before dawn Paul began persuading all the people to eat something. He said, "For the past two weeks you have been waiting and watching. You have not eaten for 14 days. [34]Now I beg you to eat something. You need it to stay alive. None of you will lose even one hair off your heads." [35]After he said this, Paul took some bread and thanked God for it before all of them. He broke off a piece and began eating. [36]All the men felt better and started eating too. [37](There were 276 people on the ship.) [38]We ate all we wanted. Then we began making the ship lighter by throwing the grain into the sea.

The Ship Is Destroyed

[39]When daylight came, the sailors saw land, but they did not know what land it was. They saw a bay with a beach and wanted to sail the ship to the beach if they could. [40]So they cut the ropes to the anchors and left the anchors in the sea. At the same time, they

---

[a] 27:18 threw some things . . . ship The men did this to make the ship lighter so that it would not sink easily.
[b] 27:28 120 feet Literally, "20 fathoms," about 40 meters.
[c] 27:28 90 feet Literally, "15 fathoms," about 30 meters.

untied the ropes that were holding the rudders. Then they raised the front sail into the wind and sailed toward the beach. [41]But the ship hit a sandbank. The front of the ship stuck there and could not move. Then the big waves began to break the back of the ship to pieces.

[42]The soldiers decided to kill the prisoners so that none of the prisoners could swim away and escape. [43]But Julius the army officer* wanted to let Paul live. So he did not allow the soldiers to kill the prisoners. He told the people who could swim to jump into the water and swim to land. [44]The others used wooden boards or pieces of the ship. And this is how all the people went safely to land.

Paul on the Island of Malta

28 [1]When we were safe on land, we learned that the island was called Malta. [2]The people who lived there were very good to us. It was raining and very cold, so they built a fire and welcomed all of us. [3]Paul gathered a pile of sticks for the fire. He was putting the sticks on the fire, and a poisonous snake came out because of the heat and bit him on the hand. [4]When the people living on the island saw the snake hanging from his hand, they said, "This man must be a murderer! He did not die in the sea, but Justice[a] does not want him to live."

[5]But Paul shook the snake off into the fire and was not hurt. [6]The people thought he would swell up or fall down dead. They waited and watched him for a long time, but nothing bad happened to him. So they changed their opinion. They said, "He is a god!"

[7]There were some fields around that same area. They were owned by a man named Publius, the most important Roman official on the island. He welcomed us into his home and was very good to us. We stayed in his house for three days. [8]Publius' father was very sick. He had a fever and dysentery,* but Paul went to him and prayed for him. He laid his hands on* the man and healed him. [9]After this happened, all the other sick people on the island came to Paul, and he healed them too.

[10-11]The people on the island gave us many honors. And after we had been there three months and were ready to leave, they provided us everything we needed for our trip.

Paul Goes to Rome

We got on a ship from Alexandria that had stayed on the island of Malta during the winter. On the front of the ship was the sign for the twin gods.[b] [12]We stopped at the city of Syracuse. We stayed there three days and then left. [13]We came to the city of Rhegium. The next day a wind began to blow from the southwest, so we were able to leave. A day later we came to the city of Puteoli. [14]We found some believers* there, who asked us to stay with them a week. Finally, we came to Rome. [15]The brothers and sisters in Rome heard about us and came out to meet us at the Market of

---

[a] **28:4 Justice** The people thought there was a goddess named Justice who would punish bad people.

[b] **28:10-11 twin gods** Statues of Castor and Pollux, Greek gods.

Appius[a] and at the Three Inns.[b] When Paul saw these believers, he thanked God and felt encouraged.

Paul in Rome

16When we came to Rome, Paul was allowed to live alone. But a soldier stayed with him to guard him.

17Three days later Paul sent for some of the most important Jews. When they came together, he said, "My brothers, I have done nothing against our people or against the customs of our fathers.* But I was arrested in Jerusalem and handed over to the Romans. 18They asked me many questions, but they could not find any reason why I should be put to death. So they wanted to let me go free. 19But the Jews there did not want that. So I had to ask to come to Rome to have my trial before Caesar.* That doesn't mean I am accusing my people of doing anything wrong. 20That is why I wanted to see you and talk with you. I am bound with this chain because I believe in the hope of Israel.*"

21The Jews answered Paul, "We have received no letters from Judea about you. None of our Jewish brothers who have traveled from there brought news about you or told us anything bad about you. 22We want to hear your ideas. We know that people everywhere are speaking against this new group."

23Paul and the Jews chose a day for a meeting. On that day many more of these Jews met with Paul at his house. He spoke to them all day long, explaining God's kingdom* to them. He used the Law of Moses* and the writings of the prophets* to persuade them to believe in Jesus. 24Some of the Jews believed what he said, but others did not believe. 25They had an argument among themselves and were ready to leave. But Paul said one more thing to them: "The Holy Spirit* spoke the truth to your fathers through Isaiah the prophet. He said,

26'Go to this people and tell them:

You will listen and you will hear,
   but you will not understand.
You will look and you will see,
   but you will not understand what you see.

27 Yes, the minds of these people are now closed.
   They have ears, but they don't listen.
   They have eyes, but they refuse to see.
If their minds were not closed,
   they might see with their eyes;
   they might hear with their ears;
   they might understand with their minds.
Then they might turn back to me and be healed.' *Isaiah 6:9–10*

28"I want you Jews to know that God has sent his salvation to the non-Jewish people. They will listen!" 29 c

30Paul stayed two full years in his own rented house. He welcomed all the people who came and visited him. 31He told them about God's kingdom and taught them about the Lord Jesus Christ. He was very bold, and no one tried to stop him from speaking.

---

a **28:15 Market of Appius** A town about 43 miles (69 km) from Rome.
b **28:15 Three Inns** A town about 30 miles (48 km) from Rome.

c **28:29** Some late copies of Acts add verse 29: "After Paul said this, the Jews left, still having a big argument with each other."

Romans

1 ¹Greetings from Paul, a servant of Christ Jesus.

God chose me to be an apostle* and gave me the work of telling his Good News.* ²God promised long ago through his prophets* in the Holy Scriptures* to give this Good News to his people. ³⁻⁴The Good News is about God's Son, Jesus Christ our Lord. As a human, he was born from the family of David,* but through the Holy Spirit*ᵃ* he was shown to be God's powerful Son when he was raised from death.

⁵Through Christ, God gave me the special work of an apostle—to lead people of all nations to believe and obey him. I do all this to honor Christ. ⁶You are some of those who have been chosen to belong to Jesus Christ.

⁷This letter is to all of you in Rome. God loves you, and he has chosen you to be his holy people.* Grace* and peace to you from God our Father and from the Lord Jesus Christ.

A Prayer of Thanks

⁸First I want to say that I thank my God through Jesus Christ for all of you. I thank him because people everywhere in the world are talking about your great faith. ⁹⁻¹⁰Every time I pray, I always remember you. God knows this is true. He is the one I serve with all my heart by telling people the Good News* about his Son. I pray that I will be allowed to come to you. It will happen if God wants it. ¹¹I want very much to see you and give you some spiritual gift to make your faith stronger. ¹²I mean that I want us to help each other with the faith that we have. Your faith will help me, and my faith will help you.

¹³Brothers and sisters, I want you to know that I have planned many times to come to you, but something always happens to change my plans. I would like to see the same good result among you that I have had from my work among the other non-Jewish people.

¹⁴I must serve all people—those who share in Greek culture and those who are less civilized,ᵇ the educated as well as the ignorant. ¹⁵That is why I want so much to tell the Good News to you there in Rome.

¹⁶I am proud of the Good News, because it is the power God uses to save everyone who believes—to save the Jews first, and now to save those who are not Jews. ¹⁷The Good News shows how God makes people right with himself. God's way of making people right

---

ᵃ **1:3–4 Holy Spirit** Literally, "spirit of holiness."

ᵇ **1:14 those who share ... civilized** Literally, "Greeks and barbarians." See "GREEK" in the Word List.

begins and ends with faith. As the Scriptures* say, "The one who is right with God by faith will live forever."*ᵃ*

All People Have Done Wrong

18God shows his anger from heaven against all the evil and wrong things that people do. Their evil lives hide the truth they have. 19This makes God angry because they have been shown what he is like. Yes, God has made it clear to them.

20There are things about God that people cannot see—his eternal power and all that makes him God. But since the beginning of the world, those things have been easy for people to understand. They are made clear in what God has made. So people have no excuse for the evil they do.

21People knew God, but they did not honor him as God, and they did not thank him. Their ideas were all useless. There was not one good thought left in their foolish minds. 22They said they were wise, but they became fools. 23Instead of honoring the divine greatness* of God, who lives forever, they traded it for the worship of idols—things made to look like humans, who get sick and die, or like birds, animals, and snakes.

24People wanted only to do evil. So God left them and let them go their sinful way. And so they became completely immoral and used their bodies in shameful ways with each other. 25They traded the truth of God for a lie. They bowed down and worshiped the things God made instead of worshiping the God who made those things. He is the one who should be praised forever. Amen.*

26Because people did those things, God left them and let them do the shameful things they wanted to do. Women stopped having natural sex with men and started having sex with other women. 27In the same way, men stopped having natural sex with women and began wanting each other all the time. Men did shameful things with other men, and in their bodies they received the punishment for those wrongs.

28People did not think it was important to have a true knowledge of God. So God left them and allowed them to have their own worthless thinking. And so they do what they should not do. 29They are filled with every kind of sin, evil, greed, and hatred. They are full of jealousy, murder, fighting, lying, and thinking the worst things about each other. They gossip 30and say evil things about each other. They hate God. They are rude, proud, and brag about themselves. They invent ways of doing evil. They don't obey their parents, 31they are foolish, they don't keep their promises, and they show no kindness or mercy to others. 32They know God's law says that anyone who lives like that should die. But they not only continue to do these things themselves, but they also encourage others who do them.

Let God Be the Judge

2 1So do you think that you can judge those other people? You are wrong. You too are guilty of sin. You judge them, but you do the same things they do. So when you judge them, you are really condemning yourself. 2God

judges all who do such things, and we know his judgment is right. ³And since you do the same things as those people you judge, surely you understand that God will punish you too. How could you think you would be able to escape his judgment? ⁴God has been kind to you. He has been very patient, waiting for you to change. But you think nothing of his kindness. Maybe you don't understand that God is kind to you so that you will decide to change your lives.

⁵But you are so stubborn! You refuse to change. So you are making your own punishment greater and greater. You will be punished on the day when God will show his anger. On that day everyone will see how right God is to judge people. ⁶He will reward or punish everyone for what they have done. ⁷Some people live for God's glory,* for honor, and for life that cannot be destroyed. They live for those things by always continuing to do good. God will give eternal life to them. ⁸But others are selfish and refuse to follow truth. They follow evil. God will show his anger and punish them. ⁹He will give trouble and suffering to everyone who does evil—to the Jews first and also to those who are not Jews. ¹⁰But he will give glory, honor, and peace to everyone who does good—to the Jews first and also to those who are not Jews. ¹¹God judges everyone the same. It doesn't matter who they are.

¹²People who have the law* and those who have never heard of the law are all the same when they sin. People who don't have the law and are sinners will be lost. And, in the same way, those who have the law and are sinners will be judged by the law. ¹³Hearing the law does not make people right with God. They will be right before him only if they always do what the law says.

¹⁴Those who are not Jews don't have the law. But when they naturally do what the law commands without even knowing the law, then they are their own law. This is true even though they don't have the written law. ¹⁵They show that in their hearts they know what is right and wrong, the same as the law commands, and their consciences agree. Sometimes their thoughts tell them that they have done wrong, and this makes them guilty. And sometimes their thoughts tell them that they have done right, and this makes them not guilty.

¹⁶All this will happen on the day when God will judge people's secret thoughts through Jesus Christ. This is part of the Good News* that I tell everyone.

The Jews and the Law

¹⁷What about you? You say you are a Jew. You trust in the law and proudly claim to be close to God. ¹⁸You know what God wants you to do. And you know what is important, because you have learned the law. ¹⁹You think you are a guide for people who don't know the right way, a light for those who are in the dark. ²⁰You think you can show foolish people what is right. And you think you are a teacher for those who are just beginning to learn. You have the law, and so you think you know everything and have all truth. ²¹You teach others, so why don't you teach yourself? You tell them not to steal, but you yourself steal.

22You say they must not commit adultery,* but you yourself are guilty of that sin. You hate idols,* but you steal them from their temples. 23You are so proud that you have God's law, but you bring shame to God by breaking his law. 24As the Scriptures* say, "People in other nations insult God because of you."*a

25If you follow the law,* then your circumcision* has meaning. But if you break the law, then it is as if you were never circumcised. 26Those who are not Jews are not circumcised. But if they do what the law says, it is as if they were circumcised. 27You have the written law and circumcision, but you break the law. So those who are not circumcised in their bodies, but still obey the law, will show that you are guilty.

28You are not a true Jew if you are only a Jew in your physical body. True circumcision is not only on the outside of the body. 29A true Jew is one who is a Jew inside. True circumcision is done in the heart. It is done by the Spirit,* not by the written law. And anyone who is circumcised in the heart by the Spirit gets praise from God, not from people.

3 1So, do Jews have anything that others don't have? Do they get any benefit from being circumcised? 2Yes, the Jews have many benefits. The most important one is this: God trusted the Jews with his teachings. 3It is true that some Jews were not faithful to God. But will that stop God from doing what he promised? 4No, even if everyone else is a liar, God will always do what he says. As the Scriptures say about him,

"You will be proved right in
   what you say,
and you will win when
   people accuse you." *Psalm 51:4*

5When we do wrong, that shows more clearly that God is right. So can we say that God does wrong when he punishes us? (That's the way some people think.) 6Of course not. If God could not punish us, how could he judge the world?

7Someone might say, "When I lie, it really gives God glory,* because my lie makes his truth easier to see. So why am I judged a sinner?" 8It would be the same to say, "We should do evil so that good will come." Many people criticize us, saying that's what we teach. They are wrong, and they should be condemned for saying that.

All People Are Guilty

9So are we Jews better than other people? No, we have already said that those who are Jews, as well as those who are not Jews, are the same. They are all guilty of sin. 10As the Scriptures* say,

"There is no one doing what is
   right, not even one.
11 There is no one who
   understands.
There is no one who is trying
   to be with God.
12 They have all turned away
   from him,
and now they are of no use
   to anyone.
There is no one who does good,
   not even one." *Psalm 14:1–3*

13 "Their words come from
   mouths that are like open
   graves.

---

a 2:24 Quote from Isa. 52:5. See also Ezek. 36:20–23.

They use their lying tongues
to deceive others."   *Psalm 5:9*

"Their words are like the
poison of snakes." *Psalm 140:3*
¹⁴ "Their mouths are full of
cursing and angry words."
Psalm 10:7

¹⁵ "They are always ready to kill
someone.
¹⁶   Everywhere they go they cause
trouble and ruin.
¹⁷ They don't know how to live
in peace."   *Isaiah 59:7–8*

¹⁸ "They have no fear or respect
for God."   *Psalm 36:1*
¹⁹What the law* says is for those
who are under the law. It stops
anyone from making excuses.
And it brings the whole world
under God's judgment, ²⁰because
no one can be made right with
God by following the law. The law
only shows us our sin.

How God Makes People Right
²¹But God has a way to make people right, and it has nothing to do
with the law. He has now shown
us that new way, which the law
and the prophets* told us about.
²²God makes people right through
their faith in*ᵃ* Jesus Christ. He does
this for all who believe in Christ.
Everyone is the same. ²³All have
sinned and are not good enough
to share God's divine greatness.*
²⁴They are made right with God
by his grace.* This is a free gift.
They are made right with God by
being made free from sin through
Jesus Christ. ²⁵⁻²⁶God gave Jesus
as a way to forgive people's sins
through their faith in him. God
can forgive them because the

blood sacrifice of Jesus pays for
their sins. God gave Jesus to show
that he always does what is right
and fair. He was right in the past
when he was patient and did not
punish people for their sins. And
in our own time he still does what
is right. God worked all this out
in a way that allows him to judge
people fairly and still make right
any person who has faith in Jesus.
²⁷So do we have any reason to
boast about ourselves? No reason at all. And why not? Because
we are depending on the way of
faith, not on what we have done
in following the law. ²⁸I mean
we are made right with God
through faith, not through what
we have done to follow the law.
This is what we believe. ²⁹God is
not only the God of the Jews. He
is also the God of those who are
not Jews. ³⁰There is only one God.
He will make Jews*ᵇ* right with
him by their faith, and he will
also make non-Jews*ᶜ* right with
him through their faith. ³¹So do
we destroy the law by following
the way of faith? Not at all! In fact,
faith causes us to be what the law
actually wants.

The Example of Abraham
4 ¹So what can we say about
Abraham,* the father of our
people? What did he learn about
faith? ²If Abraham was made right
by the things he did, he had a reason to boast about himself. But
God knew different. ³That's why
the Scriptures* say, "Abraham believed God, and because of this he
was accepted as one who is right
with God."*ᵈ*

ᵇ **3:30 Jews** Literally, "circumcision."
ᶜ **3:30 non-Jews** Literally, "uncircumcision."
ᵈ **4:3** Quote from Gen. 15:6.
ᵃ **3:22 their faith in** Or "the faithfulness of."

[4]When people work, their pay is not given to them as a gift. They earn the pay they get. [5]But people cannot do any work that will make them right with God. So they must trust in him. Then he accepts their faith, and that makes them right with him. He is the one who makes even evil people right. [6]David* said the same thing when he was talking about the blessing people have when God accepts them as good without looking at what they have done:

[7] "It is a great blessing
   when people are forgiven for
   the wrongs they have done,
   when their sins are erased!
[8] It is a great blessing when the
   Lord accepts people
   as if they are without sin!"

Psalm 32:1–2

[9]Is this blessing only for those who are circumcised*? Or is it also for those who are not circumcised? We have already said that it was because of Abraham's faith that he was accepted as one who is right with God. [10]So how did this happen? Did God accept Abraham before or after he was circumcised? God accepted him before his circumcision. [11]Abraham was circumcised later to show that God accepted him. His circumcision was proof that he was right with God through faith before he was circumcised. So Abraham is the father of all those who believe but are not circumcised. They believe and are accepted as people who are right with God. [12]And Abraham is also the father of those who have been circumcised. But it is not their circumcision that makes him their father. He is their father only if they live following the faith that our father Abraham had before he was circumcised.

God's Promise Received Through Faith

[13]Abraham* and his descendants received the promise that they would get the whole world. But Abraham did not receive that promise because he followed the law.* He received that promise because he was right with God through his faith. [14]If people could get God's promise by following the law, then faith is worthless. And God's promise to Abraham is worthless, [15]because the law can only bring God's anger on those who disobey it. But if there is no law, then there is nothing to disobey.

[16]So people get what God promised by having faith. This happens so that the promise can be a free gift. And if the promise is a free gift, then all of Abraham's people will get that promise. The promise is not just for those who live under the Law of Moses.* It is for all who live with faith as Abraham did. He is the father of us all. [17]As the Scriptures* say, "I have made you a father of many nations."[a] This is true before God, the one Abraham believed—the God who gives life to the dead and speaks of things that don't yet exist as if they are real.

[18]There was no hope that Abraham would have children, but Abraham believed God and continued to hope. And that is why he became the father of many nations. As God told him, "You will have many descendants."[b] [19]Abraham was almost a hundred years old, so he was past the age for

a 4:17 Quote from Gen. 17:5.
b 4:18 Quote from Gen. 15:5.

having children. Also, Sarah could not have children. Abraham was well aware of this, but his faith in God never became weak. 20He never doubted that God would do what he promised. He never stopped believing. In fact, he grew stronger in his faith and just praised God. 21Abraham felt sure that God was able to do what he promised. 22So that's why "he was accepted as one who is right with God."*a* 23These words ("he was accepted") were written not only for Abraham. 24They were also written for us. God will also accept us because we believe. We believe in the one who raised Jesus our Lord from death. 25Jesus was handed over to die for our sins, and he was raised from death to make us right with God.

Right With God

5 1We have been made right with God because of our faith. So we have peace with God through our Lord Jesus Christ. 2Through our faith, Christ has brought us into that blessing of God's grace* that we now enjoy. And we are very happy because of the hope we have of sharing God's glory.* 3And we are also happy with the troubles we have. Why are we happy with troubles? Because we know that these troubles make us more patient. 4And this patience is proof that we are strong. And this proof gives us hope. 5And this hope will never disappoint us. We know this because God has poured out his love to fill our hearts through the Holy Spirit* he gave us.

6Christ died for us when we were unable to help ourselves.

We were living against God, but at just the right time Christ died for us. 7Very few people will die to save the life of someone else, even if it is for a good person. Someone might be willing to die for an especially good person. 8But Christ died for us while we were still sinners, and by this God showed how much he loves us.

9We have been made right with God by the blood sacrifice of Christ. So through Christ we will surely be saved from God's anger. 10I mean that while we were God's enemies, he made friends with us through his Son's death. And the fact that we are now God's friends makes it even more certain that he will save us through his Son's life. 11And not only will we be saved, but we also rejoice right now in what God has done for us through our Lord Jesus Christ. It is because of Jesus that we are now God's friends.

Adam and Christ

12Sin came into the world because of what one man did. And with sin came death. So this is why all people must die—because all people have sinned. 13Sin was in the world before the Law of Moses.* But God does not consider people guilty of sin if there is no law. 14But from the time of Adam to the time of Moses, everyone had to die. Adam died because he sinned by not obeying God's command. But even those who did not sin that same way had to die.

That one man, Adam, can be compared to Christ, the one who was coming in the future. 15But God's free gift is not like Adam's sin. Many people died because of the sin of that one man. But the grace* that people received from

a **4:22** Quote from Gen. 15:6.

God was much greater. Many received God's gift of life by the grace of this other man, Jesus Christ. 16After Adam sinned once, he was judged guilty. But the gift of God is different. His free gift came after many sins, and it makes people right with him. 17One man sinned, and so death ruled all people because of that one man. But now some people accept God's full grace and his great gift of being made right. Surely they will have true life and rule through the one man, Jesus Christ.

18So that one sin of Adam brought the punishment of death to all people. But in the same way, Christ did something so good that it makes all people right with God. And that brings them true life. 19One man disobeyed God and many became sinners. But in the same way, one man obeyed God and many will be made right. 20The law was brought in so that more people would sin the way Adam did. But where sin increased, there was even more of God's grace. 21Sin once used death to rule us. But God gave us more of his grace so that grace could rule by making us right with him. And this brings us eternal life through Jesus Christ our Lord.

Dead to Sin but Alive in Christ

6 1So do you think we should continue sinning so that God will give us more and more grace*? 2Of course not! Our old sinful life ended. It's dead. So how can we continue living in sin? 3Did you forget that all of us became part of Christ Jesus when we were baptized*? In our baptism* we shared in his death. 4So when we were baptized, we were buried with Christ and took part in his death. And just as Christ was raised from death by the wonderful power of the Father, so we can now live a new life.

5Christ died, and we have been joined with him by dying too. So we will also be joined with him by rising from death as he did. 6We know that our old life was put to death on the cross with Christ. This happened so that our sinful selves would have no power over us. Then we would not be slaves to sin. 7Anyone who has died is made free from sin's control.

8If we died with Christ, we know that we will also live with him. 9Christ was raised from death. And we know that he cannot die again. Death has no power over him now. 10Yes, when Christ died, he died to defeat the power of sin one time—enough for all time. He now has a new life, and his new life is with God. 11In the same way, you should see yourselves as being dead to the power of sin and alive for God through Christ Jesus.

12But don't let sin control your life here on earth. You must not be ruled by the things your sinful self makes you want to do. 13Don't offer the parts of your body to serve sin. Don't use your bodies to do evil, but offer yourselves to God, as people who have died and now live. Offer the parts of your body to God to be used for doing good. 14Sin will not be your master, because you are not under law. You now live under God's grace.

Slaves of Goodness

15So what should we do? Should we sin because we are under grace* and not under law? Certainly not! 16Surely you know that you become the slaves of whatever you give yourselves to. Anything or anyone you follow will be your master. You can follow sin, or you can obey God. Following sin brings spiritual death, but obeying God makes you right with him. [17]In the past you were slaves to sin—sin controlled you. But thank God, you fully obeyed what you were taught. [18]You were made free from sin, and now you are slaves to what is right. [19]I use this example from everyday life because you need help in understanding spiritual truths. In the past you offered the parts of your body to be slaves to your immoral and sinful thoughts. The result was that you lived only for sin. In the same way, you must now offer yourselves to be slaves to what is right. Then you will live only for God.

[20]In the past you were slaves to sin, and you did not even think about doing right. [21]You did evil things, and now you are ashamed of what you did. Did those things help you? No, they only brought death. [22]But now you are free from sin. You have become slaves of God, and the result is that you live only for God. This will bring you eternal life. [23]When people sin, they earn what sin pays—death. But God gives his people a free gift—eternal life in Christ Jesus our Lord.

An Example From Marriage

7 [1]Brothers and sisters, you all understand the Law of Moses.* So surely you know that the law rules over people only while they are alive. [2]It's like what the law says about marriage: A woman must stay married to her husband as long as he is alive. But if her husband dies, she is made free from the law of marriage. [3]But if she marries another man while her husband is still alive, the law says she is guilty of adultery.* But if her husband dies, she is made free from the law of marriage. So if she marries another man after her husband dies, she is not guilty of adultery.

[4]In the same way, my brothers and sisters, your old selves died and you became free from the law* through the body of Christ. Now you belong to someone else. You belong to the one who was raised from death. We belong to Christ so that we can be used in service to God. [5]In the past we were ruled by our sinful selves. The law made us want to do sinful things. And those sinful desires controlled our bodies, so that what we did only brought us spiritual death. [6]In the past the law held us as prisoners, but our old selves died, and we were made free from the law. So now we serve God in a new way, not in the old way, with the written rules. Now we serve God in the new way, with the Spirit.*

Our Fight Against Sin

[7]You might think I am saying that sin and the law* are the same. That is not true. But the law was the only way I could learn what sin means. I would never have known it is wrong to want something that is not mine. But the law said, "You must not want what belongs to someone else."[a] [8]And sin found a way to use that command and make me want all kinds of things that weren't mine. So sin came to me because of the command. But without the law,

a 7:7 Quote from Ex. 20:17; Deut. 5:21.

sin has no power. [9]Before I knew the law, I was alive. But when I heard the law's command, sin began to live, [10]and I died spiritually. The command was meant to bring life, but for me it brought death. [11]Sin found a way to fool me by using the command to make me die.

[12]Now the law is holy,* and the command is holy and right and good. [13]Does this mean that something that is good brought death to me? No, it was sin that used the good command to bring me death. This shows how terrible sin really is. It can use a good command to produce a result that shows sin at its very worst.

The War Inside Us

[14]We know that the law* is spiritual, but I am not. I am so human. Sin rules me as if I were its slave. [15]I don't understand why I act the way I do. I don't do the good I want to do, and I do the evil I hate. [16]And if I don't want to do what I do, that means I agree that the law is good. [17]But I am not really the one doing the evil. It is sin living in me that does it. [18]Yes, I know that nothing good lives in me—I mean nothing good lives in the part of me that is not spiritual. I want to do what is good, but I don't do it. [19]I don't do the good that I want to do. I do the evil that I don't want to do. [20]So if I do what I don't want to do, then I am not really the one doing it. It is the sin living in me that does it.

[21]So I have learned this rule: When I want to do good, evil is there with me. [22]In my mind I am happy with God's law. [23]But I see another law working in my body. That law makes war against the law that my mind accepts. That

other law working in my body is the law of sin, and that law makes me its prisoner. [24]What a miserable person I am! Who will save me from this body that brings me death? [25]I thank God for his salvation through Jesus Christ our Lord!

So in my mind I am a slave to God's law, but in my sinful self I am a slave to the law of sin.

Life in the Spirit

8 [1]So now anyone who is in Christ Jesus is not judged guilty. [2]That is because in Christ Jesus the law of the Spirit* that brings life made you[a] free. It made you free from the law that brings sin and death. [3]The law* was without power because it was made weak by our sinful selves. But God did what the law could not do: He sent his own Son to earth with the same human life that everyone else uses for sin. God sent him to be an offering to pay for sin. So God used a human life to destroy sin. [4]He did this so that we could be right just as the law said we must be. Now we don't live following our sinful selves. We live following the Spirit.

[5]People who live following their sinful selves think only about what they want. But those who live following the Spirit are thinking about what the Spirit wants them to do. [6]If your thinking is controlled by your sinful self, there is spiritual death. But if your thinking is controlled by the Spirit, there is life and peace. [7]Why is this true? Because anyone whose thinking is controlled

a **8:2 you** Some Greek copies have "me." Also in the next sentence.

by their sinful self is against God. They refuse to obey God's law. And really they are not able to obey it. [8]Those who are ruled by their sinful selves cannot please God.

[9]But you are not ruled by your sinful selves. You are ruled by the Spirit, if that Spirit of God really lives in you. But whoever does not have the Spirit of Christ does not belong to Christ. [10]Your body will always be dead because of sin. But if Christ is in you, then the Spirit gives you life, because Christ made you right with God. [11]God raised Jesus from death. And if God's Spirit lives in you, he will also give life to your bodies that die. Yes, God is the one who raised Christ from death, and he will raise you to life through his Spirit living in you.

[12]So, my brothers and sisters, we must not be ruled by our sinful selves. We must not live the way our sinful selves want. [13]If you use your lives to do what your sinful selves want, you will die spiritually. But if you use the Spirit's help to stop doing the wrong things you do with your body, you will have true life.

[14]The true children of God are those who let God's Spirit lead them. [15]The Spirit that we received is not a spirit that makes us slaves again and causes us to fear. The Spirit that we have makes us God's chosen children. And with that Spirit we cry out, "*Abba*,[a] Father." [16]And the Spirit himself speaks to our spirits and makes us sure that we are God's children. [17]If we are God's children, we will get the blessings God has

for his people. He will give us all that he has given Christ. But we must suffer like Christ suffered. Then we will be able to share his glory.*

We Will Have Glory in the Future

[18]We have sufferings now, but these are nothing compared to the great glory* that will be given to us. [19]Everything that God made is waiting with excitement for the time when he will show the world who his children are. The whole world wants very much for that to happen. [20]Everything God made was allowed to become like something that cannot fulfill its purpose. That was not its choice, but God made it happen with this hope in view: [21]That the creation would be made free from ruin— that everything God made would have the same freedom and glory that belong to God's children.

[22]We know that everything God made has been waiting until now in pain like a woman ready to give birth to a child. [23]Not only the world, but we also have been waiting with pain inside us. We have the Spirit* as the first part of God's promise. So we are waiting for God to finish making us his own children. I mean we are waiting for our bodies to be made free. [24]We were saved to have this hope. If we can see what we are waiting for, that is not really hope. People don't hope for something they already have. [25]But we are hoping for something we don't have yet, and we are waiting for it patiently.

[26]Also, the Spirit helps us. We are very weak, but the Spirit helps us with our weakness. We don't know how to pray as we should, but the Spirit himself speaks to

---

[a] **8:15 Abba** An Aramaic word that was used by Jewish children as a name for their fathers.

God for us. He begs God for us, speaking to him with feelings too deep for words. [27]God already knows our deepest thoughts. And he understands what the Spirit is saying, because the Spirit speaks for his people in the way that agrees with what God wants.

[28]We know that in everything God works for the good of those who love him. These are the people God chose, because that was his plan. [29]God knew them before he made the world. And he decided that they would be like his Son. Then Jesus would be the firstborn* of many brothers and sisters. [30]God planned for them to be like his Son. He chose them and made them right with him. And after he made them right, he gave them his glory.

God's Love in Christ Jesus

[31]So what should we say about this? If God is for us, no one can stand against us. And God is with us. [32]He even let his own Son suffer for us. God gave his Son for all of us. So now with Jesus, God will surely give us all things. [33]Who can accuse the people God has chosen? No one! God is the one who makes them right. [34]Who can say that God's people are guilty? No one! Christ Jesus died for us, but that is not all. He was also raised from death. And now he is at God's right side, speaking to him for us. [35]Can anything separate us from Christ's love? Can trouble or problems or persecution* separate us from his love? If we have no food or clothes or face danger or even death, will that separate us from his love? [36]As the Scriptures* say,

"For you we are in danger of death all the time.

People think we are worth no more than sheep to be killed." *Psalm 44:22*

[37]But in all these troubles we have complete victory through God, who has shown his love for us. [38-39]Yes, I am sure that nothing can separate us from God's love—not death, life, angels, or ruling spirits. I am sure that nothing now, nothing in the future, no powers, nothing above us or nothing below us—nothing in the whole created world—will ever be able to separate us from the love God has shown us in Christ Jesus our Lord.

God and the Jewish People

9 [1]I am in Christ and I am telling you the truth. I am not lying. And my conscience, ruled by the Holy Spirit,* agrees that what I say now is true. [2]I have great sorrow and always feel much sadness [3]for my own people. They are my brothers and sisters, my earthly family. I wish I could help them. I would even have a curse on me and cut myself off from Christ if that would help them. [4]They are the people of Israel,* God's chosen children. They have the glory* of God and the agreements he made between himself and his people. God gave them the Law of Moses,* the Temple* worship, and his promises. [5]They are the descendants of our great fathers,* and they are the earthly family of the Messiah,* who is God over all things. Praise him forever![a] Amen.*

[6]I don't mean that God failed to keep his promise to the Jewish people. But only some of the

---

[a] **9:5 Messiah, who is ... forever!** Or "Messiah. May God, who rules over all things, be praised forever!"

people of Israel are really God's people.[a] [7]And only some of Abraham's* descendants are true children of Abraham. This is what God said to Abraham: "Your true descendants will be those who come through Isaac."[b] [8]This means that not all of Abraham's descendants are God's true children. Abraham's true children are those who become God's children because of the promise he made to Abraham. [9]Here is what God said in that promise: "About this time next year I will come back, and Sarah will have a son."[c]

[10]And that is not all. Rebecca also had sons, and they had the same father. He is our father Isaac. [11-12]But before the two sons were born, God told Rebecca, "The older son will serve the younger."[d] This was before the boys had done anything good or bad. God said this before they were born so that the boy he wanted would be chosen because of God's own plan. He was chosen because he was the one God wanted to call, not because of anything the boys did. [13]As the Scriptures* say, "I loved Jacob, but I hated Esau."[e]

[14]So what does this mean? That God is not fair? We cannot say that. [15]God said to Moses, "I will show mercy to anyone I want to show mercy to. I will show pity to anyone I choose."[f] [16]So God will choose anyone he decides to show mercy to, and his choice does not depend on what people want or try to do. [17]In the Scriptures God says to Pharaoh*: "I made you king so that you could do this for me. I wanted to show my power through you. I wanted my name to be announced throughout the world."[g] [18]So God shows mercy to those he wants to show mercy to and makes stubborn those he wants to make stubborn.

[19]So one of you will ask me, "If God controls what we do, why does he blame us for our sins?" [20]Don't ask that. You are only human and have no right to question God. A clay jar does not question the one who made it. It does not say, "Why did you make me like this?" [21]The one who makes the jar can make anything he wants. He uses the same clay to make different things. He might make one thing for special purposes and another for daily use.

[22]It is the same way with what God has done. He wanted to show his anger and to let people see his power. But he patiently endured those he was angry with—people who were ready to be destroyed. [23]He waited with patience so that he could make known the riches of his glory* to the people he has chosen to receive his mercy. God has already prepared them to share his glory. [24]We are those people, the ones God chose not only from the Jews but also from those who are not Jews. [25]As the Scriptures say in the book of Hosea,

"The people who are not
    mine—
I will say they are my people.
And the people I did not love—

---

a 9:6 God's people Literally, "Israel," the people God chose to bring his blessings to the world.

b 9:7 Quote from Gen. 21:12.

c 9:9 Quote from Gen. 18:10, 14.

d 9:11–12 Quote from Gen. 25:23.

e 9:13 Quote from Mal. 1:2–3.

f 9:15 Quote from Ex. 33:19.

g 9:17 Quote from Ex. 9:16.

I will say they are the people
I love."   *Hosea 2:23*

26And,
"Where God said in the past,
  'You are not my people'—
  there they will be called
  children of the living God."
     Hosea 1:10

27And Isaiah cries out about Israel:
"There are so many people
  of Israel, they are like the
  grains of sand by the sea.
But only a few of them will
  be saved.
28Yes, the Lord will quickly
  finish judging the people
  on the earth."   *Isaiah 10:22–23*

29It is just as Isaiah said:
"The Lord All-Powerful allowed
  some of our people to live.
If he had not done that,
  we would now be like Sodom,*
  and we would be like
  Gomorrah.*"   *Isaiah 1:9*

30So what does all this mean? It means that people who are not Jews were made right with God because of their faith, even though they were not trying to make themselves right. 31And the people of Israel, who tried to make themselves right with God by following the law, did not succeed. 32They failed because they tried to make themselves right by the things they did. They did not trust in God to make them right. They fell over the stone that makes people fall. 33The Scriptures talk about that stone:
"Look, I put in Zion* a stone
  that will make people
  stumble.
It is a rock that will make
  people fall.
But anyone who trusts in him
  will never be disappointed."
     Isaiah 8:14; 28:16

10 1Brothers and sisters, what I want most is for all the people of Israel to be saved. That is my prayer to God. 2I can say this about them: They really try hard to follow God, but they don't know the right way. 3They did not know the way that God makes people right with him. And they tried to make themselves right in their own way. So they did not accept God's way of making people right. 4Christ ended the law so that everyone who believes in him is made right with God.

5Moses writes about being made right by following the law. He says, "The person who obeys these laws is the one who will have life through them."*a* 6But this is what the Scriptures say about being made right through faith: "Don't say to yourself, 'Who will go up into heaven?'" (This means "Who will go up to heaven to get Christ and bring him down to earth?") 7"And don't say, 'Who will go down into the world below?'" (This means "Who will go down to get Christ and bring him up from death?")

8This is what the Scripture says: "God's teaching is near you; it is in your mouth and in your heart."*b* It is the teaching of faith that we tell people. 9If you openly say, "Jesus is Lord" and believe in your heart that God raised him from death, you will be saved. 10Yes, we believe in Jesus deep in our hearts, and so we are made right with God. And we openly say that we believe in him, and so we are saved.

11Yes, the Scriptures say, "Anyone who trusts in him will never

---

a **10:5** Quote from Lev. 18:5.
b **10:6–8** Quotes from Deut. 30:12–14.

be disappointed."[a] [12]It says this because there is no difference between those who are Jews and those who are not. The same Lord is the Lord of all people. And he richly blesses everyone who looks to him for help. [13]Yes, "everyone who trusts in the Lord[b] will be saved."[c]

[14]But before people can pray to the Lord for help, they must believe in him. And before they can believe in the Lord, they must hear about him. And for anyone to hear about the Lord, someone must tell them. [15]And before anyone can go and tell them, they must be sent. As the Scriptures say, "How wonderful it is to see someone coming to tell good news!"[d]

[16]But not all the people accepted that good news. Isaiah said, "Lord, who believed what we told them?"[e] [17]So faith comes from hearing the Good News.* And people hear the Good News when someone tells them about Christ.

[18]But I ask, "Did those people not hear the Good News?" Yes, they heard—as the Scriptures say,
"Their voices went out all
 around the world.
Their words went
 everywhere in the world."
          Psalm 19:4
[19]Again I ask, "Did the people of Israel not understand?" Yes, they did understand. First, Moses says this for God:

"I will use those who are not
 really a nation to make you
 jealous.
I will use a nation that does
 not understand to make
 you angry."   Deuteronomy 32:21
[20]Then Isaiah is bold enough to say this for God:
"The people who were not
 looking for me—
 they are the ones who found
 me.
I made myself known to those
 who did not ask for me."
          Isaiah 65:1
[21]But about the people of Israel God says,
"All day long I stood ready to
 accept those people,
but they are stubborn and
 refuse to obey me." Isaiah 65:2

God Has Not Forgotten His People

11 [1]So I ask, "Did God force his people to leave him?" Of course not. I myself am an Israelite.* I am from the family of Abraham,* from the tribe of Benjamin. [2]God chose the Israelites to be his people before they were born. And he did not force them to leave. Surely you know what the Scriptures* say about Elijah.* The Scriptures tell about Elijah praying to God against the people of Israel.* He said, [3]"Lord, they have killed your prophets* and destroyed your altars.* I am the only prophet still living, and they are trying to kill me now."[f] [4]But what answer did God give to Elijah? God said, "I have kept for myself seven thousand men who have never given worship to Baal.*"[g]

[5]It is the same now. God has chosen a few people by his grace.*

10:11 Quote from Isa. 28:16.
10:13 who trusts in the Lord Literally, who calls on the name of the Lord," meaning to show faith in him by worshiping him or praying to him for help.
10:13 Quote from Joel 2:32.
10:15 Quote from Isa. 52:7.
10:16 Quote from Isa. 53:1.

f **11:3** Quote from 1 Kings 19:10, 14.
g **11:4** Quote from 1 Kings 19:18.

⁶And if he chose them by grace, then it is not what they have done that made them his people. If they could be made his people by what they did, his gift of grace would not really be a gift.

⁷So this is what has happened: The people of Israel wanted God's blessing, but they did not all get it. The people he chose did get his blessing, but the others became hard and refused to listen to him. ⁸As the Scriptures say,

"God caused the people to fall asleep."   *Isaiah 29:10*

"God closed their eyes so that
    they could not see,
    and he closed their ears so
    that they could not hear.
This continues until now."
          Deuteronomy 29:4

⁹And David says,

"Let those people be caught
    and trapped at their own
    feasts.
Let them fall and be
    punished.
¹⁰ Let their eyes be closed so that
    they cannot see.
And let them be troubled
    forever."   *Psalm 69:22–23*

¹¹So I ask: When the Jews fell, did that fall destroy them? No! But their mistake brought salvation to those who are not Jews. The purpose of this was to make the Jews jealous. ¹²Their mistake brought rich blessings to the world. And what they lost brought rich blessings to the non-Jewish people. So surely the world will get much richer blessings when enough Jews become the kind of people God wants.

¹³Now I am speaking to you people who are not Jews. I am an apostle* to the non-Jewish people.

So while I have that work, I will do the best I can. ¹⁴I hope I can make my own people jealous. That way, maybe I can help some of them to be saved. ¹⁵God turned away from the Jews. When that happened, he became friends with the other people in the world. So when he accepts the Jews, it will be like bringing people to life after death. ¹⁶If the first piece of bread is offered to God, then the whole loaf is made holy.* If the roots of a tree are holy, the tree's branches are holy too.

¹⁷It is as if some of the branches from an olive tree have been broken off, and the branch of a wild olive tree has been joined to that first tree. If you are not a Jew, you are the same as that wild branch, and you now share the strength and life of the first tree. ¹⁸But don't act as if you are better than those branches that were broken off. You have no reason to be proud of yourself, because you don't give life to the root. The root gives life to you. ¹⁹You might say, "Branches were broken off so that I could be joined to their tree." ²⁰That is true. But those branches were broken off because they did not believe. And you continue to be part of the tree only because you believe. Don't be proud, but be afraid. ²¹If God did not let the natural branches of that tree stay, he will not let you stay if you stop believing.

²²So you see that God is kind but he can also be very strict. He punishes those who stop following him. But he is kind to you if you continue trusting in his kindness. If you don't continue depending on him, you will be cut off from the tree. ²³And if the

Jews will believe in God again, he will accept them back. He is able to put them back where they were. ²⁴It is not natural for a wild branch to become part of a good tree. But you non-Jewish people are like a branch cut from a wild olive tree. And you were joined to a good olive tree. But those Jews are like a branch that grew from the good tree. So surely they can be joined to their own tree again.

²⁵I want you to understand this secret truth, brothers and sisters. This truth will help you understand that you don't know everything. The truth is this: Part of Israel has been made stubborn, but that will change when enough non-Jewish people have come to God. ²⁶And that is how all Israel will be saved. The Scriptures say,

"The Savior will come from
    Zion*;
he will take away all evil
    from the family of Jacob.*
²⁷ And I will make this
    agreement with those
    people
when I take away their sins."

Isaiah 59:20–21; 27:9

²⁸The Jews refuse to accept the Good News,* so they are God's enemies. This has happened to help you who are not Jews. But they are still God's chosen people, and he loves them because of the promises he made to their ancestors.* ²⁹God never changes his mind about the people he calls. He never decides to take back the blessings he has given them. ³⁰At one time you refused to obey God. But now you have received mercy, because the Jews refused to obey. ³¹And now they are the ones who refuse to obey, because God showed mercy to

you. But this happened so that they can also receive mercy from him. ³²All people have refused to obey God. And he has put them all together as people who don't obey him so that he can show mercy to everyone.

Praise to God

³³Yes, God's riches are very great! His wisdom and knowledge have no end! No one can explain what God decides. No one can understand his ways. ³⁴As the Scriptures* say,

"Who can know what is on the
    Lord's mind?
Who is able to give him
    advice?"   *Isaiah 40:13*

³⁵ "Who has ever given God
    anything?
God owes nothing to
    anyone."   *Job 41:11*

³⁶Yes, God made all things. And everything continues through him and for him. To God be the glory* forever! Amen.*

Give Your Lives to God

12 ¹So I beg you, brothers and sisters, because of the great mercy God has shown us, offer your lives*ᵃ* as a living sacrifice* to him—an offering that is only for God and pleasing to him. Considering what he has done, it is only right that you should worship him in this way. ²Don't change yourselves to be like the people of this world, but let God change you inside with a new way of thinking. Then you will be able to understand and accept what God wants for you. You will be able to

ᵃ **12:1 lives** Literally, "bodies." Paul is using the language of Old Testament animal sacrifice to express the idea of a complete giving of oneself to God.

know what is good and pleasing to him and what is perfect.

3God has given me a special gift, and that is why I have something to say to each one of you. Don't think that you are better than you really are. You must see yourself just as you are. Decide what you are by the faith God has given each of us. 4Each one of us has one body, and that body has many parts. These parts don't all do the same thing. 5In the same way, we are many people, but in Christ we are all one body. We are the parts of that body, and each part belongs to all the others.

6We all have different gifts. Each gift came because of the grace* God gave us. Whoever has the gift of prophecy* should use that gift in a way that fits the kind of faith they have. 7Whoever has the gift of serving should serve. Whoever has the gift of teaching should teach. 8Whoever has the gift of comforting others should do that. Whoever has the gift of giving to help others should give generously. Whoever has the gift of leading should work hard at it. Whoever has the gift of showing kindness to others should do it gladly.

9Your love must be real. Hate what is evil. Do only what is good. 10Love each other in a way that makes you feel close like brothers and sisters. And give each other more honor than you give yourself. 11As you serve the Lord, work hard and don't be lazy. Be excited about serving him! 12Be happy because of the hope you have. Be patient when you have troubles. Pray all the time. 13Share with God's people who need help. Look for people who need help

and welcome them into your homes.

14Wish only good for those who treat you badly. Ask God to bless them, not curse them. 15When others are happy, you should be happy with them. And when others are sad, you should be sad too. 16Live together in peace with each other. Don't be proud, but be willing to be friends with people who are not important to others. Don't think of yourself as smarter than everyone else.

17If someone does you wrong, don't try to pay them back by hurting them. Try to do what everyone thinks is right. 18Do the best you can to live in peace with everyone. 19My friends, don't try to punish anyone who does wrong to you. Wait for God to punish them with his anger. It is written: "I am the one who punishes; I will pay people back,"a says the Lord. 20But you should do this:

"If you have enemies who are
        hungry,
    give them something to eat.
If you have enemies who are
        thirsty,
    give them something to
        drink.
In doing this you will make
    them feel ashamed.b"

Proverbs 25:21-22

21Don't let evil defeat you, but defeat evil by doing good.

Obey Your Government Rulers

13 1All of you must obey the government rulers. Everyone

a **12:19** Quote from Deut. 32:35.
b **12:20 you will make them feel ashamed** Literally, "you will pour burning coals on their head." People in Old Testament times often put ashes on their heads to show that they were sad or sorry.

Jesus talks to Zacchaeus
Luke 19:1-10

©WBTC2011

Jesus enters Jerusalem like a King
Luke 19:28-40

who rules was given the power to rule by God. And all those who rule now were given that power by God. ²So anyone who is against the government is really against something God has commanded. Those who are against the government bring punishment on themselves. ³People who do right don't have to fear the rulers. But those who do wrong must fear them. Do you want to be free from fearing them? Then do only what is right, and they will praise you.

⁴Rulers are God's servants to help you. But if you do wrong, you have reason to be afraid. They have the power to punish, and they will use it. They are God's servants to punish those who do wrong. ⁵So you must obey the government, not just because you might be punished, but because you know it is the right thing to do.

⁶And this is why you pay taxes too. Those rulers are working for God, and they give all their time to the work of ruling. ⁷Give everyone what you owe them. If you owe them any kind of tax, then pay it. Show respect to those you should respect. And show honor to those you should honor.

Loving Others Is the Only Law

⁸You should owe nothing to anyone, except that you will always owe love to each other. The person who loves others has done all that the law* commands. ⁹The law says, "You must not commit adultery,* you must not murder anyone, you must not steal, you must not want what belongs to someone else."ᵃ All these commands and all other commands

are really only one rule: "Love your neighborᵇ the same as you love yourself."ᶜ ¹⁰Love doesn't hurt others. So loving is the same as obeying all the law.

¹¹I say this because you know that we live in an important time. Yes, it is now time for you to wake up from your sleep. Our salvation is nearer now than when we first believed. ¹²The night* is almost finished. The day* is almost here. So we should stop doing whatever belongs to darkness.* We should prepare ourselves to fight evil with the weapons that belong to the light.* ¹³We should live in a right way, like people who belong to the day. We should not have wild parties or be drunk. We should not be involved in sexual sin or any kind of immoral behavior. We should not cause arguments and trouble or be jealous. ¹⁴But be like the Lord Jesus Christ, so that when people see what you do, they will see Christ. Don't think about how to satisfy the desires of your sinful self.

Don't Criticize Others

14 ¹Be willing to accept those who still have doubts about what believers can do. And don't argue with them about their different ideas. ²Some people believe they can eat any kind of food,ᵈ but those who have doubts eat only vegetables. ³Those who know they can eat any kind of food must not feel that they are better than

---

ᵇ **13:9 your neighbor** Or "others." Jesus' teaching in Lk. 10:25–37 makes clear that this includes anyone in need.
ᶜ **13:9** Quote from Lev. 19:18.
ᵈ **14:2 any kind of food** The Jewish law said there were some foods that Jews could not eat. When they became followers of Christ, some of them did not understand that they could now eat all foods.

ᵃ **13:9** Quote from Ex. 20:13–15, 17.

those who eat only vegetables. And those who eat only vegetables must not decide that those who eat all foods are wrong. God has accepted them. 4You cannot judge the servants of someone else. Their own master decides if they are doing right or wrong. And the Lord's servants will be right, because the Lord is able to make them right.

5Some people might believe that one day is more important than another. And others might believe that every day is the same. Everyone should be sure about their beliefs in their own mind. 6Those who think one day is more important than other days are doing that for the Lord. And those who eat all kinds of food are doing that for the Lord. Yes, they give thanks to God for that food. And those who refuse to eat some foods do that for the Lord. They also give thanks to God.

7We don't live or die just for ourselves. 8If we live, we are living for the Lord. And if we die, we are dying for the Lord. So living or dying, we belong to the Lord. 9That is why Christ died and rose from death to live again—so that he could be Lord over those who have died and those who are living.

10So why do you judge your brother or sister in Christ? Or why do you think that you are better than they are? We will all stand before God, and he will judge us all. 11Yes, the Scriptures* say,

"'As surely as I live,' says the
  Lord,
'Everyone will bow before
  me;
everyone will say that I am
  God.'"   *Isaiah 45:23*

12So each of us will have to explain to God about the things we do.

Don't Cause Others to Sin

13So we should stop judging each other. Let's decide not to do anything that will cause a problem for a brother or sister or hurt their faith. 14I know that there is no food that is wrong to eat. The Lord Jesus is the one who convinced me of that. But if someone believes that something is wrong, then it is wrong for that person.

15If you hurt the faith of your brother or sister because of something you eat, you are not really following the way of love. Don't destroy anyone's faith by eating something they think is wrong. Christ died for them. 16Don't allow what is good for you to become something they say is evil. 17In God's kingdom,* what we eat and drink is not important. Here is what is important: a right way of life, peace, and joy—all from the Holy Spirit.* 18Whoever serves Christ by living this way is pleasing God, and they will be accepted by others.

19So let's try as hard as we can to do what will bring peace. Let's do whatever will help each other grow stronger in faith. 20Don't let the eating of food destroy the work of God. All food is right to eat, but it is wrong for anyone to eat something that hurts the faith of another person. 21It is better not to eat meat or drink wine or do anything else that hurts the faith of your brother or sister.

22You should keep your beliefs about these things a secret between yourself and God. It is a blessing to be able to do what you think is right without feeling guilty. 23But anyone who eats something without being sure it is right is doing wrong. That is because they did not believe it was right. And if you do anything that you believe is not right, it is sin.

15 ¹Some of us have no problem with these things. So we should be patient with those who are not so strong and have doubts. We should not do what pleases us ²but do what pleases them and is for their good. We should do whatever helps everyone grow stronger in faith. ³Even Christ did not live trying to please himself. As the Scriptures* say about him, "Those people who insulted you have also insulted me."[a] ⁴Everything that was written in the past was written to teach us. Those things were written so that we could have hope. That hope comes from the patience and encouragement that the Scriptures give us. ⁵All patience and encouragement come from God. And I pray that God will help you all agree with each other, as Christ Jesus wants. ⁶Then you will all be joined together. And all together you will give glory* to God the Father of our Lord Jesus Christ. ⁷Christ accepted you, so you should accept each other. This will bring honor[b] to God. ⁸I tell you that Christ became a servant of the Jews to show that God has done what he promised their great ancestors.* ⁹Christ also did this so that the non-Jewish people could praise God for the mercy he gives to them. The Scriptures say,

"So I will give thanks to you
among the people of other
nations;

I will sing praise to your
name." *Psalm 18:49*

¹⁰And the Scriptures say,

"You people of other nations
should be happy together
with God's people."
Deuteronomy 32:43

¹¹The Scriptures also say,

"Praise the Lord all you people
of other nations;

all people should praise the
Lord." *Psalm 117:1*

¹²And Isaiah says,

"Someone will come from
Jesse's family.[c]

He will come to rule over the
nations,

and they will put their hope
in him." *Isaiah 11:10*

¹³I pray that the God who gives hope will fill you with much joy and peace as you trust in him. Then you will have more and more hope, and it will flow out of you by the power of the Holy Spirit.

Paul Talks About His Work

¹⁴My brothers and sisters, I know without a doubt that you are full of goodness and have all the knowledge you need. So you are certainly able to counsel each other. ¹⁵But I have written to you very openly about some things that I wanted you to remember. I did this because God gave me this special gift: ¹⁶to be a servant of Christ Jesus for those who are not Jews. I serve like a priest whose duty it is to tell God's Good News.* He gave me this work so that you non-Jewish people could be an offering that he will accept—an offering made holy* by the Holy Spirit.*

---

[a] **15:3** Quote from Ps. 69:9.
[b] **15:7 honor** Or "glory." See "GLORY" in the Word List.

[c] **15:12 Jesse's family** Jesse was the father of David, king of Israel. Jesus was from their family.

[17]That is why I feel so good about what I have done for God in my service to Christ Jesus. [18]I will not talk about anything I did myself. I will talk only about what Christ has done with me in leading the non-Jewish people to obey God. They have obeyed him because of what I have said and done. [19]And they obeyed him because of the power of the miraculous signs* and wonders* that happened—all because of the power of God's Spirit. I have told people the Good News about Christ in every place from Jerusalem to Illyricum.* And so I have finished that part of my work. [20]I always want to tell the Good News in places where people have never heard of Christ. I do this because I don't want to build on the work that someone else has already started. [21]But as the Scriptures* say,

"Those who were not told
　　about him will see,
　and those who have not
　　heard about him will
　　understand."　　*Isaiah 52:15*

Paul's Plan to Visit Rome

[22]That's what has kept me so busy and prevented my coming to see you even though I have wanted to come many times.

[23]Now I have finished my work in these areas. And for many years I have wanted to visit you. [24]So I will visit you when I go to Spain. Yes, I hope to visit you while I am traveling to Spain, and I will stay and enjoy being with you. Then you can help me continue on my trip.

[25]Now I am going to Jerusalem to help God's people there. [26]Some of them are poor, and the believers in Macedonia* and Achaia* wanted to help them. So they gathered some money to send them. [27]They were happy to do this. And it was like paying something they owed them, because as non-Jews they have been blessed spiritually by the Jews. So now they should use the material blessings they have to help the Jews. [28]I am going to Jerusalem to make sure the poor get this money that has been given for them.

After I finish that, I will leave for Spain and stop to visit you on the way. [29]And I know that when I visit you, I will bring you Christ's full blessing.

[30]Brothers and sisters, I beg you to help me in my work by praying to God for me. Do this because of our Lord Jesus and the love that the Spirit* gives us. [31]Pray that I will be saved from those in Judea who refuse to accept our message. And pray that this help I am bringing to Jerusalem will please God's people there. [32]Then, if God wants me to, I will come to you. I will come with joy, and together you and I will have a time of rest. [33]The God who gives peace be with you all. Amen.*

Paul Has Some Final Things to Say

16 [1]I want you to know that you can trust our sister in Christ, Phoebe. She is a special servant* of the church* in Cenchrea. [2]I ask you to accept her in the Lord. Accept her the way God's people should. Help her with anything she needs from you. She has helped me very much, and she has helped many others too.

[3] Give my greetings to Priscilla and Aquila, who have worked together with me for Christ Jesus. [4]They risked their own lives to save mine.

I am thankful to them, and all the non-Jewish churches are thankful to them.

5 Also, give greetings to the church that meets in their house.

Give greetings to my dear friend Epaenetus. He was the first person to follow Christ in Asia.*

6 Greetings also to Mary. She worked very hard for you.

7 And greet Andronicus and Junia. They are my relatives, and they were in prison with me. They were followers of Christ before I was. And they are some of the most important of the ones Christ sent out to do his work.ᵃ

8 Give my greetings to Ampliatus, my dear friend in the Lord, 9and to Urbanus. He has worked together with me for Christ.

Give greetings also to my dear friend Stachys 10and to Apelles, who has proved himself to be a true follower of Christ.

Give greetings to everyone in the family of Aristobulus 11and to Herodion, my relative.

Greetings to all those in the family of Narcissus who belong to the Lord 12and to Tryphaena and Tryphosa, women who work very hard for the Lord.

Greetings to my dear friend Persis. She has also worked very hard for the Lord.

13 Greetings also to Rufus, one of the Lord's chosen people,

and to his mother, who has been a mother to me too.

14 Give my greetings to Asyncritus, Phlegon, Hermes, Patrobas, Hermas, and all the brothers in Christ who are with them.

15 Give greetings to Philologus and Julia, to Nereus and his sister, to Olympas, and to all of God's people with them.

16 Give each other the special greeting of God's people.ᵇ

All the churches that belong to Christ send their greetings to you.

17Brothers and sisters, I want you to be very careful of those who cause arguments and hurt people's faith by teaching things that are against what you learned. Stay away from them. 18People like that are not serving our Lord Christ. They are only pleasing themselves. They use fancy talk and say nice things to fool those who don't know about evil. 19Everyone has heard that you do what you were taught, and I am very happy about that. But I want you to be wise about what is good and to know nothing about what is evil.

20The God who brings peace will soon defeat Satan* and give you power over him.

The grace* of our Lord Jesus be with you.

21Timothy, a worker together with me, sends you his greetings. Also Lucius, Jason, and Sosipater (these are my relatives) send their greetings.

22I am Tertius, the one writing this letter for Paul. I send you my

---

ᵃ **16:7 most important … work** Literally, "important among (or to) the apostles."

ᵇ **16:16 the special greeting of God's people** Literally, "a holy kiss."

own greetings as one who belongs to the Lord.

²³Gaius is letting me and the whole church here use his home. He sends his greetings to you. Erastus and our brother Quartus also send their greetings. Erastus is the city treasurer here. ²⁴ ᵃ

²⁵Praise God! He is the one who can make you strong in faith. He can use the Good News* that I

ᵃ **16:24** Some Greek copies add verse 24: "The grace of our Lord Jesus Christ be with you all. Amen."

teach to make you strong. It is the message about Jesus Christ that I tell people. That message is the secret truth that was hidden for ages and ages but has been made known. ²⁶It has now been shown to us. It was made known by what the prophets* wrote, as God commanded. And it has now been made known to all people so that they can believe and obey God, who lives forever. ²⁷Glory* forever to the only wise God through Jesus Christ. Amen.*

1 Corinthians

1 ¹Greetings from Paul. I was chosen to be an apostle* of Christ Jesus. God chose me because that is what he wanted. Greetings also from Sosthenes, our brother in Christ.

²To God's church* in Corinth, you who have been made holy* because you belong to Christ Jesus. You were chosen to be God's holy people* together with all people everywhere who trust in the Lord*ᵃ* Jesus Christ—their Lord and ours.

³Grace* and peace to you from God our Father and the Lord Jesus Christ.

Paul Gives Thanks to God

⁴I always thank my God for you because of the grace* that he has given you through Christ Jesus. ⁵In him you have been blessed in every way. You have been blessed in all your speaking and all your knowledge. ⁶This proves that what we told you about Christ is true. ⁷Now you have every gift from God while you wait for our Lord Jesus Christ to come again. ⁸He will keep you strong until the end so that on the day when our Lord Jesus Christ comes, you will be free from all blame. ⁹God

is faithful. He is the one who has chosen you to share life with his Son, Jesus Christ our Lord.

Stop Arguing With Each Other

¹⁰Brothers and sisters, by the authority of our Lord Jesus Christ, I beg all of you to agree with each other. You should not be divided into different groups. Be completely joined together again with the same kind of thinking and the same purpose.

¹¹My brothers and sisters, some members of Chloe's family told me that there are arguments among you. ¹²This is what I mean: One of you says, "I follow Paul," and someone else says, "I follow Apollos." Another says, "I follow Peter,*" and someone else says, "I follow Christ." ¹³Christ cannot be divided into different groups. It wasn't Paul who died on the cross for you, was it? Were you baptized* in Paul's name? ¹⁴I am thankful that I did not baptize any of you except Crispus and Gaius. ¹⁵I am thankful because now no one can say that you were baptized in my name. ¹⁶(I also baptized the family of Stephanas, but I don't remember that I myself baptized any others.) ¹⁷Christ did not give me the work of baptizing people. He gave me the work of telling the Good News.* But he sent me to tell the Good News without using clever speech, which would take away

ᵃ **1:2 who trust in the Lord** Literally, "who call on the name of the Lord," meaning to show faith in him by worshiping or praying to him for help.

the power that is in the cross[a] of Christ.

God's Power and Wisdom in Christ Jesus

[18]The teaching about the cross seems foolish to those who are lost. But to us who are being saved it is the power of God. [19]As the Scriptures* say,

"I will destroy the wisdom of
  the wise.
I will confuse the
  understanding of the
  intelligent."   *Isaiah 29:14*

[20]So what does this say about the philosopher,* the law expert, or anyone in this world who is skilled in making clever arguments? God has made the wisdom of the world look foolish. [21]This is what God in his wisdom decided: Since the world did not find him through its own wisdom, he used the message* that sounds foolish to save those who believe it.

[22]The Jews ask for miraculous signs,* and the Greeks* want wisdom. [23]But this is the message we tell everyone: Christ was killed on a cross. This message is a problem for Jews, and to other people it is nonsense. [24]But Christ is God's power and wisdom to the people God has chosen, both Jews and Greeks. [25]Even the foolishness of God is wiser than human wisdom. Even the weakness of God is stronger than human strength.

[26]Brothers and sisters, God chose you to be his. Think about that! Not many of you were wise in the way the world judges wisdom. Not many of you had great influence, and not many of you came from important families. [27]But God chose the foolish things of the world to shame the wise. He chose the weak things of the world to shame the strong. [28]And God chose what the world thinks is not important—what the world hates and thinks is nothing. He chose these to destroy what the world thinks is important. [29]God did this so that no one can stand before him and boast about anything. [30]It is God who has made you part of Christ Jesus. And Christ has become for us wisdom from God. He is the reason we are right with God and pure enough to be in his presence. Christ is the one who set us free from sin. [31]So, as the Scriptures say, "Whoever boasts should boast only about the Lord."[b]

My Message: Jesus Christ on the Cross

2 [1]Dear brothers and sisters, when I came to you, I told you the secret truth of God. But I did not use fancy words or great wisdom. [2]I decided that while I was with you I would forget about everything except Jesus Christ and his death on the cross. [3]When I came to you, I was weak and shook with fear. [4]My teaching and my speaking were not with wise words that persuade people. But the proof of my teaching was the power that the Spirit* gives. [5]I did this so that your faith would be in God's power, not in human wisdom.

God's Wisdom

[6]We teach wisdom to people who are mature, but the wisdom we teach is not from this world. It is not the wisdom of the rulers of this world, who are losing their

---

a **1:17 cross** Paul uses the cross as a picture of the Good News, the story of Christ's death to pay for people's sins. The cross (Christ's death) was God's way to save people.

b **1:31** Quote from Jer. 9:24.

power. [7]But we speak God's secret wisdom that has been hidden from everyone until now. God planned this wisdom for our glory.* He planned it before the world began. [8]None of the rulers of this world understood this wisdom. If they had understood it, they would not have killed our great and glorious Lord on a cross. [9]But as the Scriptures* say,

"No one has ever seen,
no one has ever heard,
no one has ever imagined
what God has prepared
for those who love him."

Isaiah 64:4

[10]But God has shown us these things through the Spirit.*

The Spirit knows all things. The Spirit even knows the deep secrets of God. [11]It is like this: No one knows the thoughts that another person has. Only the person's spirit that lives inside knows those thoughts. It is the same with God. No one knows God's thoughts except God's Spirit. [12]We received the Spirit that is from God, not the spirit of the world. We received God's Spirit so that we can know all that God has given us.

[13]When we say this, we don't use words taught to us by human wisdom. We use words taught to us by the Spirit. We use the Spirit's words to explain spiritual truths. [14]People who do not have God's Spirit do not accept the things that come from his Spirit. They think these things are foolish. They cannot understand them, because they can only be understood with the Spirit's help. [15]We who have the Spirit are able to make judgments about all these things. But anyone without the Spirit is not able to make proper judgments about us. [16]As the Scriptures say,

"Who can know what is on the
Lord's mind?
Who is able to give him
advice?"

Isaiah 40:13

But we have been given Christ's way of thinking.

Teachers Are Only God's Servants

3 [1]Brothers and sisters, when I was there, I could not talk to you the way I talk to people who are led by the Spirit. I had to talk to you like ordinary people of the world. You were like babies in Christ. [2]And the teaching I gave you was like milk, not solid food. I did this because you were not ready for solid food. And even now you are not ready. [3]You are still not following the Spirit. You are jealous of each other, and you are always arguing with each other. This shows that you are still following your own selfish desires. You are acting like ordinary people of the world. [4]One of you says, "I follow Paul," and someone else says, "I follow Apollos." When you say things like that, you are acting like people of the world.

[5]Is Apollos so important? Is Paul so important? We are only servants of God who helped you believe. Each one of us did the work God gave us to do. [6]I planted the seed and Apollos watered it. But God is the one who made the seed grow. [7]So the one who plants is not important, and the one who waters is not important. Only God is important, because he is the one who makes things grow. [8]The one who plants and the one who waters have the same purpose. And each one will be rewarded for his own work. [9]We are workers

together for God, and you are like a farm that belongs to God.

And you are a house that belongs to God. [10]Like an expert builder I built the foundation of that house. I used the gift that God gave me to do this. Other people are building on that foundation. But everyone should be careful how they build. [11]The foundation that has already been built is Jesus Christ, and no one can build any other foundation. [12]People can build on that foundation using gold, silver, jewels, wood, grass, or straw. [13]But the work that each person does will be clearly seen, because the Day* will make it plain. That Day will appear with fire, and the fire will test everyone's work. [14]If the building they put on the foundation still stands, they will get their reward. [15]But if their building is burned up, they will suffer loss. They will be saved, but it will be like someone escaping from a fire.

[16]You should know that you yourselves are God's temple.*a* God's Spirit* lives in you. [17]If you destroy God's temple, God will destroy you, because God's temple is holy.* You yourselves are God's temple.

[18]Don't fool yourselves. Whoever thinks they are wise in this world should become a fool. That's the only way they can be wise. [19]I say this because the wisdom of this world is foolishness to God. As the Scriptures* say, "He catches those who think they are wise in their own clever traps."*b* [20]The

Scriptures also say, "The Lord knows the thoughts of the wise. He knows that their thoughts are worth nothing."*c* [21]So there is not a person on earth that any of you should be boasting about. Everything is yours: [22]Paul, Apollos, Peter,* the world, life, death, the present, and the future—all these are yours. [23]And you belong to Christ, and Christ belongs to God.

Apostles of Christ Jesus

4 [1]You should think of us as servants of Christ, the ones God has trusted to do the work of making known his secret truths. [2]Those who are trusted with such an important work must show that they are worthy of that trust. [3]But I don't consider your judgment on this point to be worth anything. Even an opinion from a court of law would mean nothing. I don't even trust my own judgment. [4]I don't know of any wrong I have done, but that does not make me right. The Lord is the one who must decide if I have done well or not. [5]So don't judge anyone now. The time for judging will be when the Lord comes. He will shine light on everything that is now hidden in darkness. He will make known the secret purposes of our hearts. Then the praise each person should get will come from God.

[6]Brothers and sisters, I have used Apollos and myself as examples for you. I did this so that you could learn from us the meaning of the words, "Follow what the Scriptures* say." Then you will not brag about one person and criticize another. [7]Who do you think

a **3:16 temple** God's house—the place where God's people worship him. Here, it means that believers are the spiritual temple where God lives.
b **3:19** Quote from Job 5:13.

c **3:20** Quote from Ps. 94:11.

you are? Everything you have was given to you. So, if everything you have was given to you, why do you act as if you got it all by your own power?

8You think you have everything you need. You think you are rich. You think you have become kings without us. I wish you really were kings. Then we could rule together with you. 9But it seems to me that God has given me and the other apostles* the last place. We are like prisoners condemned to die, led in a parade for the whole world to see—not just people but angels too. 10We are fools for Christ, but you think you are so wise in Christ. We are weak, but you think you are so strong. People give you honor, but they don't honor us. 11Even now we still don't have enough to eat or drink, and we don't have enough clothes. We often get beatings. We have no homes. 12We work hard with our own hands to feed ourselves. When people insult us, we ask God to bless them. When people treat us badly, we accept it. 13When people say bad things about us, we try to say something that will help them. But people still treat us like the world's garbage—everyone's trash.

14I am not trying to make you feel ashamed, but I am writing this to counsel you as my own dear children. 15You may have ten thousand teachers in Christ, but you don't have many fathers. Through the Good News* I became your father in Christ Jesus. 16So I beg you to be like me. 17That is why I am sending Timothy to you. He is my son in the Lord. I love him and trust him. He will help you remember the way I live

in Christ Jesus—a way of life that I teach in every meeting of the church* wherever I am.

18Some of you are acting so proud, it seems as though you think I won't be coming there again. 19But I will come to you very soon, the Lord willing. Then I will see if these proud talkers have the power to do anything more than talk. 20God's kingdom* is not seen in talk but in power. 21Which do you want: that I come to you with punishment, or that I come with love and gentleness?

Don't Let Your People Live in Sin

5 1I don't want to believe what I am hearing—that there is sexual sin among you. And it is such a bad kind of sexual sin that even those who have never known God don't allow it. People say that a man there has his father's wife. 2And still you are proud of yourselves! You should have been filled with sadness. And the man who committed that sin should be put out of your group. 3I cannot be there with you in person, but I am with you in spirit. And I have already judged the man who did this. I judged him the same as I would if I were really there. 4Come together in the name of our Lord Jesus. I will be with you in spirit, and you will have the power of our Lord Jesus with you. 5Then turn this man over to Satan.* His sinful self^a has to be destroyed so that his spirit will be saved on the day when the Lord comes again.

6Your proud talk is not good. You know the saying, "Just a little yeast* makes the whole batch of dough rise." 7Take out all the old yeast, so that you will be a new

a **5:5 sinful self** Or "body." Literally, "flesh."

batch of dough. You really are bread without yeast—Passover bread.*a* Yes, Christ our Passover Lamb*b* has already been killed. 8So let us eat our Passover meal, but not with the bread that has the old yeast, the yeast of sin and wrongdoing. But let us eat the bread that has no yeast. This is the bread of goodness and truth.

9I wrote to you in my letter that you should not associate with people who sin sexually. 10But I did not mean the people of this world. You would have to leave the world to get away from all the people who sin sexually, or who are greedy and cheat each other, or who worship idols. 11I meant you must not associate with people who claim to be believers* but continue to live in sin. Don't even eat with a brother or sister who sins sexually, is greedy, worships idols, abuses others with insults, gets drunk, or cheats people.

12–13It is not my business to judge those who are not part of the group of believers. God will judge them, but you must judge those who are part of your group. The Scriptures* say, "Make the evil person leave your group."*c*

Judging Problems Between Believers

6 1When one of you has something against someone else in your group, why do you go to the judges in the law courts? The way they think and live is wrong. So why do you let them decide who is right? Why don't you let God's holy people* decide who is right? 2Don't you know that God's people will judge the world? So if you will judge the world, then surely you can judge small arguments like this. 3You know that in the future we will judge angels. So surely we can judge life's ordinary problems. 4So if you have such matters to be judged, why do you take them to those who are not part of the church*? They mean nothing to you. 5I say this to shame you. Surely there is someone in your group wise enough to judge a complaint between two believers.* 6But now one believer goes to court against another, and you let people who are not believers judge their case!

7The lawsuits that you have against each other show that you are already defeated. It would be better for you to let someone wrong you. It would be better to let someone cheat you. 8But you are the ones doing wrong and cheating. And you do this to your own brothers and sisters in Christ!

9–10Surely you know that people who do wrong will not get to enjoy God's kingdom.* Don't be fooled. These are the people who will not get to enjoy his kingdom: those who sin sexually, those who worship idols,* those who commit adultery,* men who let other men use them for sex or who have sex with other men, those who steal, those who are greedy, those who drink too much, those who abuse others with insults, and those who cheat. 11In the past some of you were like that. But you were washed clean, you were made holy,* and you were made right

a **5:7 Passover bread** The special bread without yeast that the Jews ate at their Passover meal. Paul means that believers are free from sin, just as the Passover bread was free from yeast.
b **5:7 Passover Lamb** Jesus was a sacrifice for his people, like a lamb killed for the Jewish Passover Feast.
c **5:12–13** Quote from Deut. 22:21, 24.

with God in the name of the Lord Jesus Christ and by the Spirit of our God.

Use Your Bodies for God's Glory

12"I am allowed to do anything," you say. My answer to this is that not all things are good. Even if it is true that "I am allowed to do anything," I will not let anything control me like a slave. 13Someone else says, "Food is for the stomach, and the stomach for food." Yes, and God will destroy them both. But the body is not for sexual sin. The body is for the Lord, and the Lord is for the body. 14And God will raise our bodies from death with the same power he used to raise the Lord Jesus. 15Surely you know that your bodies are parts of Christ himself. So I must never take what is part of Christ and join it to a prostitute! 16The Scriptures* say, "The two people will become one."ᵃ So you should know that anyone who is joined with a prostitute becomes one with her in body. 17But anyone who is joined with the Lord is one with him in spirit.

18So run away from sexual sin. It involves the body in a way that no other sin does. So if you commit sexual sin, you are sinning against your own body. 19You should know that your body is a templeᵇ for the Holy Spirit* that you received from God and that lives in you. You don't own yourselves. 20God paid a very high price to make you his. So honor God with your body.

ᵃ **6:16** Quote from Gen. 2:24.
ᵇ **6:19 temple** God's house—the place where God's people worship him. Here, it means that believers are the spiritual temple where God lives.

About Marriage

7 1Now I will discuss the things you wrote me about. You asked if it is better for a man not to have any sexual relations at all. 2But sexual sin is a danger, so each man should enjoy his own wife, and each woman should enjoy her own husband. 3The husband should give his wife what she deserves as his wife. And the wife should give her husband what he deserves as her husband. 4The wife does not have power over her own body. Her husband has the power over her body. And the husband does not have power over his own body. His wife has the power over his body. 5Don't refuse to give your bodies to each other. But you might both agree to stay away from sex for a while so that you can give your time to prayer. Then come together again so that Satan* will not be able to tempt you in your weakness. 6I say this only to give you permission to be separated for a time. It is not a rule. 7I wish everyone could be like me. But God has given each person a different ability. He makes some able to live one way, others to live a different way.

8Now for those who are not married and for the widows I say this: It is good for you to stay single like me. 9But if you cannot control your body, then you should marry. It is better to marry than to burn with sexual desire.

10Now, I have a command for those who are married. Actually, it is not from me; it is what the Lord commanded. A wife should not leave her husband. 11But if a wife does leave, she should remain single or get back together with her husband. And a husband should not divorce his wife.

¹²The advice I have for the others is from me. The Lord did not give us any teaching about this. If you have a wife who is not a believer, you should not divorce her if she will continue to live with you. ¹³And if you have a husband who is not a believer, you should not divorce him if he will continue to live with you. ¹⁴The husband who is not a believer is set apart for God through his believing wife. And the wife who is not a believer is set apart for God through her believing husband. If this were not true, your children would be unfit for God's use. But now they are set apart for him.

¹⁵But if the husband or wife who is not a believer decides to leave, let them leave. When this happens, the brother or sister in Christ is free. God chose you to have a life of peace. ¹⁶Wives, maybe you will save your husband; and husbands, maybe you will save your wife. You don't know now what will happen later.

Live as God Called You

¹⁷But each one of you should continue to live the way the Lord God has given you to live—the way you were when God chose you. I tell people in all the churches* to follow this rule. ¹⁸If a man was already circumcised* when he was chosen, he should not change his circumcision. If a man was without circumcision when he was chosen, he should not be circumcised. ¹⁹It is not important if anyone is circumcised or not. What is important is obeying God's commands. ²⁰Each one of you should stay the way you were when God chose you. ²¹If you were

a slave when God chose you, don't let that bother you. But if you can be free, then do it. ²²If you were a slave when the Lord chose you, you are now free in the Lord. You belong to the Lord. In the same way, if you were free when you were chosen, you are now Christ's slave. ²³God paid a high price for you, so don't be slaves to anyone else. ²⁴Brothers and sisters, in your new life with God, each one of you should continue the way you were when God chose you.

Questions About Getting Married

²⁵Now I write about people who are not married.ᵃ I have no command from the Lord about this, but I give my opinion. And I can be trusted, because the Lord has given me mercy. ²⁶This is a time of trouble. So I think it is good for you to stay the way you are. ²⁷If you have a wife, don't try to get free from her. If you are not married, don't try to find a wife. ²⁸But if you decide to marry, that is not a sin. And it is not a sin for a girl who has never married to get married. But those who marry will have trouble in this life, and I want you to be free from this trouble.

²⁹Brothers and sisters, this is what I mean: We don't have much time left. So starting now, those who have wives should be the same as those who don't. ³⁰It should not be important whether you are sad or whether you are happy. If you buy something, it should not matter to you that you own it. ³¹You should use the things of the world without letting them become important to

ᵃ 7:25 people who are not married Literally, "virgins."

you. This is how you should live, because this world, the way it is now, will soon be gone.

³²I want you to be free from worry. A man who is not married is busy with the Lord's work. He is trying to please the Lord. ³³But a man who is married is busy with things of the world. He is trying to please his wife. ³⁴He must think about two things—pleasing his wife and pleasing the Lord. A woman who is not married or a girl who has never married is busy with the Lord's work. She wants to give herself fully—body and spirit—to the Lord. But a married woman is busy with things of the world. She is trying to please her husband. ³⁵I am saying this to help you. I am not trying to limit you, but I want you to live in the right way. And I want you to give yourselves fully to the Lord without giving your time to other things.

³⁶A man might think that he is not doing the right thing with his fiancée. She might be almost past the best age to marry.^a So he might feel that he should marry her. He should do what he wants. It is no sin for them to get married. ³⁷But another man might be more sure in his mind. There may be no need for marriage, so he is free to do what he wants. If he has decided in his own heart not to marry his fiancée, he is doing the right thing. ³⁸So the man who marries his fiancée does right, and the man who does not marry does better.

³⁹A woman should stay with her husband as long as he lives. But if the husband dies, the woman is free to marry any man she wants, but he should belong to the Lord. ⁴⁰The woman is happier if she does not marry again. This is my opinion, and I believe that I have God's Spirit.

About Food Offered to Idols

8 ¹Now I will write about meat that is sacrificed^b to idols.* It is certainly true that "we all have knowledge," as you say. But this knowledge only fills people with pride. It is love that helps the church grow stronger. ²Those who think they know something do not yet know anything as they should. ³But whoever loves God is known by God.

⁴So this is what I say about eating meat: We know that an idol is really nothing in the world, and we know that there is only one God. ⁵It's really not important if there are things called gods in heaven or on earth—and there are many of these "gods" and "lords" out there. ⁶For us there is only one God, and he is our Father. All things came from him, and we live for him. And there is only one Lord, Jesus Christ. All things were made through him, and we also have life through him.

⁷But not all people know this. Some have had the habit of worshiping idols. So now when they eat meat, they still feel as if it belongs to an idol. They are not sure that it is right to eat this meat. So when they eat it, they feel guilty. ⁸But food will not bring us closer to God. Refusing to eat does not make us less pleasing to God, and

---

^a **7:36 She ... to marry** Or "He may have trouble controlling his desires."

^b **8:1 sacrificed** Killed and offered as a gift to show worship. Also in verse 10.

eating does not make us closer to him.

9But be careful with your freedom. Your freedom to eat anything may make those who have doubts about what they can eat fall into sin. 10You understand that it's all right to eat anything, so you can eat even in an idol's temple. But someone who has doubts might see you eating there, and this might encourage them to eat meat sacrificed to idols too. But they really think it is wrong. 11So this weak brother or sister—someone Christ died for—is lost because of your better understanding. 12When you sin against your brothers and sisters in Christ in this way and you hurt them by causing them to do things they feel are wrong, you are also sinning against Christ. 13So if the food I eat makes another believer fall into sin, I will never eat meat again. I will stop eating meat, so that I will not make my brother or sister sin.

Rights That Paul Has Not Used

9 1I am a free man. I am an apostle.* I have seen Jesus our Lord. You people are an example of my work in the Lord. 2Others may not accept me as an apostle, but surely you do. You are proof that I am an apostle in the Lord.

3Some people want to judge me. So this is the answer I give them: 4We have the right to eat and drink, don't we? 5We have the right to bring a believing wife with us when we travel, don't we? The other apostles and the Lord's brothers and Peter* all do this. 6And are Barnabas and I the only ones who must work to earn our living? 7No soldier ever serves in the army and pays his own salary. No one ever plants a vineyard* without eating some of the grapes himself. No one takes care of a flock of sheep without drinking some of the milk himself.

8These aren't just my own thoughts. God's law says the same thing. 9Yes, it is written in the Law of Moses*: "When a work animal is being used to separate grain, don't keep it from eating the grain."a When God said this, was he thinking only about work animals? No. 10He was really talking about us. Yes, that was written for us. The one who plows and the one who separates the grain should both expect to get some of the grain for their work. 11We planted spiritual seed among you, so we should be able to harvest from you some things for this life. Surely that is not asking too much. 12Others have this right to get things from you. So surely we have this right too. But we don't use this right. No, we endure everything ourselves so that we will not stop anyone from obeying the Good News* of Christ. 13Surely you know that those who work at the Temple* get their food from the Temple. And those who serve at the altar* get part of what is offered at the altar. 14It is the same with those who have the work of telling the Good News. The Lord has commanded that those who tell the Good News should get their living from this work.

15But I have not used any of these rights, and I am not trying to get anything from you. That is not my purpose for writing this. I would rather die than to have someone take away what for me

a 9:9 Quote from Deut. 25:4.

is a great source of pride. [16]It's not my work of telling the Good News that gives me any reason to boast. That is my duty—something I must do. If I don't tell people the Good News, I am in real trouble. [17]If I did it because it was my own choice, I would deserve to be paid. But I have no choice. I must tell the Good News. So I am only doing the duty that was given to me. [18]So what do I get for doing it? My reward is that when I tell people the Good News I can offer it to them for free and not use the rights that come with doing this work.

[19]I am free. I belong to no other person, but I make myself a slave to everyone. I do this to help save as many people as I can. [20]To the Jews I became like a Jew so that I could help save Jews. I myself am not ruled by the law,* but to those who are ruled by the law I became like someone who is ruled by the law. I did this to help save those who are ruled by the law. [21]To those who are without the law I became like someone who is without the law. I did this to help save those who are without the law. (But really, I am not without God's law—I am ruled by the law of Christ.) [22]To those who are weak, I became weak so that I could help save them. I have become all things to all people. I did this so that I could save people in any way possible. [23]I do all this to make the Good News known. I do it so that I can share in the blessings of the Good News.

[24]You know that in a race all the runners run, but only one runner gets the prize. So run like that. Run to win! [25]All who compete in the games use strict training. They do this so that they can win a prize*—one that doesn't last. But our prize is one that will last forever. [26]So I run like someone who has a goal. I fight like a boxer who is hitting something, not just the air. [27]It is my own body I fight to make it do what I want. I do this so that I won't miss getting the prize myself after telling others about it.

Warning From History

10 [1]Brothers and sisters, I want you to know what happened to our ancestors* who were with Moses.* They were all under the cloud,[a] and they all walked through the sea. [2]They were all baptized[b] into Moses in the cloud and in the sea. [3]They all ate the same spiritual food, [4]and they all drank the same spiritual drink. They drank from that spiritual rock that was with them, and that rock was Christ. [5]But God was not pleased with most of those people, so they were killed in the desert.

[6]And these things that happened are examples for us. These examples should stop us from wanting evil things like those people did. [7]Don't worship idols* as some of them did. As the Scriptures* say, "The people sat down to eat and drink and then got up to have a wild party."[c] [8]We should not commit sexual sins as some of them did. In one day 23,000 of

---

[a] **10:1 cloud** The cloud that led and protected the people of Israel on their journey out of Egypt, across the Red Sea, and through the wilderness. See Ex. 13:20–22; 14:19, 20.

[b] **10:2 baptized** See "BAPTIZE" in the Word List. Here, Paul seems to mean that what happened to the Jews with Moses can be compared to the baptism of a believer into Christ.

[c] **10:7** Quote from Ex. 32:6.

them died because of their sin. [9]We should not test Christ[a] as some of them did. Because of that, they were killed by snakes. [10]And don't complain as some of them did. Because they complained, they were killed by the angel that destroys.

[11]The things that happened to those people are examples. They were written to be warnings for us. We live in the time that all those past histories were pointing to. [12]So anyone who thinks they are standing strong should be careful that they don't fall. [13]The only temptations that you have are the same temptations that all people have. But you can trust God. He will not let you be tempted more than you can bear. But when you are tempted, God will also give you a way to escape that temptation. Then you will be able to endure it.

[14]So, my dear friends, stay away from worshiping idols. [15]You are intelligent people. Judge for yourselves the truth of what I say now. [16]The cup of blessing[b] that we give thanks for is a sharing in the blood sacrifice of Christ, isn't it? And the bread that we break is a sharing in the body of Christ, isn't it? [17]There is one loaf of bread, so we who are many are one body, because we all share in that one loaf.

[18]And think about what the people of Israel* do. When they eat the sacrifices,[c] they are united by sharing what was offered on the altar.* [19]So, am I saying that sacrifices to idols are the same as those Jewish sacrifices? No, because an idol is nothing, and the things offered to idols are worth nothing. [20]But I am saying that when food is sacrificed to idols, it is an offering to demons,* not to God. And I don't want you to share anything with demons. [21]You cannot drink the cup of the Lord and then go drink a cup that honors demons. You cannot share a meal at the Lord's table and then go share a meal that honors demons. [22]Doing that would make the Lord jealous.[d] Do you really want to do that? Do you think we are stronger than he is?

Use Your Freedom for God's Glory

[23]"All things are allowed," you say. But not all things are good. "All things are allowed." But some things don't help anyone. [24]Try to do what is good for others, not just what is good for yourselves.

[25]Eat any meat that is sold in the meat market. Don't ask questions about it to see if it is something you think is wrong to eat. [26]You can eat it, "because the earth and everything in it belong to the Lord."[e]

[27]Someone who is not a believer might invite you to eat with them. If you want to go, then eat anything that is put before you. Don't ask questions to see if it is something you think is wrong to eat. [28]But if someone tells you, "That food was offered to idols,*" then don't eat it. That's because some people think it is wrong, and it might cause a problem for the

---

a **10:9 Christ** Some Greek copies say, "the Lord."

b **10:16 cup of blessing** The cup of wine that believers in Christ thank God for and drink at the Lord's Supper.

c **10:18 sacrifices** Animals killed and offered as gifts to God.

d **10:22 make the Lord jealous** See Deut. 32:16, 17.

e **10:26** Quote from Ps. 24:1; 50:12; 89:11.

person who told you that. ²⁹I don't mean that you think it is wrong. But the other person might think it is wrong. That's the only reason not to eat it. My own freedom should not be judged by what another person thinks. ³⁰I eat the meal with thankfulness. So I don't want to be criticized because of something I thank God for.

³¹So if you eat, or if you drink, or if you do anything, do it for the glory* of God. ³²Never do anything that might make other people do wrong—Jews, non-Jews, or anyone in God's church.* ³³I do the same thing. I try to please everyone in every way. I am not trying to do what is good for me. I am trying to do what is good for the most people so that they can be saved.

11 ¹Follow my example, just as I follow the example of Christ.

Being Under Authority

²I praise you because you remember me in all things. You follow closely the teachings I gave you. ³But I want you to understand this: The head of every man is Christ. And the head of a woman is the man.ᵃ And the head of Christ is God.

⁴Every man who prophesies* or prays with his head covered brings shame to his head. ⁵But every woman who prays or prophesies should have her head covered. If her head is not covered, she brings shame to her head. Then she is the same as a woman who has her head shaved. ⁶If a woman does not cover her head, it is the same as cutting off all her hair. But it is shameful for a woman to cut off her hair or to shave her head. So she should cover her head.

⁷But a man should not cover his head, because he is made like God and is God's glory.* But woman is man's glory. ⁸Man did not come from woman. Woman came from man. ⁹And man was not made for woman. Woman was made for man. ¹⁰So that is why a woman should have her head covered with something that shows she is under authority.ᵇ Also, she should do this because of the angels.

¹¹But in the Lord the woman needs the man, and the man needs the woman. ¹²This is true because woman came from man, but also man is born from woman. Really, everything comes from God.

¹³Decide this for yourselves: Is it right for a woman to pray to God without something on her head? ¹⁴Even nature itself teaches you that wearing long hair is shameful for a man. ¹⁵But wearing long hair is a woman's honor. Long hair is given to the woman to cover her head. ¹⁶Some people may still want to argue about this. But we and the churches* of God don't accept what those people are doing.

The Lord's Supper

¹⁷In the things I tell you now I don't praise you. Your meetings hurt you more than they help you. ¹⁸First, I hear that when you meet together as a church* you are divided. And this is not hard to

---

ᵇ **11:10 have her head … authority** Literally, "have authority on her head." This could also be translated, "keep control of her head," meaning "do what will keep people from misunderstanding her uncovered head."

ᵃ **11:3 the man** This could also mean "her husband."

believe [19]because of your idea that you must have separate groups to show who the real believers are!

[20]When you all come together, it is not really the Lord's Supper[a] you are eating. [21]I say this because when you eat, each one eats without waiting for the others. Some people don't get enough to eat or drink, while others have too much.[b] [22]You can eat and drink in your own homes. It seems that you think God's church is not important. You embarrass those who are poor. What can I say? Should I praise you? No, I cannot praise you for this.

[23]The teaching I gave you is the same that I received from the Lord: On the night when the Lord Jesus was handed over to be killed, he took bread [24]and gave thanks for it. Then he divided the bread and said, "This is my body; it is for you. Eat this to remember me." [25]In the same way, after they ate, Jesus took the cup of wine. He said, "This cup represents the new agreement* from God, which begins with my blood sacrifice. When you drink this, do it to remember me." [26]This means that every time you eat this bread and drink this cup, you are telling others about the Lord's death until he comes again.

[27]So if you eat the bread or drink the cup of the Lord in a way that does not fit its meaning, you are sinning against the body and the blood of the Lord. [28]Before you eat the bread and drink the cup, you should examine your own attitude. [29]If you eat and drink

without paying attention to those who are the Lord's body, your eating and drinking will cause you to be judged guilty. [30]That is why many in your group are sick and weak, and many have died. [31]But if we judged ourselves in the right way, then God would not judge us. [32]But when the Lord judges us, he punishes us to show us the right way. He does this so that we will not be condemned with the world.

[33]So, my brothers and sisters, when you come together to eat, wait for each other. [34]If some are too hungry to wait, they should eat at home. Do this so that your meeting together will not bring God's judgment on you. I will tell you what to do about the other things when I come.

Gifts From the Holy Spirit

12 [1]Now, brothers and sisters, I want you to understand about spiritual gifts. [2]You remember the lives you lived before you were believers. You let yourselves be influenced and led away to worship idols*—things that have no life. [3]So I tell you that no one who is speaking with the help of God's Spirit says, "Jesus be cursed." And no one can say, "Jesus is Lord," without the help of the Holy Spirit.*

[4]There are different kinds of spiritual gifts, but they are all from the same Spirit. [5]There are different ways to serve, but we serve the same Lord. [6]And there are different ways that God works in people, but it is the same God who works in all of us to do everything.

[7]Something from the Spirit can be seen in each person. The Spirit gives this to each one to help others. [8]The Spirit gives one person

[a] **11:20 Lord's Supper** The special meal Jesus told his followers to eat to remember him. See Lk. 22:14–20.
[b] **11:21 have too much** Literally, "get drunk."

the ability to speak with wisdom. And the same Spirit gives another person the ability to speak with knowledge. [9]The same Spirit gives faith to one person and to another he gives gifts of healing. [10]The Spirit gives to one person the power to do miracles,* to another the ability to prophesy,* and to another the ability to judge what is from the Spirit and what is not. The Spirit gives one person the ability to speak in different kinds of languages, and to another the ability to interpret those languages. [11]One Spirit, the same Spirit, does all these things. The Spirit decides what to give each one.

The Body of Christ

[12]A person has only one body, but it has many parts. Yes, there are many parts, but all those parts are still just one body. Christ is like that too. [13]Some of us are Jews and some of us are not; some of us are slaves and some of us are free. But we were all baptized* to become one body through one Spirit.* And we were all given[a] the one Spirit.

[14]And a person's body has more than one part. It has many parts. [15]The foot might say, "I am not a hand, so I don't belong to the body." But saying this would not stop the foot from being a part of the body. [16]The ear might say, "I am not an eye, so I don't belong to the body." But saying this would not make the ear stop being a part of the body. [17]If the whole body were an eye, it would not be able to hear. If the whole body were an ear, it would not be able to smell anything. [18-19]If each part of the body were the same part, there

would be no body. But as it is, God put the parts in the body as he wanted them. He made a place for each one. [20]So there are many parts, but only one body.

[21]The eye cannot say to the hand, "I don't need you!" And the head cannot say to the foot, "I don't need you!" [22]No, those parts of the body that seem to be weaker are actually very important. [23]And the parts that we think are not worth very much are the parts we give the most care to. And we give special care to the parts of the body that we don't want to show. [24]The more beautiful parts don't need this special care. But God put the body together and gave more honor to the parts that need it. [25]God did this so that our body would not be divided. God wanted the different parts to care the same for each other. [26]If one part of the body suffers, then all the other parts suffer with it. Or if one part is honored, then all the other parts share its honor.

[27]All of you together are the body of Christ. Each one of you is a part of that body. [28]And in the church* God has given a place first to apostles,* second to prophets,* and third to teachers. Then God has given a place to those who do miracles,* those who have gifts of healing, those who can help others, those who are able to lead, and those who can speak in different kinds of languages. [29]Not all are apostles. Not all are prophets. Not all are teachers. Not all do miracles. [30]Not all have gifts of healing. Not all speak in different kinds of languages. Not all interpret those languages. [31]Continue to give your attention to the spiritual gifts you consider to be

a **12:13 given** Literally, "given to drink."

the greatest. But now I want to point out a way of life that is even greater.

Let Love Be Your Guide

13 [1]I may speak in different languages, whether human or even of angels. But if I don't have love, I am only a noisy bell or a ringing cymbal. [2]I may have the gift of prophecy,* I may understand all secrets and know everything there is to know, and I may have faith so great that I can move mountains. But even with all this, if I don't have love, I am nothing. [3]I may give away everything I have to help others, and I may even give my body as an offering to be burned. But I gain nothing by doing all this if I don't have love.

[4]Love is patient and kind. Love is not jealous, it does not brag, and it is not proud. [5]Love is not rude, it is not selfish, and it cannot be made angry easily. Love does not remember wrongs done against it. [6]Love is never happy when others do wrong, but it is always happy with the truth. [7]Love never gives up on people. It never stops trusting, never loses hope, and never quits.

[8]Love will never end. But all those gifts will come to an end—even the gift of prophecy, the gift of speaking in different kinds of languages, and the gift of knowledge. [9]These will all end because this knowledge and these prophecies we have are not complete. [10]But when perfection comes, the things that are not complete will end.

[11]When I was a child, I talked like a child, I thought like a child, and I made plans like a child. When I became a man, I stopped those childish ways. [12]It is the same with us. Now we see God as if we are looking at a reflection in a mirror. But then, in the future, we will see him right before our eyes. Now I know only a part, but at that time I will know fully, as God has known me. [13]So these three things continue: faith, hope, and love. And the greatest of these is love.

Use Spiritual Gifts to Help the Church

14 [1]Love should be the goal of your life, but you should also want to have the gifts that come from the Spirit.* And the gift you should want most is to be able to prophesy.* [2]I will explain why. Those who have the gift of speaking in a different language are not speaking to people. They are speaking to God. No one understands them—they are speaking secret things through the Spirit. [3]But those who prophesy are speaking to people. They help people grow stronger in faith, and they give encouragement and comfort. [4]Those who speak in a different language are helping only themselves. But those who prophesy are helping the whole church.*

[5]I would like all of you to have the gift of speaking in different languages. But what I want more is for you to prophesy. Anyone who prophesies is more important than those who can only speak in different languages. However, if they can also interpret those languages, they are as important as the one who prophesies. If they can interpret, then the church can be helped by what they say.

[6]Brothers and sisters, will it help you if I come to you speaking in different languages? No, it

will help you only if I bring you a new truth or some knowledge, prophecy,* or teaching. 7This is true even with lifeless things that make sounds—like a flute or a harp. If the different musical notes are not made clear, you can't understand what song is being played. Each note must be played clearly for you to be able to understand the tune. 8And in a war, if the trumpet does not sound clearly, the soldiers will not know it is time to prepare for fighting.

9It is the same with you. If you don't speak clearly in a language people know, they cannot understand what you are saying. You will be talking to the air! 10It is true that there are many different languages in the world, and they all have meaning. 11But if I don't understand the meaning of what someone is saying, it will just be strange sounds to me, and I will sound just as strange to them. 12That's why you who want spiritual gifts so much should prefer those gifts that help the church grow stronger.

13So those who have the gift of speaking in a different language should pray that they can also interpret what they say. 14If I pray in a different language, my spirit is praying, but my mind does nothing. 15So what should I do? I will pray with my spirit, but I will also pray with my mind. I will sing with my spirit, but I will also sing with my mind. 16You might be praising God with your spirit. But someone there without understanding cannot say "Amen*" to your prayer of thanks, because they don't know what you are saying. 17You may be thanking God

in a good way, but others are not helped.

18I thank God that my gift of speaking in different kinds of languages is greater than any of yours. 19But in the church meetings I would rather speak five words that I understand than thousands of words in a different language. I would rather speak with my understanding, so that I can teach others.

20Brothers and sisters, don't think like children. In evil things be like babies, but in your thinking you should be like full-grown adults. 21As the Scriptures*a say,

"Using those who speak a
    different language
  and using the lips of
    foreigners,
I will speak to these people.
  But even then, they will not
    obey me."   Isaiah 28:11–12
This is what the Lord says.

22And from this we see that the use of different languages shows how God deals with those who don't believe, not with those who believe. And prophecy shows how God works through those who believe, not through unbelievers. 23Suppose the whole church meets together and you all speak in different languages. If some people come in who are without understanding or don't believe, they will say you are crazy. 24But suppose you are all prophesying and someone comes in who does not believe or who is without understanding. Their sin will be shown to them, and they will be judged by everything you say. 25The secret things in their heart

a **14:21 Scriptures** Literally, "law," which sometimes means the Old Testament.

will be made known. So they will bow down and worship God. They will say, "Without a doubt, God is here with you."[a]

Your Meetings Should Be Helpful to All

26So, brothers and sisters, what should you do? When you meet together, one person has a song, another has a teaching, and another has a new truth from God. One person speaks in a different language, and another interprets that language. The purpose of whatever you do should be to help everyone grow stronger in faith. 27When you meet together, if anyone speaks to the group in a different language, it should be only two or no more than three people who do this. And they should speak one after the other. And someone else should interpret what they say. 28But if there is no interpreter, then anyone who speaks in a different language should be quiet in the church meeting. They should speak only to themselves and to God.

29And only two or three prophets* should speak. The others should judge what they say. 30And if a message from God comes to someone who is sitting, the first speaker should be quiet. 31You can all prophesy* one after the other. This way everyone can be taught and encouraged. 32The spirits of prophets are under the control of the prophets themselves. 33God is not a God of confusion but a God of peace. This is the rule for all the meetings of God's people.

34The women should keep quiet in these church* meetings. They are not allowed to speak out but should be under authority, as the Law of Moses says. 35If there is something they want to know, they should ask their own husbands at home. It is shameful for a woman to speak up like that in the church meeting.

36God's teaching did not come from you, and you are not the only ones who have received it. 37If you think you are a prophet or that you have a spiritual gift, you should understand that what I am writing to you is the Lord's command. 38If you do not accept this, you will not be accepted.

39So my brothers and sisters, continue to give your attention to prophesying. And don't stop anyone from using the gift of speaking in different languages. 40But everything should be done in a way that is right and orderly.

The Good News About Jesus Christ

15 1Now, brothers and sisters, I want you to remember the Good News* I told you. You received that Good News message, and you continue to base your life on it. 2That Good News, the message you heard from me, is God's way to save you. But you must continue believing it. If you don't, you believed for nothing.

3I gave you the message that I received. I told you the most important truths: that Christ died for our sins, as the Scriptures* say; 4that he was buried and was raised to life on the third day, as the Scriptures say; 5and that he appeared to Peter and then to the twelve apostles.* 6After that Christ appeared to more than 500 other believers* at the same time. Most of them are still living today, but some have died. 7Then he appeared to James and later to all the apostles. 8Last of all, he

---

[a] 14:25 See Isa. 45:14 and Zech. 8:23.

appeared to me. I was different, like a baby born before the normal time.

⁹All the other apostles are greater than I am. I say this because I persecuted* the church* of God. That is why I am not even good enough to be called an apostle. ¹⁰But, because of God's grace,* that is what I am. And his grace that he gave me was not wasted. I worked harder than all the other apostles. (But I was not really the one working. It was God's grace that was with me.) ¹¹So then it is not important if I told you God's message or if it was the other apostles who told you—we all tell people the same message, and this is what you believed.

We Will Be Raised From Death

¹²We tell everyone that Christ was raised from death. So why do some of you say that people will not be raised from death? ¹³If no one will ever be raised from death, then Christ has never been raised. ¹⁴And if Christ has never been raised, then the message we tell is worth nothing. And your faith is worth nothing. ¹⁵And we will also be guilty of lying about God, because we have told people about him, saying that he raised Christ from death. And if no one is raised from death, then God never raised Christ from death. ¹⁶If those who have died are not raised, then Christ has not been raised either. ¹⁷And if Christ has not been raised from death, then your faith is for nothing; you are still guilty of your sins. ¹⁸And those in Christ who have already died are lost. ¹⁹If our hope in Christ is only for this life here on earth, then people should feel more sorry for us than for anyone else.

²⁰But Christ really has been raised from death—the first one of all those who will be raised. ²¹Death comes to people because of what one man did. But now there is resurrection* from death because of another man. ²²I mean that in Adam all of us die. And in the same way, in Christ all of us will be made alive again. ²³But everyone will be raised to life in the right order. Christ was first to be raised. Then, when Christ comes again, those who belong to him will be raised to life. ²⁴Then the end will come. Christ will destroy all rulers, authorities, and powers. Then he will give the kingdom to God the Father.

²⁵Christ must rule until God puts all enemies under his control.ᵃ ²⁶The last enemy to be destroyed will be death. ²⁷As the Scriptures* say, "God put everything under his control."ᵇ When it says that "everything" is put under him, it is clear that this does not include God himself. God is the one putting everything under Christ's control. ²⁸After everything has been put under Christ, then the Son himself will be put under God. God is the one who put everything under Christ. And Christ will be put under God so that God will be the complete ruler over everything.

²⁹If no one will ever be raised from death, then what will the people do who are baptized* for those who have died? If the dead are never raised, then why are people baptized for them?

³⁰And what about us? Why do we put ourselves in danger every

ᵃ **15:25 control** Literally, "feet."
ᵇ **15:27** Quote from Ps. 8:6.

hour? ³¹I face death every day. That is true, brothers and sisters, just as it is true that I am proud of what you are because of Christ Jesus our Lord. ³²I fought wild animals in Ephesus. If I did that only for human reasons, then I have gained nothing. If we are not raised from death, "Let us eat and drink, because tomorrow we die."*a*

³³Don't be fooled: "Bad friends will ruin good habits." ³⁴Come back to your right way of thinking and stop sinning. Some of you don't know God. I say this to shame you.

What Kind of Body Will We Have?

³⁵But someone may ask, "How are the dead raised? What kind of body will they have?" ³⁶These are stupid questions. When you plant something, it must die in the ground before it can live and grow. ³⁷And when you plant something, what you plant does not have the same "body" that it will have later. What you plant is only a seed, maybe wheat or something else. ³⁸But God gives it the body that he has planned for it, and he gives each kind of seed its own body. ³⁹All things made of flesh are not the same: People have one kind of flesh, animals have another, birds have another, and fish have yet another kind. ⁴⁰Also there are heavenly bodies and earthly bodies. But the beauty of the heavenly bodies is one kind, and the beauty of the earthly bodies is another. ⁴¹The sun has one kind of beauty, the moon has another kind, and the stars have another. And each star is different in its beauty.

⁴²It will be the same when those who have died are raised to life. The body that is "planted" in the grave will ruin and decay, but it will be raised to a life that cannot be destroyed. ⁴³When the body is "planted," it is without honor. But when it is raised, it will be great and glorious. When the body is "planted," it is weak. But when it is raised, it will be full of power. ⁴⁴The body that is "planted" is a physical body. When it is raised, it will be a spiritual body.

There is a physical body. So there is also a spiritual body. ⁴⁵As the Scriptures* say, "The first man, Adam, became a living person.*b*"*c* But the last Adam*d* is a life-giving spirit. ⁴⁶The spiritual man did not come first. It was the physical man that came first; then came the spiritual. ⁴⁷The first man came from the dust of the earth. The second man came from heaven. ⁴⁸All people belong to the earth. They are like that first man of earth. But those who belong to heaven are like that man of heaven. ⁴⁹We were made like that man of earth, so we will also be made like that man of heaven.

⁵⁰I tell you this, brothers and sisters: Our bodies of flesh and blood cannot have a part in God's kingdom.* Something that will ruin cannot have a part in something that never ruins. ⁵¹But listen, I tell you this secret: We will not all die, but we will all be changed. ⁵²It will only take the time of a second. We will be changed as quickly as an eye

---

a **15:32** Quote from Isa. 22:13; 56:12.

b **15:45 person** Literally, "soul."

c **15:45** Quote from Gen. 2:7.

d **15:45 Adam** The name Adam means "man." Here, "the last Adam" refers to Christ, the "man of heaven."

blinks. This will happen when the last trumpet blows. The trumpet will blow and those who have died will be raised to live forever. And we will all be changed. [53]This body that ruins must clothe itself with something that will never ruin. And this body that dies must clothe itself with something that will never die. [54]So this body that ruins will clothe itself with that which never ruins. And this body that dies will clothe itself with that which never dies. When this happens, the Scriptures will be made true:

"Death is swallowed in victory."

Isaiah 25:8

[55]"O death, where is your
victory?
Where is your power to hurt?"

Hosea 13:14

[56]Death's power to hurt is sin, and the power of sin is the law. [57]But we thank God who gives us the victory through our Lord Jesus Christ! [58]So, my dear brothers and sisters, stand strong. Don't let anything change you. Always give yourselves fully to the work of the Lord. You know that your work in the Lord is never wasted.

The Collection for Believers in Judea

16 [1]Now, about the collection of money for God's people: Do the same as I told the Galatian churches* to do. [2]On the first day of every week, each of you should take some of your money and put it in a special place. Save up as much as you can from what you are blessed with. Then you will not have to gather it all after I come. [3]When I arrive, I will send some men to take your gift to Jerusalem. These will be the ones you all agree should go. I will send them with letters of introduction. [4]If it seems good for me to go too, we can all travel together.

Paul's Plans

[5]I plan to go through Macedonia,* so I will come to you after that. [6]Maybe I will stay with you for a time. I might even stay all winter. Then you can help me on my trip, wherever I go. [7]I don't want to come see you now, because I would have to leave to go to other places. I hope to stay a longer time with you, if the Lord allows it. [8]But I will stay in Ephesus until Pentecost.* [9]I will stay here, because a good opportunity for a great and growing work has been given to me now. And there are many people working against it.

[10]Timothy might come to you. Try to make him feel comfortable with you. He is working for the Lord the same as I am. [11]So none of you should refuse to accept Timothy. Help him continue on his trip in peace so that he can come back to me. I am expecting him to come back with the other brothers.

[12]Now about our brother Apollos: I strongly encouraged him to visit you with the other brothers. He prefers not to come now, but he will come when he has the opportunity.

Paul Ends His Letter

[13]Be careful. Hold firmly to your faith. Have courage and be strong. [14]Do everything in love. [15]You know that Stephanas and his family were the first believers in Achaia.* They have given themselves to the service of God's people. I ask you, brothers and sisters, [16]to follow the leading of people like these and others who

work hard and serve together with them.

17I am happy that Stephanas, Fortunatus, and Achaicus have come. You are not here, but they have filled your place. 18They have been a great encouragement to me and to you as well. You should recognize the value of such people.

19The churches* in Asia* send you their greetings. Aquila and Priscilla greet you in the Lord. Also the church that meets in their house sends greetings. 20All the brothers and sisters here send their greetings. Give each other the special greeting of God's people.[a]

21Here's my greeting in my own handwriting—PAUL.

22If anyone does not love the Lord, let that person be separated from God—lost forever!

Come, O Lord![b]

23The grace* of the Lord Jesus be with you.

24My love be with all of you in Christ Jesus.

---

a **16:20 the special greeting of God's people** Literally, "a holy kiss."
b **16:22 Come, O Lord** This is a translation of the Aramaic "*marana tha.*"

2 Corinthians

1 ¹Greetings from Paul, an apostle* of Christ Jesus. I am an apostle because that is what God wanted. Greetings also from Timothy our brother in Christ.

To God's church* in Corinth and to all of God's holy people* throughout Achaia.*

²Grace* and peace to you from God our Father and the Lord Jesus Christ.

Paul Gives Thanks to God

³Praise be to the God and Father of our Lord Jesus Christ. He is the Father who is full of mercy, the God of all comfort. ⁴He comforts us every time we have trouble so that when others have trouble, we can comfort them with the same comfort God gives us. ⁵We share in the many sufferings of Christ. In the same way, much comfort comes to us through Christ. ⁶If we have troubles, it is for your comfort and salvation. If we are comforted, it is so that we can comfort you. And this helps you patiently accept the same sufferings we have. ⁷Our hope for you is strong. We know that you share in our sufferings. So we know that you also share in our comfort.

⁸Brothers and sisters, we want you to know about the trouble we suffered in Asia.* We had great burdens there, which were greater than our own strength. We even gave up hope for life. ⁹In fact, it seems like God has been telling us we are going to die. But this is so that we will not trust in ourselves but in God, who raises people from death. ¹⁰He saved us from these great dangers of death, and he will continue to save us. We feel sure he will always save us. ¹¹And you can help us with your prayers. Then many people will give thanks for us—that God blessed us because of their many prayers.

The Change in Paul's Plans

¹²This is what we are proud of, and I can say with a clear conscience that it is true: In everything we have done in the world, we have done it with an honest and pure heart from God. And this is even truer in what we have done with you. We did this by God's grace,* not by the kind of wisdom the world has. ¹³We write to you only what you can read and understand. And I hope you will fully understand, ¹⁴just as you already understand many things about us. I hope you will understand that you can be proud of us, just as we will be proud of you on the day when our Lord Jesus Christ comes again.

¹⁵I was very sure of all this. That is why I made plans to visit you first. Then you could be blessed twice. ¹⁶I planned to visit you on my way to Macedonia* and again on my way back. I wanted to get help from you for my trip to Judea.

17Do you think that I made these plans without really thinking? Or maybe you think I make plans as the world does, saying yes and no at the same time.

18But if you can believe God, then you can believe that what we tell you is never both yes and no. 19The Son of God, Jesus Christ, the one that Silas, Timothy, and I told you about was not yes and no. In Christ it has always been yes. 20The yes to all of God's promises is in Christ. And that is why we say "Amen*" through Christ to the glory* of God. 21And God is the one who makes you and us strong in Christ. God is also the one who chose us for his work.a 22He put his mark on us to show that we are his. Yes, he put his Spirit* in our hearts as the first payment that guarantees all that he will give us.

23I tell you this, and I ask God to be my witness that this is true: The reason I did not come back to Corinth was that I did not want to punish or hurt you. 24I don't mean that we are trying to control your faith. You are strong in faith. But we are workers with you for your own happiness.

2 1So I decided that my next visit to you would not be another visit to make you sad. 2If I make you sad, then who will make me happy? Only you can make me happy—you, the ones I made sad. 3I wrote you a letter so that when I came to you I would not be made sad by those who should make me happy. I felt sure that all of

a **1:21 chose us for his work** Literally, "anointed us." In Greek this word is related to the title "Christ," which means "anointed one." See "ANOINT" and "CHRIST" in the Word List.

you would share my joy. 4When I wrote to you before, I was very troubled and my heart was full of sadness. I wrote with many tears. I did not write to make you sad, but to let you know how much I love you.

Forgive the Person Who Did Wrong
5Someone in your group has caused sadness—not to me, but to all of you. I mean he has caused sadness to all in some way. (I don't want to make it sound worse than it really is.) 6The punishment that most of your group gave him is enough for him. 7But now you should forgive him and encourage him. This will keep him from having too much sadness and giving up completely. 8So I beg you to show him that you love him. 9This is why I wrote to you. I wanted to test you and see if you obey in everything. 10If you forgive someone, then I also forgive them. And what I have forgiven—if I had anything to forgive—I forgave it for you, and Christ was with me. 11I did this so that Satan* would not win anything from us. We know very well what his plans are.

God Gives Us Victory Over Troubles
12I went to Troas to tell people the Good News* of Christ. The Lord gave me a good opportunity there. 13But I had no peace because I did not find my brother Titus. So I said goodbye and went to Macedonia.*

14But thanks be to God, who always leads us in victory through Christ. God uses us to spread his knowledge everywhere like a sweet-smelling perfume. 15Our offering to God is to be the perfume of Christ that goes out to those who are being saved and to those who are being lost. 16To those who are being lost, this perfume smells like death, and it brings them death. But to those who are being saved, it has the sweet smell of life, and it brings them life. So who is good enough to do this work? [17]Certainly not those who are out there selling God's message* for a profit! But we don't do that. With Christ's help we speak God's truth honestly, knowing that we must answer to him.

Servants of God's New Agreement

3 [1]Why are we beginning again to tell you all these good things about ourselves? Do we need letters of introduction to you or from you, like some other people? [2]No, you yourselves are our letter, written on our hearts. It is known and read by all people. [3]You show that you are a letter from Christ that he sent through us. This letter is not written with ink but with the Spirit* of the living God. It is not written on stone[a] tablets but on human hearts.

[4]We can say this, because through Christ we feel sure before God. [5]I don't mean that we are able to do anything good ourselves. It is God who makes us able to do all that we do. [6]He made us able to be servants of a new agreement* from himself to his people. It is not an agreement of written laws, but it is of the Spirit. The written law brings death, but the Spirit gives life.

An Agreement With Greater Glory

[7]The old agreement[b] that brought death, written with words on stone, came with God's glory.* In fact, the face of Moses* was so bright with glory (a glory that was ending) that the people of Israel* could not continue looking at his face. [8]So surely the new agreement that comes from the life-giving Spirit* has even more glory. [9]This is what I mean: That old agreement judged people guilty of sin, but it had glory. So surely the new agreement that makes people right with God has much greater glory. [10]That old agreement had glory. But it really loses its glory when it is compared to the much greater glory of the new agreement. [11]If the agreement that was brought to an end came with glory, then the agreement that never ends has much greater glory.

[12]We are so sure of this hope that we can speak very openly. [13]We are not like Moses, who put a covering over his face. He covered his face so that the people of Israel would not see it. The glory was disappearing, and Moses did not want them to see it end. [14]But their minds were closed. And even today, when those people read the writings of the old agreement,[c] that same covering hides the meaning. That covering has not been removed for them. It is taken away only through Christ. [15]Yes, even today, when they read the Law of Moses, there is a covering over their minds. [16]But when someone changes and follows the Lord, that covering is taken away. [17]The Lord is the Spirit, and where the Spirit of the Lord is, there is

---

[a] **3:3 stone** Meaning the law that God gave to Moses, which was written on stone tablets. Also in verse 7. See Ex. 24:12; 25:16.
[b] **3:7 agreement** In verses 7–11 literally, "service" or "ministry."

[c] **3:14 old agreement** See "AGREEMENT" in the Word List. Here, "old agreement" is used to mean the Law of Moses on which that agreement was based.

freedom. [18]And our faces are not covered. We all show the Lord's glory, and we are being changed to be like him. This change in us brings more and more glory, which comes from the Lord, who is the Spirit.

Spiritual Treasure in Clay Jars

4 [1]God, with his mercy, gave us this work to do, so we don't give up. [2]But we have turned away from secret and shameful ways. We don't use trickery, and we don't change the teaching of God. We teach the truth plainly. This is how we show people who we are. And this is how they can know in their hearts what kind of people we are before God. [3]The Good News* that we tell people may be hidden, but it is hidden only to those who are lost. [4]The ruler[a] of this world* has blinded the minds of those who don't believe. They cannot see the light of the Good News—the message about the divine greatness* of Christ. Christ is the one who is exactly like God. [5]We don't tell people about ourselves. But we tell people that Jesus Christ is Lord, and we tell them that we are your servants for Jesus. [6]God once said, "Let light shine out of the darkness!"[b] And this is the same God who made his light shine in our hearts to let us know that his own divine greatness is seen in the face of Christ.

[7]We have this treasure from God, but we are only like clay jars that hold the treasure. This is to show that the amazing power we have is from God, not from us. [8]We have troubles all around us, but we are not defeated. We often don't know what to do, but we don't give up. [9]We are persecuted,* but God does not leave us. We are hurt sometimes, but we are not destroyed. [10]So we constantly experience the death of Jesus in our own bodies, but this is so that the life of Jesus can also be seen in our bodies. [11]We are alive, but for Jesus we are always in danger of death, so that the life of Jesus can be seen in our bodies that die. [12]So death is working in us, but the result is that life is working in you.

[13]The Scriptures* say, "I believed, so I spoke."[c] Our faith is like that too. We believe, and so we speak. [14]God raised the Lord Jesus from death, and we know that he will also raise us with Jesus. God will bring us together with you, and we will stand before him. [15]All these things are for you. And so the grace* of God is being given to more and more people. This will bring more and more thanks to God for his glory.*

Living by Faith

[16]That is why we never give up. Our physical body is becoming older and weaker, but our spirit inside us is made new every day. [17]We have small troubles for a while now, but these troubles are helping us gain an eternal glory.* That eternal glory is much greater than our troubles. [18]So we think about what we cannot see, not what we see. What we see lasts only a short time, and what we cannot see will last forever.

5 [1]We know that our body—the tent we live in here on earth—will be destroyed. But when that happens, God will have a home

---

a **4:4 The ruler** Literally, "The god."
b **4:6 Let ... darkness** See Gen. 1:3
c **4:13** Quote from Ps. 116:10.

for us to live in. It will not be the kind of home people build here. It will be a home in heaven that will continue forever. ²But now we are tired of this body. We want God to give us our heavenly home. ³It will clothe us and we will not be naked. ⁴While we live in this tent, we have burdens and so we complain. I don't mean that we want to remove this tent, but we want to be clothed with our heavenly home. Then this body that dies will be covered with life. ⁵This is what God himself made us for. And he has given us the Spirit* as the first payment to guarantee the life to come.

⁶So we always have confidence. We know that while we live in this body, we are away from the Lord. ⁷We live by what we believe will happen, not by what we can see. ⁸So I say that we have confidence. And we really want to be away from this body and be at home with the Lord. ⁹Our only goal is to always please the Lord, whether we are living here in this body or there with him. ¹⁰We must all stand before Christ to be judged. Everyone will get what they should. They will be paid for whatever they did—good or bad—when they lived in this earthly body.

Helping People Become God's Friends

¹¹We know what it means to fear the Lord, so we try to help people accept the truth. God knows what we really are, and I hope that in your hearts you know us too. ¹²We are not trying to prove ourselves to you again. But we are telling you about ourselves. We are giving you reasons to be proud of us. Then you will have an answer for those who are proud about what

can be seen. They don't care about what is in a person's heart. ¹³If we are crazy, it is for God. If we have our right mind, it is for you. ¹⁴The love of Christ controls us, because we know that one person died for everyone. So all have died. ¹⁵He died for all so that those who live would not continue to live for themselves. He died for them and was raised from death so that they would live for him.

¹⁶From this time on we don't think of anyone as the world thinks of people. It is true that in the past we thought of Christ as the world thinks. But we don't think that way now. ¹⁷When anyone is in Christ, it is a whole new world.ᵃ The old things are gone; suddenly, everything is new! ¹⁸All this is from God. Through Christ, God made peace between himself and us. And God gave us the work of bringing people into peace with him. ¹⁹I mean that God was in Christ, making peace between the world and himself. In Christ, God did not hold people guilty for their sins. And he gave us this message of peace to tell people. ²⁰So we have been sent to speak for Christ. It is like God is calling to people through us. We speak for Christ when we beg you to be at peace with God. ²¹Christ had no sin, but God made him become sinᵇ so that in Christ we could be right with God.

6 ¹We are workers together with God. So we beg you: Don't let the grace* that you received from God be for nothing. ²God says,

ᵃ **5:17 When anyone ... world** Or "Anyone who is in Christ is a new creation."
ᵇ **5:21 sin** Or "an offering for sin."

"I heard you at the right time,
and I gave you help on the
day of salvation." *Isaiah 49:8*
I tell you that the "right time" is
now. The "day of salvation" is now.
³We don't want people to find
anything wrong with our work.
So we do nothing that will be a
problem to others. ⁴But in every
way we show that we are servants of God. We never give up,
even though we face troubles, difficulties, and problems of every
kind. ⁵We are beaten and thrown
into prison. People get upset at
us and fight against us. We work
hard, and sometimes we get no
sleep or food. ⁶We show that we
are God's servants by our pure
lives, by our understanding, by
our patience, and by our kindness.
We show it by the Holy Spirit,*
by genuine love, ⁷by speaking
the truth, and by depending on
God's power. This right way of
living has prepared us to defend
ourselves against every kind of
attack.

⁸Some people honor us, but
others shame us. Some people
say good things about us, but others say bad things. Some people
say we are liars, but we speak the
truth. ⁹To some people we are not
known, but we are well known.
We seem to be dying, but look! We
continue to live. We are punished,
but we are not killed. ¹⁰We have
much sadness, but we are always
rejoicing. We are poor, but we are
making many people rich in faith.
We have nothing, but really we
have everything.

¹¹We have spoken freely to
you people in Corinth. We have
opened our hearts to you. ¹²Our
feelings of love for you have
not stopped. It is you who have
stopped your feelings of love for
us. ¹³I speak to you as if you were
my children. Do the same as we
have done—open your hearts also.

We Are God's Temple

¹⁴You are not the same as those
who don't believe. So don't join
yourselves to them. Good and
evil don't belong together. Light
and darkness cannot share the
same room. ¹⁵How can there be
any unity between Christ and the
devil*ᵃ*? What does a believer have
in common with an unbeliever?
¹⁶God's temple*ᵇ* cannot have anything to do with idols,* and we
are the temple of the living God.
As God said,
"I will live with them and walk
with them;
I will be their God, and
they will be my people."
Leviticus 26:11–12

¹⁷ "So come away from those
people
and separate yourselves from
them, says the Lord.
Don't touch anything that is
not clean,
and I will accept you."
Isaiah 52:11

¹⁸ "I will be your father,
and you will be my sons and
daughters, says the Lord
All-Powerful." *2 Samuel 7:8, 14*

7 ¹Dear friends, we have these
promises from God. So we

ᵃ **6:15 the devil** Literally, *"beliar,"* one form
of the Hebrew word *"belial,"* which means
"worthlessness" and was used to refer to
the devil or the enemy of Christ.
ᵇ **6:16 God's temple** God's house—the
place where God's people worship him.
Here, it means that believers are the spiritual temple where God lives.

should make ourselves pure—free from anything that makes our body or our soul unclean. Our respect for God should make us try to be completely holy* in the way we live.

Paul's Joy

²Open your hearts to us. We have not done wrong to anyone or caused harm to anyone. And we have not cheated anyone. ³I do not say this to blame you. I told you before that we love you so much we would live or die with you. ⁴I feel that I can tell you anything. I am very proud of you. Even with all the troubles we have had, I am greatly encouraged and feel very happy.

⁵When we came into Macedonia,* we had no rest. We found trouble all around us. We had fighting on the outside and fear on the inside. ⁶But God encourages those who are troubled, and he certainly encouraged us by bringing Titus to us. ⁷It was so good to see him, but we were encouraged even more to hear about the encouragement you gave him. He told us that you really want to see me and that you are very sorry for what you did. And he told us how ready and willing you are to help me. When I heard this, I was so much happier.

⁸Even if the letter I wrote you made you sad, I am not sorry I wrote it. I know that letter made you sad, and I was sorry for that. But it made you sad only for a short time. ⁹Now I am happy, not because you were made sad, but because your sorrow made you decide to change. That is what God wanted, so you were not hurt by us in any way. ¹⁰The kind of sorrow God wants makes people

decide to change their lives. This leads them to salvation, and we cannot be sorry for that. But the kind of sorrow the world has will bring death. ¹¹You had the kind of sorrow God wanted you to have. Now see what that sorrow has brought you: It has made you very serious. It made you want to prove that you were not wrong. It made you angry and afraid. It made you want to see me. It made you care. It made you want the right thing to be done. You proved that you were not guilty in any part of that problem. ¹²The main reason I wrote that letter was not because of the one who did the wrong or the one who was hurt. I wrote so that you would realize, before God, how very much you care for us. ¹³And that is what was so encouraging to us.

We were greatly encouraged, but we were especially pleased to see how happy Titus was. You all made him feel so much better. ¹⁴I had bragged about you to Titus, and you didn't embarrass me. We have always told you the truth, and now what we told Titus about you has been shown to be true. ¹⁵And his love for you is stronger when he remembers that you were all ready to obey. You welcomed him with respect and fear. ¹⁶I am so happy that I can trust you fully.

Help for God's People in Judea

8 ¹And now, brothers and sisters, we want to tell you what God's grace* has done in the churches* in Macedonia.* ²These believers have been tested by great troubles, and they are very poor. But their great joy caused them to be very generous in their giving. ³I can tell you that they gave as much as they were able and even more than they could afford. No one told them to do this. It was their idea. 4But they asked us again and again—they begged us to let them share in this service for God's people. 5And they gave in a way that we did not expect: They gave themselves to the Lord and to us before they gave their money. This is what God wants.

6So we asked Titus to help you finish this special work of giving. He is the one who started this work. 7You are rich in everything—in faith, in speaking ability, in knowledge, in the willingness to help, and in the love you learned from us. So now we want you to be rich in this work of giving too.

8I am not ordering you to give, but I want to see how real your love is by comparing you with others who have been so ready and willing to help. 9You know the grace of our Lord Jesus Christ. You know that he gave up his heavenly riches for you. He gave up everything so that you could be richly blessed.

10This is what I think you should do: Last year you were the first to want to give, and you were the first who gave. 11So now finish the work you started. Then your "doing" will be equal to your "wanting to do." Give from what you have. 12If you want to give, your gift will be accepted. Your gift will be judged by what you have, not by what you don't have. 13We don't want you to have troubles while others are comforted. We want everything to be equal. 14At this time you have plenty and can provide what they need. Then later, when they have plenty, they can provide what you need. Then everyone will have an equal share. 15As the Scriptures* say,

"Those who gathered much did
    not have too much,
and those who gathered little
    did not have too little."

Exodus 16:18

Titus and His Companions

16I thank God because he gave Titus the same love for you that I have. 17Titus agreed to do what we asked. In fact, he himself wanted very much to come see you. 18We are sending with Titus the brother who is praised by all the churches.* He is praised because of his service to the Good News.* 19Also, he was chosen by the churches to go with us when we carry this gift. We are doing this service to bring honor[a] to the Lord and to show that we really want to help.

20We are being careful so that no one will criticize us about the way we are caring for this large gift. 21We are trying to do what is right. We want to do what the Lord accepts as right and also what people think is right.

22Also, we are sending with them our brother who is always ready to help. He has proved this to us in many ways. And he wants to help even more now because he has much faith in you.

23Now about Titus—he is my partner. He is working together with me to help you. And about the other brothers—they are sent from the churches, and they bring honor to Christ. 24So show these men that you really have love.

---

a **8:19 honor** Or "glory." See "GLORY" in the Word List.

Show them why we are proud of you. Then all the churches can see it.

Your Giving Is a Blessing

9 ¹I really don't need to write to you about this help for God's people. ²I know that you want to help. I have been bragging about you to the people in Macedonia.* I told them that you people in Achaia* have been ready to give since last year. And your desire to give has made most of the people here ready to give also. ³But I am sending these brothers to you. I don't want our bragging about you in this to be for nothing. I want you to be ready just as I said you would be. ⁴If any of those from Macedonia come with me, and they find that you are not ready, we will be ashamed. We will be ashamed that we were so sure of you. And you will be ashamed too! ⁵So I thought that I should ask these brothers to come there before we do. They will help in getting together the generous gift you promised. Then it will be ready when we come, and it will be seen as a blessing you are giving, not as something you were forced to do.

⁶Remember this: The one who plants few seeds will have a small harvest. But the one who plants a lot will have a big harvest. ⁷Each one of you should give what you have decided in your heart to give. You should not give if it makes you unhappy or if you feel forced to give. God loves those who are happy to give. ⁸And God can give you more blessings than you need, and you will always have plenty of everything. You will have enough to give to every good work. ⁹As the Scriptures* say,

"He gives generously to the
   poor;
his goodness will continue
   forever."   *Psalm 112:9*

¹⁰God is the one who gives seed to those who plant, and he gives bread for food. And God will give you spiritual seed and make that seed grow. He will produce a great harvest from your goodness. ¹¹God will make you rich in every way so that you can always give freely. And your giving through us will make people give thanks to God.

¹²The service you are offering helps God's people with their needs, but that is not all it does. It is also bringing more and more thanks to God. ¹³This service is a proof of your faith, and people will praise God because of it. They will praise God that you freely share what you have with them and with all people. They will praise him to see you following the Good News* about Christ that you openly accepted. They will praise God because you freely share with them and with all people. ¹⁴And when they pray, they will wish they could be with you. They will feel this way because of the great grace* that God gave you. ¹⁵Thanks be to God for his gift that is too wonderful to describe.

Paul Defends His Ministry

10 ¹I, Paul, am begging you with the gentleness and the kindness of Christ. Some say that I am bold when I am writing you from a distance, but not when I am there with you. ²They think our motives for what we do are like those of the world. I plan to be very bold against those people when I come. I hope I will not need to use that same boldness with you. ³We live in this world, but we don't fight our battles in the same way the world does. [4]The weapons we use are not human ones. Our weapons have power from God and can destroy the enemy's strong places. We destroy people's arguments, [5]and we tear down every proud idea that raises itself against the knowledge of God. We also capture every thought and make it give up and obey Christ. [6]We are ready to punish anyone there who does not obey, but first we want you to be fully obedient.

[7]You must look at the facts before you. If you feel sure you belong to Christ, you must remember that we belong to Christ the same as you do. [8]It may seem as though we boast too much about the authority the Lord gave us. But he gave us this authority to strengthen you, not to hurt you. So I will not be ashamed of whatever boasting we do. [9]I don't want you to think that I am trying to scare you with my letters. [10]Some people say, "Paul's letters are powerful and sound important, but when he is with us, he is weak and the worst speaker you have ever heard." [11]Those people should know this: When we are there with you, we will show the same power that we show now in our letters.

[12]We don't dare put ourselves in the same class with those who think they are so important. We don't compare ourselves to them. They use themselves to measure themselves, and they judge themselves by what they themselves are. This shows that they know nothing.

[13]But we will not boast about anything outside the work that was given us to do. We will limit our boasting to the work God gave us, but this work includes our work with you. [14]We would be boasting too much only if we had not already come to you. But we have come to you with the Good News* about Christ. [15]We limit our boasting to the work that is ours. We don't boast about the work other people have done. We hope that your faith will continue to grow. We hope that you will help our work to grow much larger. [16]We want to tell the Good News in the areas beyond your city. We don't want to boast about work that has already been done in someone else's area. [17]"Whoever boasts should boast only about the Lord."[a] [18]What people say about themselves means nothing. What counts is whether the Lord says they have done well.

Paul and the False Apostles

[11] [1]I wish you would be patient with me even when I am a little foolish. But you are already patient with me. [2]I am jealous for you with a jealousy that comes from God. I promised to give you to Christ. He must be your only husband. I want to give you to Christ to be his pure bride.[b] [3]But I am afraid that your minds will be led away from your true and pure following of Christ. This could happen just as Eve was tricked by that snake with his clever lies. [4]You seem to be quite patient with anyone who comes to you and tells you about a Jesus that is different from the Jesus we told you about. You seem very willing to accept a spirit or a message

a **10:17** Quote from Jer. 9:24.
b **11:2 bride** Literally, "virgin."

that is different from the Spirit* and message* that you received from us.

⁵I don't think that those "super apostles*" are any better than I am. ⁶It is true that I am not a trained speaker, but I do have knowledge. We have shown this to you clearly in every way.

⁷I did the work of telling God's Good News* to you without pay. I humbled myself to make you important. Do you think that was wrong? ⁸I accepted pay from other churches.* I took their money so that I could serve you. ⁹If I needed something when I was with you, I did not trouble any of you. The brothers who came from Macedonia* gave me all that I needed. I did not allow myself to be a burden to you in any way. And I will never be a burden to you. ¹⁰No one there in Achaia* will stop me from boasting about that. I say this with the truth of Christ in me. ¹¹And why do I not burden you? Do you think it is because I don't love you? God knows that I love you.

¹²And I will continue doing what I am doing now, because I want to stop those people from having a reason to boast. They would like to say that the work they boast about is the same as ours. ¹³They are false apostles, lying workers. They only pretend to be apostles of Christ. ¹⁴That does not surprise us, because even Satan* changes himself to look like an angel of light.ᵃ ¹⁵So it does not surprise us if Satan's servants make themselves look like servants who work for what is right. But in the end those people will get the punishment they deserve.

Paul Tells About His Sufferings

¹⁶I tell you again: No one should think that I am a fool. But if you think I am a fool, then accept me as you would accept a fool. Then I can boast a little too. ¹⁷But I am not talking the way the Lord would talk. I am boasting like a fool. ¹⁸Others are boasting about their lives in the world. So I will boast too. ¹⁹You are wise, so you will gladly be patient with fools! ²⁰I say this because you are even patient with someone who forces you to do things and uses you. You are patient with those who trick you, or think they are better than you, or hit you in the face! ²¹I am ashamed to say it, but we were too "weak" to do such things to you.

But if anyone dares to boast, I will too. (I am talking like a fool.) ²²Are those people Hebrews? So am I. Are they Israelitesᵇ? So am I. Are they from Abraham's* family? So am I. ²³Are they serving Christ? I am serving him more. (I am crazy to talk like this.) I have worked much harder than they have. I have been in prison more often. I have been hurt more in beatings. I have been near death many times.

²⁴Five times the Jews have given me their punishment of 39 lashes with a whip. ²⁵Three different times I was beaten with rods. One time I was almost killed with rocks. Three times I was in ships that were wrecked, and one of those times I spent the night and the next day in the sea. ²⁶In my constant traveling I have been in

---

ᵃ **11:14 angel of light** Messenger from God. The devil fools people so that they think he is from God.

ᵇ **11:22 Hebrews … Israelites** Other names for the Jewish people.

danger from rivers, from thieves, from my own people, and from people who are not Jews. I have been in danger in cities, in places where no one lives, and on the sea. And I have been in danger from people who pretend to be believers* but are not.

27I have done hard and tiring work, and many times I did not sleep. I have been hungry and thirsty. Many times I have been without food. I have been cold and without clothes. 28And there are many other problems. One of these is the care I have for all the churches.* I worry about each group of believers every day. 29I feel weak every time another person is weak. I feel deeply upset every time another person is led into sin.

30If I must boast, I will boast about the things that show I am weak. 31God knows that I am not lying. He is the God and Father of the Lord Jesus, and he is to be praised forever. 32When I was in Damascus, the governor under King Aretas wanted to arrest me, so he put guards around the city. 33But some friends put me in a basket. Then they put the basket through a hole in the wall and lowered me down. So I escaped from the governor.

A Special Blessing in Paul's Life

12 1There is more that I have to say about myself. It won't help, but I will talk now about visions* and revelations from the Lord. 2I know a man*a* in Christ who was taken up to the third heaven. This happened 14 years ago. I don't know if the man was in his body or out of his body, but God knows. 3–4And I know that this man was taken up to paradise.* I don't know if he was in his body or away from his body, but he heard things that he is not able to explain. He heard things that no one is allowed to tell. 5I will boast about a man like that, but I will not boast about myself. I will boast only about my weaknesses.

6But if I wanted to say more about myself, I would not be a fool, because I would be telling the truth. But I won't say any more, because I don't want people to think more of me than what they see me do or hear me say.

7But I must not be too proud of the wonderful things that were shown to me. So a painful problem*b* was given to me—an angel from Satan,* sent to make me suffer, so that I would not think that I am better than anyone else. 8I begged the Lord three times to take this problem away from me. 9But the Lord said, "My grace* is all you need. Only when you are weak can everything be done completely by my power." So I will gladly boast about my weaknesses. Then Christ's power can stay in me. 10Yes, I am glad to have weaknesses if they are for Christ. I am glad to be insulted and have hard times. I am glad when I am persecuted* and have problems, because it is when I am weak that I am really strong.

Paul's Love for the Believers in Corinth

11I have been talking like a fool, but you made me do it. You people are the ones who should say good things about me. I am

---

a **12:2 a man** In 12:2–5 Paul is probably talking about himself.

b **12:7 painful problem** Literally, "thorn in the flesh."

worth nothing, but those "super apostles*" are not worth any more than I am! [12]When I was with you, I patiently did the things that prove I am an apostle—signs,* wonders,* and miracles.* [13]So you received everything that the other churches* have received. Only one thing was different: I was not a burden to you. Forgive me for this!

[14]I am now ready to visit you for the third time, and I will not be a burden to you. I don't want any of the things you own. I only want you. Children should not have to save things to give to their parents. Parents should save to give to their children. [15]So I am happy to give everything I have for you. I will even give myself for you. If I love you more, will you love me less?

[16]It is clear that I was not a burden to you, but you think that I was tricky and used lies to catch you. [17]Did I cheat you by using any of the men I sent to you? You know I didn't. [18]I asked Titus to go to you, and I sent our brother with him. Titus did not cheat you, did he? No, you know that his actions and his attitude were the same as ours.

[19]Do you think that we have been defending ourselves to you all this time? No, we say these things in Christ and before God. You are our dear friends, and everything we do is to make you stronger. [20]I do this because I am afraid that when I come, you will not be what I want you to be. And I am afraid that I will not be what you want me to be. I am afraid that I will find arguing, jealousy, anger, selfish fighting, evil talk, gossip, pride, and confusion there. [21]I am afraid that when I come to

you again, my God will make me humble before you. I may have to cry over the loss of some who sinned before. Many of them have still not changed their hearts to be sorry for their evil lives, their sexual sins, and the shameful things they have done.

Final Warnings and Greetings

13 [1]This will be my third time to visit you. And remember, "For every complaint there must be two or three people to say that they know it is true."[a] [2]When I was with you the second time, I gave a warning to those who had sinned. I am not there now, but I am giving another warning to them and to anyone else who has sinned: When I come to you again, I will punish you. [3]You want proof that Christ is speaking through me. My proof is that he is not weak in dealing with you but is showing his power among you. [4]It is true that Christ was weak when he was killed on the cross, but he lives now by God's power. It is also true that we share his weakness, but in dealing with you, we will be alive in him by God's power.

[5]Look closely at yourselves. Test yourselves to see if you are living in the faith. Don't you realize that Christ Jesus is in you? Of course, if you fail the test, he is not in you. [6]But I hope you will see that we have not failed the test. [7]We pray to God that you will not do anything wrong. Our concern here is not for people to see that we have passed the test in our work with you. Our main concern is that you do what is right, even if it looks as if we have failed the test. [8]We cannot do anything

a **13:1** Quote from Deut. 19:15.

that is against the truth but only what promotes the truth. ⁹We are happy to be weak if you are strong. And this is what we pray— that your lives will be made completely right again. ¹⁰I'm writing this before I come so that when I am there I will not have to use my authority to punish you. The Lord gave me that authority to make you stronger, not to destroy you.

¹¹Now, brothers and sisters, be filled with joy. Try to make everything right, and do what I have asked you to do. Agree with each other, and live in peace. Then the God of love and peace will be with you.

¹²Give each other the special greeting of God's people.ᵃ All of God's holy people* here send you their greetings.

¹³I pray that you will enjoy the grace* of the Lord Jesus Christ, the love of God, and the fellowshipᵇ of the Holy Spirit.*

ᵃ **13:12 the special greeting of God's people** Literally, "a holy kiss."
ᵇ **13:13 fellowship** This can mean a sharing or participation in the Holy Spirit or the loving association and unity among believers that is created by the Spirit.

Galatians

1 ¹Greetings from Paul, an apostle.* I was chosen to be an apostle, but not by any group or person here on earth. My authority came from none other than Jesus Christ and God the Father, who raised Jesus from death. ²Greetings also from all those in God's family who are with me.

To the churches* in Galatia*a*:

³I pray that God our Father and the Lord Jesus Christ will be good to you and give you peace. ⁴Jesus gave himself for our sins to free us from this evil world we live in. This is what God our Father wanted. ⁵The glory* belongs to God forever and ever. Amen.*

There Is Only One Good News Message

⁶A short time ago God chose you to follow him. He chose you through his grace* that came through Christ. But now I am amazed that you are already turning away and believing something different from the Good News* we told you. ⁷There is no other message that is the Good News, but some people are confusing you. They want to change the Good News about Christ. ⁸We told you the true Good News message. So anyone who tells you a different message should be condemned— even if it's one of us or even an angel from heaven! ⁹I said this

---

a **1:2 Galatia** Probably the area where Paul began churches on his first missionary trip. Read Acts 13 and 14.

---

before. Now I say it again: You have already accepted the Good News. Anyone who tells you another way to be saved should be condemned!

¹⁰Now do you think I am trying to make people accept me? No, God is the one I am trying to please. Am I trying to please people? If I wanted to please people, I would not be a servant of Christ.

Paul's Authority Is From God

¹¹Brothers and sisters, I want you to know that the Good News* message I told you was not made up by anyone. ¹²I did not get my message from any other human. The Good News is not something I learned from other people. Jesus Christ himself gave it to me. He showed me the Good News that I should tell people.

¹³You have heard about my past life in the Jewish religion. I persecuted* the church* of God very much. I tried to destroy his people. ¹⁴I was becoming a leader in the Jewish religion. I did better than most other Jews my own age. I tried harder than anyone else to follow the traditions we got from our ancestors.*

¹⁵But God had special plans for me even before I was born. So he chose me through his grace.* ¹⁶It pleased him to let me see and know his Son so that I could tell the Good News about him to the non-Jewish people. I immediately

prepared to do this work without asking for advice or help from anyone. [17]I did not go to Jerusalem to see those who were apostles* before I was. But, without waiting, I went away to Arabia. Later, I went back to the city of Damascus.

[18]Three years later I went to Jerusalem to meet Peter.* I stayed with him 15 days. [19]I met no other apostles—only James, the brother of the Lord. [20]God knows there is nothing untrue in any of this. [21]Later, I went to the areas of Syria and Cilicia.

[22]No one in any of Christ's churches* in Judea had ever met me before. [23]They had only heard this about me: "This man was persecuting us. But now he is telling people about the same faith that he once tried to destroy." [24]These believers praised God because of me.

The Other Apostles Accepted Paul

2 [1]After 14 years I went back to Jerusalem with Barnabas and took Titus with me. [2]I went there because God showed me that I should go. I explained to them the message* that I tell the non-Jewish people. I also met alone with those who were considered to be the leaders. I wanted to be sure we were in agreement so that my past work and the work I do now would not be wasted.

[3]Titus, who was with me, is a Greek.* But these leaders still did not force him to be circumcised.* [4]We needed to talk about these problems, because some who pretended to be our brothers had come into our group secretly. They came in like spies to find out about the freedom we have in Christ Jesus. They wanted to make us slaves, [5]but we did not agree with anything those false brothers wanted. We wanted the truth of the Good News* to continue for you.

[6]Those men who were considered to be important did not change the Good News message I tell people. (It doesn't matter to me if they were "important" or not. To God everyone is the same.) [7]But these leaders saw that God had given me a special work, the same as Peter. God gave Peter the work of telling the Good News to the Jews. But God gave me the work of telling the Good News to the non-Jewish people. [8]God gave Peter the power to work as an apostle* for the Jewish people. God gave me the power to work as an apostle too, but for those who are not Jews. [9]James, Peter, and John seemed to be the leaders. And they saw that God had given me this special gift of ministry, so they accepted Barnabas and me. They said to us, "We agree that you should go to those who are not Jews, and we will go to the Jews." [10]They asked us to do only one thing—to remember to help those who are poor. And this was something that I really wanted to do.

Paul Shows That Peter Was Wrong

[11]When Peter came to Antioch, he did something that was not right. I stood against him, because he was wrong. [12]This is what happened: When Peter first came to Antioch, he ate and associated with the non-Jewish people. But when some Jewish men came from James, Peter separated himself from the non-Jews. He stopped eating with them, because he was afraid of the Jews who believe that all non-Jewish

people must be circumcised.* [13]So Peter was a hypocrite.* The other Jewish believers joined with him, so they were hypocrites too. Even Barnabas was influenced by what these Jewish believers did. [14]They were not following the truth of the Good News.* When I saw this, I spoke to Peter in front of everyone. I said, "Peter, you are a Jew, but you don't live like one. You live like someone who is not a Jew. So why are you trying to force those who are not Jewish to live like Jews?"

[15]We are Jews by birth. We were not born "sinners," as we call those who are not Jews. [16]But we know that no one is made right with God by following the law.* It is trusting in[a] Jesus Christ that makes a person right with God. So we have put our faith in Christ Jesus, because we wanted to be made right with God. And we are right with him because we trusted in[b] Christ—not because we followed the law. I can say this because no one can be made right with God by following the law.

[17]We Jews came to Christ to be made right with God, so it is clear that we were sinners too. Does this mean that Christ makes us sinners? Of course not. [18]But I would be wrong to begin teaching again those things that I gave up. [19]It was the law itself that caused me to end my life under the law. I died to the law so that I could live for God. I have been nailed to the cross with Christ. [20]So I am not the one living now—it is Christ living in me. I still live in my body, but I live by faith in[c] the Son of God. He is the one who loved me and gave himself to save me. [21]I am not the one destroying the meaning of God's grace.* If following the law is how people are made right with God, then Christ did not have to die.

God's Blessing Comes Through Faith

3 [1]You people in Galatia are so foolish! Why do I say this? Because I told you very clearly about the death of Jesus Christ on the cross. But now it seems as though you have let someone use their magical powers to make you forget. [2]Tell me this one thing: How did you receive the Spirit*? Did you receive the Spirit by following the law*? No, you received the Spirit because you heard the message about Jesus and believed it. [3]You began your life in Christ with the Spirit. Now do you try to complete it by your own power? That is foolish. [4]You have experienced many things. Were all those experiences wasted? I hope they were not wasted! [5]Does God give you the Spirit because you follow the law? Does God work miracles* among you because you follow the law? No, God gives you his Spirit and works miracles among you because you heard the message about Jesus and believed it.

[6]The Scriptures* say the same thing about Abraham.* "Abraham believed God, and because of this faith he was accepted as one who is right with God."[d] [7]So you should know that the true children of Abraham are those who have faith. [8]The Scriptures

---

[a] **2:16 trusting in** Or "the faithfulness of."
[b] **2:16 because we trusted in** Or "through the faithfulness of."

[c] **2:20 faith in** Or "the faithfulness of."
[d] **3:6** Quote from Gen. 15:6.

told what would happen in the future. These writings said that God would make the non-Jewish people right through their faith. God told this Good News* to Abraham before it happened. God said to Abraham, "I will use you to bless all the people on earth."[a] [9]Abraham believed this, and because he believed, he was blessed. All people who believe are blessed the same as Abraham was.

[10]But people who depend on following the law to make them right are under a curse. As the Scriptures say, "They must do everything that is written in the law. If they do not always obey, they are under a curse."[b] [11]So it is clear that no one can be made right with God by the law. The Scriptures say, "The one who is right with God by faith will live forever."[c]

[12]The law does not depend on faith. No, it says that the only way a person will find life by the law is to obey its commands.[d] [13]The law says we are under a curse for not always obeying it. But Christ took away that curse. He changed places with us and put himself under that curse. The Scriptures say, "Anyone who is hung on a tree[e] is under a curse."[f] [14]Because of what Jesus Christ did, the blessing God promised to Abraham was given to all people. Christ

died so that by believing in him we could have the Spirit that God promised.

The Law and the Promise

[15]Brothers and sisters, let me give you an example from everyday life: Think about an agreement that one person makes with another. After that agreement is made official, no one can stop it or add anything to it, and no one can ignore it. [16]God made promises to Abraham* and his Descendant.[g] The Scripture* does not say, "and to your descendants." That would mean many people. But it says, "and to your Descendant." That means only one, and that one is Christ. [17]This is what I mean: The agreement that God gave to Abraham was made official long before the law* came. The law came 430 years later. So the law could not take away the agreement and change God's promise.

[18]Can following the law give us the blessing God promised? If we could receive it by following the law, then it would not be God's promise that brings it to us. But God freely gave his blessings to Abraham through the promise God made.

[19]So what was the law for? The law was given to show the wrong things people do. The law would continue until the special Descendant of Abraham came. This is the Descendant mentioned in the promise, which came directly from God. But the law was given through angels, and the angels used Moses as a mediator* to give the law to the people. [20]But when

---

a **3:8** Quote from Gen. 12:3.

b **3:10** Quote from Deut. 27:26.

c **3:11** Quote from Hab. 2:4.

d **3:12 the only way ... commands** See Lev. 18:5.

e **3:13 hung on a tree** Deut. 21:22–23 says that when a person was killed for doing wrong, his body was hung on a tree to show shame. Paul means the cross of Jesus was like that.

f **3:13** Quote from Deut. 21:23.

g **3:16 Descendant** Literally, "seed," which could also mean "family." In that case, it would refer to the one family of God in Christ.

God gave the promise, there was no mediator, because a mediator is not needed when there is only one side, and God is one.*ᵃ*

The Purpose of the Law of Moses

²¹Does this mean that the law* works against God's promises? Of course not. The law was never God's way of giving new life to people. If it were, then we could be made right with God by following the law. ²²But this is not possible. The Scriptures* put the whole world in prison under the control of sin, so that the only way for people to get what God promised would be through faith in*ᵇ* Jesus Christ. It is given to those who believe in him.

²³Before this faith came, the law held us as prisoners. We had no freedom until God showed us the way of faith that was coming. ²⁴I mean the law was the guardian in charge of us until Christ came. After he came, we could be made right with God through faith. ²⁵Now that the way of faith has come, we no longer need the law to be our guardian.

²⁶⁻²⁷You were all baptized* into Christ, and so you were all clothed with Christ. This shows that you are all children of God through faith in Christ Jesus. ²⁸Now, in Christ, it doesn't matter if you are a Jew or a Greek,* a slave or free, male or female. You are all the same in Christ Jesus. ²⁹You belong to Christ, so you are Abraham's* descendants. You get all of God's blessings because of the promise that God made to Abraham.

4 ¹This is what I am saying: When young children inherit all that their father owned, they are still no different from his slaves. It doesn't matter that they own everything. ²While they are children, they must obey those who are chosen to care for them. But when they reach the age the father set, they are free. ³It is the same for us. We were once like children, slaves to the useless rules*ᶜ* of this world. ⁴But when the right time came, God sent his Son, who was born from a woman and lived under the law. ⁵God did this so that he could buy the freedom of those who were under the law. God's purpose was to make us his children.

⁶Since you are now God's children, he has sent the Spirit of his Son into your hearts. The Spirit* cries out, "*Abba,ᵈ* Father." ⁷Now you are not slaves like before. You are God's children, and you will receive everything he promised his children.

Paul's Love for the Galatian Believers

⁸In the past you did not know God. You were slaves to gods that were not real. ⁹But now you know the true God. Really, though, it is God who knows you. So why do you turn back to the same kind of weak and useless rules you followed before? Do you want to be slaves to those things again? ¹⁰⁻¹¹It worries me that you follow teachings about special days, months, seasons, and years. I fear that my work for you has been wasted.

¹²Brothers and sisters, I became like you. So please become like me. You were very good to me before. ¹³You know that I came

---

ᵃ **3:20** Literally, "But the mediator is not of one, but God is one."
ᵇ **3:22 faith in** Or "the faithfulness of."
ᶜ **4:3 rules** Or "powers." Also in verse 9.
ᵈ **4:6 Abba** An Aramaic word that was used by Jewish children as a name for their fathers.

to you the first time because I was sick. That was when I told the Good News* to you. [14]My sickness was a burden to you, but you did not stop showing me respect or make me leave. Instead, you welcomed me as if I were an angel from God. You accepted me as if I were Jesus Christ himself! [15]You were very happy then. Where is that joy now? I can say without a doubt that you would have done anything to help me. If it had been possible, you would have taken out your own eyes and given them to me. [16]Am I now your enemy because I tell you the truth?

[17]Those people[a] are working hard to persuade you, but this is not good for you. They want to persuade you to turn against us and work hard for them. [18]It is good for you to work hard, of course, if it is for something good. That's something you should do whether I am there or not. [19]My little children, I am in pain again over you, like a mother giving birth. I will feel this pain until people can look at you and see Christ. [20]I wish I could be with you now. Then maybe I could change the way I am talking to you. Now I don't know what to do about you.

The Example of Hagar and Sarah

[21]Some of you people want to be under the law.* Tell me, do you know what the law says? [22]The Scriptures* say that Abraham* had two sons. The mother of one son was a slave woman, and the mother of the other son was a free woman. [23]Abraham's son from the slave woman was born in the normal human way. But the son from the free woman was born because of the promise God made to Abraham.

[24]This true story makes a picture for us. The two women are like the two agreements between God and his people. One agreement is the law that God made on Mount Sinai.* The people who are under this agreement are like slaves. The mother named Hagar is like that agreement. [25]So Hagar is like Mount Sinai in Arabia. She is a picture of the earthly Jewish city of Jerusalem. This city is a slave, and all its people are slaves to the law. [26]But the heavenly Jerusalem that is above is like the free woman, who is our mother. [27]The Scriptures say,

"Be happy, woman—you who
    cannot have children.
Be glad you never gave birth.
Shout and cry with joy!
    You never felt those labor
    pains.
The woman who is alone[b] will
    have more children
than the woman who has a
    husband."   *Isaiah 54:1*

[28]My brothers and sisters, you are children who were born because of God's promise, just as Isaac was. [29]But the other son of Abraham, who was born in the normal way, caused trouble for the one who was born by the power of the Spirit.* It is the same today. [30]But what do the Scriptures say? "Throw out the slave woman and her son! The son of the free woman will receive everything his father has, but the

---

a **4:17 Those people** The false teachers who were bothering the believers in Galatia. See Gal. 1:7.

b **4:27 woman ... alone** This means her husband has left her.

son of the slave woman will receive nothing."[a] [31]So, my brothers and sisters, we are not children of the slave woman. We are children of the free woman.

Keep Your Freedom

5 [1]We have freedom now, because Christ made us free. So stand strong in that freedom. Don't go back into slavery again. [2]Listen! I, Paul, tell you that if you start following the law by being circumcised,* then Christ cannot help you. [3]Again, I warn everyone: If you allow yourselves to be circumcised, then you must follow the whole law.* [4]If you try to be made right with God through the law, your life with Christ is finished—you have left God's grace.* [5]I say this because our hope of being right with God comes through faith. And the Spirit* helps us feel sure as we wait for that hope. [6]When someone belongs to Christ Jesus, it is not important if they are circumcised or not. The important thing is faith—the kind of faith that works through love.

[7]You were doing so well. Who caused you to stop following the truth? [8]It certainly wasn't the one who chose you. [9]Be careful! "Just a little yeast* makes the whole batch of dough rise."[b] [10]I trust in the Lord that you will not believe those different ideas. Someone is trying to confuse you. Whoever it is will be punished.

[11]My brothers and sisters, I don't teach that a man must be circumcised. If I do teach circumcision, then why am I still being persecuted*? If I still taught circumcision, then my message about the cross would not be a problem. [12]I wish those people who are bothering you would add castration[c] to their circumcision.

[13]My brothers and sisters, God chose you to be free. But don't use your freedom as an excuse to do what pleases your sinful selves. Instead, serve each other with love. [14]The whole law is made complete in this one command: "Love your neighbor[d] the same as you love yourself."[e] [15]If you continue hurting each other and tearing each other apart, be careful, or you will completely destroy each other.

The Spirit and Human Nature

[16]So I tell you, live the way the Spirit* leads you. Then you will not do the evil things your sinful self wants. [17]The sinful self wants what is against the Spirit, and the Spirit wants what is against the sinful self. They are always fighting against each other, so that you don't do what you really want to do. [18]But if you let the Spirit lead you, you are not under law.[f]

[19]The wrong things the sinful self does are clear: committing sexual sin, being morally bad, doing all kinds of shameful things, [20]worshiping false gods,

---

[a] **4:30** Quote from Gen. 21:10.
[b] **5:9 "Just … rise"** A proverb meaning that a small thing (like a little wrong teaching) can make a big problem or that just one person can have a bad influence on the whole group.
[c] **5:12 castration** Paul uses a word that means "to cut off" in place of "circumcision," which means "to cut around," to show how angry he is at the false teachers for forcing non-Jewish men to be circumcised.
[d] **5:14 your neighbor** Or "others." Jesus' teaching in Lk. 10:25–37 makes clear that this includes anyone in need.
[e] **5:14** Quote from Lev. 19:18.
[f] **5:18 law** Here, a law system, like the Law of Moses.

taking part in witchcraft,* hating people, causing trouble, being jealous, angry or selfish, causing people to argue and divide into separate groups, 21being filled with envy, getting drunk, having wild parties, and doing other things like this. I warn you now as I warned you before: The people who do these things will not have a part in God's kingdom.* 22But the fruit that the Spirit produces in a person's life is love, joy, peace, patience, kindness, goodness, faithfulness, 23gentleness, and self-control. There is no law against these kinds of things. 24Those who belong to Christ Jesus have crucified their sinful self. They have given up their old selfish feelings and the evil things they wanted to do. 25We get our new life from the Spirit, so we should follow the Spirit. 26We must not feel proud and boast about ourselves. We must not cause trouble for each other or be jealous of each other.

Help Each Other

6 1Brothers and sisters, someone in your group might do something wrong. You who are following the Spirit* should go to the one who is sinning. Help make that person right again, and do it in a gentle way. But be careful, because you might be tempted to sin too. 2Help each other with your troubles. When you do this, you are obeying the law of Christ. 3If you think you are too important to do this, you are only fooling yourself. 4Don't compare yourself with others. Just look at your own work to see if you have done anything to be proud of. 5You must each accept the responsibilities that are yours.

Never Stop Doing Good

6Whoever is being taught God's word should share the good things they have with the one who is teaching them.

7If you think you can fool God, you are only fooling yourselves. You will harvest what you plant. 8If you live to satisfy your sinful self, the harvest you will get from that will be eternal death. But if you live to please the Spirit,* your harvest from the Spirit will be eternal life. 9We must not get tired of doing good. We will receive our harvest of eternal life at the right time. We must not give up. 10When we have the opportunity to do good to anyone, we should do it. But we should give special attention to those who are in the family of believers.

Paul Ends His Letter

11This is my own handwriting. You can see how big the letters are. 12Those men who are trying to force you to be circumcised* are only doing it so that their people will accept them. They are afraid they will be persecuted* if they follow only the cross*a* of Christ. 13They are circumcised, but they don't obey the law* themselves. They want you to be circumcised so that they can boast about what they did to you.

14I hope I will never boast about things like that. The cross of our Lord Jesus Christ is my only reason for boasting. Through Jesus' death on the cross the world is dead*b* to me, and I am dead to

---

a **6:12 cross** Paul uses the cross as a picture of the Good News, the story of Christ's death to pay for people's sins. The cross (Christ's death) was God's way to save people. Also in verse 14.

b **6:14 is dead** Literally, "has been crucified."

the world. ¹⁵It doesn't matter if anyone is circumcised or not. The only thing that matters is this new life we have from God.ᵃ ¹⁶Peace and mercy to those who follow this rule—to all God's people.ᵇ

¹⁷So don't give me any more trouble. I have scars on my body that showᶜ I belong to Jesus.

¹⁸My brothers and sisters, I pray that the grace* of our Lord Jesus Christ will be with your spirits. Amen.*

ᵃ **6:15 this new life ... God** Or "being the new people God has made."
ᵇ **6:16 all of God's people** Literally, "the Israel of God."

ᶜ **6:17 scars ... show** Many times Paul was beaten by people who tried to stop him from teaching about Christ. The scars were from these beatings.

Ephesians

1 ¹Greetings from Paul, an apostle* of Christ Jesus. I am an apostle because that is what God wanted.

To God's holy people* living in Ephesus,ᵃ believers who belong to Christ Jesus.

²Grace* and peace to you from God our Father and the Lord Jesus Christ.

Spiritual Blessings in Christ

³Praise be to the God and Father of our Lord Jesus Christ. In Christ, God has given us every spiritual blessing in heaven. ⁴In Christ, he chose us before the world was made. He chose us in love to be his holy people*—people who could stand before him without any fault. ⁵And before the world was made, God decided to make us his own children through Jesus Christ. This was what God wanted, and it pleased him to do it. ⁶And this brings praise to God because of his wonderful grace.* God gave that grace to us freely. He gave us that grace in Christ, the one he loves.

⁷In Christ we are made free by his blood sacrifice. We have forgiveness of sins because of God's rich grace. ⁸God gave us that grace fully and freely. With full wisdom and understanding ⁹he let us know his secret plan. This was

what God wanted, and he planned to do it through Christ. ¹⁰God's goal was to finish his plan when the right time came. He planned that all things in heaven and on earth be joined together with Christ as the head.

¹¹In Christ we were chosen to be God's people. God had already planned for us to be his people, because that is what he wanted. And he is the one who makes everything agree with what he decides and wants. ¹²We Jews were the first to hope in Christ. And we were chosen so that we would bring praise to God in all his glory.* ¹³It is the same with you. You heard the true message, the Good News* about the way God saves you. When you heard that Good News, you believed in Christ. And in Christ, God put his special mark on you by giving you the Holy Spirit* that he promised. ¹⁴The Spirit is the first payment that guarantees we will get all that God has for us. Then we will enjoy complete freedom as people who belong to him. The goal for all of us is the praise of God in all his glory.

Paul's Prayer

¹⁵⁻¹⁶That is why I always remember you in my prayers and thank God for you. I have done this ever since I heard about your faith in the Lord Jesus and your love for all of God's people. ¹⁷I always pray

---

ᵃ **1:1 in Ephesus** Some Greek copies do not have the words "in Ephesus."

to the great and glorious Father, the God of our Lord Jesus Christ. I pray that he will give you the Spirit,* who will let you know truths about God and help you understand them, so that you will know him better.

[18]I pray that God will open your minds to see his truth. Then you will know the hope that he has chosen us to have. You will know that the blessings God has promised his holy people* are rich and glorious. [19]And you will know that God's power is very great for us who believe. It is the same as the mighty power [20]he used to raise Christ from death and put him at his right side in the heavenly places. [21]He put Christ over all rulers, authorities, powers, and kings. He gave him authority over everything that has power in this world or in the next world. [22]God put everything under Christ's power and made him head over everything for the church.* [23]The church is Christ's body. It is filled with him. He makes everything complete in every way.

From Death to Life

2 [1]In the past you were spiritually dead because of your sins and the things you did against God. [2]Yes, in the past your lives were full of those sins. You lived the way the world lives, following the ruler of the evil powers* over the earth. That same spirit is now working in those who refuse to obey God. [3]In the past all of us lived like that, trying to please our sinful selves. We did all the things our bodies and minds wanted. Like everyone else in the world, we deserved to suffer God's anger just because of the way we were.

[4]But God is rich in mercy, and he loved us very much. [5]We were spiritually dead because of all we had done against him. But he gave us new life together with Christ. (You have been saved by God's grace.*) [6]Yes, it is because we are a part of Christ Jesus that God raised us from death and seated us together with him in the heavenly places. [7]God did this so that his kindness to us who belong to Christ Jesus would clearly show for all time to come the amazing richness of his grace.

[8]I mean that you have been saved by grace because you believed. You did not save yourselves; it was a gift from God. [9]You are not saved by the things you have done, so there is nothing to boast about. [10]God has made us what we are. In Christ Jesus, God made us new people so that we would spend our lives doing the good things he had already planned for us to do.

One in Christ

[11]You were not born as Jews. You are the people the Jews call "uncircumcised.[a]" Those Jews who call you "uncircumcised" call themselves "circumcised." (Their circumcision* is only something they themselves do to their bodies.) [12]Remember that in the past you were without Christ. You were not citizens of Israel,* and you did not know about the agreements[b] with the promises that God made to his people. You

---

[a] **2:11 uncircumcised** People not having the mark of circumcision like the Jews have.
[b] **2:12 agreements** The agreements with special promises that God gave at various times to people in the Old Testament. See "AGREEMENT" in the Word List.

had no hope, and you did not know God. ¹³Yes, at one time you were far away from God, but now in Christ Jesus, you are brought near to him. You are brought near to God through the blood sacrifice of Christ.

¹⁴Christ is the reason we are now at peace. He made us Jews and you who are not Jews one people. We were separated by a wall of hate that stood between us, but Christ broke down that wall. By giving his own body, ¹⁵Christ ended the law with its many commands and rules. His purpose was to make the two groups become one in him. By doing this he would make peace. ¹⁶Through the cross Christ ended the hate between the two groups. And after they became one body, he wanted to bring them both back to God. He did this with his death on the cross. ¹⁷Christ came and brought the message of peace to you non-Jews who were far away from God. And he brought that message of peace to those who were near to God. ¹⁸Yes, through Christ we all have the right to come to the Father in one Spirit.*

¹⁹So now you non-Jewish people are not visitors or strangers, but you are citizens together with God's holy people.* You belong to God's family. ²⁰You believers are like a building that God owns. That building was built on the foundation that the apostles* and prophets* prepared. Christ Jesus himself is the most important stone*a* in that building. ²¹The whole building is joined together in Christ, and he makes it

grow and become a holy temple*b* in the Lord. ²²And in Christ you are being built together with his other people. You are being made into a place where God lives through the Spirit.

Paul's Work for the Non-Jewish People

3 ¹So I, Paul, am a prisoner because I serve Christ Jesus for you who are not Jews. ²Surely you know that God gave me this work through his grace* to help you. ³God let me know his secret plan by showing it to me. I have already written a little about this. ⁴And if you read what I wrote, you can see that I understand the secret truth about Christ. ⁵People who lived in other times were not told that secret truth. But now, through the Spirit,* God has made it known to his holy apostles* and prophets.* ⁶And this is the secret truth: that by hearing the Good News,* those who are not Jews will share with the Jews in the blessings God has for his people. They are part of the same body, and they share in the promise God made through Christ Jesus.

⁷By God's special gift of grace, I became a servant to tell that Good News. He gave me that grace by using his power. ⁸I am the least important of all God's people. But he gave me this gift—to tell the non-Jewish people the Good News about the riches Christ has. These riches are too great to understand fully. ⁹And God gave me the work of telling all people about the plan for his secret truth. That secret truth has been hidden in him since the beginning of time. He

a 2:20 most important stone Literally, "cornerstone." The first and most important stone in a building.

b 2:21 temple God's house—the place where God's people worship him. Here, it means that believers are the spiritual temple where God lives.

is the one who created everything. [10]His purpose was that all the rulers and powers in the heavenly places will now know the many different ways he shows his wisdom. They will know this because of the church.* [11]This agrees with the plan God had since the beginning of time. He did what he planned, and he did it through Christ Jesus our Lord. [12]In Christ we come before God with freedom and without fear. We can do this because of our faith in Christ. [13]So I ask you not to be discouraged because of what is happening to me. My sufferings are for your benefit—for your honor and glory.*

The Love of Christ

[14]So I bow in prayer before the Father. [15]Every family in heaven and on earth gets its true name from him. [16]I ask the Father with his great glory* to give you the power to be strong in your spirits. He will give you that strength through his Spirit.* [17]I pray that Christ will live in your hearts because of your faith. I pray that your life will be strong in love and be built on love. [18]And I pray that you and all God's holy people* will have the power to understand the greatness of Christ's love—how wide, how long, how high, and how deep that love is. [19]Christ's love is greater than anyone can ever know, but I pray that you will be able to know that love. Then you can be filled with everything God has for you.

[20]With God's power working in us, he can do much, much more than anything we can ask or think of. [21]To him be glory in the church* and in Christ Jesus for all time, forever and ever. Amen.*

The Unity of the Body

4 [1]So, as a prisoner for the Lord, I beg you to live the way God's people should live, because he chose you to be his. [2]Always be humble and gentle. Be patient and accept each other with love. [3]You are joined together with peace through the Spirit.* Do all you can to continue as you are, letting peace hold you together. [4]There is one body and one Spirit, and God chose you to have one hope. [5]There is one Lord, one faith, and one baptism.* [6]There is one God and Father of us all, who rules over everyone. He works through all of us and in all of us.

[7]Christ gave each one of us a special gift. Everyone received what he wanted to give them. [8]That is why the Scriptures* say,

"He went up high into the sky;
　he took prisoners with him,
　and he gave gifts to people."
Psalm 68:18

[9]When it says, "He went up," what does it mean? It means that he first came down low to earth. [10]So Christ came down, and he is the same one who went up. He went up above the highest heaven in order to fill everything with himself. [11]And that same Christ gave these gifts to people: He made some to be apostles,* some to be prophets,* some to go and tell the Good News,* and some to care for and teach God's people.[a] [12]Christ gave these gifts to prepare God's holy people* for the work of serving, to make the body of Christ stronger. [13]This work must continue until we are all joined together in what we believe and

---

[a] **4:11 to care for . . . people** Literally, "to be shepherds and teachers."

in what we know about the Son of God. Our goal is to become like a full-grown man—to look just like Christ and have all his perfection. 14Then we will no longer be like babies. We will not be people who are always changing like a ship that the waves carry one way and then another. We will not be influenced by every new teaching we hear from people who are trying to deceive us—those who make clever plans and use every kind of trick to fool others into following the wrong way. 15No, we will speak the truth with love. We will grow to be like Christ in every way. He is the head, 16and the whole body depends on him. All the parts of the body are joined and held together, with each part doing its own work. This causes the whole body to grow and to be stronger in love.

The Way You Should Live

17I have something from the Lord to tell you. I warn you: Don't continue living like those who don't believe. Their thoughts are worth nothing. 18They have no understanding, and they know nothing because they refuse to listen. So they cannot have the life that God gives. 19They have lost their feeling of shame and use their lives to do what is morally wrong. More and more they want to do all kinds of evil. 20But that way of life is nothing like what you learned when you came to know Christ. 21I know that you heard about him, and in him you were taught the truth. Yes, the truth is in Jesus. 22You were taught to leave your old self. This means that you must stop living the evil way you lived before. That old self gets worse and worse, because people are

fooled by the evil they want to do. 23You must be made new in your hearts and in your thinking. 24Be that new person who was made to be like God, truly good and pleasing to him.

25So you must stop telling lies. "You must always speak the truth to each other,"*a* because we all belong to each other in the same body. 26"When you are angry, don't let that anger make you sin,"*b* and don't stay angry all day. 27Don't give the devil a way to defeat you. 28Whoever has been stealing must stop it and start working. They must use their hands for doing something good. Then they will have something to share with those who are poor.

29When you talk, don't say anything bad. But say the good things that people need—whatever will help them grow stronger. Then what you say will be a blessing to those who hear you. 30And don't make the Holy Spirit* sad. God gave you his Spirit as proof that you belong to him and that he will keep you safe until the day he makes you free. 31Never be bitter, angry, or mad. Never shout angrily or say things to hurt others. Never do anything evil. 32Be kind and loving to each other. Forgive each other the same as God forgave you through Christ.

5 1You are God's dear children, so try to be like him. 2Live a life of love. Love others just as Christ loved us. He gave himself for us—a sweet-smelling offering and sacrifice* to God.

3But there must be no sexual sin among you. There must not be

a **4:25** Quote from Zech. 8:16.
b **4:26** Quote from Ps. 4:4 (Greek version).

Jesus dies
John 19:16-37

©WBTC

Jesus rises from death
John 20:1-9

any kind of evil or selfishly wanting more and more, because such things are not right for God's holy people.* ⁴Also, there must be no evil talk among you. Don't say things that are foolish or filthy. These are not for you. But you should be giving thanks to God. ⁵You can be sure of this: No one will have a place in the kingdom of Christ and of God if that person commits sexual sins, or does evil things, or is a person who selfishly wants more and more. A greedy person like that is serving a false god.

⁶Don't let anyone fool you with words that are not true. God gets very angry when people who don't obey him talk like that. ⁷So don't have anything to do with them. ⁸In the past you were full of darkness,* but now you are full of light* in the Lord. So live like children who belong to the light. ⁹This light produces every kind of goodness, right living, and truth. ¹⁰Try to learn what pleases the Lord. ¹¹Have no part in the things that people in darkness do, which produce nothing good. Instead, tell everyone how wrong those things are. ¹²Actually, it is shameful to even talk about the things those people do in secret. ¹³But the light makes clear how wrong those things are. ¹⁴Yes, everything is made clear by the light. This is why we say,

"Wake up, you who are
    sleeping!
  Rise from death,
and Christ will shine on you."

¹⁵So be very careful how you live. Live wisely, not like fools. ¹⁶I mean that you should use every opportunity you have for doing good, because these are evil times. ¹⁷So don't be foolish with your lives, but learn what the Lord wants you to do. ¹⁸Don't be drunk with wine, which will ruin your life, but be filled with the Spirit.* ¹⁹Encourage each other with psalms, hymns, and spiritual songs. Sing and make music in your hearts to the Lord. ²⁰Always give thanks to God the Father for everything in the name of our Lord Jesus Christ.

Wives and Husbands

²¹Be willing to serve each other out of respect for Christ.

²²Wives, be willing to serve your husbands the same as the Lord. ²³A husband is the head of his wife, just as Christ is the head of the church.* Christ is the Savior of the church, which is his body. ²⁴The church serves under Christ, so it is the same with you wives. You should be willing to serve your husbands in everything.

²⁵Husbands, love your wives the same as Christ loved the church and gave his life for it. ²⁶He died to make the church holy.* He used the telling of the Good News* to make the church clean by washing it with water. ²⁷Christ died so that he could give the church to himself like a bride in all her beauty. He died so that the church could be holy and without fault, with no evil or sin or any other thing wrong in it.

²⁸And husbands should love their wives like that. They should love their wives as they love their own bodies. The man who loves his wife loves himself, ²⁹because no one ever hates his own body, but feeds and takes care of it. And that is what Christ does for the church ³⁰because we are parts of his body. ³¹The Scriptures* say, "That is why a man will leave his

father and mother and join his wife, and the two people will become one."*a* 32That secret truth is very important—I am talking about Christ and the church. 33But each one of you must love his wife as he loves himself. And a wife must respect her husband.

Children and Parents

6 1Children, obey your parents the way the Lord wants, because this is the right thing to do. 2The command says, "You must respect your father and mother."*b* This is the first command that has a promise with it. 3And this is the promise: "Then all will go well with you, and you will have a long life on the earth."*c*

4Fathers, don't make your children angry, but raise them with the kind of teaching and training you learn from the Lord.

Slaves and Masters

5Slaves, obey your masters here on earth with fear and respect. And do this with a heart that is true, just as you obey Christ. 6You must do this not just to please your masters while they are watching, but all the time. Since you are really slaves of Christ, you must do with all your heart what God wants. 7Do your work, and be happy to do it. Work as though it is the Lord you are serving, not just an earthly master. 8Remember that the Lord will give everyone a reward for doing good. Everyone, slave or free, will get a reward for the good things they do.

9Masters, in the same way, be good to your slaves. Don't say things to scare them. You know that the one who is your Master and their Master is in heaven, and he treats everyone the same.

Wear the Full Armor of God

10To end my letter I tell you, be strong in the Lord and in his great power. 11Wear the full armor of God. Wear God's armor so that you can fight against the devil's clever tricks. 12Our fight is not against people on earth. We are fighting against the rulers and authorities and the powers of this world's darkness. We are fighting against the spiritual powers of evil in the heavenly places. 13That is why you need to get God's full armor. Then on the day of evil, you will be able to stand strong. And when you have finished the whole fight, you will still be standing.

14So stand strong with the belt of truth tied around your waist, and on your chest wear the protection of right living. 15On your feet wear the Good News* of peace to help you stand strong. 16And also use the shield of faith with which you can stop all the burning arrows that come from the Evil One.* 17Accept God's salvation as your helmet. And take the sword of the Spirit*—that sword is the teaching of God. 18Pray in the Spirit at all times. Pray with all kinds of prayers, and ask for everything you need. To do this you must always be ready. Never give up. Always pray for all of God's people.

19Also pray for me—that when I speak, God will give me words so that I can tell the secret truth about the Good News without fear. 20I have the work of speaking for that Good News, and that is what I am doing now, here in prison.

a 5:31 Quote from Gen. 2:24.
b 6:2 Quote from Ex. 20:12; Deut. 5:16.
c 6:3 Quote from Ex. 20:12; Deut. 5:16.

Pray that when I tell people the Good News, I will speak without fear as I should.

Final Greetings

21I am sending you Tychicus, the brother we love. He is a faithful servant of the Lord's work. He will tell you everything that is happening with me. Then you will know how I am and what I am doing. 22That's why I am sending him—to let you know how we are and to encourage you.

23I pray that God the Father and the Lord Jesus Christ will give peace and love with faith to all the brothers and sisters there. 24God's grace* to all of you who love our Lord Jesus Christ with love that never ends.

Philippians

1 ¹Greetings from Paul and Timothy, servants of Jesus Christ.

To all of you in Philippi who are God's holy people* in Christ Jesus, including your elders*a* and special servants.*

²Grace* and peace to you from God our Father and the Lord Jesus Christ.

Paul's Prayer

³I thank God every time I remember you. ⁴And I always pray for all of you with joy. ⁵I thank God for the help you gave me while I told people the Good News.* You helped from the first day you believed until now. ⁶I am sure that the good work God began in you will continue until he completes it on the day when Jesus Christ comes again.

⁷I know I am right to think like this about all of you because you are so close to my heart. This is because you have all played such an important part in God's grace* to me—now, during this time that I am in prison, and whenever I am defending and proving the truth of the Good News. ⁸God knows that I want very much to see you. I love all of you with the love of Christ Jesus.

⁹This is my prayer for you:
that your love will grow
more and more; that you
will have knowledge and understanding with your love; ¹⁰that you will see the difference between what is important and what is not and choose what is important; that you will be pure and blameless for the coming of Christ; ¹¹that your life will be full of the many good works that are produced by Jesus Christ to bring glory* and praise to God.

Paul's Troubles Help the Lord's Work

¹²Brothers and sisters, I want you to know that all that has happened to me has helped to spread the Good News.* ¹³All the Roman guards and all the others here know that I am in prison for serving Christ. ¹⁴My being in prison has caused most of the believers* to put their trust in the Lord and to show more courage in telling people God's message.*

¹⁵Some people are telling the message about Christ because they are jealous and bitter. Others do it because they want to help. ¹⁶They are doing it out of love. They know that God gave me the work of defending the Good News. ¹⁷But those others tell about Christ because of their selfish ambition. Their reason for doing it is wrong. They only do it because they think it will make trouble for me in prison ¹⁸But that doesn't matter. What

a **1:1 elders** Here, literally, "overseers." See "ELDERS (NEW TESTAMENT)" in the Word List.

is important is that they are telling people about Christ, whether they are sincere or not. So I am glad they are doing it.

I will continue to be glad, [19]because I know that your prayers and the help the Spirit* of Jesus Christ gives me will cause this trouble to result in my freedom.[a] [20]I am full of hope and feel sure I will not have any reason to be ashamed. I am certain I will continue to have the same boldness to speak freely that I always have. I will let God use my life to bring more honor to Christ. It doesn't matter whether I live or die. [21]To me, the only important thing about living is Christ. And even death would be for my benefit.[b] [22]If I continue living here on earth, I will be able to work for the Lord. But what would I choose—to live or to die? I don't know. [23]It would be a hard choice. Sometimes I want to leave this life and be with Christ. That would be much better for me; [24]however, you people need me here alive. [25]I am sure of this, so I know that I will stay here and be with you to help you grow and have joy in your faith. [26]When I am there with you again, you will be bursting with pride over what Christ Jesus did to help me.

[27]Just be sure you live as God's people in a way that honors the Good News of Christ. Then if I come and visit you or if I am away from you, I will hear good things about you. I will know that you stand together with the same purpose and that you work together like a team to help others

believe the Good News. [28]And you will not be afraid of those who are against you. All of this is proof from God that you are being saved and that your enemies will be lost. [29]God has blessed you in ways that serve Christ. He allowed you to believe in Christ. But that is not all. He has also given you the honor of suffering for Christ. Both of these bring glory* to Christ. [30]You saw the difficulties I had to face, and you hear that I am still having troubles. Now you must face them too.

Be United and Care for Each Other

2 [1]Think about what we have in Christ: the encouragement he has brought us, the comfort of his love, our sharing in his Spirit,* and the mercy and kindness he has shown us. If you enjoy these blessings, [2]then do what will make my joy complete: Agree with each other, and show your love for each other. Be united in your goals and in the way you think. [3]In whatever you do, don't let selfishness or pride be your guide. Be humble, and honor others more than yourselves. [4]Don't be interested only in your own life, but care about the lives of others too.

Learn From Christ to Be Unselfish

[5]In your life together, think the way Christ Jesus thought.

[6] He was like God in every way,
   but he did not think that his
   being equal with God was
   something to use for his
   own benefit.
[7] Instead, he gave up everything,
   even his place with God.
   He accepted the role of a
   servant, appearing in
   human form.
During his life as a man,

---

[a] **1:19 freedom** Or "salvation."
[b] **1:21 death … benefit** Paul says that death would be better, because death would bring him nearer to Christ.

8 he humbled himself by being
    fully obedient to God,
    even when that caused his
    death—death on a cross.
9 So God raised him up to the
    most important place
    and gave him the name that
    is greater than any other
    name.
10 God did this so that every
    person will bow down to
    honor the name of Jesus.
    Everyone in heaven, on
    earth, and under the earth
    will bow.
11 They will all confess, "Jesus
    Christ is Lord,"
    and this will bring glory* to
    God the Father.

Be the People God Wants You to Be

12My dear friends, you always obeyed what you were taught. Just as you obeyed when I was with you, it is even more important for you to obey now that I am not there. So you must continue to live in a way that gives meaning to your salvation. Do this with fear and respect for God. 13Yes, it is God who is working in you. He helps you want to do what pleases him, and he gives you the power to do it.

14Do everything without complaining or arguing 15so that you will be blameless and pure, children of God without any fault. But you are living with evil people all around you, who have lost their sense of what is right. Among those people you shine like lights in a dark world, 16and you offer them the teaching that gives life. So I can be proud of you when Christ comes again. You will show that my work was not wasted—that I ran in the race and won.

17Your faith makes you give your lives as a sacrifice* in serving God. Maybe I will have to offer my own life with your sacrifice. But if that happens, I will be glad, and I will share my joy with all of you. 18You also should be glad and share your joy with me.

News About Timothy and Epaphroditus

19With the blessing of the Lord Jesus, I hope I will be able to send Timothy to you soon. I will be glad to learn how you are. 20I have no one else like Timothy, who genuinely cares for you. 21Others are interested only in their own lives. They don't care about the work of Christ Jesus. 22You know the kind of person Timothy is. He has served with me in telling the Good News* like a son with his father. 23I plan to send him to you quickly, as soon as I know what will happen to me. 24I am sure the Lord will help me come to you soon.

25For now, I think I must send Epaphroditus back to you. He is my brother in God's family, who works and serves with me in the Lord's army. When I needed help, you sent him to me, 26but now he wants very much to see all of you again. He is worried because you heard that he was sick. 27He was sick and near death. But God helped him and me too, so that I would not have even more grief. 28So I want very much to send him to you. When you see him, you can be happy. And I can stop worrying about you. 29Welcome him in the Lord with much joy. Give honor to people like Epaphroditus. 30He should be honored because he almost died for the work of Christ. He put his life in danger so that he could help me

This was help that you could not give me.

Christ Is More Important Than Anything

3 ¹And now, my brothers and sisters, be filled with joy in the Lord. It is no trouble for me to write the same things to you again. I want to be sure that you are prepared.

²Be careful of the dogs—those men whose work does only harm. They want to cut on everyone who isn't circumcised.ᵃ ³But we are the ones who have the true circumcisionᵇ—we who worship God through his Spirit.* We don't trust in ourselves or anything we can do. We take pride only in Christ Jesus. ⁴Even if I am able to trust in myself, still I don't do it. If anyone else thinks they have a reason to trust in themselves, they should know that I have a greater reason for doing so. ⁵I was circumcised on the eighth day after my birth. I am from the people of Israel* and the tribe of Benjamin. I am a true Jew, and so were my parents. The law* was very important to me. That is why I became a Pharisee.* ⁶I was so eager to defend my religionᶜ that I persecuted* the church.* And no one could find fault with the way I obeyed the Law of Moses.

⁷At one time all these things were important to me. But because of Christ, I decided that they are worth nothing. ⁸Not only these things, but now I think that all things are worth nothing compared with the greatness of knowing Christ Jesus my Lord. Because of Christ, I lost all these things, and now I know that they are all worthless trash. All I want now is Christ. ⁹I want to belong to him. In Christ I am right with God, but my being right does not come from following the law. It comes from God through faith. God uses my faith inᵈ Christ to make me right with him. ¹⁰All I want is to know Christ and the power that raised him from death. I want to share in his sufferings and be like him even in his death. ¹¹Then there is hope that I myself will somehow be raised from death.

Trying to Reach the Goal

¹²I don't mean that I am exactly what God wants me to be. I have not yet reached that goal. But I continue trying to reach it and make it mine. That's what Christ Jesus wants me to do. It is the reason he made me his. ¹³Brothers and sisters, I know that I still have a long way to go. But there is one thing I do: I forget what is in the past and try as hard as I can to reach the goal before me. ¹⁴I keep running hard toward the finish line to get the prize that is mine because God has called me through Christ Jesus to life up there in heaven.

¹⁵All of us who have grown to be spiritually mature should think this way too. And if there is any

---

ᵃ **3:2 want to cut on … circumcised** There is a play on words here in Greek. The key word is like "circumcision" (see "CIRCUMCISE, CIRCUMCISION" in the Word List), but it means "mutilation" or "cutting to pieces."
ᵇ **3:3 we are … circumcision** Literally, "we are the circumcision." See "CIRCUMCISE, CIRCUMCISION" in the Word List.
ᶜ **3:6 eager to defend my religion** Before Paul became a believer in Jesus as the Messiah, he thought it was his duty as a good Jew to oppose the Jews who had become Christ-followers.

ᵈ **3:9 my faith in** Or "the faithfulness of."

of this that you don't agree with, God will make it clear to you. ¹⁶But we should continue following the truth we already have.

¹⁷Brothers and sisters, join together in following my example. Also, learn by watching those who are living the way we showed you. ¹⁸There are many who live like enemies of the cross of Christ. I have often told you about them. And it makes me cry to tell you about them now. ¹⁹The way they live is leading them to destruction. They have replaced God with their own desires. They do shameful things, and they are proud of what they do. They think only about earthly things. ²⁰But the government that rules us is in heaven. We are waiting for our Savior, the Lord Jesus Christ, to come from there. ²¹He will change our humble bodies and make them like his own glorious body. Christ can do this by his power, with which he is able to rule everything.

Some Things to Do

4 ¹My dear brothers and sisters, I love you and want to see you. You bring me joy and make me proud of you. Continue following the Lord as I have told you.

²Euodia and Syntyche, you both belong to the Lord, so please agree with each other. ³For this I make a special request to my friend who has served with me so faithfully: Help these women. They worked hard with me in telling people the Good News,* together with Clement and others who worked with me. Their names are written in the book of life.ᵃ

⁴Always be filled with joy in the Lord. I will say it again. Be filled with joy.

⁵Let everyone see that you are gentle and kind. The Lord is coming soon. ⁶Don't worry about anything, but pray and ask God for everything you need, always giving thanks for what you have. ⁷And because you belong to Christ Jesus, God's peace will stand guard over all your thoughts and feelings. His peace can do this far better than our human minds.ᵇ

⁸Brothers and sisters, continue to think about what is good and worthy of praise. Think about what is true and honorable and right and pure and beautiful and respected. ⁹And do what you learned and received from me—what I told you and what you saw me do. And the God who gives peace will be with you.

Paul Thanks the Philippian Believers

¹⁰I am so happy, and I thank the Lord that you have again shown your care for me. You continued to care about me, but there was no way for you to show it. ¹¹I am telling you this, but not because I need something. I have learned to be satisfied with what I have and with whatever happens. ¹²I know how to live when I am poor and when I have plenty. I have learned the secret of how to live through any kind of situation—when I have enough to eat or when I am hungry, when I have everything I need or when I have nothing. ¹³Christ is the one who gives me the strength I need to do whatever I must do.

ᵃ **4:3 book of life** God's book that contains the names of his chosen people. See Rev. 3:5; 21:27.

ᵇ **4:7 can do ... minds** Literally, "surpasses (is better than) every mind," which could also have the meaning "is beyond all understanding."

14But it was good that you helped me when I needed help. 15You people in Philippi remember when I first told the Good News* there. When I left Macedonia,* you were the only church* that gave me help. 16Several times you sent me things I needed when I was in Thessalonica. 17Really, it is not that I want to get gifts from you. But I want you to have the benefit that comes from giving. 18I have everything I need. I have even more than I need. I have all I need because Epaphroditus brought your gift to me. Your gift is like a sweet-smelling sacrifice* offered to God.

God accepts that sacrifice and it pleases him. 19My God will use his glorious riches to give you everything you need. He will do this through Christ Jesus. 20Glory* to our God and Father forever and ever. Amen.*

21Give our greetings to God's people there—to each one who belongs to Christ Jesus. Those in God's family who are with me send you their greetings. 22And greetings to you from all of God's people here, especially those who work in the service of the emperor.*

23The grace* of the Lord Jesus Christ be with you all.

Colossians

1 ¹Greetings from Paul, an apostle* of Christ Jesus. I am an apostle because that is what God wanted. Greetings also from Timothy, our brother in Christ.

²To the holy* and faithful brothers and sisters in Christ who live in Colossae.

Grace* and peace to you from God our Father.

³In our prayers we always thank God for you. He is the Father of our Lord Jesus Christ. ⁴We thank him because we have heard about the faith you have in Christ Jesus and the love you have for all of God's people. ⁵Your faith and love continue because you know what is waiting for you in heaven— the hope you have had since you first heard the true message, the Good News* ⁶that was told to you. Throughout the world, this Good News is bringing blessings and is spreading. And that's what has been happening among you since the first time you heard it and understood the truth about God's grace. ⁷You heard it from Epaphras, our dear friend and co-worker. He is a faithful servant of Christ for us.ᵃ ⁸He also told us about the love you have from the Spirit.*

⁹Since the day we heard these things about you, we have continued praying for you. This is what we pray:

that God will make you completely sure of what he wants by giving you all the wisdom and spiritual understanding you need; ¹⁰that this will help you live in a way that brings honor to the Lord and pleases him in every way; that your life will produce good works of every kind and that you will grow in your knowledge of Godᵇ; ¹¹that God will strengthen you with his own great power, so that you will be patient and not give up when troubles come.

Then you will be happy ¹²and give thanks to the Father. He has made you able to have what he has promised to give all his holy people,* who live in the light.* ¹³God made us free from the power of darkness.* And he brought us into the kingdom of his dear Son. ¹⁴The Son paid the price to make us free. In him we have forgiveness of our sins.

The Son of God Is the Same as God
¹⁵ No one can see God,
   but the Son is exactly like God.

ᵃ **1:7 us** Many ancient Greek copies have "you."

ᵇ **1:10 that your life ... God** Or "that your knowledge of God will produce more and more good works of every kind in your life."

He rules over everything
that has been made.*a*
16 Through his power all things
were made:
things in heaven and on
earth, seen and not seen—
all spiritual rulers, lords,
powers, and authorities.
Everything was made through
him and for him.

17 The Son was there before
anything was made.
And all things continue
because of him.
18 He is the head of the body,
which is the church.*
He is the beginning of
everything else.
And he is the first among
all who will be raised from
death.*b*
So in everything he is most
important.

19 God was pleased for all of
himself to live in the Son.
20   And through him, God was
happy to bring all things
back to himself again—
things on earth and things
in heaven.
God made peace by using the
blood sacrifice of his Son on
the cross.
21At one time you were separated from God. You were his
enemies in your minds, because
the evil you did was against him.
22But now he has made you his
friends again. He did this by the
death Christ suffered while he
was in his body. He did it so that

he could present you to himself
as people who are holy,* blameless, and without anything that
would make you guilty before
him. 23And that is what will happen if you continue to believe in
the Good News* you heard. You
must remain strong and sure in
your faith. You must not let anything cause you to give up the
hope that became yours when
you heard the Good News. That
same Good News has been told to
everyone on earth, and that's the
work that I, Paul, was given to do.

Paul's Work for the Church

24I am happy in my sufferings for
you. There is much that Christ
must still suffer. And I gladly
accept my part of those sufferings in my body for the good of
his body, the church.* 25I became
a servant of the church because
God gave me a special work to do.
This work helps you. My work is
to tell the complete message of
God. 26This message is the secret
truth that was hidden since the
beginning of time. It was hidden from everyone for ages, but
now it has been made known
to God's holy people.* 27God decided to let his people know just
how rich and glorious that truth
is. That secret truth, which is for
all people, is that Christ lives in
you, his people. He is our hope
for glory.* 28So we continue to tell
people about Christ. We use all
wisdom to counsel every person
and teach every person. We are
trying to bring everyone before
God as people who have grown
to be spiritually mature in Christ.
29To do this, I work and struggle
using the great strength that
Christ gives me. That strength is
working in my life.

a 1:15 He ... made Literally, "He is the
firstborn of all creation." See "FIRSTBORN" in
the Word List.
b 1:18 first ... death Literally, "firstborn
from the dead."

2 [1]I want you to know that I am trying very hard to help you. And I am trying to help those in Laodicea and others who have never seen me. [2]I want them to be strengthened and joined together with love and to have the full confidence that comes from understanding. I want them to know completely the secret truth that God has made known. That truth is Christ himself. [3]In him all the treasures of wisdom and knowledge are kept safe.

[4]I tell you this so that no one can fool you by telling you ideas that seem good, but are false. [5]Even though I am far away, my thoughts are always with you. I am happy to see your good lives and your strong faith in Christ.

Continue to Follow Christ Jesus

[6]You accepted Christ Jesus as Lord, so continue to live following him. [7]You must depend on Christ only, drawing life and strength from him. Just as you were taught the truth, continue to grow stronger in your understanding of it. And never stop giving thanks to God.

[8]Be sure you are not led away by the teaching of those who have nothing worth saying and only plan to deceive you. That teaching is not from Christ. It is only human tradition and comes from the powers that influence[a] this world. [9]I say this because all of God lives in Christ fully, even in his life on earth. [10]And because you belong to Christ you are complete, having everything you need. Christ is ruler over every other power and authority.

[11]In Christ you had a different kind of circumcision,* one that was not done by human hands. That is, you were made free from the power of your sinful self. That is the kind of circumcision Christ does. [12]When you were baptized,* you were buried with Christ, and you were raised up with him because of your faith in God's power. God's power was shown when he raised Christ from death.

[13]You were spiritually dead because of your sins and because you were not free from the power of your sinful self. But God gave you new life together with Christ. He forgave all our sins. [14]Because we broke God's laws, we owed a debt—a debt that listed all the rules we failed to follow. But God forgave us of that debt. He took it away and nailed it to the cross. [15]He defeated the rulers and powers of the spiritual world. With the cross he won the victory over them and led them away, as defeated and powerless prisoners for the whole world to see.

Don't Follow Rules That People Make

[16]So don't let anyone make rules for you about eating and drinking or about Jewish customs (festivals, New Moon* celebrations, or Sabbath* days). [17]In the past these things were like a shadow that showed what was coming. But the new things that were coming are found in Christ. [18]Some people enjoy acting as if they are humble and love to worship angels.[b] They always talk about the visions* they have seen. Don't listen to them when they say you are wrong because you don't do these things. It is so foolish

---

[a] **2:8 powers that influence** Or "elementary rules of." Also in verse 20.

[b] **2:18 worship angels** Or "worship with angels" (that they see in visions).

for them to feel such pride, because it is all based on their own human ideas. 19They don't keep themselves under the control of the head. Christ is the head, and the whole body depends on him. Because of Christ all the parts of the body care for each other and help each other. So the body is made stronger and held together as God causes it to grow.

20You died with Christ and were made free from the powers that influence this world. So why do you act as if you still belong to the world? I mean, why do you follow rules like these: 21"Don't eat this," "Don't taste that," "Don't touch that"? 22These rules are talking about earthly things that are gone after they are used. They are only human commands and teachings. 23These rules may seem to be wise as part of a made-up religion in which people pretend to be humble and punish their bodies. But they don't help people stop doing the evil that the sinful self wants to do.

Your New Life

3 1You were raised from death with Christ. So live for what is in heaven, where Christ is sitting at the right hand of God. 2Think only about what is up there, not what is here on earth. 3Your old self has died, and your new life is kept with Christ in God. 4Yes, Christ is now your life, and when he comes again, you will share in his glory.*

5So put everything evil out of your life: sexual sin, doing anything immoral, letting sinful thoughts control you, and wanting things that are wrong. And don't keep wanting more and more for yourself, which is the same as worshiping a false god. 6God will show his anger against those who don't obey him,ᵃ because they do these evil things. 7You also did these things in the past, when you lived like them.

8But now put these things out of your life: anger, losing your temper, doing or saying things to hurt others, and saying shameful things. 9Don't lie to each other. You have taken off those old clothes—the person you once were and the bad things you did then. 10Now you are wearing a new life, a life that is new every day. You are growing in your understanding of the one who made you. You are becoming more and more like him. 11In this new life it doesn't matter if you are a Greek* or a Jew, circumcised* or not. It doesn't matter if you speak a different language or even if you are a Scythian.ᵇ It doesn't matter if you are a slave or free. Christ is all that matters, and he is in all of you.

Your New Life With Each Other

12God has chosen you and made you his holy people.* He loves you. So your new life should be like this: Show mercy to others. Be kind, humble, gentle, and patient. 13Don't be angry with each other, but forgive each other. If you feel someone has wronged you, forgive them. Forgive others because the Lord forgave you. 14Together with these things, the most important part of your new life is to love each other. Love is what holds everything together in perfect unity. 15Let the peace

ᵃ **3:6 against … him** Some Greek copies do not have these words.
ᵇ **3:11 Scythians** Known as wild and uncivilized people.

that Christ gives control your thinking. It is for peace that you were chosen to be together in one body.*a* And always be thankful.

16Let the teaching of Christ live inside you richly. Use all wisdom to teach and counsel each other. Sing psalms, hymns, and spiritual songs with thankfulness in your hearts to God. 17Everything you say and everything you do should be done for Jesus your Lord. And in all you do, give thanks to God the Father through Jesus.

Your New Life at Home
18Wives, be willing to serve your husbands. This is the right thing to do in following the Lord.

19Husbands, love your wives, and be gentle to them.

20Children, obey your parents in everything. This pleases the Lord.

21Fathers, don't upset your children. If you are too hard to please, they might want to stop trying.

22Servants, obey your masters in everything. Obey all the time, even when they can't see you. Don't just pretend to work hard so that they will treat you well. No, you must serve your masters honestly because you respect the Lord. 23In all the work you are given, do the best you can. Work as though you are working for the Lord, not any earthly master. 24Remember that you will receive your reward from the Lord, who will give you what he promised his people. Yes, you are serving Christ. He is your real Master.*b* 25Remember that

anyone who does wrong will be punished for that wrong. And the Lord treats everyone the same.

4 1Masters, give what is good and fair to your servants. Remember that you have a Master in heaven.

Some Things to Do
2Never stop praying. Be ready for anything by praying and being thankful. 3Also pray for us. Pray that God will give us an opportunity to tell people his message.* I am in prison for doing this. But pray that we can continue to tell people the secret truth that God has made known about Christ. 4Pray that I will say what is necessary to make this truth clear to everyone.

5Be wise in the way you act with those who are not believers. Use your time in the best way you can. 6When you talk, you should always be kind and wise. Then you will be able to answer everyone in the way you should.

News About Those With Paul
7Tychicus is my dear brother in Christ. He is a faithful helper and he serves the Lord with me. He will tell you everything that is happening with me. 8That is why I am sending him. I want you to know how we are, and I am sending him to encourage you. 9I am sending him with Onesimus, the faithful and dear brother from your group. They will tell you everything that has happened here.

10Aristarchus, the one here in prison with me, sends you his greetings. Mark, the cousin of Barnabas, also sends his greetings. (I have already told you what to do about Mark. If he comes, welcome him.) 11And greetings from Jesus the one who is also called Justus

a **3:15 body** Christ's spiritual body, meaning the church—his people.
b **3:24 Yes, you ... Master** Or "Serve the Lord Christ." The Greek word translated "Lord" is the same as the word for "master" in verses 22 and 23.

These are the only Jewish believers who work with me for God's kingdom.* They have been a great comfort to me.

12Epaphras, another servant of Jesus Christ from your group, sends his greetings. He constantly struggles for you in prayer. He prays that you will grow to be spiritually mature and have everything that God wants for you. 13I know that he has worked hard for you and the people in Laodicea and in Hierapolis. 14Greetings also from Demas and our dear friend Luke, the doctor.

15Give our greetings to the brothers and sisters in Laodicea. Greetings also to Nympha and to the church* that meets in her house. 16After this letter is read to you, be sure it is also read to the church in Laodicea. And you read the letter that I wrote to them. 17Tell Archippus, "Be sure to do the work the Lord gave you."

18Here's my greeting in my own handwriting—PAUL. Remember me in prison. God's grace* be with you.

1 Thessalonians

1 ¹Greetings from Paul, Silas, and Timothy.

To the church* of those in Thessalonica, who are in God the Father and the Lord Jesus Christ.

Grace* and peace be yours.

The Life and Faith of the Thessalonians

²We always remember you when we pray, and we thank God for all of you. ³Every time we pray to God our Father, we thank him for all that you have done because of your faith. And we thank him for the work you have done because of your love. And we thank him that you continue to be strong because of your hope in our Lord Jesus Christ.

⁴Brothers and sisters, God loves you. And we know that he has chosen you to be his people. ⁵When we brought the Good News* to you, we came with more than words. We brought that Good News with power, with the Holy Spirit,* and with the sure knowledge that it was true. Also you know how we lived when we were with you. We lived that way to help you. ⁶And you became like us and like the Lord. You suffered much, but still you accepted the teaching with joy. The Holy Spirit gave you that joy.

⁷You became an example to all the believers in Macedonia* and Achaia.* ⁸The Lord's teaching has spread from you throughout Greece and beyond. In fact, your faith in God has become known everywhere, so we never have to tell anyone about it. ⁹People everywhere are already telling the story about the good way you accepted us when we were there with you. They tell about how you stopped worshiping idols* and changed to serve the living and true God. ¹⁰And you began waiting for God's Son to come from heaven—the Son God raised from death. He is Jesus, who saves us from God's angry judgment that is coming.

Paul's Work in Thessalonica

2 ¹Brothers and sisters, you know that our visit to you was not a failure. ²Before we came to you, people in Philippi abused us with insults and made us suffer. You know all about that. And then, when we came to you, many people there caused trouble for us. But our God gave us the courage we needed to tell you his Good News.* ³When we encourage people to believe the Good News, it's not out of wrong motives. We are not trying to trick or fool anyone. ⁴No, we did it because God is the one who gave us this work. And this was only after he tested us and saw that we could be trusted to do it. So when we speak, we are only trying to please God, not anyone else. He is the one who can see what is in our hearts.

5You know that we never tried to influence you by saying nice things about you. We were not trying to get your money. We had no greed to hide from you. God knows that this is true. 6We were not looking for praise from people—not from you or anyone else. 7When we were with you, as apostles* of Christ we could have used our authority to make you help us. But we were very gentle[a] with you. We were like a mother caring for her little children. 8We loved you very much, so we were happy to share God's Good News with you. But not only that—we were also happy to share even our own lives with you. 9Brothers and sisters, I know that you remember how hard we worked. We worked night and day to support ourselves, so that we would not be a burden to anyone while we did the work of telling you God's Good News.

10When we were there with you believers, we were pure, honest, and without fault in the way we lived. You know, just as God does, that this is true. 11You know that we treated each one of you the way a father treats his own children. 12We encouraged you, we comforted you, and we told you to live good lives for God. He calls you to be part of his glorious kingdom.

13Also, we always thank God because of the way you accepted his message.* You heard it and accepted it as God's message, not our own. And it really is God's message. And it works in you who believe. 14Brothers and sisters, you are just like God's churches* in Judea.[b] I mean that you were treated badly by your own people, just as those believers in Christ Jesus were treated badly by other Jews— 15the same Jews who killed the Lord Jesus and the prophets.* And they forced us to leave their country. They are not pleasing to God, and they are against everyone else. 16And they are trying to stop us from teaching those who are not Jews. They don't want them to be saved. But they are just adding more and more sins to the ones they already have. Now the time has come for them to suffer God's anger.

Paul's Desire to Visit Them Again

17Brothers and sisters, we were separated from you for a short time. But even though we were not there, our thoughts were still with you. We wanted very much to see you, and we tried very hard to do this. 18Yes, we wanted to come to you. I, Paul, tried more than once to come, but Satan* stopped us. 19You are our hope, our joy, and the crown* we will be proud of when our Lord Jesus Christ comes. 20You bring us honor and joy.

3 1-2We could not come to you, but it was very hard to wait any longer. So we decided to send Timothy to you and stay in Athens alone. Timothy is our brother. He works with us for God to tell people the Good News* about Christ. We sent Timothy to strengthen and encourage you in your faith. 3We sent him so that none of you would be upset by the troubles we have now. You yourselves know

---

a **2:7 But ... gentle** Several Greek copies have "But we became babies."

b **2:14 Judea** The Jewish land where Jesus lived and taught and where the church first began.

that we must have these troubles. 4Even when we were with you, we told you that we would all have to suffer. And you know that it happened just as we said. 5This is why I sent Timothy to you, so that I could know about your faith. I sent him when I could not wait anymore. I was afraid that the devil who tempts people might have defeated you with temptations. Then our hard work would have been wasted.

6But now Timothy has come back from his visit with you and told us good news about your faith and love. He told us that you always remember us in a good way. He told us that you want very much to see us again. And it is the same with us—we want very much to see you. 7So, brothers and sisters, we are encouraged about you because of your faith. We have much trouble and suffering, but still we are encouraged. 8Our life is really full if you stand strong in the Lord. 9We have so much joy before our God because of you! So we thank God for you. But we cannot thank him enough for all the joy we feel. 10Night and day we continue praying with all our heart that we can come there and see you again. We want to give you everything you need to make your faith strong.

11We pray that our God and Father and our Lord Jesus will prepare the way for us to come to you. 12We pray that the Lord will make your love grow. We pray that he will give you more and more love for each other and for all people. We pray that you will love everyone in the same way we love you. 13This will strengthen your desire to do what is right,

and you will be holy* and without fault before our God and Father when our Lord Jesus comes with all his holy people.*

A Life That Pleases God

4 1Brothers and sisters, now I have some other things to tell you. We taught you how to live in a way that will please God. And you are living that way. Now we ask and encourage you in the Lord Jesus to live that way more and more. 2You know all that we told you to do by the authority of the Lord Jesus. 3God wants you to be holy.* He wants you to stay away from sexual sins. 4God wants each one of you to learn to control your own body. Use your body in a way that is holy and that gives honor to God.a 5Don't let your sexual desires control you like the people who don't know God. 6Never wrong any of your fellow believers* or cheat them in this way. The Lord will punish those who do that. We have already told you this and warned you about it. 7God chose us to be holy. He does not want us to live in sin. 8So anyone who refuses to obey this teaching is refusing to obey God, not us. And God is the one who gives you his Holy Spirit.*

9We don't need to write to you about having love for your brothers and sisters in Christ. God has already taught you to love each other. 10In fact, you love all the believers* in Macedonia.* We encourage you now, brothers and sisters, to show your love more and more.

11Do all you can to live a peaceful life. Mind your own business,

a 4:4 Or "God wants each of you to learn to live with your wife in a way that is holy and that gives honor to God."

and earn your own living, as we told you before. [12]If you do these things, then those who are not believers will respect the way you live. And you will not have to depend on others for what you need.

The Lord's Coming

[13]Brothers and sisters, we want you to know about those who have died. We don't want you to be sad like other people—those who have no hope. [14]We believe that Jesus died, but we also believe that he rose again. So we believe that God will raise to life through Jesus any who have died and bring them together with him when he comes.

[15]What we tell you now is the Lord's own message. Those of us who are still living when the Lord comes again will join him, but not before those who have already died. [16]The Lord himself will come down from heaven with a loud command, with the voice of the archangel,* and with the trumpet call of God. And the people who have died and were in Christ will rise first. [17]After that we who are still alive at that time will be gathered up with those who have died. We will be taken up in the clouds and meet the Lord in the air. And we will be with the Lord forever. [18]So encourage each other with these words.

Be Ready for the Lord's Coming

5 [1]Now, brothers and sisters, we don't need to write to you about times and dates. [2]You know very well that the day when the Lord comes again will be a surprise, like a thief who comes at night. [3]People will say, "We have peace and we are safe." At that time destruction will come to them quickly, like the pains of a woman giving birth. And those people will not escape.

[4]But you, brothers and sisters, are not living in darkness.* And so that day will not surprise you like a thief. [5]You are all people who belong to the light.* You belong to the day.* We don't belong to the night* or to darkness. [6]So we should not be like other people. We should not be sleeping. We should be awake and have self-control. [7]People who sleep, sleep at night. People who drink too much, drink at night. [8]But we belong to the day, so we should control ourselves. We should wear faith and love to protect us. And the hope of salvation should be our helmet.

[9]God did not choose us to suffer his anger. God chose us to have salvation through our Lord Jesus Christ. [10]Jesus died for us so that we can live together with him. It is not important if we are alive or dead when Jesus comes. [11]So encourage each other and help each other grow stronger in faith, just as you are already doing.

Final Instructions and Greetings

[12]Now brothers and sisters, we ask you to recognize the value of those who work hard among you—those who, as followers of the Lord, care for you and tell you how to live. [13]Show them the highest respect and love because of the work they do.

Live in peace with each other. [14]We ask you, brothers and sisters, to warn those who will not work. Encourage those who are afraid. Help those who are weak. Be patient with everyone. [15]Be sure that no one pays back wrong for wrong. But always try to do what is good for each other and for all people.

16Always be full of joy. 17Never stop praying. 18Whatever happens, always be thankful. This is how God wants you to live in Christ Jesus.

19Don't stop the work of the Holy Spirit.* 20Don't treat prophecy* like something that is not important. 21But test everything. Keep what is good, 22and stay away from everything that is evil.

23We pray that God himself, the God of peace, will make you pure—belonging only to him. We pray that your whole self—spirit, soul, and body—will be kept safe and be blameless when our Lord Jesus Christ comes. 24The one who chose you will do that for you. You can trust him.

25Brothers and sisters, please pray for us. 26Give all the brothers and sisters the special greeting of God's people.a 27I tell you by the authority of the Lord to read this letter to all the believers* there. 28The grace* of our Lord Jesus Christ be with you.

a 5:26 the special greeting of God's people Literally, "a holy kiss."

2 Thessalonians

1 ¹Greetings from Paul, Silas, and Timothy.

To the church* of those in Thessalonica, who are in God our Father and the Lord Jesus Christ.

²Grace* and peace to you from God the Father and the Lord Jesus Christ.

³We thank God for you always. And that's what we should do, because you give us good reason to be thankful: Your faith is growing more and more. And the love that every one of you has for each other is also growing. ⁴So we tell the other churches of God how proud we are of you. We tell them how you patiently continue to be strong and have faith, even though you are being persecuted* and are suffering many troubles.

Paul Tells About God's Judgment

⁵This is proof that God is right in his judgment. He wants you to be worthy of his kingdom.* Your suffering is for that kingdom. ⁶God will do what is right. He will punish those who are causing you trouble. ⁷And he will bring relief to you who are troubled. He will bring it to you and to us when the Lord Jesus comes from heaven for all to see, together with his powerful angels. ⁸He will come with burning fire to punish those who don't know God—those who refuse to accept the Good News* about our Lord Jesus Christ. ⁹They will be punished with a destruction that never ends. They will not be allowed to be with the Lord but will be kept away from his great power. ¹⁰This will happen on the day when the Lord Jesus comes to receive honor with his holy people.* He will be admired among all who have believed. And this includes you because you believed what we told you.

¹¹That is why we always pray for you. We ask our God to help you live the good way he wanted when he chose you. The goodness you have makes you want to do good. And the faith you have makes you work. We pray that with his power God will help you do these things more and more. ¹²Then the name of our Lord Jesus will be honored because of you, and you will be honored because of him. This can happen only by the grace* of our God and the Lord Jesus Christ.

Evil Things Will Happen

2 ¹Brothers and sisters, we have something to say about the coming of our Lord Jesus Christ. We want to talk to you about that time when we will meet together with him. ²Don't let yourselves be easily upset or worried if you hear that the day of the Lord has already come. Someone might say that this idea came from us—in something the Spirit* told us, or in something we said, or in a letter we wrote. ³Don't be fooled by anything they might say. That day of the Lord will not come until the turning away from God happens. And that day will not come until the Man of Evil appears, the one who belongs to hell.ᵃ ⁴He will stand against and put himself above everything that people worship or think is worthy of worship. He will even go into God's Templeᵇ and sit there, claiming that he is God.

⁵I told you before that all these things would happen. Remember? ⁶And you know what is stopping that Man of Evil now. He is being stopped now so that he will appear at the right time. ⁷The secret power of evil is already working in the world now. But there is one who is stopping that secret power of evil. And he will continue to stop it until he is taken out of the way. ⁸Then that Man of Evil will appear. But the Lord Jesus will kill him with the breath that comes from his mouth. The Lord will come in a way that everyone will see, and that will be the end of the Man of Evil.

⁹When that Man of Evil comes, it will be the work of Satan.* He will come with great power, and he will do all kinds of false miracles, signs, and wonders. ¹⁰The Man of Evil will use every kind of evil to fool those who are lost. They are lost because they refused to love the truth and be saved. ¹¹So God will send them something powerful that leads them away from the truth and causes them to believe a lie. ¹²They will all be condemned because they did not believe the truth and because they enjoyed doing evil.

You Are Chosen for Salvation

¹³Brothers and sisters, you are people the Lord loves. And we always thank God for you. That's what we should do, because God chose you to be some of the first peopleᶜ to be saved. You are saved by the Spirit* making you holy* and by your faith in the truth. ¹⁴God chose you to have that salvation. He chose you by using the Good News* that we told you. You were chosen so that you can share in the glory* of our Lord Jesus Christ. ¹⁵So, brothers and sisters, stand strong and continue to believe the teachings we gave you when we were there and by letter.

¹⁶⁻¹⁷We pray that the Lord Jesus Christ himself and God our Father will comfort you and strengthen you in every good thing you do and say. God loved us and gave us through his grace* a wonderful hope and comfort that has no end.

Pray for Us

3 ¹And now, brothers and sisters, pray for us. Pray that the Lord's teaching will continue to spread quickly. And pray that people will give honor to that teaching, the same as happened with you. ²And pray that we will be protected from crooked and evil people. Not everyone believes in the Lord, you know.

³But the Lord is faithful. He will give you strength and protect you from the Evil One.* ⁴The Lord gives us confidence that you are doing what we told you and that you will continue to do it. ⁵We

---

ᵃ **2:3 belongs to hell** Literally, "is the son of destruction."
ᵇ **2:4 Temple** Probably the Temple in Jerusalem. See "Temple" in the Word List.

ᶜ **2:13 to be ... people** Some Greek copies say, "from the beginning."

pray that the Lord will cause you to feel God's love and remember Christ's patient endurance.

The Obligation to Work

[6]Brothers and sisters, by the authority of our Lord Jesus Christ we tell you to stay away from any believer who refuses to work. People who refuse to work are not following the teaching that we gave them. [7]You yourselves know that you should live like we do. We were not lazy when we were with you. [8]We never accepted food from anyone without paying for it. We worked and worked so that we would not be a burden to any of you. We worked night and day. [9]We had the right to ask you to help us. But we worked to take care of ourselves so that we would be an example for you to follow. [10]When we were with you, we gave you this rule: "Whoever will not work should not be allowed to eat."

[11]We hear that some people in your group refuse to work. They are doing nothing except being busy in the lives of others. [12]Our instruction to them is to stop bothering others, to start working and earn their own food. It is by the authority of the Lord Jesus Christ that we are urging them to do this. [13]Brothers and sisters, never get tired of doing good.

[14]If there are some there who refuse to do what we tell you in this letter, remember who they are. Don't associate with them. Then maybe they will feel ashamed. [15]But don't treat them as enemies. Counsel them as fellow believers.*

Final Words

[16]We pray that the Lord of peace will give you peace at all times and in every way. The Lord be with you all.

[17]Here's my greeting in my own handwriting—Paul. I do this in all my letters to show they are from me. This is the way I write.

[18]The grace* of our Lord Jesus Christ be with you all.

1 Timothy

1 ¹Greetings from Paul, an apostle* of Christ Jesus. I am an apostle by the command of God our Savior and Christ Jesus our hope.

²To Timothy, a true son to me in the faith we share.

Grace,* mercy, and peace from God the Father and Christ Jesus our Lord.

Warnings Against False Teachings

³When I went to Macedonia,* I asked you to stay in Ephesus. Some people there are teaching things that are not true, and I want you to tell them to stop. ⁴Tell them not to give their time to meaningless stories and to long lists of names to prove their family histories. Such things only cause arguments. They don't help God's work, which is done only by faith. ⁵My purpose in telling you to do this is to promote love—the kind of love shown by those whose thoughts are pure, who do what they know is right, and whose faith in God is real. ⁶But some have missed this key point in their teaching and have gone off in another direction. Now they talk about things that help no one. ⁷They want to be teachers of the law,ᵃ but they don't know what they are talking about. They don't even understand the things they say they are sure of.

⁸We know that the law is good if someone uses it right. ⁹We also know that the law is not made for those who do what is right. It is made for those who are against the law and refuse to follow it. The law is for sinners who are against God and all that is pleasing to him. It is for those who have no interest in spiritual things and for those who kill their fathers or mothers or anyone else. ¹⁰It is for those who commit sexual sins, homosexuals, those who sell slaves, those who tell lies, those who don't tell the truth under oath, and those who are against the true teaching of God. ¹¹That teaching is part of the Good News* that our blessed God gave me to tell. In it we see his glory.*

Thanks for God's Mercy

¹²I thank Christ Jesus our Lord because he trusted me and gave me this work of serving him. He gives me strength. ¹³In the past I insulted Christ. As a proud and violent man, I persecuted his people. But God gave me mercy because I did not know what I was doing. I did that before I became a believer. ¹⁴But our Lord gave me a full measure of his grace.* And with that grace came the faith and love that are in Christ Jesus.

¹⁵Here is a true statement that should be accepted without

ᵃ **1:7 law** Probably the Jewish law that God gave to Moses on Mount Sinai. See Ex. 19 and 20. Also in verse 8.

question: Christ Jesus came into the world to save sinners, and I am the worst of them. ¹⁶But I was given mercy so that in me Christ Jesus could show that he has patience without limit. Christ showed his patience with me, the worst of all sinners. He wanted me to be an example for those who would believe in him and have eternal life. ¹⁷Honor and glory* to the King who rules forever. He cannot be destroyed and cannot be seen. Honor and glory forever and ever to the only God. Amen.*

¹⁸Timothy, you are like a son to me. What I am telling you to do agrees with the prophecies*ᵃ* that were told about you in the past. I want you to remember those prophecies and fight the good fight of faith. ¹⁹Continue to trust in God and do what you know is right. Some people have not done this, and their faith is now in ruins. ²⁰Hymenaeus and Alexander are men like that. I have given them to Satan* so that they will learn not to speak against God.

God Wants Us to Pray for Everyone

2 ¹First of all, I ask that you pray for all people. Ask God to bless them and give them what they need. And give thanks. ²You should pray for rulers and for all who have authority. Pray for these leaders so that we can live quiet and peaceful lives—lives full of devotion to God and respect for him. ³This is good and pleases God our Savior.

⁴God wants everyone to be saved and to fully understand the truth. ⁵There is only one God, and there is only one way that people can reach God. That way is through Christ Jesus, who as a man ⁶gave himself to pay for everyone to be free. This is the message that was given to us at just the right time. ⁷And I was chosen as an apostle* to tell people that message. (I am telling the truth. I am not lying.) I was chosen to teach those who are not Jews to believe and understand the truth.

Special Instructions for Men and Women

⁸I want the men everywhere to pray. Men who lift their hands in prayer must be devoted to God and pleasing to him. They must be men who keep themselves from getting angry and having arguments.

⁹And I want the women to make themselves attractive in the right way. Their clothes should be sensible and appropriate. They should not draw attention to themselves with fancy hairstyles or gold jewelry or pearls or expensive clothes. ¹⁰But they should make themselves attractive by the good things they do. That is more appropriate for women who say they are devoted to God.

¹¹A woman should learn while listening quietly and being completely willing to obey. ¹²I don't allow a woman to teach a man or tell him what to do. She must listen quietly, ¹³because Adam was made first. Eve was made later. ¹⁴Also, Adam was not the one who was tricked.*ᵇ* It was the woman who was tricked and became a sinner. ¹⁵But women will be saved in their work of having

---

ᵃ **1:18 prophecies** Things that prophets said about Timothy's life before those things happened.

ᵇ **2:14 Adam was not … tricked** The devil tricked Eve, and Eve caused Adam to sin. See Gen. 3:1–13.

children. They will be saved if they continue to live in faith, love, and holiness with sensible behavior.

Leaders in the Church

3 ¹It is a true statement that anyone whose goal is to serve as an elder*a* has his heart set on a good work. ²An elder*b* must be such a good man that no one can rightly criticize him. He must be faithful to his wife.*c* He must have self-control and be wise. He must be respected by others. He must be ready to help people by welcoming them into his home. He must be a good teacher. ³He must not drink too much, and he must not be someone who likes to fight. He must be gentle and peaceful. He must not be someone who loves money. ⁴He must be a good leader of his own family. This means that his children obey him with full respect. ⁵If a man does not know how to lead his own family, he will not be able to take care of God's church.*

⁶An elder must not be a new believer. It might make him too proud of himself. Then he would be condemned for his pride the same as the devil was. ⁷An elder must also have the respect of people who are not part of the church. Then he will not be criticized by others and be caught in the devil's trap.

Special Servants

⁸In the same way, the men who are chosen to be special servants*

must have the respect of others. They must not be men who say things they don't mean or who spend their time drinking too much. They must not be men who will do almost anything for money. ⁹They must follow the true faith that God has now made known to us and always do what they know is right. ¹⁰You should test them first. Then, if you find that they have done nothing wrong, they can be special servants.

¹¹In the same way, the women*d* must have the respect of others. They must not be women who speak evil about other people. They must have self-control and be women who can be trusted in everything.

¹²The men who are special servants must be faithful in marriage.*e* They must be good leaders of children and their own families. ¹³Those who do well as special servants are making an honorable place for themselves. And they will feel very sure of their faith in Christ Jesus.

The Secret of Our Life

¹⁴I hope I can come to you soon. But I am writing this to you now, ¹⁵so that, even if I cannot come soon, you will know how people should live in the family*f* of God. That family is the church* of the living God. And God's church is

---

d **3:11 women** Probably the women who serve as special servants (See Rom. 16:1). It could be translated, "their wives," meaning the wives of the special servants, although there is no word for "their" in the Greek text.
e **3:12 faithful in marriage** Literally, "a man of one woman."
f **3:15 family** Literally, "house." This could mean that God's people are like God's temple.

a **3:1 whose ... elder** Literally, "who aspires to supervision."
b **3:2 elder** Here, literally, "overseer." See "ELDERS (NEW TESTAMENT)" in the Word List.
c **3:2 faithful to his wife** Literally, "a man of one woman."

the support and foundation of the truth. ¹⁶Without a doubt, the secret of our life of worship is great:

Christᵃ was shown to us in human form;
the Spirit* proved that he was right;
he was seen by angels.
The message* about him was told to the nations;
people in the world believed in him;
he was taken up to heaven in glory.*

A Warning About False Teachers

4 ¹The Spirit* clearly says that in the last times some will turn away from what we believe. They will obey spirits that tell lies. And they will follow the teachings of demons.* ²Those teachings come through people who tell lies and trick others. These evil people cannot see what is right and what is wrong. It is like their conscience has been destroyed with a hot iron. ³They say that it is wrong to marry. And they say that there are some foods that people must not eat. But God made these foods, and those who believe and who understand the truth can eat them with thanks. ⁴Everything that God made is good. Nothing he made should be refused if it is accepted with thanks to him. ⁵Everything he created is made holy* by what he has said and by prayer.

Be a Good Servant of Christ Jesus

⁶Tell this to the brothers and sisters there. This will show that you are a good servant of Christ Jesus. You will show that you are made strong by the words of faith and good teaching you have followed. ⁷People tell silly stories that don't agree with God's truth. Don't follow what these stories teach. But teach yourself to be devoted to God. ⁸Training your body helps you in some ways. But devotion to God helps you in every way. It brings you blessings in this life and in the future life too. ⁹Here is a true statement that should be accepted without question: ¹⁰We hope in the living God, the Savior of all people. In particular, he is the Savior of all those who believe in him. This is why we work and struggle.

¹¹Command and teach these things. ¹²You are young, but don't let anyone treat you as if you are not important. Be an example to show the believers how they should live. Show them by what you say, by the way you live, by your love, by your faith, and by your pure life.

¹³Continue to read the Scriptures* to the people, encourage them, and teach them. Do this until I come. ¹⁴Remember to use the gift you have, which was given to you through a prophecyᵇ when the group of elders* laid their hands on* you. ¹⁵Continue to do these things. Give your life to doing them. Then everyone can see that your work is progressing. ¹⁶Be careful in your life and in your teaching. Continue to live and teach rightly. Then you will save yourself and those who listen to your teaching.

5 ¹Don't speak angrily to an older man. But talk to him as if he were your father. Treat the

---

ᵃ **3:16 Christ** Literally, "who." Some Greek copies have "God."

ᵇ **4:14 prophecy** Something said about Timothy's life before that thing happened.

younger men like brothers. 2Treat the older women like mothers. And treat the younger women with respect like sisters.

Taking Care of Widows

3Take care of widows who really need help. 4But if a widow has children or grandchildren, the first thing they need to learn is this: to show their devotion to God by taking care of their own family. They will be repaying their parents, and this pleases God. 5A widow who really needs help is one who has been left all alone. She trusts God to take care of her. She prays all the time, night and day, and asks God for help. 6But the widow who uses her life to please herself is really dead while she is still living. 7Tell the believers there to take care of their family so that no one can say they are doing wrong. 8Everyone should take care of all their own people. Most important, they should take care of their own family. If they do not do that, then they do not accept what we believe. They are worse than someone who does not even believe in God.

9To be added to your list of widows, a woman must be 60 years old or older. She must have been faithful to her husband.a 10She must be known for the good she has done: raising children, welcoming travelers into her home, serving the needsb of God's people, helping those in trouble, and using her life to do all kinds of good.

11But don't put younger widows on that list. When their strong physical needs pull them away from their commitment to Christ, they will want to marry again. 12Then they will be guilty of not doing what they first promised to do. 13Also, these younger widows begin to waste their time going from house to house. They also begin to gossip and try to run other people's lives. They say things they should not say. 14So I want the younger widows to marry, have children, and take care of their homes. If they do this, our enemy will not have any reason to criticize them. 15But some of the younger widows have already turned away to follow Satan.*

16If any woman who is a believer has widows in her family, shec should take care of them herself. Then the church* will not have that burden and will be able to care for the widows who have no one else to help them.

More About Elders and Other Matters

17The elders* who lead the church in a good way should receive double honord—in particular, those who do the work of counseling and teaching. 18As the Scriptures* say, "When a work animal is being used to separate grain, don't keep it from eating the grain."e And the Scriptures also say, "A worker should be given his pay."f

19Don't listen to someone who accuses an elder. You should listen to them only if there are two

---

a **5:9 faithful to her husband** Literally, "a woman of one man."
b **5:10 serving the needs** Literally, "washing the feet," a social custom of the first century, because people wore open sandals on very dusty roads.

c **5:16 woman ... she** Some Greek copies have "man or woman ... he/she."
d **5:17 double honor** Or "double pay."
e **5:18** Quote from Deut. 25:4.
f **5:18** Quote from Lk. 10:7.

or three others who can say what the elder did wrong. [20]Tell those who sin that they are wrong. Do this in front of the whole church so that the others will have a warning.

[21]Before God and Jesus Christ and the chosen angels, I tell you to make these judgments without any prejudice. Treat every person the same.

[22]Think carefully before you lay your hands on* anyone to make him an elder. Don't share in the sins of others. Keep yourself pure.

[23]Timothy, stop drinking only water, and drink a little wine. This will help your stomach, and you will not be sick so often.

[24]The sins of some people are easy to see. Their sins show that they will be judged. But the sins of some others are seen only later. [25]It is the same with the good things people do. Some are easy to see. But even if they are not obvious now, none of them will stay hidden forever.

Special Instructions for Slaves

6 [1]All those who are slaves should show full respect to their masters. Then God's name and our teaching will not be criticized. [2]Some slaves have masters who are believers, so they are brothers. Does this mean they should show their masters any less respect? No, they should serve them even better, because they are helping believers, people they should love.

This is what you must teach and tell everyone to do.

False Teaching and True Riches

[3]Some people will teach what is false and will not agree with the true teaching of our Lord Jesus Christ. They will not accept the teaching that produces a life of devotion to God. [4]They are proud of what they know, but they understand nothing. They are sick with a love for arguing and fighting about words. And that brings jealousy, quarrels, insults, and evil mistrust. [5]They are always making trouble, because they are people whose thinking has been confused. They have lost their understanding of the truth. They think that devotion to God is a way to get rich.

[6]Devotion to God is, in fact, a way for people to be very rich, but only if it makes them satisfied with what they have. [7]When we came into the world, we brought nothing. And when we die, we can take nothing out. [8]So, if we have food and clothes, we will be satisfied with that. [9]People who want to be rich bring temptations to themselves. They are caught in a trap. They begin to want many foolish things that will hurt them. These things ruin and destroy people. [10]The love of money causes all kinds of evil. Some people have turned away from what we believe because they want to get more and more money. But they have caused themselves a lot of pain and sorrow.

Some Things to Remember

[11]But you belong to God. So you should stay away from all those things. Always try to do what is right, to be devoted to God, and to have faith, love, patience, and gentleness. [12]We have to fight to keep our faith. Try as hard as you can to win that fight. Take hold of eternal life. It is the life you were chosen to have when you confessed your faith in Jesus—that wonderful truth that you spoke so

openly and that so many people heard. [13]Before God and Christ Jesus I give you a command. Jesus is the one who confessed that same wonderful truth when he stood before Pontius Pilate.* And God is the one who gives life to everything. Now I tell you this: [14]Do what you were commanded to do without fault or blame until the time when our Lord Jesus Christ comes again. [15]God will make that happen at the right time. God is the blessed and only Ruler. He is the King of all kings and the Lord of all lords. [16]God is the only one who never dies. He lives in light so bright that people cannot go near it. No one has ever seen him; no one is able to see him. All honor and power belong to him forever. Amen.*

[17]Give this command to those who are rich with the things of this world. Tell them not to be proud. Tell them to hope in God, not their money. Money cannot be trusted, but God takes care of us richly. He gives us everything to enjoy. [18]Tell those who are rich to do good—to be rich in good works. And tell them they should be happy to give and ready to share. [19]By doing this, they will be saving up a treasure for themselves. And that treasure will be a strong foundation on which their future life will be built. They will be able to have the life that is true life.

[20]Timothy, God has trusted you with many things. Keep these things safe. Stay away from people who talk about useless things that are not from God and who argue against you with a "knowledge" that is not knowledge at all. [21]Some people who claim to have that "knowledge" have gone completely away from what we believe.

God's grace* be with you all.

2 Timothy

1 ¹Greetings from Paul, an apostle* of Christ Jesus. I am an apostle because God wanted me to be. God sent me to tell people about the promise of life that is in Christ Jesus.

²To Timothy, a dear son to me. Grace,* mercy, and peace to you from God the Father and from Christ Jesus our Lord.

Thanksgiving and Encouragement

³I always remember you in my prayers day and night. And in these prayers I thank God for you. He is the God my ancestors* served, and I have always served him with a clear conscience. ⁴I remember that you cried for me. I want very much to see you so that I can be filled with joy. ⁵I remember your true faith. That kind of faith first belonged to your grandmother Lois and to your mother Eunice. I know you now have that same faith. ⁶That is why I want you to remember the gift God gave you. God gave you that gift when I laid my hands on* you. Now I want you to use that gift and let it grow more and more, like a small flame grows into a fire. ⁷The Spirit* God gave us does not make us afraid. His Spirit is a source of power and love and self-control.

⁸So don't be ashamed to tell people about our Lord Jesus. And don't be ashamed of me—I am in prison for the Lord. But suffer with me for the Good News.* God gives us the strength to do that.

⁹God saved us and chose us to be his holy* people, but not because of anything we ourselves did. God saved us and made us his people because that was what he wanted and because of his grace.* That grace was given to us through Christ Jesus before time began. ¹⁰And now it has been shown to us in the coming of our Savior Christ Jesus. He destroyed death and showed us the way to have life. Yes, through the Good News Jesus showed us the way to have life that cannot be destroyed.

¹¹I was chosen to tell people that message as an apostle* and teacher. ¹²And I suffer now because of that work. But I am not ashamed, because I know the one I have put my trust in. And I am sure that he is able to protect what I have put into his care*ᵃ* until that Day.*

¹³What you heard me teach is an example of what you should teach. Follow that model of right teaching with the faith and love we have in Christ Jesus. ¹⁴This teaching is a treasure that you have been trusted with. Protect it with the help of the Holy Spirit, who lives inside us.

ᵃ 1:12 what … care Or "what he has trusted me with."

¹⁵You know that everyone in Asia* has left me. Even Phygelus and Hermogenes have left me. ¹⁶I pray that the Lord will show mercy to the family of Onesiphorus. Many times Onesiphorus encouraged me. He was not ashamed that I was in prison. ¹⁷No, he was not ashamed. When he came to Rome, he looked and looked for me until he found me. ¹⁸I pray that the Lord Jesus will make sure Onesiphorus receives mercy from the Lord God on that Day. You know how many ways this brother helped me in Ephesus.

A Loyal Soldier of Christ Jesus

2 ¹Timothy, you are a son to me. Be strong in the grace* that we have because we belong to Christ Jesus. ²What you have heard me teach publicly you should teach to others. Share these teachings with people you can trust. Then they will be able to teach others these same things. ³As a good soldier of Christ Jesus, accept your share of the troubles we have. ⁴A soldier wants to please his commanding officer, so he does not spend any time on activities that are not a part of his duty. ⁵Athletes in a race must obey all the rules to win. ⁶The farmer who works hard deserves the first part of the harvest. ⁷Think about what I am saying. The Lord will help you understand it all.

⁸Remember Jesus Christ. He is from the family of David.* After Jesus died, he was raised from death. This is the Good News* that I tell people. ⁹And because I tell that message, I am suffering. I am even bound with chains like someone who has really done wrong. But God's message is not bound. ¹⁰So I patiently accept all these troubles. I do this to help the people God has chosen so that they can have the salvation that is in Christ Jesus. With this salvation comes glory* that never ends.

¹¹Here is a true statement:
If we died with him, we will also live with him.
¹² If we remain faithful even in suffering, we will also rule with him.
If we refuse to say we know him, he will refuse to say he knows us.
¹³ If we are not faithful, he will still be faithful,
because he cannot be false to himself.

A Worker Who Pleases God

¹⁴Keep on telling everyone these truths. And warn them before God not to argue about words. Such arguments don't help anyone, and they ruin those who listen to them. ¹⁵Do your best to be the kind of person God will accept, and give yourself to him. Be a worker who has no reason to be ashamed of his work, one who applies the true teaching in the right way.

¹⁶Stay away from people who talk about useless things that are not from God. That kind of talk will lead a person more and more against God. ¹⁷Their evil teaching will spread like a sickness inside the body. Hymenaeus and Philetus are men like that. ¹⁸They have left the true teaching. They say that the day when people will be raised from death has already come and gone. And they are destroying the faith of some people ¹⁹But God's strong foundation never moves, and these words are written on it: "The Lord knows

those who belong to him."[a] Also, these words are written there: "Everyone who says they believe in the Lord must stop doing wrong."

20In a large house there are things made of gold and silver. But there are also things made of wood and clay. Some of these are used for special purposes, others for ordinary jobs. 21The Lord wants to use you for special purposes, so make yourself clean from all evil. Then you will be holy,* and the Master can use you. You will be ready for any good work.

22Stay away from the evil things a young person like you typically wants to do. Do your best to live right and to have faith, love, and peace, together with others who trust in the Lord with pure hearts. 23Stay away from foolish and stupid arguments. You know that these arguments grow into bigger arguments. 24As a servant of the Lord, you must not argue. You must be kind to everyone. You must be a good teacher, and you must be patient. 25You must gently teach those who don't agree with you. Maybe God will let them change their hearts so that they can accept the truth. 26The devil has trapped them and now makes them do what he wants. But maybe they can wake up to see what is happening and free themselves from the devil's trap.

Many People Will Stop Loving God

3 1Remember this: There are some terrible times coming in the last days. 2People will love only themselves and money. They will be proud and boast about themselves. They will abuse others with insults. They will not obey their parents. They will be ungrateful and against all that is pleasing to God. 3They will have no love for others and will refuse to forgive anyone. They will talk about others to hurt them and will have no self-control. They will be cruel and hate what is good. 4People will turn against their friends. They will do foolish things without thinking and will be so proud of themselves. Instead of loving God, they will love pleasure. 5They will go on pretending to be devoted to God, but they will refuse to let that "devotion" change the way they live. Stay away from these people!

6Some of them go into homes and get control over weak women, whose lives are full of sin—women who are led into sin by all the things they want. 7These women always want to learn something new, but they are never able to fully understand the truth. 8Just as Jannes and Jambres[b] fought against Moses,* these people fight against the truth. Their thinking has been confused. The faith they have and teach is worthless. 9But they will not succeed in what they are trying to do. Everyone will see how foolish they are. That is what happened to Jannes and Jambres.

Last Instructions

10But you know all about me. You know what I teach and the way I live. You know my goal in life. You know my faith, my patience, and my love. You know that I never stop trying. 11You know about my persecutions* and my sufferings. You know all the things that happened to me in Antioch, Iconium,

b 3:8 **Jannes and Jambres** Probably the magicians who opposed Moses in Pharaoh's court. See Ex. 7:11–12, 22.

and Lystra—the persecution I suffered in those places. But the Lord saved me from all of it. [12]Everyone who wants to live showing true devotion to God in Christ Jesus will be persecuted. [13]People who are evil and cheat others will become worse and worse. They will fool others, but they will also be fooling themselves.

[14]But you should continue following the teaching you learned. You know it is true, because you know you can trust those who taught you. [15]You have known the Holy Scriptures[a] since you were a child. These Scriptures are able to make you wise. And that wisdom leads to salvation through faith in Christ Jesus. [16]All Scripture is given by God. And all Scripture is useful for teaching and for showing people what is wrong in their lives. It is useful for correcting faults and teaching the right way to live. [17]Using the Scriptures, those who serve God will be prepared and will have everything they need to do every good work.

4 [1]Before God and Jesus Christ, I give you a command. Christ Jesus is the one who will judge all people—those who are living and those who have died. He is coming again to rule in his kingdom.* So I give you this command: [2]Tell everyone God's message.* Be ready at all times to do whatever is needed. Tell people what they need to do, tell them when they are doing wrong, and encourage them. Do this with great patience and careful teaching.

[3]The time will come when people will not listen to the true

teaching. But people will find more and more teachers who please them. They will find teachers who say what they want to hear. [4]People will stop listening to the truth. They will begin to follow the teaching in false stories. [5]But you should control yourself at all times. When troubles come, accept them. Do the work of telling the Good News.* Do all the duties of a servant of God.

[6]My life is being given as an offering for God. The time has come for me to leave this life here. [7]I have fought the good fight. I have finished the race. I have served the Lord faithfully. [8]Now, a prize is waiting for me—the crown* that will show I am right with God. The Lord, the judge who judges rightly, will give it to me on that Day.* Yes, he will give it to me and to everyone else who is eagerly looking forward to his coming.

Personal Notes

[9]Do your best to come to me as soon as you can. [10]Demas loved this world too much. That is why he left me. He went to Thessalonica. Crescens went to Galatia. And Titus went to Dalmatia. [11]Luke is the only one still with me. Get Mark and bring him with you when you come. He can help me in my work here. [12]I sent Tychicus to Ephesus.

[13]When I was in Troas, I left my coat there with Carpus. So when you come, bring it to me. Also, bring my books. The books written on parchment* are the ones I need.

[14]Alexander the metalworker caused me so much harm. The Lord will punish him for what he did. [15]He fought against everything we teach. You should be

---

[a] **3:15 Holy Scriptures** Writings that Jews and followers of Christ accepted to be from God—the Old Testament.

careful that he doesn't hurt you too.

¹⁶The first time I defended myself, no one helped me. Everyone left me. I pray that God will forgive them. ¹⁷But the Lord stayed with me. The Lord gave me strength so that I could tell the Good News* everywhere. He wanted all those who are not Jews to hear that Good News. So I was saved from the lion's mouth. ¹⁸The Lord will save me when anyone tries to hurt me. He will bring me safely to his heavenly kingdom. Glory* forever and ever be the Lord's. Amen.*

Final Greetings

¹⁹Give my greetings to Priscilla and Aquila and to the family of Onesiphorus. ²⁰Erastus stayed in Corinth. And I left Trophimus in Miletus—he was sick. ²¹Try as hard as you can to come to me before winter.

Greetings to you from Eubulus, Pudens, Linus, Claudia, and all the brothers and sisters here.

²²The Lord be with your spirit. Grace* be with you.

Titus

1 ¹Greetings from Paul, a servant of God and an apostle* of Jesus Christ. I was sent to help God's chosen people have faith and understand the truth that produces a life of devotion to God. ²This faith and knowledge make us sure that we have eternal life. God promised that life to us before time began—and God does not lie. ³At the right time, God let the world know about that life. He did this through the telling of the Good News message,* and he trusted me with that work. I told people that message because God our Savior commanded me to.

⁴To Titus, a true son to me in the faith we share together.

Grace* and peace to you from God the Father and Christ Jesus our Savior.

Titus' Work in Crete

⁵I left you in Crete so that you could finish doing what still needed to be done. And I also left you there so that you could choose men to be elders* in every town. ⁶To be an elder, a man must not be guilty of living in a wrong way. He must be faithful to his wife,ᵃ and his children must be faithful to God.ᵇ They must not be known as children who are wild or don't obey. ⁷An elderᶜ has the job of taking care of God's work. So people should not be able to say that he lives in a wrong way. He must not be someone who is proud and selfish or who gets angry quickly. He must not drink too much, and he must not be someone who likes to fight. He must not be a man who will do almost anything for money. ⁸An elder must be ready to help people by welcoming them into his home. He must love what is good. He must be wise. He must live right. He must be devoted to God and pleasing to him. And he must be able to control himself. ⁹An elder must be faithful to the same true message we teach. Then he will be able to encourage others with teaching that is true and right. And he will be able to show those who are against this teaching that they are wrong.

¹⁰This is important, because there are many people who refuse to obey—people who talk about worthless things and mislead others. I am talking especially about those who say that men who are not Jews must be circumcised* to please God. ¹¹These people must be stopped, because they are destroying whole families by

---

ᵃ **1:6 faithful to his wife** Literally, "a man of one woman."

ᵇ **1:6 faithful to God** This word can mean "trustworthy" or "believers." Here, both meanings may be included. Compare this verse with 1 Tim. 3:4.

ᶜ **1:7 elder** Here, literally, "overseer." See "ELDERS (NEW TESTAMENT)" in the Word List.

teaching what they should not teach. They teach only to cheat people and make money. [12]Even one of their own prophets said, "Cretans are always liars. They are evil animals and lazy people who do nothing but eat." [13]The words that prophet said are true. So tell those people that they are wrong. You must be strict with them. Then they will become strong in the faith, [14]and they will stop paying attention to the stories told by those Jews. They will stop following the commands of those who have turned away from the truth.

[15]To people who are pure, everything is pure. But to those who are full of sin and don't believe, nothing is pure. Really, their thinking has become evil and their consciences have been ruined. [16]They say they know God, but the evil things they do show that they don't accept him. They are disgusting. They refuse to obey God and are not capable of doing anything good.

Following the True Teaching

2 [1]You, however, must tell everyone how to live in a way that agrees with the true teaching. [2]Teach the older men to have self-control, to be serious, and to be wise. They must be strong in faith, in love, and in patience.

[3]Also, teach the older women to live the way those who serve the Lord should live. They should not go around saying bad things about others or be in the habit of drinking too much. They should teach what is good. [4]By doing this they will teach the younger women to love their husbands and children. [5]They will teach them to be wise and pure, to take care of their homes, to be kind, and to be willing to serve their husbands. Then no one will be able to criticize the teaching God gave us.

[6]In the same way, tell the young men to be wise. [7]You should be an example for them in every way by the good things you do. When you teach, be honest and serious. [8]And your teaching should be clearly right so that you cannot be criticized. Then anyone who is against you will be ashamed. There will not be anything bad they can say about us.

[9]And tell this to those who are slaves: They should be willing to serve their masters at all times; they should try to please them, not argue with them; [10]they should not steal from them; and they should show their masters that they can be trusted. Then, in everything they do, they will show that the teaching of God our Savior is good.

[11]That is the way we should live, because God's grace* has come. That grace can save everyone. [12]It teaches us not to live against God and not to do the bad things the world wants to do. It teaches us to live on earth now in a wise and right way—a way that shows true devotion to God. [13]We should live like that while we are waiting for the coming of our great God and Savior Jesus Christ. He is our great hope, and he will come with glory.* [14]He gave himself for us. He died to free us from all evil. He died to make us pure—people who belong only to him and who always want to do good.

[15]These are the things you should tell people. Encourage them, and when they are wrong,

correct them. You have full authority to do this, so don't let anyone think they can ignore you.

The Right Way to Live

3 ¹Remind your people that they should always be under the authority of rulers and government leaders. They should obey these leaders and be ready to do good. ²Tell them not to speak evil of anyone but to live in peace with others. They should be gentle and polite to everyone.

³In the past we were foolish too. We did not obey, we were wrong, and we were slaves to the many things our bodies wanted and enjoyed. We lived doing evil and being jealous. People hated us and we hated each other. ⁴But then the kindness and love of God our Savior was made known. ⁵He saved us because of his mercy, not because of any good things we did. He saved us through the washing that made us new people. He saved us by making us new through the Holy Spirit.* ⁶God poured out to us that Holy Spirit fully through Jesus Christ our Savior. ⁷We were made right with God by his grace.* God saved us so that we could be his children and look forward to receiving life that never ends. ⁸This is a true statement.

And I want you to be sure that the people understand these things. Then those who believe in God will be careful to use their lives for doing good. These things are good and will help everyone.

⁹Stay away from those who have foolish arguments, who talk about useless family histories, or who make trouble and fight about what the Law of Moses teaches. These things are useless and will not help anyone. ¹⁰Give a warning to all those who cause arguments. If they continue to cause trouble after a second warning, then don't associate with them. ¹¹You know that people like that are evil and sinful. Their sins prove they are wrong.

Final Instructions and Greetings

¹²I will send Artemas and Tychicus to you. When I send them, try hard to come to me at Nicopolis. I have decided to stay there this winter. ¹³Zenas the lawyer and Apollos will be traveling from there. Do all that you can to help them prepare for their trip. Be sure that they have everything they need. ¹⁴Our people must learn to use their lives for doing good and helping anyone who has a need. Then they will not have empty lives.

¹⁵All the people with me here send you their greetings. Give my greetings to those who love us in the faith.

Grace* be with you all.

Philemon

[1]Greetings from Paul, a prisoner for Jesus Christ, and from Timothy, our brother.

To Philemon, our dear friend and worker with us. [2]Also to our sister Apphia, to Archippus, who serves with us in the Lord's army, and to the church* that meets in your home.

[3]Grace* and peace to you from God our Father and the Lord Jesus Christ.

Philemon's Love and Faith

[4]I remember you in my prayers. And I always thank my God for you. [5]I thank God because I hear about the love you have for all of God's holy people* and the faith you have in the Lord Jesus. [6]I pray that the faith you share will make you understand every blessing we have in Christ. [7]My brother, you have shown love to God's people, and your help has greatly encouraged them. What a great joy and encouragement that has been to me.

Accept Onesimus as a Brother

[8]There is something that you should do. And because of the authority I have in Christ, I feel free to command you to do it. [9]But I am not commanding you; I am asking you to do it out of love. I, Paul, am an old man now, and I am a prisoner for Christ Jesus. [10]I am asking you for my son Onesimus. He became my son while I was in prison. [11]In the past he was useless to you. But now he has become useful[a] for both you and me.

[12]I am sending him back to you, but it's as hard as losing part of myself. [13]I would like to keep him here to help me while I am still in prison for telling the Good News.* By helping me here, he would be representing you. [14]But I did not want to do anything without asking you first. Then whatever you do for me will be what you want to do, not what I forced you to do.

[15]Onesimus was separated from you for a short time. Maybe that happened so that you could have him back forever, [16]not to be just a slave, but better than a slave, to be a dear brother. That's what he is to me. And I know he will mean even more to you, both as your slave and as one who shares your faith in the Lord.

[17]If you accept me as your friend, then accept Onesimus back. Welcome him like you would welcome me. [18]If he has done any wrong to you or owes you anything, charge that to me. [19]I, Paul, am writing this in my own handwriting: I will pay back anything Onesimus owes. And I will say nothing about what you owe me for your own life. [20]So, my brother, as a follower of the Lord please

a **11 useless ... useful** Paul here makes a play on words with the name Onesimus, which means "useful."

do this favor[a] for me. It would be such a great encouragement to me as your brother in Christ. 21I write this letter knowing that you will do what I ask, and even more than I ask.

22Also, please prepare a room for me. I hope that God will answer your prayers and that I will be able to come and see you.

Final Greetings

23Epaphras is a prisoner with me for Christ Jesus. He sends you his greetings. 24Also Mark, Aristarchus, Demas, and Luke send their greetings. They are workers together with me.

25The grace* of our Lord Jesus Christ be with your spirit.

[a] **20 please do this favor** Paul here makes another wordplay on the name Onesimus, using a verb related to it.

Hebrews

God Has Spoken Through His Son

1 [1]In the past God spoke to our people through the prophets.* He spoke to them many times and in many different ways. [2]And now in these last days, God has spoken to us again through his Son. He made the whole world through his Son. And he has chosen his Son to have all things. [3]The Son shows the glory* of God. He is a perfect copy of God's nature, and he holds everything together by his powerful command. The Son made people clean from their sins. Then he sat down at the right side[a] of God, the Great One in heaven. [4]The Son became much greater than the angels, and God gave him a name that is much greater than any of their names.

[5]God never said this to any of the angels:

"You are my Son.
Today I have become your
Father." *Psalm 2:7*

God also never said about an angel,

"I will be his Father,
and he will be my son."
2 Samuel 7:14

[6]And then, when God presents his firstborn* Son to the world,[b] he says,

"Let all God's angels worship
him."[c]

[7]This is what God said about the angels:

"He changes his angels into
winds[d]
and his servants into
flaming fire." *Psalm 104:4*

[8]But this is what he said about his Son:

"God, your kingdom will last
forever and ever.
You use your authority for
justice.
[9] You love what is right and
hate what is wrong.
So God, your God, has chosen
you,
giving you more honor and
joy than anyone like you."
Psalm 45:6-7

[10]God also said,

"O Lord, in the beginning you
made the earth,
and your hands made the
sky.
[11] These things will disappear,
but you will stay.
They will all wear out like
old clothes.
[12] You will fold them up like
a coat,
and they will be changed
like clothes.

---

[a] **1:3 right side** The place of honor and authority (power).
[b] **1:6 world** This may mean the world into which Jesus was born (see Lk. 2:1–14), or it may have the same meaning as in Heb. 2:5—the world to come, to which the risen Christ is presented as king (see Php. 2:9–11).
[c] **1:6 "Let ... him"** These words are found in Deut. 32:43 in the ancient Greek version and in a Hebrew scroll from Qumran.
[d] **1:7 winds** This can also mean "spirits."

But you never change,
and your life will never end."

Psalm 102:25–27

[13]And God never said this to an angel:

"Sit at my right side
until I put your enemies
under your power.[a]"

Psalm 110:1

[14]All the angels are spirits who serve God and are sent to help those who will receive salvation.

Our Salvation Is Greater Than the Law

2 [1]So we must be more careful to follow what we were taught. We must be careful so that we will not be pulled away from the true way. [2]The teaching that God spoke through angels was shown to be true. And every time his people did something against that teaching, they were punished for what they did. They were punished when they did not obey that teaching. [3]So surely we also will be punished if we don't pay attention to the salvation we have that is so great. It was the Lord Jesus who first told people about it. And those who heard him proved to us that it is true. [4]God also proved it by using miraculous signs,* wonders,* and all kinds of miracles.* And he proved it by giving people various gifts through the Holy Spirit* in just the way he wanted.

Christ Became Like People to Save Them

[5]God did not choose angels to be the rulers over the new world that was coming. That future world is the world we have been talking about. [6]It is written some place in the Scriptures,*

"Why are people so important to you?
Why do you even think about them?
Why do you care about the son of man[b]?
Is he so important?
[7]For a short time you made him lower than the angels.
You crowned him with glory* and honor.
[8]You put everything under his control.[c]"

Psalm 8:4–6

If God put everything under his control, then there was nothing left that he did not rule. But we don't yet see him ruling over everything. [9]For a short time Jesus was made lower than the angels, but now we see him wearing a crown of glory and honor because he suffered and died. Because of God's grace,* Jesus died for everyone.

[10]God—the one who made all things and for whose glory all things exist—wanted many people to be his children and share his glory. So he did what he needed to do. He made perfect the one who leads those people to salvation. He made Jesus a perfect Savior through his suffering.

[11]Jesus, the one who makes people holy,* and those who are made holy are from the same family. So he is not ashamed to call them his brothers and sisters. [12]He says,

"God, I will tell my brothers and sisters about you.
Before all your people I will sing your praises."

Psalm 22:22

[a] **1:13 until I put … power** Literally, "until I make your enemies a footstool for your feet."
[b] **2:6 son of man** This can mean any human, but the name "Son of Man" (see "SON OF MAN" in the Word List) is often used to mean Jesus, who showed what God planned for all people to be.
[c] **2:8 control** Literally, "feet."

13He also says,
"I will trust in God." *Isaiah 8:17*
And he says,
"I am here, and with me are
the children God has given
me." *Isaiah 8:18*
14These children are people with physical bodies. So Jesus himself became like them and had the same experiences they have. Jesus did this so that, by dying, he could destroy the one who has the power of death—the devil. 15Jesus became like these people and died so that he could free them. They were like slaves all their lives because of their fear of death. 16Clearly, it is not angels that Jesus helps. He helps the people who are from Abraham.* 17For this reason, Jesus had to be made like us, his brothers and sisters, in every way. He became like people so that he could be their merciful and faithful high priest* in service to God. Then he could bring forgiveness for the people's sins. 18And now he can help those who are tempted. He is able to help because he himself suffered and was tempted.

Jesus Is Greater Than Moses

3 1So, my brothers and sisters, those chosen by God to be his holy people,* think about Jesus. He is the one we believe God sent to save us and to be our high priest.* 2God made him our high priest, and he was faithful to God just as Moses* was. He did everything God wanted him to do in God's house. 3When someone builds a house, people will honor the builder more than the house. It is the same with Jesus. He should have more honor than Moses. 4Every house is built by someone, but God built everything. 5Moses was faithful as a servant in God's whole house. He told people what God would say in the future. 6But Christ is faithful in ruling God's house as the Son. And we are God's house, if we remain confident of the great hope we are glad to say we have.

We Must Continue to Follow God

7So it is just as the Holy Spirit* says:
"If you hear God's voice today,
8 don't be stubborn as you were
in the past, when you
turned against God.
That was the day you tested
God in the desert.
9 For 40 years in the desert, your
people saw what I did.
But they tested me and my
patience.
10 So I was angry with them.
I said, 'Their thoughts are
always wrong.
They have never understood
my ways.'
11 So I was angry and made
a promise:
'They will never enter my
place of rest.'" *Psalm 95:7–11*
12So, brothers and sisters, be careful that none of you has the evil thoughts that cause so much doubt that you stop following the living God. 13But encourage each other every day, while you still have something called "today.*a*" Help each other so that none of you will be fooled by sin and become too hard to change. 14We have the honor of sharing in all that Christ has if we continue until the end to have the sure faith we had in the beginning. 15That's why the Spirit said,

a 3:13 today This word is taken from verse 7. It means it is important to do this now, while there is still opportunity.

"If you hear God's voice today,
    don't be stubborn as in the
    past when you turned
    against God."   *Psalm 95:7–8*

[16]Who were those who heard God's voice and turned against him? It was all the people Moses* led out of Egypt. [17]And who was God angry with for 40 years? He was angry with those who sinned. And their dead bodies were left in the desert. [18]And which people was God talking to when he promised that they would never enter his place of rest? He was talking to those who did not obey him. [19]So we see that they were not allowed to enter and have God's rest, because they did not believe.

4 [1]And we still have the promise that God gave those people. That promise is that we can enter his place of rest. So we should be very careful that none of you fails to get that promise. [2]Yes, the good news about it was told to us just as it was to them. But the message they heard did not help them. They heard it but did not accept it with faith. [3]Only we who believe it are able to enter God's place of rest. As God said,

"I was angry and made
    a promise:
'They will never enter my
    place of rest.'"   *Psalm 95:11*

But God's work was finished from the time he made the world. [4]Yes, somewhere in the Scriptures* he talked about the seventh day of the week. He said, "So on the seventh day God rested from all his work."[a] [5]But in the Scripture above God said, "They will never enter my place of rest."

[6]So the opportunity is still there for some to enter and enjoy God's rest. But those who first heard the good news about it did not enter, because they did not obey. [7]So God planned another special day. It is called "today." He spoke about that day through David* a long time later using the words we quoted before:

"If you hear God's voice today,
    don't be stubborn." *Psalm 95:7–8*

[8]We know that Joshua* did not lead the people into the place of rest that God promised. We know this because God spoke later about another day for rest. [9]This shows that the seventh-day rest[b] for God's people is still to come. [10]God rested after he finished his work. So everyone who enters God's place of rest will also have rest from their own work just as God did. [11]So let us try as hard as we can to enter God's place of rest. We must try hard so that none of us will be lost by following the example of those who refused to obey God.

[12]God's word[c] is alive and working. It is sharper than the sharpest sword and cuts all the way into us. It cuts deep to the place where the soul and the spirit are joined. God's word cuts to the center of our joints and our bones. It judges the thoughts and feelings in our hearts. [13]Nothing in all the world can be hidden from God. He can clearly see all things. Everything is open before him. And to him we must explain the way we have lived.

---

[b] **4:9 seventh-day rest** Literally, "Sabbath rest," meaning a sharing in the rest God began after he created the world.
[c] **4:12 God's word** God's teachings and commands.

[a] **4:4** Quote from Gen. 2:2.

Jesus Christ Is Our High Priest

¹⁴We have a great high priest* who has gone to live with God in heaven. He is Jesus the Son of God. So let us continue to express our faith in him. ¹⁵Jesus, our high priest, is able to understand our weaknesses. When Jesus lived on earth, he was tempted in every way. He was tempted in the same ways we are tempted, but he never sinned. ¹⁶With Jesus as our high priest, we can feel free to come before God's throne where there is grace.* There we receive mercy and kindness to help us when we need it.

5 ¹Every Jewish high priest is chosen from among men. That priest is given the work of helping people with the things they must do for God. He must offer to God gifts and sacrifices* for sins. ²The high priest has his own weaknesses. So he is able to be gentle with those who do wrong out of ignorance. ³He offers sacrifices for their sins, but he must also offer sacrifices for his own sins.

⁴To be a high priest is an honor. But no one chooses himself for this work. That person must be chosen by God just as Aaron* was. ⁵It is the same with Christ. He did not choose himself to have the honor of becoming a high priest. But God chose him. God said to him,

> "You are my Son.
>> Today I have become your
>> Father."   *Psalm 2:7*

⁶And in another part of the Scriptures* God says,

> "You are a priest forever—
>> the kind of priest
>> Melchizedek* was."
>   *Psalm 110:4*

⁷While Jesus lived on earth he prayed to God, asking for help from the one who could save him from death. He prayed to God with loud cries and tears. And his prayers were answered because of his great respect for God. ⁸Jesus was the Son of God, but he still suffered, and through his sufferings he learned to obey whatever God says. ⁹This made him the perfect high priest, who provides the way for everyone who obeys him to be saved forever. ¹⁰God made him high priest, just like Melchizedek.

Warning Against Falling Away

¹¹We have many things to tell you about this. But it is hard to explain because you have stopped trying to understand. ¹²You have had enough time that by now you should be teachers. But you need someone to teach you again the first lessons of God's teaching. You still need the teaching that is like milk. You are not ready for solid food. ¹³Anyone who lives on milk is still a baby and is not able to understand much about living right. ¹⁴But solid food is for people who have grown up. From their experience they have learned to see the difference between good and evil.

6 ¹⁻²So we should be finished with the beginning lessons about Christ. We should not have to keep going back to where we started. We began our new life by turning away from the evil we did in the past and by believing in God. That's when we were taught about baptisms,^a laying hands on*

a **6:1-2 baptisms** The word here may mean the baptism (brief 'burial' in water) of believers in Christ, or it may mean Jewish ceremonial washings.

people, the resurrection* of those who have died, and the final judgment. Now we need to go forward to more mature teaching. ³And that's what we will do if God allows.

⁴⁻⁶After people have left the way of Christ, can you make them change their lives again? I am talking about people who once learned the truth, received God's gift, and shared in the Holy Spirit.* They were blessed to hear God's good message* and see the great power of his new world. But then they left it all behind, and it is not possible to make them change again. That's because those who leave Christ are nailing him to the cross again, shaming him before everyone.

⁷Some people are like land that gets plenty of rain and produces a good crop for those who farm it. That kind of land has God's blessing. ⁸But other people are like land that grows only thorns and weeds. It is worthless and in danger of being cursed by God. It will be destroyed by fire.

⁹Dear friends, I am not saying this because I think it is happening to you. We really expect that you will do better—that you will do the good things that will result in your salvation. ¹⁰God is fair, and he will remember all the work you have done. He will remember that you showed your love to him by helping his people and that you continue to help them. ¹¹We want each of you to be willing and eager to show your love like that the rest of your life. Then you will be sure to get what you hope for. ¹²We don't want you to be lazy. We want you to be like those who, because of their faith and patience, will get what God has promised.

¹³God made a promise to Abraham.* And there is no one greater than God, so he made the promise with an oath* in his own name— an oath that he would do what he promised. ¹⁴He said, "I will surely bless you. I will give you many descendants."ᵃ ¹⁵Abraham waited patiently for this to happen, and later he received what God promised.

¹⁶People always use the name of someone greater than themselves to make a promise with an oath. The oath proves that what they say is true, and there is no more arguing about it. ¹⁷God wanted to prove that his promise was true. He wanted to prove this to those who would get what he promised. He wanted them to understand clearly that his purposes never change. So God said something would happen, and he proved what he said by adding an oath. ¹⁸These two things cannot change: God cannot lie when he says something, and he cannot lie when he makes an oath.

So these two things are a great help to us who have come to God for safety. They encourage us to hold on to the hope that is ours. ¹⁹This hope is like an anchor for us. It is strong and sure and keeps us safe. It goes behind the curtain.ᵇ ²⁰Jesus has already entered there and opened the way for us. He has

---

ᵃ 6:14 Quote from Gen. 22:17.
ᵇ 6:19 curtain The spiritual curtain in the heavenly temple, which was symbolized by the physical one that separated the inner sanctuary (and God's presence) from the other room in the Holy Tent and in the Jerusalem Temple. See "CURTAIN" in the Word List. Also in 10:20.

become the high priest* forever, just like Melchizedek.*

The Priest Melchizedek

7 ¹Melchizedek* was the king of Salem and a priest for God the Most High. He met Abraham* when Abraham was coming back after defeating the kings. That day Melchizedek blessed him. ²Then Abraham gave him a tenth of everything he had.

The name Melchizedek, king of Salem, has two meanings. First, Melchizedek means "king of justice." And "king of Salem" means "king of peace." ³No one knows who his father or mother was or where he came from.ᵈ And no one knows when he was born or when he died. Melchizedek is like the Son of God in that he will always be a priest.

⁴You can see that Melchizedek was very great. Abraham, our great ancestor, gave him a tenth of everything he won in battle. ⁵Now the law says that those from the tribe of Levi who become priests must get a tenth from their own people, even though they and their people are both from the family of Abraham. ⁶Melchizedek was not even from the tribe of Levi, but Abraham gave him a tenth of what he had. And Melchizedek blessed Abraham—the one who had God's promises. ⁷And everyone knows that the more important person always blesses the less important person.

⁸Those priests get a tenth, but they are only men who live and then die. But Melchizedek, who got a tenth from Abraham, continues to live, as the Scriptures* say. ⁹Now those from the family of Levi are the ones who get a tenth from the people. But we can say that when Abraham paid Melchizedek a tenth, then Levi also paid it. ¹⁰Levi was not yet born, but he already existed in his ancestor Abraham when Melchizedek met him.

¹¹The people were given the law* under the system of priests from the tribe of Levi. But no one could be made spiritually perfect through that system of priests. So there was a need for another priest to come. I mean a priest like Melchizedek, not Aaron.* ¹²And when a different kind of priest comes, then the law must be changed too. ¹³⁻¹⁴We are talking about our Lord Christ, who belonged to a different tribe. No one from that tribe ever served as a priest at the altar.* It is clear that Christ came from the tribe of Judah. And Moses* said nothing about priests belonging to that tribe.

Jesus Is a Priest Like Melchizedek

¹⁵And these things become even clearer when we see that another priest has come who is like Melchizedek.* ¹⁶He was made a priest, but not because he met the requirement of being born into the right family. He became a priest by the power of a life that will never end. ¹⁷This is what the Scriptures* say about him: "You are a priest forever—the kind of priest Melchizedek was."ᵇ

¹⁸The old rule is now ended because it was weak and worthless. ¹⁹The Law of Moses* could not

---

ᵈ **7:3 No one ... came from** Literally, "Melchizedek was without father, without mother, without genealogy."

ᵇ **7:17** Quote from Ps. 110:4.

make anything perfect. But now a better hope has been given to us. And with that hope we can come near to God.

20Also, it is important that God made a promise with an oath* when he made Jesus high priest.* When those other men became priests, there was no oath. 21But Christ became a priest with God's oath. God said to him,

"The Lord has made a promise
     with an oath
and will not change his
     mind:
'You are a priest forever.'"

Psalm 110:4

22So this means that Jesus is the guarantee of a better agreement* from God to his people.

23Also, when one of those other priests died, he could not continue being a priest. So there were many of those priests. 24But Jesus lives forever. He will never stop serving as a priest. 25So Christ can save those who come to God through him. Christ can do this forever, because he always lives and is ready to help people when they come before God.

26So Jesus is the kind of high priest we need. He is holy. He has no sin in him. He is pure and not influenced by sinners. And he is raised above the heavens. 27He is not like those other priests. They had to offer sacrifices* every day, first for their own sins, and then for the sins of the people. But Jesus doesn't need to do that. He offered only one sacrifice for all time. He offered himself. 28The law chooses high priests who are men and have the same weaknesses that all people have. But after the law, God spoke the oath that made his Son high priest. And

that Son, made perfect through suffering, will serve forever.

Jesus Our High Priest

8 1Here is the point of what we are saying: We have a high priest* like that, who sits on the right side *a* of God's throne in heaven. 2Our high priest serves in the Most Holy Place.*b* He serves in the true place of worship*c* that was made by God, not by anyone here on earth.

3Every high priest has the work of offering gifts and sacrifices* to God. So our high priest must also offer something to God. 4If our high priest were now living on earth, he would not be a priest. I say this because there are already priests here who follow the law by offering gifts to God. 5The work that these priests do is really only a copy and a shadow of what is in heaven. That is why God warned Moses* when he was ready to build the Holy Tent*: "Be sure to make everything exactly like the pattern I showed you on the mountain."*d* 6But the work that has been given to Jesus is much greater than the work that was given to those priests. In the same way, the new agreement* that Jesus brought from God to his people is much greater than the old one. And the new agreement is based on better promises.

7If there was nothing wrong with the first agreement,* then there would be no need for a

---

a **8:1 right side** The place of honor and authority (power).
b **8:2 Most Holy Place** Literally, "holies" for "holy of holies," the spiritual place where God lives and is worshiped.
c **8:2 place of worship** Literally, "Tabernacle" or "tent."
d **8:5** Quote from Ex. 25:40.

second agreement. [8]But God found something wrong with the people. He said,

> "The time is coming, says the Lord,
> when I will give a new agreement to the people of Israel* and to the people of Judah.*
> [9] It will not be like the agreement that I gave to their fathers.
> That is the agreement I gave when I took them by the hand and led them out of Egypt.
> They did not continue following the agreement I gave them,
> and I turned away from them, says the Lord.
> [10] This is the new agreement I will give the people of Israel.
> I will give this agreement in the future, says the Lord:
> I will put my laws in their minds,
> and I will write my laws on their hearts.
> I will be their God,
> and they will be my people.
> [11] Never again will anyone have to teach their neighbors or their family to know the Lord.
> All people—the greatest and the least important—will know me.
> [12] And I will forgive the wrongs they have done,
> and I will not remember their sins."   *Jeremiah 31:31–34*

[13]God called this a new agreement, so he has made the first agreement old. And anything that is old and useless is ready to disappear.

Worship Under the Old Agreement

9 [1]The first agreement* had rules for worship and a place for worship here on earth. [2]This place was inside a tent. The first area in the tent was called the Holy Place. In the Holy Place were the lamp and the table with the special bread offered to God. [3]Behind the second curtain* was a room called the Most Holy Place.* [4]In the Most Holy Place was a golden altar* for burning incense.* And also there was the Box of the Agreement.* The Box was covered with gold. Inside this Box was a golden jar of manna* and Aaron's rod—the rod that once grew leaves. Also in the Box were the flat stones with the Ten Commandments of the old agreement on them. [5]Above the Box were the Cherub angels* that showed God's glory.* These Cherub angels were over the place of mercy.[a] But we cannot say everything about this now.

[6]Everything in the tent was made ready in the way I have explained. Then the priests went into the first room every day to do their worship duties. [7]But only the high priest* could go into the second room, and he went in only once a year. Also, he could never enter that room without taking blood with him. He offered that blood to God for himself and for the sins the people committed without knowing they were sinning.

[8]The Holy Spirit* uses those two separate rooms to teach us that

---

[a] **9:5 place of mercy** Or "mercy seat," a place on top of the "Box of the Agreement," where the high priest put the blood of an animal once a year to pay for the sins of the people.

the way into the Most Holy Place[a] was not open while the first room was still there. [9]This is an example for us today. It shows that the gifts and sacrifices* the priests offer to God are not able to make the consciences of the worshipers completely clear. [10]These gifts and sacrifices are only about food and drink and special washings. They are only rules about the body. God gave them for his people to follow until the time of his new way.

Worship Under the New Agreement

[11]But Christ has already come to be the high priest.* He is the high priest of the good things we now have. But Christ does not serve in a place like the tent that those other priests served in. He serves in a better place. Unlike that tent, this one is perfect. It was not made by anyone here on earth. It does not belong to this world. [12]Christ entered the Most Holy Place only one time—enough for all time. He entered the Most Holy Place by using his own blood, not the blood of goats or young bulls. He entered there and made us free from sin forever.

[13]The blood of goats and bulls and the ashes of a cow were sprinkled on those who were no longer pure enough to enter the place of worship. The blood and ashes made them pure again—but only their bodies. [14]So surely the blood sacrifice of Christ can do much more. Christ offered himself through the eternal Spirit[b] as a perfect sacrifice* to God. His blood will make us completely clean from the evil we have done. It will give us clear consciences so that we can worship the living God.

[15]So Christ brings a new agreement* from God to his people. He brings this agreement so that those who are chosen by God can have the blessings God promised, blessings that last forever. This can happen only because Christ died to free people from sins committed against the commands of the first agreement.*

[16]When someone dies and leaves a will,* there must be proof that the one who wrote the will is dead. [17]A will means nothing while the one who wrote it is still living. It can be used only after that person's death. [18]That is why blood was needed to begin the first agreement between God and his people. [19]First, Moses* told the people every command in the law. Then he took the blood of young bulls and mixed it with water. He used red wool and a branch of hyssop* to sprinkle the blood and water on the book of the law and on all the people. [20]Then he said, "This is the blood that makes the agreement good—the agreement that God commanded you to follow."[c] [21]In the same way, Moses sprinkled the blood on the Holy Tent.* He sprinkled the blood over everything used in worship. [22]The law* says that almost everything must be made clean by blood. Sins cannot be forgiven without a blood sacrifice.

Jesus Christ Is Our Sacrifice for Sin

[23]These things are copies of the real things that are in heaven

---

[a] **9:8 Most Holy Place** Literally, "holies" for "holy of holies," the spiritual place where God lives and is worshiped. Also in verses 12, 24.

[b] **9:14 Spirit** Probably the Holy Spirit. See "HOLY SPIRIT" in the Word List.

[c] **9:20** Quote from Ex. 24:8.

These copies had to be made clean by animal sacrifices.* But the real things in heaven must have much better sacrifices. 24Christ went into the Most Holy Place. But it was not the man-made one, which is only a copy of the real one. He went into heaven, and he is there now before God to help us.

25The high priest* enters the Most Holy Place* once every year. He takes with him blood to offer. But he does not offer his own blood like Christ did. Christ went into heaven, but not to offer himself many times like the high priest offers blood again and again. 26If Christ had offered himself many times, he would have needed to suffer many times since the time the world was made. But he came to offer himself only once. And that once is enough for all time. He came at a time when the world is nearing an end. He came to take away all sin by offering himself as a sacrifice.

27Everyone must die once. Then they are judged. 28So Christ was offered as a sacrifice one time to take away the sins of many people. And he will come a second time, but not to offer himself for sin. He will come the second time to bring salvation to those who are waiting for him.

Jesus Christ—the Only Sacrifice We Need

10 1The law* gave us only an unclear picture of the good things coming in the future. The law is not a perfect picture of the real things. The law tells people to offer the same sacrifices* every year. Those who come to worship God continue to offer those sacrifices. But the law can never make them perfect. 2If the law could make people perfect, those sacrifices would have already stopped. They would already be clean from their sins, and they would not still feel guilty. 3But that's not what happens. Their sacrifices make them remember their sins every year, 4because it is not possible for the blood of bulls and goats to take away sins.

5So when Christ came into the world he said,

"You don't want sacrifices and offerings,
but you have prepared a body for me.
6 You are not pleased with the sacrifices of animals killed and burned
or with offerings to take away sins.
7 Then I said, 'Here I am, God.
It is written about me in the book of the law.
I have come to do what you want.'" *Psalm 40:6-8*

8Christ first said, "You don't want sacrifices and offerings. You are not pleased with animals killed and burned or with sacrifices to take away sin." (These are all sacrifices that the law commands.) 9Then he said, "Here I am, God. I have come to do what you want." So God ends that first system of sacrifices and starts his new way. 10Jesus Christ did the things God wanted him to do. And because of that, we are made holy* through the sacrifice of Christ's body. Christ made that sacrifice one time—enough for all time.

11Every day the priests stand and do their religious service. Again and again they offer the same sacrifices, which can never take away sins. 12But Christ offered only one sacrifice for sins, and that sacrifice is good for all time. Then he sat down at the right side of God. [13]And now Christ waits there for his enemies to be put under his power.[a] [14]With one sacrifice Christ made his people perfect forever. They are the ones who are being made holy.

[15]The Holy Spirit* also tells us about this. First he says,

[16] "This is the agreement[b] I will make with my people in the future, says the Lord.
I will put my laws in their hearts.
I will write my laws in their minds."   Jeremiah 31:33

[17]Then he says,

"I will forget their sins and never again remember the evil they have done."
                Jeremiah 31:34

[18]And after everything is forgiven, there is no more need for a sacrifice to pay for sins.

Come Near to God

[19]And so, brothers and sisters, we are completely free to enter the Most Holy Place.[c] We can do this without fear because of the blood sacrifice of Jesus. [20]We enter through a new way that Jesus opened for us. It is a living way that leads through the curtain—Christ's body. [21]And we have a great priest who rules the house of God. [22]Sprinkled with the blood of Christ, our hearts have been made free from a guilty conscience, and our bodies have been washed with pure water. So come near to God with a sincere heart, full of confidence because of our faith in Christ. [23]We must hold on to the hope we have, never hesitating to tell people about it. We can trust God to do what he promised.

Help Each Other Be Strong

[24]We should think about each other to see how we can encourage each other to show love and do good works. [25]We must not quit meeting together, as some are doing. No, we need to keep on encouraging each other. This becomes more and more important as you see the Day* getting closer.

Don't Turn Away From God's Son

[26]If we decide to continue sinning after we have learned the truth, then there is no other sacrifice* that will take away sins. [27]If we continue sinning, all that is left for us is a fearful time of waiting for the judgment and the angry fire that will destroy those who live against God. [28]Whoever refused to obey the Law of Moses* was found guilty from the testimony given by two or three witnesses. Such people were not forgiven. They were killed. [29]So think how much more punishment people deserve who show their hate for the Son of God— people who show they have no respect for the blood sacrifice that began the new agreement and once made them holy or who insult the Spirit* of God's grace. [30]We know that God said, "I will punish people for the wrongs they do; I will repay them."[d] And he also said, "The Lord will judge his

---

[a] 10:13 to be put under his power Literally, "to be made a footstool for his feet."

[b] 10:16 agreement The new and better agreement that God has given to his people through Jesus. See "AGREEMENT" in the Word List.

[c] 10:19 Most Holy Place Literally, "holies" for "holy of holies," the spiritual place where God lives and is worshiped.

[d] 10:30 Quote from Deut. 32:35.

people."*a* ³¹It is a terrible thing to face punishment from the living God.

Keep the Courage and Patience You Had

³²Remember the days when you first learned the truth. You had a hard struggle with much suffering, but you continued strong. ³³Sometimes people said hateful things to you and mistreated you in public. And sometimes you helped others who were being treated that same way. ³⁴Yes, you helped them in prison and shared in their suffering. And you were still happy when everything you owned was taken away from you. You continued to be happy, because you knew that you had something much better—something that would continue forever.

³⁵So don't lose the courage that you had in the past. Your courage will be rewarded richly. ³⁶You must be patient. After you have done what God wants, you will get what he promised you. ³⁷He says,

"Very soon now, the one who is
    coming
  will come and will not be
    late.
³⁸ The person who is right with
    me
  will live by trusting in me.
  But I will not be pleased with
    the one
  who turns back in fear."

Habakkuk 2:3–4 (Greek version)

³⁹But we are not those who turn back and are lost. No, we are the people who have faith and are saved.

Faith

11 ¹Faith is what makes real the things we hope for. It is proof of what we cannot see. ²God was

pleased with the people who lived a long time ago because they had faith like this.

³Faith helps us understand that God created the whole world by his command. This means that the things we see were made by something that cannot be seen.

⁴Cain* and Abel* both offered sacrifices* to God. But Abel offered a better sacrifice to God because he had faith. God said he was pleased with what Abel offered. And so God called him a good man because he had faith. Abel died, but through his faith he is still speaking.

⁵Enoch was carried away from this earth, so he never died. The Scriptures* tell us that before he was carried off, he was a man who pleased God. Later, no one knew where he was, because God had taken Enoch to be with him. This all happened because he had faith. ⁶Without faith no one can please God. Whoever comes to God must believe that he is real and that he rewards those who sincerely try to find him.

⁷Noah was warned by God about things that he could not yet see. But he had faith and respect for God, so he built a large boat to save his family. With his faith, Noah showed that the world was wrong. And he became one of those who are made right with God through faith.

⁸God called Abraham to travel to another place that he promised to give him. Abraham did not know where that other place was. But he obeyed God and started traveling because he had faith. ⁹Abraham lived in the country that God promised to give him. He lived there like a visitor who

did not belong. He did this because he had faith. He lived in tents with Isaac and Jacob, who also received the same promise from God. [10]Abraham was waiting for the city[a] that has real foundations. He was waiting for the city that is planned and built by God.

[11]Sarah was not able to have children, and Abraham was too old. But he had faith in God, trusting him to do what he promised. And so God made them able to have children. [12]Abraham was so old he was almost dead. But from that one man came as many descendants as there are stars in the sky. So many people came from him that they are like grains of sand on the seashore.

[13]All these great people continued living with faith until they died. They did not get the things God promised his people. But they were happy just to see those promises coming far in the future. They accepted the fact that they were like visitors and strangers here on earth. [14]When people accept something like that, they show they are waiting for a country that will be their own. [15]If they were thinking about the country they had left, they could have gone back. [16]But they were waiting for a better country—a heavenly country. So God is not ashamed to be called their God. And he has prepared a city for them.

[17–18]God tested Abraham's faith. God told him to offer Isaac as a sacrifice. Abraham obeyed because he had faith. He already had the promises from God. And God had already said to him, "It is through Isaac that your descendants will come."[b] But Abraham was ready to offer his only son. He did this because he had faith. [19]He believed that God could raise people from death. And really, when God stopped Abraham from killing Isaac, it was as if he got him back from death.

[20]Isaac blessed the future of Jacob and Esau. He did that because he had faith. [21]And Jacob, also because he had faith, blessed each one of Joseph's sons. He did this while he was dying, leaning on his rod and worshiping God.

[22]And when Joseph was almost dead, he spoke about the people of Israel* leaving Egypt. And he told them what they should do with his body. He did this because he had faith.

[23]And the mother and father of Moses* hid him for three months after he was born. They did this because they had faith. They saw that Moses was a beautiful baby. And they were not afraid to disobey the king's order.

[24–25]Moses grew up and became a man. He refused to be called the son of Pharaoh's daughter. He chose not to enjoy the pleasures of sin that last such a short time. Instead, he chose to suffer with God's people. He did this because he had faith. [26]He thought it was better to suffer for the Messiah than to have all the treasures of Egypt. He was waiting for the reward that God would give him.

[27]Moses left Egypt because he had faith. He was not afraid of the king's anger. He continued strong

---

a **11:10 city** The spiritual "city" where God's people live with him. Also called "the heavenly Jerusalem." See Heb. 12:22.

b **11:17–18** Quote from Gen. 21:12.

as if he could see the God no one can see. ²⁸Moses prepared the Passover* and spread the blood on the doorways of the people of Israel, so that the angel of death*ᵃ would not kill their firstborn* sons. Moses did this because he had faith.

²⁹And God's people all walked through the Red Sea as if it were dry land. They were able to do this because they had faith. But when the Egyptians tried to follow them, they were drowned.

³⁰And the walls of Jericho fell because of the faith of God's people. They marched around the walls for seven days, and then the walls fell.

³¹And Rahab, the prostitute, welcomed the Israelite* spies like friends. And because of her faith, she was not killed with the ones who refused to obey.

³²Do I need to give you more examples? I don't have enough time to tell you about Gideon, Barak, Samson, Jephthah, David, Samuel, and the prophets.* ³³All of them had great faith. And with that faith they defeated kingdoms. They did what was right, and God helped them in the ways he promised. With their faith some people closed the mouths of lions. ³⁴And some were able to stop blazing fires. Others escaped from being killed with swords. Some who were weak were made strong. They became powerful in battle and defeated other armies. ³⁵There were women who lost loved ones but got them back when they were raised from

death. Others were tortured* but refused to accept their freedom. They did this so that they could be raised from death to a better life. ³⁶Some were laughed at and beaten. Others were tied up and put in prison. ³⁷They were killed with stones. They were cut in half. They were killed with swords. The only clothes some of them had were sheepskins or goatskins. They were poor, persecuted,* and treated badly by others. ³⁸The world was not good enough for these great people. They had to wander in deserts and mountains, living in caves and holes in the ground.

³⁹God was pleased with all of them because of their faith. But not one of them received God's great promise. ⁴⁰God planned something better for us. He wanted to make us perfect. Of course, he wanted those great people to be made perfect too, but not before we could all enjoy that blessing together.

We Also Should Follow Jesus' Example

12 ¹We have all these great people around us as examples. Their lives tell us what faith means. So we, too, should run the race that is before us and never quit. We should remove from our lives anything that would slow us down and the sin that so often makes us fall. ²We must never stop looking to Jesus. He is the leader of our faith, and he is the one who makes our faith complete. He suffered death on a cross. But he accepted the shame of the cross as if it were nothing because of the joy he could see waiting for him. And now he is sitting at the right side of God's throne. ³Think about Jesus. He patiently endured

11:28 angel of death Literally, "the destroyer." To punish the Egyptians, God sent an angel to kill the oldest son in each home. See Ex. 12:29–32.

the angry insults that sinful people were shouting at him. Think about him so that you won't get discouraged and stop trying.

God Is Like a Father

⁴You are struggling against sin, but you have not had to give up your life for the cause. ⁵You are children of God, and he speaks words of comfort to you. You have forgotten these words:

"My child, don't think the
   Lord's discipline is worth
   nothing,
and don't stop trying when
   he corrects you.
⁶ The Lord disciplines everyone
   he loves;
he punishes everyone
   he accepts as a child."

Proverbs 3:11-12

⁷So accept sufferings like a father's discipline. God does these things to you like a father correcting his children. You know that all children are disciplined by their fathers. ⁸So, if you never receive the discipline that every child must have, you are not true children and don't really belong to God. ⁹We have all had fathers here on earth who corrected us with discipline. And we respected them. So it is even more important that we accept discipline from the Father of our spirits. If we do this, we will have life. ¹⁰Our fathers on earth disciplined us for a short time in the way they thought was best. But God disciplines us to help us so that we can be holy* like him. ¹¹We don't enjoy discipline when we get it. It is painful. But later, after we have learned our lesson from it, we will enjoy the peace that comes from doing what is right.

Be Careful How You Live

¹²You have become weak, so make yourselves strong again. ¹³Live in the right way so that you will be saved and your weakness will not cause you to be lost.

¹⁴Try to live in peace with everyone. And try to keep your lives free from sin. Anyone whose life is not holy* will never see the Lord. ¹⁵Be careful that no one fails to get God's grace.* Be careful that no one loses their faith and becomes like a bitter weed growing among you. Someone like that can ruin your whole group. ¹⁶Be careful that no one commits sexual sin. And be careful that no one is like Esau and never thinks about God. As the oldest son, Esau would have inherited everything from his father. But he sold all that for a single meal. ¹⁷You remember that after Esau did this, he wanted to get his father's blessing. He wanted that blessing so much that he cried. But his father refused to give him the blessing, because Esau could find no way to change what he had done.

¹⁸You have not come to a place that can be seen and touched, like the mountain the people of Israel* saw, which was burning with fire and covered with darkness, gloom, and storms. ¹⁹There is no sound of a trumpet or a voice speaking words like those they heard. When they heard the voice, they begged never to hear another word. ²⁰They did not want to hear the command: "If anything, even an animal, touches the mountain it must be killed with stones."ᵃ ²¹What they saw was so terrible

ᵃ **12:20** Quote from Ex. 19:12–13.

that Moses said, "I am shaking with fear."[a][b]

22But you have come to Mount Zion,* to the city of the living God, the heavenly Jerusalem.[c] You have come to a place where thousands of angels have gathered to celebrate. 23You have come to the meeting of God's firstborn[d] children. Their names are written in heaven. You have come to God, the judge of all people. And you have come to the spirits of good people who have been made perfect. 24You have come to Jesus—the one who brought the new agreement* from God to his people. You have come to the sprinkled blood[e] that tells us about better things than the blood of Abel.*

25Be careful and don't refuse to listen when God speaks. Those people refused to listen to him when he warned them on earth. And they did not escape. Now God is speaking from heaven. So now it will be worse for those who refuse to listen to him. 26When he spoke before, his voice shook the earth. But now he has promised, "Once again I will shake the earth, but I will also shake heaven."[f] 27The words "once again" clearly show us that everything that was created will be destroyed—that

is, the things that can be shaken. And only what cannot be shaken will remain.

28So we should be thankful because we have a kingdom that cannot be shaken. And because we are thankful, we should worship God in a way that will please him. We should do this with respect and fear, 29because our God is like a fire that can destroy us.

Worship That Pleases God

13 1Continue loving each other as brothers and sisters in Christ. 2Always remember to help people by welcoming them into your home. Some people have done that and have helped angels without knowing it. 3Don't forget those who are in prison. Remember them as though you were in prison with them. And don't forget those who are suffering. Remember them as though you were suffering with them.

4Marriage should be honored by everyone. And every marriage should be kept pure between husband and wife. God will judge guilty those who commit sexual sins and adultery.* 5Keep your lives free from the love of money. And be satisfied with what you have. God has said,

"I will never leave you;
 I will never run away from
  you."   *Deuteronomy 31:6*

6So we can feel sure and say,

"The Lord is my helper;
 I will not be afraid.
People can do nothing to me."
     Psalm 118:6

7Remember your leaders. They taught God's message to you. Remember how they lived and died, and copy their faith. 8Jesus Christ is the same yesterday, today, and forever. 9Don't let all kinds of

---

12:21 Quote from Deut. 9:19.
12:18–21 These verses refer to things that happened to the people of Israel in the time of Moses as described in Ex. 19.
12:22 Jerusalem Here, the spiritual city of God's people.
12:23 firstborn The first son born in a Jewish family had the most important place in the family and received special blessings. All of God's children are like that.
12:24 sprinkled blood The blood (death) of Jesus.
12:26 Quote from Hag. 2:6.

strange teachings lead you into the wrong way. Depend only on God's grace* for spiritual strength, not on rules about foods. Obeying those rules doesn't help anyone.

[10]We have a sacrifice.[a] And those priests who serve in the Holy Tent* cannot eat from the sacrifice we have. [11]The high priest* carries the blood of animals into the Most Holy Place[b] and offers that blood for sins. But the bodies of those animals are burned outside the camp. [12]So Jesus also suffered outside the city. He died to make his people holy* with his own blood. [13]So we should go to Jesus outside the camp and accept the same shame that he had. [14]Here on earth we don't have a city that lasts forever. But we are waiting for the city that we will have in the future. [15]So through Jesus we should never stop offering our sacrifice* to God. That sacrifice is our praise, coming from lips that speak his name. [16]And don't forget to do good and to share what you have with others, because sacrifices like these are very pleasing to God.

[17]Obey your leaders. Be willing to do what they say. They are responsible for your spiritual welfare, so they are always watching to protect you. Obey them so that their work will give them joy, not grief. It won't help you to make it hard for them.

[18]Continue praying for us. We feel right about what we do, because we always try to do what is best. [19]And I beg you to pray that God will send me back to you soon. I want this more than anything else.

[20-21]I pray that the God of peace will give you every good thing you need so that you can do what he wants. God is the one who raised from death our Lord Jesus, the Great Shepherd of his sheep. He raised him because Jesus sacrificed his blood to begin the new agreement* that never ends. I pray that God will work through Jesus Christ to do the things in us that please him. To him be glory* forever. Amen.*

[22]My brothers and sisters, I beg you to listen patiently to what I have said. I wrote this letter to strengthen you. And it is not very long. [23]I want you to know that our brother Timothy is out of prison. If he comes to me soon, we will both come to see you.

[24]Give my greetings to all your leaders and to all God's people. All those from Italy send you their greetings.

[25]God's grace be with you all.

---

[a] **13:10 sacrifice** Literally, "altar." Here, it means the sacrifice (offering) of Jesus. He gave his life to pay for people's sins.
[b] **13:11 Most Holy Place** Literally, "the holies," the place in the Jewish Tabernacle or Temple where God met the high priest.

James

1 ¹Greetings from James, a servant of God and of the Lord Jesus Christ.

To God's people*a* who are scattered all over the world.

Faith and Wisdom

²My brothers and sisters, you will have many kinds of trouble. But this gives you a reason to be very happy. ³You know that when your faith is tested, you learn to be patient in suffering. ⁴If you let that patience work in you, the end result will be good. You will be mature and complete. You will be all that God wants you to be.

⁵Do any of you need wisdom? Ask God for it. He is generous and enjoys giving to everyone. So he will give you wisdom. ⁶But when you ask God, you must believe. Don't doubt him. Whoever doubts is like a wave in the sea that is blown up and down by the wind. ⁷⁻⁸People like that are thinking two different things at the same time. They can never decide what to do. So they should not think they will receive anything from the Lord.

True Riches

⁹Believers who are poor should be glad that God considers them so important. ¹⁰Believers who are rich should be glad when bad things happen that humble them. Their riches won't keep them from disappearing as quickly as wildflowers. ¹¹As the sun rises and gets hotter, its heat dries up the plants, and the flowers fall off. The flowers that were so beautiful are now dead. That's how it is with the rich. While they are still making plans for their business, they will die.

Temptation Does Not Come From God

¹²Great blessings belong to those who are tempted and remain faithful! After they have proved their faith, God will give them the reward*b* of eternal life. God promised this to all people who love him. ¹³Whenever you feel tempted to do something bad, you should not say, "God is tempting me." Evil cannot tempt God, and God himself does not tempt anyone. ¹⁴You are tempted by the evil things you want. Your own desire leads you away and traps you. ¹⁵Your desire grows inside you until it results in sin. Then the sin grows bigger and bigger and finally ends in death.

¹⁶My dear brothers and sisters, don't be fooled about this. ¹⁷Everything good comes from God. Every perfect gift is from him.

1:1 God's people Literally, "the twelve tribes." Believers in Christ are like the tribes of Israel, God's chosen people in the Old Testament.

b **1:12 reward** Literally, "wreath," a ring of leaves or branches that was placed on the head of the winners of athletic contests to honor them. It was a symbol of victory and reward.

These good gifts come down from the Father who made all the lights in the sky. But God never changes like the shadows from those lights. He is always the same. [18]God decided to give us life through the true message* he sent to us. He wanted us to be the most important of all that he created.

Listening and Obeying

[19]My dear brothers and sisters, always be more willing to listen than to speak. Keep control of your anger. [20]Anger does not help you live the way God wants. [21]So get rid of everything evil in your lives—every kind of wrong you do. Be humble and accept God's teaching that is planted in your hearts. This teaching can save you.

[22]Do what God's teaching says; don't just listen and do nothing. When you only sit and listen, you are fooling yourselves. [23]Hearing God's teaching and doing nothing is like looking at your face in the mirror [24]and doing nothing about what you saw. You go away and immediately forget how bad you looked. [25]But when you look into God's perfect law that sets people free, pay attention to it. If you do what it says, you will have God's blessing. Never just listen to his teaching and forget what you heard.

The True Way to Worship God

[26]You might think you are a very religious person. But if your tongue is out of control, you are fooling yourself. Your careless talk makes your offerings to God worthless. [27]The worship that God wants is this: caring for orphans or widows who need help and keeping yourself free from the world's evil influence. This is the kind of worship that God accepts as pure and good.

Love All People

2 [1]My dear brothers and sisters, you are believers in our glorious Lord Jesus Christ. So don't treat some people better than others. [2]Suppose someone comes into your meeting wearing very nice clothes and a gold ring. At the same time a poor person comes in wearing old, dirty clothes. [3]You show special attention to the person wearing nice clothes. You say, "Sit here in this good seat." But you say to the poor person, "Stand there!" or "Sit on the floor by our feet!" [4]Doesn't this show that you think some people are more important than others? You set yourselves up as judges—judges who make bad decisions.

[5]Listen, my dear brothers and sisters. God chose the poor people in the world to be rich in faith. He chose them to receive the kingdom* God promised to those who love him. [6]But you show no respect to those who are poor. And you know that the rich are the ones who always try to control your lives. And they are the ones who take you to court. [7]And the rich are the ones who insult the wonderful name of Christ, the name by which you are known.

[8]One law rules over all other laws. This royal law is found in the Scriptures*: "Love your neighbor the same as you love yourself."[b] I you obey this law, you are doing right. [9]But if you are treating one person as more important than

a 2:8 your neighbor Or "others." Jesus' teaching in Lk. 10:25–37 makes clear that this includes anyone in need.
b 2:8 Quote from Lev. 19:18.

another, you are sinning. You are guilty of breaking God's law.

¹⁰You might follow all of God's law. But if you fail to obey only one command, you are guilty of breaking all the commands in that law. ¹¹God said, "Don't commit adultery.*"ᵃ The same God also said, "Don't kill."ᵇ So if you don't commit adultery, but you kill someone, you are guilty of breaking all of God's law.

¹²You will be judged by the law that makes people free. You should remember this in everything you say and do. ¹³Yes, you must show mercy to others. If you do not show mercy, then God will not show mercy to you when he judges you. But the one who shows mercy can stand without fear before the Judge.

Faith and Good Works

¹⁴My brothers and sisters, if a person claims to have faith but does nothing, that faith is worth nothing. Faith like that cannot save anyone. ¹⁵Suppose a brother or sister in Christ comes to you in need of clothes or something to eat. ¹⁶And you say to them, "God be with you! I hope you stay warm and get plenty to eat," but you don't give them the things they need. If you don't help them, your words are worthless. ¹⁷It is the same with faith. If it is just faith and nothing more—if it doesn't do anything—it is dead.

¹⁸But someone might argue, "Some people have faith, and others have good works." My answer would be that you can't show me your faith if you don't do anything. But I will show you my faith by

the good I do. ¹⁹You believe there is one God. That's good, but even the demons* believe that! And they shake with fear.

²⁰You fool! Faith that does nothing is worth nothing. Do you want me to prove this to you? ²¹Our father* Abraham* was made right with God by what he did. He offered his son Isaac to God on the altar.* ²²So you see that Abraham's faith and what he did worked together. His faith was made perfect by what he did. ²³This shows the full meaning of the Scriptures* that say, "Abraham believed God, and because of this faith he was accepted as one who is right with God."ᶜ Abraham was called "God's friend."ᵈ ²⁴So you see that people are made right with God by what they do. They cannot be made right by faith alone.

²⁵Another example is Rahab. She was a prostitute, but she was made right with God by something she did. She helped those who were spying for God's people. She welcomed them into her home and helped them escape by a different road.ᵉ

²⁶A person's body that does not have a spirit is dead. It is the same with faith—faith that does nothing is dead!

Controlling the Things We Say

3 ¹My brothers and sisters, not many of you should be teachers. I say this because, as you know, we who teach will be judged more strictly than others.

²We all make many mistakes. A person who never said anything wrong would be perfect. Someone

---

ᶜ **2:23** Quote from Gen. 15:6.
ᵈ **2:23** Quote from 2 Chron. 20:7; Isa. 41:8.
ᵉ **2:25 She helped ... road** The story about Rahab is found in Josh. 2:1–21.

like that would be able to control their whole body too. ³We put bits into the mouths of horses to make them obey us. With these bits we can control their whole body. ⁴It is the same with ships. A ship is very big, and it is pushed by strong winds. But a very small rudder controls that big ship. And the one who controls the rudder decides where the ship will go. It goes where he wants it to go. ⁵It is the same with our tongue. It is a small part of the body, but it can boast about doing great things.

A big forest fire can be started with only a little flame. ⁶The tongue is like a fire. It is a world of evil among the parts of our body. It spreads its evil through our whole body and starts a fire that influences all of life. It gets this fire from hell.

⁷Humans have control over every kind of wild animal, bird, reptile, and fish, and they have controlled all these things. ⁸But no one can control the tongue. It is wild and evil, full of deadly poison. ⁹We use our tongues to praise our Lord and Father, but then we curse people who were created in God's likeness. ¹⁰These praises and curses come from the same mouth. My brothers and sisters, this should not happen. ¹¹Do good water and bad water flow from the same spring? Of course not. ¹²My brothers and sisters, can a fig tree make olives? Or can a grapevine make figs? No, and a well full of salty water cannot give good water.

True Wisdom

¹³Are there any among you who are really wise and understanding? Then you should show your wisdom by living right. You should do what is good with humility. A wise person does not boast. ¹⁴If you are selfish and have bitter jealousy in your hearts, you have no reason to boast. Your boasting is a lie that hides the truth. ¹⁵That kind of "wisdom" does not come from God. That "wisdom" comes from the world. It is not spiritual. It is from the devil. ¹⁶Where there is jealousy and selfishness, there will be confusion and every kind of evil. ¹⁷But the wisdom that comes from God is like this: First, it is pure. It is also peaceful, gentle, and easy to please. This wisdom is always ready to help people who have trouble and to do good for others. This wisdom is always fair and honest. ¹⁸People who work for peace in a peaceful way get the blessings that come from right living.

Give Yourselves to God

4 ¹Do you know where your fights and arguments come from? They come from the selfish desires that make war inside you. ²You want things, but you don't get them. So you kill and are jealous of others. But you still cannot get what you want. So you argue and fight. You don't get what you want because you don't ask God. ³Or when you ask, you don't receive anything, because the reason you ask is wrong. You only want to use it for your own pleasure.

⁴You people are not faithful to God! You should know that loving what the world has is the same as hating God. So anyone who wants to be friends with this evil world becomes God's enemy. ⁵Do you think the Scriptures* mean nothing? The Scriptures say, "The Spirit* God made to live in u

wants us only for himself."[a] [6]But the kindness God shows is greater. As the Scripture says, "God is against the proud, but he is kind to the humble."[b]

[7]So give yourselves to God. Stand against the devil, and he will run away from you. [8]Come near to God and he will come near to you. You are sinners, so clean sin out of your lives.[c] You are trying to follow God and the world at the same time. Make your thinking pure. [9]Be sad, be sorry, and cry! Change your laughter into crying. Change your joy into sadness. [10]Be humble before the Lord, and he will make you great.

You Are Not the Judge

[11]Brothers and sisters, don't say anything against each other. If you criticize your brother or sister in Christ or judge them, you are criticizing and judging the law they follow. And when you are judging the law, you are not a follower of the law. You have become a judge. [12]God is the one who gave us the law, and he is the judge. He is the only one who can save and destroy. So it is not right for you to judge anyone.

Let God Plan Your Life

[13]Some of you say, "Today or tomorrow we will go to some city. We will stay there a year, do business, and make money." Listen, think about this: [14]You don't know what will happen tomorrow. Your life is like a fog. You can see it for a

short time, but then it goes away. [15]So you should say, "If the Lord wants, we will live and do this or that." [16]But now you are proud and boast about yourself. All such boasting is wrong. [17]If you fail to do what you know is right, you are sinning.

A Warning to Rich and Selfish People

5 [1]You rich people, listen! Cry and be very sad because much trouble will come to you. [2]Your riches will rot and be worth nothing. Your clothes will be eaten by moths. [3]Your gold and silver will rust, and that rust will be a proof that you were wrong. That rust will eat your bodies like fire. You saved your treasure in the last days. [4]People worked in your fields, but you did not pay them. They are crying out against you. They harvested your crops. Now the Lord All-Powerful has heard their cries.

[5]Your life on earth was full of rich living. You pleased yourselves with everything you wanted. You made yourselves fat, like an animal ready for the day of slaughter.[d] [6]You showed no mercy to good people. They were not against you, but you killed them.

Be Patient

[7]Brothers and sisters, be patient; the Lord will come. So be patient until that time. Look at the farmers. They have to be patient. They have to wait for their valuable crop to grow and produce a harvest. They wait patiently for the first rain and the last rain.[e]

4:5 "The Spirit ... himself" Other possible translations: "God strongly desires the Spirit that he made to live in us." Or "The Spirit that he made to live in us is full of envious desires." See Ex. 20:5.
4:6 Quote from Prov. 3:34.
4:8 so clean sin out of your lives Literally, "so wash your hands."

d 5:5 You made yourselves fat ... slaughter Literally, "You fattened your hearts for the day of slaughter."
e 5:7 first rain ... last rain The "first rain" came in the fall, and the "last rain" came in the spring.

8You must be patient too. Never stop hoping. The Lord is coming soon. 9Brothers and sisters, don't complain against each other. If you don't stop complaining, you will be judged guilty. And the Judge is ready to come!

10Brothers and sisters, follow the example of the prophets* who spoke for the Lord. They suffered many bad things, but they were patient. 11And we say that those who accepted their troubles with patience now have God's blessing. You have heard about Job's patience.a You know that after all his troubles, the Lord helped him. This shows that the Lord is full of mercy and is kind.

Be Careful What You Say

12My brothers and sisters, it is very important that you not use an oath when you make a promise. Don't use the name of heaven, earth, or anything else to prove what you say. When you mean yes, say only "yes." When you mean no, say only "no." Do this so that you will not be judged guilty.

The Power of Prayer

13Are you having troubles? You should pray. Are you happy? You should sing. 14Are you sick? Ask the elders* of the church* to come and rub oil on youb in the name of the Lord and pray for you. 15If such a prayer is offered in faith, it will heal anyone who is sick. The Lord will heal them. And if they have sinned, he will forgive them.

16So always tell each other the wrong things you have done. Then pray for each other. Do this so that God can heal you. Anyone who lives the way God wants can pray, and great things will happen. 17Elijah* was a person just like us. He prayed that it would not rain. And it did not rain on the land for three and a half years! 18Then Elijah prayed that it would rain. And the rain came down from the sky, and the land grew crops again.

Helping People When They Sin

19My brothers and sisters, if anyone wanders away from the truth and someone helps that person come back, 20remember this: Anyone who brings a sinner back from the wrong way will save that person from eternal death and cause many sins to be forgiven.

a 5:11 Job's patience See the book of Job in the Old Testament.

b 5:14 rub oil on you Oil was used like medicine.

Peter speaks during Pentecost
Acts 2:14-41

© WBTC 2011

Philip teaches a man from Ethiopia
Acts 8:26-40

© WBTC 2011

1 Peter

1 ¹Greetings from Peter, an apostle* of Jesus Christ.

To God's chosen people who are away from their homes—people scattered all over the areas of Pontus, Galatia, Cappadocia, Asia, and Bithynia. ²God planned long ago to choose you and to make you his holy people,* which is the Spirit's* work. God wanted you to obey him and to be made clean by the blood sacrifice*a* of Jesus Christ.

I pray that you will enjoy more and more of God's grace* and peace.

A Living Hope

³Praise be to the God and Father of our Lord Jesus Christ. God has great mercy, and because of his mercy he gave us a new life. This new life brings us a living hope through Jesus Christ's resurrection from death. ⁴Now we wait to receive the blessings God has for his children. These blessings are kept for you in heaven. They cannot be ruined or be destroyed or lose their beauty.

⁵God's power protects you through your faith, and it keeps you safe until your salvation comes. That salvation is ready to be given to you at the end of time. ⁶I know the thought of that is exciting, even if you must suffer through different kinds of troubles for a short time now. ⁷These troubles test your faith and prove that it is pure. And such faith is worth more than gold. Gold can be proved to be pure by fire, but gold will ruin. When your faith is proven to be pure, the result will be praise and glory* and honor when Jesus Christ comes.

⁸You have not seen Christ, but still you love him. You can't see him now, but you believe in him. You are filled with a wonderful and heavenly joy that cannot be explained. ⁹Your faith has a goal, and you are reaching that goal— your salvation.

¹⁰The prophets* studied carefully and tried to learn about this salvation. They spoke about the grace* that was coming to you. ¹¹The Spirit* of Christ was in those prophets. And the Spirit was telling about the sufferings that would happen to Christ and about the glory that would come after those sufferings. The prophets tried to learn about what the Spirit was showing them—when it would happen and what the world would be like at that time.

¹²It was made clear to them that their service was not for themselves. They were serving you

---

a 1:2 made clean ... sacrifice Or "sprinkled with the blood," which probably compares the beginning of the new agreement by the blood sacrifice of Christ (Mk. 14:24) with Moses' sprinkling the blood of animal sacrifices on the people of Israel to seal the agreement God made with them (Ex. 4:3–8). See also Heb. 9:15–26.

when they told about the things you have now heard. You heard them from those who told you the Good News* with the help of the Holy Spirit sent from heaven. Even the angels would like very much to know more about these things you were told.

A Call to Holy Living

13So prepare your minds for service. With complete self-control put all your hope in the grace* that will be yours when Jesus Christ comes. 14In the past you did not have the understanding you have now, so you did the evil things you wanted to do. But now you are children of God, so you should obey him and not live the way you did before. 15Be holy* in everything you do, just as God is holy. He is the one who chose you. 16In the Scriptures* God says, "Be holy, because I am holy."*a*

17You pray to God and call him Father, but he will judge everyone the same way—by what they do. So while you are visiting here on earth, you should live with respect for God. 18You know that in the past the way you were living was useless. It was a way of life you learned from those who lived before you. But you were saved from that way of living. You were bought, but not with things that ruin like gold or silver. 19You were bought with the precious blood of Christ's death. He was a pure and perfect sacrificial Lamb.* 20Christ was chosen before the world was made, but he was shown to the world in these last times for you. 21You believe in God through Christ. God is the one who raised him from death and gave honor

to him. So your faith and your hope are in God.

22You have made yourselves pure by obeying the truth. Now you can have true love for your brothers and sisters. So love each other deeply—with all your heart. 23You have been born again. This new life did not come from something that dies. It came from something that cannot die. You were born again through God's life-giving message* that lasts forever. 24The Scriptures say,

"Our lives are like the grass of
  spring,
and any glory* we enjoy
  is like the beauty of
  a wildflower.
The grass dries up and dies,
  and the flower falls to the
  ground.
25 But the word of the Lord lasts
  forever."   *Isaiah 40:6–8*
And that word is the Good News*
that was told to you.

The Living Stone and the Holy Nation

2 1So then, stop doing anything to hurt others. Don't lie anymore, and stop trying to fool people. Don't be jealous or say bad things about others. 2Like newborn babies hungry for milk, you should want the pure teaching that feeds your spirit. With it you can grow up and be saved. 3You have already tasted the goodness of the Lord.

4The Lord Jesus is the living stone.*b* The people of the world decided that they did not want this stone. But he is the one God chose as one of great value. So come to him. 5You also are like living stones, and God is using you

---

a **1:16** Quote from Lev. 11:44, 45; 19:2; 20:7.

b **2:4 stone** The most important stone in God's spiritual temple or house (his people) to build a spiritual house.*ᵃ* You are to serve God in this house as holy* priests, offering him spiritual sacrifices* that he will accept because of Jesus Christ. ⁶The Scriptures* say,

"Look, I have chosen a
  cornerstone* of great value,
  and I put that stone in Zion.*
Anyone who trusts in him
  will never be disappointed."
Isaiah 28:16

⁷So, that stone brings honor for you who believe. But for those who don't believe he is

"the stone that the builders
  refused to accept,
  which became the most
  important stone." *Psalm 118:22*

⁸For them he is also

"a stone that makes people
  stumble,
  a rock that makes people
  fall." *Isaiah 8:14*

People stumble because they don't obey what God says. This is what God planned to happen to those people.

⁹But you are his chosen people, the King's priests. You are a holy nation, people who belong to God. He chose you to tell about the wonderful things he has done. He brought you out of the darkness of sin into his wonderful light. ¹⁰ In the past you were not a
  special people,
  but now you are God's people.
Once you had not received
  mercy,
  but now God has given you
  his mercy.*ᵇ*

Live for God

¹¹Dear friends, you are like visitors and strangers in this world. So I beg you to keep your lives free from the evil things you want to do, those desires that fight against your true selves. ¹²People who don't believe are living all around you. They may say that you are doing wrong. So live such good lives that they will see the good you do, and they will give glory* to God on the day he comes.

Obey Every Human Authority

¹³Be willing to serve the people who have authority*ᶜ* in this world. Do this for the Lord. Obey the king, the highest authority. ¹⁴And obey the leaders who are sent by the king. They are sent to punish those who do wrong and to praise those who do good. ¹⁵When you do good, you stop ignorant people from saying foolish things about you. This is what God wants. ¹⁶Live like free people, but don't use your freedom as an excuse to do evil. Live as those who are serving God. ¹⁷Show respect for all people. Love your brothers and sisters in God's family. Respect God, and honor the king.

The Example of Christ's Suffering

¹⁸Slaves, be willing to serve your masters. Do this with all respect. You should obey the masters who are good and kind, and you should obey the masters who are bad. ¹⁹One of you might have to suffer even when you have done nothing wrong. If you think of God and bear the pain, this pleases God. ²⁰But if you are punished for doing wrong, there is no reason

---

2:5 house God's house—the place where God's people worship him. Here, it means that believers are the spiritual building where God lives.

2:10 In the past ... his mercy See Hos. 2:23.

ᶜ **2:13 people ... authority** Literally, "every human creation," meaning rulers, governors, presidents, or other government leaders.

to praise you for bearing that punishment. But if you suffer for doing good and you are patient, this pleases God. 21This is what you were chosen to do. Christ gave you an example to follow. He suffered for you. So you should do the same as he did:

22 "He never sinned,
    and he never told a lie."

Isaiah 53:9

23People insulted him, but he did not insult them back. He suffered, but he did not threaten anyone. No, he let God take care of him. God is the one who judges rightly. 24Christ carried our sins in his body on the cross. He did this so that we would stop living for sin and live for what is right. By his wounds you were healed. 25You were like sheep that went the wrong way. But now you have come back to the Shepherd and Protector of your lives.

Wives and Husbands

3 1In the same way, you wives should be willing to serve your husbands. Then, even those who have refused to accept God's teaching will be persuaded to believe because of the way you live. You will not need to say anything. 2Your husbands will see the pure lives that you live with respect for God. 3It is not fancy hair, gold jewelry, or fine clothes that should make you beautiful. 4No, your beauty should come from inside you—the beauty of a gentle and quiet spirit. That beauty will never disappear. It is worth very much to God.

5It was the same with the holy* women who lived long ago and followed God. They made themselves beautiful in that same way. They were willing to serve their husbands. 6I am talking about women like Sarah. She obeyed Abraham,* her husband, and called him her master. And you women are true children of Sarah if you always do what is right and are not afraid.

7In the same way, you husbands should live with your wives in an understanding way, since they are weaker than you. You should show them respect, because God gives them the same blessing he gives you—the grace* of true life. Do this so that nothing will stop your prayers from being heard.

Suffering for Doing Right

8So all of you should live together in peace. Try to understand each other. Love each other like brothers and sisters. Be kind and humble. 9Don't do wrong to anyone to pay them back for doing wrong to you. Or don't insult anyone to pay them back for insulting you. But ask God to bless them. Do this because you yourselves were chosen to receive a blessing. 10The Scriptures* say,

"If you want to enjoy true life
    and have only good days,
then avoid saying anything
    hurtful,
    and never let a lie come out
    of your mouth.
11 Stop doing what is wrong, and
    do good.
    Look for peace, and do all
    you can to help people live
    peacefully.
12 The Lord watches over those
    who do what is right,
    and he listens to their
    prayers.
    But he is against those who do
    evil."   *Psalm 34:12-16*

13If you are always trying to do good, no one can really harm you

[14]But you may suffer for doing right. If that happens, you have God's blessing. "Don't be afraid of the people who make you suffer; don't be worried."[a] [15]But keep the Lord Christ holy in your hearts. Always be ready to answer everyone who asks you to explain about the hope you have. [16]But answer them in a gentle way with respect. Keep your conscience clear. Then people will see the good way you live as followers of Christ, and those who say bad things about you will be ashamed of what they said.

[17]It is better to suffer for doing good than for doing wrong. Yes, it is better if that is what God wants. [18] Christ himself suffered when
he died for you,
and with that one death he
paid for your sins.
He was not guilty,
but he died for people who
are guilty.
He did this to bring all of you
to God.
In his physical form he was
killed,
but he was made alive by the
Spirit.*[b]
[19]And by the Spirit he went and preached to the spirits in prison. [20]Those were the spirits who refused to obey God long ago in the time of Noah. God was waiting patiently for people while Noah was building the big boat. And only a few—eight in all—were saved in the boat through the floodwater. [21]And that water is like baptism,* which now saves you. Baptism is not the washing of dirt from the body. It is asking God for a clean conscience. It saves you because Jesus Christ was raised from death. [22]Now he has gone into heaven. He is at God's right side and rules over angels, authorities, and powers.

Changed Lives

4 [1]Christ suffered while he was in his body. So you should strengthen yourselves with the same kind of thinking Christ had. The one who accepts suffering in this life has clearly decided to stop sinning. [2]Strengthen yourselves so that you will live your lives here on earth doing what God wants, not the evil things that people want to do. [3]In the past you wasted too much time doing what those who don't know God like to do. You were living immoral lives, doing the evil things you wanted to do. You were always getting drunk, having wild drinking parties, and doing shameful things in your worship of idols.

[4]Now those "friends" think it is strange that you no longer join them in all the wild and wasteful things they do. And so they say bad things about you. [5]But they will have to face God to explain what they have done. He is the one who will soon judge everyone—those who are still living and those who have died. [6]Some were told the Good News* before they died. They were criticized by others in their life here on earth. But it was God's plan that they hear the Good News so that they could have a new life through the Spirit.*[c]

3:14 Quote from Isa. 8:12.
3:18 by the Spirit Or "in the spirit." Also in verse 19.

[c] **4:6 through the Spirit** Or "in the spirit," meaning in the spiritual or heavenly realm.

Be Good Managers of God's Gifts

7The time is near when all things will end. So keep your minds clear, and control yourselves. This will help you in your prayers. 8Most important of all, love each other deeply, because love makes you willing to forgive many sins. 9Open your homes to each other and share your food without complaining. 10God has shown you his grace* in many different ways. So be good servants and use whatever gift he has given you in a way that will best serve each other. 11If your gift is speaking, your words should be like words from God. If your gift is serving, you should serve with the strength that God gives. Then it is God who will be praised in everything through Jesus Christ. Power and glory* belong to him forever and ever. Amen.*

Suffering as a Follower of Christ

12My friends, don't be surprised at the painful things that you are now suffering, which are testing your faith. Don't think that something strange is happening to you. 13But you should be happy that you are sharing in Christ's sufferings. You will be happy and full of joy when Christ shows his glory.* 14When people say bad things to you because you follow Christ, consider it a blessing. When that happens, it shows that God's Spirit, the Spirit of glory, is with you. 15You may suffer, but don't let it be because you murder, steal, make trouble, or try to control other people's lives. 16But if you suffer because you are a "Christ-follower," don't be ashamed. You should praise God for that name. 17It is time for judging to begin. That judging will begin with God's family. If it begins with us, then what will happen to those who don't accept the Good News* of God?

18 "If it is hard for even a good
    person to be saved,
  what will happen to the one
    who is against God and full
    of sin?" *Proverbs 11:31 (Greek version)*

19So if God wants you to suffer, you should trust your lives to him. He is the one who made you, and you can trust him. So continue to do good.

The Flock of God

5 1Now I have something to say to the elders* in your group. I am also an elder. I myself have seen Christ's sufferings. And I will share in the glory* that will be shown to us. I beg you to 2take care of the group of people you are responsible for. They are God's flock.*a* Watch over that flock because you want to, not because you are forced to do it. That is how God wants it. Do it because you are happy to serve, not because you want money. 3Don't be like a ruler over those you are responsible for. But be good examples to them. 4Then when Christ the Ruling Shepherd comes, you will get a crown*—one that will be glorious and never lose its beauty.

5Young people, I have something to say to you too. You should accept the authority of the elders. You should all have a humble attitude in dealing with each other.

  "God is against the proud,
    but he is kind to the
    humble."   *Proverbs 3:34*

6So be humble under God's powerful hand. Then he will lift you

---

a 5:2 **God's flock** God's people. They are like a flock of sheep that need to be cared for.

up when the right time comes. ⁷Give all your worries to him, because he cares for you.

⁸Control yourselves and be careful! The devil is your enemy, and he goes around like a roaring lion looking for someone to attack and eat. ⁹Refuse to follow the devil. Stand strong in your faith. You know that your brothers and sisters all over the world are having the same sufferings that you have.

¹⁰Yes, you will suffer for a short time. But after that, God will make everything right. He will make you strong. He will support you and keep you from falling. He is the God who gives all grace. He chose you to share in his glory in Christ. That glory will continue forever. ¹¹All power is his forever. Amen.*

Final Greetings

¹²Silas will bring this letter to you. I know that he is a faithful brother in Christ. I wrote this short letter to encourage you. I wanted to tell you that this is the true grace* of God. Stand strong in that grace.

¹³The church in Babylon*ᵃ* sends you greetings. They were chosen just as you were. Mark, my son in Christ, also sends his greetings. ¹⁴Give each other a special greeting*ᵇ* of love when you meet.

Peace to all of you who are in Christ.

ᵃ **5:13 The church in Babylon** Literally, "She in Babylon."
ᵇ **5:14 special greeting** Literally, "kiss."

2 Peter

1 ¹Greetings from Simon Peter, a servant and apostle* of Jesus Christ.

To all of you who share in the same valuable faith that we have. This faith was given to us because our God and Savior Jesus Christ always does what is good and right.

²Grace* and peace be given to you more and more, because now you know God and Jesus our Lord.

God Has Given Us Everything We Need

³Jesus has the power of God. And his power has given us everything we need to live a life devoted to God. We have these things because we know him. Jesus chose us by his glory* and goodness, ⁴through which he also gave us the very great and rich gifts that he promised us. With these gifts you can share in being like God. And so you will escape the ruin that comes to people in the world because of the evil things they want.

⁵Because you have these blessings, do all you can to add to your life these things: to your faith add goodness; to your goodness add knowledge; ⁶to your knowledge add self-control; to your self-control add patience; to your patience add devotion to God; ⁷to your devotion add kindness toward your brothers and sisters in Christ, and to this kindness add love. ⁸If all these things are in you and growing, you will never fail to be useful to God. You will produce the kind of fruit that should come from your knowledge of our Lord Jesus Christ. ⁹But those who don't grow in these blessings are blind. They cannot see clearly what they have. They have forgotten that they were cleansed from their past sins.

¹⁰My brothers and sisters, God called you and chose you to be his. Do your best to live in a way that shows you really are God's called and chosen people. If you do all this, you will never fall. ¹¹And you will be given a very great welcome into the kingdom* of our Lord and Savior Jesus Christ, a kingdom that never ends.

¹²You already know these things. You are very strong in the truth you have. But I am always going to help you remember them. ¹³While I am still living here on earth, I think it is right for me to remind you of them. ¹⁴I know that I must soon leave this body. Our Lord Jesus Christ has shown me that. ¹⁵I will try my best to make sure you remember these things even after I am gone.

We Saw Christ's Glory

¹⁶We told you about the power of our Lord Jesus Christ. We told you about his coming. The things we told you were not just clever stories that people invented. No, we saw the greatness of Jesus with our own eyes. ¹⁷Jesus heard the

voice of the great and glorious God. That was when he received honor and glory* from God the Father. The voice said, "This is my Son, the one I love. I am very pleased with him." [18]And we heard that voice. It came from heaven while we were with Jesus on the holy mountain.[a]

[19]This makes us more sure about what the prophets* said. And it is good for you to follow closely what they said, which is like a light shining in a dark place. You have that light until the day begins and the morning star brings new light to your minds. [20]Most important of all, you must understand this: No prophecy* in the Scriptures* comes from the prophet's own understanding. [21]No prophecy ever came from what some person wanted to say. But people were led by the Holy Spirit* and spoke words from God.

False Teachers

2 [1]In the past there were false prophets* among God's people. It is the same now. You will have some false teachers in your group. They will teach things that are wrong—ideas that will cause people to be lost. And they will teach in a way that will be hard for you to see that they are wrong. They will even refuse to follow the Master who bought their freedom. And so they will quickly destroy themselves. [2]Many people will follow them in the morally wrong things they do. And because of them, others will say bad things about the way of truth we follow. These false teachers only want your money. So they will use you

by telling you things that are not true. But the judgment against these false teachers has been ready for a long time. And they will not escape God who will destroy them.

[4]When angels sinned, God did not let them go free without punishment. He sent them to hell. He put those angels in caves of darkness, where they are being held until the time when God will judge them.

[5]And God punished the evil people who lived long ago. He brought a flood to the world that was full of people who were against God. But he saved Noah and seven other people with him. Noah was a man who told people about living right.

[6]God also punished the evil cities of Sodom and Gomorrah. He burned them until there was nothing left but ashes. He used those cities as an example of what will happen to people who are against God. [7]But he saved Lot, a good man who lived there. Lot was greatly troubled by the morally bad lives of those evil people. [8]This good man lived with those evil people every day, and his good heart was hurt by the evil things he saw and heard.

[9]So you see that the Lord God knows how to save those who are devoted to him. He will save them when troubles come. And the Lord will hold evil people to punish them on the day of judgment. [10]That punishment is for those who are always doing the evil that their sinful selves want to do. It is for those who hate the Lord's authority.

These false teachers do whatever they want, and they are so

1:17–18 This event is described in the Gospels. See Mt. 17:1–8; Mk. 9:2–8; Lk. 9:28–36.

proud of themselves. They are not afraid even to say bad things against the glorious ones.[a] [11]The angels are much stronger and more powerful than these beings. But even the angels don't accuse them and say bad things about them to the Lord.

[12]But these false teachers speak evil against what they don't understand. They are like animals that do things without really thinking—like wild animals that are born to be caught and killed. And, like wild animals, they will be destroyed. [13]They have made many people suffer. So they themselves will suffer. That is their pay for what they have done.

They think it is fun to do evil where everyone can see them. They enjoy the evil things that please them. So they are like dirty spots and stains among you—they bring shame to you in the meals you eat together. [14]Every time they look at a woman, they want her. They are always sinning this way. And they lead weaker people into the trap of sin. They have taught themselves well to be greedy. They are under a curse.[b]

[15]These false teachers left the right way and went the wrong way. They followed the same way that the prophet Balaam* went. He was the son of Beor, who loved being paid for doing wrong. [16]But a donkey told him that he was doing wrong. A donkey cannot talk, of course, but that donkey spoke with a man's voice and stopped the prophet from acting so crazy.

[17]These false teachers are like springs that have no water. They are like clouds that are blown by a storm. A place in the deepest darkness has been kept for them. [18]They boast with words that mean nothing. They lead people into the trap of sin. They find people who have just escaped from a wrong way of life and lead them back into sin. They do this by using the evil things people want to do in their human weakness. [19]These false teachers promise those people freedom, but they themselves are not free. They are slaves to a mind that has been ruined by sin. Yes, people are slaves to anything that controls them.

[20]People can be made free from the evil in the world. They can be made free by knowing our Lord and Savior Jesus Christ. But if they go back into those evil things and are controlled by them, then it is worse for them than it was before. [21]Yes, it would be better for them to have never known the right way. That would be better than to know the right way and then to turn away from the holy* teaching that was given to them. [22]What they did is like these true sayings: "A dog vomits and goes back to what it threw up."[c] And "After a pig is washed, it goes back and rolls in the mud again."

Jesus Will Come Again

3 [1]My friends, this is the second letter I have written to you. I wrote both letters to you to help your honest minds remember something. [2]I want you

---

[a] **2:10 the glorious ones** Literally, "the glories." These seem to be some kind of angelic beings.

[b] **2:14 under a curse** Literally, "children of a curse," meaning that God will punish them.

[c] **2:22** Quote from Prov. 26:11.

to remember the words that the holy prophets* spoke in the past. And remember the command that our Lord and Savior gave us. He gave us that command through your apostles.*

³It is important for you to understand what will happen in the last days. People will laugh at you. They will live following the evil they want to do. ⁴They will say, "Jesus promised to come again. Where is he? Our fathers have died, but the world continues the way it has been since it was made."

⁵But these people don't want to remember what happened long ago. The skies were there, and God made the earth from water and with water. All this happened by God's word. ⁶Then the world was flooded and destroyed with water. ⁷And that same word of God is keeping the skies and the earth that we have now. They are being kept to be destroyed by fire. They are kept for the day of judgment and the destruction of all people who are against God.

⁸But don't forget this one thing, dear friends: To the Lord a day is like a thousand years, and a thousand years is like a day. ⁹The Lord is not being slow in doing what he promised—the way some people understand slowness. But God is being patient with you. He doesn't want anyone to be lost. He wants everyone to change their ways and stop sinning.

¹⁰But the day when the Lord comes again will surprise everyone like the coming of a thief. The sky will disappear with a loud noise. Everything in the sky will be destroyed with fire. And the earth and everything in it will be burned up.ᵃ ¹¹Everything will be destroyed in this way. So what kind of people should you be? Your lives should be holy* and devoted to God. ¹²You should be looking forward to the day of God, wanting more than anything else for it to come soon. When it comes, the sky will be destroyed with fire, and everything in the sky will melt with heat. ¹³But God made a promise to us. And we are waiting for what he promised—a new sky and a new earth. That will be the place where goodness lives.

¹⁴Dear friends, we are waiting for this to happen. So try as hard as you can to be without sin and without fault. Try to be at peace with God. ¹⁵Remember that we are saved because our Lord is patient. Our dear brother Paul told you that same thing when he wrote to you with the wisdom that God gave him. ¹⁶That's what he says in all his letters when he writes about these things. There are parts of his letters that are hard to understand, and some people give a wrong meaning to them. These people are ignorant and weak in faith. They also give wrong meanings to the other Scriptures.* But they are destroying themselves by doing that.

¹⁷Dear friends, you already know about this. So be careful. Don't let these evil people lead you away by the wrong they do. Be careful that you do not fall from your strong faith. ¹⁸But grow in the grace* and knowledge of our Lord and Savior Jesus Christ. Glory* be to him, now and forever! Amen.*

ᵃ 3:10 will be burned up Among the other readings of this text in early Greek copies, many have "will be found," and one has "will disappear."

1 John

1 ¹We want to tell you about the Word*a* that gives life—the one who existed before the world began. This is the one we have heard and have seen with our own eyes. We saw what he did, and our hands touched him. ²Yes, the one who is life was shown to us. We saw him, and so we can tell others about him. We now tell you about him. He is the eternal life that was with God the Father and was shown to us. ³We are telling you about what we have seen and heard because we want you to have fellowship*b* with us. The fellowship we share together is with God the Father and his Son Jesus Christ. ⁴We write these things to you so that you can be full of joy with us.

God Forgives Our Sins

⁵We heard the true teaching from God. Now we tell it to you: God is light,* and in him there is no darkness.* ⁶So if we say that we share in life with God, but we continue living in darkness, we are liars, who don't follow the truth. ⁷We should live in the light, where God is. If we live in the light, we have fellowship with each other, and the blood sacrifice of Jesus, God's Son, washes away every sin and makes us clean.

⁸If we say that we have no sin, we are fooling ourselves, and the truth is not in us. ⁹But if we confess our sins, God will forgive us. We can trust God to do this. He always does what is right. He will make us clean from all the wrong things we have done. ¹⁰If we say that we have not sinned, we are saying that God is a liar and that we don't accept his true teaching.

Jesus Is Our Helper

2 ¹My dear children, I write this letter to you so that you will not sin. But if anyone sins, we have Jesus Christ to help us. He always did what was right, so he is able to defend us before God the Father. ²Jesus is the way our sins are taken away. And he is the way all people can have their sins taken away too.

³If we obey what God has told us to do, then we are sure that we know him. ⁴If we say we know God but do not obey his commands, we are lying. The truth is not in us. ⁵But when we obey God's teaching, his love is truly working in us. This is how we know that we are living in him. ⁶If we say we live in God, we must live the way Jesus lived.

---

a **1:1 Word** The Greek word is *"logos,"* meaning any kind of communication. Here, it means Christ—the way God told people about himself.

b **1:3 fellowship** Associating with people and sharing things together with them. Believers in Christ share love, joy, sorrow, faith, and other things with each other and with God. Also in verse 7.

Jesus Told Us to Love Others

⁷My dear friends, I am not writing a new command to you. It is the same command you have had since the beginning. This command is the teaching you have already heard. ⁸But what I write is also a new command. It is a true one; you can see its truth in Jesus and in yourselves. The darkness* is passing away, and the true light is already shining.

⁹Someone might say, "I am in the light,*" but if they hate any of their brothers or sisters in God's family, they are still in the darkness. ¹⁰Those who love their brothers and sisters live in the light, and there is nothing in them that will make them do wrong. ¹¹But whoever hates their brother or sister is in darkness. They live in darkness. They don't know where they are going, because the darkness has made them blind.

¹² I write to you, dear children,
    because your sins are
      forgiven through Christ.
¹³ I write to you, fathers,
    because you know the one
      who existed from the
      beginning.
  I write to you, young people,
    because you have defeated
      the Evil One.*
¹⁴ I write to you, children,
    because you know the
      Father.
  I write to you, fathers,
    because you know the one
      who existed from the
      beginning.
  I write to you, young people,
    because you are strong.
  The word of God lives in you,
    and you have defeated the
      Evil One.

¹⁵Don't love this evil world or the things in it. If you love the world, you do not have the love of the Father in you. ¹⁶This is all there is in the world: wanting to please our sinful selves, wanting the sinful things we see, and being too proud of what we have. But none of these comes from the Father. They come from the world. ¹⁷The world is passing away, and all the things that people want in the world are passing away. But whoever does what God wants will live forever.

Don't Follow the Enemies of Christ

¹⁸My dear children, the end is near! You have heard that the enemy of Christ* is coming. And now many enemies of Christ are already here. So we know that the end is near. ¹⁹These enemies were in our group, but they left us. They did not really belong with us. If they were really part of our group, they would have stayed with us. But they left. This shows that none of them really belonged with us.

²⁰You have the gift*a* that the Holy One*b* gave you. So you all know the truth. ²¹Do you think I am writing this letter because you don't know the truth? No, I am writing because you do know the truth. And you know that no lie comes from the truth.

²²So who is the liar? It is the one who says Jesus is not the Messiah.* Whoever says that is the enemy of Christ—the one who does not believe in the Father or in his Son. ²³Whoever does not believe in the

---

a **2:20 gift** Literally, "anointing." This might mean the Holy Spirit. Or it might mean teaching or truth as in verse 24. Also in verse 27.
b **2:20 Holy One** God or Christ.

Son does not have the Father, but whoever accepts the Son has the Father too.

24Be sure that you continue to follow the teaching you heard from the beginning. If you do that, you will always be in the Son and in the Father. 25And this is what the Son promised us—eternal life.

26I am writing this letter about those who are trying to lead you into the wrong way. 27Christ gave you a special gift. You still have this gift in you. So you don't need anyone to teach you. The gift he gave you teaches you about everything. It is a true gift, not a false one. So continue to live in Christ, as his gift taught you.

28Yes, my dear children, live in him. If we do this, we can be without fear on the day when Christ comes again. We will not need to hide and be ashamed when he comes. 29You know that Christ always did what was right. So you know that all those who do what is right are God's children.

We Are God's Children

3 1The Father has loved us so much! This shows how much he loved us: We are called children of God. And we really are his children. But the people in the world don't understand that we are God's children, because they have not known him. 2Dear friends, now we are children of God. We have not yet been shown what we will be in the future. But we know that when Christ comes again, we will be like him. We will see him just as he is. 3He is pure, and everyone who has this hope in him keeps themselves pure like Christ.

4Anyone who sins breaks God's law. Yes, sinning is the same as living against God's law. 5You know that Christ came to take away people's sins. There is no sin in Christ. 6So whoever lives in Christ does not continue to sin. If they continue to sin, they have never really understood Christ and have never known him.

7Dear children, don't let anyone lead you into the wrong way. Christ always did what was right. So to be good like Christ, you must do what is right. 8The devil has been sinning since the beginning. Anyone who continues to sin belongs to the devil. The Son of God came for this: to destroy the devil's work.

9Those who are God's children do not continue to sin, because the new life God gave them*a* stays in them. They cannot keep sinning, because they have become children of God. 10So we can see who God's children are and who the devil's children are. These are the ones who are not God's children: those who don't do what is right and those who do not love their brothers and sisters in God's family.

We Must Love One Another

11This is the teaching you have heard from the beginning: We must love each other. 12Don't be like Cain.* He belonged to the Evil One.* Cain killed his brother. But why did he kill him? Because what Cain did was evil, and what his brother did was good.

13Brothers and sisters, don't be surprised when the people of this world hate you. 14We know that we have left death and have come into life. We know this because

---

a 3:9 the new life God gave them Literally, "his seed."

we love each other as brothers and sisters. Anyone who does not love is still in death. [15]Anyone who hates a fellow believer* is a murderer.[d] And you know that no murderer has eternal life.

[16]This is how we know what real love is: Jesus gave his life for us. So we should give our lives for each other as brothers and sisters. [17]Suppose a believer who is rich enough to have all the necessities of life sees a fellow believer who is poor and does not have even basic needs. What if the rich believer does not help the poor one? Then it is clear that God's love is not in that person's heart. [18]My children, our love should not be only words and talk. No, our love must be real. We must show our love by the things we do.

[19-20]That's how we know we belong to the way of truth. And when our hearts make us feel guilty, we can still have peace before God, because God is greater than our hearts. He knows everything.

[21]My dear friends, if we don't feel that we are doing wrong, we can be without fear when we come to God. [22]And God gives us what we ask for. We receive it because we obey God's commands and do what pleases him. [23]This is what God commands: that we believe in his Son Jesus Christ, and that we love each other as he commanded. [24]All who obey God's commands live in God. And God lives in them. How do we know that God lives in us? We know because of the Spirit* he gave us.

John Warns Against False Teachers

4 [1]My dear friends, many false prophets* are in the world now. So don't believe every spirit, but test the spirits to see if they are from God. [2]This is how you can recognize God's Spirit. One spirit says, "I believe that Jesus is the Messiah* who came to earth and became a man." That Spirit is from God. [3]Another spirit refuses to say this about Jesus. That spirit is not from God. This is the spirit of the enemy of Christ. You have heard that the enemy of Christ is coming, and now he is already in the world.

[4]My dear children, you belong to God, so you have already defeated these false prophets. That's because the one who is in you is greater than the one who is in the world. [5]And they belong to the world, so what they say is from the world too. And the world listens to what they say. [6]But we are from God. So the people who know God listen to us. But the people who are not from God don't listen to us. This is how we know the Spirit that is true and the spirit that is false.

Love Comes From God

[7]Dear friends, we should love each other, because love comes from God. Everyone who loves has become God's child. And so everyone who loves knows God. [8]Anyone who does not love does not know God, because God is love. [9]This is how God showed his love to us: He sent his only Son into the world to give us life through him. [10]True love is God's love for us, not our love for God. He sent his Son as the way to take away our sins.

[11]That is how much God loved us, dear friends! So we also must

love each other. ¹²No one has ever seen God. But if we love each other, God lives in us. If we love each other, God's love has reached its goal—it is made perfect in us.

¹³We know that we live in God and God lives in us. We know this because he gave us his Spirit.* ¹⁴We have seen that the Father sent his Son to be the Savior of the world, and this is what we tell people now. ¹⁵Anyone who says, "I believe that Jesus is the Son of God," is a person who lives in God, and God lives in that person. ¹⁶So we know the love that God has for us, and we trust that love.

God is love. Everyone who lives in love lives in God, and God lives in them. ¹⁷If God's love is made perfect in us, we can be without fear on the day when God judges the world. We will be without fear, because in this world we are like Jesus.ᵃ ¹⁸Where God's love is, there is no fear, because God's perfect love takes away fear. It is his punishment that makes a person fear. So his love is not made perfect in the one who has fear.

¹⁹We love because God first loved us. ²⁰If we say we love God but hate any of our brothers or sisters in his family, we are liars. If we don't love someone we have seen, how can we love God? We have never even seen him. ²¹God gave us this command: If we love God, we must also love each other as brothers and sisters.

God's Children Win Against the World

5 ¹The people who believe that Jesus is the Messiah* are God's children. Anyone who loves the Father also loves the Father's children. ²How do we know that we

love God's children? We know because we love God and we obey his commands. ³Loving God means obeying his commands. And God's commands are not too hard for us, ⁴because everyone who is a child of God has the power to win against the world. ⁵It is our faith that has won the victory against the world. So who wins against the world? Only those who believe that Jesus is the Son of God.

God Told Us About His Son

⁶Jesus Christ is the one who came. He came with water and with blood.ᵇ He did not come by water only. No, Jesus came by both water and blood. And the Spirit* tells us that this is true. The Spirit is the truth. ⁷So there are three witnesses that tell us about Jesus: ⁸the Spirit, the water, and the blood. These three witnesses agree.

⁹We believe people when they say something is true. But what God says is more important. And this is what God told us: He told us the truth about his own Son. ¹⁰Whoever believes in the Son of God has the truth that God told us. But people who do not believe God make God a liar, because they do not believe what God told us about his Son. ¹¹This is what God told us: God has given us eternal life, and this life is in his Son. ¹²Whoever has the Son has life, but whoever does not have the Son of God does not have life.

We Have Eternal Life Now

¹³I write this letter to you who believe in the Son of God. I write so that you will know that you have eternal life now. ¹⁴We can come to

ᵃ **4:17 Jesus** Literally, "that one."

ᵇ **5:6 water, blood** Probably meaning the water of Jesus' baptism and the blood he shed on the cross.

God with no doubts. This means that when we ask God for things (and those things agree with what God wants for us), God cares about what we say. ¹⁵He listens to us every time we ask him. So we know that he gives us whatever we ask from him.

¹⁶Suppose you see your fellow believer* sinning (sin that does not lead to eternal death). You should pray for them. Then God will give them life. I am talking about people whose sin does not lead to eternal death. There is sin that leads to death. I don't mean that you should pray about that kind of sin. ¹⁷Doing wrong is always sin. But there is sin that does not lead to eternal death.

¹⁸We know that those who have been made God's children do not continue to sin. The Son of God keeps them safe.ᵃ The Evil One* cannot hurt them. ¹⁹We know that we belong to God, but the Evil One controls the whole world. ²⁰And we know that the Son of God has come and has given us understanding. So now we can know the one who is true, and we live in that true God. We are in his Son, Jesus Christ. He is the true God, and he is eternal life. ²¹So, dear children, keep yourselves away from false gods.

ᵃ 5:18 The Son ... safe Literally, "The one who was born from God keeps him safe" or "... keeps himself safe."

2 John

¹Greetings from the Elder.ᵃ

To the ladyᵇ chosen by God and to her children.

I truly love all of you. And I am not the only one. All those who know the truthᶜ love you in the same way. ²We love you because of the truth—the truth that lives in us. That truth will be with us forever.

³Grace,* mercy, and peace will be with us from God the Father and from his Son, Jesus Christ, as we live in truth and love.

⁴I was very happy to learn about some of your children. I am happy that they are following the way of truth, just as the Father commanded us. ⁵And now, dear lady, I tell you: We should all love each other. This is not a new command. It is the same command we had from the beginning. ⁶And loving means living the way he commanded us to live. And God's command is this: that you live a life of love. You heard this command from the beginning.

⁷Many false teachers are in the world now. They refuse to say that Jesus Christ came to earth and became a man. Anyone who refuses to accept this fact is a false teacher and the enemy of Christ. ⁸Be careful! Don't lose the reward weᵈ have worked for. Be careful so that you will receive all of that reward.

⁹Everyone must continue to follow only the teaching about Christ. Whoever changes that teaching does not have God. But whoever continues to follow the teaching about Christ has both the Father and his Son. ¹⁰Don't accept those who come to you but do not bring this teaching. Don't invite them into your house. Don't welcome them in any way. ¹¹If you do, you are helping them with their evil work.

¹²I have much to say to you. But I don't want to use paper and ink. Instead, I hope to come visit you. Then we can be together and talk. That will make us very happy. ¹³The children of your sisterᵉ who was chosen by God send you their love.

ᵃ **1 Elder** This is probably John the apostle. "Elder" means an older man or a special leader in the church (as in Titus 1:5).

ᵇ **1 lady** This might mean a woman. Or, in this letter, it might mean a church. If it is a church, then "her children" would be the people of the church. Also in verse 5.

ᶜ **1 truth** The truth or "Good News" about Jesus Christ that joins all believers together.

ᵈ **8 we** Some Greek copies have "you."

ᵉ **13 sister** Sister of the "lady" in verse 1. This might be another woman or another church.

3 John

¹Greetings from the Elder.ᵃ

To my dear friend Gaius, a person I truly love.

²My dear friend, I know that you are doing well spiritually. So I pray that everything else is going well with you and that you are enjoying good health. ³Some believers* came and told me about the truthᵇ in your life. They told me that you continue to follow the way of truth. This made me very happy. ⁴It always gives me the greatest joy when I hear that my children are following the way of truth.

⁵My dear friend, it is good that you continue to help the believers. They are people you don't even know. ⁶They told the church* about the love you have. Please help them to continue their trip. Help them in a way that will please God. ⁷They went on their trip to serve Christ. They did not accept any help from people who are not believers. ⁸So we should help them. When we help them, we share with their work for the truth.

⁹I wrote a letter to the church, but Diotrephes will not listen to what we say. He always wants to be the leader. ¹⁰When I come, I will talk with him about what he is doing. He lies and says evil things about us, but that is not all. He refuses to welcome and help the believers who travel there. And he will not let others help them. If they do, he stops them from meeting with the church anymore.

¹¹My dear friend, don't follow what is bad; follow what is good. Whoever does what is good is from God. But whoever does evil has never known God.

¹²Everyone says good things about Demetrius, and the truth agrees with what they say. Also, we say good about him. And you know that what we say is true.

¹³I have many things I want to tell you. But I don't want to use pen and ink. ¹⁴I hope to visit you soon. Then we can be together and talk. ¹⁵Peace to you. The friends here with me send their love. Please give our love to each one of the friends there.

ᵃ **1 Elder** This is probably John the apostle. "Elder" means an older man or a special leader in the church (as in Titus 1:5).
ᵇ **3 truth** The truth or "Good News" about Jesus Christ that joins all believers together. Also in verses 8, 12.

Jude

¹Greetings from Jude, a servant of Jesus Christ and a brother of James.

To those who have been chosen and are loved by God the Father and have been kept safe in Jesus Christ.

²Mercy, peace, and love be yours more and more.

God Will Punish Those Who Do Wrong

³Dear friends, I wanted very much to write to you about the salvation we all share together. But I felt the need to write to you about something else: I want to encourage you to fight hard for the faith that God gave his holy people.* God gave this faith once, and it is good for all time. ⁴Some people have secretly entered your group. These people have already been judged guilty for what they are doing. Long ago the prophets* wrote about them. They are against God. They have used the grace* of our God in the wrong way—to do sinful things. They refuse to follow Jesus Christ, our only Master and Lord.

⁵I want to help you remember some things you already know: Remember that the Lord*ᵃ* saved his people by bringing them out of the land of Egypt. But later he destroyed all those who did not believe. ⁶And remember the angels who lost their authority to rule. They left their proper home. So the Lord has kept them in darkness, bound with everlasting chains, to be judged on the great day. ⁷Also, remember the cities of Sodom* and Gomorrah* and the other towns around them. Like those angels they were full of sexual sin and involved themselves in sexual relations that are wrong. And they suffer the punishment of eternal fire, an example for us to see.

⁸It is the same way with these people who have entered your group. They are guided by dreams. They make themselves dirty with sin. They reject God's authority and say bad things against the glorious ones.*ᵇ* ⁹Not even the archangel* Michael did this. Michael argued with the devil about who would have the body of Moses.* But Michael did not dare to condemn even the devil for his false accusations. Instead, Michael said, "The Lord punish you!"

¹⁰But these people criticize things they don't understand. They do understand some things. But they understand these things not by thinking, but by feeling,

---

ᵃ **5 the Lord** Some of the oldest and best Greek manuscripts of Jude have "Jesus" here. If "Jesus" is accepted as the original reading, it should replace "the Lord" in verse 6 as well.

ᵇ **8 the glorious ones** Literally, "the glories." These seem to be some kind of angelic beings.

the way dumb animals understand things. And these are the things that destroy them. ¹¹It will be bad for them. They have followed the way that Cain* went. To make money, they have given themselves to following the wrong way that Balaam* went. They have fought against God like Korah^a did. And like Korah, they will be destroyed.

¹²These people are like dirty spots among you—they bring shame to you in the special meals you share together. They eat with you and have no fear. They take care of only themselves. They are like clouds without rain. The wind blows them around. They are like trees that have no fruit at harvest time and are pulled out of the ground. So they are twice dead. ¹³Like the dirty foam on the wild waves in the sea, everyone can see the shameful things they do. They are like stars that wander in the sky. A place in the blackest darkness has been kept for them forever.

¹⁴Enoch, the seventh descendant from Adam, said this about these people: "Look, the Lord is coming with thousands and thousands of his holy* angels ¹⁵to judge everyone. He will punish all those who are against him for all the evil they have done in their lack of respect for him. Yes, the Lord will punish all these sinners who don't honor him. He will punish them for all the evil things they have said against him."

¹⁶These people always complain and find wrong in others. They always do the evil things they want to do. They boast about themselves. The only reason they say good things about others is to get what they want.

A Warning and Things to Do

¹⁷Dear friends, remember what the apostles* of our Lord Jesus Christ said would happen. ¹⁸They told you, "In the last times there will be people who laugh at God and do only what they want to do—things that are against God." ¹⁹These are the people who divide you. They are not spiritual, because they don't have the Spirit.*

²⁰But you, dear friends, use your most holy faith to build yourselves up even stronger. Pray with the help of the Holy Spirit. ²¹Keep yourselves safe in God's love, as you wait for the Lord Jesus Christ in his mercy to give you eternal life.

²²Help those who have doubts. ²³Rescue those who are living in danger of hell's fire. There are others you should treat with mercy, but be very careful that their filthy lives don't rub off on you.^b

Praise God

²⁴God is strong and can keep you from falling. He can bring you before his glory* without any wrong in you and give you great joy. ²⁵He is the only God, the one who saves us. To him be glory, greatness, power, and authority through Jesus Christ our Lord for all time past, now, and forever. Amen.*

---

^a **11 Korah** He turned against Moses. See Num. 16:1–40.

^b **23 that ... on you** Literally, "hating even their undershirt that is defiled from the flesh."

Revelation

John Tells About This Book

1 ¹This is a revelation*a* from Jesus Christ, which God gave him to show his servants what must happen soon. And Christ sent his angel to show it to his servant John, ²who has told everything he saw. It is the truth that Jesus Christ told him; it is the message from God. ³Great blessings belong to the person who reads the words of this message from God and to those who hear this message and do what is written in it. There is not much time left.

John Writes to the Churches

⁴From John,
To the seven churches* in the province of Asia*:

Grace* and peace to you from the one who is, who always was, and who is coming; and from the seven spirits before his throne; ⁵and from Jesus Christ. Jesus is the faithful witness. He is first among all who will be raised from death. He is the ruler of the kings of the earth.

Jesus is the one who loves us and has made us free from our sins with his blood sacrifice. ⁶He made us his kingdom* and priests who serve God his Father. To Jesus be glory* and power forever and ever! Amen.*

⁷Look, Jesus is coming with the clouds! Everyone will see him, even those who pierced*b* him. All peoples of the earth will cry loudly because of him. Yes, this will happen! Amen.

⁸The Lord God says, "I am the Alpha and the Omega.*c* I am the one who is, who always was, and who is coming. I am the All-Powerful."

⁹I am John, your fellow believer.* We are together in Jesus, and we share these things: suffering, the kingdom, and patient endurance. I was on the island of Patmos*d* because I was faithful to God's message* and to the truth of Jesus. ¹⁰On the Lord's Day, the Spirit* took control of me. I heard a loud voice behind me that sounded like a trumpet. ¹¹It said, "Write down in a book what you see, and send it to the seven churches: to Ephesus, Smyrna, Pergamum, Thyatira, Sardis, Philadelphia, and Laodicea."

¹²I turned to see who was talking to me. When I turned, I saw seven golden lampstands. ¹³I saw someone among the lampstands

b 1:7 pierced When Jesus was killed, he was stabbed with a spear in the side. See Jn. 19:34.

c 1:8 Alpha ... Omega The first and last letters in the Greek alphabet, meaning the beginning and the end.

d 1:9 Patmos A small island in the Aegean Sea, near the coast of modern Turkey.

a 1:1 revelation An opening up (making known) of truth that was hidden.

who looked like the Son of Man.* He was dressed in a long robe, with a golden sash tied around his chest. ¹⁴His head and hair were white like wool—wool that is white as snow. His eyes were like flames of fire. ¹⁵His feet were like brass that glows hot in a furnace. His voice was like the noise of flooding water. ¹⁶He held seven stars in his right hand. A sharp two-edged sword came out of his mouth. He looked like the sun shining at its brightest time.

¹⁷When I saw him, I fell down at his feet like a dead man. He put his right hand on me and said, "Don't be afraid! I am the First and the Last. ¹⁸I am the one who lives. I was dead, but look, I am alive forever and ever! And I hold the keys of death and Hades.* ¹⁹So write what you see. Write the things that happen now and the things that will happen later. ²⁰Here is the hidden meaning of the seven stars that you saw in my right hand and the seven golden lampstands that you saw: The seven lampstands are the seven churches. The seven stars are the angels of the seven churches.

Jesus' Letter to the Church in Ephesus

2 ¹"Write this to the angel of the church* in Ephesus:

"Here is a message from the one who holds the seven stars in his right hand and walks among the seven golden lampstands.

²"I know what you do, how hard you work and never give up. I know that you don't accept evil people. You have tested those who say they are apostles* but are not. You found that they are liars. ³You never stop trying. You have endured troubles for my name and have not given up.

⁴"But I have this against you: You have left the love you had in the beginning. ⁵So remember where you were before you fell. Change your hearts and do what you did at first. If you don't change, I will come to you and remove your lampstand from its place. ⁶But there is something you do that is right—you hate the things that the Nicolaitans* do. I also hate what they do.

⁷"Everyone who hears this should listen to what the Spirit* says to the churches. To those who win the victory I will give the right to eat the fruit from the tree of life,* which is in God's paradise.*

Jesus' Letter to the Church in Smyrna

⁸"Write this to the angel of the church* in Smyrna:

"Here is a message from the one who is the First and the Last, the one who died and came to life again.

⁹"I know your troubles, and I know that you are poor, but really you are rich! I know the insults you have suffered from people who say they are Jews. But they are not true Jews. They are a group* that belongs to Satan.* ¹⁰Don't be afraid of what will happen to you. I tell you, the devil will put some of you in prison. He will do this to test you. You will suffer for ten days, but be faithful, even if you have to die. If you continue to be faithful, I will give you the reward* of life.

---

a **2:6 Nicolaitans** A religious group that followed wrong ideas. Also in verse 15.
b **2:9 group** Literally, "synagogue."
c **2:10 reward** Literally, "wreath," a ring of leaves or branches that was placed on the head of the winners of athletic contests to honor them. It was a symbol of victory and reward.

[11]"Everyone who hears this should listen to what the Spirit* says to the churches. Those who win the victory will not be hurt by the second death.

Jesus' Letter to the Church in Pergamum

[12]"Write this to the angel of the church* in Pergamum:

"Here is a message from the one who has the sharp two-edged sword.

[13]"I know where you live. You live where Satan* has his throne, but you are true to me. You did not refuse to tell about your faith in me even during the time of Antipas. Antipas was my faithful witness[a] who was killed in your city, the city where Satan lives.

[14]"But I have a few things against you. You have people there who follow the teaching of Balaam.* Balaam taught Balak how to make the people of Israel* sin. They sinned by eating food offered to idols* and by committing sexual sins. [15]It is the same in your group. You have people who follow the teaching of the Nicolaitans. [16]So change your hearts! If you don't change, I will come to you quickly and fight against these people with the sword that comes out of my mouth.

[17]"Everyone who hears this should listen to what the Spirit* says to the churches!

"I will give the hidden manna* to everyone who wins the victory. I will also give each one a white stone that has a new name written on it. And no one will know this name except the one who gets the stone.

Jesus' Letter to the Church in Thyatira

[18]"Write this to the angel of the church* in Thyatira:

"Here is a message from the Son of God, the one who has eyes that blaze like fire and feet like shining brass.

[19]"I know what you do. I know about your love, your faith, your service, and your patience. I know that you are doing more now than you did at first. [20]But I have this against you: You let that woman Jezebel do what she wants. She says that she is a prophet,[b] but she is leading my people away with her teaching. Jezebel leads my people to commit sexual sins and to eat food that is offered to idols.* [21]I have given her time to change her heart and turn away from her sin, but she does not want to change.

[22]"So I will throw her on a bed of suffering. And all those who commit adultery* with her will suffer greatly. I will do this now if they don't turn away from the things she does. [23]I will also kill her followers. Then all the churches will see that I am the one who knows what people feel and think. And I will repay each of you for what you have done.

[24]"But others of you in Thyatira have not followed her teaching. You have not learned the things they call 'Satan's* deep secrets.' This is what I say to you: I will not put any other burden on you. [25]Only hold on to the truth you have until I come.

[26]"I will give power over the nations to all those who win the

---

a **2:13 faithful witness** A person who speaks God's message truthfully, even in times of danger.

b **2:20 prophet** Jezebel was a false prophet. She claimed to speak for God, but she didn't really speak God's truth.

victory and continue until the end to do what I want. 27They will rule the nations with an iron rod. They will break them to pieces like clay pots.ᵃ 28They will have the same power I received from my Father, and I will give them the morning star. 29Everyone who hears this should listen to what the Spirit* says to the churches.

Jesus' Letter to the Church in Sardis

3 1"Write this to the angel of the church* in Sardis:

"Here is a message from the one who has the seven spirits and the seven stars.

"I know what you do. People say that you are alive, but really you are dead. 2Wake up! Make yourselves stronger before what little strength you have left is completely gone. I find that what you do is not good enough for my God. 3So don't forget what you have received and heard. Obey it. Change your hearts and lives! You must wake up, or I will come to you and surprise you like a thief. You will not know when I will come.

4"But you have a few people in your group there in Sardis who have kept themselves clean. They will walk with me. They will wear white clothes, because they are worthy. 5Everyone who wins the victory will be dressed in white clothes like them. I will not remove their names from the book of life. I will say that they belong to me before my Father and before his angels. 6Everyone who hears this should listen to what the Spirit* says to the churches.

Jesus' Letter to the Church in Philadelphia

7"Write this to the angel of the church* in Philadelphia:

"Here is a message from the one who is holy and true, the one who holds the key of David.* When he opens something, it cannot be closed. And when he closes something, it cannot be opened.

8"I know what you do. I have put before you an open door that no one can close. I know you are weak, but you have followed my teaching. You were not afraid to speak my name. 9Listen! There is a groupᵇ that belongs to Satan.* They say they are Jews, but they are liars. They are not true Jews. I will make them come before you and bow at your feet. They will know that you are the people I have loved. 10You followed my command to endure patiently. So I will keep you from the time of trouble that will come to the world—a time that will test everyone living on earth.

11"I am coming soon. Hold on to the faith you have, so that no one can take away your crown.* 12Those who win the victory will be pillars* in the temple of my God. I will make that happen for them. They will never again have to leave God's temple. I will write on them the name of my God and the name of the city of my God. That city is the new Jerusalem.ᶜ It is coming down out of heaven from my God. I will also write my new name on them. 13Everyone who hears this should listen to what the Spirit* says to the churches.

ᵃ 2:26–27 These verses are almost the same as Ps. 2:8–9.
ᵇ 3:9 group Literally, "synagogue."
ᶜ 3:12 new Jerusalem The spiritual city where God's people live with him.

Jesus' Letter to the Church in Laodicea

¹⁴"Write this to the angel of the church* in Laodicea:

"Here is a message from the Amen,ᵃ the faithful and true witness, the ruler of all that God has made.

¹⁵"I know what you do. You are not hot or cold. I wish that you were hot or cold! ¹⁶But you are only warm—not hot, not cold. So I am ready to spit you out of my mouth. ¹⁷You say you are rich. You think you have become wealthy and don't need anything. But you don't know that you are really miserable, pitiful, poor, blind, and naked. ¹⁸I advise you to buy gold from me—gold made pure in fire. Then you will be rich. I tell you this: Buy clothes that are white. Then you will be able to cover your shameful nakedness. I also tell you to buy medicine to put on your eyes. Then you will be able to see.

¹⁹"I correct and punish the people I love. So show that nothing is more important to you than living right. Change your hearts and lives. ²⁰Here I am! I stand at the door and knock. If you hear my voice and open the door, I will come in and eat with you. And you will eat with me.

²¹"I will let everyone who wins the victory sit with me on my throne. It was the same with me. I won the victory and sat down with my Father on his throne. ²²Everyone who hears this should listen to what the Spirit* says to the churches."

ᵃ **3:14 Amen** Used here, as a name for Jesus, it means to agree strongly that something is true.

John Sees Heaven

4 ¹Then I looked, and there before me was an open door in heaven. And I heard the same voice that spoke to me before. It was the voice that sounded like a trumpet. It said, "Come up here, and I will show you what must happen after this." ²Immediately the Spirit* took control of me, and there in heaven was a throne with someone sitting on it. ³The one sitting there was as beautiful as precious stones, like jasper and carnelian. All around the throne was a rainbow with clear colors like an emerald.

⁴In a circle around the throne were 24 other thrones with 24 elders* sitting on them. The elders were dressed in white, and they had golden crowns on their heads. ⁵Lightning flashes and noises of thunder came from the throne. Before the throne there were seven lamps burning, which are the seven Spirits of God. ⁶Also before the throne there was something that looked like a sea of glass, as clear as crystal.

In front of the throne and on each side of it there were four living beings. They had eyes all over them, in front and in back. ⁷The first living being was like a lion. The second was like a bull. The third had a face like a man. The fourth was like a flying eagle. ⁸Each of these four living beings had six wings. They were covered all over with eyes, inside and out. Day and night they never stopped saying,

"Holy, holy, holy is the Lord
   God All-Powerful.
He always was, he is, and he is
   coming."

⁹These living beings were giving

glory* and honor and thanks to the one who sits on the throne, the one who lives forever and ever. And every time they did this, [10]the 24 elders bowed down before the one who sits on the throne. They worshiped him who lives forever and ever. They put their crowns down before the throne and said, [11] "Our Lord and God!

You are worthy to receive glory
    and honor and power.
You made all things.
Everything existed and was
    made because you wanted
    it."

Who Can Open the Scroll?

5 [1]Then I saw a scroll* in the right hand of the one sitting on the throne. The scroll had writing on both sides and was kept closed with seven seals.* [2]And I saw a powerful angel, who called in a loud voice, "Who is worthy to break the seals and open the scroll?" [3]But there was no one in heaven or on earth or under the earth who could open the scroll or look inside it. [4]I cried and cried because there was no one who was worthy to open the scroll or look inside. [5]But one of the elders* said to me, "Don't cry! The Lion[a] from the tribe of Judah has won the victory. He is David's* descendant. He is able to open the scroll and its seven seals."

[6]Then I saw a Lamb* standing in the center near the throne with the four living beings around it. The elders were also around the Lamb. The Lamb looked as if it had been killed. It had seven horns and seven eyes, which are the seven spirits of God that were sent into all the world. [7]The Lamb came and took the scroll from the right hand of the one sitting on the throne. [8]After the Lamb took the scroll, the four living beings and the 24 elders bowed down before the Lamb. Each one of them had a harp. Also, they were holding golden bowls full of incense,* which are the prayers of God's holy people.* [9]And they all sang a new song to the Lamb:

"You are worthy to take the
    scroll
    and to open its seals,
because you were killed,
    and with your blood sacrifice
    you bought people for God
    from every tribe, language,
    race of people, and nation.
[10] You made them to be a
    kingdom and to be priests
    for our God.
And they will rule on the
    earth."

[11]Then I looked, and I heard the voices of many angels. The angels were around the throne, the four living beings, and the elders. There were thousands and thousands of angels—10,000 times 10,000. [12]The angels said in a loud voice,

"All power, wealth, wisdom,
    and strength belong to the
    Lamb who was killed.
He is worthy to receive
    honor, glory,* and praise!"

[13]Then I heard every created being that is in heaven and on earth and under the earth and in the sea, everything in all these places, saying,

"All praise and honor and glory
    and power forever and ever
    to the one who sits on the
    throne and to the Lamb!"

[14]The four living beings said, "Amen*!" And the elders bowed down and worshiped.

---

[a] **5:5 Lion** Used here to refer to Jesus.

The Lamb Opens the Scroll

6 [1]Then I watched as the Lamb* opened the first of the seven seals.* Then I heard one of the four living beings speak with a voice like thunder. It said, "Come!" [2]I looked, and there before me was a white horse. The rider on the horse held a bow and was given a crown.* He rode out to defeat the enemy and win the victory.

[3]The Lamb opened the second seal. Then I heard the second living being say, "Come!" [4]Then another horse came out, a red one. The rider on the horse was given power to take away peace from the earth so that people would kill each other. He was given a big sword.

[5]The Lamb opened the third seal. Then I heard the third living being say, "Come!" I looked, and there before me was a black horse. The rider on the horse held a pair of scales in his hand. [6]Then I heard something that sounded like a voice. The voice came from where the four living beings were. It said, "A quart[a] of wheat or three quarts of barley will cost a full day's pay. But don't harm the supply of olive oil and wine!"

[7]The Lamb opened the fourth seal. Then I heard the voice of the fourth living being say, "Come!" [8]I looked, and there before me was a pale-colored horse. The rider on the horse was death, and Hades* was following close behind him. They were given power over a fourth of the earth—power to kill people with the sword, by starving, by disease, and with the wild animals of the earth.

[9]The Lamb opened the fifth seal. Then I saw some souls under the altar.* They were the souls of those who had been killed because they were faithful to God's message* and to the truth they had received. [10]These souls shouted in a loud voice, "Holy and true Lord, how long until you judge the people of the earth and punish them for killing us?" [11]Then each one of them was given a white robe. They were told to wait a short time longer. There were still some of their brothers and sisters in the service of Christ who must be killed as they were. These souls were told to wait until all the killing was finished.

[12]Then I watched while the Lamb opened the sixth seal. There was a great earthquake, and the sun became as black as sackcloth.[b] The full moon became red like blood. [13]The stars in the sky fell to the earth like a fig tree dropping its figs when the wind blows. [14]The sky was split in the middle and both sides rolled up like a scroll.* And every mountain and island was moved from its place.

[15]Then all the people—the kings of the world, the rulers, the army commanders, the rich people, the powerful people, every slave, and every free person—hid themselves in caves and behind the rocks on the mountains. [16]They said to the mountains and the rocks, "Fall on us. Hide us from the face of the one who sits on the throne. Hide us from the anger of the Lamb! [17]The great day for their anger has come. No one can stand against it."

---

[a] **6:6 quart** Literally, "*choinix*," the amount of the daily ration of grain for a soldier. Equals about 1 liter.

[b] **6:12 sackcloth** Literally, "sackcloth of hair." See "SACKCLOTH" in the Word List.

The 144,000 People of Israel

7 ¹After this happened I saw four angels standing at the four corners of the earth. The angels were holding the four winds of the earth. They were stopping the wind from blowing on the land or the sea or on any tree. ²Then I saw another angel coming from the east. This angel had the seal* of the living God. The angel called out in a loud voice to the four angels. These were the four angels that God had given the power to hurt the earth and the sea. The angel said to them, ³"Don't harm the land or the sea or the trees before we mark the foreheads of those who serve our God."

⁴Then I heard how many people had God's mark on their foreheads. There were 144,000. They were from every tribe of the people of Israel*:

⁵ from the tribe of Judah	12,000
from the tribe of Reuben	12,000
from the tribe of Gad	12,000
⁶ from the tribe of Asher	12,000
from the tribe of Naphtali	12,000
from the tribe of Manasseh	12,000
⁷ from the tribe of Simeon	12,000
from the tribe of Levi	12,000
from the tribe of Issachar	12,000
⁸ from the tribe of Zebulun	12,000
from the tribe of Joseph	12,000
from the tribe of Benjamin	12,000

The Great Crowd

⁹Then I looked, and there was a large crowd of people. There were so many people that no one could count them all. They were from every nation, tribe, race of people, and language of the earth. They were standing before the throne and before the Lamb.* They all wore white robes and had palm branches in their hands. ¹⁰They shouted loudly, "Victory belongs to our God, who sits on the throne, and to the Lamb."

¹¹The elders* and the four living beings were there. All the angels were standing around them and the throne. The angels bowed down on their faces before the throne and worshiped God. ¹²They said, "Amen*! Praise, glory,* wisdom, thanks, honor, power, and strength belong to our God forever and ever. Amen!"

¹³Then one of the elders asked me, "Who are these people in white robes? Where did they come from?"

¹⁴I answered, "You know who they are, sir."

And the elder said, "These are the ones who have come out of the great suffering. They have washed their robes *a* with the blood of the Lamb, and they are clean and white. ¹⁵So now these people are before the throne of God. They worship God day and night in his temple. And the one who sits on the throne will protect them. ¹⁶They will never be hungry again. They will never be thirsty again. The sun will not hurt them. No heat will burn them. ¹⁷The Lamb in front of the throne will be their shepherd. He will lead them to springs of water

a **7:14 washed their robes** Meaning that they had believed in Jesus and had been made clean from sin by his blood sacrifice. See Rev. 5:9; Heb. 9:14; 10:14–22; Acts 22:16; 1 Jn. 1:7.

that give life. And God will wipe away every tear from their eyes."

The Seventh Seal

8 ¹The Lamb* opened the seventh seal.* Then there was silence in heaven for about half an hour. ²And I saw the seven angels who stand before God. They were given seven trumpets.

³Another angel came and stood at the altar.* This angel had a golden holder for incense.* The angel was given much incense to offer with the prayers of all God's holy people.* The angel put this offering on the golden altar before the throne. ⁴The smoke from the incense went up from the angel's hand to God. The smoke went up with the prayers of God's people. ⁵Then the angel filled the incense holder with fire from the altar and threw it down on the earth. Then there were flashes of lightning, thunder and other noises, and an earthquake.

The First of Seven Trumpet Blasts

⁶Then the seven angels with the seven trumpets prepared to blow their trumpets.

⁷The first angel blew his trumpet. Then hail and fire mixed with blood was poured down on the earth. And a third of the earth and all the green grass and a third of the trees were burned up.

⁸The second angel blew his trumpet. Then something that looked like a big mountain burning with fire was thrown into the sea. And a third of the sea became blood. ⁹And a third of the created beings in the sea died, and a third of the ships were destroyed.

¹⁰The third angel blew his trumpet. Then a large star, burning like a torch, fell from the sky. It fell on a third of the rivers and on the springs of water. ¹¹The name of the star was Bitterness.ᵃ And a third of all the water became bitter. Many people died from drinking this bitter water.

¹²The fourth angel blew his trumpet. Then a third of the sun and a third of the moon and a third of the stars were struck. So a third of them became dark. A third of the day and night was without light.

¹³While I watched, I heard an eagle that was flying high in the air. The eagle said in a loud voice, "Terrible! Terrible! How terrible for those who live on the earth! The terrible trouble will begin after the sounds of the trumpets that the other three angels will blow."

The Fifth Trumpet Begins the First Terror

9 ¹The fifth angel blew his trumpet. Then I saw a star fall from the sky to the earth. The star was given the key to the deep hole that leads down to the bottomless pit. ²Then the star opened the hole leading to the pit. Smoke came up from the hole like smoke from a big furnace. The sun and sky became dark because of the smoke from the hole.

³Then locusts* came out of the smoke and went down to the earth. They were given the power to sting like scorpions. ⁴They were told not to damage the fields of grass or any plant or tree. They were to hurt only those who did not have God's mark on their foreheads. ⁵They were not given the power to kill them but

---

ᵃ **8:11 Bitterness** Literally, "Wormwood," a very bitter plant; here, it is a symbol of bitter sorrow.

only to cause them pain for five months—pain like a person feels when stung by a scorpion. [6]During those days people will look for a way to die, but they will not find it. They will want to die, but death will hide from them.

[7]The locusts looked like horses prepared for battle. On their heads they wore something that looked like a gold crown. Their faces looked like human faces. [8]Their hair was like women's hair. Their teeth were like lions' teeth. [9]Their chests looked like iron breastplates. The sound their wings made was like the noise of many horses and chariots hurrying into battle. [10]The locusts had tails with stingers like scorpions. The power they had to give people pain for five months was in their tails. [11]They had a ruler, who was the angel of the bottomless pit. His name in Hebrew is Abaddon.[a] In Greek it is Apollyon.[b]

[12]The first terror is now past. There are still two other terrors to come.

The Sixth Trumpet Blast

[13]The sixth angel blew his trumpet. Then I heard a voice coming from the horns on the four corners of the golden altar* that is before God. [14]It said to the sixth angel who had the trumpet, "Free the four angels who are tied at the great river Euphrates." [15]These four angels had been kept ready for this hour and day and month and year. The angels were set free to kill a third of all the people on the earth. [16]I heard how many

troops on horses were in their army. There were 200,000,000.

[17]In my vision,* I saw the horses and the riders on the horses. They looked like this: They had breastplates that were fiery red, dark blue, and yellow like sulfur. The heads of the horses looked like heads of lions. The horses had fire, smoke, and sulfur coming out of their mouths. [18]A third of all the people on earth were killed by these three plagues coming out of the horses' mouths: the fire, the smoke, and the sulfur. [19]The horses' power was in their mouths and also in their tails. Their tails were like snakes that have heads to bite and hurt people.

[20]The other people on earth were not killed by these plagues. But these people still did not change their hearts and turn away from worshiping the things they had made with their own hands. They did not stop worshiping demons* and idols* made of gold, silver, bronze, stone, and wood—things that cannot see or hear or walk. [21]They did not change their hearts and turn away from killing other people or from their evil magic, their sexual sins, and their stealing.

The Angel and the Little Scroll

10 [1]Then I saw another powerful angel coming down from heaven. The angel was dressed in a cloud. He had a rainbow around his head. The angel's face was like the sun, and his legs were like poles of fire. [2]The angel was holding a small scroll.* The scroll was open in his hand. He put his right foot on the sea and his left foot on the land. [3]He shouted loudly like the roaring of

---

[a] **9:11 Abaddon** A Hebrew name meaning "death" or "destruction." See Job 26:6 and Ps. 88:11.

[b] **9:11 Apollyon** A name that means "destroyer."

a lion. After he shouted, the voices of seven thunders spoke.

⁴The seven thunders spoke, and I started to write. But then I heard a voice from heaven that said, "Don't write what the seven thunders said. Keep those things secret."

⁵Then the angel I saw standing on the sea and on the land raised his right hand to heaven. ⁶The angel made a promise by the power of the one who lives forever and ever. He is the one who made the skies and all that is in them. He made the earth and all that is in it, and he made the sea and all that is in it. The angel said, "There will be no more waiting! ⁷In the days when the seventh angel is ready to blow his trumpet, God's secret plan will be completed—the Good News* that God told to his servants, the prophets.*"

⁸Then I heard the same voice from heaven again. It said to me, "Go and take the open scroll that is in the angel's hand. This is the angel who is standing on the sea and on the land."

⁹So I went to the angel and asked him to give me the little scroll. He said to me, "Take the scroll and eat it. It will be sour in your stomach, but in your mouth it will be sweet like honey." ¹⁰So I took the little scroll from the angel's hand and ate it. In my mouth it tasted sweet like honey, but after I ate it, it was sour in my stomach. ¹¹Then I was told, "You must prophesy* again about many races of people, many nations, languages, and rulers."

The Two Witnesses

11 ¹Then I was given a measuring rod as long as a walking stick. I was told, "Go and measure the temple*ᵃ* of God and the altar,* and count the people worshiping there. ²But don't measure the yard outside the temple. Leave it alone. It has been given to those who are not God's people. They will show their power over the holy city for 42 months. ³And I will give power to my two witnesses. And they will prophesy* for 1260 days. They will be dressed in sackcloth.*"

⁴These two witnesses are the two olive trees and the two lampstands that stand before the Lord of the earth. ⁵If anyone tries to hurt the witnesses, fire comes from the mouths of the witnesses and kills their enemies. Anyone who tries to hurt them will die like this. ⁶These witnesses have the power to stop the sky from raining during the time they are prophesying. These witnesses have power to make the water become blood. They have power to send every kind of plague to the earth. They can do this as many times as they want.

⁷When the two witnesses have finished telling their message, the beast will fight against them. This is the beast that comes up from the bottomless pit. It will defeat and kill them. ⁸The bodies of the two witnesses will lie in the street of the great city. This city is named Sodom* and Egypt. These names for the city have a special meaning. This is the city where the Lord was killed. ⁹People from every race of people, tribe, language, and nation will look at

ᵃ **11:1 temple** God's house—the place where God's people worship and serve him. Here, John sees it pictured as the special building in Jerusalem for Jewish worship. Also in verse 19.

the bodies of the two witnesses for three and a half days. The people will refuse to bury them. [10]Everyone on the earth will be happy because these two are dead. They will have parties and send each other gifts. They will do this because these two prophets brought much suffering to the people living on earth.

[11]But after three and a half days, God let life enter the two witnesses again. They stood on their feet. All those who saw them were filled with fear. [12]Then the two witnesses heard a loud voice from heaven say, "Come up here!" And both of them went up into heaven in a cloud. Their enemies watched them go.

[13]At that same time there was a great earthquake. A tenth of the city was destroyed. And 7000 people were killed in the earthquake. Those who did not die were very afraid. They gave glory* to the God of heaven.

[14]The second terror is now past. The third terror is coming soon.

The Seventh Trumpet Blast

[15]The seventh angel blew his trumpet. Then there were loud voices in heaven. The voices said,

"The kingdom of the world has
    now become the kingdom
    of our Lord and of his
    Messiah.*
And he will rule forever and
    ever."

[16]Then the 24 elders* bowed down on their faces and worshiped God. These are the elders who sit on their thrones before God. [17]The elders said,

"We give thanks to you, Lord
    God All-Powerful.
You are the one who is and
    who always was.

We thank you because you
    have used your great power
    and have begun to rule.
[18] The people of the world were
    angry,
    but now is the time for your
    anger.
Now is the time for the dead
    to be judged.
It is time to reward your
    servants, the prophets,*
and to reward your holy
    people,*
    the people, great and small,
    who respect you.
It is time to destroy those
    people who destroy the
    earth!"

[19]Then God's temple in heaven was opened. The Box of the Agreement[a] could be seen in his temple. Then there were flashes of lightning, noises, thunder, an earthquake, and a great hailstorm.

The Woman Giving Birth and the Dragon

12 [1]And then a great wonder appeared in heaven: There was a woman who was clothed with the sun, and the moon was under her feet. She had a crown of twelve stars on her head. [2]She was pregnant and cried out with pain because she was about to give birth.

[3]Then another wonder appeared in heaven: There was a giant red dragon there. The dragon had seven heads with a crown on each head. It also had ten horns. [4]Its tail swept a third of

---

a 11:19 **Box of the Agreement** This is like the special box kept in the Most Holy Place of the Israelite Holy Tent and, later, the Jerusalem Temple, which contained "proof" of the agreement between God and his people. See "Box of the Agreement" in the Word List.

the stars out of the sky and threw them down to the earth. It stood in front of the woman who was ready to give birth to the baby. It wanted to eat the woman's baby as soon as it was born.

5 The woman gave birth to a son, who would rule all the nations with an iron rod. And her child was taken up to God and to his throne. 6 The woman ran away into the desert to a place that God had prepared for her. There she would be taken care of for 1260 days.

7 Then there was a war in heaven. Michael[a] and his angels fought against the dragon. The dragon and its angels fought back, 8 but they were not strong enough. The dragon and its angels lost their place in heaven. 9 It was thrown down out of heaven. (This giant dragon is that old snake, the one called the devil or Satan, who leads the whole world into the wrong way.) The dragon and its angels were thrown to the earth.

10 Then I heard a loud voice in heaven say, "The victory and the power and the kingdom of our God and the authority of his Messiah* have now come. These things have come, because the accuser of our brothers and sisters has been thrown out. He is the one who accused them day and night before our God. 11 They defeated him by the blood sacrifice of the Lamb* and by the message of God that they told people. They did not love their lives too much. They were not afraid of death. 12 So rejoice, you heavens and all who live there! But it will be terrible for the earth and sea, because the devil has gone down to you. He is filled with anger. He knows he doesn't have much time."

13 The dragon saw that he had been thrown down to the earth. So he chased the woman who had given birth to the child. 14 But the woman was given the two wings of a great eagle. Then she could fly to the place that was prepared for her in the desert. There she would be taken care of for three and a half years. There she would be away from the dragon.[b] 15 Then the dragon poured water out of its mouth like a river. It poured the water toward the woman so that the flood would carry her away. 16 But the earth helped the woman. The earth opened its mouth and swallowed the river that came from the mouth of the dragon. 17 Then the dragon was very angry with the woman. It went away to make war against all her other children. Her children are those who obey God's commands and have the truth that Jesus taught.

18 The dragon stood on the seashore.

The Beast From the Sea

13 1 Then I saw a beast coming up out of the sea. It had ten horns and seven heads. There was a crown on each of its horns. It had an evil name written on each head. 2 This beast looked like a leopard, with feet like a bear's feet. It had a mouth like a lion's mouth. The dragon gave the beast all of its power and its throne and great authority.

---

a 12:7 **Michael** The archangel—leader of God's angels. See Jude 9.

b 12:14 **dragon** Here and in verse 15 literally, "snake." See verse 9 above.

³One of the heads of the beast looked as if it had been wounded and killed, but the death wound was healed. All the people in the world were amazed, and they all followed the beast. ⁴People worshiped the dragon because it had given its power to the beast, and they also worshiped the beast. They asked, "Who is as powerful as the beast? Who can make war against it?"

⁵The beast was allowed to boast and speak insults against God. It was allowed to use its power for 42 months. ⁶The beast opened its mouth to insult God—to insult his name, the place where he lives, and all those who live in heaven. ⁷It was given power to make war against God's holy people* and to defeat them. It was given power over every tribe, race of people, language, and nation. ⁸Everyone living on earth would worship the beast. These are all the people since the beginning of the world whose names are not written in the Lamb's* book of life. The Lamb is the one who was killed.

⁹Anyone who hears these things should listen to this:
¹⁰ Whoever is to be a prisoner,
    will be a prisoner.
Whoever is to be killed with
    a sword,
will be killed with a sword.
This means that God's holy people must have patience and faith.

The Beast From the Earth

¹¹Then I saw another beast coming up out of the earth. He had two horns like a lamb, but he talked like a dragon. ¹²This beast stood before the first beast and used the same power the first beast had. He used this power to make everyone living on the earth worship the first beast. The first beast was the one that had the death wound that was healed. ¹³The second beast did great miracles.ᵈ He even made fire come down from heaven to earth while people were watching.

¹⁴This second beast fooled the people living on earth by using the miracles that he had been given the power to do for the first beast. He ordered people to make an idol* to honor the first beast, the one that was wounded by the sword but did not die. ¹⁵The second beast was given power to give life to the idol of the first beast. Then the idol could speak and order all those who did not worship it to be killed. ¹⁶The second beast also forced all people, small and great, rich and poor, free and slave, to have a mark put on their right hand or on their forehead. ¹⁷No one could buy or sell without this mark. (This mark is the name of the beast or the number of its name.)

¹⁸Anyone who has understanding can find the meaning of the beast's number. This requires wisdom. This number is the number of a man. It is 666.

God's People Sing a New Song

14 ¹Then I looked, and there before me was the Lamb,* who was standing on Mount Zion.ᵇ There were 144,000 people with him. They all had his name and his Father's name written on their foreheads.

²And I heard a sound from heaven as loud as the crashing of

ᵈ **13:13 miracles** False miracles—amazing acts done by the power of the devil.
ᵇ **14:1 Mount Zion** Another name for Jerusalem, here meaning the spiritual city where God's people live with him.

floodwaters or claps of thunder. But it sounded like harpists playing their harps. ³The people sang a new song before the throne and before the four living beings and the elders.* The only ones who could learn the new song were the 144,000 who had been bought from the earth. No one else could learn it.

⁴These are the ones who did not do sinful things with women. They kept themselves pure. Now they follow the Lamb wherever he goes. They were bought from among the people of the earth as the first to be offered to God and the Lamb. ⁵They are not guilty of telling lies; they are without fault.

The Three Angels

⁶Then I saw another angel flying high in the air. The angel had the eternal Good News* to announce to the people living on earth—to every nation, tribe, language, and race of people. ⁷The angel said in a loud voice, "Fear God and give him praise. The time has come for God to judge all people. Worship God. He made the heavens, the earth, the sea, and the springs of water."

⁸Then the second angel followed the first angel and said, "She is destroyed! The great city of Babylon is destroyed! She made all the nations drink the wine of her sexual sin and of God's anger."

⁹A third angel followed the first two angels. This third angel said in a loud voice, "God will punish all those who worship the beast and the beast's idol* and agree to have the beast's mark on their forehead or on their hand. ¹⁰They will drink the wine of God's anger. This wine is prepared with all its strength in the cup of God's anger. They will be tortured* with burning sulfur before the holy angels and the Lamb.* ¹¹And the smoke from their burning pain will rise forever and ever. There will be no rest, day or night, for those who worship the beast and its idol or who wear the mark of its name." ¹²This means that God's holy people* must be patient. They must obey God's commands and keep their faith in Jesus.

¹³Then I heard a voice from heaven. It said, "Write this: From now on there are great blessings for those who belong to the Lord when they die."

The Spirit* says, "Yes, that is true. They will rest from their hard work. What they have done will stay with them."

The Earth Is Harvested

¹⁴I looked and there before me, sitting on a white cloud, was one who looked like the Son of Man.* He had a gold crown on his head and a sharp sickle* in his hand. ¹⁵Then another angel came out of the temple. This angel called to the one who was sitting on the cloud, "Take your sickle and gather from the earth. The time to harvest has come, and the fruit on the earth is ripe." ¹⁶So the one who was sitting on the cloud swung his sickle over the earth. And the earth was harvested.

¹⁷Then another angel came out of the temple in heaven. This angel also had a sharp sickle. ¹⁸And then another angel, one with power over the fire, came from the altar.* He called to the angel with the sharp sickle and said, "Take your sharp sickle and gather the bunches of grapes from the earth's vine. The earth's grapes are ripe." ¹⁹The angel swung his sickle over the earth.

He gathered the earth's grapes and threw them into the great winepress of God's anger. 20The grapes were squeezed in the winepress outside the city. Blood flowed out of the winepress. It rose as high as the heads of the horses for a distance of 200 miles.*a*

The Angels With the Last Plagues

15 1Then I saw another wonder in heaven. It was great and amazing. There were seven angels bringing seven plagues. These are the last plagues, because after these, God's anger is finished.

2I saw what looked like a sea of glass mixed with fire. All those who had won the victory over the beast and his idol* and over the number of its name were standing by the sea. These people had harps that God had given them. 3They sang the song of Moses,* the servant of God, and the song of the Lamb*:

"Great and wonderful are the
    things you do,
    Lord God All-Powerful.
Right and true are your ways,
    Ruler of the nations.
4 All people will fear you, O Lord.
All people will praise your
    name.
    Only you are holy.
All people will come and
    worship before you,
    because it is clear that you
    do what is right."

5After this I saw the temple, the holy place of God's presence,*b* in heaven. It was opened, 6and the seven angels bringing the seven

plagues came out. They were dressed in clean, shining linen cloth. They wore golden bands tied around their chests. 7Then one of the four living beings gave seven golden bowls to the seven angels. The bowls were filled with the anger of God, who lives forever and ever. 8The temple was filled with smoke from the glory* and the power of God. No one could enter the temple until the seven plagues of the seven angels were finished.

The Bowls Filled With God's Anger

16 1Then I heard a loud voice from the temple. It said to the seven angels, "Go and pour out the seven bowls of God's anger on the earth."

2The first angel left. He poured out his bowl on the land. Then all those who had the mark of the beast and who worshiped its idol* got sores that were ugly and painful.

3The second angel poured out his bowl on the sea. Then the sea became blood like a dead man's blood. And everything living in the sea died.

4The third angel poured out his bowl on the rivers and the springs of water. The rivers and the springs of water became blood. 5Then I heard the angel of the waters say to God,

"You are the one who is and
    who always was.
You are the Holy One.
You are right in these
    judgments you have made.
6 The people have spilled the
    blood of your holy people*
    and your prophets.*
Now you have given those
    people blood to drink.
    This is what they deserve."

---

a **14:20 200 miles** Literally, "1600 *stadia*," a little less than 300 km.
b **15:5 holy place of God's presence** Literally, "tent of the testimony." See "HOLY TENT" in the Word List. Read Ex. 25:8–22.

7And I heard the altar* say,
"Yes, Lord God All-Powerful,
    your judgments are true and
    right."

8The fourth angel poured out his bowl on the sun. The sun was given power to burn the people with fire. 9The people were burned by the great heat. They cursed the name of God, who had control over these plagues. But they refused to change their hearts and lives and give glory* to God.

10The fifth angel poured out his bowl on the throne of the beast. And darkness covered the beast's kingdom. People bit their tongues because of the pain. 11They cursed the God of heaven because of their pain and the sores they had. But they refused to change their hearts and turn away from the evil things they did.

12The sixth angel poured out his bowl on the great river Euphrates. The water in the river was dried up. This prepared the way for the rulers from the east to come. 13Then I saw three evil spirits that looked like frogs. They came out of the mouth of the dragon, out of the mouth of the beast, and out of the mouth of the false prophet.* 14These evil spirits are the spirits of demons.* They have power to do miracles.ᵃ They go out to the rulers of the whole world to gather them for battle on the great day of God All-Powerful.

15"Listen! I will come at a time you don't expect, like a thief. Great blessings belong to those who stay awake and keep their clothes with them. They will not have to go without clothes and be ashamed for people to see them."

16Then the evil spirits gathered the rulers together to the place that in Hebrew is called Armageddon.

17The seventh angel poured out his bowl into the air. Then a loud voice came out of the temple from the throne. It said, "It is finished!" 18Then there were flashes of lightning, noises, thunder, and a big earthquake. This was the worst earthquake that has ever happened since people have been on earth. 19The great city split into three parts. The cities of the nations were destroyed. And God did not forget to punish Babylon the Great. He gave that city the cup filled with the wine of his terrible anger. 20Every island disappeared and there were no more mountains. 21Giant hailstones fell on the people from the sky. These hailstones weighed almost 100 poundsᵇ each. People cursed God because of this plague of the hail. It was terrible.

The Woman on the Red Beast

17 1One of the seven angels came and spoke to me. This was one of the angels that had the seven bowls. The angel said, "Come, and I will show you the punishment that will be given to the famous prostitute. She is the one sitting over many waters. 2The rulers of the earth sinned sexually with her. The people of the earth became drunk from the wine of her sexual sin."

3Then the angel carried me away by the Spirit* to the desert There I saw a woman sitting on a

---

ᵃ **16:14 miracles** False miracles—amazing acts done by the power of the devil.

ᵇ **16:21 100 pounds** Literally, "*talanton*" or "talent." A talent was about 27 to 36 kg (60 to 80 pounds).

red beast. The beast was covered with evil names. It had seven heads and ten horns. ⁴The woman was dressed in purple and red. She was shining with the gold, jewels, and pearls that she was wearing. She had a golden cup in her hand. This cup was filled with terribly evil things and the filth of her sexual sin. ⁵She had a title written on her forehead. This title has a hidden meaning. This is what was written:

THE GREAT BABYLON
MOTHER OF PROSTITUTES
AND THE EVIL THINGS
OF THE EARTH

⁶I saw that the woman was drunk. She was drunk with the blood of God's holy people.* She was drunk with the blood of those who told about their faith in Jesus.

When I saw the woman, I was fully amazed. ⁷Then the angel said to me, "Why are you amazed? I will tell you the hidden meaning of this woman and the beast she rides—the beast with seven heads and ten horns. ⁸The beast you saw was once alive, but now it is not. However, it will come up out of the bottomless pit and go away to be destroyed. The people who live on the earth will be amazed when they see the beast, because it was once alive, is no longer living, but will come again. These are the people whose names have never been written in the book of life since the beginning of the world.

⁹"You need wisdom to understand this. The seven heads on the beast are the seven hills where the woman sits. They are also seven rulers. ¹⁰Five of the rulers have already died. One of the rulers lives now, and the last ruler

is coming. When he comes, he will stay only a short time. ¹¹The beast that was once alive but is no longer living is an eighth ruler. This eighth ruler also belongs to the first seven rulers. And he will go away to be destroyed.

¹²"The ten horns you saw are ten rulers. These ten rulers have not yet received their kingdom, but they will receive power to rule with the beast for one hour. ¹³All ten of these rulers have the same purpose. And they will give their power and authority to the beast. ¹⁴They will make war against the Lamb.* But the Lamb will defeat them, because he is Lord of lords and King of kings. And with him will be his chosen and faithful followers—the people he has called to be his."

¹⁵Then the angel said to me, "You saw the waters where the prostitute sits. These waters are the many peoples, the different races, nations, and languages in the world. ¹⁶The beast and the ten horns you saw will hate the prostitute. They will take everything she has and leave her naked. They will eat her flesh and destroy her with fire. ¹⁷God put the idea in their minds to do what would complete his purpose. They agreed to give the beast their power to rule until what God has said is completed. ¹⁸The woman you saw is the great city that rules over the kings of the earth."

Babylon Is Destroyed

18 ¹Then I saw another angel coming down from heaven. This angel had great power. The angel's glory* made the earth bright. ²The angel shouted with a powerful voice,

"She is destroyed!
The great city of Babylon is
destroyed!
She has become a home for
demons.*
That city has become a place
for every unclean spirit to
live.
She is a city filled with all
kinds of unclean birds.
She is a place where every
unclean and hated animal
lives.
3 All the peoples of the earth
have drunk the wine of
her sexual sin and of God's
anger.
The rulers of the earth sinned
sexually with her,
and the merchants* of the
world grew rich from the
great wealth of her luxury."

4 Then I heard another voice
from heaven say,
"Come out of that city, my
people,
so that you will not share in
her sins.
Then you will not suffer any
of the terrible punishment
she will get.
5 That city's sins are piled up as
high as heaven.
God has not forgotten the
wrongs she has done.
6 Give that city the same as she
gave to others.
Pay her back twice as much
as she did.
Prepare wine for her that is
twice as strong as the wine
she prepared for others.
7 She gave herself much glory
and rich living.
Give her that much suffering
and sadness.
She says to herself, 'I am a
queen sitting on my throne.

I am not a widow;
I will never be sad.'
8 So in one day she will suffer
great hunger, mourning,*
and death.
She will be destroyed by fire,
because the Lord God who
judges her is powerful.
9 "The rulers of the earth who
sinned sexually with her and
shared her wealth will see the
smoke from her burning. Then
they will cry and be sad because
of her death. 10 The rulers will be
afraid of her suffering and stand
far away. They will say,
'Terrible! How terrible, O great
city,
O powerful city of Babylon!
Your punishment came in one
hour!'
11 "And the merchants of the
earth will cry and be sad for her.
They will be sad because now
there is no one to buy the things
they sell— 12 gold, silver, jewels,
pearls, fine linen cloth, purple
cloth, silk, and scarlet cloth, all
kinds of citron wood, and all
kinds of things made from ivory,
expensive wood, bronze, iron, and
marble. 13 They also sell cinnamon,
spice, incense,* frankincense,*
myrrh,* wine, olive oil, fine flour,
wheat, cattle, sheep, horses, car-
riages, and slaves—yes, even
human lives. The merchants will
cry and say,
14 'O Babylon, the good things
you wanted have left you.
All your rich and fancy things
have disappeared.
You will never have them
again.'
15 "The merchants will be afraid
of her suffering and will stand far
away from her. They are the ones
who became rich from selling

those things to her. They will cry and be sad. [16]They will say,

'Terrible! How terrible for the
     great city!
She was dressed in fine
     linen;
she wore purple and scarlet
     cloth.
She was shining with gold,
     jewels, and pearls!
[17] All these riches have been
     destroyed in one hour!'

"Every sea captain, all those who travel on ships, the sailors, and all those who earn money from the sea stood far away from Babylon. [18]They saw the smoke from her burning. They cried out, 'There was never a city like this great city!' [19]They threw dust on their heads and cried loudly to show the deep sorrow they felt. They said,

'Terrible! How terrible for the
     great city!
All those who had ships on the
     sea became rich because of
     her wealth!
But she has been destroyed
     in one hour!
[20] Be happy because of this,
     O heaven!
Be happy, God's holy people*
     and apostles* and
     prophets*!
God has punished her because
     of what she did to you.'"

[21]Then a powerful angel picked up a large rock. This rock was as big as a large millstone.* The angel threw the rock into the sea and said,

"That is how the great city of
     Babylon will be thrown
     down.
It will never be found again.
[22] O Babylon, the music of
     people playing harps and

other instruments, flutes
     and trumpets, will never be
     heard in you again.
No worker doing any job will
     ever be found in you again.
The sound of a millstone
     will never be heard in you
     again.
[23] The light of a lamp will never
     shine in you again.
The voices of a bridegroom*
     and bride will never be
     heard in you again.
Your merchants were the
     world's great people.
All the nations were tricked by
     your magic.
[24] You are guilty of the death of
     the prophets, of God's holy
     people,
and of all those who have
     been killed on earth."

People in Heaven Praise God

19 [1]After this I heard what sounded like a large crowd of people in heaven. The people were saying,
"Hallelujah[a]!
Victory, glory,* and power
     belong to our God.
[2] His judgments are true and
     right.
Our God has punished the
     prostitute.
She is the one who ruined
     the earth with her sexual
     sin.
God has punished the
     prostitute to pay her
     back for the death of his
     servants."
[3]These people also said,
"Hallelujah!
She is burning and her smoke
     will rise forever and ever."

[a] **19:1 Hallelujah** This means "Praise God!" Also in verses 3, 4, 6.

[4]Then the 24 elders* and the four living beings bowed down. They worshiped God, who sits on the throne. They said,

"Amen*! Hallelujah!"

[5]Then a voice came from the throne and said,

"Praise our God, all you who
    serve him!
Praise our God, all you small
    and great who honor him!"

[6]Then I heard something that sounded like a large crowd of people. It was as loud as crashing waves or claps of thunder. The people were saying,

"Hallelujah!
    Our Lord God rules.
    He is the All-Powerful.
[7] Let us rejoice and be happy
    and give God glory!
Give God glory, because the
    wedding of the Lamb* has
    come.
And the Lamb's bride has
    made herself ready.
[8] Fine linen was given to the
    bride for her to wear.
    The linen was bright and
    clean."

(The fine linen means the good things that God's holy people* did.)

[9]Then the angel said to me, "Write this: Great blessings belong to those who are invited to the wedding meal of the Lamb!" Then the angel said, "These are the true words of God."

[10]Then I bowed down before the angel's feet to worship him. But the angel said to me, "Don't worship me! I am a servant like you and your brothers and sisters who have the truth of Jesus. So worship God! Because the truth of Jesus is the spirit of prophecy.*"

The Rider on the White Horse

[11]Then I saw heaven open. There before me was a white horse. The rider on the horse was called Faithful and True, because he is right in his judging and in making war. [12]His eyes were like burning fire. He had many crowns on his head. A name was written on him, but he was the only one who knew its meaning. [13]He was dressed in a robe dipped in blood, and he was called the Word of God. [14]The armies of heaven were following the rider on the white horse. They were also riding white horses. They were dressed in fine linen, white and clean. [15]A sharp sword came out of the rider's mouth, a sword that he would use to defeat the nations. And he will rule the nations with a rod of iron. He will crush the grapes in the winepress of the terrible anger of God All-Powerful. [16]On his robe and on his leg was written this name:

KING OF KINGS AND
LORD OF LORDS

[17]Then I saw an angel standing in the sun. In a loud voice the angel said to all the birds flying in the sky, "Come together for the great supper of God. [18]Come together so that you can eat the bodies of rulers and army commanders and famous men. Come to eat the bodies of the horses and their riders and the bodies of all people—free, slave, small, and great."

[19]Then I saw the beast and the rulers of the earth. Their armies were gathered together to make war against the rider on the horse and his army. [20]But the beast was captured, and the false prophet was also captured. He was the

one who did the miracles*ᵈ* for the beast. He had used these miracles to trick those who had the mark of the beast and worshiped its idol.* The false prophet and the beast were thrown alive into the lake of fire that burns with sulfur. ²¹Their armies were killed with the sword that came out of the mouth of the rider on the horse. All the birds ate these bodies until they were full.

The 1000 Years

20 ¹I saw an angel coming down out of heaven. The angel had the key to the bottomless pit. The angel also held a large chain in his hand. ²The angel grabbed the dragon, that old snake, also known as the devil or Satan. The angel tied the dragon with the chain for 1000 years. ³Then the angel threw the dragon into the bottomless pit and closed it. The angel locked it over the dragon. The angel did this so that the dragon could not trick the people of the earth until the 1000 years were ended. After 1000 years the dragon must be made free for a short time.

⁴Then I saw some thrones and people sitting on them. These were the ones who had been given the power to judge. And I saw the souls of those who had been killed because they were faithful to the truth of Jesus and the message* from God. They did not worship the beast or its idol.* They did not receive the mark of the beast on their foreheads or on their hands. They came back to life and ruled with Christ for 1000 years. ⁵(The rest of the dead

did not live again until the 1000 years were ended.)

This is the first resurrection.* ⁶Great blessings belong to those who share in this first resurrection. They are God's holy people.* The second death has no power over them. They will be priests for God and for Christ. They will rule with him for 1000 years.

The Defeat of Satan

⁷When the 1000 years are ended, Satan* will be made free from his prison. ⁸He will go out to trick the nations in all the earth, the nations known as Gog and Magog. Satan will gather the people for battle. There will be more people than anyone can count, like sand on the seashore.

⁹I saw Satan's army march across the earth and gather around the camp of God's people and the city that God loves. But fire came down from heaven and destroyed Satan's army. ¹⁰And he (the one who tricked these people) was thrown into the lake of burning sulfur with the beast and the false prophet.* There they would be tortured* day and night forever and ever.

People of the World Are Judged

¹¹Then I saw a large white throne. I saw the one who was sitting on the throne. Earth and sky ran away from him and disappeared. ¹²And I saw those who had died, great and small, standing before the throne. Some books were opened. And another book was opened—the book of life. The people were judged by what they had done, which is written in the books.

¹³The sea gave up the dead who were in it. Death and Hades* gave up the dead who were in them. All these people were judged by what

---

ᵈ **19:20 miracles** False miracles—amazing acts done by the power of the devil.

they had done. ¹⁴And Death and Hades were thrown into the lake of fire. This lake of fire is the second death. ¹⁵And anyone whose name was not found written in the book of life was thrown into the lake of fire.

The New Jerusalem

21 ¹Then I saw a new heaven and a new earth. The first heaven and the first earth had disappeared. Now there was no sea. ²And I saw the holy city, the new Jerusalem,ᵃ coming down out of heaven from God. It was prepared like a bride dressed for her husband.

³I heard a loud voice from the throne. It said, "Now God's home is with people. He will live with them. They will be his people. God himself will be with them and will be their God. ⁴He will wipe away every tear from their eyes. There will be no more death, sadness, crying, or pain. All the old ways are gone."

⁵The one who was sitting on the throne said, "Look, I am making everything new!" Then he said, "Write this, because these words are true and can be trusted."

⁶The one on the throne said to me, "It is finished! I am the Alpha and the Omega,ᵇ the Beginning and the End. I will give free water from the spring of the water of life to anyone who is thirsty. ⁷All those who win the victory will receive all this. And I will be their God, and they will be my children. ⁸But those who are cowards, those who refuse to believe, those who

do terrible things, those who kill, those who sin sexually, those who do evil magic, those who worship idols,* and those who tell lies— they will all have a place in the lake of burning sulfur. This is the second death."

⁹One of the seven angels came to me. This was one of the angels who had the seven bowls full of the seven last plagues. The angel said, "Come with me. I will show you the bride, the wife of the Lamb.*" ¹⁰The angel carried me away by the Spirit* to a very large and high mountain. The angel showed me the holy city, Jerusalem. The city was coming down out of heaven from God.

¹¹The city was shining with the glory* of God. It was shining bright like a very expensive jewel, like a jasper. It was clear as crystal. ¹²The city had a large, high wall with twelve gates. There were twelve angels at the gates. On each gate was written the name of one of the twelve tribes of Israel.* ¹³There were three gates on the east, three gates on the north, three gates on the south, and three gates on the west. ¹⁴The walls of the city were built on twelve foundation stones. On the stones were written the names of the twelve apostles* of the Lamb.

¹⁵The angel who talked with me had a measuring rod made of gold. The angel had this rod to measure the city, its gates, and its wall. ¹⁶The city was built in a square. Its length was equal to its width. The angel measured the city with the rod. The city was 12,000 *stadia*ᶜ long, 12,000 *stadia*

ᵃ **21:2 new Jerusalem** The spiritual city where God's people live with him.
ᵇ **21:6 Alpha ... Omega** The first and last letters in the Greek alphabet, meaning the beginning and the end.

ᶜ **21:16 stadia** One Greek *stadion* was 600 feet, about 185 meters.

wide, and 12,000 *stadia* high. ¹⁷The angel also measured the wall. It was 144 cubits*ᵃ* high. (The angel was using the same measurement that people use.) ¹⁸The wall was made of jasper. The city was made of pure gold, as pure as glass.

¹⁹The foundation stones of the city walls had every kind of expensive jewels in them. The first foundation stone was jasper, the second was sapphire, the third was chalcedony, the fourth was emerald, ²⁰the fifth was onyx, the sixth was carnelian, the seventh was yellow quartz, the eighth was beryl, the ninth was topaz, the tenth was chrysoprase, the eleventh was jacinth, and the twelfth was amethyst. ²¹The twelve gates were twelve pearls. Each gate was made from one pearl. The street of the city was made of pure gold, as clear as glass.

²²I did not see a temple in the city. The Lord God All-Powerful and the Lamb were the city's temple. ²³The city did not need the sun or the moon to shine on it. The glory of God gave the city light. The Lamb was the city's lamp.

²⁴The peoples of the world will walk by the light given by the Lamb. The rulers of the earth will bring their glory into the city. ²⁵The city's gates will never close on any day, because there is no night there. ²⁶The greatness and the honor of the nations will be brought into the city. ²⁷Nothing unclean will ever enter the city. No one who does shameful things or tells lies will ever enter the city. Only those whose names

are written in the Lamb's book of life will enter the city.

22 ¹The angel showed me the river of the water of life, clear as crystal. The river flows from the throne of God and the Lamb. ²It flows down the middle of the street of the city. The tree of life* is on each side of the river, and it produces fruit every month, twelve times a year. The leaves of the tree are for healing the nations.

³Nothing that God judges guilty will be there in that city. The throne of God and the Lamb will be in the city. God's servants will worship him. ⁴They will see his face. God's name will be written on their foreheads. ⁵There will never be night again. People will not need the light of a lamp or the light of the sun. The Lord God will give them light. And they will rule like kings forever and ever.

⁶Then the angel said to me, "These words are true and can be trusted. The Lord, the God of the spirits of the prophets,* has sent his angel to show his servants what must happen soon: ⁷'Listen, I am coming soon! Great blessings belong to the one who obeys the words of prophecy* in this book.'"

⁸I am John. I am the one who heard and saw these things. After I heard and saw them, I bowed down to worship at the feet of the angel who showed them to me. ⁹But the angel said to me, "Don't worship me! I am a servant like you and your brothers the prophets. I am a servant like all those who obey the words in this book. You should worship God!"

¹⁰Then the angel told me, "Don't keep secret the words of prophecy in this book. The time is near for

ᵃ **21:17 cubits** A cubit is the length of a man's arm from the elbow to the tip of the little finger, about half a meter.

these things to happen. [11]Let anyone who is doing wrong continue to do wrong. Let anyone who is unclean continue to be unclean. Let anyone who is doing right continue to do right. Let anyone who is holy* continue to be holy."

[12]"Listen, I am coming soon! I will bring rewards with me. I will repay everyone for what they have done. [13]I am the Alpha and the Omega,[a] the First and the Last, the Beginning and the End.

[14]"Great blessings belong to those who have washed their robes.[b] They will have the right to eat the food from the tree of life. They can go through the gates into the city. [15]Outside the city are all those who live like dogs—those who do evil magic, those who sin sexually, those who murder, those who worship idols, and those who love to lie and pretend to be good.

[16]"I, Jesus, have sent my angel to tell you these things for the churches.* I am the descendant from the family of David.* I am the bright morning star."

[17]The Spirit and the bride say, "Come!" Everyone who hears this should also say, "Come!" All who are thirsty may come; they can have the water of life as a free gift if they want it.

[18]I warn everyone who hears the words of prophecy in this book: If anyone adds anything to these, God will give that person the plagues written about in this book. [19]And if anyone takes away from the words of this book of prophecy, God will take away that person's share of the tree of life and of the holy city, which are written about in this book.

[20]Jesus is the one who says that all of this is true. Now he says, "Yes, I am coming soon."

Amen*! Come, Lord Jesus!

[21]The grace* of the Lord Jesus be with all people.

---

[a] **22:13 Alpha ... Omega** The first and last letters in the Greek alphabet, meaning the beginning and the end.
[b] **22:14 washed their robes** Meaning that they had believed in Jesus and had been made clean from sin by his blood sacrifice. See Rev. 5:9; 7:14; Heb. 9:14; 10:14–22; Acts 22:16; 1 Jn. 1:7.

Word List

– A –

Aaron Moses' brother, who was chosen as the first high priest of Israel.

Abel The son of Adam and Eve who was killed by his brother Cain. Read Gen. 4:1–16.

Abraham The most respected ancestor of the Jewish people. Through him God promised to make a great nation and bless all the people of the earth. Read Gen. 12:1–3.

Achaia The region in the southern part of Greece where the ancient cities of Athens and Corinth were located.

Adriatic Sea The sea between Greece and Italy, including the central part of the Mediterranean Sea.

adultery Breaking a marriage promise by committing sexual sin.

agreement A contract or agreement from God to his people. The agreement that God gave his people at Mount Sinai, based on the Law of Moses, became the most important for the Israelites or Jews. It replaced or renewed all other agreements, such as that given earlier to Abraham. In the New Testament it is referred to as the "old" or "first" agreement. After Jesus Christ came and offered his life as payment for the sins of all people, God was able to offer a "new" and "better" agreement based on Christ's sacrifice.

Agreement Where this is marked, it is literally "Testimony," a word that usually refers to the flat stones with the Ten Commandments written on them, which were evidence or "proof" of the agreement between God and Israel.

Agrippa Herod Agrippa II, great-grandson of Herod the Great.

alabaster A beautiful kind of stone that can be carved.

aloes The oil from a sweet-smelling wood that was used to make perfume (Ps. 45:8; Prov. 7:17) or the bitter juice from a cactus-like plant that was used to prepare bodies for burial (Jn. 19:39).

altar A raised area, pile of stones, or table that people used to offer sacrifices on. An important altar was the one in front of the Temple in Jerusalem. See also "GOLDEN ALTAR."

Amen A Hebrew word meaning "That's right," "True," or "Yes." It is used to express strong agreement with what has been said.

ancestors Literally, "fathers," meaning a person's parents, grandparents, and all the other people that person is descended from. In the New Testament it usually refers to people who lived during Old Testament times.

anoint To pour a special oil on people or things to show that they have been chosen by God and set apart for a special work or purpose.

apostle A follower of Jesus chosen to represent him in a special way. During his earthly ministry, Jesus named twelve men as apostles. They had the specific responsibility and authority to represent him and proclaim his message throughout the world. Later, he appeared to Paul and gave him a similar commission, especially to non-Jewish people. Barnabas, Paul's missionary companion, and James, the brother of Jesus, are also called apostles, as well as several others in the New Testament. Some of these occurrences of the word, however, have the more general sense of "messenger" or "representative."

Aramaic The language of the Arameans, which became the main language of trade and diplomacy in the ancient near east during the Assyrian, the Neo-Babylonian, and Persian empires. Similar to Hebrew, it later became the common language of many Jews and is the spoken "Hebrew" referred to in the New Testament.

archangel The leader among God's angels.

Areopagus council A group of important leaders in Athens who served like judges.

army officer A centurion, a Roman army officer who had authority over 100 soldiers.

Asia The geographical area, sometimes called Asia Minor, that is now the western part of modern Turkey.

– B –

Baal A false god worshiped by the Canaanites. They believed he brought rain and storms and made the land produce good crops.

Balaam A non-Israelite prophet in the Old Testament who was hired by Balak, king of Moab, to curse his enemy Israel. Read Num. 22-24.

baptism A Greek word usually referring to the act of dipping or "burying" a person briefly in water, connected with their decision to change their life and turn to God, trusting him to forgive their sins. For people coming to faith in Jesus Christ it was an expression of their trust in his death as the sacrifice God accepted to pay for their sins. Described as a sharing in the death, burial, and resurrection of Christ, it marked the beginning of their new life in Christ as part of God's people. See Acts 2:38; Rom. 6:3, 4; Gal. 3:26-28; Col. 2:12, 13.

baptize To perform the act of baptism. See "BAPTISM."

believer Where this word is marked, it is literally "brother," a term used by followers of Jesus Christ to refer to fellow members of God's family.

Bernice King Agrippa's sister, the oldest daughter of Herod Agrippa I.

Bethsaida A town by Lake Galilee that Jesus visited during his teaching ministry and where he performed many miracles.

Box of the Agreement Or traditionally, "Ark of the Covenant." The special box kept in the Most Holy Place of the Israelite Holy Tent and, later, the Jerusalem Temple. It contained the stone tablets with the Ten Commandments written on them, which were evidence or "proof" of the agreement between God and his people. In some passages it is literally, "Box of the Testimony" or simply, "Testimony" (see "AGREEMENT"). See Ex. 25:10-22; 1 Kings 8:1-9.

bridegroom A man who is getting married.

— C —

Caesar The name or title given to the emperor (ruler) of Rome.

Cain The son of Adam and Eve who killed his brother Abel. Read Gen. 4:1-16.

Canaan The land where the Canaanites lived. In the time of Joshua the Israelites fought for this land and eventually controlled most of it. It was generally the same area that was later called Palestine and included what are now Israel and Lebanon.

Capernaum A town on the northern shore of Lake Galilee where Jesus often spent time and taught.

chariot A small, two-wheeled cart pulled by horses and used in war.

Cherub angels Winged beings like angels that serve God, usually as guards around his throne or other holy places. Two statues of these beings were on the cover of the Box of the Agreement that represented God's presence. See Ex. 25:10-22.

Chorazin A town by Lake Galilee that Jesus visited during his teaching ministry and where he performed many miracles.

Christ Literally, "Anointed," a title that comes from the Old Testament ceremony in which perfumed oil was poured or rubbed on someone being appointed to a high office, especially that of prophet, priest, or king, to show

that this person was chosen by God for that role. The Hebrew word is "Messiah," a title used for Old Testament kings and for the one God would send as prophet, priest, and king to bring people back to a good relationship with him.

church Literally, "assembly" or "community," the people who have been brought together as God's family through their common faith in Jesus Christ. The word often refers to a group of believers who meet together or who live in the same area, but it is also used to mean the worldwide community of all believers in Christ.

circumcise, circumcision Cutting off the foreskin of the male sex organ. This was done to every Jewish baby boy as a mark of the agreement God made with Abraham. Read Gen. 17:9-14. Sometimes "circumcision" is used with "heart" in the figurative sense of true devotion to God (see Jer. 9:26; Rom. 2:28). In the New Testament "circumcision" is also used in a spiritual sense to refer to the changed life of believers who have come to share in the new agreement God gave his people through Jesus. (See Php. 3:3; Col. 2:11.)

Claudius The emperor (ruler) of Rome, 41-54 A.D.

cornerstone The first and most important stone of a building.

cross The wooden post that Romans used to execute criminals. It is a symbol of shame, suffering and death. Just as Jesus was willing to suffer death on a cross for all people, so he asks his followers to be willing to give up their lives for him.

crown Literally, "wreath," a ring of leaves or branches that was placed on the head of the winners of athletic contests to honor them. It was a symbol of victory and reward.

curtain The curtain that separated the inner sanctuary (Most Holy Place) from the front room in the Tabernacle (see "HOLY TENT") and in the Jerusalem Temple. It represented the spiritual barrier that kept people from entering God's presence. When Jesus died, the curtain was torn open (Mt. 27:51), which was a symbol to show that in the heavenly temple the way into God's presence had been opened. See Heb. 10:19, 20.

– D –

darkness A symbol for the kinds of things that describe Satan's kingdom, such as sin and evil.

David Israel's greatest king, who ruled about 1000 years before Christ. Besides being a great military and political leader, he was a deeply spiritual man and a gifted musician, who wrote many of the Psalms. He made plans and arrangements for the building of the first Temple in Jerusalem ("the city of David"), which was actually completed by his son Solomon. The Scriptures said that a descendant of David would be God's chosen messiah (king), who would establish an eternal kingdom. For that reason, Jesus is sometimes called "the Son of David."

day A symbol for the kinds of things that describe God's kingdom, such as goodness and truth.

Day The day Christ will come to judge everyone and take his people to live with him.

demon An evil spirit from the devil.

divine greatness Literally, "glory," a word that refers to the special qualities of God. See "GLORY."

dysentery A very bad intestinal sickness that causes pain and diarrhea.

– E –

elders (in Revelation) The 24 elders in Revelation could be the great leaders of God's people under both the Old Testament and New Testament periods, combining the leaders of the twelve tribes of Israel and Jesus' twelve apostles. Or they could be angels as leaders of heavenly worship, corresponding to the 24 groups of priests in charge of worship in the Old Testament.

elders (New Testament) Men chosen to lead a local group of believers (church). Also called "overseers" and "pastors" (shepherds), they have the work of caring for God's people. See Acts 14:23; 20:17, 28; Eph. 4:11; Php. 1:1; 1 Tim. 3:1-7; Tit. 1:5-9; 1 Pet. 5:1-3.

Elijah A very important Israelite leader and prophet who spoke for God during a 25-year period ending about 850 B.C. In the time of Jesus, the Jews were expecting Elijah to come again before the Messiah. See Mal. 4:5-6.

Elisha A prophet who served as an assistant to the prophet Elijah and carried on Elijah's ministry after about 850 B.C.

emperor Caesar, the ruler (leader) of the Roman empire.

eunuch A man who had been castrated so that he could not have sex or one who was physically unable to have children

Often, such men were chosen to be in charge of the women in a ruler's household or served as public officials.

Evil One The devil or Satan, the ruler of demons and enemy of God.

– F –

false prophet A person who claims to speak for God but does not really speak God's truth.

fast To live without food for a time of prayer or mourning.

fathers Important ancestors of the Jewish people, especially the leaders of the tribes of Israel.

Festival of Harvest A one-day celebration of the wheat harvest in the spring, fifty days after Passover, during which the first part of the new crop was offered to God. Often called "Festival of Weeks," it was later known as "Pentecost" (from the Greek word meaning "fifty").

Festival of Shelters A special week each year when the Israelites, and later the Jews, lived in tents to remember God's protection during the time their people wandered in the desert for 40 years with Moses. Also called "Festival of Ingathering" (Ex. 23:16; 34:22). Read Lev. 23:33–36, 39–43.

Festival of Unleavened Bread An important and holy week for the people of Israel and their descendants. In the time of the Old Testament it began the day after Passover, but by New Testament times the two festivals had become one. To prepare for it, the people threw out all their yeast and ate only bread without yeast for seven days."

first agreement The contract God gave to the Israelites when he gave them the Law of Moses. See "AGREEMENT."

firstborn The first child born into a family. The first son was very important in ancient times and became the head of the family at the father's death. It can also mean a person of special importance. In reference to Christ, it means that he is the first and most important of God's children, the first to share his glory.

frankincense Special dried tree sap that was burned to make a sweet-smelling smoke and offered as a gift to God. See "INCENSE."

Free Men Jews who had been slaves or whose fathers had been slaves, but were now free.

– G –

glory A word that refers to the special qualities of God. The expression "Glory of the Lord" refers to one of the forms God used when he appeared to people. It was like a bright, shining light. In the book of Numbers, it might have been a bright light or a tall cloud. Sometimes glory means majesty or power, referring to a kind of greatness that cannot be compared to anything in human experience. It can also include the ideas of wealth, honor, fame, or respect, especially in expressions of praise.

God's kingdom The "reign" or "rule" of God over all people who accept Jesus as the Messiah (the chosen king). Jesus' life and teachings show what it means for God to be King on earth. Jesus fulfilled the King's mission of love and justice by setting people free from the control of the devil, the temporary ruler of this world. Through Jesus, God offers his enemies forgiveness for their rebellion against him. And when people are freed from their slavery to sin, they can give control of their lives to Jesus. Then they become part of God's kingdom and gladly accept his mission. Just as Jesus did, they too invite God's enemies to change their hearts and lives, become God's friends, and enjoy the benefits of his just rule, both now and in the future. (Note that in Matthew this term also translates the Greek word "kingdom" by itself or the phrase, "the kingdom of the heavens," which was used by Jews as a way to avoid saying the divine name.)

Gomorrah A city that God destroyed, together with the city of Sodom, because the people living there were so evil. See Gen. 19.

Good News In the Gospels this is usually the news about the coming of God's kingdom (see "GOD'S KINGDOM") or its representative Jesus the Messiah. In other places it is, more specifically, the news or message of God's grace—that he has made a way through Jesus Christ for people to be made right with him and enjoy his blessings now and forever.

golden altar The table made from acacia wood and covered with gold that was used in the Holy Tent for burning incense as a gift to God.

grace The love and kindness that God shows in his complete willingness to give people favors he does not owe them and blessings they don't deserve.

Greek A non-Jewish person anywhere throughout the first century world who was influenced by Greek language and culture.

– H –

Hades The Greek word for "Sheol," the home of the dead. It is often used as a metaphor for death.

hands on See "LAY HANDS ON."

Hermes A Greek god. The Greeks believed he was a messenger for the other gods.

Herod (1) Herod I (the Great), king of Judea and all of Palestine (40–4 B.C.), Mt. 2:1–22; Lk. 1:5; Acts 23:35. (2) Herod Antipas, son of Herod the Great, tetrarch (ruler) of Galilee and Perea (4 B.C.–39 A.D.), Mt. 14:1–6; Mk. 6:14–22; 8:15; Lk. 3:1, 19; 8:3; 9:7, 9; 13:31; 23:7–15; Acts 4:27; 13:1. (3) Herod Agrippa I, grandson of Herod the Great, king of Palestine (37–44 A.D.), Acts 12:1, 6–21.

Herodians Members of a Jewish political group who were supporters of Herod and cooperated with the Pharisees in finding a way to stop Jesus from teaching.

high priest The most important priest and leader of the Israelites or the Jews, God's people under the "old agreement." Under the "new agreement" the high priest for God's people is Jesus Christ. Read Heb. 7:11–8:13.

holy people Literally, "saints" or "holy ones," a term used in the New Testament to describe followers of Jesus Christ as God's special people. They are holy because they have been made pure through Christ and belong only to God. See "HOLY."

Holy Spirit Also called the Spirit of God, the Spirit of Christ, and the Comforter. In union with God and Christ, he does God's work among people in the world.

Holy Tent Or "Tabernacle," the special tent described in the Law of Moses, where God lived among his people and where the Israelite priests performed their worship duties. It was often called the "Meeting Tent" because it was where the Israelites went to meet with God. It was used until Solomon built the Temple in Jerusalem.

holy When referring to people or things, holy means set apart or chosen for a special use; especially, belonging to God or used only for him. It can also mean pure or perfect, worthy of God and fit for his service. When God is called holy, in addition to the idea of pure and perfect, it often means he is completely separate or different from and above everything else that exists. In the New Testament God's people are holy because they have been made perfect and pure through Christ and, with the help of the Holy Spirit, keep themselves away from sin and live only for God.

hypocrisy Pretending to be good while hiding wrong motives.

hypocrite A person with wrong motives who pretends to be good.

hyssop A plant with fine branches and leaves used for sprinkling blood or water in cleansing ceremonies.

– I –

idol A statue of a false god that people worship. It can also mean anything that is more important to a person than God.

Illyricum A Roman province north and west of Greece.

incense Special dried tree sap that was burned to make a sweet-smelling smoke and offered as a sacrifice.

Isaac The son of Abraham and one of the most important ancestors of the Israelites or Jews.

Israel Another name for Jacob (see Gen. 32:24–28) and for the nation God chose to accomplish his plan of blessing the world through the Messiah (see "Messiah"). The people of Israel were the descendants of Jacob's twelve sons. In the New Testament this name is sometimes used in a broader sense to mean all of God's people.

Israelite Belonging to the nation of Israel (see "Israel").

– J –

Jacob Or "Israel," ancestor of the people of Israel (also called Israelites and, later, Jews). See Gen. 32:24–28 for the story of how Jacob was given the name Israel. He was the father of twelve sons from whom the twelve tribes of Israel descended, and the name Jacob continued to be used for the nation or people of Israel.

Jeremiah A man who spoke for God about 600 B.C.

John the Baptizer The man God chose to tell people about Christ's coming and to prepare them by warning them to change their lives and by baptizing them (see "baptize") as a sign of their decision to change. Read Mt. 3; Mk. 1:1–11; Lk. 1:5–25, 57–80; 3:1–18.

John See "John the Baptizer."

Joshua The Israelite military captain who, after Moses died, took his place as the leader of the Israelites and led them into the land that God had promised them.

Judah One of the 12 sons of Jacob (Israel); also the tribe and, later, the nation named after him. Described as the "southern kingdom," it was made up of the Israelite tribes that occupied the southern part of Palestine, while the northern tribes were united into a "northern kingdom" known as Israel.

– K –

kingdom See "GOD'S KINGDOM."

– L –

Lamb A symbolic name for Jesus Christ. It means that he was an offering for sin like the lambs that were offered as a sacrifice to God in the Old Testament.

law This usually refers to God's law as it is represented in the Mosaic Law, the rules he gave to the Israelites through Moses (see Ex. 34:29–32). Sometimes it may mean the principle of law rather than a specific law or set of laws.

lay hands on This act was a way of asking God to bless people in a special way—to heal them, to cause the Holy Spirit to come into them, or to give them power for a special work.

leatherworker Or "tanner," a person who makes leather from animal skins.

leper A person who has leprosy. See "LEPROSY."

leprosy A very bad skin disease. The word in the text has a broad sense, which may include many different types of skin disease.

Levite An Israelite from the tribe of Levi. The Levites from the family of Aaron served as priests. All the other descendants of Levi served as helpers of the priests in the Holy Tent (Tabernacle) and Temple. In later periods, some Levites worked for the government as civil servants.

light A symbol for the kinds of things that describe God or his kingdom, such as goodness and truth.

locusts Insects like grasshoppers that could destroy a large crop very quickly. See Ex. 10. The Law of Moses said that locusts could be eaten. See Lev. 11:21–22.

lots Stones, sticks, or bones used like dice for making decisions. See Prov. 16:33.

– M –

Macedonia The northern part of Greece, where Thessalonica and Philippi were.

manna The special food provided by God that the Israelites gathered daily from the ground during the 40 years they wandered through the desert. See Ex. 16:4–36.

mediator A person who helps one person talk to or give something to another person.

Melchizedek A priest and king who lived in the time of Abraham. See Gen. 14:17–24.

merchant A person who earns a living by buying and selling things.

message See "GOOD NEWS."

Messiah A Hebrew word that has the same meaning as the Greek word Christ (see "CHRIST"). It was a title for the kings of God's people in the Old Testament and for the special king God promised to send as a "savior" to defeat evil and establish the reign of God. Many prophets made it clear that this new kingdom would be eternal; that is, not only would the promised Messiah bring about a time of justice and right living among God's people here on earth but also his kingdom would extend beyond this world to life forever with God. However, mos

Jews of the first century expected the Messiah to be a political ruler here on earth who would defeat the other nations and return the nation of Israel to a position of great glory and power. But God intended his Messiah to establish a new "Israel," an eternal kingdom that would bless all the nations.

mill Two large, flat rocks used for grinding grain to make flour.

millstone A large, round stone used for grinding grain.

miracle An amazing act done by the power of God.

miraculous sign An amazing act that demonstrates the power of God.

Moses One of the most important leaders of the Israelites during the time of the Old Testament. God used him to give the people his law, which is often called "the Law of Moses."

Most Holy Place Literally, "holy of holies," the most important room in the Holy Tent or the Temple, where the Box of the Agreement was kept. It was like a throne room where God sat as king of Israel and where the high priest entered into his presence on the Day of Atonement.

Mount of Olives A hill east of the city of Jerusalem from which a person could see the Temple area.

Mount Sinai The mountain located somewhere on the Sinai Peninsula (the eastern part of modern-day Egypt) where God gave his laws to Moses and the Israelites. Also called Mount Horeb. See Ex. 19 and 20.

Mount Zion See "Zion."

mourn, mourners To express sorrow for someone who has died or for something lost. In ancient Israel people often put on special clothes, cried very loudly, and put ashes on their head to show their sadness. Professional "mourners" were sometimes paid to do this at a funeral.

mustard A plant that has a very small seed but grows taller than a man.

myrrh Sweet-smelling sap from the bark of trees or other plants that was used for perfume and also to prepare bodies for burial. Mixed with wine, it was probably used to relieve pain (Mk. 15:23).

– N –

nard Very expensive oil from the root of the nard plant. It was used as a perfume.

Nazirite A person who has made a special vow of dedication to God. This name is from the Hebrew word meaning "to separate" or "to consecrate" and refers to the promise Nazirites made to separate themselves from others and dedicate themselves to God by following certain requirements. See Num. 6:1–21.

new agreement The "better agreement" that God has given to his people through Jesus Christ. See "AGREEMENT."

New Moon The first day of the month for Israelites or Jews, which they celebrated as a special day of rest and worship. The people met together and shared in the fellowship offerings like those described in Lev. 7:16–21.

night A symbol for the kinds of things that describe Satan's kingdom, such as sin and evil.

– O –

oath A strong declaration that one will tell the truth or keep a promise, often using the name of God or something else known to be real or important. It may include a wish to be punished if the promise is not kept.

– P –

paradise A wonderful place of blessing, where God's people go when they die.

parchment Something like paper made from the skins of sheep and used for writing on.

Passover A very important holy day for the people of Israel and their descendants. They ate a special meal on this day every year to remember that God made them free from slavery in Egypt in the time of Moses. The name may come from the word in Ex. 12:13, 23, 27 that means "to pass over" or "to protect."

Pentecost An Israelite or Jewish festival celebrating the wheat harvest fifty days after Passover. See "FESTIVAL OF HARVEST."

persecute To hurt, cause trouble for, or do bad things to someone, especially because of their beliefs.

persecution The act of persecuting or being persecuted. See "PERSECUTE."

Peter Where this is marked, the Greek text has "Cephas," the Aramaic name for Peter, one of Jesus' twelve apostles. Both names mean "rock."

Pharaoh A title for the king of Egypt.

Pharisee A person who belonged to a Jewish religious group that claimed to follow carefully all Jewish laws and customs.

philosopher A person who spends much time studying, thinking, talking, or writing about different ideas and trying to gain wisdom.

Pilate, Pontius The Roman governor of Judea, 26–36 A.D. Read Lk. 23:1–3.

pillar One of the tall, carved stones used to hold up the roof of a building.

Preparation day Friday, the day before the Sabbath day.

prize See "CROWN."

prophecy A message or teaching from God. Also, the ability and authority from God to speak for him.

prophesy To speak or teach things from God.

prophet A person who speaks a message from God. Many of the books in the Old Testament are messages spoken or written by "the prophets," who were some of those God chose to speak for him. God often used dreams or visions to tell or show his prophets what they should say.

prophetess A woman prophet.

– R –

resurrection Being raised from death to live again.

ruler of the evil powers See "SATAN."

ruler of this world See "SATAN."

– S –

Sabbath Saturday, the seventh day of the week and a special day for Israelites or Jews. By God's command it was set aside as a time for the people to rest and honor God.

sackcloth A rough cloth made from animal hair that people sometimes wore to show sadness.

sacrifice To offer a gift to God (or to any god) as an expression of worship, thanksgiving, or payment for sin. Also, the gift that is offered. In the Old Testament it was usually a special animal that was killed and burned on an altar. The Old Testament sacrifices offered for sins were symbolic of the perfect sacrifice that God himself would provide through Jesus Christ. Jesus gave his own life as a sacrifice to pay for the sins of all people. See Heb. 10:1–14.

Sadducees A leading Jewish religious group. They accepted only the first five books of the Old Testament and believed that people will not live again after death.

Samaritans During New Testament times, the people who lived in Samaria, the region north of Judea. They were part Jewish and followed the Law of Moses, but the Jews of Judea did not accept them as pure descendants of Israel.

Samuel The last judge (leader) and first prophet of Israel.

Satan A name for the devil meaning "the enemy," or "the accuser."

Scripture Part of the Scriptures or "Holy Writings"—the Old Testament.

scroll A long roll of paper or leather used for writing on.

seal A small stone or ring with a picture carved in it that was pressed into wet clay or hot wax to hold down the loose end of a scroll. It left a special mark, also called a seal, that was like a signature to keep anyone from opening the scroll except the right person.

sickle A tool with a curved blade for harvesting grain and other crops.

Sidon A non-Jewish city on the coast of Phoenicia (modern Lebanon).

sign See "MIRACULOUS SIGN."

silver coin Or "denarius," a Roman coin that was worth the average pay for one day's work.

Sodom A city that God destroyed, together with the city of Gomorrah, because the people living there were so evil. See Gen. 19.

Solomon's Porch An area on the east side of the Temple, covered by a roof.

Son of David A name for the Messiah (Christ) because it was prophesied that he would come from the family of David. See "DAVID."

son of David Any person from the family of David. See "DAVID."

Son of Man The name that Jesus most often used for himself. The phrase in Hebrew or Aramaic means "human being" or "mankind," but in Dan. 7:13–14 it is used of a future savior and king, and this was later understood to be the Messiah, the one God would send to save his people.

special servant The Greek word is *diakonos*, which is usually translated "servant." However, in three places (Rom. 16:1; Php. 1:2; 1 Tim. 3:8–13) the service of those so described is associated with a local church, indicating that they were chosen to serve in some special way. Compare Acts 6:1–6.

Spirit See "HOLY SPIRIT."

synagogue A place in many cities where Jews gathered for prayer, study of the Scriptures, and other public meetings.

Syrtis A shallow area in the sea near the Libyan coast.

– T –

tax collector A Jew hired by the Romans to collect taxes. Tax collectors often cheated, and the other Jews hated them.

Temple The permanent building in Jerusalem that replaced the portable "Holy Tent" that was used by the Israelites from the time of their wandering in the desert to the reign of King Solomon, when the first Temple was built. Like the Holy Tent, the Temple was the center of Israelite worship, although provision was made for it to be "a house of prayer for all nations" (Isa. 56:7).

Ten Towns Greek, "Decapolis," an area on the east side of Lake Galilee that once had ten main towns.

Tent, Holy See "HOLY TENT."

the Way A symbolic name used by followers of Jesus Christ to describe their faith as "the way" to God through Jesus.

tomb A grave dug in a wall of rock or a building where a dead body is buried. It can also be a small building made to show respect for important people who had died.

torture To hurt or cause someone pain, often to force them to say something against their will.

tree of life The tree whose fruit gives people the power to live forever. See Gen. 2:9; 3:22 and Rev. 22:1-2.

tunic A piece of clothing like a long undershirt.

Tyre A non-Jewish city on the coast of Phoenicia (modern Lebanon).

– V –

vineyard A garden or farm where grapes are grown.

virgin A woman, especially a young woman, who is not married and has never had sexual relations.

vision Something like a dream used by God to speak to people.

vow A very strong promise that a person makes, sometimes to God and often using the name of God or something else known to be real or important. It may include a wish to be punished if the promise is not kept.

vulture Or "eagle," a bird of prey that eats dead animals.

– W –

will The legal paper that people sign to give instructions about what should be done with their possessions after they die.

winepress A place dug in rock used to mash grapes and collect the juice for making wine.

wineskin A bag made from the skin of an animal and used for storing wine.

wise men Literally, "magi," probably meaning pagan religious scholars who studied the stars to predict future events.

witchcraft Using magic or the power of Satan.

wonders Miracles that cause people to react with amazement and fear of God.

– Y –

yeast The part of bread dough that makes it rise. Sometimes it is used as a symbol of bad influence

– Z –

Zealot A term used to describe Jews who had an enthusiastic desire or "zeal" to maintain the purity of Judaism—the land, the Temple, observance of the law and the traditions. This desire included a willingness to do whatever necessary to protect this purity against any outside threat such as Roman control. This kind of spirit eventually brought about the formation of a group of Jewish patriots known as the Zealots. (Note that in Mt. 10:4 and Mk. 3:18 "Zealot" is used to translate the Aramaic term, "Cananaean," which had the same meaning.)

Zeus The most important of the gods in which the ancient Greeks believed.

Zion The southeastern part of the mountain that Jerusalem is built on. Sometimes it means the city of Jerusalem, the people of God living there, or the Temple.

MAP 1   **438**

PROVINCE of SYRIA

Mediterranean Sea

• Tyre

Caesarea
Philippi

Phoenicia

Ptolemais

GALILEE

TETRARCHY
of
PHILIP

• Chorazin
Capernaum
Gennesaret
• Cana
Tiberias

• Bethsaida
• Gergesa

Lake
Galilee

• Nazaret

DECAPOLIS

• Gadara

Dor •

• Nain

Caesarea •

Salim
Aenon

• Pella

SAMARIA

Sebaste
(Samaria)
• Sychar

• Gerasa

• Antipatris

• Joppa

Arimathea

Jordan River

JUDEA

• Ephraim

PEREA

• Philadelphia

• Lydda

Jericho •

Emmaus •
Bethphage •
Bethlehem •

Jerusalem •
• Bethany

• Azotus

• Ashkelon

Dead Sea

NABATEAN KINGDOM

• Gaza

• Hebron

IDUMEA

• Masada

Palestine in
New Testament Times

▬ ▬ Political Boundaries A.D. 6–44

0   5   10   15   20 Miles

0   10   20   30   40 km

MAP 3   440

God frees Paul and Silas from jail
Acts 16:16-40

Timothy reads the Bible
2 Timothy 3:14-17

© WBTC 2011

People from all nations praise God
Revelation 7:9-17

Tyre

Caesarea Philippi

GALILEE

Mediterranean Sea

Bethsaida

Capernaum

Cana

Lake Galilee

Nazareth

Caesarea

SAMARIA

Jordan River

Jericho

JUDEA

Jerusalem

Bethany

Bethlehem

Dead Sea

To EGYPT

The land where Jesus walked

© WBTC 2011